Fodor's

EIGHTEENTH EDITION

New

Eastern and Central Europe

DISCARDED

The complete guide, thoroughly up-to-date

Packed with details that will make your trip

The must-see sights, off and on the beaten path

What to see, what to skip

Mix-and-match vacation itineraries

City strolls, countryside adventures

Smart lodging and dining options

Essential local do's and taboos

Transportation tips, distances and directions

Key contacts, savvy travel tips

When to go, what to pack

Clear, accurate, easy-to-use maps

Books to read, helpful vocabulary

Fodor's Travel Publications, Inc.
New York • Toronto • London • Sydney • Auckland
www.fodors.com

Fodor's Eastern and Central Europe

EDITOR: Jennifer J. Paull

Editorial Contributors: Eleanore H. Boyse, David Brown, Christina Knight, Ky Krauthamer, Martha Lagace, Matthew Lore, Tatiana Repková, Robert Rigney, Kristin Rimington, Helayne Schiff, Julie Tomasz, Annie Ward

Editorial Production: Tom Holton

Maps: David Lindroth, *cartographer*; Steven Amsterdam, *map editor*

Design: Fabrizio La Rocca, *creative director*; Guido Caroti, *associate art director*; Jolie Novak, *photo editor*

Production/Manufacturing: Bob Shields

Cover Photograph: David Hanson/Tony Stone Images

Copyright

Eighteenth Edition

ISBN 0–679–00011–9

Special Sales

Fodor's Travel Publications are available at special discounts for bulk purchases for sales promotions or premiums. Special editions, including personalized covers, excerpts of existing guides, and corporate imprints, can be created in large quantities for special needs. For more information, contact your local bookseller or write to Special Markets, Fodor's Travel Publications, 201 East 50th Street, New York, NY 10022. Inquiries from Canada should be directed to your local Canadian bookseller or sent to Random House of Canada, Ltd., Marketing Department, 2775 Matheson Boulevard East, Mississauga, Ontario L4W 4P7. Inquiries from the United Kingdom should be sent to Fodor's Travel Publications, 20 Vauxhall Bridge Road, London SW1V 2SA, England.

PRINTED IN THE UNITED STATES OF AMERICA

10 9 8 7 6 5 4 3 2 1

CONTENTS

Maps and Charts

ON THE ROAD WITH FODOR'S

WHEN I PLAN A VACATION, the first thing I do is cast around among my friends and colleagues to find someone who's just been where I'm going. That's because there's no substitute for a recommendation from a good friend who knows your tastes, your budget, and your circumstances, someone who's just been there. Unfortunately, such friends are few and far between. So it's nice to know that there's *Fodor's Eastern and Central Europe,* eighteenth edition.

In the first place, this book won't stay home when you hit the road. It will accompany you every step of the way, steering you away from wrong turns and wrong choices and never expecting a thing in return. Most important of all, it's written and assiduously updated by the kind of people you *would* hit up for travel tips if you knew them. They're as choosy as your pickiest friend, and they're equipped with insider's knowledge of Eastern and Central Europe. In these pages, they don't send you chasing down every town and sight in Eastern and Central Europe but have instead selected the best ones, the ones that are worthy of your time and money. To make it easy for you to put it all together in the time you have, they've created short, medium, and long itineraries and, in cities, neighborhood walks that you can mix and match in a snap. Will this be the vacation of your dreams? We hope so.

About Our Writers

Our success in helping to make your trip the best of all possible vacations is a credit to the hard work of our extraordinary writers.

Poland updater **Eleanore H. Boyse** has lived outside the U.S. for most of her life; as the daughter of an American diplomat, she was born in South Africa and spent her childhood in France and Italy. For the past dozen years she has lived with her husband (also an American diplomat) in England, Bangladesh, Russia, and Poland. During her four years in Warsaw she grew to love the city; she also traveled extensively throughout the country with her family.

Ky Krauthamer and **Martha Lagace** contributed to the Czech Republic chapter. A resident of Prague since 1992, Ky is the assistant features editor of the weekly *Prague Post;* he has also contributed to *Fodor's Pocket Prague, Fodor's Europe,* and *Fodor's Affordable Europe.* Martha is an editor on the arts and entertainment desk of the *Prague Post.* She grew up in New England, Montana, and Canada, and was a freelance journalist in New York City and Paris before moving to Prague in the spring of 1991. She has also contributed to *Fodor's Pocket Prague* and *Fodor's Europe.*

Tatiana Repková was born and raised in Slovakia; she earned her degree from the Bratislava School of Economics. After the fall of Communism, she became the publisher and editor of the independent Slovak business weekly, *Trend,* as well as the daily *Narodna Obroda.* Her groundbreaking work was a benchmark for professional reporting. Having lived abroad for most of the past few years, her update of the Slovakia chapter helped her rediscover the rapidly changing country. Since summer 1998, she has been a fellow of the Open Society Institute, working on a manual for publishing and editing newspapers in post-communist countries.

Robert Rigney is a freelance writer from West Berlin who has been living in Prague since 1996. He writes about art, culture and travel for American and European publications. Lately he has become something of a Prague shopping connoisseur; he also covered southern Moravia and northern and southern Bohemia for this edition.

A series of chance events led **Kristin Rimington** to Bucharest, where she has spent the last few years working as an English and French teacher at the American School in Bucharest. A true fan of Romanian french fries and the capital's buses, Kristin has found her time in Romania to be both enriching and humorous. Between her encounters with wild dogs and getting locked into the basement of the People's Palace, her research for

Fodor's Romania chapter was marked with adventures.

Julie Tomasz, a travel and fiction writer of Hungarian descent, updated the Hungary chapter. She lived in Budapest for three years working as a founding editor of the *Budapest Sun*, and has been writing and editing for Fodor's for nine years, covering primarily Hungary but also making a foray farther east to write parts of Fodor's India guide. Julie's extensive off-duty travels have taken her to less-trodden areas, such as Albania and Transylvania. Hopelessly in love with Budapest and having acquired Hungarian citizenship, Julie plans to divide her time between the United States and Hungary.

A native of Kansas City, Kansas, **Annie Ward** went west to Los Angeles to earn her B.A. from UCLA and an M.F.A. in screenwriting from American Film Institute. Her first short film, "Strange Habit," was the grand jury best film selection at the 1996 Aspen Film Festival. Having lived for several years in Spain, she is now a resident of Sofia, Bulgaria and a journalist for the English-language newspaper *The Sofia Independent*. She has been foiled in her attempts to secure a residence visa for more than 30 days, and so has learned to enjoy her monthly excursions to the border. Passport control officers in Greece, Serbia, Turkey, Macedonia, and Romania also seem to enjoy her visits, as they always celebrate afterwards with a bottle of western whiskey. She is currently working on a novel set in Spain and Bulgaria.

Editor **Jennifer J. Paull** would like to thank the national and local tourist offices of all six countries for their help with questions great and small. She also thanks the updating team for their tremendous efforts.

We gratefully acknowledge **Malév Hungarian Airlines** for its help with realizing the Hungary chapter.

Connections

We're pleased that the American Society of Travel Agents continues to endorse Fodor's as its guidebook of choice. ASTA is the world's largest and most influential travel trade association, operating in more than 170 countries, with 27,000 members pledged to adhere to a strict code of ethics reflecting the Society's motto, "Integrity in Travel." ASTA shares Fodor's devotion to providing smart, honest travel information and advice to travelers, and we've long recommended that our readers—even those who have guidebooks and traveling friends—consult ASTA member agents for the experience and professionalism they bring to your vacation planning.

On Fodor's Web site (www.fodors.com), check out the new Resource Center, an online companion to the Gold Guide section of this book, complete with useful hot links to related sites. In our forums, you can also get lively advice from other travelers and more great tips from Fodor's experts worldwide.

How to Use This Book
Organization

Up front is the **Gold Guide,** an easy-to-use section arranged alphabetically by topic. Under each listing you'll find tips and information that will help you accomplish what you need to in Eastern and Central Europe. You'll also find addresses and telephone numbers of organizations and companies that offer destination-related services and detailed information and publications.

The first chapter in the guide, Destination: Eastern and Central Europe helps get you in the mood for your trip. New and Noteworthy cues you in on trends and happenings, What's Where gets you oriented, Pleasures and Pastimes describes the activities and sights that make Eastern and Central Europe unique, Fodor's Choice showcases our top picks, and Festivals and Seasonal Events alerts you to special events you'll want to seek out.

Each country's chapter is divided by geographical area; within each area, towns are covered in logical geographical order, and attractive stretches of road and minor points of interest between them are indicated by the designation *En Route.* And within town sections, all restaurants and lodgings are grouped.

To help you decide what to visit in the time you have, all chapters begin with our recommended itineraries. The A to Z section that ends all chapters covers getting there and getting around. It also provides helpful contacts and resources.

At the end of the book you'll find suggestions for recommended reading and helpful vocabulary charts.

Icons and Symbols

★   Our special recommendations
✕   Restaurant
🏠   Lodging establishment
✕🏠 Lodging establishment whose restaurant warrants a special trip
☺   Good for kids (rubber duck)
☞   Sends you to another section of the guide for more information
⊠   Address
☎   Telephone number
☉   Opening and closing times
💲   Admission prices (those we give apply to adults; substantially reduced fees are almost always available for children, students, and senior citizens)

Numbers in white and black circles (e.g., ③ ❸) that appear on the maps, in the margins, and within the tours correspond to one another.

Dining and Lodging

The restaurants and lodgings we list are the cream of the crop in each price range. Price charts appear in the Pleasures and Pastimes section that follows each chapter introduction.

Hotel Facilities

We always list the facilities that are available—but we don't specify whether you'll be charged extra to use them: When pricing accommodations, always ask what's included. In addition, assume that all rooms have private baths unless noted otherwise. In addition, when you book a room, be sure to mention if you have a disability or are traveling with children, if you prefer a private bath or a certain type of bed, or if you have specific dietary needs or other concerns.

Assume that hotels operate on the **European Plan** (EP, with no meals) unless we specify that they include breakfast or other meals in the rates.

Restaurant Reservations and Dress Codes

Reservations are always a good idea; we mention them only when they're essential or are not accepted. Book as far ahead as you can, and reconfirm as soon as you arrive. Unless otherwise noted, the restaurants listed are open daily for lunch and dinner. We mention dress only when men are required to wear a jacket or a jacket and tie. Look for an overview of local dining-out habits in the Pleasures and Pastimes section that follows each chapter introduction.

Credit Cards

The following abbreviations are used: **AE,** American Express; **DC,** Diners Club; **MC,** MasterCard; and **V,** Visa.

Don't Forget to Write

You can use this book in the confidence that all prices and opening times are based on information supplied to us at press time; Fodor's cannot accept responsibility for any errors. Time inevitably brings changes, so always confirm information when it matters—especially if you're making a detour to visit a specific place.

Were the restaurants we recommended as described? Did our hotel picks exceed your expectations? Did you find a museum we recommended a waste of time? Keeping a travel guide fresh and up-to-date is a big job, and we welcome your feedback, positive *and* negative. If you have complaints, we'll look into them and revise our entries when the facts warrant it. If you've discovered a special place that we haven't included, we'll pass the information along to our correspondents and have them check it out. So send us your thoughts via e-mail at editors@fodors.com (specifying the name of the book on the subject line) or on paper in care of the Eastern and Central Europe editor at Fodor's, 201 East 50th Street, New York, New York 10022. In the meantime, have a wonderful trip!

Karen Cure

Karen Cure
Editorial Director

Eastern and Central Europe

RUSSIA

LITHUANIA

★ Minsk

BELARUS

○ Białystok

✪ Warsaw

○ Radom   ○ Lublin

○ Rzeszów

○ Przemyśl   ○ L'vov

UKRAINE

Kiev ✪

ecen

ROMANIA   Suceava

Oradea   Piatra-Neamţ   Iaşi   MOLDOVA

Tîrgu Mureş   ★ Chişinău

Cluj-Napoca   Bacău   ○ Odessa

Arad   ○ Alba Iulia   Bîrlad

Timişoara   Sibiu   Braşov   Galaţi

Reşiţa   Buzău   Brăila

Piteşti   Ploieşti   Urziceni   Hîrşova

Turnu Severin   Bucharest ✪   Black Sea

LAVIA   Craiova   Constanţa

Giurgiu

Belogradčik   Ruse

Pleven   Šumen   Varna   N

Veliko Tărnovo   Kazanlăk

BULGARIA   Jambol   Burgas

Sofia ★   Plovdiv

Rila   Pazardžik   Bačkovo

✪ Skopje

MACEDONIA   TURKEY   ○ Istanbul

KEY
— Rail Lines

0 _____ 180 miles
0 _____ 270 km

SMART TRAVEL TIPS A TO Z

Basic Information on Traveling in Eastern and Central Europe, Savvy Tips to Make Your Trip a Breeze, and Companies and Organizations to Contact

AIR TRAVEL

BOOKING YOUR FLIGHT

Price is just one factor to consider when booking a flight: frequency of service and even a carrier's safety record are often just as important. Major airlines offer the greatest number of departures. Smaller airlines—including regional and no-frills airlines—usually have a limited number of flights daily. On the other hand, so-called low-cost airlines usually are cheaper, and their fares impose fewer restrictions, such as advance-purchase requirements. Safety-wise, low-cost carriers as a group have a good history—about equal to that of major carriers.

When you book, **look for nonstop flights** and **remember that "direct" flights stop at least once.** Try to **avoid connecting flights,** which require a change of plane. Two airlines may jointly operate a connecting flight, so ask if your airline operates every segment—you may find that your preferred carrier flies you only part of the way. International flights on a country's flag carrier are almost always nonstop; U.S. airlines often fly direct.

Ask your airline if it offers electronic ticketing, which eliminates all paperwork. There's no ticket to pick up or misplace. You go directly to the gate and give the agent your confirmation number. There's no worry about waiting in line at the airport while precious minutes tick by.

CARRIERS

When flying internationally, you must usually choose between a domestic carrier, the national flag carrier of the country you are visiting, and a foreign carrier from a third country. National flag carriers have the greatest number of nonstops. Domestic carriers may have better connections to your home town and serve a greater number of gateway cities. Third-party carriers may have a price advantage.

➤ MAJOR AIRLINES: **Continental** (☎ 800/231–0856). **Delta** (☎ 800/241–4141). **Northwest** (☎ 800/447–4747). **United** (☎ 800/538–2929). In most cases, a European co-carrier provides a connecting flight from a gateway in Europe. These European national airlines offer nonstop service from the United States to their own countries and connecting flights to others: Bulgaria: **Balkan Air** (☎ 212/573–5530). The Czech Republic: **Czech Airlines** (CSA; ☎ 212/765–6022). Hungary: **Malév Hungarian Airlines** (☎ 212/757–6446). Poland: **LOT Polish Airlines,** from New York, Newark, and Chicago (☎ 212/869–1074). Romania: **Tarom Romanian Airlines** (☎ 212/687–6013).

➤ FROM THE U.K.: **British Airways** (✉ 156 Regent St., London W1R 5TA, ☎ 0181/897–4000; outside London, 0345/222–111). **British Midland** (☎ 0345/554–554) flies daily to Prague and Warsaw.

➤ REGIONAL CARRIERS: **Czech Airlines** (☞ above; ☎ 02/2010–4310 in Prague) and **Balkan Air** (☞ above; ☎ 02/684-148 in Sofia) offer flights within Eastern and Central Europe from Prague and Sofia, respectively. **Malév Hungarian Airlines** (☞ *above;* in Budapest, ☎ 1/235–3535 or 06/80–212–121 toll free; 1/235–3804 [ticketing]) has regular nonstop flights between Budapest and major Eastern and Central European cities. **LOT** (☞ above; ☎ 22/953 or 22/952 in Warsaw) has flights between Polish cities and from Warsaw to many destinations in Eastern and Central Europe. **Tarom** (☞ *above;* ☎ 01/6594125 or 01/6150499 in Romania), the Romanian national airline, provides flights to most major cities within Romania and Eastern and Central European destinations.

CHARTERS

Charters usually have the lowest fares but are the least dependable. Departures are infrequent and seldom on time, flights can be delayed for up to 48 hours or can be canceled for any reason up to 10 days before you're scheduled to leave. Itineraries and prices can change after you've booked your flight.

In the U.S., the Department of Transportation's Aviation Consumer Protection Division has jurisdiction over charters and provides a certain degree of protection. The DOT requires that money paid to charter operators be held in escrow, so if you can't pay with a credit card, **always make your check payable to a charter carrier's escrow account.** The name of the bank should be in the charter contract. If you have any problems with a charter operator, contact the DOT (☞ Airline Complaints, *below*). If you buy a charter package that includes both air and land arrangements, remember that the escrow requirement applies only to the air component.

CONSOLIDATORS

Consolidators buy tickets for scheduled international flights at reduced rates from the airlines, then sell them at prices that beat the best fare available directly from the airlines, usually without restrictions. Sometimes you can even get your money back if you need to return the ticket. Carefully read the fine print detailing penalties for changes and cancellations, and **confirm your consolidator reservation with the airline.**

➤ CONSOLIDATORS: **Cheap Tickets** (☎ 800/377–1000). **Up & Away Travel** (☎ 212/889–2345). **Discount Travel Network** (☎ 800/576–1600). **Unitravel** (☎ 800/325–2222). **World Travel Network** (☎ 800/409–6753).

COURIERS

When you fly as a courier, you trade your checked-luggage space for a ticket deeply subsidized by a courier service. It's all perfectly legitimate, but there are restrictions: You can

usually book your flight only a week or two in advance, your length of stay may be set for a certain number of days, and you probably won't be able to book a companion on the same flight.

CUTTING COSTS

The least-expensive airfares to Eastern and Central Europe are priced for round-trip travel and usually must be purchased in advance. It's smart to **call a number of airlines, and when you are quoted a good price, book it on the spot**—the same fare may not be available the next day. Airlines generally allow you to change your return date for a fee. If you don't use your ticket, you can apply the cost toward the purchase of a new ticket, again for a small charge. However, most low-fare tickets are nonrefundable. To get the lowest airfare, **check different routings.** Compare prices of flights to and from different airports if your destination or home city has more than one gateway. Also price off-peak flights, which may be significantly less expensive.

Travel agents, especially those who specialize in finding the lowest fares (☞ Discounts & Deals, *below*), can be especially helpful when booking a plane ticket. When you're quoted a price, **ask your agent if the price is likely to get any lower.** Good agents know the seasonal fluctuations of airfares and can usually anticipate a sale or fare war. However, waiting can be risky: The fare could go *up* as seats become scarce, and you may wait so long that your preferred flight sells out. A wait-and-see strategy works best if your plans are flexible. If you must arrive and depart on certain dates, don't delay.

CHECK IN & BOARDING

Airlines routinely overbook planes, assuming that not everyone with a ticket will show up, but sometimes everyone does. When that happens, airlines ask for volunteers to give up their seats. In return these volunteers usually get a certificate for a free flight and are rebooked on the next flight out. If there are not enough volunteers, the airline must choose who will be denied boarding. The first to get bumped are passengers

THE GOLD GUIDE / SMART TRAVEL TIPS

who checked in late and those flying on discounted tickets, so **get to the gate and check in as early as possible,** especially during peak periods.

Although the trend on international flights is to drop reconfirmation requirements, many airlines still ask you to reconfirm each leg of your international itinerary. Failure to do so may result in your reservation being canceled.

Always **bring a government-issued photo ID to the airport.** You may be asked to show it before you are allowed to check in.

ENJOYING THE FLIGHT

For more legroom, **request an emergency-aisle seat.** Don't sit in the row in front of the emergency aisle or in front of a bulkhead, where seats may not recline.

If you don't like airline food, **ask for special meals when booking.** These can be vegetarian, low-cholesterol, or kosher, for example.

When flying internationally, try to maintain a normal routine, to help fight jet-lag. At night, **get some sleep.** By day, **eat light meals, drink water (not alcohol), and move around the cabin** to stretch your legs.

Many carriers have prohibited smoking on all of their international flights; others allow smoking only on certain routes or certain departures, so **contact your carrier regarding its smoking policy.**

HOW TO COMPLAIN

If your baggage goes astray or your flight goes awry, complain right away. Most carriers require that you **file a claim immediately.**

➤ AIRLINE COMPLAINTS: U.S. Department of Transportation **Aviation Consumer Protection Division** (✉ C-75, Room 4107, Washington, DC 20590, ☎ 202/366–2220). **Federal Aviation Administration Consumer Hotline** (☎ 800/322–7873).

AIRPORTS

For the best way to get between the airport and your destination, *see* Arriving and Departing in the A to Z section at the end of each country

chapter, or in the A to Z section of the city you are flying into.

➤ BULGARIA: All international flights use **Sofia Airport** (☎ 02/722–414 for domestic flight information; 02/720–672 or 02/876–612 for international flight information).

➤ CZECH REPUBLIC: **Ruzyně Airport** (☎ 4202/367814 for arrival and departure times) handles nearly all international flights.

➤ HUNGARY: Hungary's only commercial airport is **Budapest Ferihegy Repülőtér** (Budapest Ferihegy Airport; ☎ 1/296–9696, 1/296–7155 for same-day flight information).

➤ POLAND: Besides the capital's airport, **Warszawa International Airport** (☎ 022/650–30–00), Poland has several regional airports: **Gdańsk-Trojmiasto** (☎ 058/41-52-51); **Kraków-Balice** (☎ 012/411–19–55); **Poznań-ławica** (☎ 061/868-15-11); **Szczecin-Goleniów** (☎ 091/18-28-64); **Wrocław-Strachowice** (☎ 071/57-39-59).

➤ ROMANIA: Bucharest's **Otopeni Airport** (☎ 01/2300042) is used for most international flights; domestic flights go through nearby **Baneasa Airport** (☎ 01/2320020).

➤ SLOVAKIA: There are internal links from Bratislava's **M. R. Štefánik Airport** (☎ 07/5773353) to the **Košice Airport** (☎ 0956/221093).

BIKE TRAVEL

BIKES IN FLIGHT

Most airlines will accommodate bikes as luggage, provided they are dismantled and put into a box. Call to see if your airline sells bike boxes (about $5; bike bags are at least $100) although you can often pick them up free at bike shops. International travelers can sometimes substitute a bike for a piece of checked luggage for free; otherwise, it will cost about $100. Domestic and Canadian airlines charge a $25–$50 fee.

BOAT & FERRY TRAVEL

➤ BOAT CARRIERS: **MAHART Tours** (International Shipping Station, Belgrád rakpart, Budapest, ☎ 1/118–1704 or 1/118–1586; in Vienna,

43–1/729–2161 or 43–1/729–2162), Hungary's national shipping company, operates hydrofoils on the Danube between Budapest and Vienna, which make stops in Bratislava on advance order. **Polferries** (Polish Baltic Shipping Company, ☎ 022/830–00–97) and **Lion Ferry** (☎ 058/665-14-14) have regular passenger and car ferries between Denmark, Sweden and Poland. Hydrofoils of Slovenská plavba dunajská travel the Danube between Vienna and Bratislava, and Budapest and Bratislava. For reservations call **Slovenská plavba dunajská** in Bratislava (☎ 07/363522 or 07/5362226). **Polske Linie Oceaniczne** (Polish Ocean Lines, ☎ 022/629–28–95) will occasionally book you (and your car) onto cargo boats to and from Scandinavian or British ports. You can cruise between Black Sea resorts in Bulgaria, as well as to Romania and Turkey. In Sofia, **Balkantourist,** (✉ 1, bul. Vitosha, ☎ 02/43-331) can provide you with schedules and make reservations.

FERRIES

Ferries offer a pleasant and cheap mode of transportation to Eastern and Central Europe, although you have to be fairly close to your destination already to hop a Europe-bound ferry or hydrofoil. Flying into the appropriate hub, however, is an option. Water bookings connect Denmark and Sweden to eastern Germany, and Copenhagen, Denmark, to Świnoujście and Gdańsk, Poland. A hydrofoil shuttles visitors from Vienna to Bratislava, Slovakia, or Budapest, Hungary. For further country-specific information, *see* Arriving and Departing in the A to Z section in Budapest (Chapter 4); Gdańsk and the Northeast (Chapter 5), and the Poland A to Z section; the Black Sea Golden Coast (Chapter 6), and the Bulgaria A to Z section; and the Black Sea Coast and Danube Delta (Chapter 7).

In Hungary, ferries operate on the Danube River and on Lake Balaton. In Poland, you can take ferries or hydrofoils between various points on the Baltic coast, two of the more popular routes being Szczecin to Świnoujście, near the German border

on the coast; and Sopot to Hel, farther east near Gdańsk. Ferries also travel daily from Gdańsk to Helsinki and to Oxelösund, Sweden.

➤ FERRY LINES: **Hungary: MAHART Tours** (✉ V, Belgrád rakpart, ☎ 1/ 118–1704) in Budapest for information. **Poland: Polske Linie Oceaniczne** (Polish Ocean Lines, ☎ 022/629–28–95); **Orbis** in the Hotel Hevelius (✉ Ul. Heweliusa 22, Gdańsk, ☎ 058/301–45–44); **Polish Baltic Shipping Co.** (✉ Ul. Przemysłowa 1, Gdańsk, ☎ 058/343–18–87). **Slovakia: Slovenská plavba dunajská** (☎ 07/363522 or 07/5362226 for reservations) in Bratislava.

BUS TRAVEL

Bus travel is generally more costly than travel by train, although this varies by country. In some instances, especially where trains are largely local (and stop seemingly every 100 feet), buses are actually speedier than rail travel. Comfort is minimal, though; roads tend to be bumpy and seats lumpy. Buses are generally tidier; train bathrooms are notoriously rank. It's a bit of a gamble; seats on buses are a rarity during prime traveling hours, and drivers don't always stop where they should, although most leave punctually (especially when you're still waiting in line for a ticket). Comfort and fares vary drastically by nation.

See Arriving and Departing by Bus in the A to Z section at the end of each country chapter.

FROM THE U.K.

Unless you latch onto a real deal on airfare, a bus ticket from London's Victoria Terminal (☎ 0171/730–0202) is probably the cheapest transit from the United Kingdom to Eastern and Central Europe, although it may take a little research, as regularly scheduled routes to all cities except Berlin and Warsaw are practically nonexistent. Check newspaper ads for eastbound passage.

BUSINESS HOURS

For country-specific opening and closing times and business hours, *see* Opening and Closing Times in the A to Z section at the end of each country chapter.

THE GOLD GUIDE / SMART TRAVEL TIPS

CAMERAS & COMPUTERS

EQUIPMENT PRECAUTIONS

Always **keep your film, tape, or computer disks out of the sun.** Carry an extra supply of batteries, and **be prepared to turn on your camera, camcorder, or laptop** to prove to security personnel that the device is real. Always **ask for hand inspection of film,** which becomes clouded after successive exposure to airport X-ray machines, and **keep videotapes and computer disks away from metal detectors.**

➤ PHOTO HELP: **Kodak Information Center** (☎ 800/242–2424). *Kodak Guide to Shooting Great Travel Pictures,* available in bookstores or from Fodor's Travel Publications (☎ 800/533–6478; $16.50 plus $4 shipping).

CAR RENTAL

The big drawback here is price— rentals can rival airfare for the most expensive transport alternative. The pluses are a freewheeling itinerary and lots of luggage space. One restriction to keep in mind: Don't plan on renting a car in Western Europe and dropping it off in Eastern or Central Europe. Such one-way rentals are usually prohibited (or prohibitively expensive). For instance, most rental companies will not allow you to take a car over a border to Poland, because of the high risk of car theft.

➤ MAJOR AGENCIES: **Avis** (☎ 800/ 331–1084, 800/879–2847 in Canada, 008/225–533 in Australia). **Budget** (☎ 800/527–0700, 0800/ 181181 in the U.K.). **Dollar** (☎ 800/ 800–4000; 0990/565656 in the U.K., where it is known as Eurodollar). **Hertz** (☎ 800/654–3001, 800/ 263–0600 in Canada, 0345/555888 in the U.K., 03/9222–2523 in Australia, 03/358–6777 in New Zealand). **National InterRent** (☎ 800/227–3876; 0345/222525 in the U.K., where it is known as Europcar InterRent).

CUTTING COSTS

To get the best deal, **book through a travel agent who is willing to shop around.**

Also **ask your travel agent about a company's customer-service record.** How has the company responded to late plane arrivals and vehicle mishaps? Are there often lines at the rental counter? If you're traveling during a holiday period, does a confirmed reservation guarantee you a car?

Be sure to **look into wholesalers,** companies that do not own fleets but rent in bulk from those that do and often offer better rates than traditional car-rental operations. Prices are best during off-peak periods. Rentals booked through wholesalers must be paid for before you leave the United States.

➤ RENTAL WHOLESALERS: **Auto Europe** (☎ 207/842–2000 or 800/223– 5555, FAX 800–235–6321). **DER Travel Services** (✉ 9501 W. Devon Ave., Rosemont, IL 60018, ☎ 800/ 782–2424, FAX 800/282–7474 for information or 800/860–9944 for brochures). **Kemwel Holiday Autos** (☎ 914/835–5555 or 800/678– 0678, FAX 914/835–5126).

INSURANCE

When driving a rented car you are generally responsible for any damage to or loss of the vehicle. Before you rent, **see what coverage you already have** under the terms of your personal auto-insurance policy and credit cards.

Collision policies that car-rental companies sell for European rentals typically do not cover stolen vehicles. Before you buy additional coverage for theft, check with your credit-card company and personal auto insurance—you may already be covered.

REQUIREMENTS

In most Eastern and Central European countries, visitors need an International Driver's Permit; U.S. and Canadian citizens can obtain one from the American or Canadian Automobile Association, respectively. In some countries, such as Hungary and the Czech Republic, many car rental agencies will accept an international license, but the formal permit is technically required. In Romania, an International Driver's Permit is required for all drivers from outside the country for stays of more than 30 days.

SURCHARGES

Before you pick up a car in one city and leave it in another, **ask about drop-off charges or one-way service fees,** which can be substantial. Note, too, that some rental agencies charge extra if you return the car before the time specified in your contract. To avoid a hefty refueling fee, **fill the tank just before you turn in the car,** but be aware that gas stations near the rental outlet may overcharge.

CAR TRAVEL

The plus side of driving is an itinerary free from the constraints of bus and train schedules and lots of trunk room for extra baggage. The negatives are many, however (☞ Car Rental, *above*), not the least of which are shabbily maintained secondary roads, the risk of theft and vandalism, and difficulty finding gas. Crowded roads and fast and/or careless drivers add to the danger element, particularly in Poland. However, car travel does make it much easier to get to out-of-the-way monasteries and other sights not easily accessible by public transportation. Good road maps are usually available.

A word of caution: If you have any alcohol whatsoever in your body, do not drive. Penalties are fierce, and the blood-alcohol limit is practically zero. (In Hungary, it *is* zero.)

AUTO CLUBS

➤ IN EASTERN AND CENTRAL EUROPE: Czech Republic: **Autoturist** (✉ Na Rybníčku 16, Prague, ☎ 02/2491–1830). Hungary: **Hungarian Automobile Club** (✉ Budapest XIV, Francia út 38/B, ☎ 088). Poland: **Polish Motoring Association** (PZMot; ☎ 022/629–83–36). Romania: Automobil Clubul Roman (ACR; ✉ Str. Take Ionescu 27, Bucharest, ☎ 01/6507076, ℻ 01/3120434). Slovakia: **Auto-Moto-Klub** (✉ Račianska 71, Bratislava, ☎ 0820/140123).

➤ IN AUSTRALIA: **Australian Automobile Association** (☎ 06/247–7311).

➤ IN CANADA: **Canadian Automobile Association** (CAA, ☎ 613/247–0117).

➤ IN NEW ZEALAND: **New Zealand Automobile Association** (☎ 09/377–4660).

➤ IN THE U.K.: **Automobile Association** (AA, ☎ 0990/500–600), **Royal Automobile Club** (RAC, ☎ 0990/722–722 for membership, 0345/121–345 for insurance).

➤ IN THE U.S.: **American Automobile Association** (☎ 800/564–6222).

FROM THE U.K.

Theoretically it's possible to travel by car from the United Kingdom to Eastern and Central Europe, although it's really not recommended due to lack of parts and mechanical know-how. However, if you do choose to drive your own vehicle, don't leave home without the car registration, third-party insurance, driver's license, and (if you're not the car's owner) a notarized letter of permission from the owner. The vehicle must bear a country ID sticker.

The best ferry ports for Eastern and Central Europe are Rotterdam, Holland, or Ostende, Belgium, from which you drive to Cologne (Köln), Germany, and then through either Dresden or Frankfurt and on to Prague.

ROADS & GASOLINE

Eastern and Central Europe's main roads are built to a fairly high standard. There are now quite substantial stretches of highway on main routes, and a lot of rebuilding is being done. Gas stations are fewer than in the West, sited at intervals of about 48 kilometers (30 miles) along main routes and on the outskirts of large towns. Very few stations remain open after 9:30 PM. At least two grades of gasoline are sold in Eastern and Central European countries, usually 90–93 octane (regular) and 94–98 octane (super). Lead-free gasoline is now available in most gas stations in Bulgaria, the Czech Republic, Hungary, Poland, Romania, and Slovakia.

For additional country-specific information relating to roads, gasoline, and insurance, *see* Getting Around by Car in the A to Z section at the end of each country chapter.

ROAD MAPS

In Sofia, **Bulgaria,** maps are plentiful at street kiosks, and you can also find them at the Balkantourist main office (⊠ 1, Vitosha Bul., Sofia, ☎ 02/43-331). Outside the capital, the many Shell gas stations along the highway usually offer a good selection of road maps. In the **Czech Republic,** Čedok, the ubiquitous travel agency, is a good first stop for city maps. In Prague, the downstairs level of the Jan Kanzelsberger bookshop on Wenceslas Square (⊠ Václavské nám. 42, ☎ 02/2421–7335) has a good selection of hiking maps and auto atlases. In **Hungary,** good maps are sold at most large gas stations. In Budapest, the Globe Térképbolt (Globe Map Store; ⊠ VI, Bajcsy-Zsilinszky út 37, ☎ 1/312–6001) has an excellent supply of domestic and foreign maps. In **Poland,** check at large bookshops for driving maps; major hotels will also supply them, and all the modern gas stations have them. Esso driving maps are available at Esso gas stations and sometimes elsewhere. For maps of **Romania** check bookstores, travel agencies, and sidewalk vendors. They may also be obtained from the Romanian National Tourist Office (ONT) (☞ Visitor Information, below). In **Slovakia,** road maps are available at most gas stations. In Bratislava, the most convenient place selling road maps is Academia Bookstore (⊠ Štúrova 9, ☎ 07/368772).

CHILDREN & TRAVEL

CHILDREN IN EASTERN AND CENTRAL EUROPE

Be sure to plan ahead and **involve your youngsters** as you outline your trip. When packing, include things to keep them busy en route. On sightseeing days try to schedule activities of special interest to your children. If you are renting a car don't forget to **arrange for a car seat** when you reserve.

➤ SUGGESTED READING: *The Adventures of Mickey, Taggy, Pupo, and Cica and How They Discover Budapest,* by Kati Rekai (Canadian Stage Arts Publications, Toronto), is an animal fantasy story set in Budapest, written by a Hungarian-born author. *The Trumpeter of Krakow* by Eric P. Kelly is a delightful, Newbery medal book set in Kraków in the early Renaissance; though first published in 1928, it was reprinted in 1992. Intricate illustrations of Prague fill Czech-American Peter Sis' *The Three Golden Keys* (Doubleday); aimed at young readers, it evokes the city of the author's childhood.

FLYING

If your children are two or older, **ask about children's airfares.** As a general rule, infants under two not occupying a seat fly at greatly reduced fares or even for free.

In general the adult baggage allowance applies to children paying half or more of the adult fare. When booking, **ask about carry-on allowances for those traveling with infants.** In general, for babies charged 10% of the adult fare you are allowed one carry-on bag and a collapsible stroller, which may have to be checked; you may be limited to less if the flight is full.

Experts agree that it's a good idea to use safety seats aloft for children weighing less than 40 pounds. Airlines, however, can set their own policies: U.S. carriers allow FAA-approved models but usually require that you buy a ticket, even if your child would otherwise ride free, since the seats must be strapped into regular seats. Airline rules vary, so it's important to **check your airline's policy about using safety seats during takeoff and landing.** Safety seats cannot obstruct the movement of other passengers in the row, so get an appropriate seat assignment as early as possible.

When making your reservation, **request children's meals or a free-standing bassinet** if you need them; the latter are available only to those seated at the bulkhead, where there's enough legroom. Remember, however, that bulkhead seats may not have their own overhead bins, and there's no storage space in front of you—a major inconvenience.

GROUP TRAVEL

When planning to take your kids on a tour, look for companies that specialize in family travel.

➤ FAMILY-FRIENDLY TOUR OPERATORS: **Grandtravel** (✉ 6900 Wisconsin Ave., Suite 706, Chevy Chase, MD 20815, ☎ 301/986–0790 or 800/247–7651) for people traveling with grandchildren ages 7–17. **Families Welcome!** (✉ 92 N. Main St., Ashland, OR 97520, ☎ 541/482–6121 or 800/326–0724, FAX 541/482–0660).

HOTELS

Most hotels in Eastern and Central Europe allow children under a certain age to stay in their parents' room at no extra charge, but others charge them as extra adults; be sure to **ask about the cutoff age for children's discounts.**

The **Novotel** chain, which has hotels in Budapest, Warsaw, and five other Polish cities, allows up to two children under 12 to stay free in their parents' room. The same policy theoretically holds for Novotel branches in Sofia and Plovdiv in Bulgaria, but you will have to ask or even bargain. For Novotel branches in Poland, the cutoff age is 16. The **Budapest Hilton** has an unusual policy allowing children of any age—even middle-aged adults—to stay for free in their parents' room. In Bratislava, Slovakia, there are a few hotels with discounts, the Danube Hotel allows kids under 3 to stay free in their parents' room, and gives a 50% discount for children between 3 and 10. The Perugia Hotel will add a children's bed in the parents' room, charging an additional $30 for the entire stay.

Young visitors to the Czech Republic will enjoy staying at one of Prague's picturesque floating "botels." For further information contact Čedok (☞ Visitor Information, *below*).

➤ BEST CHOICES: **Novotel** (☎ 800/221–4542). **Budapest Hilton** (☎ 1/214–3000 in Budapest).

CONSUMER PROTECTION

Whenever possible, **pay with a major credit card** so you can cancel payment or get reimbursed if there's a problem, provided that you can provide documentation. This is the best way to pay, whether you're buying travel arrangements before your trip or shopping at your destination.

If you're doing business with a particular company for the first time, **contact your local Better Business Bureau and the attorney general's offices** in your state and the company's home state, as well. Have any complaints been filed?

Finally, if you're buying a package or tour, always **consider travel insurance** that includes default coverage (☞ Insurance, *below*).

➤ LOCAL BBBs: **Council of Better Business Bureaus** (✉ 4200 Wilson Blvd., Suite 800, Arlington, VA 22203, ☎ 703/276–0100, FAX 703/525–8277).

CUSTOMS & DUTIES

When shopping, **keep receipts** for all of your purchases. Upon reentering the country, **be ready to show customs officials what you've bought.** If you feel a duty is incorrect, appeal the assessment. If you object to the way your clearance was handled, get the inspector's badge number. In either case, first ask to see a supervisor, then write to the appropriate authorities, beginning with the port director at your point of entry.

IN EASTERN AND CENTRAL EUROPE

You may import duty-free into Slovakia, Hungary, Poland, or Bulgaria 250 cigarettes or the equivalent in tobacco, 1 liter of spirits, and 2 liters of wine (in Poland, ½ liter of spirits and 2 liters of wine). In addition to the above, you are permitted to import into Hungary gifts valued up to 27,000 Ft; into Poland, gifts valued at up to $200; into Slovakia, gifts valued at up to 1,000 Sk (approximately $30). You may import duty-free into the Czech Republic 200 cigarettes, 100 cigarillos, 250 grams of tobacco, or 50 cigars, 1 liter of spirits, and 2 liters of wine, as well as gifts and personal items valued at up to 3,000 Kč (about $85). On arrival in Romania, you may bring in a personal computer and printer, two cameras, 10 rolls of film, one small video camera and VCR, 10 videocassette tapes, one typewriter, binoculars, one radio/tape recorder, one small television set, one bicycle, one child's stroller, 200 cigarettes, 2 liters of liquor, and 4 liters of wine or beer. Gifts are permitted, though you may be charged duty on some electronic goods.

If you are bringing into any of these countries any valuables or foreign-made equipment from home, such as cameras, it's wise to carry the original receipts with you or register the items with U.S. Customs before you leave (Form 4457). Otherwise you could end up paying duty upon your return. When traveling to Romania and Bulgaria, you should declare video cameras, personal computers, and expensive jewelry upon arrival. Be aware that leaving the country without expensive items declared upon entering can present a huge hassle with airport police.

IN AUSTRALIA

Australia residents who are 18 or older may bring back A$400 worth of souvenirs and gifts (including jewelry), 250 cigarettes or 250 grams of tobacco, and 1,125 ml of alcohol (including wine, beer, and spirits). Residents under 18 may bring back A$200 worth of goods.

➤ INFORMATION: **Australian Customs Service** (Regional Director, ✉ Box 8, Sydney, NSW 2001, ☎ 02/9213–2000, FAX 02/9213–4000).

IN CANADA

Canadian residents who have been out of Canada for at least 7 days may bring in C$500 worth of goods duty-free. If you've been away less than 7 days but more than 48 hours, the duty-free allowance drops to C$200; if your trip lasts 24–48 hours, the allowance is C$50. You may not pool allowances with family members. Goods claimed under the C$500 exemption may follow you by mail; those claimed under the lesser exemptions must accompany you. Alcohol and tobacco products may be included in the 7-day and 48-hour exemptions but not in the 24-hour exemption. If you meet the age requirements of the province or territory through which you reenter Canada, you may bring in, duty-free, 1.14 liters (40 imperial ounces) of wine or liquor or 24 12-ounce cans or bottles of beer or ale. If you are 16 or

older you may bring in, duty-free, 200 cigarettes and 50 cigars.

You may send an unlimited number of gifts worth up to C$60 each duty-free to Canada. Label the package UNSOLICITED GIFT—VALUE UNDER $60. Alcohol and tobacco are excluded.

➤ INFORMATION: **Revenue Canada** (✉ 2265 St. Laurent Blvd. S, Ottawa, Ontario K1G 4K3, ☎ 613/993–0534, 800/461–9999 in Canada).

IN NEW ZEALAND

Although greeted with a "Haere Mai" ("Welcome to New Zealand"), home-ward-bound residents with goods to declare must present themselves for inspection. If you're 17 or older, you may bring back $700 worth of souvenirs and gifts. Your duty-free allowance also includes 4.5 liters of wine or beer; one 1,125-ml bottle of spirits; and either 200 cigarettes, 250 grams of tobacco, 50 cigars, or a combo of all three up to 250 grams.

➤ INFORMATION: **New Zealand Customs** (✉ Custom House, ✉ 50 Anzac Ave., Box 29, Auckland, New Zealand, ☎ 09/359–6655, ☎ 09/309–2978).

IN THE U.K.

From countries outside the EU, including those covered in this book, you may import, duty-free, 200 cigarettes or 50 cigars; 1 liter of spirits or 2 liters of fortified or sparkling wine or liqueurs; 2 liters of still table wine; 60 milliliters of perfume; 250 milliliters of toilet water; plus £136 worth of other goods, including gifts and souvenirs.

➤ INFORMATION: **HM Customs and Excise** (✉ Dorset House, ✉ Stamford St., London SE1 9NG, ☎ 0171/202–4227).

IN THE U.S.

U.S. residents may bring home $400 worth of foreign goods duty-free if they've been out of the country for at least 48 hours (and if they haven't used the $400 allowance or any part of it in the past 30 days).

U.S. residents 21 and older may bring back 1 liter of alcohol duty-free. In addition, regardless of your age, you are allowed 200 cigarettes and 100 non-Cuban cigars. Antiques, which the U.S. Customs Service defines as objects more than 100 years old, enter duty-free, as do original works of art done entirely by hand, including paintings, drawings, and sculptures.

You may also send packages home duty-free: up to $200 worth of goods for personal use, with a limit of one parcel per addressee per day (and no alcohol or tobacco products or perfume worth more than $5); label the package PERSONAL USE, and attach a list of its contents and their retail value. Do not label the package UNSOLICITED GIFT, or your duty-free exemption will drop to $100. Mailed items do not affect your duty-free allowance on your return.

➤ INFORMATION: **U.S. Customs Service** (Inquiries, ✉ Box 7407, Washington, DC 20044, ☎ 202/927–6724; complaints, Office of Regulations and Rulings, ✉ 1301 Constitution Ave. NW, Washington, DC 20229; registration of equipment, Resource Management, ✉ 1301 Constitution Ave. NW, Washington DC 20229, ☎ 202/927–0540).

DINING

For country-specific dining information, *see* Dining *in* Pleasures and Pastimes at the beginning of each country chapter. Additional city-specific dining information may also be found at the start of a city's dining listings.

DISABILITIES & ACCESSIBILITY

ACCESS IN EASTERN AND CENTRAL EUROPE

Provisions for travelers with disabilities in Eastern and Central Europe are extremely limited; probably the best solution is to travel with a nondisabled companion. While many hotels, especially large American or international chains, offer some wheelchair-accessible rooms, special facilities at museums, restaurants, and on public transportation are difficult to find. In Poland wheelchairs are available at all airports, and most trains have special seats designated for people with disabilities, but it is wise to notify ahead. Generally speaking, neither Bulgaria nor Romania is very friendly toward travelers with disabilities.

Some of the newer hotels are wheelchair accessible, but beyond that, a traveler with a disability will have a difficult time here.

➤ LOCAL RESOURCES: Visitors to the Czech Republic may contact **Sdružení zdravotné postižených** (Association of Disabled Persons; ✉ Karlínské nám. 12, Prague 8, ☎ 02/2481–5915). In Hungary, contact the **Mozgáskorlátozottak Egyesületeinek Országos Szövetsége** (National Association of People with Mobility Impairments, or MEOSZ; ✉ 1032 Budapest, San Marco u. 76, ☎ 1/388–8951) for information on special services and accommodations. In Slovakia, contact **Slovenský zväz telesne postihnutých** (Slovak Association of People with Mobility Impairments; ✉ Bratislava, Jakubovo nám. 12, ☎ 07/363284), which can provide information in a foreign language only through an interpreter ordered in advance.

MAKING RESERVATIONS

When discussing accessibility with an operator or reservations agent, **ask hard questions.** Are there any stairs, inside *or* out? Are there grab bars next to the toilet *and* in the shower/tub? How wide is the doorway to the room? To the bathroom? For the most extensive facilities meeting the latest legal specifications, **opt for newer accommodations,** which are more likely to have been designed with access in mind. Older buildings or ships may have more limited facilities. Be sure to **discuss your needs before booking.**

TRANSPORTATION

➤ COMPLAINTS: **Disability Rights Section** (✉ U.S. Department of Justice, Civil Rights Division, ✉ Box 66738, Washington, DC 20035–6738, ☎ 202/514–0301 or 800/514–0301, TTY 202/514–0383 or 800/514–0383, FAX 202/307–1198) for general complaints. **Aviation Consumer Protection Division** (☞ Air Travel, *above*) for airline-related problems. **Civil Rights Office** (✉ U.S. Department of Transportation, Departmental Office of Civil Rights, S-30, ✉ 400 7th St. SW, Room 10215, Washington, DC, 20590, ☎ 202/366–4648, FAX 202/366–9371) for problems with surface transportation.

THE GOLD GUIDE / SMART TRAVEL TIPS

TRAVEL AGENCIES & TOUR OPERATORS

As a whole, the travel industry has become more aware of the needs of travelers with disabilities. In the U.S., the Americans with Disabilities Act requires that travel firms serve the needs of all travelers. Note, though, that some agencies and operators specialize in making travel arrangements for individuals and groups with disabilities.

➤ TRAVELERS WITH MOBILITY PROBLEMS: **Access Adventures** (✉ 206 Chestnut Ridge Rd., Rochester, NY 14624, ☎ 716/889–9096), run by a former physical-rehabilitation counselor. **Flying Wheels Travel** (✉ 143 W. Bridge St., Box 382, Owatonna, MN 55060, ☎ 507/451–5005 or 800/535–6790, FAX 507/451–1685), a travel agency specializing in customized tours and itineraries worldwide. **Hinsdale Travel Service** (✉ 201 E. Ogden Ave., Suite 100, Hinsdale, IL 60521, ☎ 630/325–1335), a travel agency that benefits from the advice of wheelchair traveler Janice Perkins.

DISCOUNTS & DEALS

Be a smart shopper and **compare all your options** before making any choice. A plane ticket bought with a promotional coupon may not be cheaper than the least expensive fare from a discount ticket agency. For high-price travel purchases, such as packages or tours, keep in mind that what you get is just as important as what you save. Just because something is cheap doesn't mean it's a bargain.

CLUBS & COUPONS

Many companies sell discounts in the form of travel clubs and coupon books, but these cost money. You must use participating advertisers to get a deal, and only after you recoup the initial membership cost or book price do you begin to save. If you plan to use the club or coupons frequently, you may save considerably. Before signing up, find out what discounts you get for free.

➤ DISCOUNT CLUBS: **Entertainment Travel Editions** (✉ 2125 Butterfield Rd., Troy, MI 48084, ☎ 800/445–4137; $20–$51, depending on destination). **Great American Traveler** (✉ Box 27965, Salt Lake City, UT 84127, ☎ 801/974–3033 or 800/548–2812; $49.95 per year). **Moment's Notice Discount Travel Club** (✉ 7301 New Utrecht Ave., Brooklyn, NY 11204, ☎ 718/234–6295; $25 per year, single or family). **Privilege Card International** (✉ 237 E. Front St., Youngstown, OH 44503, ☎ 330/746–5211 or 800/236–9732; $74.95 per year). **Sears's Mature Outlook** (✉ Box 9390, Des Moines, IA 50306, ☎ 800/336–6330; $19.95 per year). **Travelers Advantage** (✉ CUC Travel Service, ✉ 3033 S. Parker Rd., Suite 1000, Aurora, CO 80014, ☎ 800/548–1116 or 800/648–4037; $59.95 per year, single or family). **Worldwide Discount Travel Club** (✉ 1674 Meridian Ave., Miami Beach, FL 33139, ☎ 305/534–2082; $50 per year family, $40 single).

CREDIT-CARD BENEFITS

When you use your credit card to make travel purchases you may get free travel-accident insurance, collision-damage insurance, and medical or legal assistance, depending on the card and the bank that issued it. American Express, MasterCard, and Visa provide one or more of these services, so **get a copy of your credit card's travel-benefits policy.** If you are a member of an auto club, always **ask hotel and car-rental reservations agents about auto-club discounts.** Some clubs offer additional discounts on tours, cruises, and admission to attractions.

DISCOUNT RESERVATIONS

To save money, **look into discount-reservations services** with toll-free numbers, which use their buying power to get a better price on hotels, airline tickets, even car rentals. When booking a room, always **call the hotel's local toll-free number** (if one is available) rather than the central reservations number—you'll often get a better price. Always ask about special packages or corporate rates.

When shopping for the best deal on hotels and car rentals, **look for guaranteed exchange rates,** which protect you against a falling dollar. With your rate locked in, you won't pay more, even if the price goes up in the local currency.

➤ AIRLINE TICKETS: ☎ 800/FLY–4–LESS.

➤ HOTEL ROOMS: **Hotels Plus** (☎ 800/235–0909). **International Marketing & Travel Concepts** (☎ 800/790–4682). **Steigenberger Reservation Service** (☎ 800/223–5652). **Travel Interlink** (☎ 800/888–5898).

PACKAGE DEALS

Packages and guided tours can save you money, but don't confuse the two. When you buy a package, your travel remains independent, just as though you had planned and booked the trip yourself. Fly/drive packages, which combine airfare and car rental, are often a good deal. If you **buy a rail/drive pass,** you'll save on train tickets and car rentals. All Eurail- and Europass holders get a discount on Eurostar fares through the Channel Tunnel.

ELECTRICITY

To use your U.S.-purchased electric-powered equipment, **bring a converter and adapter.** The electrical current in Eastern and Central Europe is 220 volts, 50 cycles alternating current (AC); wall outlets generally take plugs with two round prongs.

If your appliances are dual-voltage, you'll need only an adapter. Don't use 110-volt outlets, marked FOR SHAVERS ONLY, for high-wattage appliances such as blow-dryers. Most laptops operate equally well on 110 and 220 volts and so require only an adapter.

EMERGENCIES

For country-specific emergency numbers, *see* Emergencies in the A to Z section at the end of each country chapter. For medical emergency contacts, *see also* Health, *below.*

GAY & LESBIAN TRAVEL

Throughout Eastern and Central Europe, gay and lesbian resources are thin on the ground, if not underground. While the level of tolerance varies, the region is generally conservative; strongly Catholic countries are the most intolerant.

The **Czech Republic** is one of the most liberal countries. Prague fosters a growing gay and lesbian scene; the English-language *Prague Post* includes gay and lesbian clubs in its regular club listings. **Hungary** is also relatively open-minded, though even in Budapest, the gay population keeps a fairly low profile. Budapest's thermal baths are popular meeting places, as are the city's several gay bars and clubs, which you can find listed in English-language newspapers and the monthly magazine, *Mások.*

Though gays and lesbians are gaining acceptance in **Bulgaria,** they do not have any national organizations. Social steps towards acceptance are quite new; the first openly gay disco opened in Sofia in 1997. In general, attitudes towards homosexuality throughout the Bulgarian interior are hostile, while at the more cosmopolitan Black Sea coast resorts people tend to be more open-minded. Gay and lesbian organization is a relatively new thing in **Poland,** and clubs and meeting points change addresses frequently. One of the longest-standing gay organizations is Lambda. In **Slovakia** resources are limited; the Ganymedes hotline (☎ 0905/618291) operates on Tuesdays and Thursdays from 6–8 PM.

In **Romania,** homosexuality is considered illegal; any meeting places or groups are highly secretive.

➤ LOCAL RESOURCES: In **Budapest,** *Budapest Week* and the *Budapest Sun,* both English-language weekly newspapers, include gay clubs in their nightlife listings; *Mások* is a monthly gay magazine in Hungarian that may be helpful as well. In **Poland,** contact Lambda (✉ Ul. Śniadeckich 1/15, Warszawa, ☎ 022/628–52–22).

➤ GAY- AND LESBIAN-FRIENDLY TRAVEL AGENCIES: **Corniche Travel** (✉ 8721 Sunset Blvd., Suite 200, West Hollywood, CA 90069, ☎ 310/854–6000 or 800/429–8747, FAX 310/659–7441). **Islanders Kennedy Travel** (✉ 183 W. 10th St., New York, NY 10014, ☎ 212/242–3222 or 800/988–1181, FAX 212/929–8530). **Now Voyager** (✉ 4406 18th St., San Francisco, CA 94114, ☎ 415/626–1169 or 800/255–6951,

FAX 415/626–8626). **Yellowbrick Road** (✉ 1500 W. Balmoral Ave., Chicago, IL 60640, ☎ 773/561–1800 or 800/642–2488, FAX 773/561–4497). **Skylink Travel and Tour** (✉ 3577 Moorland Ave., Santa Rosa, CA 95407, ☎ 707/585–8355 or 800/225–5759, FAX 707/584–5637), serving lesbian travelers.

HEALTH

You may gain weight, but there are few other serious health hazards for the traveler in Eastern and Central Europe. Tap water tastes bad but is generally drinkable; when it runs rusty out of the tap or the aroma of chlorine is overpowering, it might help to have some iodine tablets or bottled water handy. Vegetarians and those on special diets may have a problem with the heavy local cuisine, which is based almost exclusively on pork and beef. To prevent your vitamin intake from dropping to danger levels, buy fresh fruits and vegetables at seasonal street markets—regular grocery stores often don't sell them. Milk in Romania or Bulgaria may not be pasteurized and can make Westerners sick; stick to cheese to satisfy calcium cravings. In Bulgaria, mayonnaise-based salads are very common; avoid them, especially any mayonnaise-based products served from street kiosks.

No vaccinations are required for entry into any of the Eastern and Central European countries covered in this book, but selective vaccinations are recommended. Those traveling in forested areas of most Eastern and Central European countries should consider vaccinating themselves against Central European, or tick-borne, encephalitis. Tick-borne Lyme disease is also a risk in the Czech Republic. If you plan to travel for an extended period of time in rural Bulgaria, it is a good idea to consider a vaccination for hepatitis spread through food and water. Schedule vaccinations well in advance of departure because some require several doses, and others may cause uncomfortable side effects.

To avoid problems clearing customs, diabetic travelers carrying needles and syringes should have on hand a letter from their physician confirming their need for insulin injections.

In Romania you should avoid drinking tap water, as it is often contaminated with such things as cholera. When traveling with children, be especially cautious, as there is a heavy lead content. In Bulgaria and Poland, faulty plumbing, especially in cities, ruins the water quality. Buy bottled water, particularly if staying in an older home or a hotel.

➤ EMERGENCY CONTACTS: In Sofia, **Bulgaria,** the Pirogov Accident and Emergency Hospital (✉ Tsar Boris, 3rd Bul., ☎ 150 for an ambulance) has English speaking doctors in the crisis center. In the **Czech Republic,** the best resources are in Prague, including the Foreigners' Department of Na Homolce Hospital (✉ Roentgenova 2, ☎ 02/5292–2146 weekdays, 02/5721–1111 or 02/5292–2191 evenings and weekends); First Medical Clinic of Prague (✉ Vyšehradská 35, ☎ 02/292–286, 2421–6200, or 02/0601–225050 24-hr emergency mobile phone); American Medical Center (✉ Janovského 48, ☎ 02/807–756 weekdays). In Warsaw, **Poland,** the American Medical Center (☎ 022/622–74–55) is open 24 hours a day. Medical care in **Romania** is still not up to Western expectations, though there are a few Western-style facilities in Bucharest (☞ Emergencies *in* Bucharest A to Z). You should look into evacuation insurance; your private health provider can usually make a recommendation. For minor difficulties your embassy or consulate may be able to help you. For an emergency in Bratislava, **Slovakia,** you can call (☎ 07/394949), but it's not always possible to find a doctor who speaks English.

MEDICAL PLANS

No one plans to get sick while traveling, but it happens, so **consider signing up with a medical-assistance company.** Members get doctor referrals, emergency evacuation or repatriation, 24-hour telephone hot lines for medical consultation, cash for emergencies, and other personal and legal assistance. Coverage varies by plan, so **review the benefits of each carefully.**

➤ MEDICAL-ASSISTANCE COMPANIES:
International SOS Assistance (✉ 8
Neshaminy Interplex, Suite 207,
Trevose, PA 19053, ☎ 215/245–
4707 or 800/523–6586, FAX 215/
244–9617; ✉ 12 Chemin Riant-
bosson, 1217 Meyrin 1, Geneva,
Switzerland, ☎ 4122/785–6464,
FAX 4122/785–6424; ✉ 10 Anson
Rd., 14-07/08 International Plaza,
Singapore, 079903, ☎ 65/226–3936,
FAX 65/226–3937).

HOLIDAYS

For country-specific holidays, *see*
National Holidays in the A to Z
section at the end of each country
chapter.

INSURANCE

Travel insurance is the best way to
protect yourself against financial loss.
The most useful plan is a comprehensive policy that includes coverage for
trip cancellation and interruption,
default, trip delay, and medical expenses (with a waiver for preexisting
conditions).

Without insurance, you will lose all
or most of your money if you cancel
your trip, regardless of the reason.
Default insurance covers you if your
tour operator, airline, or cruise line
goes out of business. Trip-delay
covers unforeseen expenses that you
may incur due to bad weather or
mechanical delays. It's important to
compare the fine print regarding trip-
delay coverage when comparing
policies.

For overseas travel, one of the most
important components of travel
insurance is its medical coverage.
Supplemental health insurance will
pick up the cost of your medical bills
should you get sick or injured while
traveling. U.S. residents should note
that Medicare generally does not
cover health-care costs outside the
United States, nor do many privately
issued policies. Residents of the
United Kingdom can buy an annual
travel-insurance policy valid for most
vacations taken during the year in
which the coverage is purchased. If
you are pregnant or have a preexisting condition, make sure you're
covered. British citizens should buy
extra medical coverage when travel-

ing overseas, according to the Association of British Insurers. Australian
travelers should buy travel insurance,
including extra medical coverage,
whenever they go abroad, according
to the Insurance Council of Australia.

Always **buy travel insurance directly
from the insurance company;** if you
buy it from a cruise line, airline, or
tour operator that goes out of business you probably will not be covered
for the agency or operator's default, a
major risk. Before you make any
purchase, **review your existing health
and home-owner's policies** to find out
whether they cover expenses incurred
while traveling.

➤ TRAVEL INSURERS: In the U.S., **Access
America** (✉ 6600 W. Broad St., Richmond, VA 23230, ☎ 804/285–3300
or 800/284–8300). **Travel Guard
International** (✉ 1145 Clark St.,
Stevens Point, WI 54481, ☎ 715/345–
0505 or 800/826–1300). In Canada,
Mutual of Omaha (✉ Travel Division,
✉ 500 University Ave., Toronto,
Ontario M5G 1V8, ☎ 416/598–
4083, 800/268–8825 in Canada).

➤ INSURANCE INFORMATION: In the
U.K., **Association of British Insurers**
(✉ 51 Gresham St., London EC2V
/HQ, ☎ 0171/600–3333). In Australia, the **Insurance Council of Australia** (☎ 613/9614–1077, FAX 613/
9614–7924).

LANGUAGE

For country-specific information
about language issues, *see* Language
in the A to Z section at the end of
each country chapter.

LODGING

If your experience of Eastern and
Central European hotels is limited to
capital cities such as Prague and
Budapest, you may be pleasantly
surprised. There are baroque mansions turned guest houses and elegant
high-rise resorts, not to mention bed-
and-breakfast inns presided over by
matronly babushkas. Many facilities
throughout the region are being
upgraded.

Outside major cities, hotels and inns
are more rustic than elegant. Standards of service generally do not
suffer, but in most rural areas the

definition of "luxury" includes little more than a television and a private bathroom. In some instances, you may have no choice but to stay in one of the cement high-rise hotels that scar skylines from Poland to the Czech Republic. Huge, impersonal, concrete hotels are part of the Communist legacy, and it may take a few more years to exorcise or "beautify" these ubiquitous monsters. However, even in Bulgaria, where changes are very slow, new, luxurious hotels can be found in most regions of the country, if you're willing to pay Western prices.

In rural Eastern and Central Europe, you may have difficulty parting with more than $25–$30 per night for lodgings. Reservations are vital if you plan to visit Prague, Budapest, Warsaw, or most other major cities during the summer season. Reservations are a good idea but aren't imperative if you plan to strike out into the countryside.

For country-specific lodging information, *see* Lodging *in* Pleasures and Pastimes at the beginning of each country chapter. Additional city-specific lodging information may also be found at the start of a city's lodging listings.

APARTMENT & VILLA RENTALS

If you want a home base that's roomy enough for a family and comes with cooking facilities, **consider a furnished rental.** These can save you money, especially if you're traveling with a large group of people. Home-exchange directories list rentals (often second homes owned by prospective house swappers), and some services search for a house or apartment for you (even a castle if that's your fancy) and handle the paperwork. Some send an illustrated catalog; others send photographs only of specific properties, sometimes at a charge. Up-front registration fees may apply.

➤ RENTAL AGENTS: **Europa-Let/Tropical Inn-Let** (⊠ 92 N. Main St., Ashland, OR 97520, ☎ 541/482–5806 or 800/462–4486, ℻ 541/482–0660). **Interhome** (⊠ 124 Little Falls Rd., Fairfield, NJ 07004, ☎ 973/882–6864 or 800/882–6864, ℻ 973/

808–1742). **Property Rentals International** (⊠ 1008 Mansfield Crossing Rd., Richmond, VA 23236, ☎ 804/378–6054 or 800/220–3332, ℻ 804/379–2073). **Rent-a-Home International** (⊠ 7200 34th Ave. NW, Seattle, WA 98117, ☎ 206/789–9377 or 800/488–7368, ℻ 206/789–9379). **Hideaways International** (⊠ 767 Islington St., Portsmouth, NH 03801, ☎ 603/430–4433 or 800/843–4433, ℻ 603/430–4444; membership $99) is a club for travelers who arrange rentals among themselves.

HOSTELS

No matter what your age, you can **save on lodging costs by staying at hostels.** In some 5,000 locations in more than 70 countries around the world, Hostelling International (HI), the umbrella group for a number of national youth hostel associations, offers single-sex, dorm-style beds and, at many hostels, "couples" rooms and family accommodations. Membership in any HI national hostel association, open to travelers of all ages, allows you to stay in HI-affiliated hostels at member rates (one-year membership is about $25 for adults; hostels run about $10–$25 per night). Members also have priority if the hostel is full; they're eligible for discounts around the world, even on rail and bus travel in some countries.

➤ HOSTEL ORGANIZATIONS: **Hostelling International—American Youth Hostels** (⊠ 733 15th St. NW, Suite 840, Washington, DC 20005, ☎ 202/783–6161, ℻ 202/783–6171). **Hostelling International—Canada** (⊠ 400-205 Catherine St., Ottawa, Ontario K2P 1C3, ☎ 613/237–7884, ℻ 613/237–7868). **Youth Hostel Association of England and Wales** (⊠ Trevelyan House, ⊠ 8 St. Stephen's Hill, St. Albans, Hertfordshire AL1 2DY, ☎ 01727/855215 or 01727/845047, ℻ 01727/844126); membership in the U.S. $25, in Canada C$26.75, in the U.K. £9.30).

MAIL

For country-specific mail information, *see* Mail in the A to Z section at the end of each country chapter.

MONEY

COSTS & CURRENCY

For country-specific money information, *see* Money and Expenses in the A to Z section at the end of each country chapter.

CREDIT & DEBIT CARDS

Should you use a credit card or a debit card when traveling? Both have benefits. A credit card allows you to delay payment and gives you certain rights as a consumer (☞ Consumer Protection, *above*). A debit card, also known as a check card, deducts funds directly from your checking account and helps you stay within your budget. When you want to rent a car, though, you may still need an old-fashioned credit card. Although you can always *pay* for your car with a debit card, some agencies will not allow you to *reserve* a car with a debit card.

Otherwise, the two types of plastic are virtually the same. Both will get you cash advances at ATMs worldwide if your card is properly programmed with your personal identification number (PIN). For use in Eastern Europe, your PIN must be four digits long. Both offer excellent, wholesale exchange rates. And both protect you against unauthorized use if the card is lost or stolen. Your liability is limited to $50, as long as you report the card missing.

➤ ATM LOCATIONS: Cirrus (☎ 800/424–7787). Plus (☎ 800/843–7587) for locations in the U.S. and Canada, or visit your local bank.

EXCHANGING MONEY

In many Eastern and Central European countries, you should **change money at banks** for the most favorable exchange rate. Although fees charged for ATM transactions may be higher abroad than at home, Cirrus and Plus exchange rates are excellent, because they are based on wholesale rates offered only by major banks. You often won't do as well at exchange booths in airports or rail and bus stations, in hotels, in restaurants, or in stores, although you may find their hours more convenient. Romania is an exception; exchange bureaus

have the best rates, especially in Bucharest. In Bulgaria, many banks are temporarily closed; you'll have to rely on the exchange bureaus, which generally have good rates and don't charge a commission. To avoid lines at airport exchange booths, **get a bit of local currency before you leave home.**

➤ EXCHANGE SERVICES: Chase *Currency To Go* (☎ 800/935–9935; 935–9935 in NY, NJ, and CT). International Currency Express (☎ 888/842–0880 on the East Coast, 888/278–6628 on the West Coast). Thomas Cook Currency Services (☎ 800/287–7362 for telephone orders and retail locations).

TRAVELER'S CHECKS

Do you need traveler's checks? It depends on where you're headed. The general rule is: If you're going to rural areas and small towns, go with cash; traveler's checks are best used in cities. However, traveler's checks are virtually useless in Bulgaria, and are rarely accepted in Romania.

Lost or stolen checks can usually be replaced within 24 hours. To ensure a speedy refund, buy your own traveler's checks—don't let someone else pay for them: irregularities like this can cause delays. The person who bought the checks should make the call to request a refund.

PACKING

LUGGAGE

How many carry-on bags you can bring with you is up to the airline. Most allow two, but the limit is often reduced to one on certain flights. Gate agents will take excess baggage—including bags they deem oversize—from you as you board and add it to checked luggage. To avoid this situation, make sure that everything you carry aboard will fit under your seat. Also, get to the gate early, and request a seat at the back of the plane; you'll probably board first, while the overhead bins are still empty. Since big, bulky baggage attracts the attention of gate agents and flight attendants on a busy flight, make sure your carry-on is really a carry-on. Finally, a carry-on that's long and narrow is more likely to remain unnoticed than one that's wide and squarish.

If you are flying internationally, note that baggage allowances may be determined not by piece but by weight—generally 88 pounds (40 kilograms) in first class, 66 pounds (30 kilograms) in business class, and 44 pounds (20 kilograms) in economy.

Airline liability for baggage is limited to $1,250 per person on flights within the United States. On international flights it amounts to $9.07 per pound or $20 per kilogram for checked baggage (roughly $640 per 70-pound bag) and $400 per passenger for unchecked baggage. You can buy additional coverage at check-in for about $10 per $1,000 of coverage, but it excludes a rather extensive list of items, shown on your airline ticket.

Before departure, **itemize your bags' contents** and their worth, and label the bags with your name, address, and phone number. (If you use your home address, cover it so that potential thieves can't see it readily.) Inside each bag, **pack a copy of your itinerary.** At check-in, **make sure that each bag is correctly tagged** with the destination airport's three-letter code. If your bags arrive damaged or fail to arrive at all, file a written report with the airline before leaving the airport.

PACKING LIST

Don't worry about packing lots of formal clothing. Fashion was all but nonexistent under 40 years of Communist rule, although residents of Budapest, Prague, and even Bucharest—catching up with their counterparts in other European capitals—are considerably more fashionably dressed than even a few years ago. Still, Western dress of virtually any kind is considered stylish: A sports jacket for men and a dress or pants for women are appropriate for an evening out. Everywhere else, you'll feel comfortable in casual pants or jeans.

Eastern and Central Europe enjoy all the extremes of an inland climate, so plan accordingly. In the higher elevations winter can last until April, and even in summer the evenings will be on the cool side.

Many areas are best seen on foot, so take a pair of sturdy walking shoes and be prepared to use them. High heels will present considerable problems on the cobblestone streets of Prague, Sofia, Warsaw, and towns in Hungary, or the potholed streets in Romania. If you plan to visit the mountains, make sure your shoes have good traction and ankle support, as some trails can be quite challenging.

Some items that you take for granted at home are occasionally unavailable or of questionable quality in Eastern and Central Europe, though the situation has been steadily improving. Toiletries and personal-hygiene products have become relatively easy to find, but it's always a good idea to bring necessities when traveling in rural areas. If you're heading to Bulgaria, make sure you have a flashlight with you at all times. Streetlights are rare, even in city centers, and often interior hallways are unlit.

In your carry-on luggage **bring an extra pair of eyeglasses or contact lenses** and **enough of any medication you take** to last the entire trip. You may also want your doctor to write a spare prescription using the drug's generic name, since brand names may vary from country to country. **Never put prescription drugs or valuables in luggage to be checked.** To avoid customs delays, carry medications in their original packaging. And don't forget to copy down and carry addresses of offices that handle refunds of lost traveler's checks.

PASSPORTS & VISAS

When traveling internationally, **carry a passport even if you don't need one** (it's always the best form of I.D.), and make **two photocopies of the data page** (one for someone at home and another for you, carried separately from your passport). If you lose your passport, promptly call the nearest embassy or consulate and the local police.

ENTERING EASTERN AND CENTRAL EUROPE

➤ AUSTRALIANS: Australian citizens need a visa and a valid passport to visit Bulgaria, the Czech Republic,

Hungary, Poland, Romania and Slovakia.

➤ CANADIANS: You need a valid passport to enter Romania for stays of up to 30 days, to enter Bulgaria, Hungary, Slovakia, and Poland for stays of up to 90 days, and to enter the Czech Republic for stays up to six months. Canadians also need a visa to enter Romania; these can be obtained at the border or at Canadian embassies or consulates.

➤ U.K. CITIZENS: Citizens of the United Kingdom need a valid passport to enter Bulgaria, Hungary, and Poland for stays of up to 90 days, and to enter the Czech Republic and Slovakia for stays up to six months. To enter Romania, you must have both a valid passport and a visa. EC citizens no longer require a visa to enter Bulgaria.

➤ NEW ZEALAND CITIZENS: New Zealand citizens need a valid passport to enter the Czech Republic for stays of up to one month; for travel to Bulgaria, Romania, Hungary, Poland and Slovakia you must have both a visa and a passport.

➤ U.S. CITIZENS: All U.S. citizens, even infants, need a valid passport to enter Bulgaria, the Czech Republic, Romania, or Slovakia for stays of up to 30 days, and to enter Hungary or Poland for stays of up to 90 days. U.S. citizens must pay an entry tax of $23 to enter Bulgaria.

PASSPORT OFFICES

The best time to apply for a passport or to renew is during the fall and winter. Before any trip, be sure to check your passport's expiration date and, if necessary, renew it as soon as possible. (Some countries won't allow you to enter on a passport that's due to expire in six months or less.)

➤ AUSTRALIAN CITIZENS: **Australian Passport Office** (☎ 131–232).

➤ CANADIAN CITIZENS: **Passport Office** (☎ 819/994–3500 or 800/567–6868).

➤ NEW ZEALAND CITIZENS: **New Zealand Passport Office** (☎ 04/494–0700 for information on how to apply, 0800/727–776 for information on applications already submitted).

➤ U.K. CITIZENS: **London Passport Office** (☎ 0990/21010), for fees and documentation requirements and to request an emergency passport.

➤ U.S. CITIZENS: **National Passport Information Center** (☎ 900/225–5674; calls are charged at 35¢ per minute for automated service, $1.05 per minute for operator service).

SAFETY

Crime rates are still relatively low in Eastern and Central Europe, but travelers should beware of pickpockets in crowded areas, especially on public transportation, at railway stations, and in big hotels. In general, always keep your valuables with you—in open bars and restaurants, purses hung on or placed next to chairs are easy targets. Make sure your wallet is safe in a buttoned pocket, or watch your handbag.

Keep a sharp eye out for pickpockets in **Bulgaria** and be very careful with your passport. (The black market price for an American or Canadian passport is around $1,000, which is almost the average yearly salary.) Ironically, you are required by Bulgarian law to carry your passport on your person at all times. In urban areas, you should also watch out for packs of stray dogs. In **Hungary,** pickpocketing and car theft are the main concerns. While a typical rental car is less likely to be stolen, expensive German makes such as Audi, BMW, and Mercedes are hot targets for car thieves. An unusual program recently started in Budapest; beginning in summer 1998, multilingual students have been posted in the capital's most touristed areas to help visitors communicate with police. At press time, translators were expected to be stationed in the Lake Balaton region as well.

In the **Czech Republic,** there has been a small but worrying trend of attacks against people of color. Crime rates have been rising in major cities in **Poland;** besides watching out for the omnipresent pickpockets, you should observe the usual urban rules of caution: be extra attentive and stick to well-lit, well-trafficked areas at night. In **Romania,** the streets are generally safe, if not well-lit. The black market should be definitely be avoided.

SENIOR-CITIZEN TRAVEL

To qualify for age-related discounts, **mention your senior-citizen status up front** when booking hotel reservations (not when checking out) and before you're seated in restaurants (not when paying the bill). Note that discounts may be limited to certain menus, days, or hours. When renting a car, **ask about promotional car-rental discounts,** which can be cheaper than senior-citizen rates.

➤ LOCAL DISCOUNTS: In Hungary, non-Hungarian senior citizens (men over 60, women over 55) are eligible for a 20% discount on rail travel. Contact or visit **MÁV Passenger Service** (✉ Andrassy út 35, Budapest VI, ☎ 1/322–8275) for information. In Poland, travelers over 60 receive discounts up to 40% on LOT air tickets.

➤ EDUCATIONAL PROGRAMS: **Elderhostel** (✉ 75 Federal St., 3rd floor, Boston, MA 02110, ☎ 617/426–8056). **Interhostel** (✉ University of New Hampshire, ✉ 6 Garrison Ave., Durham, NH 03824, ☎ 603/862–1147 or 800/733–9753, FAX 603/862–1113).

STUDENT TRAVEL

For country-specific student and youth travel information, *see* Student and Youth Travel in the A to Z section at the end of each country chapter.

TRAVEL AGENCIES

To save money, **look into deals available through student-oriented travel agencies.** To qualify you'll need a bona fide student I.D. card. Members of international student groups are also eligible.

➤ STUDENT I.D.s & SERVICES: **Council on International Educational Exchange** (✉ CIEE, ✉ 205 E. 42nd St., 14th floor, New York, NY 10017, ☎ 212/822–2600 or 888/268–6245, FAX 212/822–2699), for mail orders only, in the United States. **Travel Cuts** (✉ 187 College St., Toronto, Ontario M5T 1P7, ☎ 416/979–2406 or 800/667–2887) in Canada.

➤ STUDENT TOURS: **Contiki Holidays** (✉ 300 Plaza Alicante, Suite 900, Garden Grove, CA 92840, ☎ 714/740–0808 or 800/266–8454, FAX 714/740–2034).

TAXES

Most Eastern and Central European countries have some form of value-added tax (VAT); rebate rules vary by country, but you'll need to present your receipts on departure.

For country-specific tax and VAT information, *see* Customs and Duties and Money and Expenses in the A to Z section at the end of each country chapter.

TELEPHONES

COUNTRY CODES

Country and select city codes are as follows: Bulgaria (359), Sofia (2); Czech Republic (420), Prague (2); Hungary (36), Budapest (1); Poland (48), Warsaw (22); Romania (40), Bucharest (1); Slovakia (421), Bratislava (7).

For additional country-specific telephone information, *see* Telephones in the A to Z section at the end of each country chapter.

INTERNATIONAL CALLS

AT&T, MCI, and Sprint international access codes make calling the United States relatively convenient, but you may find the local access number blocked in many hotel rooms. First ask the hotel operator to connect you. If the hotel operator balks, ask for an international operator, or dial the international operator yourself. One way to improve your odds of getting connected to your long-distance carrier is to travel with more than one company's calling card (a hotel may block Sprint, for example, but not MCI). If all else fails, call from a pay phone in the hotel lobby.

➤ ACCESS CODES: **AT&T Direct** (008000010 in Bulgaria; 0042000101 in the Czech Republic and Slovakia; 0080001111 in Hungary; 008001111111 in Poland; 018004288 in Romania; ☎ 800/435–0812 for other areas). **MCI WorldPhone** (008000001 in Bulgaria; 0042000112 in the Czech

Republic; 0080001411 in Hungary; 008001112122 in Poland; 018001800 in Romania; 0042100112 in Slovakia; ☎ 800/444–4141 for other areas). **Sprint International Access** (008001010 in Bulgaria; 0042087187 in the Czech Republic; 0080001877 in Hungary; 008001113115 in Poland; 018000877 in Romania; 0042187187 in Slovakia; ☎ 800/877–4646 for other areas).

TOUR OPERATORS

Buying a prepackaged tour or independent vacation can make your trip to Eastern and Central Europe less expensive and more hassle-free. Because everything is prearranged, you'll spend less time planning.

Operators that handle several hundred thousand travelers per year can use their purchasing power to give you a good price. Their high volume may also indicate financial stability. But some small companies provide more personalized service; because they tend to specialize, they may also be more knowledgeable about a given area.

BOOKING WITH AN AGENT

Travel agents are excellent resources. In fact, large operators accept bookings made only through travel agents. But it's a good idea to **collect brochures from several agencies,** because some agents' suggestions may be influenced by relationships with tour and package firms that reward them for volume sales. If you have a special interest, **find an agent with expertise in that area;** ASTA (☞ Travel Agencies, *below*) has a database of specialists worldwide.

Make sure your travel agent knows the accommodations and other services. Ask about the hotel's location, room size, beds, and whether it has a pool, room service, or programs for children, if you care about these. Has your agent been there in person or sent others you can contact?

Do some homework on your own, too: Local tourism boards can provide information about lesser-known and small-niche operators, some of which may sell only direct.

BUYER BEWARE

Each year consumers are stranded or lose their money when tour opera-

tors—even very large ones with excellent reputations—go out of business. So **check out the operator.** Find out how long the company has been in business, and ask several travel agents about its reputation. If the package or tour you are considering is priced lower than in your wildest dreams, **be skeptical.** Try to **book with a company that has a consumer-protection program.** If the operator has such a program, you'll find information about it in the company's brochure. If the operator you are considering does not offer some kind of consumer protection, then ask for references from satisfied customers.

In the U.S., members of the National Tour Association and United States Tour Operators Association are required to set aside funds to cover your payments and travel arrangements in case the company defaults. It's also a good idea to choose a company that participates in the American Society of Travel Agent's Tour Operator Program (TOP). This gives you a forum if there are any disputes between you and your tour operator; ASTA will act as mediator.

➤ TOUR-OPERATOR RECOMMENDATIONS: American Society of Travel Agents (☞ Travel Agencies, *below*). **National Tour Association** (✉ NTA, ✉ 546 E. Main St., Lexington, KY 40508, ☎ 606/226–4444 or 800/755–8687). **United States Tour Operators Association** (✉ USTOA, ✉ 342 Madison Ave., Suite 1522, New York, NY 10173, ☎ 212/599–6599 or 800/468–7862, ℻ 212/599–6744).

COSTS

The more your package or tour includes, the better you can predict the ultimate cost of your vacation. Make sure you know exactly what is covered, and **beware of hidden costs.** Are taxes, tips, and service charges included? Transfers and baggage handling? Entertainment and excursions? These can add up.

Prices for packages and tours are usually quoted per person, based on two sharing a room. If traveling solo, you may be required to pay the full double-occupancy rate. Some operators eliminate this surcharge if you agree to be matched with a roommate of the same sex, even if one is not found by departure time.

GROUP TOURS

Among companies that sell tours to Eastern and Central Europe, the following are nationally known, have a proven reputation, and offer plenty of options. The classifications used below represent different price categories, and you'll probably encounter these terms when talking to a travel agent or tour operator. The key difference is usually in accommodations, which run from budget to better, and better-yet to best.

➤ SUPER-DELUXE: **Abercrombie & Kent** (✉ 1520 Kensington Rd., Oak Brook, IL 60521-2141, ☎ 630/954–2944 or 800/323–7308, FAX 630/954–3324). **Travcoa** (✉ Box 2630, 2350 S.E. Bristol St., Newport Beach, CA 92660, ☎ 714/476–2800 or 800/992–2003, FAX 714/476–2538).

➤ DELUXE: **Globus** (✉ 5301 S. Federal Circle, Littleton, CO 80123-2980, ☎ 303/797–2800 or 800/221–0090, FAX 303/347–2080). **Maupintour** (✉ 1515 St. Andrews Dr., Lawrence, KS 66047, ☎ 785/843–1211 or 800/255–4266, FAX 785/843–8351). **Tauck Tours** (✉ Box 5027, 276 Post Rd. W, Westport, CT 06881-5027, ☎ 203/226–6911 or 800/468–2825, FAX 203/221–6866).

➤ FIRST-CLASS: **Brendan Tours** (✉ 15137 Califa St., Van Nuys, CA 91411, ☎ 818/785–9696 or 800/421–8446, FAX 818/902–9876). **Caravan Tours** (✉ 401 N. Michigan Ave., Chicago, IL 60611, ☎ 312/321–9800 or 800/227–2826, FAX 312/321–9845). **Čedok Travel** (✉ 10 E. 40th St., #3604, New York, NY 10016, ☎ 212/725–0948 or 800/800–8891). **Collette Tours** (✉ 162 Middle St., Pawtucket, RI 02860, ☎ 401/728–3805 or 800/340–5158, FAX 401/728–4745). **DER Tours** (✉ 9501 W. Devon St., Rosemont, IL 60018, ☎ 800/937–1235, FAX 847/692–4141 or 800/282–7474, 800/860–9944 for brochures). **General Tours** (✉ 53 Summer St., Keene, NH 03431, ☎ 603/357–5033 or 800/221–2216, FAX 603/357–4548). **Insight International Tours** (✉ 745 Atlantic Ave., #720, Boston, MA 02111, ☎ 617/482–2000 or 800/582–8380, FAX 617/482–2884 or 800/622–5015). **Trafalgar Tours** (✉ 11 E. 26th St., New York, NY 10010, ☎ 212/689–8977 or 800/854–0103, FAX 800/457–6644).

➤ BUDGET: **Cosmos** (☞ Globus, *above*). **Trafalgar Tours** (☞ *above*).

PACKAGES

Like group tours, independent vacation packages are available from major tour operators and airlines. The companies listed below offer vacation packages in a broad price range.

➤ AIR/HOTEL: **Continental Vacations** (☎ 800/634–5555). **DER Tours** (☞ Group Tours, *above*). **General Tours** (☞ Group Tours, *above*).

THEME TRIPS

➤ BALLOONING: **Buddy Bombard European Balloon Adventures** (✉ 333 Pershing Way, West Palm Beach, FL 33401, ☎ 561/837–6610 or 800/862–8537, FAX 561/837–6623).

➤ BARGE/RIVER CRUISES: **KD River Cruises of Europe** (✉ 2500 Westchester Ave., Purchase, NY 10577, ☎ 914/696–3600 or 800/346–6525, FAX 914/696–0833).

➤ BEER/WINE: **MIR Corporation** (✉ 85 S. Washington St., #210, Seattle, WA 98104, ☎ 206/624–7289 or 800/424–7289, FAX 206/624–7360).

➤ BICYCLING: **Backroads** (✉ 801 Cedar St., Berkeley, CA 94710-1800, ☎ 510/527–1555 or 800/462–2848, FAX 510-527–1444). **Butterfield & Robinson** (✉ 70 Bond St., Toronto, Ontario, Canada M5B 1X3, ☎ 416/864–1354 or 800/678–1147, FAX 416/864–0541). **Euro-Bike Tours** (✉ Box 990, De Kalb, IL 60115, ☎ 800/321–6060, FAX 815/758–8851). **Uniquely Europe** (✉ 1940 116th Ave. NE, Bellevue, WA 98004, ☎ 425/455–4445 or 800/927–3876, FAX 425/455–2111).

➤ CRUISING: **EuroCruises** (✉ 303 W. 13th St., New York, NY 10014-1207, ☎ 800/688–3876, FAX 212/366–4747).

➤ HISTORY & ART: **IST Cultural Tours** (✉ 225 W. 34th St., New York, NY 10122-0913, ☎ 212/563–1202

THE GOLD GUIDE / SMART TRAVEL TIPS

or 800/833–2111, FAX 212/594–6953). **Smithsonian Study Tours and Seminars** (✉ 1100 Jefferson Dr. SW, Room 3045, MRC 702, Washington, DC 20560, ☎ 202/357–4700, FAX 202/633–9250).

➤ NATURAL HISTORY: **Earthwatch** (✉ Box 9104, 680 Mount Auburn St., Watertown, MA 02272, ☎ 617/926–8200 or 800/776–0188, FAX 617/926–8532) for research expeditions. **Questers** (✉ 381 Park Ave. S, New York, NY 10016, ☎ 212/251–0444 or 800/468–8668, FAX 212/251–0890). **Victor Emanuel Nature Tours** (✉ ✉ Box 33008, Austin, TX 78764, ☎ 512/328–5221 or 800/328–8368, FAX 512/328–2919).

➤ PERFORMING ARTS: **Dailey-Thorp Travel** (✉ 330 W. 58th St., #610, New York, NY 10019-1817, ☎ 212/307–1555 or 800/998–4677, FAX 212/974–1420).

➤ SINGLES AND YOUNG ADULTS: **Club Europa** (✉ 802 W. Oregon St., Urbana, IL 61801, ☎ 217/344–5863 or 800/331–1882, FAX 217/344–4072). **Contiki Holidays** (✉ 300 Plaza Alicante, #900, Garden Grove, CA 92640, ☎ 714/740–0808 or 800/266–8454, FAX 714/740–0818).

➤ SPAS: **Great Spas of the World** (✉ 55 John St., New York, NY 10038, ☎ 212/267–5500 or 800/772–8463, FAX 212/571–0510). **Spa-Finders** (✉ 91 5th Ave., #301, New York, NY 10003-3039, ☎ 212/924–6800 or 800/255–7727).

➤ TRAIN TOURS: **Abercrombie & Kent** (☞ Group Tours, *above*).

➤ WALKING/HIKING: **Backroads** (☞ Bicycling, *above*). **Himalayan Travel** (✉ 110 Prospect St., Stamford, CT 06901, ☎ 203/359–3711 or 800/225–2380, FAX 203/359–3669). **Mountain Travel-Sobek** (✉ 6420 Fairmount Ave., El Cerrito, CA 94530, ☎ 510/527–8100 or 800/227–2384, FAX 510/525–7710). **Uniquely Europe** (☞ Bicycling, *above*).

TRAIN TRAVEL

Although standards have improved during the past few years, on the whole they are far short of what is acceptable in the West. Trains are very busy, and it is rare to find one running less than full or almost so. All six countries operate their own dining, buffet, and refreshment services. Always crowded, they tend to open and close at the whim of the staff. In Bulgaria, Hungary, and Slovakia, couchette cars are second class only and can be little more than a hard bunk without springs and adequate bed linen. In Romania, there are first class couchettes (though they are comparable to second or third class compartments in more Westernized countries); these have room for two people and are relatively safe and clean. First class couchettes are also available on Czech trains, and there are two types of second class couchettes. The cheapest (*lehatko*) has six hard beds per compartment; the slightly more expensive *lůžko* has three beds and a sink, and are sex-segregated. Some of the most comfortable trains are the express trains in the Czech Republic, Hungary, and Poland—they're normally less crowded and more comfortable (you should make a reservation).

Although trains in Eastern and Central Europe can mean hours of sitting on a hard seat in a smoky car, traveling by rail is very inexpensive (it's much cheaper than renting a car in this part of Europe). Rail networks in all the Eastern and Central European countries are very extensive, though trains can be infuriatingly slow. You'll invariably enjoy interesting and friendly traveling company, however; most Eastern and Central Europeans are eager to hear about the West and to discuss the enormous changes in their own countries.

DISCOUNT PASSES

To save money, **look into rail passes.** But be aware that if you don't plan to cover many miles, you may come out ahead by buying individual tickets.

You can use the **European East Pass** on the national rail networks of Austria, the Czech Republic, Hungary, Poland, and Slovakia. The pass covers five days of unlimited first-class travel within a one-month period for $199. Additional travel days may be purchased.

You can also combine the East Pass with a national rail pass. The Bulgarian Flexipass costs $70 for three days of unlimited first-class travel within a one-month period. A pass for the Czech Republic costs $69 for five days of train travel within a 15-day period. The Hungarian Flexipass costs $55 for five days of unlimited first-class train travel within a 15-day period or $69 for 10 days within a one-month period. The Romanian Pass costs $60 for three days of first-class train travel in a 15-day period.

The **Balkan Flexipass** covers first-class train travel through Bulgaria and Romania, as well as Greece, Macedonia, Turkey, and Yugoslavia; there are passes for 5, ten, or fifteen travel days in a one-month period for $152, $264, and $317 respectively.

Hungary is one of 17 countries in which you can **use Eurailpasses,** which provide unlimited first-class rail travel, in all of the participating countries, for the duration of the pass. If you plan to rack up the miles, get a standard pass. These are available for 15 days ($538), 21 days ($698), one month ($864), two months ($1,224), and three months ($1,512).

In addition to standard Eurailpasses, **ask about special rail-pass plans.** Among these are the Eurail Youthpass (for those under age 26), the Eurail Saverpass (which gives a discount for two or more people traveling together), a Eurail Flexipass (which allows a certain number of travel days within a set period), the Euraildrive Pass and the Europass Drive (which combines travel by train and rental car). Whichever pass you choose, remember that you must **purchase your pass before you leave** for Europe.

Many travelers assume that rail passes guarantee them seats on the trains they wish to ride. Not so. You need to **book seats ahead even if you are using a rail pass;** seat reservations are required on some European trains, particularly high-speed trains, and are a good idea on trains that may be crowded—particularly in summer on popular routes. You will also need a reservation if you purchase sleeping accommodations.

➤ INFORMATION AND PASSES: **Rail Europe** (✉ 500 Mamaroneck Ave., Harrison, NY 10528, ☎ 914/682–5172 or 800/438–7245, FAX 800/432–1329; ✉ 2087 Dundas E, Suite 106, Mississauga, Ontario L4X 1M2, ☎ 800/361–7245, FAX 905/602–4198). **DER Travel Services** (✉ 9501 W. Devon Ave., Rosemont, IL 60018, ☎ 800/782–2424, FAX 800/282–7474 for information or 800/860–9944 for brochures). **CIT Tours Corp.** (✉ 15 West 44th Street, 10th Floor, New York, NY 10036, ☎ 212/730–2400 or 800/248–7245 in the U.S., 800/387–0711 or 800/361–7799 in Canada).

FROM THE U.K.

There are no direct trains from London. You can take a direct train from Paris to Warsaw or via Frankfurt to Prague (daily) or from Berlin to Warsaw or via Dresden to Prague (6 times a day). Vienna is a good starting point for Prague, Brno, or Bratislava. There are three trains a day to Prague from Vienna's Südbahnhof (South Station) via Brno (5 hours). Bratislava can be reached from Vienna by a 67-minute shuttle service, which runs every two hours during the day. You should check out times and routes before leaving. Sofia has service to Bucharest, Budapest and Vienna, but for travelers without the necessary visas, it can be a long, out-of-the-way journey to skirt Serbia.

TRAVEL AGENCIES

A good travel agent puts your needs first. Look for an agency that has been in business at least five years, emphasizes customer service, and has someone on staff who specializes in your destination. In addition, **make sure the agency belongs to a professional trade organization,** such as ASTA in the United States. If your travel agency is also acting as your tour operator, *see* Buyer Beware *in* Tour Operators, *above*).

➤ LOCAL AGENT REFERRALS: **American Society of Travel Agents** (ASTA, ☎ 800/965–2782 24-hr hot line, FAX 703/684–8319). **Association of Canadian Travel Agents** (✉ Suite 201, 1729 Bank St., Ottawa, Ontario K1V 7Z5, ☎ 613/521–0474, FAX 613/521–0805). **Association of British**

Travel Agents (✉ 55–57 Newman St., London W1P 4AH, ☎ 0171/637–2444, FAX 0171/637–0713). **Australian Federation of Travel Agents** (☎ 02/9264–3299). **Travel Agents' Association of New Zealand** (☎ 04/499–0104).

TRAVEL GEAR

Travel catalogs specialize in useful items, such as compact alarm clocks and travel irons, that can **save space when packing.** They also offer dual-voltage appliances, currency converters, and foreign-language phrase books.

➤ CATALOGS: **Magellan's** (☎ 800/962–4943, FAX 805/568–5406). **Orvis Travel** (☎ 800/541–3541, FAX 540/343–7053). **TravelSmith** (☎ 800/950–1600, FAX 800/950–1656).

U.S. GOVERNMENT

Government agencies can be an excellent source of inexpensive travel information. When planning your trip, **find out what government materials are available.**

➤ ADVISORIES: **U.S. Department of State** (✉ Overseas Citizens Services Office, ✉ Room 4811 N.S., Washington, DC 20520; ☎ 202/647–5225 or FAX 202/647–3000 for interactive hot line; ☎ 301/946–4400 for computer bulletin board); enclose a self-addressed, stamped, business-size envelope.

➤ PAMPHLETS: **Consumer Information Center** (✉ Consumer Information Catalogue, Pueblo, CO 81009, ☎ 719/948–3334 or 888/878–3256) for a free catalog that includes travel titles.

VISITOR INFORMATION

➤ BULGARIA: **Balkan USA/Affordable Europe Vacations** (✉ 20 E. 46th St., New York, NY 10017, ☎ 212/338–6838, FAX 212/338–6830); in the U.K. **Balkan Tourist** (✉ Osbourne Hills, 111 Bartholomew Rd., London NW5 2BJ, ☎ 0171/485–5280, FAX 0171/485–5864).

➤ CZECH REPUBLIC: The tourist desk of the **Czech Tourist Authority**, a state-run information service, dispenses brochures, maps, and the like. In the United States: ✉ 1109–1111

Madison Ave., New York, NY 10028 , ☎ 212/288–0830, FAX 212/288–0971. In Canada: ✉ Box 198, Exchange Tower, 2 First Canadian Place, 14th floor, Toronto, Ontario M5X 1A6 , ☎ 416/367–3432, FAX 416/367–3492. In the United Kingdom: (✉ 95 Great Portland St., London W1N 5RA , ☎ 0171/291–9920, FAX 0171/436–8300).

➤ HUNGARY: **Hungarian National Tourist Office** In the United States and Canada: **IBUSZ**, ✉ 150 E. 58th St., New York, NY 10155 , ☎ 212/355–0240, FAX 212/207–4103. In Canada, contact the **Hungarian Consulate General Office** (✉ 121 Bloor St. E, Suite 1115, Toronto M4W3M5, Ontario , ☎ 416/923–8981, FAX 416/923–2732). In the United Kingdom: **Hungarian National Tourist Board** c/o Embassy of the Republic of Hungary, Commercial Section (✉ 46 Eaton Pl., London, SW1X 8AL , ☎ 0171/823–1032 or 0171/823–1055, FAX 0171/823–1459).

➤ POLAND: **Polish National Tourist Office**: In the U.S. and Canada, ✉ 275 Madison Ave., Suite 1711, New York, NY 10016 , ☎ 212/338–9412, FAX 212/338–9283. In the United Kingdom: ✉ Remo House, 1st floor, 310–312 Regent St., London W1R 5AJ, ☎ 0171/580–8811, FAX 0171/580–8866.

➤ ROMANIA: **In the United States and Canada:** ✉ 14 East 38th St., 12th floor, New York, NY 10016, ☎ 212/545–8484, FAX 212/251–0429. **In the United Kingdom:** ✉ 83A Marylebone High St., London W1M 3DE , ☎ FAX 0171/224–3692.

➤ SLOVAKIA: In the United States: **The Slovak Information Center** (✉ 406 E. 67th St., New York, NY 10021, ☎ 212/737–3971, FAX 212/737–3454) has a walk-in information center and can also provide travel information via phone, fax, or e-mail. In Canada: **Slovak Culture and Information Center** (✉ 12 Birch Ave., Toronto, Ontario M4V 1C8, ☎ 416/925–0008, FAX 416/925–0009). In the United Kingdom: **Embassy of the Slovak Republic** (✉ Information Dept., 25 Kensington Palace Gardens, London W8 4QY, ☎ 0171/243–0803, FAX 0171/

727–5824), operates Monday–
Friday between 10 AM–12:30 PM.

WHEN TO GO

The tourist season generally runs from
April or May through October; spring
and fall combine good weather with a
more bearable level of tourism. The
ski season lasts from mid-December
through March. Outside the mountain
resorts you will encounter few other
visitors; you'll have the opportunity to
see the region covered in snow, but
many of the sights are closed, and it
can get very, very cold. If you're not a
skier, try visiting the Giant Mountain
of Bohemia or the High Tatras in
Slovakia and Poland in late spring or
fall; the colors are dazzling, and you'll
have the hotels and restaurants pretty
much to yourself. Bear in mind that
many attractions are closed November
through March.

Prague and Budapest are beautiful
year-round, but avoid midsummer
(especially July and August) and the
Christmas and Easter holidays, when
the two cities are choked with visitors. Warsaw, too, suffers a heavy
influx of tourists during the summer
season, though not on quite the same
grand scale. Lake Balaton in Hungary
becomes a mob scene in July and
August. In Bulgaria, the best summer
destinations are the gorgeous Black
Sea fishing villages, or the medieval
mountain towns in the interior, where
cool breezes and sports opportunities
make for a refreshing, if rugged,
summer holiday. At the opposite end
of the spectrum, Bucharest and Sofia
are rarely crowded, even at the height
of summer. In July and August, however, the weather in these capitals
sometimes borders on stifling.

For additional country-specific information, *see* When to Tour following
the Great Itineraries at the beginning
of each country chapter.

CLIMATE

The following are the average daily
maximum and minimum temperatures for major cities in the region.

BRATISLAVA

Jan.	36F	2C	May	70F	21C	Sept.	72F	22C
	27	– 3		52	11		54	12
Feb.	39F	4C	June	75F	24C	Oct.	59F	15C
	28	– 2		57	14		45	7
Mar.	48F	9C	July	79F	26C	Nov.	46F	8C
	34	1		61	16		37	3
Apr.	61F	16C	Aug.	79F	26C	Dec.	39F	4C
	43	6		61	16		32	0

BUCHAREST

Jan.	34F	1C	May	74F	23C	Sept.	78F	25C
	19	– 7		51	10		52	11
Feb.	38F	4C	June	81F	27C	Oct.	65F	18C
	23	– 5		57	14		43	6
Mar.	50F	10C	July	86F	30C	Nov.	49F	10C
	30	– 1		60	16		35	2
Apr.	64F	18C	Aug.	85F	30C	Dec.	39F	4C
	41	5		59	15		26	– 3

BUDAPEST

Jan.	34F	1C	May	72F	22C	Sept.	73F	23C
	25	– 4		52	11		54	12
Feb.	39F	4C	June	79F	26C	Oct.	61F	16C
	28	– 2		59	15		45	7
Mar.	50F	10C	July	82F	28C	Nov.	46F	8C
	36	2		61	16		37	3
Apr.	63F	17C	Aug.	81F	27C	Dec.	39F	4C
	25	– 4		61	16		30	– 1

PRAGUE

Jan.	36F	2C	May	66F	19C	Sept.	68F	20C
	25	− 4		46	8		50	10
Feb.	37F	3C	June	72F	22C	Oct.	55F	13C
	27	− 3		52	11		41	5
Mar.	46F	8C	July	75F	24C	Nov.	46F	8C
	32	0		55	13		36	2
Apr.	58F	14C	Aug.	73F	23C	Dec.	37F	3C
	39	4		55	13		28	− 2

SOFIA

Jan.	35F	2C	May	69F	21C	Sept.	70F	22C
	25	− 4		50	10		52	11
Feb.	39F	4C	June	76F	24C	Oct.	63F	17C
	27	− 3		56	14		46	8
Mar.	50F	10C	July	81F	27C	Nov.	48F	9C
	33	1		60	16		37	3
Apr.	60F	16C	Aug.	79F	26C	Dec.	38F	4C
	42	5		59	15		28	− 2

WARSAW

Jan.	32F	0C	May	68F	20C	Sept.	66F	19C
	21	− 6		48	9		50	10
Feb.	32F	0C	June	73F	23C	Oct.	55F	13C
	21	− 6		54	12		41	5
Mar.	43F	6C	July	75F	24C	Nov.	43F	6C
	28	− 2		59	15		34	1
Apr.	54F	12C	Aug.	73F	23C	Dec.	36F	2C
	37	3		57	14		27	− 3

➤ FORECASTS: **Weather Channel Connection** (☎ 900/932–8437), 95¢ per minute from a Touch-Tone phone.

1 Destination: Eastern and Central Europe

WHAT'S WHERE

Bulgaria

The southernmost frontier of Eastern and Central Europe, Bulgaria borders Turkey to the south and the Black Sea to the east; to the west are the territories of the former Yugoslavia. Covering a territory of approximately 111,000 square km (43,000 square mi), Bulgaria has a population of about 9 million. **Sofia,** the bustling, cosmopolitan capital, sits on the so-called Sofia Plain in western Bulgaria and is surrounded by rugged mountain ranges. The wooded and mountainous interior is sprinkled with attractive "museum" villages and ancient towns. In the **Balkan Range** in the north is the old Bulgarian capital of **Veliko Târnovo.** South of there, in the foothills of the Balkan Range, you'll find the verdant Valley of Roses and beyond that, **Plovdiv,** the country's second-largest city, and reputed intellectual center. The sunny, sandy beaches of Bulgaria's **Black Sea coast** attract visitors from all over Europe; the historic port city of **Varna** makes a good base for exploring the region.

Czech Republic

Planted firmly in the heart of Central Europe—Prague is some 320 km (200 mi) north*west* of Vienna—the Czech Republic is culturally and historically more closely linked to Western, particularly Germanic, culture than any of its former East-bloc brethren. Encompassing some 79,000 square km (30,500 square mi), the Czech Republic is made up of the regions of Bohemia in the west (sharing long borders with Germany and Austria) and Moravia in the east. Moravia's White Carpathian Mountains (Bílé Karpaty) form the border with the young Slovak Republic, which broke its 74-year-old union with the Czechs in 1993 to establish itself as an independent nation. With a population of over 10 million, the Czech Republic is one of the most densely populated countries of Eastern and Central Europe.

The capital city of **Prague** sits on the Vltava (Moldau) River, roughly in the middle of Bohemian territory. A stunning city of human dimensions, Prague offers the traveler a lesson in almost all the major architectural styles of Western European history; relatively unscathed by major wars, most of Prague's buildings are remarkably well preserved. **Southern Bohemia** is dotted with several stunning walled towns retaining much of their medieval appearance, many of which played important roles in the Hussite religious wars of the 15th century. The two most notable towns are Tábor and Český Krumlov. **Western Bohemia,** especially the far western hills near the German border, remains justly famous for its mineral springs and spa towns, in particular Karlovy Vary, Mariánské Lázně, and Františkový Lázně. **Northern Bohemia,** with its rolling hills and the not-so-giant **Krkonoše** (Giant Mountains), is a hiker's and camper's delight.

Hungary

Sandwiched between Slovakia and Romania, Hungary was the Austro-Hungarian Empire's eastern frontier. Measuring approximately 93,000 square km (36,000 square mi), with a population of more than 10 million, it is the geographical link between the Slavic regions of Central Europe and the Black Sea region's amalgam of Orthodox and Islamic cultures. The heart of the nation is **Budapest,** in the northwest on the Danube, just an hour from Bratislava in Slovakia and two hours from Vienna. Just north of Budapest, the Danube River forms a gentle, heart-shape curve along which lie the romantic and historic towns of the region called the **Danube Bend.** Southwest of Budapest are the vineyards, quaint villages, and popular, developed summer resorts around **Lake Balaton,** the largest lake in Central Europe. The more rural and gently mountainous stretch of **northern Hungary** also includes the handsome, vibrant town of Eger and the famous wine village of Tokaj; the contrastingly flat and dry expanses of the Great Plain, in the east, are spiced with legendary traditions of horsemanship and agriculture and anchored by the interesting and lively cities of Kecskemét and Debrecen. The verdant, rolling countryside of **Transdanubia** stretches west of the Danube to the borders of Austria, Slovenia, and Croatia; in the northern hills nestle the gemlike, beautifully restored towns of Sopron and

Kőszeg and, in the south, the culturally rich, dynamically beautiful city of Pécs.

Poland

The northernmost country in Central Europe, Poland has a long coastline on the Baltic Sea. A vast nation of 313,000 square km (121,000 square mi), Poland is made up primarily of a great plain in the north and central region and a small but dramatic stretch of mountainous territory to the south (on its border with Slovakia and the Czech Republic). **Warsaw,** just to the east of the country's center, has rebuilt itself several times over the course of its tumultuous history and since the end of communism has been changing faster than any other city or region in Poland.

Travelers interested in art and architecture shouldn't miss **Kraków** in the south (it's one of UNESCO's 12 great historic cities of the world) and the historic small towns of the surrounding region known as Little Poland. Outdoor enthusiasts will want to move on to the west and south, to the **Podhale** region and the **Tatra Mountains.** Many of the natural wonders and recreational areas of these two regions are within two hours' drive of downtown Kraków.

Gdańsk and the north offer wide-open vistas, long stretches of coast, great lakes dotting large stretches of forest, and historic cities and castles rising up from the plain. This is a great area for enjoying water sports, hiking, and camping. **Lublin** and the east offer a trip back into the traditional way of life of rural Central Europe: small towns, whose great age was in the Renaissance but which have slept since, vast palaces of the nobility, and gently varied countryside where the tractor has not yet replaced the horse.

Apart from the far southwest and a few park areas around **Poznań** and **Wrocław,** the countryside of western Poland is flat and somewhat monotonous—lots of dairy farms and hay fields. Poznań and Wrocław have fine historic centers and a thriving cultural life.

Romania

Romania is one of the poorest countries in Europe, second only to Albania, but it's also one of the most beautiful. The same factors that kept Romania from developing economically during the Communist era also helped to preserve the country as one of the last bastions of medieval Europe. The country covers approximately 238,000 square km (92,000 square mi). **Bucharest,** the capital city, in the southeast just two hours or so from the Black Sea coast, was once known as the "Paris of the East." From Bucharest you can set out on a journey of the villages of **Transylvania.** Many of the towns here have preserved their medieval core and still show traces of the Latin and Germanic traders who passed through on their way to the Black Sea.

Bucovina, a remote region in the north, provides an unspoiled view of medieval Europe: Farmers still tend fields with handmade plows and hoes, and horse-drawn wagons are as numerous as cars. This region is home to the painted churches, a collection of monasteries built during the Middle Ages notable for their vividly colored frescoes.

In contrast to the rest of Romania, the **Black Sea** region has always been a major center of tourism. The main attraction here is the warm beaches. The area is also studded with ruins dating to the conquest of the region during the period of the Roman Empire. From the coast travelers can journey to the **Danube Delta,** Europe's largest wetland and home to 300 bird species.

Slovakia

Having declared its independence from the Czech Republic in 1993, the smaller and more agrarian Slovak Republic has been struggling to revive its economic life and adjust to new post–Cold War realities. The 49,000 square km (19,000 square mi) of Slovak territory are both less urbanized and less industrialized than that of the country's Moravian and Bohemian neighbors to the west. **Bratislava,** the capital, lies on the Danube in the southwestern corner of the country, just a few miles away from both the Austrian and Hungarian borders. Its small Old Town is charming and contains several buildings and churches of interest (especially to those interested in the history of the Austrio-Hungarian Empire), but Slovakia's real assets are to the north and east. **Central Slovakia,** a hilly region crossed by hiking trails, is rich in folklore and traces of medieval history. The **High Tatra Mountains** attract skiers, campers, and mountaineers from all across

Europe; these days they are a real meeting ground for tourists from east and west. And relatively undiscovered **eastern Slovakia** lures travelers with its country lanes—watch out for herds of sheep and gaggles of geese—fairy-tale-like villages, castles, and wooden churches.

NEW AND NOTEWORTHY

Bulgaria

In the last year alone, so much has changed in Bulgaria that even the locals are bewildered. Suddenly the old coins are obsolete, the price of bread quadrupled, and neon signs glow with the names of foreign companies. For citizens of this small Balkan country recovering from a *peaceful* revolution in 1997, recent times have been hard and chaotic—from a historical perspective, undoubtedly interesting.

In January 1997, a national uprising paralyzed the country for a full month before ousting the Socialist government from parliament two years before the end of their term under accusations of rampant corruption. At press time, many of the former Bulgarian Socialist Party leaders were under house arrest, awaiting trial for crimes against the State. The country is now struggling forward under the leadership of the opposition party, the Union of Democratic Forces (UDF).

Despite economic hardships, the **tourism industry is developing rapidly**—especially since tourism is the most immediate hope for incoming revenue. Most cities now have privately owned luxury hotels, and restaurants, bars, and discos echo the standards of the West. Prices remain low, so Bulgaria is a great destination for bargain hunters.

The pace of change is fastest in Sofia, where new businesses (and Western franchises) have established a beachhead. A **new telephone system** is being installed in Sofia and its suburbs; many numbers are changing with the adoption of digital lines. The **Sofia subway,** once slated for a 1996 grand opening, is still a muddy eyesore, the events of 1997 having stopped work on the project. Though locals are skeptical, officials say it will open in fall 1998.

Czech Republic

The Czech Republic continues along its path of economic and cultural revitalization, which began with the peaceful revolution of 1989 and accelerated following the breakup of the Czechoslovak state in 1993. Far from hurting the country, the Czech-Slovak split has freed officials to concentrate on the rapid economic changes of Bohemia and Moravia without having to worry about Slovakia. Their eventual goal is **incorporation into the European Union** (EU). In 1997 the Czech Republic, along with Poland, Hungary, Estonia, Slovenia, and Cyprus, began the long process of integration into the legal and economic framework of the EU. Pointedly, Slovakia was not invited to join this most recent wave of would-be union members, nor to the talks that will lead to **NATO membership** for the Czech Republic, Poland, and Hungary in 1999.

One tangible impact of the country's economic reforms has been an acceleration in the pace of architectural renovations. Many hotels, old private houses, and churches are installing new fixtures and applying a fresh coat of paint. This is most noticeable in the capital, but everywhere, castles, palaces, and dusty old museums are spiffing themselves up and throwing open their doors to visitors. The fiscal shocks of 1997, a year when the Czech crown lost more than 20% of its value against the U.S. dollar, could not shut the doors on several **major museum projects** planned for Prague for 1998. These include the private Mucha Museum, the Prague Municipal House's collection of 20th-century Czech art, and the long-awaited reopening of the Prague Castle Picture Gallery.

The number of **hotels and restaurants** keeps pace with the growing number of visitors. This is even true of Prague, which has become one of Europe's leading tourist destinations. Like the number of new large hotels, the number of smaller, privately owned hotels and pensions is also on the rise. The arrival of visitors and long-term residents from all over the world has brought forth new restaurants offering Cajun, Indian, vegetarian, and other exotic fare alongside the traditional ones serving pork and dumplings.

Prague's cultural life continues to thrive, and the city in particular is a dream for classical-music lovers and opera fans. The annual mid-May–early June Prague Spring Music Festival, which even before the collapse of the Communist government was one of the great events on the European calendar, is attracting record numbers of music lovers. The less-hyped Prague Autumn festival has begun to bring in equally strong performers and orchestras.

Hungary

With **NATO membership** imminent and an invitation into the European Union on the more distant, but likely, horizon, Hungary continues to strengthen both its international position and its internal assets. Anticipation is running high for the year 2000, especially since it will coincide with the **Magyar Millennium**, the 1,000th anniversary of Hungary's founding as a state. Continuing the celebratory restorations in honor of another recent national anniversary in 1996—the 1,100th anniversary of the Magyar settlement of the Carpathian Basin—restoration work on important sites throughout the country will be finished in the year 2000. A new National Theater will be built in Budapest, and several other new cultural institutions are planned, including a Hungarian literature institute.

Grand old **Budapest** is seeing more and more improvements and development, from private restoration of crumbling buildings to city-funded projects, such as the increase in pedestrian-only zones and the construction of a fourth metro line through southern Buda, begun in late 1998.

Slowly but surely, Hungary continues to **improve its infrastructure.** Over the next several years, major highways will be upgraded and extended, the airport in Budapest will undergo a major expansion, and the antiquated telephone system will be overhauled. Travelers may witness these changes taking place but should not expect to reap their full benefits for some time to come.

National elections in May 1998 brought to Hungary's helm a **new government** and a new prime minister: In a surprise victory, the center-right FIDESZ (Alliance of Young Democrats–Hungarian Civic Party), led by Viktor Orbán, beat the ruling MSZP (Hungarian Socialist Party). By voting out the Socialist party, composed largely of the former Communists, the nation has placed its trust in a fresh generation.

At press time, Hungary's annual inflation rate had decreased from more than 25% to 16%, and with continued significant devaluation of the forint, exchange rates keep improving for visitors. Yet, while Hungary remains a bargain compared to Western Europe, strictly rock-bottom prices are a thing of the past.

Poland

Poland's political and economic profile is becoming easy on the international eye. Along with the Czech Republic and Hungary, the country is readying itself to be part of **NATO's expansion** eastward in 1999. It also stands a good chance to become part of the **European Union.**

Transportation both to and within Poland has been on a steady upswing. The second terminal at Warsaw airport, opened in the early 1990s, has greatly improved the speed and comfort of arrival at Poland's capital; LOT now also offers more domestic flights—at least one daily to most major cities from Warsaw. **New terminals** have also opened at most other major airports. Public transportation has been expanded by a network of Express buses that serve the bigger cities. Major highways are being widened and improved, albeit slowly, and major car-rental companies are competing to offer better prices.

The financial services and banking sectors have been slower to change, but **credit cards** are now accepted in almost all tourist-class hotels, restaurants, and large stores. In major cities it is also becoming much easier to cash **traveler's checks** and to use cash cards (like American Express or Eurocheque) in the growing network of ATMs. At press time, Poland planned to replace its government tourist office with a national tourism board partially supported by the private sector. The new organization should be in place by late 1999.

Romania

Romania, and especially the capital, Bucharest, has experienced great change since the revolution of 1989. With the much-awaited election of Romania's first democratic government in November 1996, the country has slowly begun to move away from the destructive era identified with the dictatorship of Nicolae Ceauşescu. Unfortunately, daily life for most Romanians is still scarred with the disastrous effects of its past, oppressive government. Inflation averaged 151% in 1998, and unemployment is expected to reach 10%. However, Romania hopes to join NATO and to become a member of the EU, and the strict admission guidelines have pushed the country in a positive direction, forcing it to begin plotting a stable future course.

Due to tight investment constraints, Romania lags considerably behind the rest of Eastern Europe in terms of privatization and foreign investment. Despite these difficulties, the **number of private establishments is increasing** at a steady pace. With the help of governmental decisions in favor of tourism, including the agreement to discourage the long-standing policy of charging foreigners higher rates than Romanians, tourists should become a more frequent sight in Romania.

The increasing warmth toward private businesses has resulted in slowly improving standards overall—including a better selection of hotels and restaurants. Romania may not be an easy place to travel, but it is an unadulterated place to adventure.

Slovakia

Slovakia continues steadily along the path to economic and democratic restructuring, with the eventual goal of incorporation into the EU. New hotels, pensions, and restaurants are springing up all over the country—but not fast enough to eliminate the shabby government-owned establishments that still dominate certain parts of the scene. Almost all cities now have pensions, often housed in beautifully renovated historic buildings. Eastern Slovakia, known for its natural beauty and unusual architecture, remains uncharted territory but can now offer accommodations that are up to Western standards.

FODOR'S CHOICE

Dining

Bulgaria

★ **Nad Aleyata, Zad Shkafut, Sofia.** You can dine among diplomats in this old

brick house; the menu shares the clientele's international bent. $$$$

★ **La Gondola Vinarna, Sofia.** In this cellar wine-tasting house, you can indulge in a hearty buffet and an excellent selection of domestic wines. $$$

Czech Republic

★ **V Zátiši, Prague.** In one of the city's oldest and calmest squares—the restaurant's name means "still life," or "in a quiet corner"—this refined dining room offers tantalizing international specialties and wonderful service. $$$$

★ **Lobkovická, Prague.** This atmospheric, 17th-century wine bar has an imaginative menu and an enticing roster of Moravian wines. $$$

★ **Slávia kavárna, Prague.** To lap up some of the artistic scene, come to this Art Deco café; the views of the Prague Castle and the National Theater aren't too shabby either. $

Hungary

★ **Gundel, Budapest.** Established at the turn of the century, Budapest's most famous restaurant continues its legacy of Old World grandeur and elegant cuisine. $$$$

★ **Művészinas, Budapest.** The chef at this romantic, bustling bistro in downtown Pest has a flair for taking typical Hungarian dishes to new heights. $$$

★ **Aranysárkány, Szentendre.** This small size and turbulent open kitchen give it a decidedly convivial atmosphere. $$

★ **Hortobágyi Csárda, Hortobágy.** A favorite of wayfarers since it opened in 1699, the Great Plain's legendary old inn consistently serves excellent, traditional fare. $

Poland

★ **Belvedere, Warsaw.** It doesn't get much more romantic than this; exquisitely prepared Polish cuisine in an elegant candlelit orangerie in Warsaw's serene Łazienki Park. $$$$

★ **Wierzynek, Kraków.** Poland's most famous restaurant, in a room glittering with chandeliers and silver, has a reputation for fine food that goes back to the 14th century. $$$$

★ **Pod Łososiem, Gdańsk.** This historic Old Town inn is named for its strong suit: fish (though there's also fowl on the menu). *$$$*

Romania
★ **Coliba Haiducilor, Poina Braşov.** This updated version of a traditional Romanian hunting lodge specializing in bear, venison, and chicken served flaming on a stake will make you feel as if you've just returned from a wild-boar hunt. *$$–$$$*

★ **Bistro Atheneu, Bucharest.** Though the atmosphere leans toward Paris, the menu is staunchly Romanian here. Live classical music adds to the experience. *$$*

Slovakia
★ **Kláštorná vináreň, Bratislava.** Sample the best of the happy—and spicy—merger of Hungarian and Slovak cuisines at this dark and intimate monastery wine cellar not far from the banks of the Danube. *$$$*

★ **Restaurant Koliba, Starý Smokovec.** This charming, rustic spot on the slopes of the Tatra Mountains serves up grilled specialties to the accompaniment of Gypsy folk music. *$$*

★ **Slovenská Reštauracia, Poprad.** The very best of eastern Slovakian comfort food is served in a cheery village-style atmosphere. *$*

Lodging

Bulgaria
★ **Grand Hotel Varna, Sveti Konstantin.** The best hotel on Bulgaria's Black Sea coast, the Varna offers its guests spa services in addition to lodging. *$$$$*

★ **Sheraton Sofia Hotel Balkan, Sofia.** It's hard to beat the central location of this first-class hotel. *$$$$*

Czech Republic
★ **Dům U Červeného Lva, Prague.** Spare decor sets off beautiful antiques and painted-beam ceilings in this polished Baroque building. *$$$$*

★ **Dvořák, Karlovy Vary.** This elegant hotel right in the center of a beautiful spa town has all the modern amenities but plenty of Old World charm to spare. *$$$$*

★ **Růže, ČeskýKrumlov.** Some rooms in this refurbished monastery on a hill facing Krumlov Castle afford stunning views of the loveliest of Bohemian towns. *$$$*

★ **Bican Pension, Tábor, Bohemia.** This lovely family-run pension dates from the 14th century but has all the modern conveniences you've come to expect at the end of the 20th; its cool cellar lounge provides a perfect retreat on scorching summer days. *$–$$*

Hungary
★ **Danubius Hotel Gellért, Budapest.** This grand 1918 Art Nouveau hotel on the Danube at the foot of Gellért Hill is the pride of Budapest. Housing an extensive, elegant complex of marble bathing facilities fed by ancient curative springs, it is also one of Europe's most famous Old World spas. *$$$$*

★ **Epona Rider Village, Máta.** You don't have to rough it to spend a night out on the wide open spaces of Hungary's Great Plain; this luxurious modern complex offers sparkling facilities and world-class equestrian entertainment. *$$$$*

★ **Hotel Palota, Miskolc-Lillafüred.** This turreted castle in a magical setting in the forested hills of northern Hungary provides comfortable lodging and a perfect base for walking and fishing. *$$$*

★ **Kulturinov, Budapest.** Set on one of historic Castle Hill's most famous cobblestone squares, this neo-Baroque castle houses budget accommodations in a priceless location. *$*

Poland
★ **Bristol, Warsaw.** Warsaw's only truly legendary hotel, the Bristol has emerged from a decade of extensive refurbishing and is once again pampering guests with luxurious service. *$$$$*

★ **Sheraton, Warsaw.** This American-run hotel has much to recommend it: outstanding service, the best health club in the city, and a great location near parks and downtown Warsaw. *$$$$*

★ **Grand Hotel, Sopot.** This legendary late-19th-century luxury hotel fronts directly onto Sopot Beach and stands in its own gorgeous gardens. *$$$*

★ **Pod Różą, Kraków.** One of Kraków's oldest hotels, this property has bright, modern guest rooms and a prime location. *$$*

Romania
★ **Athenęe Palace Hilton, Bucharest.** Reopened in 1997, this hotel retains its

shine with immaculate rooms and a grand lobby. $$$$

★ **Mara Sinaia, Sinaia.** This is quite possibly the grandest hotel outside the capital, with stunning mountain views and an extremely good restaurant. $$$$

★ **Casa Viorel, Poiana Brașov.** Perhaps the best-kept secret in Romania, this pleasant family-run hotel has clean-as-a-whistle rooms, a fantastic mountain view, and an excellent breakfast. $$

Slovakia

★ **Danube, Bratislava.** This gleaming French-run hotel on the banks of the Danube has all the comforts of a modern, international chain. $$$$

★ **Grandhotel Praha, Tatranská Lomnica.** This multiturreted mansion in the foothills of the Tatras has retained the elegance and gentility of an earlier age. $$$

★ **Arkada Hotel, Levoča.** The bright and comfortable rooms in this boutique hotel belie the building's 13th-century origins. $$

Castles and Churches

Bulgaria

★ **Hram-pametnik Alexander Nevski (Alexander Nevski Memorial Cathedral), Sofia.** A modern, neo-Byzantine structure with glittering onion domes, this memorial to the Bulgarians' Russian neighbors-liberators can hold some 5,000 worshipers; the Crypt Museum holds an outstanding collection of icons and religious artifacts.

Czech Republic

★ **Chrám svatého Víta (St. Vitus Cathedral), Prague.** Soaring above the castle walls and dominating the city at its feet, St. Vitus Cathedral is among the most beautiful sights in Europe. Its stained-glass windows are particularly brilliant.

★ **Chrám svaté Barbory (St. Barbara's Cathedral), Kutná Hora.** Arguably the best example of the Gothic impulse in Bohemia, St. Barbara's Cathedral lifts the spirit and gives the town of Kutná Hora its unmistakable skyline.

★ **Týn Church, Staré Město, Prague.** The exterior of this 15th-century cathedral, with its twin gold-tipped, jet-black spires, is a sterling example of Prague Gothic.

★ **Vranov Castle, Vranov, Moravia.** You'll admire or wince at this multicolored mix of Gothic, Renaissance, and Baroque styles; the eclectic effect always sparks an opinion.

Hungary

★ **Bazilika (cathedral), Esztergom** The imposing neoclassical dome of Hungary's largest church looming over the village and river below is one of the Danube Bend's best sights.

★ **Eszterházy Palace, Fertöd.** Known as the Hungarian Versailles, this yellow, 18th-century Baroque palace near Sopron in northern Transdanubia was a residence of the noble Eszterházy family.

★ **Fellegvár (Citadel), Visegrád.** This 13th-century, hilltop fortress was once the seat of Hungarian kings. The hike up will reward you with gorgeous, panoramic views of the Danube Bend.

★ **Festetics Kastély (Festetics Palace), Keszthely.** A tremendous library, lush park, and distinctive tower make this one of the finest Baroque complexes in Hungary.

★ **Mátyás Templom (Matthias Church), Budapest.** Castle Hill's soaring Gothic church is colorfully ornate inside with lavishly frescoed Byzantine pillars.

★ **Nagy Zsinagóga (Great Synagogue), Budapest.** This giant Byzantine-Moorish beauty (Europe's largest synagogue) underwent a massive restoration after being ravaged by Hungarian and German Nazis during World War II.

★ **Pécs Bazilika (Pécs Basilica), Pécs.** This four-spired cathedral is one of Europe's most magnificent, its breathtaking interior resplendent with shimmering frescoes and ornate statuary.

★ **Szent István Bazilika (St. Stephen's Basilica), Budapest.** Inside this massive neo-Renaissance beauty, the capital's biggest church, is a rich collection of mosaics and statuary, as well as the mummified right hand of Hungary's first king and patron saint, St. Stephen.

Poland

★ **Kaplica Trójcy Świetej (Chapel of the Holy Trinity), Lublin.** This stunning 14th-century chapel recently reopened after decades of restoration; it's filled with Byzantine-style murals.

★ **Klasztor Paulinów (Pauline monastery), Częstochowa.** The 14th-century church in this monastic complex holds Poland's holiest religious image, the famous Black Madonna of Częstochowa, a destination for pilgrims from around the world.

★ **Kościół Mariacki (Church of Our Lady), Kraków.** This church on Kraków's central marketplace holds a magnificent wooden altarpiece with more than 200 carved figures, works of the 15th-century master Wit Stwosz.

★ **Kościół Najświętszej Marii Panny (Church of Our Lady), Gdańsk.** Climbing up the tower of the largest church in Poland results in breathtaking views.

★ **Łańcut Palace, Rzeszów.** This aristocratic residence is truly grandiose; there are extensive gardens, an impressive art collection, and even a small, private theater.

★ **Pałac Wilanowski (Wilanów Palace), Warsaw.** A Baroque gem on the outskirts of the capital, this palace was home to several Polish kings and queens; when you get tired of royal portraits and gilt, explore the Romantic gardens with their pagodas, summerhouses, and bridges overlooking a lake.

★ **Zamek Królewski (Royal Castle), Kraków.** Stroll the courtyards and chambers of Krakow's 14th-century Royal Castle, built when Kraków was Poland's capital, to get a compact lesson in the trials and tribulations of Polish history and to view fine collections of artwork, arms and armor, and tapestries.

Romania

★ **Biserica Stavropoleos (Stavropoleos Church), Bucharest.** Inside this Orthodox church are superb examples of Romanian folk-style wood-and-stone carvings and a richly ornate iconostasis.

★ **Voroneţ Monastery, Bucovina.** The walls of the church at the most famous of all of the Bucovina monasteries are lined with detailed and vivid frescoes depicting scenes from the Bible; the peculiarly deep and penetrating shade of blue used in the frescoes is known to art historians and artists as "voroneţ blue."

Slovakia

★ **Dóm svätej Alžbety (Cathedral of St. Elizabeth), Košice.** Inside this 15th-century Gothic cathedral—the largest in Slovakia— stands a monumental piece of wood carving, the 35-ft Altar of the Holy Elizabeth.

★ **Kostol svätého Jakuba (St. Jacob Church), Levoča.** This is the most impressive memorial to Gothic art in Eastern Europe; front and center on the main altar is wood-carver Pavol of Levoča's breathtaking masterpiece *The Last Supper.*

★ **Krásna Hôrka, Krásnohradské Podhradie.** Visible from miles around, this fairy-tale castle on a hill is one of Slovakia's best-preserved medieval fortifications.

★ **Wooden churches of eastern Slovakia.** Even the nails are made of wood in these handsome structures that combine elements of Byzantine and Baroque styles; religious paintings and icons line the interior walls of many.

Museums

Bulgaria

★ **Natzionale Archeologicheski Musei (National Archaeological Museum), Sofia.** Housed in the former Great Mosque, this collection is devoted to the various peoples who have inhabited Bulgarian territory over the centuries.

★ **Natzionalen Istoricheski Musei (National History Museum), Sofia.** Considered the city's most important museum, it houses priceless Thracian treasures, Roman mosaics, and enameled jewelry from the First Bulgarian Kingdom.

Czech Republic

★ **Národní galérie (National Gallery), Prague.** Spread among a half dozen branches around the city, the National Gallery's collections span most major periods of European art, from medieval and Baroque masters to a vast constructivist gallery of 20th-century Czech and European works.

★ **Židovské muzeum v Praze (Prague Jewish Museum), Prague.** Actually a collection of several must-see sights and exhibits, the Jewish Museum includes the Old Jewish Cemetery, crowded with tombstones, and several historic synagogues.

★ **Malá Pevnost (Small Fortress), Terezín.** The grounds and buildings of the most notorious Nazi concentration camp on Czech territory have been preserved as a testament to the horrific legacy of the Holocaust.

Hungary

★ **Néprajzi Múzeum (Museum of Ethnography), Budapest.** A majestic 1890s structure across from the Parliament building—the lavish marble entrance hall alone is worth a visit—houses an impressive exhibit on Hungary's historic folk traditions.

★ **Szépművészeti Múzeum (Museum of Fine Arts), Budapest.** Hungary's best collection of fine art includes esteemed works by Dutch and Spanish old masters, as well as exhibits on major Hungarian artists.

★ **Zsolnay Múzeum (Zsolnay Museum), Pécs.** Pécs's oldest surviving building houses an extensive collection of the world-famous Zsolnay family's exquisite porcelain art.

Poland

★ **Czartoryski Collection, Kraków.** Part of the National Museum's holdings, housed in Municipal Arsenal, this is one of the best art collections in Poland; among its highlights are works by Leonardo, Raphael, and Rembrandt.

★ **Muzeum Narodowe (National Museum), Warsaw.** This is a remarkable collection of contemporary Polish and European paintings and ceramics, as well as Gothic icons and works from antiquity.

★ **Oświęcim (Auschwitz-Birkenau), near Kraków.** A million Jews, Gypsies, and others were killed by the Nazis at this concentration camp, which more than any other has come to be seen as the epicenter of the moral collapse of the West; it has been preserved as a museum.

Romania

★ **Muzeul Satului Romanesc (Village Museum), Bucharest.** This fascinating open-air museum near Herăstrău Lake comprises some 300 authentic, fully furnished peasants' houses.

★ **Muzeul Țăranului Român (Peasant Museum), Bucharest.** You can catch an evocative glimpse of Romanian peasantry through these beautifully displayed costumes, icons, carpets, and other items of rural life.

Slovakia

★ **Múzeum Židovskej Kultúry (Museum of Jewish Culture in Slovakia), Bratislava.** Housed in a mid-17th-century Renaissance mansion, this exhibition covers the history of Jews in Slovakia from the time of the Great Moravian Empire to the present.

★ **Šariš (Icon Museum), Bardejov.** The myth of St. George and the dragon is one of the favorite themes in this captivating collection of Russian Orthodox artwork from the region's churches.

★ **Warhol Family Museum of Modern Art, Medzilaborce.** In this tiny town, view original Andy Warhol silkscreens, including two from the famous Campbell's Soup series, as well as portraits of Lenin and singer Billie Holiday.

Towns and Villages

Bulgaria

★ **Koprivshtitsa (Inland Bulgaria).** Situated among mountain pastures and pine forests in the Sredna Gora Range, Koprivshtitsa is a showcase of the Bulgarian Renaissance style, where buildings are covered in brightly painted designs and ornate carvings.

Czech Republic

★ **Český Krumlov, Bohemia.** The repainted Renaissance facades and the new shops and pensions that now crowd the lanes have banished much of Krumlov's charming old decay, but the hard-earned dignity of the houses and the sweet melancholy of the streetscapes abide in this lovely southern Bohemian town.

★ **Telč, Moravia.** The perfectly preserved town square, clustered with superb examples of Gothic, Renaissance, and Baroque architecture, is almost preternaturally perfect.

★ **Mariánské Lázně, Bohemia.** In this genteel spa town, you can take the waters while strolling under gracious colonnades.

Hungary

★ **Pécs, Transdanubia.** This vibrant, cultured city's numerous museums—among the best in the country—glorious basilica, and picturesque location in the Mecsek Hills make it one of Hungary's lesser-known gems.

★ **Szentendre, the Danube Bend.** A tremendously popular day-trip destination from Budapest, this quaint town offers cobblestone streets for strolling and numerous art galleries for browsing and buying.

★ **Szigliget, Lake Balaton.** A tranquil, delightfully picturesque little village on the lakeshore, Szigliget is a collection of traditional thatched-roof houses clustered together on narrow streets at the base of a hill crowned by a 13th-century fortress; the views of the lake from the ruins are exceptional.

Poland

★ **Kazimierz Dolny, eastern Poland.** Perched on a steep, hilly bank above the Vistula River, Kazimierz Dolny is a cluster of whitewashed facades and red-tiled roofs; known in an earlier incarnation as the "Pearl of the Renaissance," the town is something of an artists' colony.

★ **Toruń, western Poland.** One of the few cities to come through World War II unscathed, Tonuń is a lovely blend of medieval, Baroque, Gothic, and Renaissance buildings.

★ **Zamość, eastern Poland.** The main square of this fortified town is a graceful, arcaded plaza punctuated by a Baroque town hall.

Romania

★ **Sighişoara, Transylvania.** The birthplace of Vlad Ţepeş, the real Dracula, Sighişoara has hardly been developed as a tourist attraction, which makes its medieval citadel particularly inviting.

Slovakia

★ **Levoča, eastern Slovakia.** The medieval capital of the Spiš region seems frozen in time; between the 14th and 17th centuries it flourished as an important center of trade, crafts, and art.

FESTIVALS AND SEASONAL EVENTS

Bulgaria

For exact dates of annual events or other information, check with any local tourist agency or contact Balkan Holidays International (✉ 5 Triaditsa, Sofia, ☎ 02/86–861) or Balkantourist (✉ 1, bul. Vitosha, ☎ 02/43–331). These agencies generally have an English-speaking staff member on hand who will have the most up-to-date information.

DECEMBER–JANUARY➤ **Sofia International New Year's Music Festival** is a winter version of the summer Music Days (☞ *below*). Parties on New Year's Eve turn almost every *mehana* (folk restaurant) in the mountain towns of Bansko, Pamporovo, and Borovets into must-see Bulgarian folk spectacles.

MAY–JUNE➤ **Sofia Music Days,** focusing on classical and contemporary orchestral repertoire, attracts internationally recognized musicians, conductors, orchestras, and choruses. Concerts are held at the Bulgaria Concert Hall and the National Palace of Culture. The **Albena Chess Festival and International Masters' Tournament** is held annually at the Black Sea resort of Albena. The **Rose Festival** in the Valley of the Roses is held in the town of Kazanlak. Dancers and singers perform after the predawn gathering of rosebuds by "rose maidens." In Stara Zagora, in May, you can spend a week learning to appreciate Bulgarian theater fine arts during the **Festival of Opera and Ballet,** or in the first weekend of June,

check out the newly instituted **Festival of Folk Arts.** At the end of June Plovdiv hosts the **International Chamber Music Festival,** when many intimate concerts are held in the small churches of the Old Town.

JUNE–JULY➤ **Varna Summer International Music Festival** is held in Varna and Golden Sands. It also incorporates the **International Ballet Festival,** held in July. A variant of **Sofia Music Days,** focusing on modern and international music, continues through the end of July in the capital. On June 16, the border town of Rousse holds a folk festival called **Golden Rebec,** featuring singing, crafts, and feasts with a slight Romanian influence.

JUNE–AUGUST➤ The **International Windsurfing Regatta** takes place at the Black Sea resorts of Golden Sands, Sunny Beach, and Sozopol.

AUGUST➤ **Rozhen Sings National Fair,** held in Rozhen near the Pamporovo mountain resort, features Bulgarian folk singers, dancers, and revelers outfitted in traditional costumes. A similar gathering can be found at the end of the month on the Black Sea in the city of Burgas. Plovdiv also has a **Folk Festival** held on the last weekend in August. The most popular August event is the **Golden Orpheus,** an international festival of Bulgarian pop music. It has been drawing crowds to Sunny Beach, or Slanchev Bryag, from August 28 to September 3, for the last 30 years.

SEPTEMBER➤ Probably the most famous and popular festival in all of Bulgaria, the **Apollonia Festival of the Arts** is held in Sozopol, including art exhibitions, theater, poetry readings, and street events. At the end of the month, the cosmopolitan crowds move to Varna for the **Golden Rose International Film Festival.** Though the event has taken place annually for more than 40 years, it has only recently begun to feature some of the best and brightest filmmakers in Eastern Europe and farther abroad.

OCTOBER➤ Rousse attracts jazz lovers to its **International Jazz Forum,** with concerts in the larger performance venues as well as a tight schedule of back-to-back jazz in bars and clubs.

NOVEMBER➤ **KINOMANIA,** roughly translated as Film Fever, turns Sofia's National Palace of Culture into a giant film complex for three weeks. With the newest and best Bulgarian and international films of the year playing all day long in all 15 theaters, it is a movie lover's extravaganza.

Czech Republic

DECEMBER➤ **Christmas fairs and programs** take place in most towns and cities; among those particularly worth catching are **Christmas in Valašsko,** in Rožnov pod Radhoštěm, and the **Arrival of Lady Winter Festival,** in Prachatice.

JANUARY➤ Prague hosts the **FebioFest International**

Film, Television and Video Festival.

MARCH➤ The Czech Republic's **Cross-country Skiing Championships** take place in Špindlerův Mlýn; Prague holds **St. Matthew's Fair,** an annual children's fair in honor of St. Matthew.

APRIL➤ Several international music festivals are held in the capital: **Classical Easter,** and two festivals of sacred music, **Musica Ecumenica** and **Musica Sacra Praga.** Prague is also the site of **Days of European Film.** Brno puts on an **Easter Spiritual Music Festival.**

MAY➤ There are events both athletic and artistic in Prague; there's the **Prague Spring International Music Festival** as well as the **Prague Marathon.** Major writers from around the world present readings during the **Prague Writers' Festival.** An **International Children's Film Festival** is held in Zlín, while the **Antonín Dvořák Music Festival** takes place in Vysoká, near Příbram. For music in a Bohemian spa town, head to the **Karlovy Vary International Jazz Festival.**

JUNE➤ The international dance festival **Tanec Praha** hits the capital. Nelahozeves hosts the **Dvořák Music Summer**; there's an **international folklore festival** in the Moravian town Strážnice.

JULY➤ Karlovy Vary has its own **International Film Festival. Chrudim Puppeteering** is a puppet theater festival; Telč puts on a folk music festival, **Holidays in Telčfolk.**

AUGUST➤ This is a great month for music of all

kinds. Prague's **Verdi Festival** is staged at the State Opera; Mariánské Lázně holds a **Chopin Festival.** For something more musically ornate, visit the **Baroque Opera Festival** in Valtice. Český Krumlov has an **International Music Festival,** and Strakonice hosts the **International Bagpipe Festival.**

SEPTEMBER➤ You'll need to book a hotel room well in advance for Brno's **International Engineering Fair**; on a lighter note, the city also has a **Beer Days** celebration. Prague holds several arts festivals: the **Autumn International Music Festival,** the **Bedřich Smetana Festival,** and the **Festival of German-Language Theater.** Events celebrating new vintages begin, such as the **Mikulov Vintage Wine Festival** and the **Mělník Vintage Wine Festival.**

OCTOBER➤ The capital continues its run of cultural events, including an **International Jazz Festival,** the **Festival of Progressive Personalities in European Dance Theater, Musica Iudaica,** a festival of Jewish music, and the **Festival of 20th Century Music.** The **Velká Pardubická Steeplechase** is considered one of Europe's toughest racing events.

NOVEMBER➤ Prague focuses on visual arts with the **Festival of Independent Film** and the **Czech Press Photo** annual exhibition.

Hungary

For contact information about most of these festivals, *see* the city or town's Nightlife and the Arts section or inquire at the Budapest Tourinform

office or the local visitor information center.

MID-MARCH TO EARLY APRIL➤ The season's first and biggest arts festival, the **Budapest Spring Festival,** showcases Hungary's best opera, music, theater, fine arts, and dance, as well as visiting foreign artists. Other towns—including Kecskemét, Szentendre, and Szombathely—also participate.

MAY➤ The **Balaton Festival** in Keszthely features high-caliber classical concerts and other festivities held in venues around town and outdoors on Kossuth Lajos utca.

JUNE➤ The **World Music Festival** in Budapest, held in early June, has several days of world music concerts by local and international artists. Kőszeg's biggest cultural event, held mid-month, is the annual **East West Folk Festival**—a weekend of open-air international folk music and dance performances. Szombathely's gala **Savaria International Dance Competition** (one day in early June) features a full day of elegant ballroom dancing by competing pairs from around the world. The monthlong **Sopron Festival Weeks,** beginning in mid-June, brings music, dance, and theater performances and art exhibits to churches and venues around town.

LATE JUNE–EARLY JULY➤ Pécs's **Nemzetközi Színházi Fesztivál** (International Theater Festival) presents performances by local and international artists.

JULY➤ The **Szentendre Summer Days** festival offers open-air theater performances and jazz and classical concerts.

Equestrian fans will not want to miss the **Horto-bágy International Horse Show,** held in Máta (and in neighboring Horto-bágy) annually the first week of July.

Jazz fans can enjoy local and international ensembles during the **Debrecen Jazz Festival** in mid-July; around the same time, the **Visegrád International Palace Games** includes medieval jousting tournaments and festivities. Late in the month, Balaton-füred's **Anna Ball** is a traditional ball and beauty contest. In Vác the last weekend in July, the **Váci Világi Vigalom** (Vác World Jamboree) festival is held, with folk dancing, music, crafts fairs, and other festivities.

Every two years in early July (the next scheduled for 2000), Kecskemét hosts a giant children's festival, **Európa Jövője Gyermektalálkozó** (Future of Europe Children's Convention), during which children's groups from some 25 countries put on colorful folk-dance and singing performances. Debrecen's biannual **Béla Bartók International Choral Festival,** scheduled for early July 2000, is an international choir competition.

JULY–AUGUST➤ Established in the 1930s, the annual **Szegedi Szabadtéri Napok** (Open-Air Days) offers a gala series of dramas, operas, operettas, classical concerts, and folk-dance performances by Hungarian and international artists. Tickets are always hot commodities; plan far ahead.

AUGUST➤ Early in the month, Budapest hosts a

Formula 1 car race, while the weeklong **BudaFest** opera and ballet festival takes place mid-month at the opera house after the opera season ends. During the first two weeks of August, the **Celebration Weeks** festival in Baroque Eger presents classical concerts, dance, and other arts programs. **St. Stephen's Day** (August 20) is a major national holiday. Two highlights are the fireworks in Budapest and Debrecen's **Flower Carnival,** which features a festive parade of flower-encrusted floats and carriages. Held annually around August 20, **Hortobágy Bridge Fair** brings horse shows, a folk-art fair, ox roasts, and festive crowds to the plot beneath the famous Nine-Arch Bridge.

Every two years Esztergom hosts the **Nemzetközi Gitár Fesztivál** (International Guitar Festival), during which renowned classical guitarists from around the world hold master classes and workshops for participants. The festival runs for two weeks early in the month; the next one will be held in 1999.

SEPTEMBER➤ The **Eger Harvest Festival** early in the month celebrates the grape harvest with a traditional parade and wine tastings.

EARLY OCTOBER➤ Tokaj's annual **Szüreti Hét** (Harvest Week) celebrates the autumn grape harvest with a parade, street ball, folk-art markets, and a plethora of wine-tasting opportunities from the local vintners' stands set up on and around the main square.

Poland

DECEMBER➤ **St. Nicholas Day** (December 6) is prevalent in the south; children receive gifts and dress as mummers. Kraków's **Christmas crèche competition** displays handmade nativity crèches.

JANUARY➤ Warsaw holds a Polish theater festival, **Warsawskie Spotkania Teatralne.**

MAY➤ Spring starts off with plenty of music; there's a **Chamber Music Festival** in Łańcut, an **International Jazz Festival "Jazz on the Oder"** in Wrocław, and the **International Festival of Music** in Częstochowa. The **Warsaw International Book Fair** is Central and Eastern Europe's largest fair of books, magazines, and manuscripts.

MAY–JUNE➤ The **International Festival of Short Feature Films** (Kraków) presents hundreds of short, video, documentary, animated, and experimental films.

JUNE➤ Kraków has a **Festival of Jewish Culture.** The **International Oratorios and Cantata Festival "Wratislavia Cantans"** is staged in Wrocław. Warsaw's **midsummer ceremonies** (June 23) include throwing candlelit wreaths into the Vistula; the capital also has Sunday morning and afternoon **open-air Chopin concerts** at the Chopin Memorial in Łazienki Park and **Chopin concerts** at Żelazowa Wola (these run until October). For **folk music and dance,** head to the festival in Kazimierz Dolny.

JUNE–JULY➤ Warsaw offers a **Mozart Festival.** There are two **interna-**

tional festivals of organ, choir, and chamber music, one in Gdańsk–Oliwa, the other in Kamien Pomorski, near Szczecin. Poznan's **International Theater Festival** offers performances in various outdoor venues.

JULY➤ The **music of Karol Szymanowski** is celebrated in Zakopane, the village where the Polish composer lived during the 1920s.

AUGUST➤ Artisans, folk dancers, and musicians take over the streets of Gdańsk for the **Dominican Fair and Festival,** the annual commemoration of St. Dominic. The **International Festival of Highland Folklore** in Zakopane celebrates highland cultures with folk-art and costume exhibits, poetry competitions, and musical concerts. The **International Country Music Festival** in Mrągowo features local and foreign performers. Other August festivals include the **International Song Festival** (Sopot), **International Festival of Choir Songs**(Międzyzdroje), the **International Chopin Festival** (Duszniki Zdrój) and the **Knights and Crossbow Tournament for the Sword of John III Sobieski** (Gniew).

SEPTEMBER➤ **Wratislavia Cantans** in Wrocław features oratorio and cantata music. The **"Warsaw Autumn" festival of contemporary music** showcases symphony and chamber concerts, opera, ballet, and electronic-music performances.

Krynica presents the **Jan Kiepura Festival of Opera Songs,** and during the last week of September, the archaeological site of **Biskupin** has a festival, including historic reenactments.

OCTOBER➤ **Warsaw's Jazz Jamboree** is the oldest jazz festival in Europe. Kraków hosts its own **Jazz Festival.** The world famous **Chopin competition,** which takes place every five years, will be held in Warsaw in the year 2000.

NOVEMBER➤ Thousands of candles are placed on graves in cemeteries on **All Saints' Day** (November 1).

Romania

JULY➤ The **Golden Stag,** Braşov's annual music festival, attracts local and international musicians for a weeklong series of performances.

SEPTEMBER➤ Though the **Medieval Festival** of Sighişoara has lost some of its traditional focus over the years, it is still a vibrant, popular celebration. Many young people set up tents inside the citadel and camp out for the weekend.

EARLY OCTOBER➤ In a nod to its Germanic ancestry, the town of Braşov holds an annual **Octoberfest,** with food, local and imported beer, and traditional folk activities.

Slovakia

In addition to hosting the events noted below, many

villages also have annual folklore festivals, usually on a weekend in late summer or early fall, which are often filled with singing, dancing, and drinking. For more information, look for the English-language annual events calendar put out by the Slovak Ministry of Economy; it's available in travel agencies and tourist information centers.

DECEMBER➤ **Christmas at the Castle** is in Bojnice. Visiting children are presented with Christmas gifts by local historical characters.

MARCH➤ Bardejov has a **Musical Spring** performance series; Liptovský Mikuláš has a **Folk Song Festival.**

APRIL➤ The **International Festival of Ghosts and Phantoms** is held every year at the end of April in the striking castle in Bojnice.

MAY➤ **Košice Musical Spring** takes place in May.

JUNE➤ An **International Folklore Festival** is held in Košice.

JULY➤ **Folklore Festival Východná** takes place in Eastern Slovakia.

SEPTEMBER➤ A **Vintage Festival** takes place in Pezinok, near Bratislava.

OCTOBER➤ The **Bratislava Music Festival** attracts national and international musicians to venues throughout the capital late in the month. The capital also hosts the **Jazz Days Festival.**

2 The Czech Republic

Faster and with greater success than any other former Soviet-bloc country, the Czech Republic has matured into a showcase democracy that offers visitors some of Central Europe's most alluring attractions. The "hundred-spired" capital city of Prague—one of the world's best-preserved architectural cityscapes—offers world-class cultural performances and increasingly distinctive dining and shopping. In the countryside beyond, medieval castles perch quietly near lost-in-time Baroque and Renaissance villages. Pine forests and gentle green mountains beckon outdoor enthusiasts with a multitude of pleasures.

By Mark Baker

Updated by Ky
Krauthamer,
Martha
Lagace, and
Robert Rigney

AVICTIM OF ENFORCED OBSCURITY throughout much of the 20th century, the Czech Republic, comprising the provinces of Bohemia and Moravia (but no longer Slovakia), is once again in the spotlight. In a world where revolution was synonymous with violence, and in a country where truth was quashed by the tanks of Eastern-bloc socialism, in November 1989 Václav Havel's sonorous voice proclaimed the victory of the "Velvet Revolution" to enthusiastic crowds on Wenceslas Square and preached the value of "living in truth." Recording the dramatic events of the time, television cameras panned across Prague's glorious skyline and fired the world's imagination with the image of political renewal superimposed on somber Gothic and voluptuous Baroque.

Travelers have rediscovered the country, and Czechs and Moravians have rediscovered the world. Not so long ago, the visitor was unhindered by crowds of tourists but had to struggle with a creeping sensation of melancholy and neglect that threatened to eclipse the country's beauty. Combined with a truly frustrating lack of services in every branch of the tourist industry, a trip to Czechoslovakia was always an adventure in the full sense of the word.

At least on the surface, the atmosphere is changing rapidly. The stagnant "normalization" of the Husák era, which froze the country out of the developments of the late 20th century, is giving way to the dynamic and the cosmopolitan. The revolution brought enthusiasm and such conveniences as English-language newspapers and attentive service.

The revolution inspired one other thing: nationalism. Unable to unite on a common course of economic renewal, Czechs and Slovaks peacefully agreed to dissolve their 74-year-old federal state on January 1, 1993. Though the division was greeted with sadness by outsiders, and internal political developments have moved the nations far apart on many issues, visitors to either country are not likely to notice much difference save the hassle of an extra border and the need now to change money when traveling back and forth.

The drab remnants of socialist reality are still omnipresent on the back roads of Bohemia and Moravia. But many of the changes made by the Communists were superficial—adding ugliness but leaving the society's core more or less intact. The colors are less jarring, not designed to attract the moneyed eye; the fittings are as they always were, not adapted to the needs of a new world.

The experience of visiting the Czech Republic still involves stepping back in time. Even in Prague, now deluged by tourists two-thirds of the year, the sense of history—stretching back through centuries of wars, empires, and monuments to everyday life—remains uncluttered by the trappings of modernity. The peculiar melancholy of Central Europe, less tainted now by the oppressive political realities of the postwar era, still lurks in narrow streets and forgotten corners. Crumbling facades, dilapidated palaces, and treacherous cobbled streets both shock and enchant the visitor used to a world where what remains of history has been spruced up for tourist eyes.

The arrival of designer boutiques, chain restaurants, and shopping malls—not only in Prague but increasingly in the larger provincial towns—does mean that the country has lost some of the "feel" it had just a few years ago. At the same time, the seemingly unstoppable transition of the economy signals an increasing harmonization of Czechs' way of life with that of Western Europe. But the process goes slowly,

Czech Republic (Česká Republika)

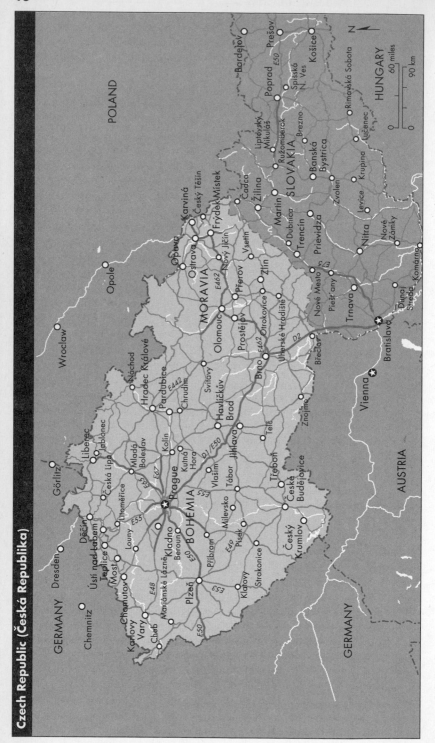

and the heavy blows of 1997—the fall of the currency, devastating floods, and the scandal-marred end of Prime Minister Václav Klaus' government—may retard it for several years. The good news is that the country is on track to join the NATO alliance in 1999 and to become a European Union member state sometime in the next decade. The Czech Republic still looks like a post-Communist success story, though one coming to know the hard facts of modern life, from corruption to unemployment. Economic and social integration into the "common European home," which in the postrevolutionary euphoria seemed possible within a few years, must now be measured in decades.

However, the strange, Old World, and at times frustratingly bureaucratic atmosphere of the Czech Republic is not all a product of the Communist era. Many of the everyday rituals are actually remnants of the Hapsburg Empire and are also to be found, perhaps to a lesser degree, in Vienna and Budapest. The *šatna* (coatroom), for example, plays a vivid role in any visit to a restaurant or theater at any time of year other than summer. Coats must be given with a few coins to the attendant, usually an old lady with a sharp eye for ignorant or disobedient tourists. The attendant often also plays a role in controlling the rest room; the entrance fee entitles the visitor to a small roll of paper, ceremoniously kept on the attendant's table. Another odd institution associated with this part of the world is the *Tabák-Trafik*, a newsstand that sells two things connected for no apparent reason: tobacco products and public-transportation tickets.

Outside the capital, for those willing to put up with the inconveniences of shabby hotels and mediocre restaurants, the sense of rediscovering a neglected world is even stronger. And the range is startling, from imperial spas, with their graceful colonnades and dilapidated villas, to the hundreds of arcaded town squares, modestly displaying the passing of time with each splendid layer of once contemporary style. Gothic towers, Renaissance facades, Baroque interiors, and aging modern supermarkets merge. Between the man-made sights, the visitor is rewarded with glorious mountain ranges and fertile rolling countryside laced with carp ponds and forests.

The key to enjoying the country is to relax. There is no point in demanding high levels of service or quality. And for the budget-conscious traveler, this is Central Europe at its most beautiful, at prices that are several times below those of Austria and even Hungary.

Pleasures and Pastimes

Castles and Châteaus

More than 2,000 castles, manor houses, and châteaus collectively form a precious and not-to-be-missed part of the country's cultural and historical heritage. Grim ruins glower from craggy hilltops, and fantastical Gothic castles guard ancient trade routes. Hundreds of noble houses—Renaissance, Baroque, Empire, and their many compounds—dot the countryside. Their former bourgeois and aristocratic owners were expelled in the anti-German reaction of 1945–1946 or forced out by the Communists. Many of their valuable old seats now stand in near ruin, though some have been returned to the original owners while others remain in state hands. While not one, perhaps, will ever be as it once was, more sights than ever before are open to the public. Picture galleries, rooms full of historic furniture, exquisite medieval stonework, and Baroque chapels—all speak of a vanished way of life whose remnants survive in every town and village of Bohemia and Moravia.

Dining

The quality of restaurant cuisine and service in the Czech Republic remains uneven, but many excellent private restaurants have sprung up in Prague in recent years. The traditional dishes—roast pork or duck with dumplings, or broiled meat with sauce—can be light and tasty when well prepared. Often in smaller towns the hotel restaurant is still the only dining option available. An annoying "cover charge" usually makes its way onto restaurant bills, seeming to subsidize the salt and pepper shakers; in any case, you should discreetly check the addition, since a few unscrupulous proprietors still overcharge foreigners.

Restaurants generally fall into three categories. A *pivnice,* or beer hall, usually offers a simple menu of goulash or pork with dumplings at very low prices. The atmosphere tends to be friendly and casual; you can expect to share a table. More attractive (and more expensive) are the *vinárna* (wine cellars) and *restaurace* (restaurants), which serve a full range of dishes. Wine cellars, some occupying Romanesque basements, can be a real treat. A fourth dining option, the *lahůdky* (snack bar or deli), is the quickest and cheapest option.

Lunch, usually eaten between noon and 2, is the main meal for Czechs and offers you the best deal. Many restaurants put out a special luncheon menu (*denní lístek*), usually printed only in Czech, with more appetizing selections at better prices. If you don't see it, ask your waiter. Dinner is usually served from 5 until 9 or 10, but don't wait too long to eat. First of all, most Czechs eat only a light meal in the evening. Second, restaurant cooks frequently knock off early on slow nights, and the later you arrive, the more likely it is that the kitchen will be closed. In general, dinner menus do not differ substantially from lunch offerings, except the prices are higher.

CATEGORY	PRAGUE*	OTHER AREAS*
$$$$	over $40	over $35
$$$	$25–$40	$20–$35
$$	$15–$25	$10–$20
$	under $15	under $10

per person for a three-course meal, excluding wine and tip

Hiking

The Czech Republic is a hiker's paradise, with 40,000 km (25,000 mi) of well-kept, -marked, and -signposted trails both in the mountainous regions and leading through beautiful countryside from town to town. The best areas are the Beskydy range in northern Moravia and the Krkonoše range (Giant Mountains) in northern Bohemia. The rolling Šumava Hills of southern Bohemia are also excellent hiking territory, and the environment there is the purest in the country. You'll find the colored markings denoting trails on trees, fences, walls, rocks, and elsewhere. The main paths are marked in red, others in blue and green, while the least important trails are marked in yellow. Hiking maps covering the entire country can be found in almost any bookstore; look for the large-scale *Soubor turistických* maps.

Lodging

The number of hotels and pensions has increased dramatically throughout the Czech Republic, in step with the influx of tourists. Finding a suitable room should pose no problem, although it is highly recommended that you book ahead during the peak tourist season (July and August, and the Christmas and Easter holidays). Hotel prices, in general, remain high. This is especially true in Prague and in the spa towns of western Bohemia. Better value can often be found at private pensions and with individual homeowners offering rooms to let. In the outlying towns, the best strategy is to inquire at the local tourist information office or simply fan out around the town and look for room-for-rent signs on houses (usually in German: ZIMMER FREI or PRIVAT ZIMMER).

Outside Prague and the major tourist centers, hotels tend to fall into two categories: the old-fashioned hotel on the main square, with rooms above a restaurant, no private bathrooms, and a very low price; and the modern, impersonal, and often ugly high-rise with all the basic facilities and a reasonable price. Nevertheless, clean rooms are the rule, and some hotels (of both varieties) can be quite pleasant. Hostels are understood to mean dormitory rooms and are probably best avoided. In the mountains you can often find little *chaty* (chalets), where pleasant surroundings compensate for a lack of basic amenities. *Autokempink* parks (campsites) generally have a few bungalows.

The Czech Republic's official hotel classification now follows the international star system. These ratings correspond closely to our categories as follows: deluxe or five-star plus four-star ($$$$); three-star ($$$); two-star ($$). The $ category will most often be met by private rooms. Often you can book rooms—both at hotels and in private homes—through Čedok or visitor bureaus. Otherwise, try calling or writing the hotel directly. Keep in mind that in many hotels, except at the deluxe level, a "double" bed means two singles that can be pushed together. (Single-mattress double beds are generally not available.)

The prices quoted below are for double rooms during high season; generally, breakfast is included in the room rate. At certain periods, such as Easter and during festivals, prices can jump 15%–25%; as a rule, always ask the price before taking a room.

As for camping, there are hundreds of sites for tents and trailers throughout the country, but most are open only in summer (May to mid-September). You can get a map from Čedok of all the sites, with addresses, opening times, and facilities. Camping outside official sites is prohibited. Some campgrounds also offer bungalows. Campsites are divided into Categories A and B according to facilities, but both have hot water and toilets.

CATEGORY	PRAGUE*	OTHER AREAS*
$$$$	over $200	over $100
$$$	$100–$200	$50–$100
$$	$50–$100	$25–$50
$	under $50	under $25

All prices are for a standard double room during peak season, including breakfast.

Outdoor Activities and Sports

Bicycling: Czechs are avid cyclists. The flatter areas of southern Bohemia and Moravia are ideal for biking. Outside the larger towns, quiet roads stretch out for miles. The hillier terrain of northern Bohemia makes it popular with mountain-biking enthusiasts. Not many places rent bikes, though. Inquire at Čedok or at your hotel for rental information. **Boating and Sailing:** The country's main boating area is the enormous series of dams and reservoirs along the Vltava south of Prague. The most popular lake is Slapy, where it is possible to rent small paddleboats as well as to relax and swim on a hot day. Rowboats are available for rent along Prague's Vltava in summertime. **Skiing:** The two main skiing areas in the Czech Republic are the Krkonoše range in northern Bohemia and the Šumava hills of southern Bohemia (lifts at both operate from January through March). In both areas you'll find a number of organizations renting skis—although supplies may be limited and lines may be long. Both places are also good for cross-country skiing.

Shopping

In Prague, Karlovy Vary, and elsewhere in Bohemia, look for elegant and unusual crystal and porcelain. Bohemia is also renowned for the quality and deep-red color of its garnets; keep an eye out for beautiful garnet rings and brooches, set in either gold or silver. You can also find excellent ceramics, especially in Moravia, as well as other folk artifacts, such as printed textiles, lace, hand-knit sweaters, and painted eggs. There are attractive crafts stores throughout the Czech Republic. Karlovy Vary is blessed with a variety of unique items to buy, including the strange pipelike drinking mugs used in the spas; vases left to petrify in the mineral-laden water; and *Becherovka,* a tasty herbal aperitif that makes a nice gift to take home.

Wine and Beer

Czechs are reputed to drink more beer per capita than any people on earth; small wonder, as many connoisseurs rank Bohemian lager-style beer as the best in the world. This cool, crisp brew was invented in Plzeň (Pilsen) in 1842, although Czech beer had already been brewed for centuries prior to that time. Aside from the world-famous *Plzeňský Prazdroj* (Pilsner Urquell) and milder *Budvar* (the original Budweiser) brands, some typical beers are the slightly bitter *Krušovice,* fruity *Radegast,* and the sweeter, Prague-brewed *Staropramen. Světlé pivo,* or golden beer, is most common, although many pubs also serve *černé* (dark) which is often slightly sweeter than the light variety.

Czechs also produce quite drinkable wines: peppy, fruity whites and mild, versatile reds. Southern Moravia, with comparatively warm summers and rich soil, grows the bulk of the wine harvest; look for the Mikulov and Znojmo regional designations. Favorite white varietals are *Müller Thurgau,* with a fine muscat bouquet and light flavor, and *Neuburské,* yellow-green in color and with a dry, smoky bouquet. *Rulandské bílé,* a semidry Burgundy-like white, has a flowery bouquet and full-bodied flavor. Belying the notion that northerly climes are more auspicious for white than red grapes, northern Bohemia's scant few hundred acres of vineyards produce reliable reds and the occasional jewel. *Frankovka* is fiery red and slightly acidic, while the cherry-red *Rulandské červené* is an excellent, drier choice. *Vavřinecké* is dark and slightly sweet.

Exploring the Czech Republic

The stunning silhouette of Prague is undeniably one of the country's strongest magnets, but there are plenty of beautiful vistas, spired castles, and peaceful town squares beyond the capital. Bohemia, for centuries its own kingdom, spreads around Prague to the borders of Germany and Austria. This region is rich with spa towns in the west, walled towns and castles to the south, and moving reminders of World War II in the north. Moravia, the area east of Prague, is anchored by Brno. This relatively modern city is surrounded by smaller, traditional towns, some tied to the wine trade; to the north a stretch of rural hills leads to the Tatra mountains.

Great Itineraries

Numbers in the text correspond to numbers in the margin and on the Exploring Prague, Prague Castle [Pražský hrad] and Bohemia maps.

IF YOU HAVE 3 DAYS

Make ⚞ **Prague** ①–㊻ your base. This will allow you plenty of time to explore the beauties and wonders of the Old Town and Hradčany, as well as to make a day trip to one of the country's fascinating smaller cities: the splendid spa town of **Karlovy Vary** ㊻, nestled in the western Bohemia hills, makes a good one-day destination.

Plan to spend three full days exploring Prague. You could easily spend a day each in the Old Town, Malá Strana, and the castle and the other two days visiting the well-preserved medieval mining town of **Kutná Hora** ⑤⑥ and the unforgettable concentration camp **Terezín** ⑦③. Or you could spend a day amid the Renaissance charm of **Český Krumlov** ⑥②.

When to Tour

Prague is beautiful year-round, but avoid midsummer (especially July and August) and the Christmas and Easter holidays, when the city is overrun with tourists. Spring and fall generally combine good weather with a more bearable level of tourism. In winter you'll encounter fewer other visitors and have the opportunity to see Prague breathtakingly covered in snow; but it can get very cold. The same guidelines generally apply to traveling in the rest of Bohemia and Moravia, although even in August, the peak of the high season, the number of visitors to these areas is far smaller than in Prague. The Giant Mountains of Bohemia come into their own in winter (December–February). If you're not a skier, try visiting the mountains in late spring (May or June) or fall, when the colors are dazzling and you'll have the hotels and restaurants nearly to yourself. Bear in mind that most castles, and some museums outside Prague, are closed November through March.

PRAGUE

In the nine years since Prague's students took to the streets to help bring down the 40-year-old Communist regime, the city has enjoyed an unparalleled cultural renaissance. Much of the energy has come from planeloads of idealistic young foreigners, but the enthusiasm has been shared in near-equal measure by their Czech counterparts. Amid Prague's cobblestone streets and gold-tipped spires, new galleries, cafés, and clubs teem with bright-eyed "expatriates" and ever more locals. New shops and, perhaps most noticeably, scads of new restaurants have opened, expanding the city's culinary reach far beyond the traditional roast pork and dumplings. Many have something to learn in the way of presentation and service, but Praguers still marvel at a variety that was unthinkable not so many years ago.

The arts and theater are also thriving in the "new" Prague. Young playwrights, some writing in English, regularly stage their own works. Weekly poetry readings are standing room only. The city's dozen or so rock clubs are jammed nightly; bands play everything from metal and psychedelic to garage and grunge.

All of this frenetic activity plays well against a stunning backdrop of towering churches and centuries-old bridges and alleyways. Prague achieved much of its present glory in the 14th century, during the long reign of Charles IV, king of Bohemia and Moravia and Holy Roman Emperor. It was Charles who established a university in the city and laid out the New Town (Nové Město), charting Prague's growth.

During the 15th century, the city's development was hampered by the Hussite Wars, a series of crusades launched by the Holy Roman Empire to subdue the fiercely independent Czech noblemen. The Czechs were eventually defeated in 1620 at the Battle of White Mountain (Bílá Hora) near Prague and were ruled by the Hapsburg family for the next 300 years. Under the Hapsburgs, Prague became a German-speaking city and an important administrative center, but it was forced to play second fiddle to the monarchy's capital of Vienna. Much of the Lesser Town (Malá Strana), across the river, was built up at this time, becoming home to Austrian nobility and its Baroque tastes.

Prague regained its status as a national capital in 1918, with the creation of the modern Czechoslovak state, and quickly asserted itself in the interwar period as a vital cultural center. Although the city escaped World War II essentially intact, Czechoslovakia fell under the political and cultural domination of the Soviet Union until the 1989 popular uprisings. The election of dissident playwright Václav Havel to the post of national president set the stage for the city's renaissance, which has since proceeded at a dizzying, quite Bohemian rate.

Exploring Prague

The spine of the city is the River Vltava (also known by its German name, Moldau), which runs through the city from south to north with a single sharp curve to the east. Prague originally comprised five independent towns, represented today by its main historic districts: **Hradčany** (Castle Area), **Malá Strana** (Lesser Quarter), **Staré Město** (Old Town), **Nové Město** (New Town), and **Josefov** (the Jewish Quarter).

Hradčany, the seat of Czech royalty for hundreds of years, has as its center the **Pražský Hrad** (Prague Castle), which overlooks the city from its hilltop west of the Vltava. Steps lead down from Hradčany to Malá Strana, an area dense with ornate mansions built by 17th- and 18th-century nobility.

Karlův Most (Charles Bridge) connects Malá Strana with Staré Město. Just a few blocks east of the bridge is the focal point of the Old Town, **Staroměstské náměstí** (Old Town Square). Staré Město is bounded by the curving Vltava and three large commercial avenues: **Revoluční** to the east, **Na Příkopě** to the southeast, and **Národní třída** to the south. Josefov is northwest of Staroměstské náměstí, bordered by the streets 17 listopadu, Na Františku, and Kozí.

Beyond lies the Nové Město; several blocks south is **Karlovo náměstí,** the city's largest square. Roughly 1 km (½ mi) farther south is **Vyšehrad,** an ancient castle high above the river.

On a promontory to the east of Wenceslas Square stretches **Vinohrady,** once the favored neighborhood of well-to-do Czechs; below Vinohrady lie the crumbling neighborhoods of **Žižkov** to the north and **Nusle** to the south. On the west bank of the Vltava south and east of Hradčany lie many older residential neighborhoods and enormous parks. About 3 km (2 mi) from the center in every direction, Communist-era housing projects begin their unsightly sprawl.

Numbers in the text correspond to numbers in the margin and on the Exploring Prague map.

Staré Město (the Old Town)
A GOOD WALK

Václavské náměstí ①, marked by the **Statue of St. Wenceslas** ② and convenient to hotels and transportation, is an excellent place to begin a tour of the Old Town. A long, gently sloping boulevard rather than a square in the usual sense, Václavské náměstí is bounded at the top (the southern end) by the **Národní Muzeum** ③ and at the bottom by the pedestrian shopping areas of Národní třída and Na Příkopě. Today Václavské náměstí comprises Prague's liveliest street scene. Don't miss the dense maze of arcades tucked away from the street in buildings that line both sides. You'll find an odd assortment of cafés, discos, ice cream parlors, and movie houses, all seemingly unfazed by the passage of time. At night the square changes character somewhat as dance music pours out from the crowded discos. One eye-catching building on the square is the **Hotel Europa** ④, at No. 25, a riot of Art Nouveau that recalls the glamorous world of turn-of-the-century Prague.

To begin the approach to the Old Town proper, walk past the tall, Art Deco Koruna complex and turn right onto the handsome pedestrian zone of Na Příkopě. Turn left onto Havířská ulice and follow this small alley to the glittering green-and-cream splendor of the 18th-century **Stavovské Divadlo** ⑤.

Return to Na Příkopě, turn left, and continue to the end of the street. On weekdays between 8 AM and 5 PM, it's well worth taking a peek at the stunning interior of the Živnostenská banka (Merchant's Bank), at No. 20.

Na Příkopě ends abruptly at the **Náměstí Republiky** ⑥, an important New Town transportation hub (with a metro stop). The severe depression-era facade of the Česká Národní banka (at Na Příkopě 30) makes the building look more like a fortress than the nation's central bank. Close by stands the stately **Prašná brána,** its festive Gothic spires looming above the square. Adjacent to the dignified Prašná brána, the **Obecní dům** looks decidedly decadent.

Walk through the arch at the base of Prašná brána and down the formal **Celetná ulice,** the first leg of the so-called Royal Way. Monarchs favored this route primarily because it has a stunning entry into Staroměstské náměstí and because the houses along Celetná were among the city's finest, providing a suitable backdrop to the coronation procession. The pink **U Sixtu** ⑦, at Celetná 2, sports one of the street's handsomest, if restrained, Baroque facades.

Staroměstské náměstí ⑧, at the end of Celetná, is dazzling, thanks partly to the double-spired **Kostel Panny Marie před Týnem** ⑨, which rises over the square from behind a row of patrician houses. To the immediate left of this church, at No. 13, is Dům U Kamenného zvonu, a Baroque structure that has been stripped down to its original Gothic elements.

Next door stands the gorgeous pink-and-ocher **Palác Kinských.** At this end of the square, you can't help noticing the expressive **Jan Hus monument** ⑩. Opposite the Kostel Panny Marie před Týnem is the Gothic **Staroměstská radnice** ⑪, which with its impressive 200-ft tower, gives the square its sense of importance. As the hour approaches, join the crowds milling below the tower's 15th-century **astronomical clock** for a brief but spooky spectacle taken straight from the Middle Ages, every hour on the hour.

Walk north along the edge of the small park beside Town Hall to reach the Baroque **Kostel svatého Mikuláše** ⑫, not to be confused with the Lesser Town's Chrám svatého Mikuláše on the other side of the river (☞ A Good Walk *in* Karlův most [Charles Bridge] and Malá Strana [Lesser Quarter], *below*). For a small detour, head down Kaprova street to the **Rudolfinum** concert hall and gallery; across the street is the Uměleckoprůmyslové muzeum (Museum of Decorative Arts). Both are notable neo-Renaissance buildings.

Returning to Staroměstské náměstí, you'll find **Výstava Franze Kafky** just to the left of Kostel svatého Mikuláše on U radnice. A small plaque can be found on the side of the house. Continue southwest from Staroměstské náměstí until you come to Malé náměstí, a nearly perfect ensemble of facades dating from the Middle Ages. Look for tiny Karlova ulice, which begins in the southwest corner of Malé náměstí, and take another quick right to stay on it (watch the signs—this medieval street seems designed to confound the visitor). Turn left at the

Exploring Prague

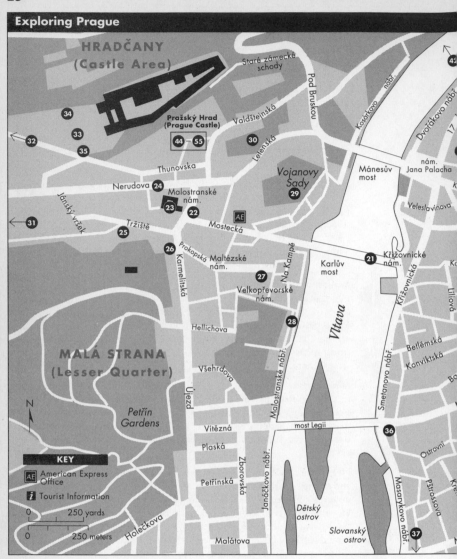

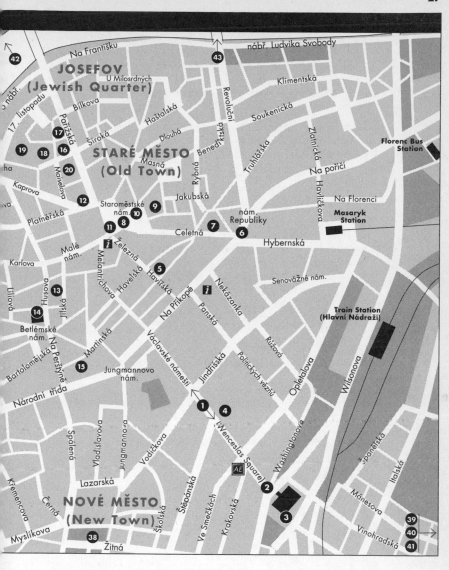

JOSEFOV
(Jewish Quarter)

STARÉ MĚSTO
(Old Town)

NOVÉ MĚSTO
(New Town)

Na Františku

nábř. Ludvíka Svobody

U Milosrdných

Klimentská

17. listopadu

Bílkova

Soukenická

Haštalská

Pařížská

Dlouhá

Revoluční

Široká

Benediktská

Truhlářská

Zlatnická

Na poříčí

Masná

Rybná

Na Florenci

Kaprova

Maiselova

Jakubská

Havlíčkova

Platnéřská

Staroměstské
nám.

nám.
Republiky

Celetná

Hybernská

Malé
nám.

Železná

Senovážné nám.

Karlova

Melantrichova

Havelská

Havířská

Na Příkopě

Nekázanka

Panská

Liliova

Husova

Jilská

Na Příkopě

Růžová

Opletalova

Wilsonova

Betlémské
nám.

Martinská

Václavské náměstí

Jindřišská

Politických vězňů

Bartolomějská

Na Perštýně

Jungmannovo
nám.

Národní třída

Washingtonova

Spálená

Vladislavova

Jungmannova

Vodičkova

Štěpánská

Ve Smečkách

Krakovská

Mánesova

Španělská

Italská

Lazarská

Černá

Vinohradská

Myslíkova

Žitná

Školská

Florenc Bus
Station

Masaryk
Station

Train Station
(Hlavní Nádraží)

42 43 17 19 18 16 20 12 10 9 11 8 7 6 5 13 14 15 1 4 2 3 38 39 40 41

AE

T intersection where Karlova seems to end in front of the České muzeum výtvarných umění (Czech Museum of Fine Arts) and continue left down the quieter Husova ulice, veer to the right for the Karlův most and the other side of the river). Pause and inspect the exotic Clam-Gallas palác (Clam-Gallas Palace) at Husova 20; it's now the municipal archives and rarely open to visitors. You'll recognize it easily: Look for the Titans in the doorway holding up what must be a very heavy Baroque facade.

Return to the T and continue down Husova. For a glimpse of a less successful Baroque reconstruction, take a close look at the **Kostel svatého Jiljí** ⑬, across from No. 7.

Continue walking along Husova ulice to Na Perštýně and turn right at tiny Betlémská ulice. The alley opens up onto a quiet square of the same name (Betlémská náměstí) and upon the most revered of all Hussite churches in Prague, the **Betlémská kaple** ⑭.

Return to Na Perštýně and continue walking to the right. As you near the back of the buildings of the busy Národní třída (National Boulevard), turn left at Martinská ulice. At the end of the street, the forlorn but majestic church **Kostel svatého Martina ve zdi** ⑮ stands like a post-war ruin. Walk around the church to the left and through a little archway of apartments onto the bustling Národní třída. To the left, a five-minute walk away, lies Václavské náměstí and the starting point of the walk.

TIMING

Václavské náměstí and Staroměstské náměstí are busy with activity around-the-clock almost all year round. If you're in search of a little peace and quiet, you will find the streets at their most subdued on early weekend mornings or right after a sudden downpour. The streets in this walking tour are reasonably close together and can be covered in half a day, or in a full day if you have more time. Remember to be in the Staroměstské náměstí just before the hour if you want to see the astronomical clock in action.

SIGHTS TO SEE

⑭ **Betlémská kaple** (Bethlehem Chapel). The church's elegant simplicity is in stark contrast to the diverting Gothic and Baroque of the rest of the city. The original structure dates from the end of the 14th century, and the Czech religious reformer Jan Hus was a regular preacher here from 1402 until his exile in 1412. After the Thirty Years' War the church fell into the hands of the Jesuits and was finally demolished in 1786. Excavations carried out after World War I uncovered the original portal and three windows, and the entire church was reconstructed during the 1950s. Although little remains of the first church, some remnants of Hus's teachings can still be read on the inside walls. ⊠ *Betlémské nám. 5.* 🎫 *30 Kč.* ☉ *Apr.–Sept., daily 9–6; Oct.–Mar., daily 9–5.*

Celetná ulice (Celetna Street). Most of the facades indicate the buildings are from the 17th or 18th century, but appearances are deceiving: Many of the houses in fact have foundations dating from the 12th century or earlier. U Sixtu (Sixt House), at Celetná 2, dates from the 12th century—its Romanesque vaults are still visible in the wine restaurant in the basement.

❹ **Hotel Europa.** An Art Nouveau gem, it has elegant stained glass and mosaics in the café and restaurant. The terrace is an excellent spot for people-watching. ⊠ *Václavské nám. 25.*

❿ **Jan Hus monument.** Few memorials have elicited as much controversy as this one, which was dedicated in July 1915, exactly 500 years after

Hus was burned at the stake in Constance, Germany. Some maintain that the monument's Secessionist style (the inscription seems to come right from turn-of-the-century Vienna) clashes with the Gothic and Baroque of the square. Others dispute the romantic depiction of Hus, who appears here in flowing garb as tall and bearded. The real Hus, historians maintain, was short and had a baby face. Still, no one can take issue with the influence of this fiery preacher, whose ability to transform doctrinal disputes, both literally and metaphorically, into the language of the common man made him into a religious and national symbol for the Czechs. ⊠ *Staroměstské nám.*

★ ❾ **Kostel Panny Marie před Týnem** (Týn Church). The exterior of Týn Church is one of the best examples of Prague Gothic; it is in part the work of Peter Parler, architect of the Charles Bridge and St. Vitus Cathedral. Construction of its twin jet-black spires was begun by King Jiří of Poděbrad in 1461, during the heyday of the Hussites. Jiří had a gilded chalice, the symbol of the Hussites, proudly displayed on the front gable between the two towers. Following the defeat of the Hussites by the Catholic Hapsburgs, the chalice was removed and eventually replaced by a Madonna. As a final blow, the chalice was melted down and made into the Madonna's glimmering halo (you still can see it by walking into the center of the square and looking up between the spires). The entrance to Týn Church is through the arcades, under the house at No. 604.

Much of the interior, including the tall nave, was rebuilt in the Baroque style in the 17th century. Some Gothic pieces remain, however: Look to the left of the main altar for a beautifully preserved set of early Gothic carvings. Before leaving the church, look for the grave marker (tucked away to the right of the main altar) of the great Danish astronomer Tycho Brahe, who came to Prague as "Imperial Mathematicus" in 1599 under Rudolf II. As a scientist, Tycho had a place in history that is assured: Johannes Kepler (another resident of the Prague court) used Tycho's observations to formulate his laws of planetary motion. But it is myth that has endeared Tycho to the hearts of Prague residents: The robust Dane, who was apparently fond of duels, lost part of his nose in one (take a closer look at the marker). He quickly had a wax nose fashioned for everyday use but preferred to parade around on holidays and festive occasions sporting a bright silver one. ⊠ *Celetná 5,* ☎ *no phone.* ◷ *Daily 10–6.*

⓮ **Kostel svatého Jiljí** (Church of St. Giles). This Baroque church was another important outpost of Czech Protestantism in the 16th century. The exterior is a powerful example of Gothic architecture, including the buttresses and a characteristic portal; the interior, surprisingly, is Baroque. The church is only open for evening concerts, held several times a week. ⊠ *Across from Husova 7.*

⓯ **Kostel svatého Martina ve zdi** (St. Martin-in-the-Wall). It was here in 1414 that Holy Communion was first given to the Bohemian laity—with both bread and wine, in defiance of the Catholic custom of the time, which dictated that only bread was to be offered to the masses, with wine reserved for the priests and clergy. From then on, the chalice came to symbolize the Hussite movement. The church is open for evening concerts, held several times each week. ⊠ *Martinská ul.*

⓬ **Kostel svatého Mikuláše** (Church of St. Nicholas). Designed in the 18th century by Prague's own master of late Baroque, Kilian Ignaz Dientzenhofer, this church is probably less successful than its namesake across town, the Chrám svatého Mikuláše, in capturing the style's lyric exuberance. Still, Dientzenhofer utilized the limited space to create a well-balanced structure. The interior is compact, with a beautiful but small chandelier and an enormous black organ that seems to overwhelm the rear of the church. The church often hosts afternoon and evening concerts. ⊠ *Staroměstské nám.*

Mucha Museum. For decades it was almost impossible to find an Alfons Mucha original in the homeland of this famous Czech artist. In February 1998 this museum opened with nearly 100 works from his long career. What you'd expect to see is here—the theater posters of actress Sarah Bernhardt; the magazine covers; the luscious, sinuous Art Nouveau designs—but there are also paintings, photographs taken in Mucha's studio (one shows Paul Gauguin playing the piano in his underwear), and even Czechoslovak banknotes designed by the artist. ⊠ *Panská 7,* ☎ *02/628–4162.* ▣ *100 Kč.* ۞ *Daily 10–6.*

Na Příkopě. The name means "at the moat," harking back to the time when the street was indeed a moat separating the Old Town on the left from the New Town on the right. Today the pedestrian zone Na Příkopě is prime shopping territory, its boutiques rivaling the often elegant shops on Wenceslas Square. But don't expect much real high fashion here: It will take time to recover from 40 years of communism.

❻ Náměstí Republiky (Republic Square). Although an important New Town transportation hub (with a metro stop), the square has never really come together as a vital public space, perhaps because of its jarring architectural eclecticism. Taken one by one, each building is interesting in its own right, but the ensemble is less than the sum of the parts.

❸ Národní Muzeum (Czech National Museum). This imposing structure, designed by Prague architect Josef Schulz and built between 1885 and 1890, does not come into its own until it is bathed in nighttime lighting. By day the grandiose edifice seems an inappropriate venue for a musty collection of stones and bones, minerals, and coins. This museum is only for dedicated fans of the genre. ⊠ *Václavské nám. 68,* ☎ *02/2449–7111.* ▣ *60 Kč.* ۞ *Daily 9–5; closed 1st Tues. of month.*

Obecní dům (Municipal House). After several years of on-again, off-again reconstruction, this building has been reinstated as a center for concerts, rotating art exhibits, and café society. Much of the interior bears the work of the Art Nouveau master Alfons Mucha and other leading Czech artists. Mucha decorated the main Hall of the Lord Mayor upstairs; his impressive, magical frescoes depict Czech history. The beautiful Smetana Hall, which hosts concerts by the Prague Symphony Orchestra as well as international guests, is on the second floor. The ground-floor café is lovely but overpriced; you should pass on the two restaurants (one French and one Czech) as the food is decidedly disappointing. ⊠ *Nám. Republiky 5,* ☎ *02/2200–2100.* ۞ *Daily 9–6.*

NEED A BREAK?   If you prefer subtle elegance, head around the corner to the café at **Hotel Paříž** (⊠ U Obecního domu 1, ☎ 02/2422–2151), a Jugendstil jewel tucked away on a relatively quiet street.

Palác Kinských (Kinský Palace). This exuberant building, built in 1765, is considered one of Prague's finest late-Baroque structures. With its exaggerated pink overlay and numerous statues, the facade looks extreme when contrasted with the more staid Baroque elements of other nearby buildings. (The interior, however, was "modernized" under communism.) The palace once housed a German school—where Franz Kafka was a student for nine misery-laden years—and presently contains the National Gallery's graphics collection. The main exhibition room is on the second floor; exhibits change every few months and are usually worth seeing. It was from this building that Communist leader Klement Gottwald, flanked by his comrade Clementis, first addressed the crowds after seizing power in February 1948—an event recounted in the first chapter of Milan Kundera's novel *The Book of Laughter and Forgetting*. ⊠ *Staroměstské nám. 12.* 🎫 *70 Kč.* ⊙ *Tues.–Sun. 10–6.*

Prašná brána (Powder Tower). Construction of the tower, one of the city's 13 original gates, was begun by King Vladislav II of Jagiello in 1475. At the time, the kings of Bohemia maintained their royal residence next door (on the site of the current Obecní dům; ☞ *above*), and the tower was intended to be the grandest gate of all. But Vladislav was Polish and thus heartily disliked by the rebellious Czech citizens of Prague. Nine years after he assumed power, fearing for his life, he moved the royal court across the river to Prague Castle. Work on the tower was abandoned, and the half-finished structure was used for storing gunpowder—hence its odd name—until the end of the 17th century. The oldest part of the tower is the base; the golden spires were not added until the end of the last century. The climb to the top affords a striking view of the Old Town and Prague Castle in the distance. ⊠ *Nám. Republiky.* 🎫 *20 Kč.* ⊙ *Apr.–Oct., daily 9–6.*

Rudolfinum. Thanks to a thorough makeover and exterior sandblasting, this neo-Renaissance monument designed by Josef Zítek and Josef Schulz presents the cleanest, brightest stonework in the city. Now the Czech Philharmonic has its home base here; the 1,200-seat **Dvořákova síň** (Dvořák Hall) has superb acoustics. The box office is on the right-hand side of the building. ⊠ *Náměstí Jana Palacha,* ☎ *02/2489–3352.*

Behind Dvořák Hall is a set of large exhibition rooms, the **Galerie Rudolfinum,** an innovative, state-supported gallery for rotating shows of contemporary art. Four or five large shows are mounted here annually, showcasing excellent Czech work along with international artists such as photographer Cindy Sherman. It remains to be seen to what extent the country's fiscal crisis of 1997 will affect this and other public arts institutions. ⊠ *Alšovo nábřeží 12,* ☎ *02/2489–3205.* 🎫 *40 Kč.* ⊙ *Tues.–Sun. 10–6.*

★ ⑧ **Staroměstské náměstí** (Old Town Square). Dazzling. Long the heart of the Old Town, the square grew to its present proportions when the city's original marketplace was moved away from the river in the 12th century. Its shape and appearance have changed little over the years—during the day the square has a festive atmosphere as musicians vie for the favor of onlookers and artists display renditions of Prague street scenes. If you come back to the square at night, the unlit shadowy towers of the Týn Church (to your right as you enter the square) rise ominously over the glowing Baroque facades. The crowds thin out, and the ghosts of the square's stormy past return.

During the 15th century the square was the focal point of conflict between Czech Hussites and German Catholics. In 1422 the radical Hussite preacher Jan Želevský was executed here for his part in storming the New Town's town hall. Three Catholic consuls and seven German citizens were thrown out of the window in the ensuing fray—the first of Prague's many famous defenestrations. Within a few years, the Hussites had taken over the town, expelled the Germans, and set up their own administration.

★ ⑪ **Staroměstská radnice** (Old Town Hall). This is one of Prague's magnets; hundreds of people gravitate to it to see the hour struck by the mechanical figures of the **astronomical clock.** Just before the hour, look to the upper part of the clock, where a skeleton begins by tolling a death knell and turning an hourglass upside down. The Twelve Apostles parade momentarily, and then a cockerel flaps its wings and crows, piercing the air as the hour finally strikes. To the right of the skeleton, the dreaded Turk nods his head, seemingly hinting at another invasion like those of the 16th and 17th centuries.

The Town Hall has served as the center of administration for the Old Town since 1338, when King Johann of Luxembourg first granted the city council the right to a permanent location. The impressive 200-ft **Town Hall Tower**, where the clock is mounted, was first built in the 14th century and given its current late-Gothic appearance around 1500 by the master Matyáš Rejsek. For a rare view of the Old Town and its maze of crooked streets and alleyways, climb to the top of the tower. The climb is not strenuous, but steep stairs at the top unfortunately prevent people with disabilities from enjoying the view. Enter through the door to the left of the tower.

Just in front of the hall, look for the 27 white crosses on the ground. These mark the spot where 27 Bohemian noblemen were killed by the Hapsburgs in 1621 during the dark days following the defeat of the Czechs at the Battle of White Mountain. The grotesque spectacle, designed to quash any further national or religious opposition, took some five hours to complete, as the men were put to the sword or hanged one by one. If you walk around the hall to the left, you'll see it's actually a series of houses jutting into the square; they were purchased over the years and successively added to the complex. The most interesting is the **U Minuty,** the corner building to the left of the clock tower, with its 16th-century Renaissance sgraffiti of biblical and classical motifs.

Immediately after the hour, guided tours in English and German (German only in winter) of the Town Hall depart from the main desk inside. However, the only notable features inside are the fine Renaissance ceilings and the Gothic Council Room. ⊠ *Staroměstské nám.* ☒ *All sights 40 Kč.* ☽ *Daily 9–6 (until 5 in winter).*

....

NEED A   Staroměstské náměstí is a convenient spot for refreshments. **Tchibo,** at
BREAK?   No. 6 (☏ 02/2481-1026), has tasty sandwiches and pastries, excellent coffee, and an outdoor terrace in season.

....

❷ **Statue of St. Wenceslas.** In 1848 citizens protested Hapsburg rule at this statue in front of the National Museum. In 1939 residents gathered to oppose Hitler's takeover of Bohemia and Moravia. It was here also, in 1969, that the student Jan Palach set himself on fire to protest the bloody invasion of his country by the Soviet Union and other Warsaw Pact countries in August of the previous year. The invasion ended the "Prague Spring," a cultural and political movement emphasizing free expression, which was supported by Alexander Dubček, the popular leader at the time. Although Dubček never intended to dismantle Communist authority completely, his political and economic reforms proved too daring for fellow comrades in the rest of Eastern Europe. In the months following the invasion, conservatives loyal to the Soviet Union were installed in all influential positions. The subsequent two decades were a period of cultural stagnation. Thousands of residents left the country or went underground; many more resigned themselves to lives of minimal expectations and small pleasures. ⊠ *Václavské nám.*

❺ **Stavovské Divadlo** (Estates Theater). Built in the 1780s in the classical style and reopened in 1991 after years of renovation, this handsome theater was for many years a beacon of Czech-language culture in a city long dominated by the German variety. It is probably best known as the site of the world premiere of Mozart's opera *Don Giovanni* in October 1787, with the composer himself conducting. Prague audiences were quick to acknowledge Mozart's genius: The opera was an instant hit here, though it flopped nearly everywhere else in Europe. Mozart wrote most of the opera's second act in Prague at the Villa Bertramka (☞ *below*), where he was a frequent guest. ⊠ *Ovocný trh.*

❶ **Václavské náměstí** (Wenceslas Square). You may recognize this spot from your television set, for it was here that some 500,000 students and citizens gathered in the heady days of November 1989 to protest the policies of the former Communist regime. The government capitulated after a week of demonstrations, without a shot fired or the loss of a single life, bringing to power the first democratic government in 40 years (under playwright-president Václav Havel). Today this peaceful transfer of power is proudly referred to as the "Velvet" or "Gentle" Revolution (*něžná revolucia*). It was only fitting that the 1989 revolution should take place on Wenceslas Square; throughout much of Czech history, the square has served as the focal point for popular discontent. Although Wenceslas Square was first laid out by Charles IV in 1348 as the center of the New Town (Nové Město), few buildings of architectural merit line the square today.

Výstava Franze Kafky (Franz Kafka's birthplace). For years this memorial to Kafka's birth (July 3, 1883) was the only public acknowledgment of the writer's stature in world literature, reflecting the traditionally ambiguous attitude of the Czech government to his work. The Communists were always too uncomfortable with Kafka's themes of bureaucracy and alienation to sing his praises loudly, if at all. As a German and a Jew, moreover, Kafka could easily be dismissed as standing outside the mainstream of Czech literature. Following the 1989 revolution, however, Kafka's popularity soared, and his works are now widely available in Czech. Only the portal of the original house remains; inside the building is a fascinating little exhibit (mostly photographs) on Kafka's life, with commentary in English. ⊠ *U radnice 5.* 🕮 *50 Kč.* ☉ *Tues.–Fri. 10–6, Sat. 10–5 (until 7 in summer).*

Josefov (The Jewish Ghetto)

Prague's Jews survived centuries of discrimination, but two unrelated events of modern times have left their historic ghetto little more than a collection of museums. Around 1900, city officials decided for hygienic purposes to raze the ghetto and pave over its crooked streets. Only the synagogues, the town hall, and a few other buildings survived this early attempt at urban renewal. The second event was the Holocaust. Under Nazi occupation, a staggering percentage of the city's Jews were deported or murdered in concentration camps. Of the 35,000 Jews living in the ghetto before World War II, only about 1,200 returned to resettle the neighborhood after the war. The community is still quite small; there are now roughly 5,000 Jews living in the quarter.

A GOOD WALK

To reach **Josefov,** the Jewish ghetto, leave Old Town Square via the handsome Pařížská and head north toward the river. The festive atmosphere changes suddenly as you enter the area of the ghetto. The buildings are lower here and older; the mood is hushed. Treasures and artifacts of the ghetto are now the property of the **Židovské muzeum v Praze,** a complex comprising the Old Jewish Cemetery and the collections of the remaining individual synagogues. On Maiselova ulice is the **Židovská radnice** ⑯, now home to the Jewish Community Center. The **Staronová synagóga** ⑰ across the street at Červená 2 is the oldest standing synagogue in Europe.

Červená becomes the little U starého hřbitova (At the Old Cemetery Street). The **main museum ticket office** is at the **Klausová synagóga** at No. 3a. Just to the right is the **Obřadní síň,** which exhibits traditional Jewish funeral objects.

Return to Maiselova and follow it to Široká. Turn right to find the **Pinkasova synagóga** ⑱, a handsome Gothic structure that houses the restored memorial to Czech Jews murdered by the Nazis and a moving exhibition of drawings made by children held at the Nazi concentration camp at Terezín (Theresienstadt), in northern Bohemia. Here also is the entrance to the Jewish ghetto's most astonishing sight, the **Starý židovský hřbitov** ⑲.

Return to Maiselova once more and turn right in the direction of the Old Town, crossing Široká. Look in at the enormous collection of silver articles of worship in the **Maiselova synagóga** ⑳.

TIMING

The Jewish ghetto is one of the most popular visitor destinations in Prague, especially in the height of summer, when its tiny streets are jammed to bursting with tourists almost all the time. The best time for a quieter visit would be early morning when the museums and cemetery first open. The area itself is very compact, and a basic walkthrough should take only half a day. Travelers who'd like to linger in the museums could easily spend two days or more exploring this area.

SIGHTS TO SEE

Klausová synagóga (Klaus Synagogue). This Baroque former synagogue was built at the end of the 17th century in the place of three small buildings (a synagogue, school, and ritual bath) which were destroyed in a fire in the ghetto in 1689. The main ticket office for the Jewish museum is now here; it also displays an exhibition of Czech Jewish traditions and hosts occasional art shows. ☒ *U starého hřbitova 3a,* ☎ *02/2481–0099.*

⑳ **Maiselova synagóga** (Maisel Synagogue). This houses a huge number of silver articles of worship confiscated by the Nazis from synagogues throughout Central Europe. Here you'll find the Jewish Museum's finest collection of Torah wrappers and mantles, silver pointers, breastplates, spice boxes, candleholders (the eight-branched *Hanukkiah* and the seven-branched menorah), and Levite washing sets. ☒ *Maiselova 10.* ☜ *For admission information to this and other synagogues, see entry under Židovské muzeum v Praze, below.*

Obřadní síň (Ceremony Hall). After reopening in spring 1998, this space focuses on rather grim subjects; there are displays of Jewish funeral paraphernalia, old gravestones, and medical instruments. ☒ *U starého hřbitova 3a.* ☜ *For admission information, see entry under Židovské muzeum v Praze, below.*

⑱ **Pinkasova synagóga** (Pinkas Synagogue). This synagogue has two particularly moving testimonies to the appalling crimes perpetrated against the Jews during World War II. One tribute can astound by sheer numbers; the inside walls are covered with nearly 80,000 names of Bohemian and Moravian Jews murdered by the Nazis. Among them are the names of the paternal grandparents of U.S. Secretary of State Madeleine Albright, who learned of their fate only in 1997. There is also an exhibition of drawings made by children at the Nazi concentration camp Terezín. During the early years of the war the Nazis used the camp for propaganda purposes to demonstrate their "humanity" toward the Jews, and prisoners were given relative freedom to lead "normal" lives. Transports to death camps in Poland began in earnest in the final months of the war, however, and many thousands of Terezín prisoners, including many of these children, eventually perished. Enter the synagogue from Široká Street. ⊠ *Široká 3.* ☜ *For admission information to this and other synagogues,* see *entry under Židovské muzeum v Praze,* below.

⑰ **Staronová synagóga** (Old-New Synagogue). Dating from the mid-13th century, it is one of the most important works of early Gothic in Prague. The odd name recalls the legend that the synagogue was built on the site of an ancient Jewish temple and that stones from the temple were used to build the present structure. The synagogue has not only survived fires and the razing of the ghetto at the end of the last century but also emerged from the Nazi occupation intact; it is still in active use. The oldest part of the synagogue is the entrance, with its vault supported by two pillars. Note that men are required to cover their heads inside and that during services men and women sit apart. ⊠ *Červená 2.* ☜ *For admission information,* see *entry under Židovské muzeum v Praze,* below.

★ ⑲ **Starý židovský hřbitov** (Old Jewish Cemetery). This unforgettably melancholy sight not far from the busy city was, from the 14th century to 1787, the final resting place for all Jews living in Prague. Some 12,000 graves in all are piled atop one another in layers. Walk the paths amid the gravestones; the relief symbols you'll see represent the name or profession of the deceased. The oldest marked grave belongs to the poet Avigdor Kara, who died in 1439. The best-known marker is probably that of Jehuda ben Bezalel, the famed Rabbi Loew, who is credited with having created the mythical Golem in 1573. Even today, small scraps of paper bearing wishes are stuffed into the cracks of the rabbi's tomb in the hope he will grant them. Loew's grave lies just a few steps from the entrance, near the western wall of the cemetery. ☜ *For admission information,* see *entry under Židovské muzeum v Praze,* below.

★ ⑯ **Židovská radnice** (Jewish Town Hall). The hall was the creation of Mordecai Maisel, an influential Jewish leader at the end of the 16th century. It was restored in the 18th century and given its clock and bell tower at that time. A second clock, with Hebrew numbers, keeps time counterclockwise. Now home to the Jewish Community Center, the building also houses Prague's only kosher restaurant, Shalom. ⊠ *Maiselova 18.*

Židovské muzeum v Praze (Prague Jewish Museum). All the synagogues and the Old Jewish Cemetery are under the auspices of this museum. (The Old-New Synagogue [☞ *above*] which is a functioning house of worship, technically does not belong to the museum, but the Prague Jewish Community oversees both.) Ironically, the holdings' abundance can be credited to Hitler, who had planned to open a museum here documenting the lifestyle of what he had hoped would be an "extinct" people. The cemetery and most of the synagogues are open to the public. Each synagogue specializes in certain artifacts, and you can buy tickets for all the buildings at either Maisel Synagogue, Pinkas Synagogue, or Klausova synagóga. ☎ *02/231–7191.* ☜ *Combined ticket to Jewish Museum collections 450 Kč; museum collections only 250 Kč; Old-New Synagogue only 200 Kč.* ☉ *Apr.–May, Sun.–Fri. 9–6; June–Oct., Sun.–Fri. 9–6:30; Nov.–Mar., Sun.–Fri. 9–4; closed Sat. and Jewish holidays. Old-New Synagogue closes 2 hrs early on Fri.*

Karlův Most (Charles Bridge) and Malá Strana (Lesser Quarter)

A GOOD WALK

Prague's Malá Strana (the so-called Lesser Quarter, or Little Town) is not for the methodical traveler. Its charm lies in the tiny lanes, the sudden blasts of bombastic architecture, and the soul-stirring views that emerge for a second before disappearing behind the sloping roofs.

Begin the tour on the Old Town side of **Karlův most** ㉑, which you can reach by foot in about 10 minutes from the Old Town Square. Rising above it is the majestic **Staroměstská mostecká věž**; the climb of 138 steps is worth the effort for the views it affords of the Old Town and, across the river, of the Lesser Quarter and Prague Castle.

It's worth pausing to take a closer look at some of the statues as you walk across the Karlův most toward the Lesser Quarter. You'll see the Kampa Island below you, separated from the mainland by an arm of the Vltava known as Čertovka (Devil's Stream).

By now you are almost at the end of the bridge. In front of you is the striking conjunction of the two Malá Strana bridge towers, one Gothic, the other Romanesque. Together they frame the Baroque flamboyance of Chrám svatého Mikuláše in the distance. At night this is an absolutely wondrous sight.

Walk under the gateway of the towers into the little uphill street called Mostecká ulice. You have now entered the Malá Strana. Follow Mostecká ulice up to the rectangular **Malostranské náměstí** ㉒, now the district's traffic hub rather than its heart. On the left side of the square stands **Chrám svatého Mikuláše** ㉓.

Nerudova ulice ㉔ runs up from the square toward Prague Castle. Lined with gorgeous houses (and in recent years an ever-larger number of places to spend money), it's sometimes burdened with the moniker "Prague's most beautiful street." A tiny passageway at No. 13, on the left-hand side as you go up, leads to **Tržiště ulice** and the **Schöbornský palác** ㉕, once Franz Kafka's home, now the embassy of the United States. The street winds down to the quarter's noisy main street, Karmelitská, where the famous "Infant Jesus of Prague" resides in the **Kostel Panny Marie vítězné**. A few doors away, closer to Tržiště ulice, is the **Vrtbovská zahrada** ㉖. Tiny Prokopská ulice leads off of Karmelitská, past the former Church of St. Procopius, now converted, oddly, into an apartment block, and into Maltézské náměstí (Maltese Square), a characteristically noble compound. Nearby, **Velkopřevorské náměstí** ㉗ boasts even grander palaces.

A tiny bridge at the cramped square's lower end takes you across a small water channel called Čertovka to **Kampa** ㉘ island and its broad lawns, cafés, and river views. Winding your way underneath the Karlův most and along the street U lužického semináře brings you to a quiet walled garden, **Vojanovy sady** ㉙. Another, more formal garden, with an unbeatable view of Prague Castle looming above, the **Zahrada Valdštejnského paláca** ㉚ hides itself off busy Letenská ulice near the Malostranská metro station.

TIMING

The area is at its best in the evening, when the softer light hides the crumbling facades and brings you into a world of glimmering beauty. The basic walk described here could take as little as half a day—longer if you'd like to explore the area's lovely nooks and crannies.

SIGHTS TO SEE

★ ㉓   **Chrám svatého Mikuláše** (St. Nicholas Church). With its dynamic curves, this church is one of the purest and most ambitious examples of high Baroque. The celebrated architect Christoph Dientzenhofer began the Jesuit church in 1704 on the site of one of the more active Hussite churches of 15th-century Prague. Work on the building was taken over by his son Kilian Ignaz Dientzenhofer, who built the dome and pres-

bytery; Anselmo Lurago completed the whole in 1755 by adding the
bell tower. The juxtaposition of the broad, full-bodied dome with the
slender bell tower is one of the many striking architectural contrasts
that mark the Prague skyline. Inside, the vast pink-and-green space is
impossible to take in with a single glance; every corner bristles with
movement, guiding the eye first to the dramatic statues, then to the hec-
tic frescoes, and on to the shining faux-marble pillars. ✉ *Malostranské nám.* 🚇 *30 Kč.* ☉ *Daily 9–4 (until 5 or 6 in summer).*

㉘ Kampa. Prague's largest island is cut off from the "mainland" by the
narrow Čertovka streamlet. The name Čertovka translates as Devil's Stream
and reputedly refers to a cranky old lady who once lived on Maltese Square
(given the river's present filthy state, however, the name is ironically appropriate). The unusually well kept lawns of the **Kampa Gardens** that
occupy much of the island are one of the few places in Prague where sitting on the grass is openly tolerated. If it's a warm day, spread out a blanket and bask for a while in the sunshine. The row of benches that line
the river is also a popular spot from which to contemplate the city. At
night this stretch along the river is especially romantic.

★ ㉑ Karlův most (Charles Bridge). The view from the foot of the bridge on
the Old Town side is nothing short of breathtaking, encompassing the
towers and domes of the Lesser Quarter and the soaring spires of St.
Vitus Cathedral to the northwest. This heavenly vision, one of the most
beautiful in Europe, changes subtly in perspective as you walk across
the bridge, attended by the host of Baroque saints that decorate the
bridge's peaceful Gothic stones. At night its drama is spellbinding: St.
Vitus Cathedral lit in a ghostly green, the castle in monumental yellow, and the Church of St. Nicholas in a voluptuous pink, all viewed
through the menacing silhouettes of the bowed statues and the Gothic
towers. If you do nothing else in Prague, you must visit the Charles
Bridge at night. During the day the pedestrian bridge buzzes with activity. Street musicians vie with artisans hawking jewelry, paintings, and
glass for the hearts and wallets of the passing multitude. At night the
crowds thin out a little, the musicians multiply, and the bridge becomes
a long block party—nearly everyone brings a bottle.

When the Přemyslide princes set up residence in Prague in the 10th century, there was a ford across the Vltava at this point, a vital link along
one of Europe's major trading routes. After several wooden bridges
and the first stone bridge had washed away in floods, Charles IV appointed the 27-year-old German Peter Parler, the architect of St. Vitus
Cathedral, to build a new structure in 1357. After 1620, following the
defeat of Czech Protestants by Catholic Hapsburgs at the Battle of White
Mountain, the bridge and its adornment became caught up in the
Catholic–Hussite (Protestant) conflict. The many Baroque statues that
began to appear in the late 17th century, commissioned by Catholics,
eventually came to symbolize the totality of the Austrian (hence
Catholic) triumph.

The religious conflict is less obvious nowadays, leaving only the artistic tension between Baroque and Gothic that gives the bridge its allure. It's worth pausing to take a closer look at some of the statues as
you walk toward the Lesser Quarter. The eighth statue on the right,
St. John of Nepomuk, is the oldest of all; it was designed by Johann
Brokoff in 1683. On the left-hand side, sticking out from the bridge
between the 9th and 10th statues (the latter has a wonderfully expressive
vanquished Satan), stands a Roland (Brunvík) statue. This knightly figure, bearing the coat of arms of the Old Town, was once a reminder
that this part of the bridge belonged to the Old Town before Prague
became a unified city in 1784.

In the eyes of most art historians, the most valuable statue is the 12th, on the left. Mathias Braun's statue of St. Luitgarde depicts the blind saint kissing Christ's wounds. The most compelling grouping, however, is the second from the end on the left, a work of Ferdinand Maximilien Brokoff from 1714. Here the saints are incidental; the main attraction is the Turk, his face expressing extreme boredom while guarding Christians imprisoned in the cage at his side. When the statue was erected, just 29 years after the second Turkish invasion of Vienna, it scandalized the Prague public, who smeared the statue with mud. St. Luitgarde and all but five of the other Baroque sculptures on the bridge are 20th-century copies; in addition, a half dozen of the 30 bridge sculptures are 19th-century replacements for originals damaged in wars or fallen into the river in 1784 during a flood. Most of the surviving Baroque originals have been removed to safer quarters, protected from Prague's acidic air; several can be viewed in the Lapidarium museum at Výstaviště exhibition grounds in Prague 7 and in a man-made cavern at Vyšehrad (☞ Nové město (New Town) and Vyšehrad, *below*).

Kostel Panny Marie vítězné (Church of Our Lady Victorious). This comfortably ramshackle church makes the unlikely home of one of Prague's best-known religious artifacts, the *Pražské Jezulátko* (Infant Jesus of Prague). Originally brought to Prague from Spain in the 16th century, this tiny porcelain doll (now bathed in neon lighting straight out of Las Vegas) is renowned worldwide for showering miracles on anyone willing to kneel before it and pray. ⊠ *Karmelitská 9a.* 🖾 *Free.* ☉ *Mon.– Sat. 10–5:30, Sun. 1–5.*

Ledeburská zahrada (Ledeburg Garden). Among the row of steeply banked Baroque gardens behind the palaces of Valdštejnská ulice, this is the only one presently open to the public. It's a pleasant spot for a rest amid shady arbors and niches. The garden with its frescoes and statuary was restored in 1995 with support from a fund headed by Czech president Václav Havel and Charles, Prince of Wales. ⊠ *Entrance at Valdštejnské nám. 3; in summer also from the South Gardens of Prague Castle.* 🖾 *25 Kč.* ☉ *Daily 10–6.*

㉒ Malostranské náměstí (Lesser Quarter Square). The arcaded houses on the east and south sides, dating from the 16th and 17th centuries, exhibit a mix of Baroque and Renaissance elements. The Czech Parliament resides partly in the gaudy yellow-and-green palace on the square's north side, partly in the street behind the palace, Sněmovní. Now the square buzzes with restaurants, street vendors, clubs, and shops; the huge bulk of St. Nicholas Church divides the lower, busier section from the quieter upper part. ⊠ *Mostecká ul., Letenská ul., and Karmelitská ul. lead into square.*

㉔ Nerudova ulice. This steep little street used to be the last leg of the Royal Way, walked by the king before his coronation, and it is still the best way to get to Prague Castle. Until Joseph II's administrative reforms in the late 18th century, house numbering was unknown in Prague. Each house bore a name, depicted on the facade, and these are particularly prominent on Nerudova ulice. House No. 6, **U červeného orla** (At the Red Eagle), proudly displays a faded painting of a red eagle. No. 12 is known as **U tří housliček** (At the Three Violins). In the early 18th century, three generations of the Edlinger violin-making family lived here. Joseph II's scheme numbered each house according to its position in Prague's separate "towns" (here the Lesser Quarter) rather than according to its sequence on the street. The red plates record these original house numbers; the blue ones are the numbers used in addresses today—except, oddly enough, in some of the newer suburbs—while, to confuse the tourist, many architectural guides refer to the old, red-number plates.

NEED A
BREAK? Nerudova ulice is filled with little restaurants and snack bars and offers
something for everyone. **U zeleného čaje,** at No. 19, is a fragrant little
tearoom, offering fruit and herbal teas as well as light salads and
sweets. **U Kocoura,** at No. 2, is a traditional pub that hasn't caved in to
touristic niceties.

Two palaces break the unity of the burghers' houses on Nerudova ulice.
Both were designed by the adventurous Baroque architect Giovanni
Santini, one of the Italian builders most in demand by wealthy nobles
of the early 18th century. The **Morzin Palace,** on the left at No. 5, is
now the Romanian Embassy. The fascinating facade, with an allegory
of night and day, was created in 1713 and is the work of Ferdinand
Brokoff of Charles Bridge statue fame. Across the street at No. 20 is
the **Thun-Hohenstein Palace,** now the Italian Embassy. The gateway
with two enormous eagles (the emblem of the Kolovrat family, who
owned the building at the time) is the work of the other great Charles
Bridge statue sculptor, Mathias Braun.

㉕ Schönbornský palác (Schönborn Palace). Franz Kafka had an apartment in this massive Baroque building at the top of **Tržiště ulice** from
March through August 1917, after moving out from Zlatá ulička
(Golden Lane) (☞ Pražský hrad (Prague Castle) *below*). The U.S. Embassy now occupies this prime location. ⊠ *Tržiště at Vlašská.*

Staroměstská mostecká věž (Old Town Bridge Tower). This was where
Peter Parler (the architect of St. Vitus Cathedral) began his bridge
building. The carved facades he designed for the sides of the bridge
were destroyed by Swedish soldiers in 1648, at the end of the Thirty
Years' War. The sculptures facing the square, however, are still intact
(although some are recent copies); they depict an old and gout-ridden
Charles IV with his son, who later became Wenceslas IV. Above them
are two of Bohemia's patron saints: Adalbert (Vojtěch) and Sigismund.
Inside the tower is a small exhibit of antique musical instruments. ☎
20 Kč. ☉ *Daily 9–7.*

㉗ Velkopřevorské náměstí (Grand Priory Square). The palace fronting
the square is considered one of the finest Baroque buildings in the Lesser
Quarter, though it is now part of the Embassy of the Knights of Malta
and no longer open to the public. Opposite is the flamboyant orange-
and-white stucco facade of the Buquoy Palace, built in 1719 by Giovanni Santini and the present home of the French Embassy. The
so-called **John Lennon Peace Wall,** leading to a bridge over the Čertovka stream, was once a kind of monument to youthful rebellion, emblazoned with a large painted head of the former Beatle, lyrics from
his songs, and other messages of peace. It has lost much social signif-
icance, not to mention attractiveness, since the years around the 1989
revolution when graffiti actually meant something in Prague. ⊠
Lázeňská ulice leads into square.

㉙ Vojanovy sady (Vojan Park). Once the gardens of the Monastery of
the Discalced Carmelites, later taken over by the Order of the English
Virgins, and now part of the Ministry of Finance, this walled garden,
with its weeping willows, fruit trees, and benches, makes another
peaceful haven in summer. Exhibitions of modern sculptures are often
held here, contrasting sharply with the two Baroque chapels and the
graceful Ignaz Platzer statue of John of Nepomuk standing on a fish
at the entrance. ⊠ *U lužického semináře, between Letenská and
Míšeňská ul.* ☉ *Nov.–Mar. 8–5, Apr.–Oct. 8–7.*

★ ㉖ Vrtbovská zahrada (Vrtba Garden). An unobtrusive door on noisy
Karmelitská hides the entranceway to a fascinating oasis which also

affords one of the best views over the Lesser Quarter. The street door opens onto the intimate courtyard of the Vrtbovský palác (Vrtba Palace), which is now private housing. Two Renaissance wings flank the courtyard, the one to the left built in 1575, the one to the right in 1591. The owner of the latter house was one of the 27 Bohemian nobles executed by the Hapsburgs in 1621 before the Old Town Hall. The house was given as confiscated property to Count Sezima of Vrtba, who bought the neighboring property and turned the buildings into a late-Renaissance palace. The Vrtba Garden, created a century later, reopened in summer 1998 after an excruciatingly long renovation. This is the most elegant of the Lesser Quarter's public gardens, built in five levels rising from behind the courtyard in a wave of statuary-bedecked staircases and formal terraces to reach a seashell-decorated pavilion at the top. (The fenced-off garden immediately behind and above belongs to the U.S. Embassy.) The powerful stone figure of Atlas that caps the entranceway in the courtyard, as well as most of the other classically derived statues, are from the workshop of Mathias Braun, perhaps the best of Czech Baroque sculptors. ⊠ *Karmelitská ul. 25.* 🖾 *20 Kč.* ☉ *Garden open Apr.–Oct., daily 10–6.*

OFF THE
BEATEN PATH   **VILLA BERTRAMKA** – Mozart fans won't want to pass up a visit to this villa, where the great composer lived during a couple of his visits to Prague. The small, well-organized museum is packed with memorabilia, including the program from that exciting night in 1787 when *Don Giovanni* had its world premiere in Prague. Also on hand is one of the master's pianos. Take Tram No. 12 from Karmelitská south to the Anděl metro station (or ride Metro Line B), walk down Plzeňská ulice a few hundred yards, and take a left at Mozartova ulice. ⊠ *Mozartova ul. 169, Prague 5 (Smíchov),* ☎ *02/543893.* 🖾 *60 Kč.* ☉ *Daily 10–5.*

★ ③⓪ **Zahrada Valdštejnského paláca** (Wallenstein Palace Gardens). Albrecht von Wallenstein, onetime owner of the house and gardens, began a meteoric military career in 1622 when the Austrian emperor Ferdinand II retained him to save the empire from the Swedes and Protestants during the Thirty Years' War. Wallenstein, wealthy by marriage, offered to raise 20,000 men at his own cost and lead them personally. Ferdinand II accepted and showered Wallenstein with confiscated land and titles. Wallenstein's first acquisition was this enormous area. Having knocked down 23 houses, a brick factory, and three gardens, in 1623 he began to build his magnificent palace with its idiosyncratic high-walled gardens and superb, vaulted Renaissance *sala terrena* (room opening onto a garden). Walking around the formal paths, you'll come across numerous statues, an unusual fountain with a woman spouting water from her breasts, and a lava-stone grotto along the wall. Most of the palace itself now serves the Czech Senate as meeting space and offices. The only part open to the public is an exhibition devoted to the 17th-century Moravian Protestant divine and educational philosopher Jan Amos Komenský, known to the world as Comenius. The palace's cavernous former *Jízdárna,* or riding school, now hosts occasional art exhibitions. ⊠ *Komenský Museum entrance at Valdštejnská 20. Garden entrance at Letenská 10.* 🖾 *Garden free; museum 6 Kč.* ☉ *Garden May–Sept., daily 9–7; Apr. and Oct, daily 10–6; Nov.–March, daily 10–5. Museum Tues.– Sun. 10–12:30 and 1–5.*

Hradčany (The Castle District)

To the west of Prague Castle is the residential **Hradčany** (Castle District), the town that during the early 14th century emerged out of a collection of monasteries and churches. The concentration of history packed into one small area makes Prague Castle and the Castle District challenging objects for visitors not versed in the ups and downs of Bohemian kings, religious uprisings, wars, and oppression. The picturesque area surrounding Prague Castle, with its breathtaking vistas of the Old Town and the Lesser Quarter, is ideal for just wandering; but the castle itself, with its convoluted history and architecture, is difficult to appreciate fully without investing a little more time.

A GOOD WALK

Begin on **Nerudova ulice** ㉔, which runs east–west a few hundred yards south of Prague Castle. At the western (upper) end of the street, look for a flight of stone steps guarded by two saintly statues. The stairs lead up to Loretánská ulice, affording panoramic views of St. Nicholas Church and the Lesser Quarter. At the top of the steps, turn left and walk a couple hundred yards until you come to a dusty elongated square named Pohořelec (Scene of Fire), which suffered tragic fires in 1420, 1541, and 1741. Go through the inconspicuous gateway at No. 8 and up the steps, and you'll find yourself in the courtyard of one of the city's richest monasteries, the **Strahovský klášter** ㉛.

Retrace your steps to Loretánské náměstí, the square at the head of Loretánská ulice, which is flanked by the feminine curves of the Baroque church, **Loreta** ㉜. Across the road, the 29 half pillars of the Černínský palác (Chernin Palace) now mask the Czech Ministry of Foreign Affairs. At the bottom of Loretánské náměstí, a little lane trails to the left into the area known as **Nový Svět**; the name means "new world," though the district is as Old World as they come. Turn right onto the street Nový Svět. Around the corner you get a tantalizing view of the cathedral through the trees. Walk past the Austrian Embassy to Kanovnická ulice, a winding street lined with the dignified but melancholy Kostel svatého Jana Nepomuckého (Church of St. John of Nepomuk). At the top of the street on the left, the rounded, Renaissance corner house Martinický palác catches the eye with its detailed sgraffito decorations. Martinický palác opens onto **Hradčanské náměstí** ㉝, with its grandiose gathering of Renaissance and Baroque palaces. To the left of the bright yellow Arcibiskupský palác (Archbishop's Palace) on the square is an alleyway leading down to the **Národní galerie** ㉞ and its collections of European art. Across the square, the handsome sgraffito sweep of **Schwarzenberský palác** ㉟ beckons; this is the building you saw from the back side at the beginning of the tour.

TIMING

Brisk-paced sightseers could zip through Hradčany in an hour, but to do it justice, allow at least an hour just for ambling and admiring the passing buildings and views of the city. The Strahovský klášter halls need about a half hour to take in, more if you tour the small picture gallery there, and the Loreta and its treasures at least that length of time. The National Gallery in the Šternberský palác deserves at least a couple of hours. Keep in mind that several places are not open on Mondays.

SIGHTS TO SEE

㉝ **Hradčanské náměstí** (Hradčany Square). With its fabulous mixture of Baroque and Renaissance housing, topped by the castle itself, the square featured prominently (ironically, disguised as Vienna) in the film *Amadeus,* directed by the then-exiled Czech director Miloš Forman. Forman used the flamboyant rococo **Arcibiskupský palác** (Archbishop's Palace), at the top of the square on the left, as the Viennese archbishop's palace. The plush interior, shown off in the film, is open to the public only on Maundy Thursday. ✉ *Loretánská ul. and Kanovnická ul. lead into square.*

㉜ **Loreta** (Loreto Church). The church's seductive lines were a conscious move on the part of Counter-Reformation Jesuits in the 17th century who wanted to build up the cult of Mary and attract the largely Protestant Bohemians back to the church. According to legend, angels had carried Mary's house from Nazareth and dropped it in a patch of laurel trees in Ancona, Italy; known as *Loreto* (from the Latin for laurel), it immediately became a center of pilgrimage. The Prague Loreto was one of many symbolic reenactments of this scene across Europe, and it worked: Pilgrims came in droves. The graceful facade, with its voluptuous tower, was built in 1720 by Kilian Ignaz Dientzenhofer, the architect of the two St. Nicholas churches in Prague. Most spectacular of all is a small exhibition upstairs displaying the religious treasures presented to Mary in thanks for various services, including a monstrance studded with 6,500 diamonds. ⊠ *Loretánské nám. 7,* 🖃 *80 Kč (priests, monks, and nuns admitted free).* ☉ *Tues.–Sun. 9–12:15 and 1–4:30.*

★ ㉞ **Národní galerie** (National Gallery). Housed in the 18th-century **Šternberský palác** (Sternberg Palace), this collection is small but impressive. During the time when Berlin, Dresden, and Vienna were building up superlative old-master galleries, Prague languished, neglected by her Viennese rulers—one reason why the city's museums lag behind. On the first floor there's an exhibition of icons and other religious art from the 3rd through the 14th centuries. Up a second flight of steps is an entire room full of Cranachs and an assortment of paintings by Holbein, Dürer, Brueghel, Van Dyck, Canaletto, and Rubens. Other branches of the National Gallery are scattered around town, notably the modern art collections in the Veletržní palác (☞ Letná and Holešovice, *below*). ⊠ *Hradčanské nám. 15,* 🕾 *02/2051–4634.* 🖃 *70 Kč.* ☉ *Tues.–Sun. 10–6.*

Nový Svět. This picturesque, winding little alley, with facades from the 17th and 18th centuries, once housed Prague's poorest residents; now many of the homes are used as artists' studios. The last house on the street, No. 1, was the home of the Danish-born astronomer Tycho Brahe. Living so close to the Loreto, so the story goes, Tycho was constantly disturbed during his nightly stargazing by the church bells. He ended up complaining to his patron, Emperor Rudolf II, who instructed the Capuchin monks to finish their services before the first star appeared in the sky.

㉟ **Schwarzenberský palác** (Schwarzenberg Palace). This boxy palace with its extravagant sgraffito facade contains the **Vojenské historické muzeum** (Military History Museum), one of the largest of its kind in Europe. A dim, old-fashioned collection, it concentrates on pre-20th century Czech military history. Of more general interest are the jousting tournaments held in the courtyard in summer. ⊠ *Hradčanské nám. 2.* 🖃 *20 Kč.* ☉ *Apr.–Oct., Tues.–Sun. 10–6.*

★ ㉛ **Strahovský klášter** (Strahov Monastery). Founded by the Premonstratensian order in 1140, the monastery remained in their hands until 1952, when the Communists suppressed all religious orders and turned the entire complex into the **Památník národního písemnictví** (Museum of National Literature). The major building of interest is the **Strahov Library**, with its collection of early Czech manuscripts, the 10th-century Strahov New Testament, and the collected works of famed Danish astronomer Tycho Brahe. Also of note is the late-18th-century **Philosophical Hall.** Engulfing its ceilings is a startling sky-blue fresco which depicts an unusual cast of characters, including Socrates' nagging wife Xanthippe, Greek astronomer Thales with his trusty telescope, and a collection of Greek philosophers mingling with Descartes, Diderot, and Voltaire. Also on the premises is the order's small art gallery, highlighted by late-Gothic altars and paintings from Rudolf II's time. You can arrange for a tour in English with several days' advance notice. ✉ *Strahovské nádvoří 1/132, tour arrangements* ☎ *02/2051–6671.* 🎫 *Library tour 20 Kč, gallery 25 Kč.* ⏲ *Library daily 9–noon and 1–5; gallery Tues.–Sun. 9–noon and 12:30–5.*

OFF THE BEATEN PATH

PETŘÍN – For a superb view of the city—from a mostly undiscovered, tourist-free perch—stroll over from the Strahov Monastery along the paths toward Prague's own miniature version of the Eiffel Tower. You'll find yourself in a hilltop park, laced with footpaths, with several buildings clustered together near the tower—just keep going gradually upward till you reach the tower's base. The tower and its breathtaking view, the hall of mirrors, or *bludiště*, in a small structure near the tower's base, and the seemingly abandoned sv. Vavřinec (St. Lawrence) church are beautifully peaceful and well worth an afternoon's wandering. You can also walk up from Karmelitská ulice or Újezd down in the Lesser Quarter or ride the funicular railway from U lanové dráhy ulice, off Újezd. Regular public-transportation tickets are valid. For the descent, take the funicular or meander on foot down through the stations of the cross on the pathways leading back to the Lesser Quarter.

Pražský hrad (Prague Castle)

Numbers in the text correspond to numbers in the margin and on the Prague Castle (Pražský hrad) map.

Despite its monolithic presence, Pražský hrad (Prague Castle) is a collection of buildings dating from the 10th to the 20th century, all linked by internal courtyards. The most important structures are **Chrám svatého Víta** ㊿, clearly visible soaring above the castle walls, and the **Královský palác** (51), the official residence of kings and presidents and still the center of political power in the Czech Republic. The castle is compact and easy to navigate in. Be forewarned: In summer, Chrám svatého Víta and Zlatá ulička take the brunt of the heavy sightseeing traffic, while all of the castle is hugely popular.

TIMING

The castle is at its mysterious best in early morning and late evening, and it is incomparable when it snows. The cathedral deserves an hour, as does the Královský palác, while you can easily spend an entire day taking in the museums, the views of the city, and the hidden nooks of the castle. Remember that some sights, such as the Lobkovický palác, are not open on Monday.

SIGHTS TO SEE

(52) **Bazilika svatého Jiří** (St. George's Basilica). This church was originally built in the 10th century by Prince Vratislav I, the father of Prince (and St.) Wenceslas. It was dedicated to St. George (of dragon fame), who it was believed would be more agreeable to the still largely pagan people. The outside was remodeled during early Baroque times, although the striking rusty-red color is in keeping with the look of the Romanesque edifice. The interior looks more or less as it did in the 12th century and is the best-preserved Romanesque relic in the country. The effect is at once barnlike and peaceful, the warm golden yellow of the stone walls and the small triplet arched windows exuding a sense of enduring harmony. The house-shape painted tomb at the front of the church holds the remains of the founder, Vratislav I. Up the steps, in a chapel to the right, is the tomb Peter Parler designed for St. Ludmila, the grandmother of St. Wenceslas. ✉ *Náměstí U sv. Jiří.* 🎫 *For admission information,* see *Informační středisko,* below. ⏲ *Apr.–Oct., daily 9–5; Nov.–Mar., daily 9–4.*

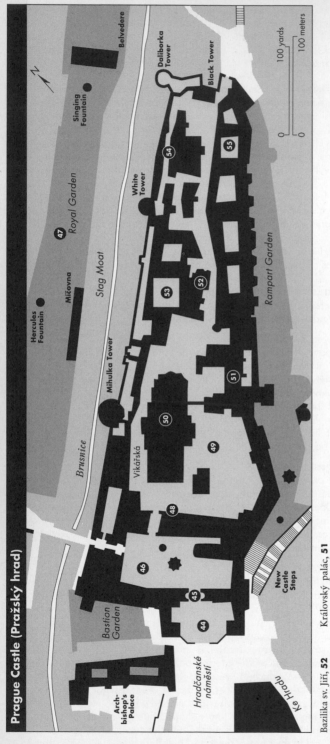

Prague Castle (Pražský hrad)

44

Arch-bishop's Palace

Hradčanské náměstí

Ke Hradu

Bastion Garden

Brusnice

Hercules Fountain

Mičovna

Stag Moat

Royal Garden

Singing Fountain

Belvedere

Mihulka Tower

Vikářská

White Tower

Daliborka Tower

Black Tower

Rampart Garden

New Castle Steps

0 — 100 yards

0 — 100 meters

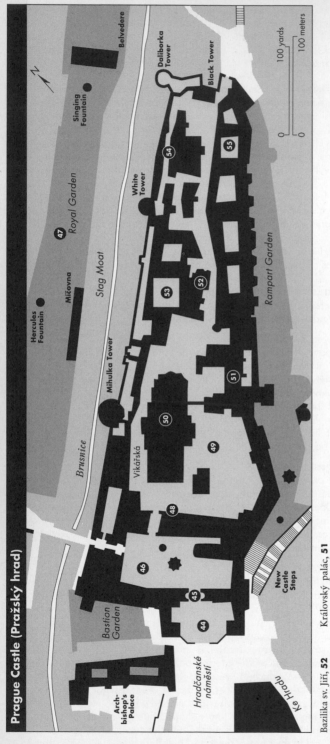

Bazilika sv. Jiří, **52**
Chrám sv. Víta, **50**
Druhé nádvoří, **46**
Informační středisko, **48**
Klášter sv. Jiří, **53**
Královská zahrada, **47**

Královský palác, **51**
Lobkovický palác, **55**
Matyášova brána, **45**
První nádvoří, **44**
Třetí nádvoří, **49**
Zlatá ulička, **54**

★ ㊿ **Chrám svatého Víta** (St. Vitus Cathedral). With its graceful, soaring towers, this Gothic cathedral—among the most beautiful in Europe— is the spiritual heart not only of Prague Castle, but of the entire country. It has a long and complicated history, beginning in the 10th century and continuing to its completion in 1929. If you want to hear its history in depth, English-speaking guided tours of the cathedral and the Královský palác (☞ *below*) can be arranged at the information office across from the cathedral entrance (☞ *above*).

Once you enter the cathedral, pause to take in the vast but delicate beauty of the Gothic and neo-Gothic interior glowing in the colorful light that filters through the startlingly brilliant stained-glass windows. This western third of the structure, including the facade and the two towers you can see from outside, was not completed until 1929. The six stained-glass windows to your left and right and the large rose window behind are modern masterpieces. Take a good look at the third window up on the left. The familiar Art Nouveau flamboyance, depicting the blessing of the 9th-century St. Cyril and St. Methodius (missionaries to the Slavs and creators of the Cyrillic alphabet), is the work of the Czech father of the style, Alfons Mucha. He achieved the subtle coloring by painting rather than staining the glass.

If you walk halfway up the right-hand aisle you will find the exquisitely ornate **Svatováclavská kaple** (Chapel of St. Wenceslas). With a 14th-century tomb holding the saint's remains, this square chapel is the ancient heart of the cathedral. Wenceslas (the "good king" of Christmas-carol fame) was a determined Christian in an era of widespread paganism. In 925, as prince of Bohemia, he founded a rotunda church dedicated to St. Vitus on this site. But the prince's brother, Boleslav, was impatient to take power and ambushed Wenceslas four years later near a church at Stará Boleslav, northeast of Prague. Wenceslas was originally buried in that church, but his grave produced so many miracles that he rapidly became a symbol of piety for the common people, something that greatly irritated the new Prince Boleslav. In 931 Boleslav was finally forced to honor his brother by reburying the body in the St. Vitus Rotunda. Shortly afterward, Wenceslas was canonized.

The rotunda was replaced by a Romanesque basilica in the late 11th century. Work was begun on the existing building in 1344; for the first few years the chief architect was the Frenchman Mathias d'Arras, but after his death in 1352, the work was continued by the 22-year-old German architect Peter Parler, who went on to build the Charles Bridge and many other Prague treasures.

The small door in the back of the chapel leads to the **Korunní komora** (Crown Chamber), the repository of the Bohemian crown jewels. It remains locked with seven keys held by seven different people and is definitely not open to the public.

A little beyond the Wenceslas Chapel on the same side, stairs lead down to the underground **royal crypt,** interesting primarily for the information it provides about the cathedral's history. As you descend the stairs, you'll see parts of the old Romanesque basilica and portions of the foundations of the rotunda. Moving around into the second room, you'll find a rather eclectic group of royal remains ensconced in new sarcophagi dating from the 1930s. In the center is Charles IV, who died in 1378. Rudolf II, patron of Renaissance Prague, is entombed at the rear in the original tin coffin. To his right is Maria Amalia, the only child of Maria Theresa to reside in Prague. Ascending the wooden steps back into the cathedral, you'll come to the white-marble **Kralovské mausoleum** (Royal Mausoleum), atop which lie stone statues of the first two Hapsburg kings to rule in Bohemia, Ferdinand I and Maximilian II.

You can't fail to catch sight of the ornate silver **sarcophagus of St. John of Nepomuk.** According to legend, when Nepomuk's body was exhumed in 1721 to be reinterred, the tongue was found to be still intact and pumping with blood. These strange tales sadly served a highly political purpose. The Catholic Church and the Hapsburgs were seeking a new folk hero to replace the Protestant forerunner Jan Hus, whom they despised. The late Father Nepomuk was sainted and reburied a few years later with great ceremony in the 3,700-pound silver tomb, replete with angels and cherubim; the tongue was enshrined in its own reliquary.

The eight chapels around the back of the cathedral are the work of the original architect, Mathias d'Arras. Since the last century, **Valdštejnská kaple** (Wallenstein Chapel) has housed the Gothic tombstones of its two architects, d'Arras and Peter Parler, who died in 1352 and 1399, respectively. If you look up to the balcony, you can just make out the busts of these two men, designed by Parler's workshop. The other busts around the triforium depict various Czech kings.

The Hussite wars in the 15th century put an end to the first phase of the cathedral's construction. During the short era of illusory peace before the Thirty Years' War, lack of money quashed any idea of finishing the building, and the cathedral was closed by a wall built across from the Wenceslas Chapel. Not until the 20th century was the western side of the cathedral, with its two towers, completed according to Parler's original plans.

A key element of the cathedral's teeming, rich exterior decoration is the **Last Judgment mosaic** above the ceremonial entrance, called the Golden Portal, on the south side. The use of mosaic is quite rare in countries north of the Alps; this work, dating from the 1370s, is made of 1 million glass and stone chunks. It's currently undergoing an extensive, desperately needed restoration led by the Getty Conservation Institute. Just visible are the faded central image of Christ in glory, adored by Charles IV, his wife, and several saints; the risen dead and attendant angels to the left; and on the right, Satan surrounded by the flames of Hell. ⊠ *St. Vitus Cathedral.* ⌦ *Western section free; chapels, crypt, and tower accessible with castle-wide ticket (see Informační středisko, below).* ☉ *Apr.–Oct., daily 9–5; Nov.–Mar., daily 9–4.*

㊺ **Druhé nádvoří** (Second Courtyard). Empress Maria Theresa's court architect, Nicolò Pacassi, received the imperial approval to remake the castle in the 1760s, as the castle was badly damaged by Prussian shelling during the War of the Austrian Succession in 1757. The Second Courtyard was the main victim of Pacassi's attempts at imparting classical grandeur to what had been a picturesque collection of Gothic and Renaissance styles. This courtyard also houses the reliquary of Charles IV inside the **Kaple svatého Kříže** (Chapel of the Holy Cross). Displays include Gothic silver busts of the major Bohemian patron saints as well as bones and vestments that supposedly belonged to various saints. However, except for the view of the spires of St. Vitus Cathedral, there's little for the eye to feast upon here.

Built in the late-16th and early 17th centuries, the Second Courtyard was originally part of a reconstruction program commissioned by Rudolf II, under whom Prague enjoyed a period of unparalleled cultural development. Once the Prague court was established, the emperor gathered around him some of the world's best craftsmen, artists, and scientists, including the brilliant astronomers Johannes Kepler and Tycho Brahe.

Rudolf also amassed a large and famed collection of fine and decorative art, scientific instruments, philosophic and alchemical books, natural wonders, coins, and everything else under the sun. The bulk of the collection was looted by the Swedes during the Thirty Years' War, removed to Vienna when the imperial capital returned there after Rudolf's death, or auctioned off during the 18th century, but a small part of the painting hoard was rediscovered in unused castle rooms in the 1960s. Renaissance and Baroque paintings, for the most part acquired after Rudolf's time, are displayed in the **Obrazárna** (Picture Gallery), on the left side of the courtyard as you face St. Vitus. It reopened at long last in summer 1998, elegantly redecorated by the official castle architect, Bořek Šípek. The passageway by the gallery entrance forms the northern entrance to the castle and leads out over a luxurious ravine known as the **Jelení příkop** (Stag Moat). ⊠ *North side of Second Courtyard.* 🎫 *100 Kč.* ☉ *Daily 10–6.*

48 **Informační středisko** (Castle Information Office). This is the place to come for entrance tickets, guided tours, headphones for listening to recorded tours in English, tickets to cultural events held at the castle, and money changing. Tickets are valid for three consecutive days and allow admission to the older parts of St. Vitus Cathedral, the Královský palác, St. George's Basilica (but not the adjacent National Gallery exhibition), and a medieval bastion called Mihulka with an exhibition on alchemy. These sights may be visited only on the three-day ticket (the 20th-century section of the cathedral is free). Buy tickets to other castle sights at the door. If you just want to walk through the castle grounds, note that the gates close at midnight from April through October, at 11 PM the rest of the year, while the gardens are open from April through October only. ⊠ *Třetí nádvoří, across from the entrance to Chrám svatého Víta.* ☏ *02/2437–3368.* 🎫 *3-day tickets 100 Kč (English-language guided tours 50 Kč per person, minimum 5 people), grounds and gardens free.* ☉ *Apr.–Oct., daily 9–5; Nov.–Mar., daily 9–4.*

53 **Klášter svatého Jiří** (St. George's Convent). The first convent in Bohemia, founded in 973 next to the even older St. George's Basilica (☞ *above*) now houses the Old Bohemian Collection of the **Národní galerie** (Czech National Gallery). The works run through the history of Czech art from the Middle Ages to the rather more secular themes of the Mannerist school and the voluptuous work of the court painters of Rudolf II. This is the best place in Prague to gain an overview of Czech art during the medieval and Hapsburg periods. ⊠ *Nám. U sv. Jiří,* ☏ *02/5732–0536.* 🎫 *70 Kč.* ☉ *Tues.–Sun. 10–6.*

47 **Královská zahrada** (Royal Garden). This peaceful swath of greenery affords an unusually lovely view of St. Vitus Cathedral and the castle's walls and bastions. Originally laid out in the 16th century, it endured devastation in war, neglect in times of peace, and many redesigns, reaching its present parklike form early this century. Luckily, its Renaissance treasures survive. The garden front of the **Míčovna** (Ball Game Hall), built by Bonifaz Wohlmut in 1568, is completely covered by a dense tangle of allegorical sgraffiti.

The **Královský letohrádek** (Royal Summer Palace, also known as the Belvedere), at the garden's eastern end, deserves its usual description as one of the most beautiful Renaissance structures north of the Alps. Italian architects began it; Wohlmut finished it off in the 1560s with a copper roof like an upturned boat's keel riding above the graceful arcades of the ground floor. The Renaissance-style *giardinetto* (little garden) adjoining the summer palace centers on another masterwork, the Italian-designed, Czech-cast *Singing Fountain*, which resonates to the sound of falling water. ⊠ *Garden entrances from U Prašného mostu ul. and Mariánské hradby ul. near Chotkovy Sady Park.* 🖼 *Free.* ⊙ *Apr.–Oct., daily 10–5:45.*

51 **Královský palác** (Royal Palace). The palace is a congeries of styles and add-ons accumulated over many centuries. The best way to grasp its size is from within the **Vladislavský sál** (Vladislav Hall), the largest secular Gothic interior space in Central Europe. The enormous hall was completed in 1493 by Benedict Ried, who was to late-Bohemian Gothic what Peter Parler was to the earlier version. The room imparts a sense of space and light, softened by the sensuous lines of the vaulted ceilings and brought to a dignified close by the simple oblong form of the early Renaissance windows. In its heyday, the hall was the site of jousting tournaments, festive markets, banquets, and coronations. In more recent times, it has been used to inaugurate presidents, from the Communist Klement Gottwald in 1948 to Václav Havel in 1989, 1993, and 1998.

From the front of the hall, turn right into the rooms of the **Česká kancelář** (Bohemian Chancellery). This wing was built by the same Benedict Ried only 10 years after the hall was completed, but it shows a much stronger Renaissance influence. Pass through the Renaissance portal into the last chamber of the chancellery. This room was the site of the second defenestration of Prague, in 1618, an event that marked the beginning of the Bohemian rebellion and, ultimately, of the Thirty Years' War. This peculiarly Bohemian method of expressing protest (throwing someone out a window) had first been used in 1419 in the New Town Hall, an event that formed part of the lead-up to the Hussite wars. Two hundred years later the same conflict was reexpressed in terms of Hapsburg-backed Catholics versus Bohemian Protestants. Rudolf II had reached an uneasy agreement with the Bohemian nobles, allowing them religious freedom in exchange for financial support. But his next-but-one successor, Ferdinand II, was a rabid opponent of Protestantism and disregarded Rudolf's tolerant "Letter of Majesty." Enraged, the Protestant nobles stormed the castle and chancellery and threw two Catholic officials and their secretary, for good measure, out the window. Legend has it they landed on a mound of horse dung and escaped unharmed, an event the Jesuits interpreted as a miracle. The square window in question is on the left as you enter the room.

At the back of the Vladislav Hall, a staircase leads up to a gallery of the **Kaple všech svatých** (All Saints' Chapel). Little remains of Peter Parler's original work, but the church contains some fine works of art. The large room to the left of the staircase is the **Stará sněmovna** (council chamber), where the Bohemian nobles met with the king in a kind of prototype parliament. The descent from Vladislav Hall toward what remains of the **Romanský palác** (Romanesque palace) is by way of a wide, shallow set of steps. This **Jezdecké schody** (Riders' Staircase) was the entranceway for knights who came for the jousting tournaments. ⊠ *Royal Palace, Třetí nádvoří.* 🖼 *For admission information,* see *Castle Information Office,* above. ⊙ *Apr.–Oct., daily 9–5; Nov.–Mar., daily 9–4.*

55 **Lobkovický palác** (Lobkowicz Palace). From the beginning of the 17th century until the 1940s, this building was the residence of the powerful Catholic Lobkowicz family. It was supposedly to this house that the two defenestrated officials escaped after landing on the dung hill in 1618. During the 1970s the building was restored to its early Baroque appearance and now houses the National Museum's permanent exhibition on Czech history. If you want to get a chronological understanding of Czech history from the beginnings of the Great

Moravian Empire in the 9th century to the Czech national uprising in 1848, this is the place. Copies of the crown jewels are on display here; but it is the rich collection of illuminated Bibles, old musical instruments, coins, weapons, royal decrees, paintings, and statues that makes the museum well worth visiting. Detailed information on the exhibits is available in English. ✉ *Jiřská ul.* 🎫 *40 Kč.* ☉ *Tues.–Sun. 9–5.*

45 **Matyášova brána** (Matthias Gate). Built in 1614, the stone gate once stood alone in front of the moats and bridges that surrounded the castle. Under the Hapsburgs, the gate survived by being grafted as a relief onto the palace building. As you go through it, notice the ceremonial white-marble entrance halls on either side, which lead up to President Václav Havel's reception rooms (only rarely open to the public).

44 **První nádvoří** (First Courtyard). The main entrance to Prague Castle from Hradčanské náměstí is a little disappointing. Going through the wrought-iron gate, guarded at ground level by Czech soldiers and from above by the ferocious *Battling Titans* (a copy of Ignaz Platzer's original 18th-century statues), you'll enter this courtyard, built on the site of old moats and gates that once separated the castle from the surrounding buildings and thus protected the vulnerable western flank. The courtyard is one of the more recent additions to the castle, designed by Maria Theresa's court architect, Nicolò Pacassi, in the 1760s. Today it forms part of the presidential office complex. Pacassi's reconstruction was intended to unify the eclectic collection of buildings that made up the castle, but the effect of his work is somewhat flat.

49 **Třetí nádvoří** (Third Courtyard). The contrast between the cool, dark interior of St. Vitus Cathedral (☞ *above*) and the brightly colored Pacassi facades of the Third Courtyard just outside is startling. The courtyard's clean lines are the work of Slovenian architect Jože Plečnik in the 1930s, but the modern look is a deception. Plečnik's paving was intended to cover an underground world of house foundations, streets, and walls dating from the 9th through the 12th centuries—rediscovered when the cathedral was completed. (You can see a few archways through a grating in a wall of the cathedral.)

54 **Zlatá ulička** (Golden Lane). An enchanting collection of tiny, ancient, brightly colored houses crouches under the fortification wall, looking remarkably like a set for *Snow White and the Seven Dwarfs.* Legend has it that these were the lodgings of the international group of alchemists whom Rudolf II brought to the court to produce gold. The truth is a little less romantic: The houses were built during the 16th century for the castle guards, who supplemented their income by practicing various crafts outside the jurisdiction of the powerful guilds. By the early 20th century, Golden Lane had become the home of poor artists and writers. Franz Kafka, who lived at No. 22 in 1916 and 1917, described the house on first sight as "so small, so dirty, impossible to live in and lacking everything necessary." But he soon came to love the place. As he wrote to his fiancée: "Life here is something special . . . to close out the world not just by shutting the door to a room or apartment but to the whole house, to step out into the snow of the silent lane." The lane now houses tiny stores selling books, music, and crafts.

☾ Above Golden Lane runs a timber-roofed corridor within the walls, lined with replica suits of armor and weapons (some of it for sale), mock torture chambers, and the like (entrance between house No. 23 and No. 24). 🎫 *Free.* ☉ *Tues.–Sun. 10–6, Mon. 1–6.*

Nové město (New Town) and Vyšehrad

To this day, Charles IV's building projects are tightly woven into the daily lives of Praguers. His most extensive scheme, Nové město (the

New Town), is still such a lively, vibrant area you may hardly realize that its streets, Gothic churches, and squares were planned as far back as 1348. With Prague fast outstripping its Old Town parameters, Charles IV extended the city's fortifications; a high wall surrounded the newly developed 1½-square-mi (2½-square-km) area south and east of the Old Town, tripling the walled territory on the Vltava's right bank. The wall extended south to link with the fortifications of the citadel called Vyšehrad. In the mid-19th century, new building in the New Town boomed in a welter of Romantic and neo-Renaissance styles, particularly on Wenceslas Square and avenues such as Vodičkova, Na Poříčí, and Spálená. One of the most important structures was the Národní divadlo (National Theater), meant to symbolize in stone the revival of Czechs' history, language, and sense of national pride. Both preceding and following Czechoslovak independence in 1918, modernist architecture entered the mix, particularly on the outer fringes of the Old Town and in the New Town. One of modernism's most unexpected products was Cubist architecture, a form unique to Prague, which produced four notable examples at the foot of ancient Vyšehrad.

A GOOD WALK

Start at the **Národní divadlo** ㉟ and follow the embankment, Masarykovo nábřeží, south toward Vyšehrad. Below the Národní divadlo on Masarykovo nábřeží, note the Art Nouveau architecture of No. 32, the amazingly eclectic design by Kamil Hilbert at No. 26, and the tile-decorated Hlahol building at No. 16. Straddling an arm of the river at Myslíkova ulice are the modern Galerie Mánes (1928–1930) and its attendant 15th-century water tower, where, from a lookout on the sixth floor, Communist-era secret police used to observe Václav Havel's apartment at Rašínovo nábřeží 78. This building, still part-owned by the president, and the adjoining **Tančící dům** ("Dancing House") by Frank Gehry and Vlado Milunić, are on the far side of Jiráskovo náměstí. From the square, Resslova street leads uphill four blocks to **Karlovo náměstí** ㊳.

A convenient place to rejoin the riverfront is Palackého náměstí via Na Moráni street at the southern end of Karlovo náměstí. This square, with its (melo)dramatic monument to the 19th-century historian František Palacký, "awakener of the nation," lies 1 km (½ mi) south of the Národní divadlo. The view of the Benedictine Klášter Emauzy from here is lovely. The houses grow less attractive south of here, so you may wish to hop a tram (tram no. 3, 16 or 17 at the stop on Rašínovo nábřeží) and ride one stop to Výtoň, at the base of the **Vyšehrad** ㊲ citadel. Walk under the railroad bridge on Rašínovo nábřeží to find the closest of four nearby **Cubist buildings.** Another lies a few dozen yards farther along the embankment; two more are a couple of minutes' walk "inland" along Vnislavova to Neklanova. Alternatively, just before reaching Neklanova, veer right onto Vratislavova, an ancient road that runs tortuously up into the heart of Vyšehrad.

It's about 2¼ km (1½ mi) between Národní divadlo and the Vyšehrad. Note that tram No. 17 travels the length of the embankment, if you'd like to make a quicker trip between the two points.

TIMING

A leisurely stroll from the Národní divadlo to Vyšehrad may easily absorb two hours, as may an exploration of Karlovo náměstí and the Klášter Emauzy. Vyšehrad is open every day, year-round, and the views are stunning on a clear day or evening, but keep in mind that there is little shade along the river walk on hot afternoons.

SIGHTS TO SEE

Cubist buildings. Born of zealous modernism, Prague's Cubist architecture followed a great Czech tradition in that it fully embraced new ideas while adapting them to existing artistic and social contexts. Between 1912 and 1914, Josef Chochol (1880–1956) designed several of the city's dozen or so Cubist projects. His apartment house **Neklanova 30**, on the corner of Neklanova and Přemyslova streets, is magnificent. The pyramidal, kaleidoscopic window mouldings and roof cornices are completely novel while making an expressive link to Baroque forms; the faceted corner balcony column elegantly alludes to Gothic forerunners. On the same street, at **Neklanova 2**, is another apartment house attributed to Chochol; like the building at Neklanova 30, it uses pyramidal shapes and the suggestion of Gothic columns. ⊠ *Neklanova 30 and Neklanova 2, Prague 2.*

Chochol's **villa,** on the embankment at Libušina 3, has an undulating effect created by smoothly articulated forms. The wall and gate around the back of the house are superb as well, using triangular moldings and metal grating to create an effect of controlled energy. The **three-family house,** about 100 yards away from the villa at Rašínovo nábřeží 6–10, was completed slightly earlier, when Chochol's Cubist style was still developing. Here, the design is touched with Baroque and neoclassical influence, with a mansard roof and end gables.

㊳ Karlovo náměstí (Charles Square). This square began life as a cattle market, a function chosen by Emperor Charles IV when he established the New Town in 1348. The Horse Market (now Wenceslas Square) quickly overtook it as a livestock-trading center, and an untidy collection of shacks accumulated here until the mid-1800s, when it became a green park named for its patron. ⊠ *Vodičkova ul., Spálená ul., Resslova ul., and Na Moráni ul. lead into square.*

Novoměstská radnice (New Town Hall), at the northern edge of the square, has a late-Gothic tower similar to that of the Old Town Hall and three superb, tall Renaissance gables. The "First Defenestration of Prague" occurred here on July 30, 1419; a mob of townspeople, followers of the martyred religious reformer Jan Hus, hurled Catholic town councillors out the windows. Historical exhibitions and contemporary arts shows are held regularly, and you may climb the tower for a view of the New Town. (Admission to the exhibits varies.) ⊠ *Karlovo náměstí at Vodi kova, Prague 2.* 🎟 *Tower: 20 Kč.* ☉ *Tower June 1– Sept. 30, Tues.–Sun. 10–6.*

On the east side of the square, south of Ječná street, the glowing white-and-gold Jesuit church of St. Ignatius and adjoining plain lines of a hospital building that was once a Jesuit college form a continuous long facade. The south end of Charles Square is dominated by the Faustův dům (Faust House), said to have been a residence of the legendary Doctor Faustus, who sold his soul to the devil. Next door is the almost always locked gate to Kilian Dientzenhofer's dynamic Kostel sv. Jana Nepomuckého (Church of St. John of Nepomuk), called *na skalce* (on the rock), for a self-evident reason—perched on a rock above ground level, it has two exterior staircases leading down to the street.

Just south of the square and across from St. John of Nepomuk lies another of Charles IV's gifts to the city: the Benedictine **Klášter Emauzy** (Emmaus Monastery). It is often called Na Slovanech, literally "At the Slavs'," in reference to its purpose when established in 1347: the emperor invited Croatian monks here to celebrate mass in Old Slavonic and thus cultivate religion among the Slavs in a city largely controlled by Germans. The abbey church suffered heavy damage from a February 14, 1945, raid by Allied bombers that may have mistaken Prague for 121-km- (75-mi-) distant Dresden. The church lost its spires and the interior remains a blackened shell. Some years after the war two arcing concrete "spires" were set atop the church. ⊠ *Vyšehradská 49 (cloister entrance is on the left at the rear of the church), Prague 2.* 🖼 *10 Kč.* ⊘ *Weekdays 10–6.*

㊱ Národní divadlo (National Theater). The idea for a Czech national theater began during the revolutionary decade of the 1840s. In a telling display of national pride, donations to fund the plan poured in from all over the country, from people of every socioeconomic stratum. The cornerstone was laid in 1868; the "National Theater generation" who designed the neo-Renaissance structure became the architectural and artistic establishment for decades to come. Its designer, Josef Zítek (1832–1909), was the leading neo-Renaissance architect in Bohemia. The nearly finished interior was gutted by a fire in 1881, and Zítek's onetime student Josef Schulz (1840–1917) saw the reconstruction through to completion two years later. Statues representing Drama and Opera rise above the riverfront side entrances; two gigantic chariots flank figures of Apollo and the nine Muses above the main facade. The performance space itself is filled with gilding, voluptuous plaster figures, and plush upholstery. Next door is the modern (1970s–1980s) Nová scéna (New Stage), where the popular Magic Lantern black-light shows are staged. The Národní divadlo is one of the best places to see a performance; ticket prices here start as low as 30 Kč. ⊠ *Národní třída 2,* ☎ *02/2491–3437.*

Tančící dům (Dancing House). This whimsical building was partnered into life in 1996 by architect Frank Gehry (he of the Guggenheim-Museum-in-Bilbao fame) and his Croatian-Czech collaborator Vlado Milunić. A wasp-waisted glass-and-steel tower sways into the main structure as though they were a couple on the dance floor—a "Fred and Ginger" effect that gave the wacky, yet somehow appropriate, building its nickname. A French restaurant occupies the top floors (☞ La Perle de Prague *in* Dining, *below*), and there is a café at street level. ⊠ *Rašínovo nábřeží 80, Prague 2.*

㊲ Vyšehrad. Bedřich Smetana's symphonic poem *Vyšehrad* opens with four stirring harp chords; these bardic notes seem to echo the legendary associations with Vyšehrad's ancient fortifications. Today, the flat-topped bluff standing over the right bank of the Vltava is a green, tree-dotted expanse showing few signs that splendid medieval monuments once made it a landmark to rival Prague Castle. The Kapitulní kostel sv. Petra a Pavla dominates the plateau as it has since the 11th century; next to the church lies the burial ground of the nation's revered cultural figures. Most of the buildings still standing are from the 19th century; scattered among them are a few older structures and some foundation stones of the medieval palaces. Surrounding the ruins are gargantuan, excellently preserved brick fortifications built in the 17th to the mid-19th centuries; their broad tops allow strollers to take in sweeping vistas up- and downriver.

The historical father of Vyšehrad, the "High Castle," is Vratislav II (1061–1092), a Přemyslide duke who became first king of Bohemia. He made the fortified hilltop his capital, but, under subsequent rulers, it fell into disuse until the 14th century, when Charles IV transformed the site into an ensemble of palaces, the Gothicized Kapitulní kostel sv. Petra a Pavla, battlements, and a massive gatehouse called Špička, whose scant remains are on V Pevnosti street. By the 17th century royalty had long since departed, most of the structures they built were crumbling, and Vyšehrad became a fortress.

Vyšehrad's place in the modern Czech imagination is largely thanks to the National Revivalists of the 19th century, particularly writer Alois Jirásek (1851–1930), who mined medieval chronicles for legends and facts to glorify the early Czechs. In his rendition, Vyšehrad was the court of the prophetess-ruler Libuše, who had a vision of her husband-to-be, the ploughman Přemysl—father of the Přemyslide line—and of "a city whose glory shall reach the heavens" called Praha. (In truth, the Czechs first came to Vyšehrad around the beginning of the 900s, slightly later than the building of Prague Castle.)

A concrete result of the National Revival was the establishment of the **Hřbitov** (cemetery) in the 1860s; it peopled the fortress with the remains of luminaries from the arts and sciences. The grave of Smetana faces the **Slavín,** a mausoleum for more than 50 honored men and women including Alfons Mucha, sculptor Jan Štursa, inventor František Křižík, and the opera diva Ema Destinnová—all guarded by a winged genius who hovers above the inscription AČ ZEMŘELI, JEŠTĚ MLUVÍ ("Although they have died, they yet speak"). Antonín Dvořák (1841–1904) rests in the arcade along the north wall. Among the many writers buried here are Jan Neruda, Božena Němcová, Karel Čapek, and the Romantic poet Karel Hynek Mácha, whose grave was visited by students on their momentous November 17, 1989 protest march.

Traces of the citadel's distant past do remain. A heavily restored **Romanesque rotunda,** built by Vratislav II, stands on the east side of the compound. Foundations and a few embossed floor tiles from the late-10th-century **Basilika sv. Vavřince** (St. Lawrence Basilica) are in a structure on Soběslavova street (if it is locked, you can ask for the key at the refreshment stand just to the left of the basilica entrance; admission is 5 Kč). Part of the medieval fortifications stand next to the surprisingly confined foundation mounds of a medieval palace overlooking a ruined watchtower called Libuše's Bath. A statue of Libuše and her consort Přemysl is nearby in a plot of grass next to the Kapitulní kostel sv. Petra a Pavla (☞ *below*), one of four large sculpted images of couples from Czech legend by J. V. Myslbek (1848–1922), the sculptor of the St. Wenceslas monument.

The stone spires of the **Kapitulní kostel sv. Petra a Pavla** (Chapter Church of Sts. Peter and Paul) are visible from all over Prague. Founded by Vratislav II and rebuilt several times, the church owes its present appearance to the re-Gothicizing carried out at the turn of the 20th century. The other standing buildings are also mainly neo-Gothic; some are used by the Catholic chapter established by Vratislav in 1070.

The military history of the fortress and the city is covered in a small exposition inside the **Cihelná brána** (Brick Gate). Here also is the entrance to the casemates—a long, dark passageway within the walls that ends at a dank hall used to store several original pollution-scarred Charles Bridge sculptures. A guided tour into the casemates and the statue storage room starts at the military history exhibit (10 Kč admission to exposition; tour 20 Kč). ⊠ *Entrances on Vratislavova and V Pevnosti Sts., Prague 2.* ☉ *Grounds: daily. Military history exhibit, casemates, St. Lawrence Basilica Apr.–Oct., daily 9:30–5:30; Nov.–Mar., daily 9:30–4:30. Cemetery Apr.–Oct., daily 8–6; Nov.–Mar., daily 9–5.*

Vinohrady

From Riegrovy sady and its sweeping view of the city from above the National Museum, the elegant residential neighborhood called Vinohrady extends its streets of eclectic apartment houses and villas eastward and southward. The pastel-tinted ranks of turn-of-the-century apartment houses—many crumbling after years of neglect—are slowly but unstoppably being transformed into upscale flats, slick offices, eternally packed new restaurants, and a range of shops unthinkable only a half decade ago. Much of the development lies on or near Vinohradská, the main street, which extends from the top of Wenceslas Square to a belt of enormous cemeteries about 3 km (2 mi) eastward. Yet the flavor of daily life persists: Smoky old pubs still ply their trade on the quiet side streets; the stately theater, Divadlo na Vinohradech, keeps putting on excellent shows as it has for decades; and on the squares and in the parks nearly everyone still practices Prague's favorite form of outdoor exercise—walking the dog.

㊴ Kostel Nejsvětějšího Srdce Páně (Church of the Most Sacred Heart). If you've had your fill of Romanesque, Gothic, and Baroque, take the metro to the Jiřího z Poděbrad station (Line A) for a look at a startling Art Deco edifice. Designed in 1927 by Slovenian architect Josip Plečnik (the same architect commissioned to update Prague Castle), the church resembles a luxury ocean liner more than a place of worship. The effect was conscious; during the 1920s and '30s, the avant-garde imitated mammoth objects of modern technology. You may be able to find someone at the back entrance of the church who will let you walk up the long ramp into the fascinating glass clock tower. ⊠ *Nám. Jiřího z Poděbrad, Prague 3,* ☎ *no phone.* ◷ *Daily 10–5.*

NEED A BREAK?

The cool and quiet basement café of one of the city's best English-language bookstores, **U knihomola,** serves delicious and wholesome light meals as well as fabulous carrot cake and a variety of coffees—perfect for a lazy Sunday with the newspapers. Often there's live acoustic music as well. ⊠ *Mánesova 79, Prague 2,* ☎ *02/627-7770.*

Židovský hřbitov (Jewish Burial Ground). In an odd visual juxtaposition, this small cemetery huddles at the foot of the soaring rocket ship–like television tower that broke ground in the last years of communism and used to be mockingly called "Big Brother's Finger." The stones date back as far as the 17th century; a little neoclassical mausoleum stands forlornly just outside the fence. The cemetery gate is almost always locked, but the bars are widely spaced enough for small people to squeeze through (the cemetery is unsupervised). ⊠ *Fibichova at Kubelíkova, Prague 3.*

㊶ Pavilon (Vinohrady Pavilion market hall). This gorgeous, turn-of-the-century, neo-Renaissance, three-story market hall is one of the most attractive sites in Vinohrady. It used to be a major old-style market, a vast space filled with stalls selling all manner of foodstuffs, plus the requisite grimy pub. After being spiffed up several years ago, its settled into life as an upscale shopping mall. ⊠ *Vinohradská 50, Prague 2,* ☎ *02/2209-7111.*

NEED A BREAK?

A symbol of this bucolic neighborhood's intellectual leanings, the literary café **Literární kavárna** serves coffees and light desserts in a well-lit and welcoming shop brimming with books, newspapers, and magazines (most in Czech). Several nights a week, the café hosts readings as well as intimate concerts of folk, jazz, or Romany (Gypsy) music. ⊠ *Čerchovská 4, Prague 2,* ☎ *02/627-3332.*

㊵ Nový Židovský hřbitov (New Jewish Cemetery). Tens of thousands of Czechs find eternal rest in Vinohrady's cemeteries. In this, the newest of the city's half dozen Jewish cemeteries, you'll find the modest **tombstone of Franz Kafka,** which seems grossly inadequate to Kafka's stature but oddly in proportion to his own modest ambitions. The cemetery is usually open, although guards sometimes inexplicably seal off the grounds. Men may be required to wear a yarmulke (you can buy one there). Turn right at the main cemetery gate and follow the wall for about 100 yards. Kafka's thin, white tombstone lies at the front of Section 21. ⊠ *Vinohradská at Jana Želivského, Prague 3 (metro station Želivského).* ⚎ *Free.* ☉ *June–Aug. Sun.–Thurs. 8–5; Sept.– May Mon.–Thurs. 9–4, Sun. 9–3.*

Letná and Holešovice

From above the Vltava's left bank, the large, grassy plateau called Letná affords one of the classic views of the Old Town and the many bridges crossing the river. (To get to Letná from the Old Town above Parizska street, cross the Čechův Bridge and climb the stairs.) Beer gardens, tennis, and Frisbee attract people of all ages, while amateur soccer players emulate the professionals of Prague's top team, Sparta, which plays in the stadium just across the road. Ten minutes' walk from Letná, down into the residential neighborhood of Holešovice, brings you to a massive, gray-blue building whose cool exterior gives no hint of the treasures of Czech and French modern art that line its corridors. Just north along Dukelských hrdinů street is Stromovka—a royal hunting preserve turned gracious park.

Numbers in the margin correspond to numbers on the Exploring Prague map.

㊷ Letenské sady (Letna Gardens). Come to this large, shady park for an unforgettable view of Prague's bridges. From the enormous cement pedestal at the center of the park, the largest statue of Stalin in Eastern Europe once beckoned to citizens on the Old Town Square far below. The statue was ripped down in the 1960s, when Stalinism was finally discredited. On sunny Sundays expatriates often meet up here to play ultimate Frisbee. ⊠ *Bordered by Milady Horákové, Nad Štolou, and Badeniho Sts., Prague 7.*

㊸ Veletržní palác sbírka moderního a soucasného umění (Veletržní palác Museum of Modern Art). The National Gallery's newest museum, housed in a trade-fair hall in the Holešovice neighborhood, set off a furor when it opened in 1995. The lighting, the exhibit design, the unused empty spaces in the building's two enormous halls, even the selection of paintings and sculpture—all came under critics' scrutiny. The discouraging voices couldn't deny, though, that the palace—itself a key work of constructivist architecture—serves a vital purpose in permanently displaying long-neglected pieces of 20th-century Czech art. The collection of 19th- and 20th-century French art, including an important group of early Cubist paintings by Picasso and Braque, is also here, moved from the Šternberský Palace (☞ The Castle District, *above*). ⊠ *Veletržní at Dukelských hrdinů, Prague 7,* ☎ *02/2430–1111.* ⚎ *120 Kč.* ☉ *Tues.–Wed. and Fri.–Sun. 10–6, Thurs. 10–9.*

Dining

Dining choices in Prague have increased greatly in the past decade as hundreds of new places have opened to cope with the soaring tourist demand. Quality and price vary widely, though. Be wary of tourist traps, especially on Old Town Square; cross-check prices of foreign-language menus with Czech versions, and even in the better restaurants it's always wise to take a close look at the addition in your bill at the end of a meal before simply paying up. Also ask if there is a *denní lístek* (daily menu). These menus, usually written only in Czech, generally list cheaper and often fresher selections (though many places provide daily menus for the midday meal only). Special local dishes worth making a beeline for include *cibulačka* (onion soup), *kulajda* (potato soup

Prague Dining and Lodging

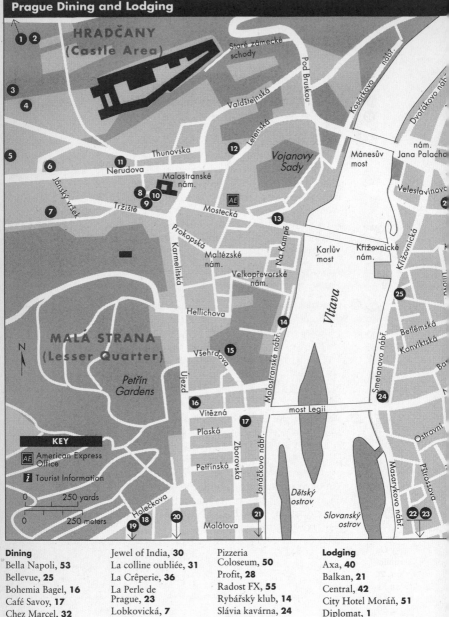

Dining

Bella Napoli, **53**
Bellevue, **25**
Bohemia Bagel, **16**
Café Savoy, **17**
Chez Marcel, **32**
Circle Line Brasserie, **8**
Dolly Bell, **22**
Fakhreldine, **37**
Fromin, **49**

Jewel of India, **30**
La colline oubliée, **31**
La Crêperie, **36**
La Perle de Prague, **23**
Lobkovická, **7**
Lotos, **29**
Mailsi, **45**
Myslivna, **56**
Novoměstský pivovar, **52**
Pasha, **12**
Pizzeria Azzurra, **33**

Pizzeria Coloseum, **50**
Profit, **28**
Radost FX, **55**
Rybářský klub, **14**
Slávia kavárna, **24**
U Mecenáše, **9**
U Počtů, **35**
U ševce Matouše, **6**
U Tří Zlatých Hvězd, **10**
U Zlaté Hrušky, **4**
V Krakovské, **54**
V Zátiší, **26**

Lodging

Axa, **40**
Balkan, **21**
Central, **42**
City Hotel Moráň, **51**
Diplomat, **1**
Dům U Červeného Lva, **11**
Grand Hotel Bohemia, **43**
Harmony, **39**
Hotel Bern, **46**
Hotel Olšanka, **47**
Kampa, **15**

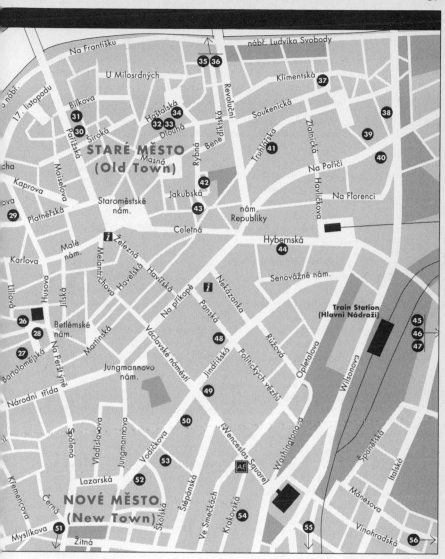

Na Františku
nábř. Ludvíka Svobody
35 36
U Milosrdných
Klimentská 37
Revoluční
17. listopadu
nábř.
Bílkova
Soukenická
38
31
Haštalská 34
Benediktská
Zlatnická
30 Široká
32 33 Dlouhá
39
Pařížská
Masná
Truhlářská 41
STARÉ MĚSTO
(Old Town)
Na Poříčí
40
Rybná
Kaprova
Maiselova
Platnéřská
42
Na Florenci
Havlíčkova
29
Jakubská
Staroměstské
nám.
43
Coletná
nám.
Republiky
Karlova
Malé
nám.
Železná
Hybernská
44
Melantrichova
Havelská
Havířská
Senovážné nám.
Train Station
(Hlavní Nádraží)
Liliová
Karlova
Na příkopě
Nekázanka
Husova
Jilská
45
46
47
Betlémské
nám.
26
Panská
Martinská
Václavské náměstí
Růžová
Opletalova
Wilsonova
28
Bartolomějská
27
Na Perštýně
48
Politických vězňů
Jungmannovo
nám.
Jindřišská
Národní třída
49
Washingtonova
Spálená
50
Vodičkova
Jungmannova
Vladislavova
Opatovická
Štěpánská
[Wenceslas Square]
Španělská
Italská
Mánesova
53
AE
Lazarská
52
Školská
NOVÉ MĚSTO
(New Town)
Ve Smečkách
Krakovská
54
Vinohradská
55
56
Kremencova
Černá
Myslíkova
51
Žitná

Kinsky Garden, **18**
Maximilian, **34**
Mepro, **20**
Meteor Plaza, **44**
Opera, **38**
Palace, **48**
Pension Unitas, **27**
Pension U Raka, **3**
Penzion Sprint, **2**
Petr, **19**
Salvator, **41**
Savoy, **5**
U Tří Pštrosů, **13**

with sour cream), *svíčková* (beef sirloin in cream sauce), and *ovocné knedlíky* (fruit dumplings).

The crush of visitors has placed tremendous strain on the more popular restaurants. The upshot: Reservations are nearly always required, especially during peak tourist periods. If you don't have reservations, try arriving a little before standard meal times: 11:30 AM for lunch or 5:30 PM for dinner.

For a cheaper and quicker alternative to the sit-down establishments listed below, try a light meal at one of the city's growing number of street stands and fast-food places. Look for stands offering *párky* (hot dogs) or *smažený syr* (fried cheese). For more exotic fare, try a gyro (made from pork) at the stand on Old Town Square or the very good vegetarian fare at **Country Life** (✉ Melantrichova ul. 15, ☎ 02/2421–3366), open Sunday–Friday. The German coffeemaker **Tchibo** has teamed up with a local bakery and now offers tasty sandwiches and excellent coffee at convenient locations on Old Town Square and at the top of Wenceslas Square.

Old Town (Staré Město)

$$$$ ✕ **Bellevue.** The first choice for visiting dignitaries and businesspeople blessed with expense accounts, Bellevue has creative, freshly prepared cuisine, more nouvelle than Bohemian—and the elegant setting not far from Charles Bridge doesn't hurt. Look for the lamb carpaccio with fresh rosemary, garlic, and extra-virgin olive oil, or the wild berries marinated in port and cognac, served with vanilla and walnut ice cream. Window seats afford stunning views of Prague Castle. There is a small, mostly Czech, vintage wine list. ✉ *Smetanovo nábřeží 18,* ☎ *02/2422–7614. AE, DC, MC, V.*

$$$$ ✕ **Jewel of India.** Although generally Asian cooking of any stripe is not Prague's forte, here is a sumptuous spot well worth seeking out for Northern Indian tandooris and other moderately spiced specialties, including some delicious vegetarian dishes. ✉ *Pařížská 20 (near metro Staroměstská), Prague 1,* ☎ *02/2481–1010. AE, MC, V.*

$$$$ ✕ **V Zátiší.** White walls and casual grace accentuate the subtle flavors
★   of smoked salmon, plaice, beef Wellington, and other non-Czech specialties. Order the house *Rulandské červené,* a fruity Moravian red wine that meets the exacting standards of the food. In behavior unusual for the city, the benign waiters fairly fall over each other to serve diners. ✉ *Liliová 1, Betlémské nám.,* ☎ *02/2422–8977. AE, DC, MC, V.*

$$ ✕ **Chez Marcel.** At this authentic French bistro on a quiet, picturesque street, you can get a little taste of that *other* riverside capital. French owned and operated, Chez Marcel has an extensive menu suitable for lingering over a three-course meal—try deciding among salads, pâtés, cheeses, rabbit, and some of the best steaks in Prague. ✉ *Haštalská 12,* ☎ *02/231–5676. No credit cards.*

$$ ✕ **La colline oubliée.** In "The Forgotten Hill," remember to try *brik* (spicy ratatouille or ground meat in pastry) or the all-you-can-eat couscous. Indecisive diners may be whisked into the kitchen by one of the charming North African team for a convincing sample. The Old Town location is ideal, just off Pařížská street. ✉ *Elišky Krásnohorské 11,* ☎ *02/232–9522. AE, V.*

$ ✕ **Lotos.** Banana ragout with polenta and broccoli strudel are two favorites at what is undoubtedly the best of the city's scant selection of all-vegetarian restaurants. Blond-wood tables and billowing tie-dyed fabric set an informal yet elegant atmosphere. The salads and soups are wonderful. ✉ *Platnéřská 13,* ☎ *02/232–2390. AE, MC, V.*

$ ✕ **Pizzeria Azzurra.** This bright and spacious pizzeria is just a couple of blocks from Old Town Square, yet it remains relatively undiscovered by all but hungry locals. Whet your appetite by watching the pizza bake in the kiln; toppings may include grilled eggplant or prosciutto. An extensive array of pastas is also available; the lasagna is especially good. ⊠ *Dlouhá 35,* ☎ *02/2481–5613. No credit cards.*

$ ✕ **Profit.** The unfortunate name masks a clean, spacious pub that serves such excellent Czech standbys as goulash and pork with dumplings and sauerkraut at astonishingly reasonable prices. The central location could hardly be better. ⊠ *Betlémské nám. 8,* ☎ *02/2421–8557. No credit cards.*

$ ✕ **Slávia kavárna.** This legendary hangout for the best and brightest
★ in Czech arts—from composer Bedřich Smetana and poet Jaroslav Seifert to then-dissident Václav Havel—is back in business after being held hostage in absurd real-estate wrangles for most of the '90s. Its Art Deco decor is a perfect backdrop for people-watching, and the vistas (the river and Prague Castle on one side, the National Theater on the other) are a compelling reason to linger for hours over an espresso. Although the Slavia is principally a café, you can also get a light meal, such as a small salad with Balkan cheese or an open-face sandwich. And despite what the old-guard coat-check lady will tell you on your way in, it is not obligatory to check your coat with her. ⊠ *Smetanovo nábřeží 1012/2,* ☎ *02/2422–0957. No credit cards.*

New Town (Nové Město)

$$$$ ✕ **La Perle de Prague.** Delicious Parisian cooking awaits at the top of the curvaceous "Fred and Ginger" building. The restaurant's interior is washed with soft tones of lilac and sea green . . . and a quiet sense of humor (parading elephants are the motif for one table setting). The semiprivate dining room at the very top affords a view so riveting diners might almost forget they were enjoying red snapper Provençal, freshwater pike-perch (*candát*), tournedos of beef Béarnaise, and other classic French dishes. Make reservations as early as you can; this is also a good reason to unpack your tie. ⊠ *Rašínovo nábřeží 80,* ☎ *02/2198–4160. AE, DC, MC, V. Closed Sun. No lunch Mon.*

$$$ ✕ **Fakhreldine.** This elegant Lebanese restaurant, crowded with diplomats who know where to find the real thing, has an excellent range of Middle Eastern dishes, such as *kibbey bisayniyeh* (lamb and ground pine-nut patty), *warakinab* (stuffed grape leaves) and three kinds of baklava. For a moderately priced meal, try several appetizers—hummus and garlic yogurt, perhaps—instead of a main course. ⊠ *Klimentská 48,* ☎ *02/232–7970. AE, DC, MC, V.*

$$ ✕ **Bella Napoli.** The decor may be a little much, but the food is gen-
★ uine and the price-to-quality ratio is hard to beat. Close your eyes to the alabaster Venus de Milos astride shopping-mall fountains and head straight for the antipasto bar, which will distract you with fresh olives, eggplant, squid, and mozzarella. For your main course, go with any of a dozen superb pasta dishes or splurge with shrimp or chicken parmigiana. The Italian-American chef hails from Brooklyn and knows his stuff. ⊠ *V jámě 8,* ☎ *02/2422–7315. No credit cards.*

$$ ✕ **Fromin.** Come dressed to the teeth—flourishing your mobile phone, preferably—for dinner at this so-chic loft high above Wenceslas Square. The food is better than average, with entrées unusual for hereabouts, such as turkey *piccata,* lamb chops, and fresh tuna steaks. The upstairs café is quiet in the mornings; then at 10 PM it becomes a disco whose doorman will turn away unstylishly dressed guests. ⊠ *Václavské nám. 21,* ☎ *02/2423–2319. AE, MC, V.*

$ ✕ **Novoměstský pivovar.** It's easy to lose your way in this crowded microbrewery-restaurant; there's a maze of rooms, some painted in mock-medieval style, others covered with murals of Prague street scenes. *Vepřové koleno* (pork knuckle) is a favorite dish. The beer is the cloudy, fruity "fermented" style. ⊠ *Vodičkova 20, Prague 1,* ☎ *02/ 2423–3533. AE, MC, V.*

$ ✗ **Pizzeria Coloseum.** Of the swarms of pizzerias that have cropped up in the past few years, most spots have proved to be mediocre, but this one has kept its popularity, due largely to its position right off Wenceslas Square. Location doesn't have everything to do with it, though; the pizzas have a wonderfully thin, crisp crust, and the pasta with Gorgonzola sauce will have you blessing Italian cows. Long picnic tables make this an ideal spot for an informal lunch or dinner. There's a salad bar, too. ⊠ *Vodičkova 32,* ☎ *02/2421–4914. AE, MC, V.*

$ ✗ **Radost FX.** Colorful and campy in design, this lively café is a streetlevel adjunct to the popular dance club Radost and CD shop next door. It's a vegetarian heaven for both Czechs and expatriates: The rotating tofu special is bound to be good, and there are usually creative specials of a Mexican or Italian persuasion. If you suddenly find yourself craving a brownie, this is the place to get a fudge-fix. Another plus: It's open until 4 AM. ⊠ *Bělehradská 120,* ☎ *02/2425–4776. No credit cards.*

$ ✗ **V Krakovské.** At this clean, proper pub close to the major tourist sights, the food is traditional and hearty; this is the place to try *svíčková na smetaně* (thinly sliced sirloin beef in cream sauce) paired with an effervescent Krušovice beer. ⊠ *Krakovská 20,* ☎ *02/2221–0204. No credit cards.*

Lesser Quarter (Malá Strana)

$$$$ ✗ **Circle Line Brasserie.** Bypass the sister restaurant, Avalon, on the ground-floor level as you enter the building (the food and service are nothing special for the price) and head straight downstairs for the fresh, delicious seafood of Circle Line. The decor here is sophisticated without being stuffy, and the service can't be faulted. There are creative seasonal specials such as the warm foie gras with cherries, but be sure to save room for the *cokoládový talíř* (chocolate plate) for dessert. ⊠ *Malostranské nám. 12,* ☎ *02/530308. AE, DC, MC, V.*

$$$$ ✗ **Pasha.** This inviting Middle Eastern spot at the foot of Prague Castle hits just the right notes of luxury and easiness. The à la carte menu includes luscious *adana kebab* (skewer of minced lamb), pilaf, and shish kebab. Baklava served with fresh mint tea makes a splendid dessert. ⊠ *Letenská 1,* ☎ *02/549773. AE, DC, MC, V. Closed Mon.*

$$$ ✗ **Lobkovická.** This dignified *vinárna* (wine hall) set inside a 17th-century town palace serves innovative, imaginative dishes by Prague standards. Chicken breast with crabmeat and curry sauce is an excellent main dish and typical of the kitchen's approach to sauces and spices. Deep-red carpeting sets the perfect mood for enjoying bottles of Moravian wine. ⊠ *Vlašská 17,* ☎ *02/530185. AE, MC, V.*

$$$ ✗ **U Mecenáše.** A fetching Renaissance inn from the 17th century, with dark, high-backed benches in the front room and cozy, elegant sofas and chairs in back, this is a place to splurge. From the aperitifs to the specialty steaks or beef Wellington and the cognac (swirled lovingly in oversize glasses), the presentation is seamless. ⊠ *Malostranské nám. 10,* ☎ *02/533881. AE, MC, V.*

$$ ✗ **U Tří Zlatých Hvězd.** The "Three Golden Stars" is a perfect spot for a romantic evening; the cuisine is hearty, classic Czech with thoughtful European touches, such as roast duck Bohemian style with apples, bacon, dumplings, and red cabbage. ⊠ *Malostranské nám. 8,* ☎ *02/ 539–660. AE, MC, V.*

$ ✗ **Bohemia Bagel.** It's not New York, but the friendly, Americanowned Bohemia Bagel still serves up a plentiful assortment of fresh bagels from raisin walnut to "supreme," with all kinds of toppings. Their thick soups are among the best in Prague for the price, and the bottomless cups of coffee are a further draw. ⊠ *Újezd 16,* ☎ *02/531002. No credit cards.*

$ ✕ **Café Savoy.** Opened in 1887 as a grand café, the Savoy lasted only a few years before the long, airy room was divided up to be made into shops. In 1992 the café was reborn, and best of all, the painted and stuccoed ceiling that had long been covered over was restored. It's best as a spot for coffee, a drink, or a fine apple strudel; typical meat dishes such as pork steak with horseradish are also available. ⊠ *Vítězná 5,* ☎ *02/535000. AE, DC, MC, V.*

$ ✕ **Rybářský klub.** The "Fishing Club" restaurant shares its building with
★ a real fishing club's headquarters; it's a great place to try a wide variety of freshwater fish. Perch, eel, barbel, and the esteemed pike-perch (*candát*) are served at picnic-style tables or by the water in summer. ⊠ *U Sovových mlýnů 1, Kampa Island,* ☎ *02/530–223. No credit cards.*

Hradčany

$$$$ ✕ **U Zlaté Hrušky.** At this bustling bistro perched on one of Prague's prettiest cobblestone streets, slide into one of the cozy dark-wood booths and let the cheerful staff advise on wines and specials. Among the regular offerings are a superb leg of venison with pears and millet gnocchi and an excellent appetizer of duck liver in wine sauce. After dinner, stroll to the castle for an unforgettable panorama. ⊠ *Nový Svět 3,* ☎ *02/2051–4778. Jacket and tie. AE, DC, MC, V.*

$$ ✕ **U ševce Matouše.** Steaks are the raison d'être at this former shoemaker's shop; the gold shoe still hangs from the ceiling of the arcade outside to guide patrons into the vaulted dining room. Appetizers are hit-and-miss; stick with the dozen or so tenderloins and filet mignons. ⊠ *Loretánské nám. 4,* ☎ *02/2051–4536. MC, V.*

Vinohrady

$$ ✕ **Myslivna.** The name means "hunting lodge," and the cooks at this neighborhood eatery certainly know their way around venison, quail, and boar. Attentive staff can advise on wines: Try Vavřinecké, a hearty red that holds its own with any beast. The stuffed quail and the leg of venison with walnuts both get high marks. A cab from the city center to Myslivna should cost under 200 Kč. ⊠ *Jagellonská 21, Prague 3,* ☎ *02/627–0209. No credit cards.*

Letná and Holešovice

$ ✕ **La Crêperie.** Run by a Czech-French couple, this creperie near the Globe Bookstore (☞ Shopping, *below*) and Veletržní palá Museum of Modern Art serves all manner of crepes (thin pancakes), both sweet and savory. (It make take at least three or four to satisfy a hearty appetite.) Make sure to leave room for the dessert crepe with cinnamon-apple purée layered with lemon cream. The owner's nationalities are reflected in the wine list, which has both French and Hungarian wines. ⊠ *Janovského 4, Holešovice,* ☎ *02/878040. No credit cards.*

$ ✕ **U Počtů.** This is a charmingly old-fashioned neighborhood eatery with comparatively skilled service. Garlic soup and chicken livers in wine sauce are flawlessly rendered, and the grilled trout is delicious. ⊠ *Milády Horakové 47, Letná,* ☎ *02/3337–1419. AE, MC, V.*

Žižkov

$ ✕ **Mailsi.** Funky paintings of Arabian Nights–type scenes in a low-ceil-
★ ing cellar make for a casual, cheerful setting at this Pakistani restaurant—normal in some other cities but practically unique in Prague. The menu offers beef, chicken, lamb, and vegetable curries, and delicious nan bread, and a tasty *murgh tikka* appetizer of thin-sliced marinated chicken. Take tram 5, 9, or 26 to the Lipanská stop, and then walk one block uphill. ⊠ *Lipanská 1,* ☎ *02/0603/466–626. No credit cards.*

Vyšehrad

$$ ✕ **Dolly Bell.** This restaurant's whimsical design, with upside-down ta-
★   bles hanging from the ceiling, provides a clever counterpoint to the ex-
tensive selection of well-prepared Yugoslav dishes. There's an emphasis
on meat and seafood—try the corn bread (polenta) with Balkan cheese,
čevapčiči (pork sausage), and *tufahija* (baked apple with a smooth nut
filling). ✉ *Neklanova 20,* ☎ *02/298–815. AE, DC, MC, V.*

Lodging

A slow rise in lodging standards continues, but at all but the most ex-
pensive hotels standards lag behind those of Germany and Austria—
as do prices. In most of the $$$$ and $$$ hotels, you can expect to
find a restaurant and an exchange bureau on or near the premises. Dur-
ing the summer season reservations are absolutely imperative; for the
remainder of the year they are highly recommended. Some hotels lower
their rates between November and March, excluding the Christmas–
to–New Year holiday season; a few hotels in the higher price categories
also drop their rates in July to off-season levels.

A cheaper and often more interesting alternative to Prague's generally mediocre hotels are private rooms and apartments. Prague is full
of travel agencies offering such accommodations; sacrificing a little
privacy is the only drawback. Room-finding services flourish at the
main train station (Hlavní nádraží), Holešovice station (Nádraží
Holešovice), and at Ruzyně Airport. These bureaus normally have em-
ployees with a basic level of English and they open between 6 and 9
AM; several stay open until 9 PM or later. Most can book rooms in hotels and pensions as well as private accommodation. Rates for private
rooms start at around $15 per person per night and can go much higher
for better-quality rooms. In general, there is no fee, but you may need
to try several bureaus in search of an accommodation you want. Ask
to see a photo of the room before accepting it, and be sure to pin-
point its location on a map. Prague is divided into 10 administrative
districts; only Prague 1 and part of Prague 2 lie entirely within the
historic center. Other districts have pleasant neighborhoods but can
extend out to far-flung suburbs; you don't want to end up in an in-
conveniently distant location. You may also be approached by (usually) men in the stations hawking rooms; while these deals aren't an
automatic ripoff, you should be wary of them. **Prague Information
Service** (PIS; ☞ Visitor Information *in* Prague A to Z, *below*) arranges
lodging from all of its central-city offices, including the branch in the
main train station, in the booth marked TURISTICKÉ INFORMACE by the
stairs down to the metro platform, on the left side of the main hall as
you exit the station (✉ Hlavní nádraží, ☎ 02/2423–9258). Between
April and October, this branch is open weekdays 9–7 and weekends
9–4; between November and March, it's open weekdays 9–6 and Saturday 9–3.

Other helpful room-finding agencies include **Hello Ltd.** (✉ Senovážné
nám. 3, Nové Město, ☎ 🖷 02/2421–2647 or 02/2421–4212), open
daily 9 AM–9 PM; it's a 10-minute walk from the main train station.
The bluntly named **Accommodation Service** (✉ Haštalská 7, Staré
Město, ☎ 02/231–0202, 🖷 02/231–6640), open daily between
April and October from 10–noon and 1–7 and from November to
March 9–1 and 2–6, specializes in Old Town rooms and apartments from 1,800 Kč for double occupancy. If all else fails, just take
a walk through the Old Town: The number of places advertising AC-
COMMODATION (often written in German as UNTERKUNFT) is as-
tounding.

Old Town (Staré Město)

$$$$ ⊞ **Grand Hotel Bohemia.** This beautifully refurbished Art Nouveau town palace, probably the most expensive hotel in Prague, is just a stone's throw from Old Town Square. The Austrian owners opted for a muted, modern decor in the rooms but left the sumptuous public areas just as they were. Sweeping, long drapes frame spectacular views of the Old Town; each room's amenities include a fax, trouser press, and answering machine. ⊠ *Králodvorská 4, 110 00 Prague 1,* ☎ *02/2480–4111,* 𝔽𝔸𝕏 *02/232–9545. 73 rooms, 5 suites. Restaurant, bar, café, minibars, in-room safes. AE, DC, MC, V.*

$$$ ⊞ **Maximilian.** Oversize beds, French cherry-wood Art Nouveau furniture, and thick drapes make for a relaxing stay in this luxurious hotel. A relatively new property (opened in 1995), it's located on a peaceful square, well away from traffic, noise, and crowds, yet within easy walking distance to Old Town Square and Pařížská street. There are fax machines and satellite TVs in every room. ⊠ *Haštalská 14, 113 03 Prague 1,* ☎ *02/2180–6111,* 𝔽𝔸𝕏 *02/2180–6110. 72 rooms. Minibars, in-room safes. AE, DC, MC, V.*

$$ ⊞ **Central.** Quite conveniently, this hotel lives up to its name, with a site on a relatively quiet sidestreet near Celetná Street and Republic Square. Rooms are sparely furnished, but all have baths, and the English-speaking concierge is very helpful and accommodating. The Baroque glories of the Old Town are steps away. ⊠ *Rybná 8, 110 00 Prague 1,* ☎ *02/2481–2041,* 𝔽𝔸𝕏 *02/232–8404. 62 rooms, 4 suites. Restaurant, bar. AE, DC, MC, V.*

$ ⊞ **Pension Unitas.** Now operated by the Christian charity Unitas, the spartan rooms of this former convent used to serve as interrogation cells for the Communist secret police. (Václav Havel was once a "guest.") Conditions are much more comfortable nowadays, if far from luxurious. There's a common (but clean) bathroom on each floor. You'll need to reserve well in advance, even in off season. Note that there is an adjacent three-star hotel, Cloister Inn, using the same location and phone number; when calling, just specify the pension. ⊠ *Bartolomějská 9, 110 00 Prague 1,* ☎ *02/232–7700,* 𝔽𝔸𝕏 *02/232–7709. 40 rooms, none with bath. Restaurant. AE, MC, V.*

New Town (Nové Město)

$$$$ ⊞ **Palace.** For the well-heeled, this is Prague's most coveted address—a beautiful Art Nouveau–style building perched on a busy corner only a block from Wenceslas Square. The hotel's spacious, well-appointed rooms, each with a white-marble bathroom, are fitted in velvety pinks and greens cribbed straight from an Alfonse Mucha print. All have satellite TV. Two rooms are set aside for travelers with disabilities. ⊠ *Panská 12, 111 21 Prague 1,* ☎ *02/2409–3120,* 𝔽𝔸𝕏 *02/2422–1240. 114 rooms, 10 suites. 2 restaurants, piano bar, 2 no-smoking floors, sauna. AE, DC, MC, V.*

$$$ ⊞ **Axa.** Funky and functional, this 1932 high-rise was a mainstay of the budget-hotel crowd until a makeover forced substantial price hikes several years ago. The rooms, now with color television sets and modern plumbing, are certainly improved; however, the lobby and public areas are still decidedly tacky, with plastic flowers, lots of mirrors, and glaring lights. However, the scores of free weights in Axa's gym make it one of the best in Prague. ⊠ *Na Poříčí 40, 113 03 Prague 1,* ☎ *02/2481–2580,* 𝔽𝔸𝕏 *02/232–2172. 109 rooms. Restaurant, bar, pool, exercise room, nightclub. AE, DC, MC, V.*

$$$ ⊞ **City Hotel Morán.** This renovated 19th-century town house has a bright, inviting lobby, made over in an updated Jugendstil style. The modern, if slightly bland, rooms are a cut above the Prague standard for convenience and cleanliness; some on the top floors afford a good view of Prague Castle. ⊠ *Na Moráni 15 (corner of Václavská), 120 00 Prague 2,* ☎ *02/2491–5208,* ℻ *02/297–533. 57 rooms. Restaurant. AE, DC, MC, V.*

$$$ 🖭 **Harmony.** This is one of the renovated, formerly state-owned standbys. A stern 1930s facade clashes with the bright, nouveau riche–type 1990s interior, but cheerful receptionists, comfortably casual rooms, and an easy 10-minute walk to the Old Town compensate for the aesthetic flaws. Ask for a room away from the bustle of one of Prague's busiest streets, which during the day is a major route for trams. ⊠ *Na Poříčí 31, 110 00 Prague 1,* ☎ *02/232–0016,* ℻ *02/231–0009. 60 rooms. Restaurant, snack bar. AE, DC, MC, V.*

$$$ 🖭 **Meteor Plaza.** This popular hotel, operated by the Best Western chain, combines modern conveniences with historical ambience (Empress Maria Theresa's son, Joseph II, stayed here when he was passing through in the 18th century). The setting is ideal: a Baroque building that is only five minutes on foot from downtown. For a better sense of the hotel's age, visit the original 14th-century wine cellar. ⊠ *Hybernská 6, 110 00 Prague 1,* ☎ *02/2419–2111,* ℻ *02/2421–3005. 90 rooms, 6 suites. Restaurant, exercise room. AE, DC, MC, V.*

$$$ 🖭 **Opera.** Once the lodging of choice for divas performing at the nearby State Theater, the Opera greatly declined under the Communists. The mid-'90s saw the grand fin-de-siècle facade rejuvenated with a perky pink-and-white exterior paint job; this exuberance is still strictly on the outside, though, as the rooms have easy-on-the-eyes, modern decor. In the off-season a double room can be had for around 2,800 Kč. ⊠ *Těšnov 13, 110 00 Prague 1,* ☎ *02/231–5609,* ℻ *02/231–1477. 66 rooms. Restaurant, bar. AE, DC, MC, V.*

$$ 🖭 **Salvator.** An efficiently run establishment just outside the Old Town, this pension offers more comforts than most in its class, including satellite TV and minibars in most rooms, and a breakfast room–cum–bar with a billiard table. Rooms are pristine if plain, with the standard narrow beds; those without private bath also lack TVs but are good value nonetheless. Parking (for a 200 Kč a day fee) is available in the courtyard. ⊠ *Truhlářská 10 (near metro Náměstí Republiky), 110 00 Prague 1,* ☎ *02/231–2234,* ℻ *02/231–6355. 13 rooms, 9 with bath, 7 suites. Breakfast room, bar, parking (fee). AE (in high season only).*

Lesser Quarter (Malá Strana)

$$$$ 🖭 **Dům U Červeného Lva.** On Mala Strana's main, historic thoroughfare, a five-minute walk from Prague Castle's front gates, the Baroque ★ House at the Red Lion is an intimate, immaculately kept hotel. The spare but comfortable guest rooms have parquet floors, 17th-century painted-beam ceilings, superb antiques, and all-white bathrooms with brass fixtures. The two top-floor rooms can double as a suite. Note: There is no elevator, and stairs are steep. ⊠ *Nerudova 41, 118 00 Prague 1,* ☎ *02/537–239 or 02/538–192,* ℻ *02/538–193. 11 rooms. 2 restaurants, bar. AE, MC, V.*

$$$ 🖭 **Kampa.** This early Baroque armory turned hotel is tucked away on ★ a leafy corner at the southern end of Malá Strana. The rooms are clean, if sparse; the bucolic setting and comparatively low rates make up for any discomforts. Note the late-Gothic vaulting in the massive dining room. ⊠ *Všehrdova 16, 118 00 Prague 1,* ☎ *02/5732–0508,* ℻ *02/5732–0262. 85 rooms. Restaurant. AE, MC, V.*

$$$ 🖭 **U Tří Pštrosů.** The location could not be better—a romantic corner just a stone's throw from the river and within arms' reach of the Charles Bridge. The airy rooms of the centuries-old building still have their original oak-beamed ceilings and antique furniture; many also have views over the river. Massive walls keep out the noise of the crowds on the bridge. An excellent in-house restaurant serves traditional Czech

dishes to guests and nonguests alike. (It does not accept credit cards.) Rates drop slightly in July and August—probably because there's no air-conditioning, though the building's thick walls help keep it cool. ⊠ *Dražického nám. 12, 118 00 Prague 1,* ☎ *02/5732–0565,* FAX *02/ 5732–0611. 14 rooms, 4 suites. Restaurant. AE, MC, V.*

Hradčany

$$$$ 🏨 **Savoy.** A restrained yellow Jugendstil facade conceals one of the city's
★ most luxurious small hotels, whose extra touches include in-room breakfast and complimentary afternoon tea in the small library. The erstwhile budget hotel was gutted and lavishly refurbished in the mid-1990s; rooms have spacious bathrooms, harmonious maroon and brown color schemes, and fax machines. Some are purely modern, while others have a faux-Rococo flourish. The only drawback: Although Prague Castle is just up the road, none of the rooms have a view of it. ⊠ *Keplerova 6, 118 00 Prague 6,* ☎ *02/2430–2430,* FAX *02/2430–2128. 55 rooms, 6 suites. Restaurant, café, exercise room, sauna, meeting rooms. AE, DC, MC, V.*

$$$ 🏨 **Pension U Raka.** This private guest house, since 1997 a member of
★ the Romantik Hotels & Restaurants organization, has a quiet location on the ancient, winding streets of Nový Svět, just behind the Loreto Church and a 10-minute walk from Prague Castle. One side of the 18th-century building presents a rare example of half-timbering; the rooms carry on the country feel with heavy furniture reminiscent of a Czech farmhouse. There are only six rooms, but if you can get a reservation (try at least a month in advance), you will nab a wonderful base for exploring Prague. ⊠ *Černínská 10/93, 118 00 Prague 1,* ☎ *02/2051–1100,* FAX *02/2051– 0511. 5 rooms, 1 suite. Breakfast room. AE, MC, V.*

Smíchov

$$$ 🏨 **Kinsky Garden.** You could walk the mile or so from this hotel to Prague Castle entirely on the tree-lined paths of Petřín, the hilly park that starts across the street. Opened in 1997, the hotel takes it name from a garden established by Count Rudolf Kinsky in 1825 on the southern side of Petřín. The public spaces and some rooms are not spacious, but everything is tasteful and comfortable; try to get a room on one of the upper floors for a view of the park. The management and restaurant are Italian. ⊠ *Holečkova 7, 150 00 Prague 5,* ☎ *02/5731–1173,* FAX *02/5731–1184. 60 rooms. Restaurant, bar, meeting room. AE, DC, MC, V.*

$$ 🏨 **Mepro.** Standard rooms and service and a reasonably central location make this small hotel worth considering. The Smíchov neighborhood offers a good range of restaurants (for one, the U Mikuláše Dačického wine tavern, across the street from the hotel) and nice strolls along the river or up the Petřín hill. ⊠ *Viktora Huga 3, 150 00 Prague 5,* ☎ *02/5721–5263,* FAX *02/527–343. 26 rooms. Snack bar. AE, MC, V.*

$$ 🏨 **Petr.** Set in a quiet part of Smíchov, just a few minutes' stroll from Malá Strana, this is an excellent value. As a "garni" hotel, it does not have a full-service restaurant, but it does serve breakfast (included in the price). The rooms are simply but adequately furnished. It's a 10-minute walk from metro Anděl, Line B. ⊠ *Drtinova 17, 150 00 Prague 5 ,* ☎ *02/5731–4068,* FAX *02/5731–4072. 37 rooms, 2 suites. AE, MC, V.*

$ 🏨 **Balkan.** One of the few central hotels that can compete in cost with private rooms, the spartan Balkan is on a busy street, not far from Malá Strana and the National Theater. Room prices do not include breakfast. ⊠ *Svornosti 28, 150 00 Prague 5,* ☎ FAX *02/540777, 02/540196, or 02/540670. 24 rooms. Restaurant. AE.*

Žižkov

$$ ⌸ **Hotel Bern.** The cream-colored Bern is a comfortable alternative to staying in the city center. Although geographically the hotel is rather far out, it is situated on a series of city bus routes that run frequently even on evenings and weekends; there are two direct bus routes to the Old Town and the ride takes about 10 minutes. Rooms are decorated in faux–Art Nouveau black and white. ⊠ *Koněvova 28, 130 00 Prague 3,* ☎ *02/697–5807,* 𝔽𝔸𝕏 *02/697–4420. 26 rooms with shower. Restaurant, bar. AE, DC, MC, V.*

$$ ⌸ **Hotel Olšanka.** The main calling card of this boxy modern hotel is its outstanding 50-meter swimming pool and modern sports center, which includes a pair of tennis courts and aerobics classes. Rooms are clean and, though basic, have the most important hotel amenities. There's also a relaxing sauna with certain nights reserved for men, women, or both. (Please note that the sports facilities may be closed for August.) The neighborhood is nondescript, but the Old Town is only 10 minutes away by direct tram. ⊠ *Táboritská 23, 130 87 Prague 3,* ☎ *02/ 6709–2202,* 𝔽𝔸𝕏 *02/273–386 or 02/278–434. 225 rooms. Restaurant, bar, pool, health club. AE, DC, MC, V.*

Western Suburbs

$$$$ ⌸ **Diplomat.** This sprawling complex opened in 1990 and remains pop-
★   ular with business travelers thanks to its location between the airport and downtown. The city center is easily reached by metro (the closest stop is Metro Dejvická on line A). The modern rooms may not exude much character, but they are tastefully furnished and quite comfort-able. Many of the hotel staff members speak English. You can drive a miniature racing car at the indoor track next door. ⊠ *Evropská 15, 160 00 Prague 6,* ☎ *02/2439–4111,* 𝔽𝔸𝕏 *02/2439–4215. 369 rooms, 13 suites. 2 restaurants, bar, café, no-smoking floor, exercise room, sauna, nightclub, meeting room. AE, DC, MC, V.*

$ ⌸ **Penzion Sprint.** Straightforward, no-surprises rooms, most of which have their own bathroom (however tiny), make the Sprint a fine choice. This pension is located on a quiet residential street, next to a large track and soccer field, in the outskirts of Prague about 20 minutes from the airport. Tram 18 rumbles directly to the Old Town, and the closest stop (Batérie) is just two blocks away. ⊠ *Cukrovárnická 62, 160 00 Prague 6,* ☎ *02/312–3338,* 𝔽𝔸𝕏 *02/312–1797. 12 rooms, 9 with bath. AE, MC, V.*

Nightlife and the Arts

The fraternal twins of the performing arts and nightlife are having an exhilarating growth spurt. Except for Czech-language theater—which is suffering from severe state budget cuts—the number of concerts, art exhibitions, and the like is on the rise. Some venues in the city center pitch themselves to tourists, but there are dozens of places where you can join the local crowds for music, dancing, or the rituals of beer and conversation. For details of cultural and nightlife events, look for the En-glish-language newspaper the *Prague Post* or the monthly *Prague Guide,* (also in English) available at hotels, tourist offices, and newsstands.

Nightlife

CABARET

For adult stage entertainment (with some nudity) try the **Varieté Praga** (⊠ Vodičkova ul. 30, ☎ 02/2421–5945).

DISCOS

Dance clubs come and go regularly. The longtime favorite is **Radost FX** (⊠ Bělehradská 120, ☎ 02/251210), with imported DJs playing the latest dance music and techno from London. **Lávka** (⊠ Novotného lávká 1, ☎ 02/2421–4797), near the Charles Bridge, has open-air dancing by the bridge on summer nights; there's also the **Corona Club and Latin Café** (⊠ Novotného lávká, ☎ 02/2108–2357), which highlights Latin, Gypsy, and other dance-friendly live music. Discos catering to a very young crowd blast sound onto lower Wenceslas Square.

JAZZ CLUBS

Jazz gained notoriety under the Communists as a subtle form of protest, and the city still has some great jazz clubs, featuring everything from swing to blues and modern. The following clubs have a cover charge. **Reduta** (⊠ Národní 20, ☎ 02/2491–2246) features a full program of local and international musicians. **AghaRTA** (⊠ Krakovská 5, ☎ 02/2221–1275) offers a variety of jazz acts in an intimate café-nightclub atmosphere. Music starts around 9 PM, but come earlier to get a seat. **Jazz Club Železná** (⊠ Železná 16, ☎ 02/2421–2541) mixes its jazz acts with world music. **Jazz Club U staré paní** (⊠ Michalská 9, ☎ 02/264–920) has a rotating list of tried-and-true Czech bands; **Jazz & Blues Café** (⊠ Na Příkopě 23, ☎ 02/2422–8788) is in the same vein.

PUBS, BARS, AND LOUNGES

Bars or lounges are not traditional Prague fixtures, but bars catering to a young, often foreign, crowd have elbowed their way in over the past few years. Still, most social life of the drinking variety takes place in pubs (*pivnice* or *hospody*), which are liberally sprinkled throughout the city's neighborhoods. Tourists are welcome to join in the evening ritual of sitting around large tables and talking, smoking, and drinking beer. Before venturing in, however, it's best to familiarize yourself with a few points of pub etiquette. Always ask if a chair is free before sitting down (*Je tu volno?*). To order a beer (*pivo*), do not wave the waiter down or shout across the room; he will usually assume you want beer—most pubs serve one brand—and bring it over to you without asking. He will also bring subsequent rounds to the table without asking. To refuse, just shake your head or say no thanks (*ne, děkuju*). At the end of the evening, usually around 10:30 or 11, the waiter will come to tally the bill. There are plenty of popular pubs in the city center, such as **U Medvídků** (⊠ Na Perštýně 7, ☎ 02/2422–0930), which was a brewery at least as long ago as the 15th century. Beer is no longer made on the premises; rather, draft Budvar is shipped from České Budějovice, the South Bohemian town known as Budweis to Germans, who call the beer Budweiser—but this is not the stuff made in St. Louis. **U Sv. Tomáše** (⊠ Letenská 12, ☎ 02/5732–0101) brewed beer for Augustinian monks starting in 1358. Now they serve commercially produced dark beer in a tourist-friendly mock-medieval hall in Malá Strana. **U Zlatého Tygra** (⊠ Husova ul. 17, ☎ 02/2422–9020) is famed as one of the three best Prague pubs for Pilsner Urquell, the original and perhaps the greatest of the pilsners. It was also a hangout for such raffish types as the writer Bohumil Hrabal, who died in 1997. All can get impossibly crowded.

One of the oddest phenomena of Prague's post-1989 renaissance is the sight of travelers and tour groups from the United States, Britain, Australia, and even Japan descending on this city to experience the life of—American expatriates. There are a handful of bars guaranteed to ooze Yanks and other native English speakers. The **James Joyce Pub** (⊠ Liliová 10, ☎ 02/2424–8793) is authentically Irish (it has Irish owners), with Guinness on tap and excellent food of the fish-and-chips persuasion. **Jo's Bar** (⊠ Malostranské nám. 7, ☎ no phone) is a haven for younger expats, serving bottled beer, mixed drinks, and good Mexican food. **U Malého Glena** (⊠ Karmelitská 23, ☎ 02/535–8115) puts on live jazz, folk, and rock; lots of expat groups perform here. The major hotels also run their own bars and nightclubs. The **Piano Bar** in the Palace hotel (☞ Lodging, *above*) is the most pleasant of the lot; jacket and tie are suggested.

ROCK CLUBS

Prague's rock scene is thriving. Hard-rock enthusiasts should check out the **Rock Café** (⊠ Národní 20, ☎ 02/2491–4416); you can also slouch into the **Lucerna Music Bar** (⊠ Vodičkova 3, ☎ 02/2421–7108). For dance tracks, hip locals congregate at **Roxy** (⊠ Dlouhá 33, ☎ 02/2481–0951). **Malostranská Beseda** (⊠ Malostranské nám. 21, ☎ 02/539–024) is a dependable bet for sometimes bizarre but always good musical acts from around the country. The cavernous **Palác Akropolis** (⊠ Kubelíkova 27, ☎ 02/9000–2310) has top Czech acts and major international world-music performers; as the name suggests, the space has an Acropolis theme.

The Arts

Prague's cultural flair is legendary, and performances are sometimes booked far in advance by all sorts of Praguers. The concierge at your hotel may be able to reserve tickets for you. Otherwise, for the cheapest tickets go directly to the theater box office a few days in advance or immediately before a performance. The biggest ticket agency, **Ticketpro,** has outlets all over town and accepts all major credit cards (main branch: ⊠ Salvátorská 10, ☎ 02/2481–4020). **Bohemia Ticket International** (⊠ Na Příkopě 16, ☎ 02/2421–5031; ⊠ Václavské nám. 25, ☎ 02/2422–7253) sells tickets for major cultural events, though at semi-inflated prices. Tickets can also be purchased at **American Express** (☞ Travel Agencies *in* Prague A to Z, *below*).

FILM

If a film was made in the United States or Britain, the chances are good that it will be shown with Czech subtitles rather than dubbed. (Film titles, however, are usually translated into Czech, so your only clue to the movie's country of origin may be the poster used in advertisements.) Movies in the original language are normally indicated with the note "*českými titulky*" (with Czech subtitles). Popular cinemas are **Blaník** (⊠ Václavské nám. 56, ☎ 02/2421–6698), **Lucerna** (⊠ Vodičkova 36, ☎ 02/2421–6972), **Praha** (⊠ Václavské nám. 17, ☎ 02/262–035), and **Světozor** (⊠ Vodičkova 39, ☎ 02/263616). Prague's English-language publications carry film reviews and full timetables.

MUSIC

Classical concerts are held all over the city throughout the year. One of the best orchestral venues is the resplendent Art Nouveau **Obecní dům** (⊠ Smetana Hall, Nám Republiky 5, ☎ 02/2200–2336), home of the Prague Symphony Orchestra. **Dvořák Hall** (⊠ In the Rudolfinum, nám. Jana Palacha, ☎ 02/2489–3111) is home to one of Central Europe's best orchestras, the Czech Philharmonic, which has been racked in recent years by bitter disputes among players, conductors, and management but still plays sublimely.

Performances also are held regularly at many of the city's palaces and churches, including the **Garden on the Ramparts** below Prague Castle (where the music comes with a view); the two **churches of St. Nicholas** (☞ Exploring Prague, *above*); the **Church of Sts. Simon and Jude** (⊠ Dušní ul., Old Town); the **Church of St. James** (⊠ Malá Štupartská, near Old Town Square); the **Zrcadlová kaple** (⊠ Mirror Chapel, Klementinum, Mariánské náměstí, Old Town); and the **Lobkowicz Palace** at Prague Castle. Classical ensembles are the most common finds, and the standard of performance ranges from adequate to superb, though the programs tend to take few risks. Serious fans of Baroque music may have the opportunity to hear works of little-known Bohemian composers at these concerts. Some of the best chamber ensembles are the **Talich Chamber Orchestra,** the **Guarneri Trio,** the **Wihan Quartet,** the **Czech Piano Trio,** and the **Agon** contemporary music group.

Concerts at the **Villa Bertramka** (☞ Karlův most [Charles Bridge] and Malá Strana [Lesser Quarter]*in* Exploring Prague, *above*) emphasize the music of Mozart and his contemporaries.

If you're organ-music buff, you'll most likely have your pick of recitals held in Prague's historic halls and churches. Popular programs are offered at **St. Vitus Cathedral** in Hradčany, U Křížovníků (⊠ Křižovnické nám., ☎ no phone) near the Charles Bridge, the **Church of St. Nicholas** in Malá Strana, and the **Church of St. James** (☞ *above*), where the organ plays amid a complement of Baroque statuary.

OPERA AND BALLET

The Czech Republic has a strong operatic tradition, and performances at the **Národní divadlo** (National Theater; ⊠ Národní třída 2, ☎ 02/2421–5001) and the **Statní Opera Praha** (State Opera House; ⊠ Wilsonova 4, ☎ 02/265–353), near the top of Wenceslas Square, can be excellent. It's always worthwhile to buy a cheap ticket (for as little as 30 Kč) just to take a look at these stunning 19th-century halls. Now, unlike during the Communist period, operas are almost always sung in their original tongue, and the repertoire offers plenty of Italian favorites and the Czech national composers Janaček, Dvořák, and Smetana. These two theaters also often stage ballets. The historic **Stavovské divadlo** (Estates' Theater; ⊠ Ovocný trh. 1, ☎ 02/2421–5001), where *Don Giovanni* premiered in the 18th century, plays host to a mix of operas and dramatic works. Simultaneous translation into English via a microwave transmitter and headsets is sometimes offered at drama performances. Appropriate attire is recommended for all venues; the National and Estates' theaters instituted a "no jeans" rule in 1998.

PUPPET SHOWS

This traditional form of Czech popular entertainment has been given new life thanks to the productions mounted at the **Národní divadlo marionet** (National Marionette Theater; ⊠ Žatecká 1, ☎ 02/232–2536) and **Divadlo v Celetné** (⊠ Celetná 17, ☎ 02/232–6843). Children and adults alike can enjoy the hilarity and pathos of these performances; one long-running show was a version of *Don Giovanni.*

THEATER

A dozen or so professional theater companies play in Prague to ever-packed houses; the language barrier can't obscure the players' artistry. Tourist-friendly, nonverbal theater abounds as well, notably "Black Light Theater," a melding of live acting, mime, video, and stage trickery, which continues to draw crowds despite signs of fatigue. The famous **Laterna Magika** (Magic Lantern) puts on a similar extravaganza (⊠ Národní třída 4, ☎ 02/2491–4129). Performances usually begin at 7 or 7:30 PM. The popular **Archa Theater** (⊠ Na Poříčí 26, ☎ 02/232–8800) offers avant-garde and experimental theater, music, and dance and has hosted world-class visiting ensembles such as the Royal Shakespeare Company. Several English-language theater groups operate sporadically; pick up a copy of the *Prague Post* for complete listings.

Outdoor Activities and Sports

Fitness Clubs

The best fitness clubs in the city are at the **Forum Hotel** (⊠ Kongresova ul. 1, ☎ 02/6119–1111; Vyšehrad metro station), which has a well-equipped weight room and a pool; the more centrally located **Hilton Hotel** (⊠ Pobřežní 1, ☎ 02/2484–1111; Florenc metro station) with its lap pool and weight machines; and the much less costly **Axa** hotel (⊠ Na Poříčí 40). All three are open to nonguests, but call first to inquire about rates.

Golf

You can golf year-round, weather permitting, at Prague's only course, located in the western suburbs at the **Hotel Golf** (⊠ Plzeňská ul. 215, ☎ 02/523251). Take a taxi to the hotel or Tram 4, 7, or 9 from metro station Anděl to the Hotel Golf stop.

Jogging

The best place for jogging is the **Letenské sady,** the large park east of the Royal Garden at Prague Castle, across Chotkova street. Cross the Svatopluka Çecha Bridge, climb the stairs, and turn to the right for a good, long run far away from the car fumes. For safety's sake, unaccompanied women should avoid the more obscure corners of this park. The **Riegrový sady,** a park in Vinohrady behind the main train station, is also nice, but it is small and a bit out of the way.

Spectator Sports

Prague plays host to a wide variety of spectator sports, including world-class ice hockey, soccer, and tennis. The best place to find out what's going on (and where) is the weekly sports page of the *Prague Post,* or you can inquire at your hotel.

SOCCER

National and international matches are played regularly at the Sparta Stadium in Letná, behind the Letenské Sady (☞ Jogging, *above*). To reach the stadium, take Tram 1, 25, or 26 to the Sparta stop. Prague's other first-division clubs are Slavia, whose Slavia Stadium is in the Vršovice neighborhood (Prague 10), and Victoria Žižkov, who play in a tiny park in the working-class Žižkov quarter.

Swimming

The best public swimming pool in Prague is at the **Podolí Swimming Stadium** in Podolí, easily reached in 15 minutes or less from the city center via Tram 3 or 17 to the Kublov stop. The indoor pool is 50 meters long, and the complex also includes two open-air pools, a sauna, a steam bath, and a wild-ride water slide. (A word of warning: Podolí, for all its attractions, is notorious as a local hot spot of petty thievery; don't entrust any valuables to the lockers—it's best either to check them in the safe with the *vrátnice* [superintendent], or better yet, don't bring them at all.) The pool at the **Hilton Hotel** (☞ Fitness Clubs, *above*) is smaller, but the location is more convenient. Another pool to try is in the **Hotel Olšanka** (⊠ Táboritská 23, ☎ 6709–2202).

Tennis

There are public courts at the **Strahov Stadium** in Břevnov. Take Bus 176 from Karlovo náměstí in the New Town, or Bus 143 from the Dejvická metro station (Line A) to the Stadion Strahov stop. The **Hilton Hotel** (☞ Fitness Clubs, *above*) has two public indoor courts.

Shopping

Despite the relative shortage of quality clothes—Prague has a long way to go before it can match shopping meccas Paris and Rome—the capital is a great place to pick up gifts and souvenirs. Bohemian crystal and porcelain deservedly enjoy a worldwide reputation for quality, and plenty of shops offer excellent bargains. The local market for antiques and artworks is still relatively undeveloped, while dozens of antiquarian bookstores can yield some excellent finds, particularly German and Czech books and graphics.

Shopping Districts

The major shopping areas are **Národní třída,** running past Můstek to Na Příkopě, and the area around **Old Town Square. Pařížská ulice, Karlova ulice** (on the way to the Charles Bridge), and the area just south of the **Jewish Quarter** are also good places to find boutiques and antiques shops. In the Malá Strana, try **Nerudova ulice,** the street that runs up to the Castle Hill district.

Department Stores

These are not always well stocked and often have everything except the one item you're looking for, but a stroll through one may yield some interesting finds and bargains. **Bilá Labuť** (⊠ Na poříčí 23, ☎ 02/2481–1364) has a decent selection, but the overall shabbiness harkens back to socialist times. **Kotva** (⊠ Nám. Republiky 8, ☎ 02/2480–1111) is comparatively upscale; it's got a nice stationary shop and a basement supermarket with good wine and cheese sections. **Krone**'s (⊠ Václavské nám. 21, ☎ 02/2423–0477) main virtues are its basement supermarket and its location near the Mustek metro. Otherwise it is cramped and poorly stocked, with a bewildering layout to boot. The centrally located **Tesco** (⊠ Národní třída 26, ☎ 02/2200–3111) is generally the best place for one-stop shopping—especially if you're caving in to homesickness. It's got same-day film developing, a news agent stocking English-language newspapers and magazines, American-brand toiletries, a supermarket with Western groceries (if you're dying for corn chips, you'll find them here), and a multilingual staff.

Street Markets

For fruits and vegetables, the best street market in central Prague is on **Havelská ulice** in the Old Town. You'll need to arrive early in the day if you want something a bit more exotic than tomatoes and cucumbers. The best market for nonfood items is the flea market in **Holešovice,** north of the city center, although there isn't really much of interest here outside of cheap tobacco and electronics products. Take the metro Line C to the Vltavská station and then ride any tram heading east (running to the left as you exit the metro station). Exit at the first stop and follow the crowds.

Specialty Stores

ANTIQUES

For antiques connoisseurs, Prague can be a bit of a letdown. Even in comparison with other former Communist capitals like Budapest, the choice of antiques in Prague might seem depressingly slim, as the city lacks large stores with a diverse selection of goods. The typical Prague *Starožitnosti* (antiques shop) tends to be a small, one-room jumble shop selling old glass and bric-a-brac. The good ones distinguish themselves by focusing on one particular specialty. On the pricey end of the scale is the Prague affiliate of the Austrian **Dorotheum** auction house (⊠ Havelsk 19, ☎ 02/2489–2921) in the Old Town. It is an elegant pawnshop that specializes in small things: jewelry, porcelain knickknacks, and standing clocks as well as the odd military sword. The small **JHB Starožitnosti** (⊠ Panská 1, ☎ 02/261–425) in the New Town is the place for old clocks: everything from rococo to Empire standing clocks and Bavarian cuckoo clocks. The shop also has a wide array of antique pocket watches. **Nostalgie Antique** (⊠ Jánský Vršek 8, ☎ 02/532–628) specializes in old textiles and jewelry. Most of the textiles are pre–WWII and include clothing, table linens, curtains, hats, and laces. **Papillio** (⊠ Ungelt 1, ☎ 02/2489–5454), in the courtyard behind Tyn church, is probably one of the best antiques shops in Prague, offering furniture, paintings, and especially museum-quality antique glass. Here you can find colorful Biedermeier goblets by Moser and wonderful Art Nouveau Loetz vases. **Zlatnictví** (✉ Vomáčka Ná prstkova 9, ☎ 02/295–2525) is a jumble shop that redeems itself with its selection of old jewelry in a broad price range, including rare Art Nouveau rings and antique garnet brooches.

ART GALLERIES

The best galleries in Prague are quirky and eclectic affairs, places to sift through artworks rather than browse at arms' length. Many galleries are also slightly off the beaten track and away from the main tourist thoroughfares. Prague's as-yet-untouristed Novy Svět neighborhood is something of a miniature artist's quarter and home to two of Prague's more interesting galleries. One is **Galerie Gambra** (✉ Černinska 5, ☎ 02/2051–4527), owned by the surrealist animator Jan Švankmayer, which displays Švankmayer's bizarre collages as well as his wife's anthropomorphic ceramics. Books and magazines focusing on Czech surrealist art are also for sale. There's also **Galerie Novy Svět** (✉ Novy Svě 5, ☎ 02/2051–4611), a small gallery displaying interesting paintings and drawings by somewhat obscure Czech artists, as well as ceramics, glass, and art books. At the higher end is **Galerie Lichtenfels** (✉ Michalská 12, ☎ 02/2422–7680) in the Old Town, which specializes in modern Czech art. Paintings, prints, and drawings crowd the walls and are propped against glass cases and window sills. Rifle through works by Czech Cubists, currently fetching high prices at international auctions.

BOOKS AND PRINTS

By the same token as antiques shops, Prague's rare book shops, or *antikvariáts,* were once part of a massive state-owned consortium that since privatization has split up and diversified. Now, while appealing to varied interests, most shops tend to cultivate their own specialties. Some places do have a small English-language section displaying a motley blend of potboilers, academic texts, classics, and tattered paperbacks; books in German, on the other hand, can be found in abundance.

Antikvariát Makovský and Gregor (✉ Kaprova 9, ☎ 02/232–8835) is a great all-around bookstore as attested by the constant traffic of philosophy students from the nearby Charles University. The art section is particularly good hunting ground, where you could turn up the Memoirs of Casanova with illustrations by Aubrey Beardsley or a book on Leni Reifenstahl's mountaineering movies. If you'd just like a good read, be sure to check out the **Globe Bookstore and Coffeehouse** (✉ Janovského 14, ☎ 02/6671–2610), which is a magnet for the local English-speaking community.

U Karlova Mostu (✉ Karlova ul. 2, Staré Město, ☎ 02/2422–9205) is the preeminent Prague bookstore. In a suitably bookish location opposite the National Library, it's the place to go if you are looking for that elusive 15th-century manuscript. In addition to housing ancient books too precious to be leafed through, the store has a good selection of books on local subjects, a small foreign-language section, and a host of prints, maps, drawings, and paintings. **U Knihomola Bookstore and Café** (✉ Mánesova 79, ☎ 02/627–7770) is a close contender to the Globe for the best place to find the latest in English literature; it also stocks the best selection of new English-language art books and guidebooks. It's near the metro stop Jiřího z Poděbrad.

FUN THINGS FOR CHILDREN

Nearly every stationery store has beautiful watercolor and colored-chalk sets available at rock-bottom prices. The Czechs are also master illustrators, and the books they've made for young "pre-readers" are some of the world's loveliest. For delightful wooden toys, look in at **Obchod Vším Možným** (⊠ Nerudova 45, ☎ 02/536941). **Object** (⊠ U lužického semináře 19, ☎ 02/900–5544) also stocks wooden toys as well as handsome art and school supplies. For older children and teens, it's worth considering a Czech or Eastern European watch, telescope, or set of binoculars. The quality/price ratio is unbeatable.

GLASS

Glass has traditionally been Bohemia's biggest export, and it was one of the few products manufactured during Communist times that managed to retain an artistically innovative spirit. Today Prague has plenty of shops selling Bohemian glass, much of it tourist kitsch. A good spot is the stylish **Galerie A** (⊠ Na Perštýné, ☎ 02/261–334), which stocks Art Nouveau, Biedermeier, and medieval replica glass in Art Deco vitrines from the 1920s. For purely artistic glass check out **Galerie Mozart** (⊠ Platyz 1, ☎ 02/2421–1127), off Národní Třidda, which offers glass sculptures as well as some colorful vases and bowls. Much more contemporary and decidedly less practical is **Galerie 'Z'** (⊠ U luzickeho semináře 7, ☎ 02/2161–1555), which sells limited-edition mold-melted and blown glass. **Moser** (⊠ Na Příkopě 12, ☎ 02/2421–1293), the flagship store for the world-famous Karlovy Vary glassmaker, offers the widest selection of traditional glass.

HOME DESIGN

Czech design is wonderfully rich both in quality and imagination, emphasizing old-fashioned craftsmanship while often taking an offbeat, even humorous approach. Strained relations between Czech designers and producers has reined in the potential selection, but there are nevertheless a handful of places showcasing Czech work. **Fast** (⊠ Sázavská 32, Vinohrady, ☎ 02/242–50538) is a little bit off the beaten track but worth the trek. Besides ultramodern furniture, there are ingenious (and more portable) pens, binders, and other office accoutrements. **Genia Loci** (⊠ Ujezd 11, ☎ 02/539–468) is one of Prague's hippest design shops; you can find irreverent things like a Kafka themed coffee service. **Tekton Gallery** (⊠ Truhlářska 20, ☎ 02/231–7743) is a father-and-son operation focusing exclusively on Czech-made furniture. Look for Jaroslav Dubsky's intaglio jewelry cases with inset gemstones.

JEWELRY

Alfons Mucha is perhaps most famous for his whiplash Art Nouveau posters, but he also designed furniture, lamps, clothing, and jewelry. **Art Décoratif** (⊠ U Obecního domu, ☎ 02/2200–2350), right next door to the Art Nouveau Obecní Dum, sells Mucha-inspired designs—the jewelry is especially remarkable. The Old Town's **Granát** (⊠ Dlouhá 30, ☎ 02/231–5612) has a comprehensive selection of garnet jewelry, plus contemporary and traditional pieces set in gold and silver. **Hlada** (⊠ Karlova 25, ☎ 02/24238928) offers sleek, Czech-designed silver jewelry; an affiliate shop at Na Příkopé 16 specializes in gold, diamonds, and pearls.

MARIONETTES

Marionettes have a long tradition in Bohemia, going back to the times when traveling troupes used to entertain children with morality plays on town squares. Now, while this art form survives, it's become yet another tourist lure; you'll continually stumble across stalls selling hand-carved marionettes. However, the marionettes at **Manhartský Dùm** (⊠ Celetná 7, ☎ 02/2480–9156) are the real thing. These puppets—knights, princesses, and cloven-hoofed devils—are made by the same artists who work for the Theater Institute. Prices may be higher than for the usual stuff on the street, but the craftsmanship is well worth it.

SPORTS EQUIPMENT

Sport Centrum (✉ Revoluční 1, ☎ 02/2180–3311) is a sprawling shop selling everything from ski-equipment to climbing gear.

Prague A to Z

Arriving and Departing

BY BUS

The Czech complex of regional bus lines known collectively as **ČSAD** operates its dense network from the sprawling main bus station on Křižíkova (metro stop: Florenc, Lines B or C). For information about routes and schedules call 02/1034, consult the confusingly displayed timetables posted at the station, or visit the information window, situated at the bus unloading area, open weekdays 6–7:45, Saturday 6–4, and Sunday 8–6.

BY CAR

Prague is well served by major roads and highways from anywhere in the country. On arriving in the city, simply follow the signs to CENTRUM (city center). During the day, traffic can be stop-and-go. Pay particular attention to the trams, which have the right-of-way in every situation. Note that parts of the historic center of Prague, including Wenceslas Square and Old Town Square, are closed to private vehicles.

Parking is permitted in the center of town on a growing number of streets with parking meters or in the few small lots within walking distance of the historic center. An underground lot is at Náměstí Jana Palacha, near Old Town Square.

BY PLANE

Ruzyně Airport, 20 km (12 mi) northwest of the downtown area, is small but easily negotiated. Allow yourself plenty of time when departing Prague because the airport is still too small to handle the large numbers of travelers who move through it, and you may encounter long lines at customs and check-in.

ČSA (the Czech national carrier) offers direct flights all over the world from Ruzyně. Major airlines with offices in Prague are **Air France** (☎ 02/2422–7164); **Alitalia** (☎ 02/2481–0079 or 02/232–5966); **Austrian Airlines** (☎ 02/231–1872); **British Airways** (☎ 02/2211–4444); **British Midland** (☎ 02/2423–9280); **ČSA** (☎ 02/2010–4310); **Delta** (☎ 02/2423–3638); **KLM** (☎ 02/2422–8678); **Lufthansa** (☎ 02/2481–1007); **SAS** (☎ 02/2421–4749); and **Swissair** (☎ 02/2481–2111).

Between the Airport and Downtown: The **Cedaz** minibus shuttle links the airport with Republic Square (just off the Old Town). It runs hourly, more often at peak periods, between 6 AM and 9:30 PM daily and makes an intermediate stop at the Dejvická metro station. The one-way fare is 90 Kč. Regular municipal bus service (Bus 119) also connects the airport and the Dejvická metro stop; the fare is 12 Kč. From Dejvická you can take a subway to the city center. To reach Wenceslas Square, get off at the Můstek station.

Taxis offer the easiest and most convenient way of getting downtown. The trip is a straight shot down Evropská Boulevard and takes approximately 20 minutes. The road is not usually busy, but anticipate an additional 20 minutes during rush hour (7 AM–9 AM and 3 PM–6 PM). The ride costs about 500 Kč.

BY TRAIN

International trains arrive at and depart from either the main station, **Hlavní nádraží** (✉ Wilsonova ulice, about 500 yards east of Wenceslas Square); or the suburban **Nádraží Holešovice** (✉ About 2 km/1 mi north of the city center).This is an unending source of confusion—always make certain you know which station your train is using. Prague's other train station, **Masarykovo nádraží** (✉ Hybernská 13, ☎ 02/2461–5156), is used for local trains. While these local trains can get you to small outlying towns like Nelahozeves, they're not very practical for longer trips. For train times, consult timetables in stations or get in line at the **information offices** (☎ 02/2422–4200, 02/2461–4030, or 02/2461–4031) upstairs at the main station or downstairs near the exits under the ČD Centrum sign. Both offices are open daily 6 AM–10 PM. The **Čedok** office at Na Příkopě 18 (☞ Visitor Information, *below*) also provides train information and issues tickets.

Wenceslas Square is a convenient five-minute walk from the main station, or you can take the subway (Line C) one stop in the Haje direction to Muzeum. A taxi ride from the main station to the center will cost about 100 Kč. To reach the city center from Nádraží Holešovice, take the subway (Line C) four stops to Muzeum. A taxi ride should cost roughly 200 Kč–250 Kč.

Getting Around

To see Prague properly, there is no alternative to walking, especially since much of the city center is off-limits to cars. And the walking couldn't be more pleasant—most of it along the beautiful bridges and cobblestone streets of the city's historic core. Before venturing out, however, be sure you have a good map. The city is divided into 10 administrative districts; Prague 1 and part of Prague 2 lie entirely within the historic center.

BY BUS AND TRAM

Prague's extensive bus and streetcar network allows for fast, efficient travel throughout the city. Tickets are the same as those used for the metro, although you validate them at machines inside the bus or streetcar. Tickets (*jízdenky*) can be bought at hotels, newsstands, and from dispensing machines in the metro stations. The price of a ticket increased in 1998 from 10 Kč to 12 Kč; the tickets permit one hour's travel throughout the metro, tram, and bus network between 5 AM and 8 PM on weekdays, or 90 minutes' travel between 8 PM and midnight and on weekends. You can also buy a one-day pass allowing unlimited use of the system for 70 Kč, a three-day pass for 180 Kč, a seven-day pass for 250 Kč, and a 15-day pass for 280 Kč. The passes can be purchased at the main metro stations and at some newsstands in the center. A pass is not valid until stamped in the orange machines in metro stations or aboard trams *and* the required information is entered on the back (instructions are provided in English). A refurbished old tram, No. 91, plies a route in the Old Town and Lesser Quarter on summer weekends. Trams 50–59 and Buses 500 and above run all night, after the metro shuts down at midnight. All night-tram routes intersect at the corner of Lazarská and Spálená streets in the New Town near the Národní Třída metro station.

BY SUBWAY

Prague's subway system, the metro, is clean and reliable; the stations are marked with red "M" signs. Trains run daily from 5 AM to midnight. Validate the tickets at the orange machines before descending the escalators; tickets are valid on trams and buses as well (☞ *above*). Trains are patrolled often; the fine for riding without a valid ticket is 200 Kč. Beware of pickpockets, who often operate in large groups on crowded trams and metro cars.

BY TAXI

Dishonest taxi drivers are the shame of the nation. Luckily you probably won't need to rely on taxis for trips within the city center (it's usu-

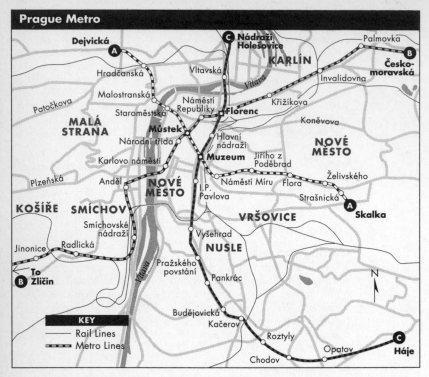

Prague Metro

ally easier to walk or take the subway). Typical scams include drivers doctoring the meter or simply failing to turn the meter on and then demanding an exorbitant sum at the end of the ride. In an honest cab, the meter starts at 25 Kč and increases by 17 Kč per km (½ mi) or 2 Kč per minute at rest. (Taxis operating from, but not to, the airport have a monopoly and charge slightly higher rates.) Most rides within town should cost no more than 80 Kč–100 Kč. To minimize the chances of getting ripped off, avoid taxi stands in Wenceslas Square, Old Town Square, and other heavily touristed areas. The best alternative is to phone for a taxi in advance. Some reputable firms are **AAA Taxi** (☎ 02/1080) and **Profitaxi** (☎ 02/1035). Many firms have English-speaking operators.

Contacts and Resources

CAR RENTALS
The following rental agencies are based in Prague:

Alamo Rent a Car (⊠ Revoluční 25, ☎ 231–0122 or 231–6947). **Avis** (⊠ Klimentská 46, ☎ 02/2185–1225). **Budget** (⊠ Hotel Inter-Continental, nám. Curieových 5, ☎ 02/2418–0777 or 02/2061–0095). **Rent-A-Car** (⊠ Washingtonova 9, ☎ 02/2421–1587 or 02/2422–9848). **Hertz** (⊠ Karlovo nám. 28, ☎ 02/291851 or 02/290122).

EMBASSIES
United States (⊠ Tržiště 15, Malá Strana, ☎ 02/5732–0663). **United Kingdom** (⊠ Thunovská 14, Malá Strana, ☎ 02/5732–0355). **Canada** (⊠ Mickiewiczova 6, Hradčany, ☎ 02/2431–1108). There are no Australian or New Zealand embassies.

EMERGENCIES
Police (☎ 158). **Ambulance** (☎ 155). **Medical emergencies: Foreigners' Department of Na Homolce Hospital** (⊠ Roentgenova 2, ☎ 02/

5292–2146 weekdays, ☎ 02/5721–1111 or 02/5292–2191 evenings and weekends); **First Medical Clinic of Prague** (✉ Vyšehradská 35, ☎ 02/292–286, 2421–6200, or ☎ 02/0601–225050 24-hr emergency mobile phone); **American Medical Center** (✉ Janovského 48, ☎ 02/807–756 weekdays). Be prepared to pay in cash for medical treatment, whether you are insured or not. **Dentists** (✉ Palackého 5, ☎ 02/2421–6032 for 24-hr emergency service).

Lost credit cards: American Express (☎ 02/2421–9978 or 02/2421–9992); **Diners Club, Visa** (☎ 02/2412–5353); **MasterCard** (☎ 02/2442–3135).

ENGLISH-LANGUAGE BOOKSTORES

In the central city these are too numerous to list. *See* Shopping, *above*, for a few recommended bookstores a bit off the tourist routes. Street vendors on Wenceslas Square and Na Příkopě carry leading foreign newspapers and periodicals. For hiking maps and auto atlases, try the downstairs level of the **Jan Kanzelsberger** bookstore on Wenceslas Square (✉ Václavské nám. 42, ☎ 02/2421–7335).

GUIDED TOURS

Čedok's (☞ Visitor Information, *below*; ☎ 02/231–8255 for tour information) three-hour "Historical Prague" tour, offered year-round, is a combination bus-walking venture that covers all the major sights with commentary in English. It departs daily at 10 AM and 2 PM from the Čedok office at Pařížská 6 (near the Inter-Continental Hotel), and the price is 590 kč. Between May and October, "Panoramic Prague," an abbreviated version of the above tour, departs Wednesday, Friday, and Saturday at 11 AM from the Čedok office at Na Příkopě 18. The price is 300 Kč. On Friday Čedok also offers "Prague on Foot," a slower-paced, three-hour walking tour that departs at 10 AM from Na Příkopě 18. The price is 300 Kč. More tours are offered, especially in summer, and the above schedule may well vary according to demand. Prices may also go up in high season.

Many private firms now offer combination **bus-walking tours** of the city that typically last two or three hours and cost 300 Kč–400 Kč or more. For more information, check with any of the dozen operators with booths on Wenceslas Square, Old Town Square (near the Jan Hus monument), or Republic Square (near the Obecní Dům).

Personal Guides: You can contact the Čedok office at Na Příkopě 18 (☞ Visitor Information, *below*) to arrange a personalized walking tour. Times and itineraries are negotiable; prices start at around 500 Kč per hour.

LATE-NIGHT PHARMACIES

There are two 24-hour pharmacies close to the city's center, both called **Lékárna** (✉ Štefánikova 6, ☎ 02/537039 or 02/5732–0918; ✉ Belgická 37, ☎ 02/2423–7207 or 02/258189).

TRAVEL AGENCIES

American Express (✉ Václavské nám. 56, ☎ 02/2421–9992, FAX 02/2211–1131); **Thomas Cook** (✉ Národní třída 28, ☎ 02/2110–5276).

For bus tickets to just about anywhere in Europe, try **Bohemia Tour** (✉ Zlatnická 7, ☎ 02/232–877) or Čedok's main office (☞ Visitor Information, *below*).

VISITOR INFORMATION

There are three central offices for the municipal **Prague Information Service** (PIS; ✉ Staroměstské nám. 22, ☎ 02/2448–2018; ✉ Na Příkopě 20, ☎ 02/264–020; ✉ Hlavní nádraží, lower hall, ☎ 02/2423–

9258). The Staroměstské náměstí (Old Town Square) branch is open weekdays 9–6 and weekends 9–5, while the Na Příkopě office, just a few doors down from Čedok's main office, is open weekdays 9–6 and Saturday 9–3. From April to October, the Hlavní nádraží branch is open on weekdays 9–7, weekends 9–4; from November to March, it's open weekdays 9–6 and Saturday 9–3. PIS locates lodging, offers city maps and general tourist information, sells tickets to cultural events, and arranges group and individual tours.

Čedok, the ubiquitous travel agency, also provides general tourist information and city maps. Čedok will also exchange money, book accommodations, arrange guided tours, and book passage on airlines, buses, and trains. You can pay for Čedok services, including booking rail tickets, with any major credit card. Note limited weekend hours. ⊠ *Main office: Na Příkopě 18,* ☎ *02/2419–7111,* ℻ *02/2422–5339.* ◷ *Weekdays 8:30–6, Sat. 9–1. Other downtown offices:* ⊠ *Rytířská 16,* ☎ *02/262–714,* ◷ *weekdays 9–6;* ⊠ *Pařížská 6,* ☎ *02/231–4302,* ◷ *weekdays 9–6, Sat. 9–noon.*

The **Czech Tourist Authority** (⊠ Národní třída 37, ☎℻ 02/2421–1458) can provide information on tourism outside Prague but does not sell tickets or book accommodations.

To find out what's on for the month and to get the latest tips for shopping, dining, and entertainment, consult Prague's weekly English-language newspaper, the **Prague Post.** It prints comprehensive entertainment listings and can be bought at most downtown newsstands as well as in major North American and European cities. The monthly **Prague Guide,** available at newsstands and tourist offices for about 25 Kč, provides a good overview of major cultural events and has listings of restaurants, hotels, and organizations offering traveler assistance.

SOUTHERN BOHEMIA

With Prague at its heart and Germany and the former Austro-Hungarian Empire on its mountainous borders, the kingdom of Bohemia was for centuries buffeted by religious and national conflicts, invasions, and wars. But its position also meant that Bohemia benefited from the cultural wealth and diversity of Central Europe. The result is a glorious array of history-laden castles, walled cities, and spa towns set in a gentle, rolling landscape.

Southern Bohemia (separate sections on the northern and western areas follow) is particularly famous for its involvement in the Hussite religious wars of the 15th century, which revolved around the town of Tábor. But the area also has more than its fair share of well-preserved and stunning walled towns, built up by generations of noble families, who left behind layers of Gothic, Renaissance, and Baroque architecture (particularly notable in Çeský Krumlov). Farther north and an easy drive east of Prague is the old silver-mining town of Kutná Hora, once a rival to Prague for the royal residence.

The major towns of southern Bohemia offer some of the best accommodations in the Czech Republic. (This is also true of western Bohemia; ☞ *below*) but here, as in many other parts of Bohemia, the only real options for dining are the restaurants and cafés at the larger hotels and resorts.

Numbers in the margin correspond to numbers on the Bohemia map.

Bohemia

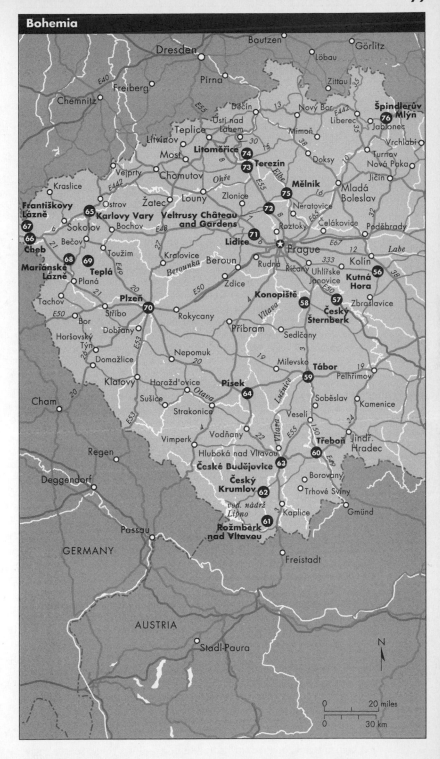

GERMANY

AUSTRIA

N

0   20 miles

0   30 km

Kutná Hora

🗺 *70 km (44 mi) east of Prague.*

The approach to Kutná Hora looks much as it has for centuries. The long economic decline of this town, once Prague's chief rival in Bohemia for wealth and beauty, spared it the postwar construction that has blighted the outskirts of so many other Czech cities. Though it is undeniably beautiful, with an intact Gothic and Baroque townscape, Kutná Hora feels a bit melancholy. The town owes its illustrious past to silver, discovered here during the 12th century. For some 400 years the mines were worked with consummate efficiency, the wealth going to support grand projects throughout Bohemia. As the silver began to run out during the 16th and 17th centuries, however, Kutná Hora's importance faded. What remains is the paradox you see today: poor inhabitants dwarfed by the splendors of the Middle Ages.

★ Forget the town center for a moment and walk to the **Chrám svaté Barbory** (St. Barbara's Cathedral), a 10-minute stroll from the main Palackého náměstí along Barborská ulice. The approach to the cathedral, overlooking the river, is magnificent. Statues line the road, and the Baroque houses vie with each other for attention. In the distance, the netted vaulting of the cathedral resembles a large, magnificent tent more than a religious center. St. Barbara's is undoubtedly Kutná Hora's masterpiece and a high point of the Gothic style in Bohemia. Built in the 14th and 15th centuries, it drew on the talents of the Peter Parler workshop as well as on other Gothic luminaries, such as Matthias Rejsek and Benedikt Ried.

St. Barbara is the patron saint of miners, and silver-mining themes dominate the interior. Gothic frescoes depict angels carrying shields with mining symbols. The town's other major occupation, minting, can be seen in frescoes in the **Minciř kaple** (Mintner's Chapel). A statue of a miner, donning the characteristic smock and dating from 1700, stands proudly in the nave. But the main attraction of the interior is the vaulting itself—attributed to Ried—which carries the eye effortlessly upward. ⊠ *Barborská ul.* 🎟 *20 Kč.* ⊙ *Tues.–Sun. 9–noon and 2–4.*

The romantic view over the town from the cathedral area, marked by the visibly tilting 260-ft tower of St. James Church, is impressive, and few modern buildings intrude. As you descend into town along Barborská ulice, you'll pass the **Hrádek** (Little Castle), which was once part of the town's fortifications and now houses a museum of mining and coin production and a claustrophobic medieval mine tunnel. ⊠ *Barborská ul.* 🎟 *20 Kč.* ⊙ *Apr.–Oct., Tues.–Sun. 9–noon and 1–5.*

NEED A   The **Café U Hrádku** is a pleasant place to stop for refreshments or a light
BREAK?   home-cooked meal. Lamps and furnishings from the 1920s add a period
           touch. ⊠ *Barborská ul. 33,* 🕾 *0327/512741.* ⊙ *Tues.–Sun. 10–5. No
           credit cards.*

You'll easily find the **Vlašský dvůr** (Italian Court), the old mint, by following the signs through town. Coins were first minted here in 1300, struck by Italian artisans brought in from Florence—hence the mint's odd name. It was here that the Prague groschen, one of the most widely circulated coins of the Middle Ages, was minted until 1726 and here, too, that the Bohemian kings stayed on their frequent visits. A **coin museum,** open in spring and summer, allows you to see the small, silvery groschen being struck and gives you a chance to buy replicas. ⊠ *Havlíčkovo nám.* 🎟 *30 Kč.* ⊙ *Apr.–Oct., daily 10–6; Nov.–Mar., daily 10–4.*

If the door to the **Chrám svatého Jakuba** (St. James Church) next door is open, peek inside. Originally a Gothic church dating from the early 1400s, the structure was almost entirely transformed into Baroque during the 17th and 18th centuries. The characteristic onion dome on the tower was added in 1737. The paintings on the wall include works of the best Baroque Czech masters; the *Pietà* is by the 17th-century painter Karel Škréta. ⊠ *Havlíčkovo nám.*

Before leaving the city, stop in the nearby suburb of Sedlec for a bone-chilling sight: a chapel decorated with the bones of some 40,000 people. The Kaple Všech Svatých Hřbitov (All Saints' Cemetery Chapel), or **Horní kaple kostnice** (Bone Church) at the site of the former Sedlec Monastery, came into being in the 14th century, when development forced the clearing of a nearby graveyard. Monks of the Cistercian order came up with the bright idea of using the bones for decoration; the most recent creations date from the end of the last century. ▨ *20 Kč.* ⊙ *Daily 9–noon and 2–4.*

Lodging

$$$ ⊞ **Medínek.** This is one of the few hotels in town with modern conveniences, so book in advance or risk being squeezed out by German and Austrian tour groups. The location, on the main square, puts you at an easy stroll from the sights, and the ground-floor restaurant offers decent Czech cooking in an atmosphere more pleasant than that found in the local beer halls. Unfortunately, the 1960s architecture blights the surrounding square. ⊠ *Palackého nám. 316, 284 01 Kutná Hora,* ☎ *0327/2741,* ☒ *0327/512743. 90 rooms, 43 with bath. Restaurant, café. AE, MC, V.*

$$ ⊞ **U Hrnčíře.** This is a picturesque little inn situated next to a potter's shop near the town center. The postcard setting doesn't make up for the very plain rooms, but the friendly staff gives the hotel a decidedly homey feel. The restaurant in the back garden has a beautiful view overlooking the valley. ⊠ *Barborská 24, 284 01 Kutná Hora,* ☎ *0327/ 512113. 5 rooms. Restaurant. AE, MC, V.*

Český Šternberk

⑤⑦ *40 km (24 mi) from Kutná Hora, 24 km (15 mi) from Benešov.*

At night this 13th-century castle looks positively forbidding, occupying a forested knoll over the Sázava River. By daylight, the structure, last renovated in the 17th century, is less haunting but still impressive. In season, you can tour some of the rooms fitted out with period furniture (mostly rococo); little of the early Gothic has survived the many renovations. ⊠ *Český Šternberk,* ☎ *0303/55101.* ▨ *95 Kč.* ⊙ *May–June and Sept., Tues.–Sun. 9–5; July–Aug., Tues.–Sun. 9–6; Apr. and Oct., weekends 9–4.*

Konopiště

⑤⑧ *25 km (15 mi) west of Český Šternberk, 45 km (27 mi) southeast of Prague.*

Given its remote location, Český Šternberk is ill equipped for a meal or an overnight stay. Instead, continue on to the superior facilities of Konopiště (via the industrial town of Benešov). Konopiště is best known for its 14th-century castle, which served six centuries later as the residence of the former heir to the Austrian crown, Franz Ferdinand d'Este. Scorned by the Austrian nobility for having married a commoner, Franz Ferdinand wanted an impressive summer residence to win back the envy of his peers, and he spared no expense in restoring the castle to its original Gothic form, filling its 82 rooms with outlandish paintings, statues, and curiosities. Franz Ferdinand's dream came to a fateful end in 1914 when he was assassinated at Sarajevo, an event that precipitated World War I. The Austrian defeat in the war ultimately led to the fall of the Hapsburgs. Ironically, the destiny of the Austrian Empire had been sealed at the castle a month before the assassination, when Austrian emperor Franz Joseph I met with Germany's Kaiser Wilhelm II and agreed to join forces with him in the event of war.

★ To visit **Zámek Konopiště** (Konopiště Castle), start from the Konopiště Motel, about 1 km (½ mi) off Route 3, and walk straight for about 2 km (1 mi) along the trail through the woods. Before long, the rounded, neo-Gothic towers appear through the trees, and you reach the formal garden with its almost mystical circle of classical statues. Built by the wealthy Beneschau family, the castle dates from around 1300 and for centuries served as a bastion of the nobility in their struggle for power with the king. At the end of the 14th century, Catholic nobles actually captured the weak King Wenceslas (Václav) IV in Prague and held him prisoner in the smaller of the two rounded towers. To this day the tower is known affectionately as the Václavka. Several of the rooms, reflecting the Archduke Franz Ferdinand's extravagant taste and lifestyle, are open to the public during the high season. A valuable collection of weapons from the 16th to 18th century can be seen in the Weapons Hall on the third floor. Less easy to miss are the hundreds of stuffed animals, rather macabre monuments to the archduke's obsession with hunting. The interior is only open to tours; while the guides don't speak English, there are English texts available. ⊠ *Zá mek Konopiště, Benešov (about 3 km/2 mi west of train and bus stations on red- or yellow-marked paths).* 🖼 *Each tour 90 Kč–200 Kč.* ☉ *Apr. and Oct., Tues.–Sun. 9–3; May–Aug., Tues.–Sun. 9–5; Sept., Tues.–Sun. 9–4.*

Dining and Lodging

$$$$ ✕ **Stodola.** This little cabin, next to the Konopiště Motel (☞ *below*), has a reputation as one of the best exemplars of Bohemian-style grilled meats, chicken, and fish dishes. Try the Moravian roast beef with smoked bratwurst, bacon, and onions, or roast pheasant with mushroom sauce. The live folk music in the evenings is romantic rather than obtrusive; the wines and service are excellent. ⊠ *Benešov,* ☎ *0301/22732. AE, MC, V. No lunch.*

$$$ 🏨 **Konopiště Motel.** Long a favorite with Prague-based diplomats, who come for the fresh air and outdoor sports, the motel is about 2 km (1 mi) from Konopiště Castle, on a small road about 1 km (½ mi) from the main Prague–Tábor highway (Route 3). Rooms are small but well appointed (ask for one away from the main road). ⊠ *256 01 Benešov,* ☎ *0301/22732,* 🖷 *0301/22053. 40 rooms. 2 restaurants, minigolf, free parking. AE, DC, MC, V.*

Tábor

🟢 *40 km (25 mi) south of Konopiště down Route 3.*

It's hard to believe this dusty Czech town was built to receive Christ on his return to Earth in the Second Coming. But that's what the Hussites intended when they flocked here by the thousands in 1420 to construct a society modeled on the communities of the early Christians. Tábor's fascinating history is unique among Czech towns—it started out as a combination utopia and fortress.

Following the execution of Jan Hus, a vociferous religious reformer who railed against the Catholic Church and the nobility, reform priests drawing on the support of poor workers and peasants took to the hills of southern Bohemia. These hilltop congregations soon grew into permanent settlements, wholly outside the feudal order. The most important settlement, on the Lužnice River, became known in 1420 as Tábor. Tábor quickly evolved into the symbolic and spiritual center of the Hussites (now called Taborites) and, together with Prague, served as the bulwark of the reform movement.

The early 1420s in Tábor were heady days for religious reformers. Private property was denounced, and the many poor who made the pilgrimage to Tábor were required to leave their possessions at the town gates. Some sects rejected the doctrine of transubstantiation (the belief that the Eucharist becomes the Body and Blood of Christ), making Holy Communion into a bawdy, secular feast of bread and wine. Still other reformers considered themselves superior to Christ—who by dying had shown himself to be merely mortal. Few, however, felt obliged to work for a living, and the Taborites had to rely increasingly on raids of neighboring villages for survival.

War fever in Tábor at the time ran high, and the town became one of the focal points of the ensuing Hussite wars (1419–1434), which pitted reformers against an array of foreign crusaders, Catholics, and noblemen. Under the brilliant military leadership of Jan Žižka, the Taborites enjoyed early successes, but the forces of the established church proved too mighty in the end. Žižka was killed in 1424, and the Hussite uprising ended at the rout of Lipany 10 years later. Still, many of the town's citizens resisted recatholicization. Fittingly, following the Battle of White Mountain in 1620 (the final defeat for the Czech Protestants), Tábor was the last city to succumb to the conquering Hapsburgs.

Begin exploring the town at the **Žižkovo náměstí** (Žižka Square), named for the gifted Hussite military leader; a large 19th-century bronze statue of Žižka dominates the square. The stone tables in front of the Gothic town hall and the house at No. 6 date from the 15th century and were used by the Hussites to give daily communion to the faithful. Follow the tiny streets around the square, which seemingly lead nowhere. They curve around, branch off, and then stop; few lead back to the main square. The confusing street plan was purposely laid during the 15th century to thwart incoming invasions.

The **Muzeum Hussitského Hnutí** (Museum of the Hussite Movement), just behind the town hall, documents the history of the reformers. You can visit an elaborate network of tunnels carved by the Hussites below the Old Town for protection in case of attack. ⊠ *Křivkova ul. 31.* ☎ *20 Kč.* ⊙ *Daily 8:30–5; closed weekends Nov.–Mar. and Mon. Apr.–Oct.*

Pražská ulice, a main route to the newer part of town, is lined with beautiful Renaissance facades. If you turn right at Divadelní and head to the Lužnice River, you'll see the remaining walls and fortifications of the 15th century, irrefutable evidence of the town's vital function as a stronghold. **Kotnov hrad** (Kotnov Castle), rising above the river in the distance, dates from the 13th century and was part of the earliest fortifications. The large pond to the northeast of Tábor was created as a reservoir in 1492; since it was used for baptism, the fervent Taborites named the lake Jordan.

Dining and Lodging

$$ ▦ **Palcát.** A 10-minute walk from the Old Town Square, the slightly run-down Palcát is quite a contrast. The architecture is overwhelmingly drab, but the rooms, though plain, are bright and comfortable; those on the upper floors have a dazzling view of the Old Town. Breakfast is included in the rates. ⊠ *Tř. 9, Května 2467, 390 01,* ☎

0361/252–901, FAX 0361/252–905. 65 rooms with shower. Restaurant,
bar, café, meeting room. AE, MC, V.

$–$$ ☒ **Bican Pension.** At this lovely family-run pension, the staff couldn't
  ★   be nicer, nor could the view from either side of the pension: One side
        faces the Old Town, while the other offers a soothing view of the river.
        The premises date from the 14th century, and the Bicans will gladly
        show you the house's own catacombs. The chilly basement lounge is
        a godsend on sweltering summer days. Breakfast is included, and you'll
        also have the use of the kitchen. ☒ Hradební 189/16, 390 01, ☎ 0361/
        252–109. 6 rooms. Sauna. No credit cards.

Třeboň

⑥ 48 km (28 mi) south of Tábor.

Amid a plethora of ponds rests another jewel of a town with a far different historical heritage than Tábor's. Třeboň was settled during the 13th century by the Wittkowitzes (later called the Rosenbergs), once Bohemia's noblest family. From 1316 to the end of the 16th century, the dynasty dominated southern Bohemia; they amassed their wealth through silver and real estate. You can see their emblem, a five-petaled rose, on castles, doorways, and coats of arms all over the region. Their official residence was 40 km (25 mi) to the southwest, in Český Krumlov (☞ below), but Třeboň was an important second residence and repository of the family archives.

Thanks to the Rosenberg family, this unlikely landlocked town has become the center of the Czech Republic's fishing industry. During the 15th and 16th centuries, the Rosenbergs peppered the countryside with 6,000 enormous ponds, partly to drain the land and partly to breed fish. Carp breeding is still big business, and if you are in the area in the late autumn, you may be lucky enough to witness the great carp harvests, when tens of thousands of the glittering fish are netted. The **Rybnik Svět** (Svět Pond) is closest to town, along the southern edge; try to fit in a stroll along its banks. Třebon is also a Greenways access point, with hiking and horseback trails leading around the area's ponds and peat bogs; for specific information, contact the tourist bureau (☞ Visitor Information *in* Southern Bohemia A to Z, *below*).

The intact town walls, built during the 16th century, are among the best in the Czech Republic. Near the first of the town's three gates, there's an 18th-century brewery, still producing outstanding beer; first brewed in 1379, as the redbrick tower proudly boasts, beer enjoys nearly as long a tradition here as in Plzeň or České Budějovice. Masarykovo náměstí (Masaryk Square), the main square, has a typical collection of arcaded Renaissance and Baroque houses. Look for the **Bílý Koníček** (Little White Horse), the best-preserved Renaissance house on the square, dating from 1544.

NEED A   Sample some of the excellent local beer at the **Bílý Koníček** (☎ 0333/
BREAK?   2818), now a modest hotel and restaurant on Masaryk Square.

The entrance to **Zámek Třeboň** (Třeboň Château) lies at the southwest corner of the square. From the outside it looks plain and sober, with its stark white walls, but the rooms (open to the public) are sumptuous re-creations of 16th-century life, and the walls of the interior courtyard are covered with sgraffito. The castle also houses a permanent exhibition of pond building. The last of the Rosenbergs died in 1611, and the castle eventually became the property of the Schwarzenberg family, who built their family tomb in a grand park on the other side of Svět Pond. It is now a monumental neo-Gothic destination for

Sunday-afternoon picnickers. ⊠ *Masarykovo nám.*, ☎ *0333/721–193.* 🎫 *70 Kč.* ⊙ *Apr. and Oct., weekends 9–4; May and Sept., Tues.–Sun. 9–4; June–Aug., Tues.–Sun. 9–5.*

In the **Augustýnský klašter** (Augustine Monastery), adjacent to the castle, take a look at the finely carved Altar of the Masters of Wittingau (Wittingau is the German name for Třebon), dating from the late 14th century. The paintings themselves, the most famous example of Bohemian Gothic art, are now in the National Gallery in Prague. This was the first hall church in Bohemia (the aisles being about as high as the nave) and it set the style for other churches in the region.

Lodging

$ 🏨 **Bílý Koníček.** This old-style hotel occupies one of the most striking Renaissance buildings on the main square. With the nearby Zlatá Hvězda being remodeled, it's an acceptable alternative. The rooms fail to measure up to the splendid facade but are suitably clean. ⊠ *Masarykovo nám. 97, 37901,* ☎ *0333/721–213,* 🅵🅰🆇 *0333/721–136. 10 rooms. Restaurant. V.*

Outdoor Activities and Sports

You can swim in most of the larger carp ponds around town. The Svět Pond is particularly appealing because of its little sandy beaches, although these are generally crowded in summer.

Rožmberk nad Vltavou

★ ⑥① *60 km (36 mi) southwest of Třeboň.*

This little village, just a few miles from the former Iron Curtain, was forgotten in the postwar years. It seems like a ghost town, especially at night with the darkened **Rosenberg hrad** (Rosenberg Castle) keeping lonely vigil atop the hill overlooking the Vltava River. The slender tower, the Jakobinka, dates from the 13th century, when the Rosenberg family built the original structure. Most of the exterior, however, is 19th-century neo-Gothic. In summer you can tour some of the rooms, admiring the weapons and Bohemian paintings. ⊠ *Rožmberk nad Vltavou,* ☎ *0337/9838.* 🎫 *50 Kč.* ⊙ *Apr. and Oct., weekends 9–3; May and Sept., Tues.–Sun. 9–3:15; June–Aug., Tues.–Sun. 9–4:15.*

Český Krumlov

★ ⑥② *22 km (13 mi) north of Rožmberk nad Vltavou.*

Český Krumlov, the official residence of the Rosenbergs for some 300 years, is an eye-opener: None of the surrounding towns or villages, with their open squares and mixtures of old and new buildings, will prepare you for the beauty of the Old Town. Here the Vltava works its wonders as nowhere else but in Prague itself, swirling in a nearly complete circle around the town. Across the river stands the proud castle, rivaling any in the country in size and splendor.

For the moment, Český Krumlov's beauty is still intact, even though the dilapidated buildings that lend the town its unique atmosphere are slowly metamorphosizing into boutiques and expensive pensions. In peak months, the existing facilities for visitors can be woefully overburdened. But overlook any minor inconveniences and enjoy a rare, unspoiled trip through time. Greenways trails lead to and from the town; for details, contact the tourist office (☞ Visitor Information *in* Southern Bohemia A to Z, *below*).

The town's main square, **Svornosti náměstí** (Unity Square), is a bit disappointing; the arcades hide the richness of the buildings' architecture.

The **town hall,** at No. 1, built in 1580, is memorable for its Renaissance friezes and Gothic arcades. Tiny alleys fan out from the square
in all directions. Horní ulice begins just opposite the Hotel Krumlov.
A quick visit to the **Městské muzeum** (City Museum) at No. 152 is a
good way to familiarize yourself with the rise and fall of the Rosenberg dynasty.

Just opposite the City Museum, at No. 154, are the Renaissance facades, complete with lively sgraffiti, of the former **Jesuitska Škola** (Jesuit school)—now the semiluxurious Růže hotel (☞ Dining and
Lodging, *below*). It owes its abundance of Renaissance detailing to its
location on the main trading routes to Italy and Bavaria—a perfect site
for absorbing incoming fashions. The tower of the late-Gothic **Kostel
Svateho Víta** (St. Vitus Church), built in the late 1400s, rises from its
position on Kostelní ulice to offset the larger, older tower of the castle across the river. The view over the Old Town and castle is at its most
spectacular from here.

☚ To get to **Krumlov hrad** (Krumlov Castle), cross the peaceful Vltava
via the main street, Radniční, and enter at one of two gates along La-
trán street. The oldest and most striking part of the castle is the round
12th-century tower, renovated in the 16th century to look something
like a minaret, with its delicately arcaded Renaissance balcony. The tower
is part of the old border fortifications, guarding the Bohemian frontiers from Austrian incursion.

The castle passed out of the Rosenbergs' hands when the last of the
line, the dissolute Petr Vok, sold castle and town to Rudolf II in 1601
to pay off his debts. The castle's Renaissance and Baroque features and
its most sumptuous furnishings were added later by the Eggenberg and
Schwarzenberg families.

As you enter the castle area, look into the old moats, where two playful brown bears now reside—unlikely to be of much help in protect-
ing the castle from attack. In season, the castle rooms are open to the
public. The **Maškarní Sal** (Hall of Masks) is the most impressive interior, with its richly detailed 18th-century frescoes. After proceeding
through a series of courtyards, you'll come to a wonderfully romantic elevated passageway with spectacular views of the huddled houses
of the Old Town. The Austrian expressionist painter Egon Schiele
often stayed in Český Krumlov in the early 1900s and liked to paint
this particular view over the river, calling his now famous Krumlov series *The Dead Town*. From the river down below, the elevated passageway is revealed in all its Renaissance glory as part of a network
of tall arches, looking like a particularly elaborate Roman viaduct. On
top runs a narrow three-story residential block (still inhabited), dressed
in gray and white Renaissance stripes. At the end of the passageway
you'll come to the luxuriously appointed castle gardens (open only June
through August). In the middle is an open-air theater, one of Bohemia's
first such theaters and remarkable for its still-intact gilded stage. Performances are held here in July and August. ✉ *Český Krumlov hrad,*
☎ *0337/3135.* ☞ *70 Kč.* ☉ *Apr. and Oct., Tues.–Sun. 9–noon and
1–3; May–Aug., Tues.–Sun. 9–noon and 1–5, Sept., Tues.–Sun. 9–
noon and 1–4.*

The **Egon Schiele Center** exhibits the work of Schiele and other 20th-
century German and Austrian artists in a rambling Renaissance brewery near the river. ✉ *Široká 70–72.* ☞ *100 Kč.* ☉ *Daily 10–6.*

Dining and Lodging

Český Krumlov is crammed with pensions and private rooms for rent,
many priced around $20 per person per night. The best place to look

is along the tiny Parkán ulice, which parallels the river just off the main street. A safe bet is the house at Parkán No. 107 (☎ 0337/4396), blessed with several nice rooms and friendly management.

$ ★ ✕🏨 **Na louži.** Wood floors and exposed-beam ceilings lend a traditional touch to this warm, inviting, family-run pub. The food is unfussy and satisfying; look for the *pstruh* (Vltava trout) with potatoes. The rooms upstairs are equally country-style, small but comfortable. ✉ *Kájovská 66, 381 01,* ☎ FAX *0337/5495. 5 rooms. Restaurant. No credit cards.*

$$$ ★ 🏨 **Růže.** This Renaissance monastery has been transformed into an excellent luxury hotel, only a five-minute walk from the main square. The rooms are spacious—some also have drop-dead views of the town below, so ask to see several before choosing. The restaurant, too, is top-rate; the elegant dining room is formal without being stuffy. ✉ *Horní ul. 153, 381 01,* ☎ *0337/2245,* FAX *0337/61742. 53 rooms, 36 with bath. Restaurant, nightclub. AE, MC, V.*

Nightlife and the Arts

The outdoor theater in the Krumlov Castle gardens (☞ *above*) is a popular venue for plays and concerts throughout the summer.

Çeské Budějovice

63 *22 km (13 mi) from Çeský Krumlov: Follow Route 159, then Route 3.*

After the glories of Çeský Krumlov, any other town would be a letdown—and Çeské Budějovice, known as Budweis under the Hapsburgs and famous primarily for its beer, is no exception. The major attraction of what is basically an industrial town is the enormously proportioned main square, Náměstí Přemysla Otakara II, lined with arcaded houses and worth an hour or two of wandering. For a bite to eat and a sampling of locally brewed Budwar beer in an atmospheric setting, stop by Masné Krámy on Krajinska 13, two blocks north of the square.To get a good view over the city, you can climb the 360 steps up to the Renaissance gallery of the **Černá Věž** (Black Tower), at the northeast corner of the square next to St. Nicholas Cathedral. 🎫 *10 Kč.* ⏲ *Apr.–Oct., Tues.–Sun. 9–5.*

Lodging

$$$ 🏨 **Gomel.** This modern high-rise, a 15-minute walk from the main square along the road to Prague, is probably best suited to business travelers. The rooms are plain, but the hotel does offer a reasonable range of facilities and has an English-speaking staff. Breakfast is included. ✉ *Pražská tř. 14, 307 01,* ☎ *038/7311390,* FAX *038/7311365. 188 rooms with bath or shower. 3 restaurants, café, nightclub, meeting room. AE, DC, MC, V.*

$$$ 🏨 **Zvon.** Old-fashioned, well kept, and comfortable, the Zvon has an ideal location right on the main town square. The rooms are bright, and the period bathrooms have large bathtubs. The price is high, however, for the level of facilities. ✉ *Nám. Přemysla Otakara II 28, 307 01,* ☎ *038/731–1383,* FAX *038/731–1385. 75 rooms. Restaurant. AE, DC, MC, V.*

Hluboká nad Vltavou

★ *9 km (5½ mi) north of Çeské Budějovice.*

This is one of the Czech Republic's most curious castles. Although the structure dates from the 13th century, what you see is pure 19th-century excess, perpetrated by the wealthy Schwarzenberg family as proof of their "good taste." If you think you've seen it somewhere before, you're probably thinking of Windsor Castle, near London, on which it was carefully modeled. Take a tour; the rather pompous interior reflects the no-holds-barred tastes of the time, but many individual pieces are interesting in their own right. The wooden Renaissance ceiling in the large dining room was removed by the Schwarzenbergs from the castle at Çeský Krumlov and brought here. Also look for the beautiful late-Baroque bookshelves in the library. If your interest in Czech painting wasn't satisfied in Prague, have a look at the **Galerie Mikoláše Aleše** (Aleš Art Gallery) in the Riding Hall, hung with the works of southern Bohemian painters from the Middle Ages to the present. The collection is the second largest in Bohemia. ⊠ *At intersection of routes 105 and 146,* ☎ *038/965–340.* 🎫 *Castle and gallery 100 Kč.* ☉ *Apr., daily 9–4:30, May and Sept.–Oct., Tues.–Sun. 9–4:30, June–Aug., daily 9–5.*

If you're in the mood for a brisk walk, follow the yellow trail signs 2 km (1 mi) to the **Ohrada Lovecka Chata** (Ohrada hunting lodge), which houses a museum of hunting and fishing and also has a small zoo for children. ☎ *038/965–340.* ☉ *Apr. and Sept.–Oct., daily 9–noon and 1–4; May–Aug., daily 1–5.*

Písek

64 *60 km (37 mi) northwest of České Budějovice.*

If it weren't for Písek's 700-year-old **Gothic bridge,** peopled with Baroque statues, you could easily bypass the town and continue on to Prague. After the splendors of Český Krumlov or even Třeboň, Písek's main square, Velké náměstí, is admittedly plain, despite its many handsome Renaissance and Baroque houses. The bridge, a five-minute walk from the main square along Karlovo ulice, was commissioned in 1254 by Přemysl Otakar II, who sought a secure crossing over the difficult Otava River for his salt shipments from nearby Prachatice. Originally one of the five major Hussite strongholds, as early as the 9th century Písek stood at the center of one of the most important trade routes to the west, linking Prague to Passau and the rest of Bavaria. The statues of saints were not added until the 18th century.

In the town square, look for the 240-ft tower of the early-Gothic **Mariánský chrám** (Church of Mary). Construction was started at about the time the bridge was built. The tower was completed in 1487 and got its Baroque dome during the mid-18th century. On the inside, look for the *Madonna from Písek,* a 14th-century Gothic altar painting. On a middle pillar is a rare series of early Gothic wall paintings dating from the end of the 13th century. ⊠ *Velké nám. 114,* ☎ *0362/214–731.* 🎫 *20 Kč.* ☉ *May–early Nov. Tues.–Sun. 9–6.*

OFF THE
BEATEN PATH

ZVÍKOV – If you've got room for still another castle, head for Zvíkov Castle, about 18 km (11 mi) north of town along route 138. The castle, at the confluence of the Otava and Vltava rivers, is impressive for its authenticity. Unlike many other castles in Bohemia, Zvíkov survived the 18th and 19th centuries unrenovated and still looks just as it did 500 years ago.

Southern Bohemia A to Z

Arriving and Departing

Prague is the main gateway to southern Bohemia (☞ Arriving and Departing *in* Prague A to Z, *above*). Several trains a day run from Vienna to Prague; most of these travel via Třeboň and Tábor. To drive from Vienna, take the E49 from Gmünd.

Getting Around

BY BUS

All the major sights are reachable from Prague using ÇSAD's dense bus network. Service between the towns, however, is far less frequent and will require advance planning.

BY CAR

Car travel affords the greatest ease and flexibility in this region. The major road from Prague south to Tábor and Çeské Budějovice, though often crowded, is in relatively good shape. Route 3 is the main road through the area.

BY TRAIN

Benešov (Konopiště), Tábor, and Třeboň all lie along the major southern line in the direction of Vienna, and train service to these cities from Prague is frequent and comfortable. Good connections also exist from Prague to Çeské Budějovice. For other destinations, you may have to combine the train and bus.

Contacts and Resources

EMERGENCIES

Police (☎ 158). **Ambulance** (☎ 155).

GUIDED TOURS

Čedok (☎ 02/2419–7111) offers several specialized tours that include visits to Çeské Budějovice, Hluboka Castle, Çeský Krumlov, Kutná Hora, and Çeský Šternberk. Čedok also offers a full-day excursion to Moser, the oldest glassworks in Central Europe, south of Prague. Prague departure points include the Čedok offices at Na příkopě 18 and Bílkova ulice 6 and the Panorama, Forum, and Hilton hotels.

VISITOR INFORMATION

Čedok is the first stop for general tourist information and city maps·

České Budějovice (⊠ Nám. Přemysla Otakára II 39, ☎ 038/635–2128). **Český Krumlov** (⊠ Čedok, Latrá 79, ☎ 0337/2189; ⊠ Infocentrum, Nám. Svornosti 1, ☎ 0337/5670). **Kutná Hora** (⊠ Kulturni a Informační Centrum, Palackého 377, ☎ 0327/515–796). **Písek** (⊠ Čedok, Velké nám. 1, ☎ 0362/212–988). **Tábor** (⊠ Kvetna 9, ☎ 0361/252–2235). **Třeboň** (⊠ Informační středisko, Masarykovo nám. 103, ☎ 0333/721–169).

WESTERN BOHEMIA

Until World War II, western Bohemia was the playground of Central Europe's rich and famous. Its three well-known spas, Karlovy Vary, Mariánské Lázně, and Františkový Lázně (better known by their German names: Karlsbad, Marienbad, and Franzensbad, respectively), were the annual haunts of everybody who was anybody—Johann Wolfgang von Goethe, Ludwig van Beethoven, Karl Marx, and England's King Edward VII, to name but a few. Although strictly "proletarianized" in the Communist era, the spas still exude a nostalgic aura of a more elegant past and, unlike most of Bohemia, offer a basic tourist infrastructure that makes dining and lodging a pleasure.

Karlovy Vary

★ ⑥ *132 km (79 mi) due west on Route 6 (E48) from Prague. By car the trip takes about two hours.*

Karlovy Vary, better known outside the Czech Republic by its German name, Karlsbad, is the most famous Bohemian spa. It is named for Emperor Charles (Karl) IV, who allegedly happened upon the springs in

1358 while on a hunting expedition. As the story goes, the emperor's hound—chasing a harried stag—fell into a boiling spring and was scalded. Charles had the water tested and, familiar with spas in Italy, ordered baths to be established in the village of Vary. The spa reached its heyday in the 19th century, when royalty came here from all over Europe for treatment. The long list of those who "took the cure" includes Goethe (no fewer than 13 times, according to a plaque on one house in the Old Town), Schiller, Beethoven, and Chopin. Even Karl Marx, when he wasn't decrying wealth and privilege, spent time at the resort and wrote some of *Das Kapital* here between 1874 and 1876.

The shabby streets of modern Karlovy Vary, though, are vivid reminders that those glory days are long over. After decades of neglect under the Communists, many of the buildings are crumbling behind their beautiful facades. Today officials face the daunting task of carving out a new role for Karlovy Vary, in an era when few people can afford to set aside weeks or months at a time for a leisurely cure. To raise some quick cash, many sanatoriums have turned to offering short-term accommodations to foreign visitors (at rather expensive rates). It's even possible at some spas to receive "treatment," including carbon-dioxide baths and massage. For most visitors, though, it's enough simply to stroll the streets and parks and allow the eyes to feast awhile on the splendors of the past.

Whether you're arriving by bus, train, or car, your first view of the town on the approach from Prague will be of the ugly new section on the banks of the Ohře River. Don't despair: Continue along the main road—following the signs to the Grandhotel Pupp—until you reach the lovely main street of the older spa area, situated gently astride the banks of the little Teplá River. The walk from the New Town to the spa area is about 20 minutes; take a taxi if you're carrying a heavy load. The **Historická čtvrt** (Historic District) is still largely intact. Tall 19th-century houses, boasting decorative and often eccentric facades, line the spa's proud, if dilapidated, streets. Throughout you'll see colonnades full of people sipping the spa's hot sulfuric water from odd pipe-shape drinking cups. At night the streets fill with steam escaping from cracks in the earth, giving the town a slightly macabre feel.

Karlovy Vary's jarringly modern **Vřídlo** (Vřídlo Colonnade), home of the spring of the same name, is the town's hottest and most dramatic spring. The Vřídlo is indeed unique, shooting its scalding water to a height of some 40 ft. Walk inside the arcade to watch the hundreds of patients here take the famed Karlsbad drinking cure. You'll recognize them promenading somnambulistically up and down, eyes glazed, clutching a drinking glass filled periodically at one of the five "sources." The waters are said to be especially effective against diseases of the digestive and urinary tracts. They're also good for the gout-ridden (which probably explains the spa's former popularity with royals!). If you want to join the crowds and take a sip, you can buy your own spouted cup from vendors within the colonnade.

Walk in the direction of the New Town, past the wooden **Tržni kolonáda** (Market Colonnade). Continue down the winding street until you reach the **Mlýnská kolonáda** (Mill Colonnade). This neo-Renaissance pillared hall, built in 1871–1881, has four springs: Rusalka, Libussa, Prince Wenceslas, and Millpond. If you continue down the valley, you'll soon arrive at the very elegant **Sádová kolonáda** (Park Colonnade), a white, wrought-iron, 19th-century construction.

The 20th century emerges at its most disturbing a little farther along the valley across the river, in the form of the huge, bunkerlike **Thermal**

Hotel, built in the late 1960s. Although the building is a monstrosity, the view of Karlovy Vary from the rooftop pool is nothing short of spectacular. (The pool is open from 8 AM to 8 PM.) Even if you don't feel like a swim, it's worth taking the winding road up to the baths for the view. ✉ *I.P. Pavlova.*

The **Imperial** (Imperial Sanatorium) is a perfect example of turn-of-the-century architecture, with its white facade and red-roofed tower. The Imperial was once the haunt of Europe's wealthiest financiers. Under the Communists, though, the sanatorium was used to house visiting Soviet dignitaries. The Imperial has recently reopened as a private hotel, but it will be many years before it can again assume its former role. ✉ *Libušina 18.*

Across the little Gogol Bridge, you'll find the steep road **Zámecký vrch,** which will lead you to a handful of other sights. Walk uphill until you come to the redbrick **Kostel sv. Lukáše** (Victorian Church) at the intersection of Zámecký vrch and Petra Velikeho; it was once used by the local English community. A few blocks farther along Petra Velikeho street, you'll come to a splendid **Kostel sv. Petra a Pavla** (Russian Orthodox church), once visited by Czar Peter the Great. Return to the English church and take a sharp right uphill on the redbrick road. Then turn left onto a footpath through the woods, following the signs to Jeleni Skok (Stag's Leap). After a while you'll see steps leading up to a bronze statue of a deer looking over the cliffs, the symbol of Karlovy Vary. From here a winding path leads up to **Altán Jeleni Skok,** a little red gazebo opening onto a fabulous panorama.

NEED A BREAK?

Reward yourself for making the climb to Stag's Leap with a light meal at the nearby restaurant **Jeleni Skok.** You may have to pay an entrance fee if there is a live band (but you'll also get the opportunity to polka). If you don't want to walk up, you can drive up a signposted road from the Victorian church.

Diagonally across from the Grandhotel Pupp (☞ Dining and Lodging, *below*), behind a little park, is the pompous Fellner and Helmer **Imperial Spa,** now known as **Lázně I** and housing the local casino. If you walk back toward the town center along the river on Stará louka, you'll pass a variety of interesting stores, including the Moser glass store and the Elefant, one of the last of a dying breed of sophisticated coffeehouses in the Czech Republic.

To the right of the Vřídlo Colonnade (☞ *above*) are steps up to the white **Kostel svatej Maři Magdaleny** (Church of Mary Magdalene). Designed by Kilian Dientzenhofer (architect of the two St. Nicholas churches in Prague), this church is the best of the few Baroque buildings still standing in Karlovy Vary. ✉ *Moravská ul.,* ☎ *no phone.* ☉ *Weekends 10–5.*

Dining and Lodging

$$$ ✕ **Embassy.** This cozy, sophisticated wine restaurant, conveniently located near the Grandhotel Pupp, serves an innovative menu: Tagliatelle with smoked salmon in cream sauce makes an excellent main course, as does roast duck with cabbage and dumplings. Highlights of the varied dessert menu include plum dumplings with *fromage blanc* (a soft, fresh cream cheese). On the wine list, look for Czech wines like Rulandské bílé and Ryzlink Rýnský. ✉ *Nová Louka 21,* ☎ *017/322–3049,* ℻ *017/322–3146. AE, DC, MC, V.*

$$ ✕ **Karel IV.** Its location atop an old castle not far from the Market Colon-★ nade affords diners the best view in town. Good renditions of traditional Czech standbys—*bramborák* (potato pancake) and chicken

breast with peaches—are served in small, secluded dining areas that are particularly intimate after sunset. ⊠ *Zámecký vrch 2,* ☎ *017/322–7255. AE, MC.*

$$$$ ▦ **Dvořák.** Consider a splurge here if you're longing for Western stan-
★ dards of service and convenience. Opened in late 1990, this Austrian-owned hotel occupies three renovated town houses that are just a five-minute walk from the main spas. The staff is helpful, and the rooms are spotlessly clean. If possible, request a room with a bay-window view of the town. Breakfast is included. ⊠ *Nová Louka 11, 360 21,* ☎ *017/322–4145,* ☎ *017/322–2814. 87 rooms. Restaurant, café, pool, beauty salon, massage, sauna, exercise room. AE, DC, MC, V.*

$$$–$$$$ ▦ **Grandhotel Pupp.** This enormous 300-year-old hotel is one of
★ Karlovy Vary's landmarks—it's also one of Central Europe's most fa-mous resorts. Standards and service slipped under the Communists (when the hotel was known as the Moskva-Pupp), but the highly professional management has more than made up for the decades of neglect. Ask for a room furnished in 19th-century period style. The food in the ground-floor restaurant is decent, but it's the elegant setting that makes the hotel worth a splurge. Every July, the Pupp becomes a temporary home base for international movie stars who come to the Karlovy Vary International Film Festival. (The adjacent Parkhotel Pupp, under the same management, is an affordable alternative to the Grandhotel.) Break-fast is included. ⊠ *Mírové nám. 2, 360 91,* ☎ *017/310–9111,* ☎ *017/310–9620 or 017/322–4032. 214 rooms, 10 suites. 4 restaurants, lounge, sauna, exercise room, 2 nightclubs. AE, DC, MC, V.*

$$$ ▦ **Elwa.** Renovations have successfully integrated modern comforts into this older, elegant spa resort located midway between the Old and New Towns. Modern features include clean, comfortable rooms (most with television) with contemporary furnishings like overstuffed chairs. There's also an on-site fitness center. Breakfast is included. ⊠ *Zahradní 29, 360 21,* ☎ *017/322–8472,* ☎ *017/322–8473. 30 rooms. Restau-rant, bar, beauty salon, health club. AE, DC, MC, V.*

Nightlife and the Arts

In Karlovy Vary, the action centers on the two nightclubs of the **Grand-hotel Pupp** (☞ Dining and Lodging, *above*). The "little dance hall" is open daily 8 PM–1 AM. The second club is open Wednesday through Sunday 7 PM–3 AM; it spins pop music. **Club Propaganda** (⊠ Jaltska 7, ☎ no phone) is Karlovy Vary's best venue for live rock and new music.

Outdoor Activities and Sports

Karlovy Vary's warm open-air public pool on top of the **Thermal Hotel** (☞ Exploring *above*) offers the unique experience of swimming com-fortably even in the coolest weather; the view over the town is out-standing.

Shopping

In western Bohemia, Karlovy Vary is best known to glass enthusiasts as home of **Moser** (⊠ Tržiště 7, ☎ 017/323–5303), one of the world's leading producers of crystal and decorative glassware. A number of outlets for lesser-known, although also high-quality, makers of glass and porcelain can also be found along Stará Louka.

For excellent buys in porcelain, try **Karlovarský porcelán** (⊠ Tržiště 27, ☎ 017/322–5660).

A cheaper but nonetheless unique gift from Karlovy Vary would be a bottle of the ubiquitous bittersweet (and potent) **Becherovka,** a liqueur produced by the town's own Jan Becher distillery. Another neat gift would be one of the pipe-shape ceramic drinking cups used to take the drinking cure at spas; you can find them at the colonnades in Karlovy Vary and Mariánské Lázně. You can also buy boxes of tasty Oplatky wafers, sometimes covered with chocolate, at shops in all of the spa towns.

Cheb

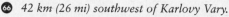 *42 km (26 mi) southwest of Karlovy Vary.*

Known for centuries by its German name of Eger, the old town of Cheb lies on the border with Germany in the far west of the Czech Republic. The town has been a fixture of Bohemia since 1322 (when the king purchased the area from German merchants), but as you walk around the beautiful medieval square, it's difficult not to think you're in Germany. The tall merchants' houses surrounding the main square, with their long, red-tiled sloping roofs dotted with windows like droopy eyelids, are more Germanic in style than anything else in Bohemia. You'll also hear a lot of German on the streets—but more from the many German visitors than from the town's residents.

Germany took full possession of the town in 1938 under the terms of the notorious Munich Pact. But following World War II, virtually the entire German population was expelled, and the Czech name of Cheb was officially adopted. A more notorious German connection has emerged in the years following the 1989 revolution; Cheb has quickly become the unofficial center of prostitution for visiting Germans. Don't be startled to see young women, provocatively dressed, lining the highways and bus stops on the roads into town.

In the bustling central square, **Náměstí Krále Jiřího z Poděbrad,** the ubiquitous Vietnamese vendors have reestablished its original marketplace function. The statue in the middle, similar to the Roland statues you see throughout Bohemia and attesting to the town's royal privileges, represents the town hero, Wastel of Eger. Look carefully at his right foot, and you'll see a small man holding a sword and a head—this denotes the town had its own judge and executioner.

On the lower part of Náměstí Krále Jiříhoz Poděbrad are two rickety groups of timbered medieval buildings, 11 houses in all, divided by a narrow alley. The houses, forming the area known as **Špalíček,** date from the 13th century and were home to many Jewish merchants. Židovská ulice (Jews' Street), running uphill to the left of the Špalíček, served as the actual center of the ghetto. Note the small alley running off to the left of Židovská. This calm street, with the seemingly inappropriate name ulička Zavražděných (Lane of the Murdered), was the scene of an outrageous act of violence in 1350. Pressures had been building for some time between Jews and Christians. Incited by an anti-Semitic bishop, the townspeople finally chased the Jews into the street, closed off both ends, and massacred them. Now only the name attests to the slaughter.

NEED A BREAK?

Cheb's main square abounds with cafés and little restaurants, all offering a fairly uniform menu of schnitzel and sauerbraten aimed at visiting Germans. The **Kavárna Špalíček,** nestled in the Špalíček buildings, is one of the better choices and has the added advantage of a unique architectural setting.

History buffs, particularly those interested in the Hapsburgs, will want to visit the **Chebský muzeum** (Cheb Museum) in the Pachelbel House on the main square. It was in this house that the great general of the Thirty Years' War, Albrecht von Wallenstein (Valdštejn), was murdered in 1634 on the orders of his own emperor, the Hapsburg Ferdinand II, who was provoked by Wallenstein's increasing power and rumors of treason. According to legend, Wallenstein was on his way to the Saxon border to enlist support to fight the Swedes when his own officers barged into his room and stabbed him through the heart with a stave. The stark bedroom with its four-poster bed and dark-red velvet curtains has been left as it was in his memory. (The story also inspired playwright Friedrich Schiller to write the *Wallenstein* trilogy; he planned the work while living at No. 2, at the top of the square.) The museum is interesting in its own right: It has a section on the history of Cheb and a collection of minerals (including one discovered by Goethe). ⊠ *Nám. Krále Jiřího z Poděbrad,* ☎ *0166/422–386.* 🎫 *40 Kč.* ☉ *Tues.–Sun. 9–noon and 1–5.*

The **art gallery** in the bright-yellow Baroque house near the top of the square offers an excellent small collection of Gothic sculpture from western Bohemia and a well-chosen sampling of modern Czech art. One of the country's best-known private galleries of photography, **Gallery G4** (☎ 0166/422–838) is just off the square at Kamenná 2. ⊠ *Nám. Krále Jiřího z Poděbrad 16,* ☎ *0166/422–450.*

In the early 1820s, Goethe often stayed in the **Gabler House,** on the corner of the main square near the Cheb Museum. He shared a passionate interest in excavation work with the town executioner, and they both worked on the excavation of the nearby extinct volcano Komorní Hůrka. The house is not open to the public. ⊠ *Nám. Krále Jiřího z Poděbrad.*

The plain but imposing **Kostel svatého Mikuláše** (St. Nicholas Church) was begun in 1230, when the church belonged to the Order of the Teutonic Knights. You can still see Romanesque windows under the tower; renovations throughout the centuries added an impressive Gothic portal and a Baroque interior. Just inside the Gothic entrance is a wonderfully faded plaque commemorating the diamond jubilee of Hapsburg emperor Franz Josef in 1908. ⊠ *Kostelní náměstí,* ☎ *no phone.*

Follow Křižovnická, behind St. Nicholas Church, up to **Chebský hrad** (Cheb Castle), which stands on a cliff overlooking the Ohře River. The castle—now a ruin—was built in the late 12th century for Holy Roman Emperor Frederick Barbarossa. The square black tower was built with blocks of lava taken from the nearby Komorní Hůrka volcano; the red-brick walls were added during the 15th century. Inside the castle grounds is the carefully restored double-decker chapel, built in the 12th century. The rather dark ground floor, still in Romanesque style, was used by commoners. The bright, ornate top floor, with pointed Gothic windows, was reserved for the emperor and his family and has a wooden bridge leading to the royal palace. ⊠ *Hradní ul,* ☎ *0166/422– 942.* 🎫 *20 Kč.* ☉ *Apr. and Oct., Tues.–Sun. 9–4; May and Sept., Tues.– Sun. 9–5; June–Aug., Tues.–Sun. 9–6.*

Dining and Lodging

$$ ✕ **Eva.** Of the many restaurants opened on and around the main square since the tourism boom began in the early 1990s, Eva is certainly one of the best. A decent array of mostly Czech and German dishes is served in a stylish, contemporary setting that is carefully maintained by a troop of attentive waiters. ⊠ *Jateční 4,* ☎ *0166/422– 498. No credit cards.*

Cheb's hotels have failed to keep pace with the times. For a short stay, a room in a **private home** is a better bet. The city tourist information center (☞ Visitor Information *in* Western Bohemia A to Z, *below*) can arrange accommodations. Several houses along Přemysla Otakara street north of the city have rooms available, and the hotels in Františkovy Lázně (☞ *below*) are just a short drive away.

Františkovy Lázně

67 *6 km (4 mi) from Cheb.*

This little spa town couldn't make a more distinct contrast to nearby Cheb's slightly seedy, hustling air and medieval streetscapes. You might like to ease the transition by walking the red-marked path from Cheb's main square, westward along the river and then north past **Komorní Hůrka.** The extinct volcano is now a tree-covered hill, but excavations on one side have laid bare the rock, and one tunnel is still open. Goethe instigated and took part in the excavations, and you can still barely make out a relief of the poet carved into the rock face.

Františkovy Lázně, or Franzensbad, the smallest of the three main Bohemian spas, isn't really in the same league as the other two (Karlovy Vary and Mariánské Lázně). Built on a more modest scale at the start of the 19th century, the town's ubiquitous kaiser-yellow buildings have been prettified after their neglect under the previous regime and now present cheerful facades, almost too bright for the few strollers. Overall, a pleasing torpor reigns in Františkovy Lázně. There is no town to speak of, just **Národní ulice,** the main street, which leads down into the spa park. The waters are used primarily for curing infertility—hence the large number of young women wandering the grounds.

The most interesting sight in town may be the small **Lázeňský muzeum** (Spa Museum), just off Národní ulice. There is a wonderful collection of spa-related antiques, including copper bathtubs and a turn-of-the-century exercise bike called a Velotrab. The guest books (*Kurbuch*) provide an insight into the cosmopolitan world of pre–World War I Central Europe. The book for 1812 contains the entry "Ludwig van Beethoven, composer from Vienna." ⊠ *Ul. Doktora Pohoreckého 8,* ☎ *0166/542–344.* ▣ *30 Kč.* ☉ *Oct.–May, weekdays 9–noon and 2–5; June–Sept., weekdays 9–noon and 2–5, weekends 9–4.*

The main spring, **Františkuv prameň,** is under a little gazebo filled with brass pipes. Walk along the path to the left until you come to the *Lázeňská poliklinika* (spa clinic), where you can arrange for a day's spa treatment for around 350 Kč. ⊠ *Národní ul.*

....

NEED A BREAK? Only insipid pop music (the scourge of eating and drinking places everywhere in the country) interrupts the cheerful atmosphere of the little café of the **Hotel Slovan** (☞ *below*) on Národní. The tiny gallery and lively frescoes make it a great spot for cake, coffee, or drinks.

....

Dining and Lodging

$$$ ✕▥ **Slovan.** This gracious place is the perfect complement to this re-
★ laxed little town. The eccentricity of the original turn-of-the-century design survived a thorough renovation during the 1970s; the airy rooms are clean and comfortable, and some have a balcony overlooking the main street. The main-floor restaurant serves above-average Czech dishes such as tasty *svíčková* (beef sirloin in a citrusy cream sauce); consider a meal here even if you're staying elsewhere. ⊠ *Národní 5, 35101,* ☎ *0166/542–841,* ℻ *0166/542–843. 25 rooms, 19 with bath. Restaurant, bar, café. DC, V.*

$$$ ▥ **Centrum.** Renovations have left the rooms clean and well appointed if a bit sterile. Still, it is among the best-run hotels in town and only a short walk from the main park and central spas. ⊠ *Anglická 41, 351*

01, ☎ *0166/543–156 or 543–157,* ℻ *0166/542–843. 30 rooms. Restaurant, bar. MC, V.*

$$$ 🏨 **Tři Lilie.** Reopened in 1995 after an expensive refitting, this place once accommodated the likes of Goethe and Metternich. Though too new to have developed a style of its own, the "Three Lilies" has certainly become the best-equipped hotel in town. Spa treatments are conducted off-premises. For reservations, you need to go through the town's spa management. ✉ *Národní 3,* ☎ *0166/542–415. 31 rooms. Restaurant, brasserie, café. No credit cards. Reservations: Obchodní oddělení, Lázně Františkovy Lázně a.s., Jiráskova 17, 351 01,* ☎ *0166/542–063,* ℻ *0166/542–970.*

$$ 🏨 **Bajkal.** This is an offbeat, older hotel with acceptably clean rooms and a friendly staff. It is on the far side of the park from the main spas, roughly a 10-minute walk from the city center. The travel agency in the building also books private accommodations. ✉ *Americká ul. 84/ 4, 351 01,* ☎ *0166/542–501,* ℻ *0166/542–503. 25 rooms, 17 with bath. Restaurant. V.*

Mariánské Lázně

★ **⑥⑧** *30 km (18 mi) southeast of Cheb, 47 km (29 mi) south of Karlovy Vary.*

Your expectations of what a spa resort should be may come nearest to full reality here. It's far larger and better maintained than Františkovy Lázně and is greener and quieter than Karlovy Vary (☞ *above*). This was the spa favored by Britain's Edward VII; Goethe and Chopin, among other luminaries, also repaired here frequently. Mark Twain, on a visit to the spa in 1892, labeled the town a "health factory" and couldn't get over how new everything looked. Indeed, at that time everything was new. The sanatoriums, all built in the middle of the 19th century in a confident, outrageous mixture of "neo" styles, fan out impressively around a finely groomed oblong park. Cure takers and curiosity seekers alike parade through the two stately colonnades, both placed near the top of the park. Buy a spouted drinking cup (available at the colonnades) and join the rest of the sippers taking the drinking cure. Be forewarned, though: The waters from the Rudolph, Ambrose, and Caroline springs, though harmless, all have a noticeable diuretic effect. For this reason they're used extensively in treating disorders of the kidney and bladder. Several spa hotels offer more extensive treatment, including baths and massage. Prices are usually reckoned in U.S. dollars or German marks. For more information, inquire at the main spa offices (✉ Masarykova 22, ☎ 0165/623–061). A stay in Mariánské Lázně, however, can be healthful even without special treatment. Special walking trails of all difficulty levels surround the resort in all directions. The best advice is simply to put on comfortable shoes, buy a hiking map, and head out. One of the country's few golf courses lies 3 or 4 km (2 or 3 mi) from town to the east. Hotels can also help to arrange special activities, such as tennis and horseback riding. For the less intrepid, a simple stroll around the gardens, with a few deep breaths of the town's famous air, is enough to restore a healthy sense of perspective.

Dining and Lodging

$$ ✕ **Filip.** This bustling wine bar is where locals come to find relief from the sometimes large horde of tourists. There's a tasty selection of traditional Czech dishes—mainly pork, grilled meats, and steaks. ✉ *Poštovní 96,* ☎ *0165/626–161. No credit cards.*

$$ ✕ **Koliba.** This combination hunting lodge and wine tavern, set in the
★ woods roughly 20 minutes on foot from the spas, is an excellent alternative to the hotel restaurants in town. Grilled meats and shish kebabs, plus tankards of Moravian wine (try the cherry-red Rulandské

Červené), are served with traditional gusto. ⊠ *Dusíkova, Route 24 in direction of Karlovy Vary,* ☎ *0165/90144. AE, DC, MC, V.*

The best place to look for private lodgings is along Paleckého ulice and Hlavní třída, south of the main spa area. Private accommodations can also be found in the neighboring villages of Zádub and Závišín and along roads in the woods to the east of Mariánské Lázně.

$$$$ 🏨 **Excelsior.** This lovely older hotel is on the main street and is convenient to the spas and colonnade. Rooms have traditional cherry-wood furniture and marble bathrooms, and the views over the town are enchanting. The staff is friendly and multilingual. While the food in the adjoining restaurant is only average, the romantic setting provides adequate compensation. ⊠ *Hlavní tř. 121, 353 01,* ☎ *0165/622–705,* FAX *0165/625–346. 64 rooms. Restaurant, café. AE, DC, MC, V.*

$$$$ 🏨 **Hotel Golf.** Book in advance to secure a room at this stately villa situated 3½ km (2 mi) out of town on the road to Karlovy Vary. A major renovation in the 1980s left the large, open rooms with a cheery, modern look. The restaurant on the main floor is excellent, but the big draw is the 18-hole golf course on the premises, one of the few in the Czech Republic. ⊠ *Zádub 55, 353 01,* ☎ *0165/622–651 or 0165/622–652,* FAX *0165/622655. 25 rooms. Restaurant, pool, 18-hole golf course, tennis court. AE, DC, MC, V.*

$$$ 🏨 **Bohemia.** At this spa resort, beautiful crystal chandeliers in the
★ main hall set the stage for a comfortable and elegant stay. The crisp beige-and-white rooms let you spread out and *really* unpack; they're spacious and high-ceilinged. (If you want to indulge, request one of the enormous suites overlooking the park). ⊠ *Hlavní třída 100, 353 01,* ☎ *0165/623–251,* FAX *0165/622–943. 73 rooms, 4 suites. 2 restaurants, café. AE, DC, MC, V.*

Nightlife and the Arts

Mariánske Lázně sponsors a **music festival** each June, with numerous concerts featuring Czech and international composers and orchestras. The town's annual Chopin festival each autumn brings in fans of the Polish composer's work from around the world.

Mariánské Lázně's **Casino Marienbad** (⊠ Anglická 336, ☎ 0165/ 623–292) is open daily 6 AM–2 AM. For late-night drinks, try the **Hotel Golf** (☞ Dining and Lodging, *above*), which has a good nightclub with dancing in season.

Teplá

⑥⑨ *15 km (9 mi) from Mariánské Lázně.*

It is worth making a detour to the little town of Teplá and its 800-year-old **Klášter premonstrátu Teplá** (Monastery of the Premonstrates), which once played an important role in Christianizing pagan Central Europe. If you don't have a car, a special bus departs daily in season from Mariánské Lázně; inquire at the information office in front of the Excelsior hotel (☞ Visitor Information *in* Western Bohemia A to Z, *below*). The sprawling monastery, founded by the Premonstratensian order of France in 1193 (the same order that established Prague's Strahov Monastery), once controlled the farms and forests in these parts for miles around. The order even owned the spa facilities at Mariánské Lázně and until 1942 used the proceeds from the spas to cover operating expenses. The complex you see before you today, however, betrays none of this earlier prosperity. Over the centuries, the monastery was plundered dozens of times during wars and upheavals, but history reserved its severest blow for the night of April 13, 1950, when security forces employed by the Communists raided the grounds and imprisoned the brothers. The monastery's property was given over to the Czech army, and for the next 28 years the buildings were used as barracks to house soldiers. In 1991 the government returned the monastery buildings and immediate grounds (but not the original land holdings) to the order, and the brothers began the arduous task of picking up the pieces—physically and spiritually.

The most important building on the grounds from an architectural point of view is the Romanesque **basilica** (1197), with its unique triple nave. The rest of the monastery complex was originally Romanesque, but it was rebuilt in 1720 by Baroque architect K. I. Dientzenhofer. There are several wall and ceiling paintings of interest here, as well as some good sculpture. The most valuable collection is in the **Nová knihovna** (New Library), where you will find illuminated hymnals and rare Czech and foreign manuscripts, including a German translation of the New Testament that predates Luther's by some 100 years. Tours of the church and library are given daily on the hour (English notes are available); if you'd like an English-speaking guide, try to call in advance. The monastery also offers short-term accommodations (inquire directly at the monastery offices on the grounds). ⊠ *Klášter, 364 61,* ☎ *0169/ 392–264 or 0169/392–691.* 🖾 *Monastery and library 90 Kč.* 🕓 *Sept.–May daily 9–3, June–Aug. 9–4:30.*

Plzeň

⑦ *92 km (55 mi) from Prague.*

The sprawling industrial city of Plzeň is hardly a tourist mecca, but it's worth stopping off for an hour or two on the way back to Prague. Two sights here are of particular interest to beer fanatics. The first is the **Pilsner-Urquell Brewery,** to the east of the city near the railway station. Group tours in English and German of the 19th-century redbrick building are offered weekdays at 12:30 PM, during which you can taste the valuable brew, exported around the world. The beer was created in 1842 using the excellent Plzeň water, a special malt fermented on the premises, and hops grown in the region around Žatec. (You can only visit via the tour.) ⊠ *U Prazdroje 7,* ☎ *019/706–1111.* 🖾 *70 Kč.*

NEED A BREAK? — You can continue drinking and find some cheap traditional grub at the large **Na Spilce** beer hall just inside the brewery gates. The pub is open daily from 10 AM to 10 PM.

The second stop on the beer tour is the **Pivovarské muzeum** (Brewery Museum), in a late-Gothic malt house one block northeast of Náměstí Republiky (☞ *below*). There are all kinds of paraphernalia tracing the region's brewing history, including the horse-drawn carts used to haul the kegs. There are no materials in English. ⊠ *Veleslavinova ul. 6,* ☎ *019/723–5574.* 🖾 *40 Kč.* 🕓 *Sept.–May Tues.–Sun. 10–6, June–Aug. daily 10–6.*

The city's architectural attractions center on the main square, **Náměstí Republiky** (Republic Square). The square is dominated by the enormous Gothic **Chrám svatého Bartoloměja** (Church of St. Bartholomew). Both the square and the church towers hold size records: The former is the largest in Bohemia and the latter, at 335 ft, the highest in the Czech Republic. Around the square, mixed in with its good selection of stores, are a variety of other architectural jewels, including the town hall, adorned with sgraffiti and built in the Renaissance style by Italian architects during the town's heyday in the 16th century.

Dining and Lodging

$$$ ✕☷ **Continental.** Just five minutes on foot from the main square, the fin-de-siècle Continental remains the best hotel in Plzeň, a relative compliment considering the hotel is slightly run-down and the rooms, though large, are exceedingly plain. The restaurant, however, serves dependably satisfying traditional Czech dishes such as *cibulka* (onion soup) and *svíčková* (beef sirloin in a citrusy cream sauce). Breakfast is included. ⊠ *Zbojnická 8, 305 31,* ☎ *019/723–6477 or 019/723–5292,* 🖷 *019/722–1746. 46 rooms, 23 with bath or shower. Restaurant, café. AE, DC, MC, V.*

$$$ ☷ **Central.** This angular 1960s structure is recommendable for its sunny rooms, friendly staff, and great location, right on the main square. Indeed, even such worthies as Czar Alexander of Russia stayed here in the days when the hotel was a charming inn known as the Golden Eagle. ⊠ *Nám. Republiky 33, 305 31,* ☎ *019/722–6757,* 🖷 *019/722–6064. 77 rooms with shower. Restaurant, bar, café. AE, DC, MC, V.*

$$ ☷ **Slovan.** A gracious off-white facade, sweeping stairways, and large, elegant rooms attest to the Slovan's former grandeur, and there's a pleasant, English-speaking staff to boot. The restaurant still occupies the once beautiful ballroom, but the experience is tarnished by mediocre food and the rock-music accompaniment. The hotel's best asset may be its location, on a lovely square of its own, a short walk from the main square. Breakfast is included. ⊠ *Smetanový Sady 1, 305 31,* ☎ *019/722–7256,* 🖷 *019/722–7012. 100 rooms, 20 with bath. Restaurant, café. AE, DC, MC, V.*

Western Bohemia A to Z

Arriving and Departing

Prague is the main gateway to western Bohemia (☞ Arriving and Departing *in* Prague A to Z, *above*). Major trains from Munich and Nürnberg stop at Cheb and some of the spa towns. It is also an easy drive across the border from Bavaria on the E48 to Cheb and from there to any of the spas.

Getting Around

Good, if slow, train service links all the major towns west of Prague. The best stretches are from Františkovy Lázně to Plzeň and from Plzeň to Prague. The Prague–Karlovy Vary run takes far longer than it should but has a romantic charm all its own. Frequent bus service between Prague and Karlovy Vary, by contrast, makes the journey only about two hours each way. Note that most trains heading west to Germany (in the direction of Nürnberg) stop at Mariánské Lázně. Most trains leave from Prague's Hlavní nádraží (main station), but be sure to check on which station if in doubt. If you're driving, you can take the E48 directly from Prague to Karlovy Vary. Roads in the area tend to be in good condition, though they can sometimes be quite narrow.

Contacts and Resources

EMERGENCIES

Police (☎ 158). **Ambulance** (☎ 155).

GUIDED TOURS

Čedok (☎ 02/2419–7111) offers several specialized tours covering western Bohemia's major sights. Tour "G–O" combines a trip to Lidice in northern Bohemia (☞ *below*) with a visit to the spa town of Karlovy Vary. The trip takes a full day and departs three times weekly. Prague departure points are at the Čedok offices at Na Příkopě 18 and Bílkova ulice 6, and the Panorama, Forum, and Hilton hotels.

VISITOR INFORMATION
Cheb (⊠ Nám. Krále Jiřího 33, ☎ 0166/434–385). **Karlovy Vary** (⊠ Ul. Dr. Bechera 21–23, ☎ 017/22281). **Mariánské Lázně** (⊠ Třebízského 2/101, ☎ 0165/2254; Infocentrum, ⊠ Hlavní 47, ☎ 0165/5330, 0165/5892, 0165/3757).

NORTHERN BOHEMIA

Northern Bohemia is a paradox: While much of it was despoiled over the past 40 years by rampant, postwar industrialization, here and there you can still find areas of great natural beauty. Particularly along the Labe (Elbe) River, rolling hills, perfect for walking, guard the country's northern frontiers with Germany and Poland. Hikers and campers head for the Krkonoše (Giant Mountains) on the Polish border (the only region that has good hotels); this range is not so giant, actually, though it is very pretty. As you move toward the west, the interest is more historical, in an area where the influence of Germany was felt in less pleasant ways than in the spas. You needn't drive too far to reach the Sudetenland, the German-speaking border area that was ceded to Hitler by the British and French in 1938. The landscape here is riddled with the tragic remains of the Nazi occupation of Czech lands from 1939 to 1945. Most drastically affected was Terezín, better known as the infamous concentration camp, Theresienstadt.

In the area around Terezín and Litoměřice, tourist amenities are practically nonexistent; if you do choose to stay overnight, you'll generally be able to find a room in a primitive inn or a rather unwelcoming modern hotel. In many parts of Bohemia the only real options for dining are the restaurants and cafés at the larger hotels and resorts.

Lidice

🔞 *18 km (11 mi) from Prague on Route 7 (the road to Ruzyně Airport). Head in the direction of Slaný. Turn off at the Lidice exit and follow the country road for 3 km (2 mi).*

The **Lidice museum and monument** are unforgettable sights. The empty field to the right, with a large cross at the bottom, is where the town of Lidice stood until 1942, when it was viciously razed by the Nazis in retribution for the assassination of German district leader Reinhard Heydrich.

The Lidice story really begins with the notorious Munich Pact of 1938, according to which the leaders of Great Britain and France permitted Hitler to occupy the largely German-speaking border regions of Czechoslovakia (the so-called Sudetenland). Less than a year later, in March 1939, Hitler used his forward position to occupy the whole of Bohemia and Moravia, making the area into a protectorate of the German Reich. To guard his new possessions, Hitler appointed ruthless Nazi Reinhard Heydrich as Reichsprotektor. Heydrich immediately implemented a campaign of terror against Jews and intellectuals while currying favor with average Czechs by raising rations and wages. As a result, the Czech army-in-exile, based in Great Britain, soon began planning Heydrich's assassination. In the spring of 1942 a small band of parachutists was flown in to carry out the task.

The assassination attempt took place just north of Prague on May 27, 1942, and Heydrich died from his injuries on June 4. Hitler immediately ordered the little mining town of Lidice, west of Prague, "removed from the face of the earth," since it was alleged (although later found untrue) that some of the assassins had been sheltered by villagers there.

On the night of June 9, a Gestapo unit entered Lidice, shot the entire adult male population (199 men), and sent the 196 women to the Ravensbruck concentration camp. The 103 children in the village were sent either to Germany to be "Aryanized" or to death camps. On June 10, the entire village was razed. The assassins and their accomplices were found a week later in the Orthodox Church of Sts. Cyril and Methodius in Prague's New Town, where they committed suicide after a shootout with Nazi militia.

The monument to these events is a sober place. The arcades are graphic in their depiction of the deportation and slaughter of the inhabitants. The museum itself is dedicated to those killed, with photographs of each person and a short description of his or her fate. You'll also find reproductions of the German documents ordering the village's destruction, including the Gestapo's chillingly bureaucratic reports on how the massacre was carried out and the peculiar problems encountered in Aryanizing the deported children. The exhibits highlighting the international response (a suburb of Chicago was even renamed for the town) are heartwarming. An absorbing 18-minute film in Czech (worthwhile even for non-Czech speakers) tells the Lidice story. ⊠ *Museum: ul. 10. června 1942.* ▣ *20 Kč.* ☉ *Daily 9–5.*

Lidice was rebuilt after the war on the initiative of a group of miners from Birmingham, England, who called their committee "Lidice Must Live." Between New Lidice and the museum is a rose garden with some 3,000 bushes sent from all over the world. The wooden cross in the field to the right of the museum, starkly decorated with barbed wire, marks the place in Old Lidice where the men were executed. Remains of brick walls are visible here, left over from the Gestapo's dynamite and bulldozer exercise. Still, Lidice is a sad town, not a place to linger.

Veltrusy Château and Gardens

⑫ *25 km (15 mi) north of Prague.*

The aristocratic retreat of Veltrusy contrasts vividly with the ordinariness of nearby Kralupy, an industrial town better left unexplored. The mansion's late-Baroque splendor lies hidden in a carefully laid out English park full of old and rare trees and scattered with 18th-century architectural follies. Until the end of World War II the château belonged to the Chotek family, whose most famous scion was Sophie Chotek, wife of Archduke Franz Ferdinand. Today the palace is given over to a museum showcasing the cosmopolitan lifestyle of the imperial aristocracy, displaying Japanese and Chinese porcelain, English chandeliers, and 16th-century tapestries from Brussels. ⊠ *Off Route 101.* ▣ *20 Kč.* ☉ *Apr. and Oct.–Dec., weekends 9–4; May–Aug., Tues.–Sun. 8–5; Sept., Tues.–Sun. 9–5.*

Nelahozeves

2½ km (1½ mi) on foot by marked paths from Veltrusy Château. By car: Turn right out of Veltrusy onto Route 101 and over the Vltava river; then make a sharp left back along the river to Nelahozeves.

Nelahozeves was the birthplace of Antonín Dvořák (1841–1904), the Czech Republic's greatest composer, who was known for weaving folk influences into Romantic music. Dvořák's pretty corner house on the main road (No. 12), with its tidy windows and arches, has a small **memorial museum.** In Dvořák's time, the house was an inn run by his parents, and it was here that he learned to play the violin. ⊠ *Across from train station.* ▣ *Free.* ☉ *Tues.–Thurs. and weekends 9–noon and 2–5.*

For those not enamored of the spirit of Dvořák's youth, the main attraction in town is the brooding Renaissance **château,** with its black-and-white sgraffito, once the residence of the powerful Lobkowitz family. The castle now houses an excellent collection of fine art, including paintings by Brueghel, Rubens, and Velázquez. ☎ *0205/22995.* 🖃 *80 Kč.* ☉ *June–Aug. Tues.–Sun. 9–5, Sept.–May Tues.–Sun. 9–4.*

Terezín

㉓ *36 km (22 mi) from Nelahozeves on Route 8.*

★ The old garrison town of Terezín gained notoriety under the Nazis as the nefarious Nazi concentration camp **Theresienstadt,** though the enormity of Theresienstadt's role in history is difficult to grasp at first. The Czechs have put up few signs to tell you what to see; the town's buildings, parks, and buses resemble those of any of a hundred other unremarkable places, built originally by the Austrians and now inhabited by Czechs. You could easily pass through it and never learn any of the town's dark secrets.

Part of the problem is that **Malá Pevnost** (Small Fortress), the actual prison and death camp, is 2 km (1 mi) south of Terezín. In the strange redbrick complex you'll see the prison more or less as it was when the Nazis left it in 1945. About 32,000 inmates came through the fortress, mostly POWs or political prisonors; those that did not die here were shipped off to other concentration camps. Above the entrance to the main courtyard stands the cynical motto ARBEIT MACHT FREI (Work will make you free). Take a walk around the various rooms, still housing a sad collection of rusty bed frames, sinks, and shower units. At the far end of the fortress, opposite the main entrance, is the special wing built by the Nazis when space became tight. The windowless cells are horrific; try going into one and closing the door—and then imagine being crammed in with 14 other people. In the center of the fortress is a museum and a room where films are shown. ☎ *0416/92225.* 🖃 *90 Kč.* ☉ *June–Aug. daily 8–5, Sept.–May daily 8–4.*

During World War II, Terezín served as a detention center for thousands of Jews and was used by the Nazis as an elaborate prop in a nefarious propaganda ploy. The large barracks buildings around town, once used in the 18th and 19th centuries to house Austrian soldiers, became living quarters for thousands of interred Jews. But in 1942, to placate international public opinion, the Nazis cynically decided to transform the town into a showcase camp—to prove to the world their "benevolent" intentions toward the Jews. To give the place the image of a spa town, the streets were given new names such as Lake Street, Bath Street, and Park Street. Numerous elderly Jews from Germany were taken in by the deception and paid large sums of money to come to the new "retirement village." Just before the International Red Cross inspected the town in early 1944, Nazi authorities began a beautification campaign: painted the buildings, set up stores, laid out a park with benches in front of the town hall, and arranged for concerts and sports. The map just off the main square shows the town's street plan as the locations of various buildings between 1941 and 1945. The Jews here were able, with great difficulty, to establish a cultural life of their own under the limited "self-government" that was set up in the camp. The inmates created a library and a theater, and lectures and musical performances were given on a regular basis.

Once it was clear that the war was lost, however, the Nazis dropped any pretense and quickly stepped up transport of Jews to the Auschwitz death camp in Poland. Transports were not new to the ghetto; to keep the population at around 30,000, a train was sent off every few months or so "to the east" to make room for incoming groups. In the fall of 1944, these transports were increased to one every few days. In all, some 87,000 Jews were murdered in this way, and another 35,000 died from starvation or disease. The town's horrific story is told in words and pictures at the **Ghetto Museum,** just off the central park in town. ⊠ *U dolní vodní brané 117,* ☎ *0416/782–168.* ⌨ *90 Kč.* ☉ *June– Aug. daily 8–5, Sept.–May daily 8–4.*

For all its history, Terezín is no place for an extended stay. Locals have chosen not to highlight the town's role during the Nazi era, and hence little provision has been made for visitors.

Litoměřice

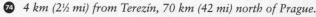 **74** *4 km (2½ mi) from Terezín, 70 km (42 mi) north of Prague.*

The decrepit state of the houses and streets belies this riverside town's medieval status as one of Bohemia's leading towns and a rival to Prague. It has remained largely untouched by modern development. Even today, although there are several factories in the surrounding area, much of central Litoměřice is like a living museum.

The best way to get a feel for Litoměřice is to start at the excellent **Městské muzeum** (City Museum), on the corner of the main square and Dlouhá ulice in the Old Town Hall building. The building itself deserves notice as one of the first examples of the Renaissance style in Bohemia, dating from 1537–1539. Unfortunately, the museum's exhibits are described in Czech (with written commentary in German available from the ticket seller); but even if you don't understand the language, you'll find this museum fascinating. Despite its position near the old border with Germany, Litoměřice was a Czech and Hussite stronghold, and one of the museum's treasures is the brightly colored, illuminated gradual, or hymn book, depicting Hus's burning at the stake in Constance. Note also the golden chalice nearby, the old symbol of the Hussites. Farther on you come to an exquisite Renaissance pulpit and altar decorated with painted stone reliefs. On the second floor the most interesting exhibit is from the Nazi era, when Litoměřice became a part of Sudeten Germany and a border town of the German Reich, providing soldiers for nearby Theresienstadt. There's a German commemorative dish marked with the words "*Wir sind frei*" (We are free), celebrating the Nazi annexation of the Sudetenland, and a yellow Star of David patch from Terezin. ⊠ *Mírové nám.* ⌨ *10 Kč.* ☉ *Tues.–Sun. 10–5.*

Mírové náměstí, the central square, has a range of architectural styles from Renaissance arcades to Baroque gables and a Gothic bell tower. The town's trademark is the chalice-shaped tower at No. 7, the **Chalice House,** built in the 1560s for an Utraquist patrician. The Utraquists were moderate Hussites who believed that laymen should receive wine as well as bread in the sacrament of Holy Communion. On the left-hand corner of the Old Town Hall is a replica of a small and unusual Roland statue (the original is in the museum) on a high stone pedestal. These statues, found throughout Bohemia, signify the town as a "royal free town," due all the usual privileges of such a distinction. This particular statue is unique because instead of showing the usual handsome knight, it depicts a hairy caveman wielding a club. Even in the 15th century, it seems, Czechs had a sense of humor.

A colorful, two-story Baroque house with a facade by the 18th-century Italian master builder Octavio Broggio houses the **Galerie výtvarného umění** (Art Gallery). Its strong collection of Czech art from the Gothic to the Baroque, including a 16th-century St. Anthony by

Lucas Cranach, makes it one of the country's best provincial art museums. The extensive collection of naive painting and wood sculpture across the courtyard is also worth a gander. ⊠ *Michalská 7.* ☜ *16 Kč.* ☯ *Mar.–Oct. Tues.–Sun. 10–6, Nov.–Apr. Tues.–Sun. 10–5.*

More of Broggio's work can be seen in the facade and interior of the **Kostel všechní svaté** (All Saints' Church), while the church's high tower keeps its 16th-century appearance. Broggio also remade the monastery **Church of St. Jacob** (⊠ Ul. Velká Dominikánská), whose exterior sorely needs restoration. His most beautiful work, though, is the small **Kostel svatého Václava** (St. Wenceslas Chapel), squeezed into an unwieldy square to the north of town on the cathedral hill and now an Orthodox church. Built in the late 17th century, it's in ripe Baroque style, filled with lush, curving forms.

Dóm svatého Štěpána (St. Stephen's Cathedral) is monumental but uninspired. Its one real treasure is a Lucas Cranach painting of St. Anthony—but unfortunately the cathedral door is often locked owing to a spate of thefts. Try ringing the bell at the bishop's residence around the corner; someone should let you in.

Lodging

$$ ⊞ **Roosevelt.** The Secession-style town bathhouse was converted into a small hotel in 1994, adding to this area's limited supply of decent accommodations. Rooms have modern, no-surprises, wood furniture. It's on a 19th-century residential street, a couple minutes' walk from the town center. ⊠ *Rooseveltova 18, 412 01,* ☎ *0416/733–596,* ℻ *0416/733–593. 30 rooms. Restaurant. AE, MC, V.*

OFF THE BEATEN PATH	**STŘEKOV CASTLE –** The Vltava River north of Litoměřice flows through a long, unspoiled, winding valley, packed in by surrounding hills. As you near heavily industrialized Ústí nad Labem, your eyes are suddenly assaulted by the towering mass of Střekov Castle, perched precariously on huge cliffs and rising abruptly above the right bank. The fortress was built in 1319 by King Johann of Luxembourg to control the rebellious nobles of northern Bohemia. During the 16th century it became the residence of Wenceslas of Lobkowicz, who rebuilt the castle in the Renaissance style. The lonely ruins have inspired many German artists and poets, including Richard Wagner, who came here on a moonlit night in the summer of 1842 and was inspired to write his romantic opera *Tannhäuser.* But if you arrive on a dark night, about the only classic that comes to mind is Mary Shelley's *Frankenstein.* Inside there is a small historical exhibit relating to the Lobkowicz family, which owns the castle, and on wine making. ⊠ *400 03, Ústí nad Labem,* ☎ *047/31553.* ☜ *30 Kč.* ☯ *Apr.–Oct., Tues.–Sun. 9–5.*

Mělník

🜨 *50 km (31 mi) south from Střekov, about 30 km (20 mi) north of Prague.*

Mělník is a lively town, known best perhaps as the source of the special Ludmila wine, the country's only decent wine not produced in southern Moravia. If coming by car, park on the small streets just off the pretty but hard-to-find main square (head in the direction of the towers to find it). The town's **zámek,** a smallish castle a few blocks from the main square, majestically guards the confluence of the Labe (Elbe) River with two arms of the Vltava. The view here is stunning, and the sunny hillsides are covered with vineyards. As the locals tell it, Emperor Charles IV was responsible for bringing wine production to the area. Having a good eye for favorable growing conditions, he encouraged vintners from Burgundy to come here and plant their vines.

The courtyard's three dominant architectural styles, reflecting alterations to the castle over the years, fairly jump out at you. On the north side, note the typical arcaded Renaissance balconies, decorated with sgraffiti; to the west, a Gothic tract is still easy to make out. The southern wing is clearly Baroque (although also decorated with arcades). Inside the castle at the back, you'll find a *vinárna* with mediocre food but excellent views overlooking the rivers. On the other side is a museum devoted to wine making and folk crafts. ⌖ *Museum 20 Kč.* ☉ *May and Sept.–Oct., Tues.–Sun. 10–5, June–Aug., Tues.–Sun. 10–6.*

Lodging

$$ ⊞ **Ludmila.** Though the hotel is an inconvenient 4 km (2½ mi) outside town, the pleasant English-speaking staff keeps the plain rooms impeccably clean, and the restaurant is better than many you will find in Mělník itself. Breakfast is included. ⊠ *Pražská 2639,* ☎ *0206/622-423. 79 rooms with bath or shower. Restaurant. AE, MC, V.*

Špindlerův Mlýn and the Krkonoše Range

⑦⑥ *About 150 km (90 mi) northeast of Prague.*

If you're not planning to go to the Tatras in Slovakia but nevertheless want a few days in the mountains, head for the **Krkonoše range**—the so-called Giant Mountains—near the Polish frontier. Here you'll find the most spectacular scenery in Bohemia, although it's something of an exaggeration to call these rolling hills "giant" (the highest point is 5,256 ft). Not only is the scenery beautiful, but the local architecture is refreshingly rural after all the towns and cities; the steep-roofed timber houses, painted in warm colors, look just right pitched against sunlit pinewoods or snowy pastures. **Špindlerův Mlýn** is attractively placed astride the rippling Labe (Elbe) River, here in its formative stages; it's a good town to use as a hiking base.

Dining and Lodging

$$ ✕⊞ **Savoy.** This Tudor-style chalet, over a century old, has a com-
★ fortable, fresh-air feeling—its cozy reception area is more typical of a family inn than a large hotel. The rooms, although on the smallish side and sparsely furnished, are immaculately clean. The restaurant serves fine traditional Czech dishes in a mellow setting. Breakfast is included. ⊠ *54351 Špindlerův Mlýn,* ☎ *0438/93521,* ⅏ *0438/93641. 50 rooms with bath or shower. Restaurant, bar. AE, DC, MC, V.*

$$$ ⊞ **Montana.** This "modern" 1970s hotel is ill suited to the rustic setting, and the rooms are quite spartan (though they have TVs); but the service is attentive, and the staff can offer good advice for planning walks around this popular resort town. Breakfast is included. ⊠ *54351 Špindlerův Mlýn,* ☎ *0438/93551,* ⅏ *0438/93556. 70 rooms. Restaurant, bar, café. AE, DC, MC, V.*

$ ⊞ **Nechanicky.** At this private, older hotel near the bridge in the center of town, the management is working to improve the structure's somewhat tarnished appearance. Rooms are bright, clean, and well proportioned; modern furniture was installed in 1997. Front-facing rooms enjoy an excellent view overlooking the town. Breakfast is included. ⊠ *54351 Špindlerův Mlýn,* ☎ *0438/93263,* ⅏ *0438/93315. 16 rooms. Restaurant, wine bar. MC, V.*

Outdoor Activities and Sports

Janské Lázně (another spa), **Pec pod Sněžkou,** and **Špindlerův Mlýn** are the principal resorts of the area, the last the most sophisticated in its accommodations and facilities. To get out and experience the mountains, a good trip is to take a bus from Špindlerův Mlýn via Janské Lázně to Pec pod Sněžkou—a deceptively long journey by road of around 50 km (31 mi). From there, embark on a two-stage chairlift to the top of **Sněžka** (the area's highest peak) and then walk along a ridge overlooking the Polish countryside, eventually dropping into deep, silent pinewoods and returning to Špindlerův Mlýn. If you walk over the mountain instead of driving around it, the return trip is just 11 km (7 mi)—a comfortable walk of about three to four hours. The path actually takes you into Poland at one point; you won't need a visa, but take your passport along just in case.

The source of the Labe also springs from the heights near the Polish border. From the town of **Harrachov,** walkers can reach it by a marked trail. The distance is about 10 km (6 mi). From Špindlerův Mlýn, a beautiful but sometimes steep trail follows the Labe Valley up to the source near Labská Bouda. Allow about three hours for this walk and take good shoes and a map.

Northern Bohemia A to Z

Arriving and Departing

Prague is the gateway to northern Bohemia (☞ Arriving and Departing *in* Prague A to Z, *above*). There are good bus connections from the capital, including links to Špindlerův Mlýn and Pec pod Sněžkou. If you are driving, the E55 leads directly into the Czech Republic from Dresden and winds down to Prague via the old spa town of Teplice. The main road between Prague and the Krkonoše range is the E65.

Getting Around

Motorists driving through northern Bohemia are rewarded with a particularly picturesque drive on Route 261 along the Labe (Elbe) River on the way to Střekov Castle near Ústí nad Labem (☞ *above*). Train connections in the north are spotty at best; bus is the preferred means of travel. Regular train service connects Prague with Ústí nad Labem, but to reach other towns you'll have to take slower local trains or the bus.

Contacts and Resources

EMERGENCIES
Police (☎ 158). **Ambulance** (☎ 155).

GUIDED TOURS
Čedok (☎ 02/2419–7111) offers several specialized tours covering the major sights in northern Bohemia. Tour "G-O" combines a trip to Lidice with a visit to the spa town of Karlovy Vary. The trip takes a full day and departs three times weekly. Prague departure points are the Čedok offices at Na příkopě 18 and Bílkova ulice 6, and the Panorama, Forum, and Hilton hotels.

Several private companies also offer trips to Lidice and Terezín (Theresienstadt) in northern Bohemia. For the latter, try **Wittmann Tours** (☎ 02/2481–2325 or 02/251–235). Bus tours leave Prague from Pařížska 28 daily at 10 AM, returning around 5 PM, with a fare of 950 Kč.

VISITOR INFORMATION
Northern Bohemia's main tourist center is the **Litoměřice Infocentrum** (✉ Mírové nám., ☎ 0416/2136). It's open daily April through September, and open Monday through Saturday October through March.

SOUTHERN MORAVIA

Lacking the turbulent history of Bohemia to the west or the stark natural beauty of Slovakia farther east, Moravia, the easternmost province of the Czech Republic, is frequently overlooked as a travel destination. Still, although Moravia's cities do not match Prague for beauty, and its gentle mountains hardly compare with Slovakia's strikingly rugged Tatras, Moravia's colorful villages and rolling hills certainly do merit a few days of exploration. Come here for the good wine, the folk music, the friendly faces, and the languid pace.

Moravia has a bit of both Bohemia and Slovakia. It is closer culturally to Bohemia: The two were bound together as one kingdom for some 1,000 years, following the fall of the Great Moravian Empire (Moravia's last stab at Slavonic statehood) at the end of the 10th century. All the historical and cultural movements that swept through Bohemia, including the religious turbulence and long period of Austrian Hapsburg rule, were felt strongly here as well. But, oddly, in many ways Moravia resembles Slovakia more than its cousin to the west. The colors come alive here in a way that is seldom seen in Bohemia: The subdued earthen pinks and yellows in towns such as Telč and Mikulov suddenly erupt into the fiery reds, greens, and purples of the traditional folk costumes farther to the east. Folk music, all but gone in Bohemia, is still very much alive in Moravia.

Southern Moravia's highlands define the "border" with Bohemia. Here, towns such as Jihlava and Telč are virtually indistinguishable from their Bohemian counterparts. The handsome squares, with their long arcades, bear witness to the prosperity enjoyed by this part of Europe several hundred years ago. In the south along the frontier with Austria—until recently a heavily fortified expanse of the Iron Curtain—life is just starting to return to normal, as the towns and people on both sides of the border seek to reestablish ties going back centuries. One of their common traditions is wine making; and Znojmo, Mikulov, and Valtice are to the Czech Republic what the small towns of the *Weinviertel* on the other side of the border are to Austria.

Don't expect gastronomic delights in Moravia. The food—especially outside Brno—is reasonably priced, but the choices are usually limited to roast pork, sauerkraut, and dumplings or fried pork and french fries. Moravia's hotels are only now beginning to recover from 40 years of state ownership. In many larger towns, private rooms are preferred. In mountainous areas inquire locally about the possibility of staying in a *chata* (cabin). These are abundant and often a pleasant alternative to the faceless modern hotels. Many lack modern amenities, though, so be prepared to rough it.

Numbers in the margin correspond to numbers on the Moravia map.

Jihlava

⑦ *100 km (62 mi) from Prague.*

On the Moravian side of the rolling highlands that mark the border between Bohemia and Moravia, and just off the main highway from Prague to Brno, lies the old mining town of Jihlava, a good place to begin an exploration of Moravia. If the silver mines here had held out just a few more years, the townspeople claim, Jihlava could have become a great European city. Indeed, during the 13th century, the town's enormous main square, **Náměstí Míru** (Square of Peace), was one of the largest in Europe, rivaled in size only by those in Cologne and Kraków. But history can be cruel: The mines went bust during the 17th

Moravia

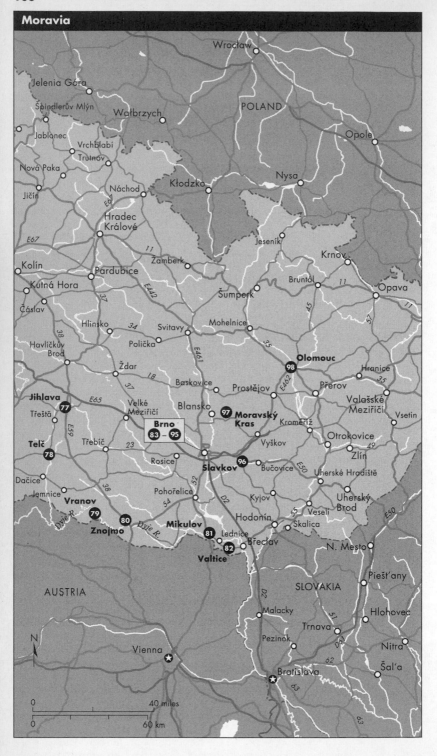

century, and the square today bears witness only to the town's once oversize ambitions.

There are several interesting churches clustered on or around Náměstí Míru. The **Kostel svatého Ignáce** (St. Ignace Church) in the northwest corner of the square is relatively young for Jihlava, built at the end of the 17th century, but look inside to see a rare Gothic crucifix, created during the 13th century for the early Bohemian king Přemysl Otakar II. The town's most striking structure is the Gothic **Kostel svatého Jakuba** (St. James Church) to the east of the main square, down the Farní ulice. The church's exterior, with its uneven towers, is Gothic; the interior is Baroque; and the font is a masterpiece of the Renaissance style, dating from 1599. Note also the Baroque Chapel of the Holy Virgin, sandwiched between two late-Gothic chapels, with its oversize 14th-century pietà. Two other Gothic churches worth a look are the **Kostel svatého Kříža** (Church of the Holy Cross), north of the main square, and the **Minoritský kostel** (Minorite Church), to the west of the square. Just next to the latter is the last remaining of the original five medieval town gates.

Dining and Lodging

$$ ✕⌂ **Zlatá Hvězda.** Centrally located on the main square, this reconstructed old hotel in a beautiful Renaissance house is comfortable and surprisingly elegant. In keeping with the building, rooms are modestly harmonious, with wood ceilings and down comforters. You're a short walk from Jihlava's restaurants and shops, though the on-site café and wine bar are among the best in town. The restaurant's menu is heavy with beef and pork; the Moravian goulash is a good choice. Breakfast is included. ⊠ *Nám. Míru 32, 58601,* ☎ *066/29421,* ⅎ̄Ⅺ *066/29426. 17 rooms, 1 apartment. Restaurant, bar, café. AE, MC, V.*

Telč

★ **⑦⑧** *30 km (19 mi) to the south from Jihlava, via Route 406.*

The little town of Telč has an even more impressive main square than that of Jihlava—but what strikes the eye most here is not its size but the unified style of the buildings. On the lowest levels are beautifully vaulted Gothic halls, just above are Renaissance floors and facades, and all of it is crowned with rich Baroque gables. The square is so perfect you feel more as if you've entered a film set rather than a living town. The town allegedly owes its architectural unity to Zacharias of Neuhaus, for whom the main square is now named: **Náměstí Zachariase z Hradce.** During the 16th century, so the story goes, the wealthy Zacharias had the castle—originally a small fort overlooking the Bohemian border with Hungary—rebuilt in the Renaissance style. But the contrast between the new castle and the town's rather ordinary buildings was so great that Zacharias had the square rebuilt to match the castle's splendor. Luckily for architecture fans, the Neuhaus dynasty died out shortly thereafter, and succeeding nobles had little interest in refashioning the town according to the vogue of the day.

It's best to approach Telč's main square on foot. If you've come by car, park outside the main walls on the side south of town and walk through the **Great Gate,** part of the original fortifications dating to the 13th century. As you approach on Palackého ulice, the square unfolds nobly in front of you, with the castle at the northern end and beautiful houses, bathed in pastel reds and golds, gracing both sides. If you're a fan of Renaissance reliefs, note the black-and-white sgraffito corner house at No. 15, which dates from the middle of the 16th century. The house at No. 61, across from the Černý Orel Hotel, is also noteworthy for its fine detail.

The **château** forms a complex with the former **Jesuit college** and Kostel Svatého Jakuba (St. James Church). The château, originally Gothic, was built during the 14th century, when Telč first gained importance as a town bordering the old Hungarian kingdom. It was given its current Renaissance appearance by Italian masters between 1553 and 1568. In season, you can tour the castle and admire the rich Renaissance interiors. Given the reputation of nobles for lively banquets lasting for hours, the sgraffito relief in the dining room depicting gluttony (in addition to the six other deadly sins) seems odd indeed. Other interesting rooms with sgraffiti include the Treasury, the Armory, and the Blue and Gold chambers. A curious counterpoint to all this Renaissance splendor is the castle's permanent exhibit of paintings by leading Czech modernist Jan Zrzavý. ☎ 066/962–943. ☞ 100 Kč. ⊙ May–Sept. Tues.–Sun. 9–5.

<table>
<tr><td>NEED A
BREAK?</td><td>If you're looking for sweets, you can get good homemade cakes at a little private café, **Cukrárna u Matěje**, at Na baště 2.</td></tr>
</table>

The tiny Palackého ulice leading off the main square takes you to the 160-ft Romanesque tower of the **Kostel svatého Ducha** (Church of the Holy Ghost). This is the oldest standing structure in Telč, dating from the first quarter of the 13th century. The interior, however, is a stylistic hodgepodge, as it was given a late-Gothic makeover and then, due to fire damage, refashioned through the 17th century.

Dining and Lodging

$$ ✕▦ **Černý Orel.** Here you'll get a very rare treat: an older, refined hotel
★   that puts modern amenities in a traditional setting. The public areas mix architectural details such as vaulted ceilings with plush, contemporary armchairs, and the basic but inviting rooms are well balanced and comfortably furnished. The hotel, with its Baroque facade, is a perfect foil to the handsome main square outside; ask for a room overlooking it. Even if you don't stay here, take a meal at the excellent hotel restaurant; it's a great spot for straightforward beef or pork dishes. Breakfast is included. ☒ Nám. Zachariase z Hradce 7, 588 56, ☎ FAX 066/ 962–220. 30 rooms, 25 with bath. Restaurant, bar. AE, DC, MC, V.

$$ ▦ **Telč.** This is a slightly upscale alternative to the Černý Orel, even though the bright, polished appearance of the reception area doesn't quite carry over to the functional but pleasant rooms. (Some rooms open onto a courtyard.) The location, in a corner of the main square, is ideal. Breakfast is included. ☒ Na Můstku 37, 588 56, ☎ 066/962– 109, FAX 066/96887. 10 rooms. Restaurant. AE, MC, V.

<table>
<tr><td>OFF THE
BEATEN PATH</td><td>**MORAVIAN WINE COUNTRY –** Going south of Telč takes you into the heart of Moravian wine country. Follow the signs first to the picturesque little town of Dačice, then along Route 408 through Jemnice, and finally to the chain of recreation areas along the man-made lakes of the Dyje (Thaya) River. Turn right at Šumná and follow the signs to the little town of Vranov, nestled snugly between hill and river.</td></tr>
</table>

Vranov

㊼ 55 km (34 mi) southeast of Telč.

As a swimming and boating center for southern Moravia, Vranov would be a good place to stop in its own right. But what makes the town
★   truly noteworthy is the enormous and colorful **Vranovský Hrad** (Vranov Castle), rising 200 ft from a rocky promontory. For nearly 1,000 years, this was the border between Bohemia and Austria and therefore

required a fortress of these dimensions. You'll either love or hate this proud mongrel of a building as its multicolored Gothic, Renaissance, and Baroque elements vie for your attention. In the foreground, the solemn Renaissance tower rises over some Gothic fortifications. The structure is shored up on its left by a golden Baroque church, with a beautiful pink-and-white Baroque dome to the back. Each unit is spectacular, but the overall effect of so many styles mixed together is jarring.

Take your eyes off the castle's motley exterior and tour its mostly Baroque (and more harmonious) interior. The most impressive room is certainly the 43-ft-high elliptical **Hall of Ancestors,** the work of the Viennese master Johann Bernhard Fischer von Erlach (builder of the Clam-Gallas Palace in Prague and the Hofburg in Vienna). Look inside the **castle church** as well. The rotunda, altar, and organ were designed by Fischer von Erlach at the end of the 17th century. ☎ *0624/296–215.* 🖭 *100 Kč.* ⊘ *Apr.–May, weekends 9–6; June–Oct., Tues.–Sun. 9–6.*

Znojmo

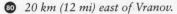 *20 km (12 mi) east of Vranov.*

Znojmo enjoys a long history as an important frontier town between Austria and Bohemia and is the cultural center of southern Moravia. The Přemyslide prince Břetislav I had already built a fortress here in the 11th century, and in 1226 Znojmo became the first Moravian town (ahead of Brno) to receive town rights from the king. But, alas, modern Znojmo, with its many factories and high-rises, isn't really a place for lingering. Plan on spending no more than a few hours walking through the Old Town and visiting the remaining fortifications and churches that stand between the New Town and the river.

Znojmo's tumbledown **main square,** now usually filled with peddlers selling everything from butter to cheap souvenirs, isn't what it used to be when it was crowned by Moravia's most beautiful **town hall.** Unfortunately, the 14th-century building was destroyed in 1945, just before the end of the war, and all that remains of the original structure is the 250-ft Gothic tower you see at the top of the square—looking admittedly forlorn astride the modern department store that now occupies the space.

Follow the run-down Zelinářská ulice, which trails from behind the town hall's tower to the southwest in the direction of the Old Town and the river. The grand, Gothic **Kostel svatého Mikuláše** (St. Nicholas Church), on the tiny Staré Město (Old Town square), dates from 1338, but its neo-Gothic tower was not added until the 19th century. If you can get into the church (it's often locked), look for the impressive sacraments house, which was built around 1500 in late-Gothic style.

The curious, two-layered **Kostel svatého Václava** (St. Wenceslas Church), built at the end of the 15th century, stands just behind St. Nicholas. The upper level of this tiny white church is dedicated to St. Anne, the lower level to St. Martin. Along the medieval ramparts that separate the town from the river stands the original 11th-century **Rotunda svatej Kateřiny** (St. Catherine's Rotunda), still in remarkably good condition. Step inside to see a rare cycle of restored frescoes from 1134 depicting various members of the early Přemyslide dynasty.

The **Jihomoravské Muzeum** (South Moravian Museum), just across the way in the former castle, houses an extensive collection of artifacts from the area, dating from the Stone Age to the present. Unless you're a big fan of museums, though, there's little point in making a special visit to this one; and unless you can read Czech, you'll have difficulty making sense of the collection. ⊠ *Přemyslovců ul. 6,* ☎ *0625/224–961.* 🎫 *10 Kč.* ☉ *Tues.–Sun. 9–5; closed weekends Nov.–Apr..*

Dining and Lodging

Znojmo's other claims to fame have endeared the town to the hearts (and palates) of Czechs everywhere. The first is the Znojmo gherkin, first cultivated in the 16th century. You'll find this tasty accompaniment to meals at restaurants all over the country. Just look for the *Znojmo* prefix—as in *Znojemský guláš,* a tasty stew spiced with pickles. Znojmo's other treat is wine. As the center of the Moravian wine industry, this is an excellent place to pick up a few bottles of your favorite grape. But don't expect to learn much about a wine from its label: Oddly, you'll search in vain for the vintage or even the name of the vineyard on labels, and about the only information you can gather is the name of the grape and the city in which the wine was bottled. The best towns to look for, in addition to Znojmo, are Mikulov and Valtice. Some of the best varieties of grapes are Rulandské and Vavřinecké (for red) and Ryslink and Müller Thurgau (for white).

$$ 🏨 **Pension Inka.** Rather than stay in a hotel, you might consider staying in this tiny, family-run pension not far from the center of town. The facilities are modest, but the rooms are bright and well kept. The kitchen is available for the use of guests. ⊠ *Jarošova ul. 27, 669 02,* ☎ *0624/224059. 3 rooms. No credit cards.*

$ 🏨 **Pension Havelka.** Though it is tiny, the charms of this family-run
★   pension's tastefully folksy furnishings and ideal location in the center of Old Town can only be topped by its friendly, obliging management. They'll gladly set you up at one of the family's two other pensions if this one happens to be full. Breakfast is included. ⊠ *Nám. Mikulásské 3, 669 02,* ☎ 🖷 *0624/220–138. 2 rooms with shared bath. Restaurant, café. No credit cards.*

Mikulov

⑧⑴ *54 km (34 mi) east of Znojmo.*

Mikulov is known today chiefly as the border crossing on the Vienna–Brno road. If you want to leave the Czech Republic for a day to stock up on Western supplies, this is the place to do it. The nearest Austrian town, Poysdorf, is just 7 km (4½ mi) away.

In many ways, Mikulov is the quintessential Moravian town. The soft pastel pinks and yellows of its buildings look almost mystical in the afternoon sunshine against the greens of the surrounding hills. But aside from the busy wine industry, not much goes on here. The main sight is the striking **château,** which dominates the tiny main square and surrounding area. The château started out as the Gothic residence of the noble Liechtenstein family in the 13th century and was given its current Baroque appearance some 400 years later. The most famous resident was Napoléon, who stayed here in 1805 while negotiating peace terms with the Austrians after winning the battle of Austerlitz (Slavkov, near Brno). Sixty-one years later, Bismarck used the castle to sign a peace treaty with Austria. The castle's darkest days came at the end of World War II, when retreating Nazi SS units set the town on fire. In season, take a walk from the main square up around the side of the castle into the **Museum výroby vína** (museum of wine making). The most remarkable exhibit is a wine cask made in 1643, with a capacity of more than 22,000 gallons. This was used for collecting the vintner's obligatory tithe. 🎫 *20 Kč.* ☉ *Apr.–May and Sept.–Oct., Tues.–Sun. 9–4, June–Aug. Tues.–Sun. 9–5.*

If you happen to arrive at grape-harvesting time in October, head for one of the many private *sklípeks* (wine cellars) built into the hills surrounding the town. The tradition in these parts is simply to knock on the door; more often than not, you'll be invited in by the owner to taste a recent vintage. If you visit in early September, try to hit Mikulov's renowned wine harvest festival, which is celebrated with traditional music, folk dancing, and much quaffing of local Riesling.

OFF THE
BEATEN PATH

PAVLOV – This little mountain town, a short drive or bus ride from Mikulov or Valtice, has several wine cellars built into the hills and makes for a good refreshment stop. At **U Venuše** (✉ Česká 27, ☎ 0625/515–230), be sure to sample some of the owner's wine, which comes from his private *sklípek* across the lake in Strachotín. After dinner, stroll around the village, perched romantically overlooking a man-made lake.

Dining and Lodging

$$$
★

✕🖫 **Rohatý Krokodýl.** This is a prim, nicely renovated hotel on a quaint street in the Old Town; the rooms are small but squeaky clean. The standards and facilities are the best in Mikulov, particularly the ground-floor restaurant, which serves a typical but delicately prepared selection of traditional Czech dishes—the tender *svíčová knedlíky* (sirloin with cream sauce and dumplings) is particularly good. Breakfast is included. ✉ *Husova 8, 692 00,* ☎ *0625/2692,* 🖷 *0625/3695. 13 rooms. Restaurant. MC, V.*

Shopping

The secret of Moravian wine is only now beginning to extend beyond the country's borders. A vintage bottle from one of the smaller but still excellent vineyards in Bzenec, Velké Pavlovice, or Hodonín would be appreciated by any wine connoisseur.

Valtice

㉒ *9 km (5½ mi) to the east of Mikulov along Route 414.*

This small town would be wholly nondescript except for the fascinating **château,** just off the main street, built by the Liechtenstein family in the 19th century. Next to the town's dusty streets, with their dilapidated postwar storefronts, the castle looks positively grand, a glorious if slightly overexuberant holdover from a long-lost era. There are some 365 windows, painted ceilings, and much ornate woodwork. But best of all is the lure of spending the night—a rare practice in the Czech Republic. The left wing of the castle has been converted into the Hubertus Hotel (☞ Dining and Lodging, *below*). A small museum on the ground floor demonstrates how the town and castle have changed over the years according to aristocratic and political whim. The Valtice winery is behind and to the right of the castle, but it is not open to the public. ☎ *0627/352–423.* 🖾 *60 Kč.* ☉ *Apr.–Oct., Tues.–Sun. 9–4.*

OFF THE
BEATEN PATH

HLOHOVEC – An abandoned summer palace lies just to the north of Valtice, not far from the tiny town of Hlohovec. In winter you can walk or skate across the adjoining Hlohovec Pond to the golden-yellow building; otherwise follow the tiny lane to Hlohovec, just off Route 422 outside Valtice. Emblazoned across the front of the palace is the German slogan ZWISCHEN ÖSTERREICH UND MÄHREN (Between Austria and Moravia), another reminder of the proximity of the border and the long history that these areas share. Consult Greenways maps for scenic horseback and automobile tours of the area.

Dining and Lodging

$$ ★ ✕▥ **Hubertus.** This comfortable hotel is not hard to find. Just look for the only palace in town; the hotel is on the left-hand side. Though the rooms are neither palatial nor furnished in period style, they are nevertheless inviting, with high ceilings and fresh flowers. The restaurant, with garden terrace, has a strong selection of fish, including carp, trout, and pike. Book ahead in summer, as the hotel is popular with Austrians who like to slip across the border for an impromptu holiday. Breakfast is included. ✉ *Zámek, 69142,* ☎ *0627/352–537,* ▥ *0627/94538. 62 rooms, 13 rooms with bath. Restaurant, bar. AE, MC, V.*

Lednice

7 km (4½ mi) northwest of Valtice.

The Liechtenstein family peppered the countryside with neoclassical temples and follies, such as Lednice, throughout the 19th century as a display of their wealth and taste. The extravagantly neo-Gothic **château** at Lednice, though obviously in disrepair, has a sumptuous interior; particularly resplendent are the blue-and-green silk wall coverings embossed with the Moravian eagle in the formal dining room and bay-windowed drawing room. The grounds, now a pleasant park open to the public, have a 200-ft minaret and a massive greenhouse filled with exotic flora. ✉ *Zámek,* ☎ *0627/352–537.* 🎫 *100 Kč.* ☉ *Apr.–May and Sept.–Oct., Tues.–Sun. 9–4, June–Aug. Tues.–Sun. 9–6.*

Dolní Věstonice

18 km (11 mi) northwest from Lednice.

The tiny town of Dolní Věstonice is perched alongside another giant artificial lake. Although the town has little going for it today, some 20,000 to 30,000 years ago the area was home to a thriving prehistoric settlement, judging from ivory and graves found here by archaeologists in 1950. Some of the world's earliest ceramics were also discovered, among them a curvaceous figurine of ash and clay that has become known as the Venus of Věstonice. The original is kept in Brno, but you can see replicas, real mammoth bones, and much else of archaeological interest at the excellent **museum** in the center of town along the main road. 🎫 *20 Kč.* ☉ *Apr.–Sept., Tues.–Sun. 8–noon and 1–4.*

Outdoor Activities and Sports

For walking enthusiasts, the **Pavlovské vrchy** (Pavlov Hills), where the settlement remains were found, offer a challenging climb. Start out by ascending the **Děvín Peak** (1,800 ft), just south of Dolní Věstonice. A series of paths then follows the ridges the 10 km (6 mi) to Mikulov. Trails are clearly marked.

Southern Moravia A to Z

Arriving and Departing

BY BUS

Bus connections from Prague to Jihlava are excellent and inexpensive and, in lieu of a car, the best way to get to Moravia. Southern Moravian destinations are also well served from Bratislava and other points in Slovakia.

BY CAR

Southern Moravia is within easy driving distance of Prague, Bratislava, and eastern Slovakia. Jihlava, the starting point for touring the region, is 124 km (78 mi) southeast of Prague along the excellent D1 freeway.

From here, it's easy to take route E65 to Brno, or the E59, which goes down to Vranov and Znojmo. Southern Moravia is also easily reached by car from Austria; there are major border crossings at Háté (below Znojmo) and Mikulov.

Getting Around

The easiest way to explore this region is by car. In general, buses run sporadically, especially on weekends. If you're planning a day trip or two, Mikulov may be the best base. Not only is it the most lively southern Moravian town, but Lednice, Pavlov, and Valtice are each less than 20 km (12 mi) away, and there is regular bus service from Mikulov to all three towns. There are also bike paths to Lednice and Valtice; you can get detailed maps and bike rental information at Pálava Tours (☞ Visitor Information, *below*).

Contacts and Resources

EMERGENCIES

Police (☎ 158). **Ambulance** (☎ 155). **Breakdowns** (☎ 154 or 123 [in some areas 0123]).

VISITOR INFORMATION

Jihlava (✉ Masarykova nm., ☎ 066/731–1926). **Mikulov** (Pálava Tours; ✉ Náměstí 32, ☎ 0625/3572). **Valtice** (Greenways Center; ✉ Zámek 2, ☎ 0627/94635).

BRNO

Moravia's cultural and geographic center, Brno (pronounced *burr*-no) grew rich in the 19th century and has a different feel than any other Czech or Slovak city. Beginning with a textile industry imported from Germany, Holland, and Belgium, Brno became the industrial heartland of the Austro-Hungarian Empire during the 18th and 19th centuries—hence its nickname Manchester of Moravia. You'll search in vain for an extensive old town; you'll also find few of the traditional arcaded storefronts that typify other historic Czech towns. What you will see instead are fine examples of Empire and neoclassical styles, their formal, geometric facades more in keeping with the conservative tastes of the 19th-century middle class.

In the early 20th century, the city became home to the best young architects working in the cubist and constructivist styles. And experimentation wasn't restricted to architecture. Leoš Janáček, an important composer of the early modern period, also lived and worked in Brno, as did Austrian novelist Robert Musil. The modern tradition continues even today, and the city is considered to have the best theater and performing arts in Moravia, as well as a small but thriving café scene.

It's best to avoid Brno at trade-fair time (the biggest are in early spring and early autumn), when hotel and restaurant facilities are strained. If the hotels are booked, Čedok or the accommodation services at the town hall or main station will help you find a room.

Numbers in the text correspond to numbers in the margin and on the Brno map.

Exploring Brno

A Good Walk

Begin the walking tour at the triangular **Náměstí Svobody** ⑬ in the heart of the commercial district. Then walk up the main Masarykova ulice toward the train station and make a right through the little arcade at No. 6 to see the animated Gothic portal of the **Stará radnice** ⑭. Leave

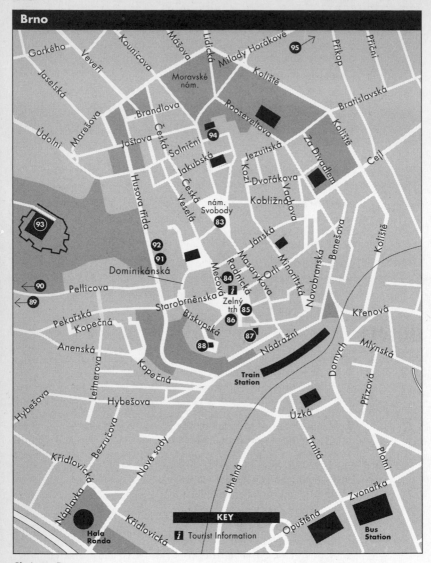

Brno

Chrám sv. Petra a
Pavla, **88**
Dietrichštejnský
Palác, **86**
Kostel Nalezení
svatého Kříže, **87**
Místodržitelský
palác, **94**
Náměstí Svobody, **83**
Pražkův palác, **92**
Špilberk hrad, **93**
Stará radnice, **84**
Starobrnénský
Klášter, **90**
Uměleckoprůmyslové
muzeum, **91**
Villa Tugendhat, **95**
Výstaviště, **89**
Zelný trh, **85**

the town hall by Pilgram's portal and turn right into the old **Zelný trh** ⑧⑤. On the far side of the market, dominating the square, stands the severe Renaissance **Dietrichštejnský Palác** ⑧⑥ at No. 8. From the garden, walk down the stairs to the Baroque **Kostel Nalezení svatého Kříže** ⑧⑦.

Towering above the church and market is the **Chrám sv. Petra a Pavla** ⑧⑧, Brno's main church and a fixture of the skyline. The best way to get to the cathedral is to return to Zelný trh (via the little street off the Kapucínské náměstí), make a left at the market, and walk up the narrow Petrská ulice, which begins just to the right of the Dietrichštejnský Palác. Before leaving the cathedral area, stroll around the pretty park and grounds. Continue walking down the continuation of Petrská ulice to Biskupská ulice. Turn left at the Starobrněnská ulice and cross the busy Husova třída onto Pekařská ulice. At the end of the street are the Mendlovo náměstí and a monastery, **Starobrnénský Klášter** ⑨⓪.

Continue the tour along the busy and somewhat downtrodden Úvoz ulice. Take the first right and climb the stairs to the calmer residential street of Pellicova. If there's a unique beauty to Brno, it's in neighborhoods such as this one, with its attractive houses, each in a different architectural style. Many houses incorporate cubist and geometric elements of the early modern period (1920s and '30s). Begin the ascent to **Špilberk hrad** ⑨③. There is no direct path to the castle; just follow your instincts (or a detailed map) upward, and you'll get there. From the top, look over to the west at the gleaming Art Deco pavilions of the Brno **Výstaviště** ⑧⑨ in the distance. The earliest buildings were completed in 1928, in time to hold the first cultural exhibition to celebrate the 10th anniversary of the Czech state. The grounds are now the site of annual trade fairs. After taking in the view, stroll back down one of the windy paths to Husova třída and have a look in two of Czech Republic's finest museums: the **Uměleckoprůmyslové museum** ⑨① and Brno's modern art museum, the **Pražkův palác** ⑨②. For old art culled from Moravian churches and estates make sure to pay a visit to the **Místodržitelský palác** ⑨④. Also try to visit Ludwig Mies van der Rohe's **Villa Tugendhat** ⑨⑤, the city's most famous work of architecture. The house is a bit off the beaten track so you will need to travel there by car, taxi, or tram.

TIMING

The tour should take two to three hours at a leisurely pace. Allow an extra hour to explore Špilberk hrad. Museum enthusiasts could easily spend a half day or more browsing the city's many collections.

Sights to See

⑧⑧ **Chrám sv. Petra a Pavla** (Cathedral of Sts. Peter and Paul). Sts. Peter and Paul is one church that probably looks better from a distance. The interior, a blend of Baroque and Gothic, is light and tasteful but hardly mind-blowing. Still, the slim neo-Gothic twin spires, added in this century to give the cathedral more of its original Gothic dignity, are a nice touch. Don't be surprised if you hear the noon bells ringing from the cathedral at 11 o'clock. The practice dates from the Thirty Years' War, when Swedish troops were massing for an attack outside the town walls. Brno's resistance had been fierce, and the Swedish commander decreed that he would give up the fight if the town could not be taken by noon the following day. The bell ringer caught wind of the decision and the next morning, just as the Swedes were preparing a final assault, rang the noon bells—an hour early. The ruse worked, and the Swedes decamped. Ever since, the midday bells have been rung an hour early as a show of gratitude. While the city escaped, the cathedral caught a Swedish cannon shot and suffered severe damage in the resulting fire. ✉ *Petrov at Petrská.* ✆ *Free.* ☉ *Daylight hrs; closed during services.*

86 Dietrichštejnský Palác (Dietrichstein Palace). The building was once home to Cardinal Count Franz von Dietrichstein, who led the Catholic Counter-Reformation in Moravia following the Battle of White Mountain in 1620. Today the palace and the adjoining **Biskupský dvůr** (Bishop's Court) house the **Moravské muzeum** (Moravian Museum), with its mundane exhibits of local history, artifacts, and wildlife. To enter the Bishop's Court, walk through the little gate to the left of the Dietrichstein Palace and then through the lovely Renaissance garden. Note the arcades, the work of 16th-century Italian craftsmen. ⊠ *Zelný trh 8,* ☎ *05/4232–1205.* ▨ *20 Kč.* ۞ *Tues.–Sun. 9–5 .*

87 Kostel Nalezení svatého Kříže (Church of the Holy Cross). Formerly part of the Capuchin Monastery, this church combines a Baroque silhouette with a rather stark facade. If you've ever wondered what a mummy looks like without its bandages, then enter the door to the monastery's *hrobka* (crypt). In the basement are the mummified remains of some 200 nobles and monks from the late 17th and the 18th century, ingeniously preserved by a natural system of air circulating through vents and chimneys. The best-known mummy is Colonel František Trenck, commander of the brutal Pandour regiment of the Austrian army, who, at least in legend, spent several years in the dungeons of Špilberk hrad before finding his final rest here in 1749. Even in death the hapless colonel has not found peace—someone made off with his head several years ago. A note of caution about the crypt: The graphic displays may frighten small children, so ask at the admission desk for the small brochure (10 Kč) with pictures that preview what's to follow. ⊠ *Kapucínské nám.* ▨ *20 Kč.* ۞ *Tues.–Sat. 9–11:45 and 2–4:30, Sun. 11–11:45 and 2–4:30.*

94 Místodržitelský palác (Místodržitelský Palace). Moravia had much stronger artistic ties to Austria than Bohemia did, as can be seen in the impressive collection of Gothic, Baroque, and 19th-century painting and sculpture found in this splendid Baroque palace. Particularly fetching are Austrian painter Franz Anton Maulbertsch's ethereal rococo pageants. ⊠ *Moravské náměstí 1a,* ☎ *05/4232–1100.* ▨ *50 Kč.* ۞ *Tues.–Sun. 10–6.*

83 Náměstí Svobody (Freedom Square). The square itself is architecturally undistinguished, but here and along the adjoining streets you'll find the city's best stores and shopping opportunities. Anyone who has been to Vienna might experience a feeling of déjà vu here, as many of the buildings were built by 19th century Austrian architects. Especially noteworthy is the stolid Klein Palace (Náměstí Svobody 10), built by Theophil Hansen and Ludwig Forster, both prominent for their work on Vienna's Ringstrasse.

92 Pražkův palác (Pražkův Palace). Second to the Veletržní palác in Prague, this handsome, 19th-century neo-Renaissance building houses the largest collection of native modern and contemporary art in the Czech Republic. While works by many of the same artists represented in Prague can be seen here, the emphasis is on Moravian artists, who tended to prefer rural themes—their avant-garde concoctions have a certain folksy flavor. ⊠ *Husova Třída 18,* ☎ *05/4232–1250.* ▨ *50 Kč.* ۞ *Tues.–Sun. 10–6.*

93 Špilberk hrad (Špilberk Castle). Once among the most feared places in the Hapsburg Empire, this fortress-cum-prison still broods over the town from behind its menacing walls. Špilberk's advantageous location was no secret to the early kings, who moved here during the 13th century from neighboring Petrov Hill. Successive rulers gradually converted the old castle into a virtually impregnable fortress. Indeed, it successfully withstood the onslaughts of Hussites, Swedes, and Prussians over the centuries; only Napoléon, in 1809, succeeded in occupying the fortress. But the castle is best known for its gruesome history as a prison for the Austro-Hungarian monarchy and, later, for the Nazis in World War II. Although tales of torture during the Austrian period are probably legendary (judicial torture had been prohibited prior to the first prisoners' arrival in 1784), conditions for the hardest offenders were hellish: shackled day and night in dark, dank catacombs and fed only bread and water. The most brutal corrections ended with the death of the harsh, rationalist ruler Joseph II in 1790. The casemates (passages within the walls of the castle) have been turned into an exhibition of the late-18th-century prison and their Nazi-era use as an air-raid shelter. Parents should note that young children can easily become lost in the spooky, dim casemates. More dangerous, the low parapets atop the castle walls near the restaurant provide little security for overcurious climbers. At press time, there were plans for more displays on the German occupation during World War II. In summertime, temporary historical exhibitions are installed in the west wing. ☎ 05/4221–4145. 🎫 Casemates 20 Kč. ☉ Oct.–May., Tues.–Sun. 9–4:45, June–Sept., Tues.–Sun. 9–6.

NEED A BREAK?	After a long walk and a good climb, what could be better than one of the best beers you'll ever have? The **Stopkova pivnice,** at Česka 5, will set you up with one, or a soft drink. If you're hungry, try the house goulash, a tangy mixture of sausage, beef, rice, egg, and dumpling. For something more substantial, head for the restaurant on the second floor.

84 **Stará radnice** (Old Town Hall). The oldest secular building in Brno has an important Gothic portal. The door is the work of Anton Pilgram, architect of Vienna's St. Stephen's Cathedral; it was completed in 1510, but the building itself is about 200 years older. Look above the door to see a badly bent pinnacle that looks as if it wilted in the afternoon sun. This isn't the work of vandals but was apparently done by Pilgram himself out of revenge against the town. According to legend, Pilgram had been promised an excellent commission for his portal, but when he finished, the mayor and city councillors reneged on their offer. So angry was Pilgram at the duplicity that he purposely bent the pinnacle and left it poised, fittingly, over the statue of justice.

Just inside the door are the remains of two other famous Brno legends, the **Brno Dragon** and the **wagon wheel.** The dragon—a female alligator, to be anatomically correct—apparently turned up at the town walls one day in the 17th century and began eating children and livestock. A gatekeeper came up with the novel idea of filling a sack with limestone and placing it inside a freshly slaughtered goat. The dragon devoured the goat, swallowing the limestone as well, and went to quench its thirst at a nearby river. The water mixed with the limestone, bursting the dragon's stomach (the scars on the preserved dragon's stomach are still clearly visible). The story of the wagon wheel, on the other hand, concerns a bet placed some 400 years ago that a young wheelwright, Jiří Birk, couldn't chop down a tree, fashion the wood into a wheel, and roll it from his home at Lednice (33 mi/53 km away) to the town walls of Brno—all between sunup and sundown. The wheel stands as a lasting tribute to his achievement (the townspeople, however, became convinced that Jiří had enlisted the help of the devil to win the bet, so they stopped frequenting his workshop; poor Jiří died penniless).

No longer the seat of the town government, the Old Town Hall holds exhibitions and performances. To find out what's on, look for a sign on the door of the exhibition room. The view from the top of the tower is one of the best in Brno, but the climb (five flights) is strenuous. What catches the eye is not so much any single building—although the cathedral does look spectacular—but the combination of old and new that defines modern Brno. In the distance, next to the crooked roofs and Baroque onion domes, a power plant looks startlingly out of place. ⊠ *Radnická ul. 8.* 🎟 *Tower 10 Kč.* 🕙 *Apr.–Sept., daily 9–5.*

⑨⓪ Starobrněnský Klášter (Monastery of Staré Brno). The uninspiring location seems to confirm the adage that genius can flourish anywhere, for in the 19th century this was home to Gregor Mendel, the shy monk who became the father of modern genetic research. If you recall from high-school science, it was Mendel's experiments with crossing pea and bean plants, from which he figured out dominant and recessive traits, that led to the first formulations of the laws of heredity. A small statue to his memory can be found in the garden behind the monastery. ⊠ *Mendlovo nám. 1.* 🕙 *Sept.–May, weekdays 8–5; June–Aug., daily 9–6.*

⑨① Uměleckoprůmyslové muzeum (Museum of Decorative Arts). Housed in one of city's finest neo-Renaissance buildings, this is doubtless the best arts-and-crafts museum in the Czech Republic, with an assemblage of artifacts far more extensive than the truncated collection in Prague's decorative arts museum. The collection includes Gothic work, Art Nouveau and Secessionist pieces, and an excellent, comprehensive overview of Bohemian and Moravian glasswork. Keep an eye out for the elegant furniture from Josef Hoffmann's Wiener Werkstätte (Vienna Workshop); a jagged, candy-color table by Milan Knížák is a striking example of contemporary work. Explanatory texts in English are available. ⊠ *Husova Třída 14,* 🕾 *05/4232–1250.* 🎟 *50 Kč.* 🕙 *Tues.–Sun. 10–6.*

⑨⑤ Villa Tugendhat. Designed by Ludwig Mies van der Rohe and completed in 1930, this austere, white Bauhaus villa counts among the most important works of the modern period. The emphasis here is on function and the use of geometric forms, but you be the judge as to whether the house fits the neighborhood. The Tugendhat family fled before the Nazis, and their original furnishings vanished during the war or the house's subsequent heavy-handed remodeling. Replicas of Mies's cool, functional designs have been installed in the downstairs living area. Some of the original exotic wood paneling and an eye-stopping onyx screen remain in place. The best way to get there is to take a taxi or Tram 3, 5, or 11 to the Dětská nemocnice stop and then walk up the unmarked Černopolní Street for 10 minutes or so. ⊠ *Černopolní 45,* 🕾 *05/4521–2118.* 🎟 *80 Kč.* 🕙 *Wed.–Sun. 10–5.*

⑧⑨ Výstaviště (exhibition grounds). The earliest buildings were completed in 1928, in time to hold the first cultural exhibition to celebrate the 10th anniversary of the Czech state. The Brno-born modern architect Adolf Loos designed the interior of the 19th-century mansion on the grounds; his cool functionality blends with luxurious marble-clad walls and friezes. Bohuslav Fuchs—another modernist linked to Brno—created the City of Brno Pavilion, an airy network of vaulted glass halls. The enormous circular Pavilion Z dates from 1959. The grounds are now the site of annual trade fairs and may be closed between fairs. ⊠ *Výstaviště 1,* 🕾 *05/4115–3101. From main train station, take Tram 1 or 18 west to the 5th stop.*

⑧⑤ Zelný trh (Cabbage Market). The only place where Brno begins to look like a typical Czech town, the Cabbage Market is immediately recognizable, not just for the many stands from which farmers still sell vegetables but also for the unique **Parnassus Fountain** that adorns its center. This Baroque outburst (you either love it or hate it) couldn't be more out of place amid the formal elegance of most of the buildings on the square. But when Johann Bernhard Fischer von Erlach created the fountain in the late 17th century, it was important for a striving town like Brno to display its understanding of the classics and of ancient Greece. Thus, Hercules slays a three-headed dragon, while Amphitrite awaits the arrival of her lover—all incongruously surrounded by farmers hawking turnips and onions.

OFF THE **MORAVSKÝ KRUMLOV** – Admirers of Art Nouveau meister Alfons Mucha
BEATEN PATH may want to make a short detour off the main highway linking Mikulov and Brno. The town museum is the unlikely home of one of Mucha's most celebrated works, his 20-canvas *Slav Epic*. This enormous work, which tells the story of the emergence of the Slav nation, was not well received when it was completed in 1928; painters at the time were more interested in imitating modern movements and considered Mucha's representational art to be old-fashioned. *Museum:* ⊠ *Zámecká 1,* ☎ *0621/2789-2225.* ☉ *Apr.–Oct., Tues.–Sun. 9–noon and 1–4.*

Dining and Lodging

$$$$ ✕ **U Královny Elišky.** Few restaurants can match this 14th-century wine cellar for historical atmosphere. Local specialties including wild game and fish are served in rooms with names like "The Musketeer" and "The Napoleon." In summer you can sit in the garden and order roast suckling pig or lamb while watching fencers in historical dress cross swords. ⊠ *Mendlovo náměstí 1,* ☎ *4321–2578. MC, V.*

$$$ ✕ **Černý Medvěd.** Undoubtedly Brno's most comfortable dining room, it has plush red upholstery and, weather permitting, a fire crackling on the open hearth. Wild game is the key ingredient in a traditionally Czech menu. ⊠ *Jakubské nám. 1,* ☎ *05/4221–4548. MC, V.*

$$ ✕ **Baroko vinárna.** This 17th-century wine cellar in a Minorite monastery offers excellent cooking in a fun, if touristy, setting. Try the roast beef Slavkov (cooked with onions and red wine and served with potatoes or sweet chestnuts), named for the site of Napoléon's triumph not far from Brno. "Mystery of Magdalene" is a potato pancake stuffed with pork, liver, mushrooms, and presumably anything else the cook could get his hands on. ⊠ *Orlí 17,* ☎ *05/4221–1344. No credit cards. No lunch.*

$$ ✕ **Maccaroni.** Delicious pastas and pizzas (a welcome alternative to the heavy local fare) are served here in an unhurried setting. Take a taxi, walk the 15 minutes from the center, or ride Tram 5 or 6 to the stop called Nemocnice u sv. Anny. ⊠ *Pekařská 80,* ☎ *05/4321–4528. MC.*

$$ ✕ **Modrá Hvězda.** Liberal opening hours (from 11:30 AM to 11 PM) and a convenient location just to the west of Náměstí Svobody make this cheery restaurant a good choice for a quick lunch or off-hours snack. House specialties include roast duck with dumplings and sauerkraut. ⊠ *Starobrněnská 20,* ☎ *05/4221–5292. AE, DC, MC, V.*

$$ ✕ **Zeman.** This contemporary recreation of a 1920s coffeehouse (the original was razed by the Communists to make way for a theater) is extremely stylish. Everything from the light fixtures to the furniture is faithfully copied from the original interior. The lofty ceilings provide pleasant, lilting acoustics, and the food isn't bad either: Czech with a dash of French, like a pepper steak with fries. ⊠ *Jezuitská 5,* ☎ *05/ 4221–8095. No credit cards.*

$$$$ ⊡ **Grand.** Though not really grand, this hotel, built in 1870 and thoroughly remodeled in 1988, is certainly comfortable and the best in Brno.

High standards are maintained through the hotel's association with an Austrian chain. The reception and public areas are clean and modern; service is attentive; and the rooms, though small, are well appointed, with coffered ceilings, leather sofas, and minibars. Ask for a room at the back, overlooking the town, as the hotel is on a busy street opposite the railroad station. ⊠ *Benešova 18/20, 657 83,* ☎ *05/4232–1287,* ℻ *05/4221–0345. 113 rooms. 3 restaurants, minibars, casino, nightclub. AE, DC, MC, V.*

$$$$ ☷ **Holiday Inn.** Opened in 1993, this handsome representative of the American chain has become the hotel of choice for business travelers in town for a trade fair. It has all you'd expect for the price, including a well-trained, multilingual staff. There are two classes of rooms, standard and executive; the main difference is that standard rooms lack air-conditioning. Executive rooms also have some extra perks, such as a modem line and trouser press. The location, at the exhibition grounds about a mile from the city center, is inconvenient for those who don't have a car. ⊠ *Křížkovského 20, 603 00,* ☎ *05/4312–2111,* ℻ *05/4115–9081. 205 rooms. Restaurant, café, sauna, meeting rooms. AE, DC, MC, V.*

$$$ ☷ **Pegas.** This little inn makes an excellent choice given its reasonable
★ price and central location. The plain rooms are snug and clean, with wood paneling and down comforters, and the staff is helpful and friendly (and speaks English). Even if you don't stay here, be sure to have a meal and home-brewed beer at the house microbrewery. ⊠ *Jakubská 4, 602 00 Brno,* ☎ *05/4221–0104,* ℻ *05/4221–1232. 15 rooms. Restaurant. AE, DC, MC, V.*

$$$ ☷ **Slavia.** The century-old Slavia, just off the main Česká ulice, was thoroughly renovated in 1987; the grace of the fin-de-siècle facade and stucco-ceilinged lobby are now oddly paired with utilitarian (though relatively spacious) rooms. The café, with adjacent terrace, is a good place to enjoy a cool drink on a warm afternoon. ⊠ *Solniční 15/17, 622 16,* ☎ *05/4221–5080,* ℻ *05/4221–1769. 81 rooms with bath or shower. Restaurant, café, minibars, free parking. AE, DC, MC, V.*

$$$ ☷ **Slovan.** For anyone wanting to get the full flavor of Brno functionalism, this hotel just outside the Old Town is an option. Rooms are predictably plain, verging on the ascetic. The hotel restaurant and the Bugatti bar, which strives for a '20s avant-garde elegance, offer some consolation. One drawback is that the hotel lies on a busy street with a noisy tram line. ⊠ *Lidická 23, 65989,* ☎ *05/4132–1207,* ℻ *05/4121–1137. 100 rooms with bath or shower. Restaurant, bar, night club, meeting rooms. AE, MC, V.*

$$ ☷ **U svatého Jakuba.** Little seems to have changed here for several decades, including the behavior of the staff (who operate on the premise that the customer may always be right—but should also be grateful for any services rendered). It used to be classed as a "moderate" hotel, but the cheaper establishments of the central city have vanished into the precapitalist past, leaving this one to keep up tradition by offering basic accommodation at reasonable rates. ⊠ *Jakubské nám. 6, 602 00,* ☎ *05/4221–0795,* ℻ *05/4221–0797. 37 rooms, 10 with bath. Restaurant, bar. MC, V.*

Nightlife and the Arts

Brno is renowned throughout the Czech Republic for its theater and performing arts. There are a couple of main venues for jacket-and-tie cultural events. The **Mahen Theater** (⊠ Rooseveltova 21, ☎ 05/4232–1285) is the principal space for drama; opera and ballet productions are held next door at the modern **Janáček Theater** (⊠ Rooseveltova, ☎ 05/4232–1285). Both are slightly northwest of the center of town, just off Rooseveltova ulica. Check the schedules at the theater or pick up a copy of *KAM*, Brno's monthly bulletin of cultural events. Buy tickets directly at the theater box office 30 minutes before showtime. One of the country's best-known fringe theater companies, **Divadlo Husa na provázku** (Goose on a String Theater), has its home where Petrská Street enters Zelný trh (⊠ Zelný trh 9, ☎ 05/4221–1630).

For more sophisticated entertainment than a conversational evening at the local *pivnice* or *vinárna,* head for the **casinos** at the **Grand Hotel** (☞ Dining and Lodging, *above*) and the **International Hotel** (⊠ Husova 16, ☎ 05/4212–2111); the tables usually stay open until 3 AM or 4 AM. Both hotels also have bars that serve drinks until very late. The "casinos" on Náměstí Svobody are glorified video gambling parlors with a mixed clientele of clueless tourists and all-too-streetwise locals.

Klub Alterna (⊠ Kounicova 48, a few blocks north of the city center, ☎ 05/4121–2091) puts on good Czech jazz and folk performers.

Shopping

Moravia produces very attractive folk pottery, painted with bright red, orange, and yellow flower patterns. You can find these products in stores and hotel gift shops throughout the region. For more sophisticated artwork, including paintings, stop by **Dílo** (⊠ Kobližná 4, ☎ 05/4221–4930). **Merkuria** (⊠ Kobližná 10, ☎ 05/4121–2781) stocks a beautiful selection of crystal and porcelain from Karlovy Vary. You can buy English paperbacks, including a huge range of travel guidebooks (should Central America suddenly seem more alluring than Central Europe), at **Zahraniční literatura** (⊠ Nám. Svobody 18). For rare books, art monographs, old prints, and a great selection of avant-garde 1920s periodicals, stop by **Antikvariát Alfa** (⊠ Jánská 11, 05/4221–1947).

Brno A to Z

Arriving and Departing

BY BUS

Bus connections from Prague to Brno are excellent and inexpensive and, in lieu of a car, the best way to get here. Buses also run daily between Brno's main bus station (Ustřední autobusové nádraží Brno Zvonařka; ⊠ Zvonařka 1, ☎ 05/4321–7733) and Vienna's Wien-Mitte station, leaving Brno at 7:30 AM and 5:30 PM. Round-trip tickets cost about $27.

BY CAR

Brno, within easy driving distance of Prague, Bratislava, and eastern Slovakia, is 196 km (122 mi) from Prague and 121 km (75 mi) from Bratislava. The main route from Prague is the E65; take the D2 from Bratislava.

BY PLANE

The private carrier **Air Ostrava** links Prague with Brno and Ostrava (⊠ Prague, ☎ 02/2403–2731 or 02/0601–533003 mobile phone). The distances between the cities are short, however, and it's ultimately cheaper and quicker to drive or take a bus. During the two large Brno trade fairs, in April and September, foreign carriers also connect the city with Frankfurt and Vienna. These flights are usually crowded with businesspeople, so you'll have to book well in advance.

BY TRAIN

Several trains daily make the three-hour run from Prague to Brno's station, **Hlavní nádraží** (⊠ Nádraží 1, ☎ 05/4221–4803). Most use Prague's **Hlavní nádraží** (main station), but some depart from and arrive at the suburban station Holešovice nádraží (Holešovice station) or at Masarykovo nádraží (Masaryk station), on Hybernská ulice in the city center. Trains leaving Prague for Budapest and Bucharest (and some Vienna-bound trains) also frequently stop in Brno (check timetables to be sure).

Getting Around

BY BUS OR TRAM

Trams are the best way to get around the city; tickets cost about 12 Kč, and are available at newsstands. The Brno bus station (Ústřední autobusové nádraží Brno Zvonařka) is a 10-minute walk behind the train station. To find it, simply go to the train station and follow the signs to ČSAD. These buses head out to peripheral parts of the city.

Contacts and Resources

B&B RESERVATION AGENCIES

If you've arrived at Brno's main station and are stuck for a room, try the accommodations service on the far left of the main hall, open Monday through Saturday from 8 AM to 8 PM, and 8 AM to 10 AM on Sunday; you can place a sports bet there, too.

EMERGENCIES

Police (☎ 158). **Ambulance** (☎ 155). **Breakdowns** (☎ 154 or 123 [in some areas 0123]).

LATE-NIGHT PHARMACIES

Brno has a 24-hour pharmacy at Kobližná ulice 7.

TRAVEL AGENCIES

CKM (youth travel bureau; ✉ Česká 11, ☎ 05/4221–2677).

VISITOR INFORMATION

Čedok (✉ Nádražní 10/12, ☎ 05/4232–1267); **Kulturní a informační Centrum** (✉ Radnická 8 [Old Town Hall], ☎ 05/4221–1090). For further information, *see* Visitor Information *in* Czech Republic A to Z, *below.*

NORTHERN MORAVIA

Just north of Brno is the Moravský Kras, a beautiful wilderness area with an extensive network of caves, caverns, and underground rivers. Many caves are open to the public, and some tours even incorporate underground boat rides. Farther to the north lies Moravia's "second capital," Olomouc, an industrial but still charming city with a long history as a center of learning. Paradoxically, despite its location far from the Austrian border, Olomouc remained a bastion of support for the Hapsburgs and the empire at a time when cries for independence could be heard throughout Bohemia and Moravia. In 1848, when revolts everywhere threatened to bring the monarchy down, the Hapsburg family fled here for safety. Franz Joseph, who went on to personify the stodgy permanence of the empire, was even crowned here as Austrian emperor that same year.

The green foothills of the Beskydy range begin east of Olomouc, perfect for a day or two of walking in the mountains. Farther to the east you'll find the spectacular peaks of the Tatras, a good jumping-off point for exploring eastern Slovakia or southern Poland.

Slavkov

96 *20 km (12 mi) east of Brno.*

Slavkov, better known as **Austerlitz,** was the scene of one of the great battlefields of European history, where the armies of Napoléon met and defeated the combined forces of Austrian emperor Franz II and Czar Alexander I in 1805. If you happen to have a copy of *War and Peace* handy, you will find no better account of it anywhere. Scattered about the rolling agricultural landscapes are a museum, a garden, and the memorial chapel of the impressive **Cairn of Peace**. In the town of Slavkov itself, the Baroque **château** houses more memorabilia about the battle; it's well worth visiting. ✉ *Slavkov U Brna*, ☎ *05/4422– 1685*. ⊙ *Apr.–Oct., Tues.–Sun. 9–4.*

Moravský Kras

👋 ⑨⑦ *30 km (19 mi) north of Brno.*

If it's scenic rather than military tourism you want, take a short trip north from Brno up the Svitava Valley and into the Moravský Kras (Moravian Karst), an area of limestone formations, underground sta- lactite caves, rivers, and tunnels. The most interesting part is near **Blansko** and includes the **Kateřinská jeskyně** (Catherine Cave), **Punkevní jeskyně** (Punkva Cave), and the celebrated **Macocha Abyss**, the deep- est drop of the karst (more than 400 ft). Several **caves** can be visited: Eight kilometers (5 miles) from the outskirts of Blansko is the Skalní Mlýn Hotel and nearby Catherine Cave, set amid thickly forested ravines. Try the 90-minute Punkva tour, which includes a boat trip along an underground river. On this tour, the *Eco-Express* train links the Skalní Mlýn Hotel to the Punkva Cave, from where a funicular (*lanovka*) climbs to the lip of Macocha Abyss. Only the Punkva Cave is normally open year-round; check with the information office for up-to-date information (☞ Visitor Information *in* Northern Moravia A to Z, *below*). It's al- ways advisable to arrive at least an hour before scheduled closing time in order to catch the day's last tour. ✉ *Catherine Cave 25 Kč, Punkva Cave (including underground boat ride) 70 Kč.* ⊙ *Catherine Cave May– Sept., daily 8:20–4, Oct. 8:20–2; usually closed Nov.–Apr. Punkva Cave June–Sept., daily 8:20–3:50, Oct.–May, daily 8:20–2.* ✉ *Fu- nicular 40 Kč.* ⊙ *Daily early Oct.–Apr. 8–5 (mid-Oct.–Mar. opera- tion depends on the number of visitors).*

Hiking

Underground or on the surface, the walking is excellent in the karst, and if you miss one of the few buses running between the town of Blan- sko and the cave region, you may have to hoof it anyway. Try to ob- tain a map in Brno or from the Moravian Karst information office (☞ Visitor Information *in* Northern Moravia A to Z, *below*) in the set- tlement of Skalní Mlýn. Look out for Devil's Bridge (*Čertův most*), a natural bridge high over the road just past the entrance to Catherine Cave; or follow the yellow-marked path from the cave for another cou- ple of miles to the Macocha Abyss. Before setting out, check with the information office or at the bus station for current bus schedules; for much of the year the last bus from Skalní Mlýn back to Blansko leaves at around 3 PM.

Olomouc

★ ⑨⑧ *77 km (48 mi) northeast of Brno.*

Olomouc is a paradox—so far from Austria yet so supportive of the empire. The Hapsburgs always felt at home here, even when they were being violently opposed by Czech nationalists and Protestants through- out Bohemia and much of Moravia. During the revolutions of 1848, when the middle class from all over the Austro-Hungarian Empire seemed ready to boot the Hapsburgs out of their palace, the royal family fled to Olomouc.

Despite being overshadowed by Brno, Olomouc, with its proud square and prim 19th-century buildings, still retains something of a provincial imperial capital, not unlike similarly sized cities in Austria. The Old Town, situated on a slight rise over a tributary of the river Morava, luckily managed to escape damage during the July 1997 floods that inundated a huge swath of Moravia, Poland, and eastern Germany. The focal point here is the triangular **Horní náměstí** (Upper Square), marked at its center by the bright and almost flippantly colored Renaissance **radnice** (town hall) with its 220-ft tower. The tower was begun in the late 14th century and given its current appearance in 1443; the astronomical clock on the outside was built in 1422, but its inner mechanisms and modern mosaic decorations date from immediately after World War II. Be sure to look inside at the beautiful Renaissance stairway. There's also a large Gothic banquet room in the main building, with scenes from the city's history, and a late-Gothic chapel. Tours of the tower and chapel are given a few times daily for a 10 Kč fee; contact the tourist office (☞ Visitor Information *in* Northern Moravia A to Z, *below*), which is in the same building.

The eccentric **Morový sloup** (Trinity Column), in the northwest corner of the square, is the largest of its kind in the Czech Republic and houses a tiny chapel. Four Baroque fountains, depicting Hercules (1687), Caesar (1724), Neptune (1695), and Jupiter (1707), dot the main square and the adjacent **Dolní náměstí** (Lower Square) to the south.

NEED A BREAK?

The wooden paneling and floral upholstery in the **Café Mahler** recall the taste of the 1880s, when Gustav Mahler briefly lived just around the corner while working as a conductor at the theater on the other side of the Upper Square. It makes a good spot for ice cream, cake, or coffee. ☒ *Horní nám. 11.*

Just north of the Horní náměstí, along the small Jana Opletalova ulice, stands the **Chrám svatého Mořice** (Church of St. Maurice), the town's best Gothic building. Construction began in 1412, but a fire 40 years later badly damaged the structure; its current fierce, gray exterior dates from the middle of the 16th century. The Baroque organ inside, the largest in the Czech Republic, originally contained 2,311 pipes until it was repaired and expanded in the 1960s to more than 10,000 pipes.

The interior of triple-domed **Kostel svatého Michala** (St. Michael's Church) casts a dramatic spell. The frescoes; the high, airy central dome; and the shades of rose, beige, and gray trompe-l'oeil marble on walls and arches blend to a harmonious, if dimly glimpsed, whole. The decoration followed a 1709 fire, which came 30 years after the original construction. Architect and builder are not known, but it's surmised they are the same team that put up the Church of the Annunciation on Svatý Kopeček (Holy Hill), a popular Catholic pilgrimage site just outside Olomouc. ☒ *Žerotínovo nám., 1 block uphill from the Upper Square along Školní ul.*

Between the main square and the **Dóm svatého Václava** (Cathedral of St. Wenceslas) lies a peaceful neighborhood given over to huge buildings, mostly belonging either to the university or the archbishopric. As it stands today, the cathedral is just another example of the overbearing neo-Gothic enthusiasm of the late 19th century, having passed through just about every other architectural fad since its true Gothic days. ☒ *Václavské náměstí.* ☉ *Daily 9–6.*

Next to the cathedral is the entrance to the **Palác Přemyslovců** (Přemyslide Palace), now a museum, where you can see early 16th-century wall paintings decorating the Gothic cloisters and, upstairs, a wonderful series of two- and three-arched Romanesque windows. This part of the building was used as a schoolroom some 700 years ago, and you can still make out drawings of animals engraved on the walls by early vandals. You can get an oddly phrased English-language pamphlet at the entrance to help you around the building. ⊠ *Dómská ul.* ☜ *20 Kč.* ☉ *Apr.–Oct., Tues.–Sun. 9–12:30 and 1–5.*

The **Děkanství** (deacon's house), opposite the cathedral, now part of Palacký University, has two unusual claims to fame. Here, in 1767, the young musical prodigy Wolfgang Amadeus Mozart, age 11, spent six weeks recovering from a mild attack of chicken pox. The 16-year-old King Wenceslas III suffered a much worse fate here in 1306, when he was murdered, putting an end to the Přemyslide dynasty. ⊠ *Václavské náměstí.*

Dining and Lodging

$$$ 🍽 **Flora.** Don't expect luxury at this 1960s cookie-cutter high-rise, about a 15-minute walk from the town square. To its credit, the staff is attentive (English is spoken), and the pleasant, if anonymous, rooms are certainly adequate for a short stay. ⊠ *Krapkova ul. 34, 779 00,* ☎ *068/412–021,* 𝔽𝔸𝕏 *068/412–221. 150 rooms, 4 suites, all with bath or shower. Restaurant. AE, DC, MC, V.*

$$ 🍽 **Národní Dům.** Built in 1885 and a block from the main square, this hotel is able to evoke a little of Olomouc's 19th-century history. The handsome building recalls the era's industriousness, as does the large, gracious café on the main floor. Standards have slipped in the intervening years; you can count on a clean room, but expect a measure of mild shabbiness. ⊠ *Třída 8. května 21, 772 00,* ☎ *068/522–4806,* 𝔽𝔸𝕏 *068/522–4808. 55 rooms, 45 with bath or shower, 2 suites. Restaurant, café, snack bar. AE, DC, MC, V.*

$$ 🍽 **U Dómu sv. Václava.** This pleasant place represents a new class of Czech hotel and pension; you'll find modernized fittings installed in the old house. This pension's six small suites all have kitchenettes. It's just down the street from the sleepy Václavské náměstí. ⊠ *Dómská 4, 772 00,* ☎ *068/522–0502,* 𝔽𝔸𝕏 *068/522–0501. 6 rooms. Kitchenettes. MC, V.*

Outdoor Activities and Sports

The gentle, forested peaks of the **Beskydy Mountains** are popular destinations for hill walking, berry picking, and cross-country skiing; several resorts have ski lifts as well. The year-round resort town of Rožnov pod Radhoštěm has bus connections to all major cities in the country. Stay the night at one of the modest but comfortable mountain chalets in the area. You'll find a good one, the **Chata Soláň,** along the road between Rožnov and Velké Karlovice (⊠ Velké Karlovice756 06, ☎ 0657/94365). The latter settlement lies at the end of a rail line from Vsetín. But be sure to take along a good map; some roads may be closed during the winter.

Northern Moravia A to Z

Arriving and Departing

Brno is the gateway to northern Moravia, whether by bus, car, plane, or train (☞ Arriving and Departing *in* Brno A to Z, *above*).

Getting Around

Comparatively good trains run frequently on the Prague–Olomouc–Vsetín main lines. In any event, you'll sometimes have to resort to the bus to reach the smaller, out-of-the-way places throughout northern Moravia (☞ Getting Around *in* the Czech Republic A to Z, *below*). Smaller roads and rail lines in this region were hit particularly hard by the floods of 1997, and some mountain rail lines may never be repaired. At this point, however, you shouldn't encounter serious obstacles.

Contacts and Resources

EMERGENCIES
Police (☎ 158). **Ambulance** (☎ 155). **Breakdowns** (☎ 154 or 123 [in some areas 0123]).

VISITOR INFORMATION
Olomouc Information Center (✉ Horní nám. [Town Hall], ☎ 068/551–3385). **Moravian Karst Ústřední informační služba SJMK** (Central Information Service of the Moravian Karst Caves; ✉ Across from the Skalní Mlýn Hotel, Skalní Mlýn, Blansko 678 25, ☎ 0506/55379).

THE CZECH REPUBLIC A TO Z

Arriving and Departing

By Bus

Several bus companies run direct services between London and Prague. Two with almost daily service are Kingscourt Express (☎ 0181/673–7500 in London) and Eurolines (☎ 0171/730–3466 in London), both operating out of London's Victoria Coach Station. The trip takes 20–24 hours and costs around $75 one-way.

By Car

The most convenient ferry ports for Prague are Hoek van Holland and Ostend. To reach Prague from either ferry port, drive first to Cologne (Köln) and then through either Dresden or Frankfurt.

By Plane

FROM NORTH AMERICA
Nearly all international flights to the Czech Republic fly into Prague's **Ruzyně Airport** (☎ 02/2011–1111), about 20 km (12 mi) northwest of downtown. The airport is small and easy to negotiate.

ČSA (Czech Airlines; ☎ 212/765–6022 in New York; 02/2010–4310 in Prague), the Czech and Slovak national carrier, maintains regular direct flights to Prague from New York and twice-weekly flights from Montréal.

Several other international airlines, including Delta, Lufthansa, SAS, KLM, and Air France, have good connections from cities in the United States and Canada to European bases and from there to Prague. **British Airways** (☎ 800/247–9297) flies daily via London; and **Swissair** (☎ 718/995–8400), daily via Zurich.

From New York, a nonstop flight to Prague takes eight hours; with a stopover, the journey will take at least 10 hours. From Montreal nonstop it is 7½ hours; from Los Angeles with a stopover, 14–16 hours.

FROM THE UNITED KINGDOM
British Airways (☎ 0171/897–4000) has daily nonstop service to Prague from London (with connections to major British cities); **ČSA** (☎ 0171/255–1898) flies daily nonstop from London. The flight takes around two hours.

By Train

There are no direct trains from London. You can take a direct train from Paris via Frankfurt to Prague (daily) or from Berlin via Dresden to Prague (six times a day). Vienna is a good starting point for Prague, Brno, or Bratislava. There are three trains a day from Vienna's Südbahnhof (South Station) via Brno (five hours).

Getting Around

Navigation is relatively simple once you know the basic street sign words: *ulice* (street, abbreviated to ul.; note that common usage often drops ulice in a printed address), *náměstí* (square, abbreviated to nám.), and *třída* (avenue). In most cases, the *blue* tags on buildings mark the street address.

By Bus

The Czech Republic's extremely comprehensive state-run bus service, **ČSAD,** is usually much quicker than the normal trains and more frequent than express trains, unless you're going to the major cities. Prices are quite low—essentially the same as those for second-class rail tickets. Buy your tickets from the ticket window at the bus station or directly from the driver on the bus. Long-distance buses can be full, so you might want to book a seat in advance; Čedok will help you do this. The only drawback to traveling by bus is figuring out the timetables. They are easy to read, but beware of the small letters denoting exceptions to the time given. If in doubt, inquire at the information window or ask someone for assistance.

By Car

Traveling by car is the easiest and most flexible way of seeing the Czech Republic—other than Prague. If you intend to visit only the capital, you can do without a car. The city center is congested and difficult to navigate, and you'll save yourself a lot of hassle by sticking to public transportation.

A permit is required to drive on expressways and other four-lane highways. They cost 800 Kč and are sold at border crossings, some service stations, and all post offices.

For accidents, call the **emergency number** (☎ 154). In case of breakdown, get in touch with the 24-hour **Yellow Angel** road service (☎ 123 [in some areas, 0123]). Autoturist offices throughout the Czech Republic (main office: ⊠ Na Rybníčku 16, ☎ 02/2491–1830) can provide motoring information of all kinds.

PARKING

There's little problem except in Prague. There, parking spaces are scarce, but parking meters have been installed in the city center, significantly easing the competition. The meters with green stripes let you park up to six hours; an orange stripe means two hours is allowed. (Use change in the meters). Signs with a blue circle outlined in red with a diagonal red slash indicate a no-parking zone. Avoid the blue-marked spaces, which are reserved for local residents. Violaters may find a "boot" immobilizing their vehicle.

ROAD CONDITIONS

There are few four-lane highways, but most of the roads are in reasonably good shape, and traffic is usually light. Roads can be poorly marked, however, so before you start out, buy one of the multilingual, inexpensive auto atlases available at any bookstore.

RULES OF THE ROAD

The Czech Republic follows the usual Continental rules of the road. A right turn on red is permitted only when indicated by a green arrow. Signposts with yellow diamonds indicate a main road where drivers have the right of way. The speed limit is 110 kph (68 mph) on four-lane highways, 90 kph (56 mph) on open roads, and 50 kph (30 mph) in built-up areas. The fine for speeding is 300 Kč, payable on the spot. Seat belts are compulsory, and drinking before driving is absolutely prohibited. Passengers under 12 years of age, or less than 150 cm (5 ft) in height, must ride in the back seat.

By Plane

Air Ostrava flies to Ostrava and Brno (Prague, ☎ 02/2011–3406). **ČSA** (Czech Airlines) flies to the North Moravian city of Ostrava. Reservations can be made through **Čedok offices** abroad or ČSA in Prague (✉ V Celnici [off Náměstí Republiky], ☎ 02/2010–4310).

By Train

The state-run rail system is called **Česká draha** (☎ 2422–3887 or 2421–7040 for information). Trains vary in speed, but it's not really worth taking anything less than an express (*rychlík*) train, marked in red on the timetable. Tickets are relatively cheap; first class is considerably more spacious and comfortable and well worth the 50% increase over standard tickets. A small supplement is charged for the excellent EuroCity (EC) and InterCity (IC) trains. If you haven't bought a ticket in advance at the station, it's easy to buy one on the train for a small extra charge. On timetables, departures (*odjezd*) appear on a yellow background; arrivals (*příjezd*) are on white. It is possible to book sleepers (*lůžkový*) or the less-roomy couchettes (*lehátkový*) on most overnight trains.

Contacts and Resources

B&B Reservation Agencies

Most offices of Čedok and local information offices also book rooms in hotels, pensions, and private accommodations. Travelers usually do not need to resort to reservation agencies and fare quite well by simply keeping a sharp eye out for room-for-rent signs reading ZIMMER FREI or UBYTOVÁNÍ. In Britain **Czechbook Agency** (✉ Jopes Mill, Trebrownbridge, near Liskeard, Cornwall PL14 3PX, ☎ FAX 01503/240629) arranges stays in B&Bs, self-catering apartments, and hotels.

Car Rentals

There are no special requirements for renting a car in the Czech Republic, but be sure to shop around, as prices can differ greatly. **Avis** and **Hertz** offer Western makes starting at around $70 per day or $400 per week, which includes insurance, damage waiver, and VAT; cars equipped with automatic transmission and air-conditioning are available, but it's best to reserve well in advance if you have special needs—try calling the firm's U.S. reservation number before you leave home (☞ Car Rental *in* the Gold Guide). It may be less expensive to reserve from home as well. Smaller local companies, on the other hand, can rent Czech cars for significantly less, but the service and insurance coverage may be inferior. A surcharge of 5% to 12% applies to rental cars picked up at Prague's Ruzyně Airport.

Customs and Duties

ON ARRIVAL

You may import duty-free into the Czech Republic 200 cigarettes, 100 cigarillos, 250 grams of tobacco, or 50 cigars, 1 liter of spirits, 2 liters of wine, and 50 grams of perfume. Other personal items are exempt up to a value of 3,000 Kč.

If you take into the Czech Republic valuables or foreign-made equipment from home, such as cameras, carry the original receipts with you or register the items with U.S. Customs before you leave (Form 4457). Otherwise you could end up paying duty upon your return.

ON DEPARTURE

The export of items considered to have historical value is not allowed. Antiques, rare craft items, and the like must have an export certificate.

Reputable shops should be willing to advise customers on how to comply with the regulations. If the shop can't provide proof of the item's suitability for export, be suspicious—if you aren't, the customs agent at the border will be. Theft of antiques—particularly Baroque religious pieces—is big business.

Emergencies

Police (☎ 158). **Ambulance** (☎ 155). **Breakdowns** (☎ 154 or 123 [in some areas, 0123]).

Guided Tours

Several Prague-based companies offer tours of the capital and other regions of the country. **Čedok** (✉ Main office: Na Příkopě 18, ☎ 2419–7111) has a large range of tours, including trips to Bohemia and Moravia. You can also contact **Wolff Travel** (✉ Na Prikope 24, ☎ 02/ 279–063, FAX 02/278–727) for regional and capital tours; it can make reservations and issue international transportation tickets as well. **Sportturist Special** (✉ Narodni trida 33, ☎ 02/2422–8518, FAX 02/263– 359) provides similar services, though it offers more outdoors-oriented tours. It is also the local office for Western Union. Both companies have English-speaking guides.

Language

Czech, a Slavic language closely related to Slovak and Polish, is the official language of the Czech Republic. Learning English is popular among young people, but German is still the most useful language for tourists.

Mail

POSTAL RATES

Postcards to the United States and Canada cost 7 Kč; letters up to 20 grams in weight, 11 Kč. Postcards to Great Britain cost 6 Kč; a letter, 10 Kč. You can buy stamps at post offices, hotels, and shops that sell postcards.

RECEIVING MAIL

If you don't know where you'll be staying, **American Express** mail service is a great convenience, available at no charge to anyone holding an American Express credit card or carrying American Express traveler's checks. The American Express office is at Václavské náměstí 56 (Wenceslas Square) in central Prague. You can also have mail held *poste restante* (general delivery) at post offices in major towns, but the letters should be marked *Pošta 1,* to designate the city's main post office. The poste restante window is at the main post office in Prague (✉ Jindřišská ul. 14). You will be asked for identification when you collect your mail.

Money and Expenses

COSTS

Despite rising inflation, the Czech Republic is still generally a bargain by Western standards. Prague remains the exception, however. Hotel prices in particular are often higher than the standard of facilities would warrant. Nevertheless, you can still find bargain private accommodations. The prices at tourist resorts outside the capital are lower and, in the outlying areas and off the beaten track, very low. Tourists can now legally pay for hotel rooms in crowns, although some hotels still insist on payment in "hard" (i.e., Western) currency. It is an unfortunate fact that many venues such as galleries, museums, castles, and certain clubs charge a higher entrance fee for foreigners than they charge for Czechs. The entrance fees are usually posted, with the Czech citizens' rate written in words rather than figures. Ticket vendors can be quite militant about defending this policy, which is legally acceptable in the Czech Republic, and protesting such discrimination when it happens will usually get you nowhere.

The unit of currency in the Czech Republic is the koruna, or crown (Kč), which is divided into 100 haléř, or hellers. There are (little-used) coins of 10, 20, and 50 hellers; coins of 1, 2, 5, 10, 20, and 50 Kč; and notes of 20, 50, 100, 200, 500, 1,000, 2,000, and 5,000 Kč. Notes of 1,000 Kč and up may not always be accepted for small purchases.

Try to avoid exchanging money at hotels or private exchange booths, including the ubiquitous Čekobanka and Exact Change booths. They routinely take commissions of 8%–10%. The best places to exchange are at bank counters, where the commissions average 1%–3%, or at ATMs. The koruna became fully convertible late in 1995 and can now be purchased outside the country and exchanged into other currencies. Ask about current regulations when you change money, however, and keep your receipts. At press time the exchange rate was around 35 Kč to the U.S. dollar, 24 Kč to the Canadian dollar, and 58 Kč to the pound sterling.

A cup of coffee will cost about 30 Kč; museum or castle entrance, 20 Kč–300 Kč; a good theater seat, up to 500 Kč; a cinema seat, 60 Kč–100 Kč; ½ liter (pint) of beer, 15 Kč–25 Kč; a 2-km (1-mi) taxi ride, 60 Kč–100 Kč; a bottle of Moravian wine in a good restaurant, 140 Kč–320 Kč; a glass (2 deciliters or 7 ounces) of wine, 35 Kč–45 Kč.

National Holidays

January 1; Easter Monday; May 1 (Labor Day); May 8 (Liberation Day); July 5 (Sts. Cyril and Methodius); July 6 (Jan Hus); October 28 (Czech National Day); and December 24, 25, and 26.

Opening and Closing Times

Though hours vary, most banks are open weekdays 8–5. Private exchange offices usually have longer hours. Museums are usually open daily except Monday (or Tuesday) 9–5; they tend to stop selling tickets an hour before closing time. Outside the large towns, many sights, including most castles, are open daily except Monday only from May through September and in April and October are open only on weekends and holidays. Stores are open weekdays 9–6; some grocery stores open at 6 AM. Department stores often stay open until 7 PM. On Saturday, most stores close at noon. Nearly all stores are closed on Sunday.

Outdoor Activities and Sports

Čedok offices and local tourist bureaus are the best places to inquire about equipment rentals, trail networks, and other sports information. Besides bicycles, rental sports equipment is still relatively hard to find.

Rada Českého rybářského svazu (Council of Czech Fishing Associations; ⊠ Nad Olšinami 31, 110 00 Prague 10, ☎ 02/781–1751).

Klub českých turistů (Czech Hiking Club; ⊠ Mezi stadiony, Box 40, 160 17 Prague 6, ☎ 02/2051–1991). Note that the usual Czech word for walker or hiker is *turist*. *See* Pleasures and Pastimes *above* for more information.

Český tenisový svaz (Czech Tennis Association; ⊠ CTD Štvanice 38, 170 00 Prague 7, ☎ 02/2481–0238).

Passports and Visas

United States, Canadian, and British citizens require only a valid passport to visit the Czech Republic as tourists. U.S. citizens may stay for 30 days without a visa; British and Canadian citizens, six months. Canadians may be required to register with the police if staying with friends or family. It's advisable to contact the Czech Embassy (✉ Embassy of the Czech Republic, 541 Sussex Dr., Ottawa, Ontario K1N 6Z6, ☎ 613/562–3875, ℻ 613/562–3878) about changes to the rules regarding Canadian citizens. U.S. citizens can receive additional information from the Czech Embassy (✉ 3900 Spring of Freedom St. NW, Washington, DC 20008, ☎ 202/274–9100, ℻ 202/966–8540).

Rail Passes

Since tickets are so inexpensive, most rail passes cost more than what you'd spend buying tickets on the spot. The **European East Pass** is good for unlimited first-class travel on the national railroads of Austria, the Czech Republic, Slovakia, Hungary, and Poland. The pass allows five days of travel within a one-month period ($199). Additional travel days may be purchased. Apply through your travel agent or through **Rail Europe** (✉ 226–230 Westchester Ave., White Plains, NY 10604, ☎ 914/682–2999 or 800/848–7245, ℻ 800/432–1329; ✉ 2087 Dundas E, Suite 106, Mississauga, Ontario L4X 1M2, ☎ 800/361–7245, ℻ 905/602–4198). The **EurailPass** and **Eurail Youthpass** are not valid for travel within the Czech Republic. The **InterRail Pass,** available only to European citizens at budget travel offices and Čedok, is valid for 22 days of unlimited train travel in the Czech Republic, Slovakia, Poland, Hungary, and Croatia. If purchased in the Czech Republic it costs 10,600 Kč, or 7,500 Kč for travelers under 26. For more information, *see* Train Travel *in* the Gold Guide.

Student and Youth Travel

CKM (Youth Travel Service; ✉ Jindřišská 28, Prague 1, ☎ 02/2423–0218) provides information on travel bargains within the Czech Republic and abroad to students, travelers under 26, and teachers. **KMC** (Young Travelers' Club; ✉ Karoliny Světlé 30, Prague 1, ☎ 02/2423 0633) issues IYH cards (50 Kč for those under 26, 200 Kč for others) and books hostel beds throughout the country. For general information about student identity cards, work-abroad programs, and youth hostels, *see* Student Travel *in* the Gold Guide.

Telephones

The country code for the Czech Republic is 420. When dialing a number in the Czech Republic from abroad, drop the initial zero from the regional area code.

INTERNATIONAL CALLS

To reach an English-speaking operator in the United States, call **AT&T** (☎ 00–420–00101), **MCI** (☎ 00–420–00112), or **Sprint** (☎ 00–420–87187). For **CanadaDirect,** dial 00–420–00151; for **B.T.Direct** to the United Kingdom, call 00–420–04401. The operator will connect your collect or credit-card call at the carrier's standard rates. In Prague, many phone booths allow direct international dialing; if you can't find one, the telephone office of the **main post office** (Hlavní pošta, ✉ Politických věznu 4), open 24 hours, is the best place to try. Once inside, follow signs for "Telegraf/Telefax." The international dialing code is 00. Rates to the U.S. are roughly 42 Kč per minute; a call to the U.K. costs about 25 Kč per minute. For international inquiries, dial 0132 for the United States, Canada, or the United Kingdom. Otherwise, ask the receptionist at any hotel to put a call through for you, though beware: The more expensive the hotel, the more expensive the call will be.

LOCAL CALLS

The few remaining coin-operated telephones take 2- and 5-Kč coins. Most newer public phones operate only with a special telephone card, available from newsstands and tobacconists in denominations of 150 Kč, 240 Kč, and 300 Kč. A call within Prague costs 2 Kč from a coin-operated phone or the equivalent of 3 Kč (1 unit) from a card-operated phone. The dial tone is a series of short and long buzzes.

Tipping

Service is usually not included in restaurant bills. Round the bill up to the next multiple of 10 (if the bill comes to 83 Kč, for example, give the waiter 90 Kč); 10% is considered appropriate in all but the most expensive places. Tip porters who bring bags to your rooms 40 Kč total. For room service, a 20-Kč tip is enough. In taxis, round the bill up by 10%. Give tour guides and helpful concierges between 50 Kč and 100 Kč for services rendered.

Travel Agencies

Prague's **American Express** (☞ Travel Agencies *in* Prague A to Z, *above*) provides full travel services in addition to changing money and selling traveler's checks. Local Czech travel agencies offer extensive information on regional activities and tours; contact either **Wolff Travel** or **Sportturist Special** (☞ Guided Tours, *above*). **Čedok** will supply you with hotel and travel information and book air and rail tickets, but except in their main Prague office (☞ Visitor Information *in* Prague A to Z) don't expect much in the way of general information.

Visitor Information

Čedok (☞ Travel Agencies, *above*), the former state-run travel bureau, went private in 1995 and is now a travel agent rather than a tourist information office.

Most major towns have a local or private information office, usually in the central square and identified by a lowercase "i" on the facade. These offices are often good sources for maps and historical information and can usually help you book hotel and private accommodations. Most are open during normal business hours, with limited hours on Saturday (until noon), and are closed on Sunday and holidays. Out-of-season hours are severely reduced. For individual centers, *see* Visitor Information *in* each of this chapter's A to Z sections, *above*.

The official provider of tourist information, the **Czech Tourist Authority** (☞ Visitor Information *in* the Gold Guide), has offices in the United States, Canada, Great Britain, other countries of Europe, and Japan, as well as Prague (✉ Národní třída 37, ☎ FAX 02/2421–1458). Besides stocking brochures and information on attractions throughout the Czech Republic, they can book accommodations anywhere in the country.

3 Slovakia

Despite a long period of common statehood with the Czechs (which ended in 1993), Slovakia (Slovensko) differs from the Czech Republic in many aspects. Its mountains are higher and more rugged, its veneer less sophisticated, its folklore and traditions richer. Observers of the two regions like to link the Czech Republic geographically and culturally with the orderly Germans, while they put Slovakia with Ukraine and Russia, firmly in the east. This is a simplification, yet it contains more than a little bit of truth.

By Mark Baker

Updated by
Tatiana
Repková

SLOVAKIA BECAME AN INDEPENDENT STATE on January 1, 1993, when Czechoslovakia—formerly composed of what is today Slovakia and the Czech Republic—ceased to exist. To the east of the Czech Republic, Slovakia is about one-third as large as its neighbor. Although the Slovaks speak a language closely related to Czech, they managed to maintain a strong sense of national identity throughout the more than 70 years of common statehood. Though united with the Czechs in the 9th century as part of the Great Moravian Empire, the Slovaks were conquered a century later by the Magyars and remained under Hungarian and Hapsburg rule. Following the Tartar invasions in the 13th century, many Saxons were invited to resettle the land and develop the economy, including the region's rich mineral resources. In the 15th and 16th centuries, Romanian shepherds migrated from Wallachia through the Carpathians into Slovakia, and the merging of these varied groups with the resident Slavs bequeathed to the region a rich folk culture and some unique forms of architecture, especially in the east.

In the end, it was this very different history that split the Slovaks from the Czechs, ending the most successful experiment in nation building to follow World War I.

For many Slovaks, the 1989 revolution provided for the first time an opportunity not only to bring down the Communists but also to establish a fully independent state. Although few Slovaks harbored any real resentment toward the Czechs, Slovak politicians were quick to recognize and exploit the deep, inchoate longing for independence. Slovak nationalist parties won more than 50% of the vote in the crucial 1992 Czechoslovak elections, and once the results were in, the end came quickly.

There is something hopeful to be seen in the peaceful nature of the separation. For the visitor, the changes may in fact be positive. The Slovaks have been long overshadowed by their cousins to the west; now they have the unfettered opportunity to tell their story to the world.

Most visitors to Slovakia head first for the great peaks of the High Tatras (Vysoké Tatry). The tourist infrastructure here is very good, catering especially to hikers and skiers. Visitors who come to admire the peaks, however, often overlook the exquisite medieval towns of Spiš, in the plains and valleys below the High Tatras, and the beautiful 18th-century country churches farther east. (Removed from main centers, these areas are short on tourist amenities, so if creature comforts are important to you, stick to the High Tatras.)

Bratislava, the capital of Slovakia, may well be a disappointment at first. The last 40 years of communism left a clear mark on the city, hiding its ancient beauty with hulking, and now dilapidated, futurist structures. Yet despite its gloomy appearance, Bratislava tries hard to project the cosmopolitanism of a European capital. The Old Town, though still needing more renovation, is beginning to recapture some of its lost charm.

Pleasures and Pastimes

Bicycling

The flatter areas to the south and east of Bratislava and along the Danube are ideal for biking. A special bike trail links Bratislava and Vienna, paralleling the Danube for much of its 40-km (25-mi) length. For the more adventurous bikers, the Low Tatras (Nízke Tatry) have scenic biking trails along the small, secluded rivers surrounding Banská Bystrica.

Not many places rent bikes, however; inquire at tourist information centers or at your hotel for rental information.

Camping

There are hundreds of camping sites for tents and trailers throughout Slovakia, but most are open only in summer (May to mid-September). You can get a map of all the sites, with addresses, opening times, and facilities, from Satur travel offices. Campsites are divided into Categories A and B according to facilities, but both have hot water (though unreliable) and toilets (though primitive).

Dining

Slovak food is an amalgam of its neighbors' cuisines. As in Bohemia and Moravia, the emphasis is on meat, particularly pork and beef. But the Slovaks, revealing their long link to Hungary, prefer to spice things up a bit, usually with paprika and red peppers. Roast potatoes or french fries are often served, although occasionally you'll find a side dish of tasty *halušky* (noodles similar to Italian gnocchi or German spaetzle) on the menu. *Bryndzové halušky,* the country's unofficial national dish, is a tasty and filling mix of halušky, sheep's cheese, and a little bacon fat for flavor. Vegetarians don't have a lot of options, though vegetable salads are normally available. For dessert, the emphasis comes from Vienna: pancakes, poppy-seed dumplings, and strudel.

Slovaks don't eat out often, particularly since prices have risen markedly in the past few years. As a result, you will find relatively few restaurants about, and those that do exist generally cater to foreigners or a wealthy business clientele. Restaurants known as *vináreň* specialize in serving wines, although you can order beer virtually anywhere. Red wines in particular complement the country's filling, spicy food; look for *Frankovka,* which is fiery and slightly acidic. *Vavrinecké,* a relatively new arrival, is dark and semisweet and stands up well to red meats.

Lunch, usually eaten between noon and 2, is the main meal for Slovaks. Many restaurants put out a special luncheon menu (*ponuka dňa* or *špecialita šéfkuchára*). Dinner is usually served from 5 until 9 or 10, but cooks frequently knock off early on slow nights.

CATEGORY	COST*
$$$$	over $20
$$$	$15–$20
$$	$7–$15
$	under $7

per person for a three-course meal, excluding wine and tip

Festivals and Seasonal Events

Many villages host annual folklore festivals, usually in late summer or early fall (☞ Festivals and Seasonal Events *in* the Gold Guide). These frequently take place in the town center and are accompanied by lots of singing, dancing, and drinking. Every year, the Slovak Ministry of Economy puts out a calendar of events in English, available in travel agencies and tourist information centers.

Fishing

There are hundreds of lakes and rivers suitable for fishing, often amid striking scenery. Demänovská dolina, a picturesque valley near Liptovský Mikuláš in central Slovakia, offers some excellent places to catch trout. Bring your own tackle or be prepared to buy it locally because rental equipment is scarce. To cast a line legally, you must have a fishing license (valid for one year) plus a fishing permit (valid for a day, week, month, or year for the particular body of water on which you plan to fish). Both are available from Satur offices.

Hiking

Slovakia is a hiker's paradise, with more than 20,000 km (15,000 mi) of well-kept, -marked, and -signposted trails in both the mountainous regions and the agricultural countryside. You'll find the colored markings denoting trails on trees, fences, walls, rocks, and elsewhere. The colors correspond to the path marking on the large-scale Súbor turistických maps available at many bookstores and tobacconists. The best areas for ambitious mountain walkers are the Low Tatras in the center of the country near Banská Bystrica and the High Tatras to the north. Slovenský Raj, or Slovak Paradise, in eastern Slovakia is an ideal place for hikers—a wild, romantic area, where you'll see cliffs, caves, and waterfalls.

Lodging

Few new hotels have been built since the Velvet Revolution, and many of the older establishments are still mostly owned by the state and often give shabby service; overall, there's still a shortage of good, inexpensive accommodations. On the bright side, small, private hotels and pensions in beautifully renovated buildings have been springing up all over the country.

In general, hotels can be divided into two categories: edifices built in the 1960s or '70s that offer modern amenities but not much character; and older, more central establishments that are heavy on personality but may lack basic conveniences. Most modern hotels have apartments (a bedroom and living room) and suites (two bedrooms and living room) as well as standard rooms. Hostels are understood to be cheap dormitory rooms and are best avoided. In the mountainous areas, you can often find little *chata* (chalets), where pleasant surroundings compensate for a lack of basic amenities. Campsites generally have a few bungalows available.

Slovakia's official hotel classification, based on letters (Deluxe, A, B, C), is gradually being changed over to the international star system, although it will be some time before the old system is completely replaced. These ratings correspond closely to our categories as follows: Deluxe or five-star ($$$$); A or four-star ($$$); B or three- to two-star ($$–$). We've included C hotels in our listings where accommodations are scarce or when the particular hotel has redeeming qualities. Unless otherwise noted, all rooms have bath.

Slovakia is a bargain by Western standards, particularly in the outlying areas. In Bratislava, however, hotel rates often meet or exceed both U.S. and Western European averages.

The prices quoted below are for double rooms, generally not including breakfast. Prices at the lower end of the scale apply to low season. At certain periods, such as Christmas, Easter, and during festivals, there may be an increase of 15%–25%.

CATEGORY	COST*
$$$$	over $100
$$$	$50–$100
$$	$15–$50
$	under $15

All prices are for a standard double room, including tax and service.

Shopping

Among the most interesting finds in Slovakia are batik-painted Easter eggs, corn-husk figures, delicate woven table mats, hand-knit sweaters, and folk pottery. The best buys are folk-art products sold at stands along the roads and in Slovart or folk art stores in most major towns.

There are also several Dielo stores, which sell paintings, some wooden toys, and great ceramic pieces by Slovak artists at very reasonable prices.

Skiing

Slovakia is one of the best countries in the region for downhill skiers, both amateurs and experts. The two main skiing areas are the Low Tatras and the High Tatras. The High Tatras offer more reliable conditions (good snow throughout winter) and superior facilities, including places where you can rent equipment. Lifts in both regions generally operate from January through March, though cross-country skiing is a popular alternative.

Exploring Slovakia

Slovakia can best be divided into four regions of interest to tourists: Bratislava, the High Tatra Mountains, central Slovakia, and eastern Slovakia. Despite being the capital, Bratislava, in the western part of the country, is probably the least alluring. The country's true beauty lies among the peaks of the High Tatras in the northern part of central Slovakia.

Great Itineraries

Numbers in the text correspond to numbers in the margin and on the Slovakia and Bratislava maps.

Although Slovakia is relatively small, its mountains and poor roads make it difficult to explore in a short period of time. Driving or taking the train from Bratislava to the eastern town of Košice will take you a minimum of seven hours. A more convenient option is to fly. From Košice, it's easy to explore the surrounding region, with the High Tatras less than three hours away.

IF YOU HAVE 3 DAYS

If you only have a few days to see Slovakia, spend a maximum of a few hours walking through the Old Town and the castle in **Bratislava** ①– ⑱; then head straight for the **High Tatras.** Once you get to the mountains, you can settle down in a comfortable hotel or a pension in one of the resort towns. ⛺ **Smokovec** ⑳ and ⛺ **Tatranská Lomnica** ㉒ are probably the most convenient places from which to explore the area and go hiking in summer or skiing in winter. If you can pull yourself away from the High Tatras on the second day, take a brief excursion slightly south to the beautiful Spiš town of ⛺ **Levoča** ㉙. Spend the night here, and on your last day, head back to Bratislava via **Poprad** ⑲ and **Banská Bystrica** ㉓.

IF YOU HAVE 5 DAYS

Follow the three-day itinerary up to ⛺ **Levoča** ㉙. From here, you can also explore the Spiš Castle and the caves and gorges in the area. The following day, head south toward ⛺ **Košice** ㉘. Take a look at some of the historic sights in the Old Town of this region's capital. On your last day, make your way back home. From Košice, it's possible to fly to Bratislava or to take a direct day or night train to Bratislava or Prague.

When to Tour Slovakia

The High Tatras are loveliest in winter (January–March). A smaller summer season in the mountains attracts mostly walkers and hikers. Because of the snow, many hiking trails, especially those that cross the peaks, are open only between June and October. Note that temperatures are always much cooler in the mountains; even in summer, expect to wear a sweater or jacket.

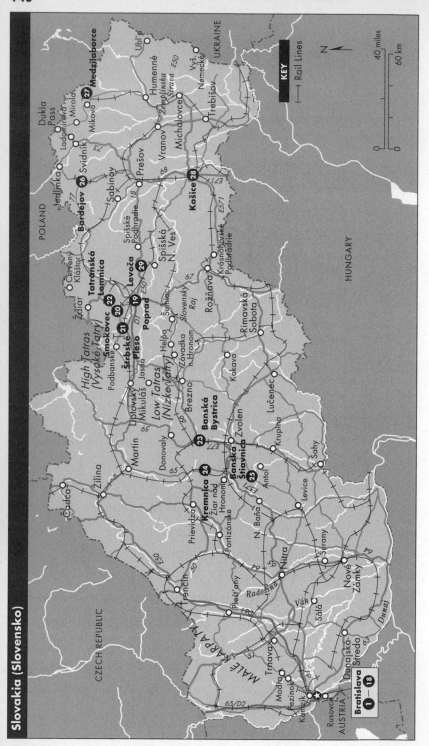

Slovakia (Slovensko)

Bratislava is at its best in the temperate months of spring and autumn. July and August, though not especially crowded, can be unbearably hot, while winter generally brings a great deal of snow and rain.

BRATISLAVA

You may get a bit of a sinking feeling when you first see Europe's newest capital city, Bratislava—or "Blava" as it is affectionately known by residents. Expecting a Slovak version of Prague or Vienna, you'll discover instead a busy industrial city that seems to embody the Communists' blind faith in modernity. The problem, of course, is that Bratislava has more than its fair share of high-rise housing projects and less-than-inspiring monuments to carefully chosen acts of heroism.

The jumble of modern Bratislava, however, masks a long and regal history that rivals Prague's in importance and complexity. Settled by a variety of Celts and Romans, the city became part of the Great Moravian Empire around the year 900 under Prince Břetislav. After a short period under the Bohemian Premysl princes, Bratislava was brought into the Hungarian kingdom by Stephan I at the end of the 10th century and given royal privileges in 1217. Following the Tartar invasion in 1241, the Hungarian kings brought in German colonists to repopulate the town. The Hungarians called the town Pozsony; the German settlers referred to it as Pressburg; and the original Slovaks called it Bratislava after Prince Břetislav.

When Pest and Buda were occupied by the Turks, in 1526 and 1541 respectively, the Hungarian kings moved their seat to Bratislava, which remained the Hungarian capital until 1784 and the coronation center until 1835. At this time, with a population of almost 27,000, it was the largest Hungarian city. Only in 1919, when Bratislava became part of the first Czechoslovak republic, did the city regain its Slovak identity. In 1939, with Germany's assistance, Bratislava infamously exerted its yearnings for independence by becoming the capital of the puppet Slovak state, under the fascist leader Jozef Tiso. In 1945 it became the provincial capital of Slovakia, still straining under the powerful hand of Prague (Slovakia's German and Hungarian minorities were either expelled or repressed). Leading up to the 1989 revolution, Bratislava was the site of numerous anti-Communist demonstrations; many of these were carried out by supporters of the Catholic Church, long repressed by the regime then in power. Following the "Velvet Revolution" in 1989, Bratislava gained importance as the capital of the Slovak Republic within the new Czech and Slovak federal state, but rivalries with Prague persisted. It was only following the breakup of Czechoslovakia on January 1, 1993, that the city once again became a capital in its own right.

Exploring Bratislava

To discover Bratislava's charms, travel the city by foot. Imagination is also helpful, as some of the Old Town's more potentially interesting streets are often in various stages of reconstruction.

Numbers in the text correspond to numbers in the margin and on the Bratislava map.

A Good Walk

Begin your tour at the modern square **Námestie SNP** ①. From here walk up the square toward Hurbanovo námestie, where you can glance at the **Kostol svätej Trojice** ②. Across the road, unobtrusively located between a shoe store and a bookstore, is the enchanting entrance to the

142

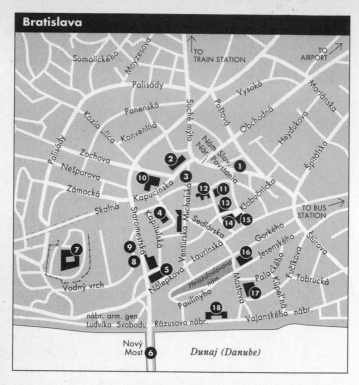

Old Town. After passing through the first archway, you'll come to the narrow promenade of Michalská ulica (Michael Street). In front of you is **Michalská brána** ③. Walk through the gate, and take a stroll down Michalská ulica. Many of the more interesting buildings along the street are undergoing renovation, but notice the eerie blue Kaplnka svätej Kataríny (Chapel of St. Catherine) at No. 6 on the left, built in 1311 but now graced with a sober classical facade. Opposite, at No. 7, is the Renaissance Segnerova kúria (Segner House), built for a wealthy merchant in 1648. Farther down on the right is the Palác Uhorskej kráľovskej komory (Hungarian Royal Chamber), a Baroque palace that housed the Hungarian nobles' parliament from 1802 until 1848; it is now the University Library. Go through the arched passageway at the back of the building, and you'll emerge in a tiny square dominated by the 14th-century **Kostol Klarisiek** ④, which is now the Slovak Pedagogical Library.

Follow Farská ulica up to the corner and turn left on Kapitulská ulica (noticing the paving stone depicting two kissing lizards). Ahead of you on the right is the side wall of the **Dóm svätého Martina** ⑤, one of the more impressive churches in the city.

As you leave the church and walk around to the front, the first thing you see is the freeway leading to the futuristic spaceship bridge, **Nový Most** ⑥, formerly called Most SNP (Bridge of the Slovak National Uprising). When the highway was built, a row of old houses and a synagogue in the former Jewish quarter outside the city walls were destroyed. The only good thing to be said for the road is that its construction led to the discovery of remnants of the city's original walls, which have been partially restored and now line the freeway on the right. Follow the steps under the passageway and up the other side in the direction of the castle.

Continue up the steps, through a Gothic arched gateway built in 1480, and climb up to the **hrad** ⑦ area. From the top, on a clear day, you can see over to Austria to the right. Leave the castle by the same route, but instead of climbing the last stairs by the Arkadia restaurant, continue down Old World Beblavého ulica.

At the bottom of the street on the right is the **Múzeum umeleckých remesiel** ⑧. Next, go around the House at the Good Shepherd and continue along Židovská ulica (Jews' Street)—the street name recalls that this area was the former Jewish ghetto. You can visit the **Múzeum Židovskej Kultúry** ⑨ in a Renaissance mansion.

Continue on Židovská ulica until you come to a thin concrete bridge that crosses the freeway to the reconstructed city walls. Standing in the middle of this bridge, looking toward the river, you'll get one of the best views of the city's incongruous and contradictory jumble of buildings. If you turn left and walk along the city walls, you will come, after negotiating a series of steps, to the main road, Kapucínska ulica.

On the left is the small, golden-yellow **Kostol kapucínov** ⑩. Cross the street and take the steps leading down into the Old Town. Turn left at the bottom into little Baštová ulica. Go through the arch at the end, and you'll find yourself back at Michael's Gate. Continue straight along Zámočnícka ulica, which turns right heading in the direction of Františkánske námestie. To the left is the oldest preserved building in Bratislava, the **Františkánsky kostol** ⑪. Across from the church is the beautifully detailed rococo **Mirbachov palác** ⑫, which today houses the Municipal Gallery.

Go across the Františkánske námestie onto the adjoining square, Hlavné námestie. The latter is lined with old houses and palaces representing a spectrum of architectural styles, from Gothic (No. 2), Baroque (No. 4), and rococo (No. 7) to a wonderfully decorative example of Art Nouveau at No. 10. To your immediate left as you come into the square is the richly decorated **Jezuitský kostol** ⑬. Next to the church is the colorful agglomeration of old bits and pieces of structures that make up the **Stará radnica** ⑭.

Leaving by the back entrance of the Stará radnica, you'll come to the Primaciálne námestie (Primates' Square), dominated by the glorious pale-pink **Primaciálny palác** ⑮. Then walk down Uršulínska ulica and turn right at the bottom onto Laurinská ulica. If you continue to the left down Rybárska brána, you will emerge into the more modern part of the Old Town at the Hviezdoslavovo námestie (Hviezdoslav Square). To your right is the **Slovenské národné divadlo** ⑯, Bratislava's opera house. Behind the theater you can buy tickets to performances.

Across the Hviezdoslav Square, on the corner of Mostová ulica and Palackého ulica, is the **Reduta** ⑰, home to the Slovak Philharmonic Orchestra. Continue down Mostová ulica to the banks of the Danube. To the right is the Baroque onetime barracks, transformed by the Communists to house the modern **Slovenská národná galéria** ⑱, which has a conglomeration of past and present works by Slovak artists.

TIMING
If you get an early morning start, you can complete a leisurely walking tour of the Old Town in a day (make sure you have on comfortable shoes). With the exception of the Slovenská národná galéria, which deserves some time, most of the museums are small and won't detain you long. Avoid touring on Mondays, as many sights are closed. On other days, plan to break around lunchtime, because many museums close between noon and 1.

SIGHTS TO SEE

⑤ Dóm svätého Martina (St. Martin's Cathedral). This massive Gothic church, consecrated in 1452, hosted the coronations of 17 Hungarian royals between the 16th and 19th centuries. Numerous additions made over the centuries were unfortunately removed in the 19th century, when the church was re-Gothicized. Nowadays, the three equal-size naves give an impression of space and light, but the uplifting glory found in Bohemia's Gothic cathedrals is definitely missing. ⊠ *Rudnayovo nám.,* ☎ *07/5331359.* ⊙ *Weekdays 10–11:30 and 2–6, Sat. 10–noon, Sun. 2–4:30.*

⑪ Františkánsky kostol (Franciscan Church). In this 13th-century church, only the presbytery is still in early Gothic style, the rest having been destroyed in an earthquake in the 17th century and rebuilt in a mixture of Baroque and Gothic. Just around the corner, built onto the church, is another quite different and much more stunning Gothic building, the 14th-century **Kaplnka svätého Jána Evangelistu** (Chapel of St. John the Evangelist). Art historians believe that Peter Parler, architect of Prague's Charles Bridge, may have worked on this gem. You can take a look around before or after services at 7 AM and 5 PM. ⊠ *Františkánske nám.*

⑦ Hrad (castle). Bratislava's castle has been continually rebuilt since its foundations were laid in the 9th century. The Hungarian kings expanded it into a large royal residence, and the Hapsburgs further developed its fortifications, turning it into a very successful defense against the Turks. The existing castle had to be completely rebuilt after a disastrous fire in 1811. Inside you'll find the **Slovenské národné múzeum** (Slovak National Museum), with exhibits on furniture, crafts, folklore costumes, and minting. ⊠ *Zámocká ul.,* ☎ *07/5311444.* 🎫 *Castle and museum: 40 Sk.* ⊙ *Tues.–Sun. 9–5.*

⑬ Jezuitský kostol (Jesuit Church). This church was originally built by Protestants who, in 1636, were granted an imperial concession to build a place of worship on the strict condition that it have no tower. The Jesuits took over the towerless church in 1672 and, to compensate for its external simplicity, went wild with Baroque detailing on the inside. ⊠ *Hlavné nám.* ☎ *No phone.* ⊙ *Service at 4:30.*

⑩ Kostol kapucínov (Capuchin Chapel). A pillar of Mary, which commemorates the plague, stands in front of this small 18th-century chapel. You can sneak a peek inside the chapel before or after the services held early in the morning or in the evening from 5 to 7. ⊠ *Kapucínska ul.*

④ Kostol Klarisiek (Klariský Church). This 14th-century church is simple but inspiring, with a wonderfully peaceful early Gothic interior. The small High Gothic steeple was added in an unusually secondary position at the back of the church during the 15th century; as a mendicant order, the Poor Clares were forbidden to build a steeple atop the church, so they sidestepped the rules and built it against a side wall. The church is now a concert hall—and usually locked, but you may be able to get in for a concert or during rehearsals. ⊠ *Farská ul.*

② Kostol svätej Trojice (Church of the Holy Trinity). This golden-yellow Baroque church has space-expanding frescoes on the ceiling, which are the work of Antonio Galli Bibiena from the early 18th century. ⊠ *Hurbanovo nám.* ⊙ *Services at 9 and 6.*

③ Michalská brána (Michael's Gate). This is the last remaining of the city's three original gates. The bottom part of the adjoining tower, built in the 14th century, retains its original Gothic design; the copper onion tower, topped with a statue of St. Michael, was added in the 18th century. The *veža* (tower) has a good view over the city. ✉ *Michalská ul. 24,* ☏ *07/5333044.* 🎟 *20 Sk.* ⊙ *Wed.–Mon. 10–4:30.*

⑫ **Mirbachov palác** (Mirbach Palace). This rococo palace with original stucco decor was built in 1770. Today it houses the **Municipal Gallery,** which has a small collection of 18th- and 19th-century Slovak and European art. ✉ *Františkánske nám.,* ☏ *07/5331556.* 🎟 *20 Sk.* ⊙ *Tues.–Sun. 10–5.*

⑧ **Múzeum umeleckých remesiel** (Handicraft Museum). In a Baroque burgher house, this tiny museum displays a few nice works of arts and crafts from the 12th to 18th centuries, including ceramics, silverware, and furniture. ✉ *Beblavého ul. 1,* ☏ *07/5312784.* 🎟 *20 Sk.* ⊙ *Wed.– Mon. 10–5.*

★ ⑨ **Múzeum Židovskej Kultúry** (Museum of Jewish Culture in Slovakia). This small but stirring museum celebrates the history and culture of the Jews living on the territory of Slovakia since the Great Moravian Empire. There's a collection of religious objects from around the country, many from synagogues in Eastern Slovakia. A section is devoted to the victims of the Holocaust in Slovakia. ✉ *Židovská ul. 17,* ☏ *07/ 5318507.* 🎟 *40 Sk.* ⊙ *Sun.–Fri. 11–5.*

❶ **Námestie SNP** (SNP Square). The square, formerly known as Stalinovo námestie (Stalin Square), was and still remains the center for demonstrations in Slovakia. SNP stands for Slovenské Národné Povstanie (Slovak National Uprising), an anti-Nazi resistance movement. In the middle of the square are three larger-than-life statues: a dour partisan with two strong, sad women in peasant clothing.

❻ **Nový Most** (New Bridge). Although it would make a splendid site for an alien flick, the modern bridge is a bit of an eyesore for anyone who doesn't appreciate futuristic designs. The bridge is difficult to miss if you're anywhere near the Danube River.

NEED A BREAK?
Unless you are squeamish about heights, have a coffee at the **Vyhliad- ková Kaviareň** (☏ 07/817746) on Nový Most. This spaceshiplike café—reached via speedy glass-faced elevators for a minimal charge— is perched on top of pylons, 262 ft above the Danube River. Be warned that during stronger winds the café does sway.

⑮ **Primaciálny palác** (Primates' Palace). This is one of the most valuable architectural monuments in Bratislava. Don't miss the dazzling Hall of Mirrors, with its six 17th-century English tapestries depicting the legend of the lovers Hero and Leander. In this room Napoléon and Hapsburg emperor Francis I signed the Bratislava Peace of 1805, following Napoléon's victory at the Battle of Austerlitz. In the revolutionary year of 1848, when the citizens of the Hapsburg lands revolted against the imperial dominance of Vienna, the rebel Hungarians had their headquarters in the palace; ironically, following the failed uprising, the Hapsburg general Hainau signed the rebels' death sentences in the very same room. ✉ *Primaciálne nám. 1,* ☏ *07/5331407.* 🎟 *20 Sk.* ⊙ *Tues.–Sun. 10–5.*

⑰ **Reduta.** Bratislava's classical musical center, this extravagantly decorated building is home to the Slovak Philharmonic Orchestra. Built in neo-Baroque style but dating from 1914, the Reduta deserves a visit. ✉ *Medená ul. 3,* ☏ *07/5333351.*

⑱ **Slovenská národná galéria** (Slovak National Gallery). This gallery is in a conspicuously modern restoration of old 18th-century barracks. The museum itself has an interesting collection of Slovak Gothic,

Baroque, and contemporary art, along with a small number of European masters. ⊠ *Rázusovo nábrežie 2,* ☎ *07/5332081.* ☜ *30 Sk.* ⊙ *Tues.–Sun. 10–6.*

⑯ Slovenské národné divadlo (Slovak National Theater). You can see performances of Bratislava's opera, ballet, and theater at this striking theater, which was built in the 1880s by the famous Central European architectural duo of Hermann Helmer and Ferdinand Fellner. ⊠ *Hviezdoslavovo nám. 1,* ☎ *07/5333083 or 07/5333890.*

⑭ Stará radnica (Old Town Hall). One of the more interesting buildings in Bratislava, it developed gradually over the 13th and 14th centuries out of a number of burghers' houses. During the summer concerts are held here. You may want to stop in the **Mestské múzeum** (City Museum) here, which documents Bratislava's varied past. ⊠ *Primaciálne nám. 3,* ☎ *07/5335800.* ☜ *20 Sk.* ⊙ *Tues.–Sun. 10–5.*

Dining

Prague may have its Slovak rival beat when it comes to architecture, but when it's time to eat, you can thank your lucky stars that you're in Bratislava. The long-shared history with Hungary gives Slovak cuisine an extra fire that Czech cooking admittedly lacks. Geographic proximity to Vienna, moreover, has lent something of grace and charm to the city's eateries. Prepare for a variety of shish kebabs, grilled meats, steaks, and pork dishes, all spiced to warm the palate and served (if you're lucky) with those special noodles Slovaks call halušky.

$$$$ ✗ **Rybársky cech.** The name means Fisherman's Guild, and fish is the unchallenged specialty at this refined but comfortable eatery on a quiet street by the Danube. Freshwater fish is served upstairs, with pricier saltwater varieties offered on the ground floor. ⊠ *Žižkova 1,* ☎ *07/5313049. AE, DC, MC, V.*

$$$ ✗ **Kláštorná vináreň.** This restaurant is in the wine cellar of a former
★ monastery—hence the shadowy intimacy and wine-barrel-shape booths. The Hungarian-influenced spiciness of traditional Slovak cooking comes alive in such dishes as *Cikós tokáň,* a fiery mixture of pork, onions, and peppers; or try the milder *Bravčové ražniči,* a tender pork shish kebab served with fried potatoes. ⊠ *Františkánska ul. 2,* ☎ *07/ 5330430. AE, MC, V. Closed Sun.*

$$ ✗ **Modrá Hviezda.** The first of a new breed of small, family-owned
★ wine cellars, this popular eatery serves old Slovak specialties from the village as well as some imaginative dishes; try the sheep's-cheese pie. ⊠ *Beblavého 14,* ☎ *07/5332747. No credit cards. Closed Sun.*

$ ✗ **Gremium.** This trendy restaurant caters to the coffee-and-cigarette crowd and to anyone in search of an uncomplicated light meal. Choose from a small menu of pastries, sandwiches, and some local specialties, including *brynzové halušky* (tasty noodles with goat cheese) and *pytliacky guláš* (creamy goulash with halušky topped with blueberries)— though a bizarre combination, it's scrumptious. ⊠ *Gorkého 11,* ☎ *07/ 321818. Reservations not accepted. AE, MC, V.*

$ ✗ **Pekná Brána.** With more than 75 main-course meals to choose
★ from, this is not the place to go if you have trouble making up your mind. The menu includes Chinese and vegetarian dishes and traditional Slovak cuisine. You can also dine in the cellar, which is open until sunrise. The restaurant is open daily 9 AM to midnight. ⊠ *Vysoká ul. 39,* ☎ *07/323008. AE, MC, V.*

$ ✗ **Stará Sladovňa.** To Bratislavans, this gargantuan beer hall is known
★ lovingly, and fittingly, as *mamut* (mammoth). Locals come here for the Bohemian brews on tap, but it is also possible to get an inexpensive and filling meal. ⊠ *Cintorínska 32,* ☎ *07/321151. No credit cards.*

Lodging

The lodging situation in Bratislava is improving, though not fast enough to rid the city of some pretty shabby establishments. Luckily, small, privately owned hotels and pensions continue to materialize. Make reservations in advance or arrive in Bratislava before 4 PM and ask tourist information (☞ Contacts and Resources *in* Bratislava A to Z, *below*) for help finding a room. If all decent hotels are booked, consider renting an apartment. Beware of individuals offering apartments at train stations, or you may be going back home with a much lighter load.

$$$$ ☷ **Danube.** Opened in 1992, this French-run hotel on the banks of the
★ Danube has quickly developed a reputation for superior facilities and service. The modern rooms are decorated in pastel colors; the gleaming public areas are everything you expect from an international hotel chain. ✉ *Rybné nám. 1,* ☎ *07/5340000,* FAX *07/5314311. 264 rooms, 4 apartments, 12 suites. 2 restaurants, pool, sauna, health club, nightclub, convention center. AE, DC, MC, V.*

$$$ ☷ **Hotel Pension No. 16.** This cozy pension in a quiet residential haven
★ close to the castle is a nice alternative to the big chain hotels—it provides all the conveniences, but with character. Rooms are warmed with wooden floors and ceilings; the apartments, which have kitchenettes, are a good deal for families. Breakfast is included. ✉ *Partizánska ul. 16a,* ☎ *07/5311672,* FAX *07/5311298. 11 rooms, 5 apartments. Breakfast room. AE, MC, V.*

$$$ ☷ **Perugia.** This stunning postmodern jewel is in a renovated building in the center of Old Town. The clean, colorful rooms are an eyeopener. Breakfast is included. ✉ *Zelená 5,* ☎ *07/5330719,* FAX *07/ 5331821. 13 rooms, 1 suite. Restaurant. AE, DC, MC, V.*

$$ ☷ **Hotel Echo.** This small, pink, modern hotel, not far from the center of Bratislava, looks more like a health club than a hotel, but it's a great place to stay, especially if you have a car. It has a friendly staff and large bright rooms; at press time, it was going to be privatized in the not-too-distant future. ✉ *Prešovská ul. 39,* ☎ *07/5669170,* FAX *07/ 5669174. 32 rooms with shower, 2 apartments. Restaurant. MC, V.*

Nightlife and the Arts

Bratislava does not have a roaring nightlife scene, but you can definitely find a place to settle in for a few drinks or some classical music. The English-language *Slovak Spectator,* a Bratislava-based newspaper, is a good place to check for listings on the city's cultural life. At press time, the *Spectator* came out biweekly, with plans to begin printing on a weekly basis in fall 1998. It's available at international chain hotels and many newsstands. For performance schedules and tickets, you can call BIS or Satur (☞ Contacts and Resources *in* Bratislava A to Z, *below*).

Nightlife

BARS AND LOUNGES

Bratislava doesn't offer much in the way of bars and lounges; after-dinner drinking takes place mostly in wine cellars and beer halls such as Kláštorná vináreň and Stará Sladovňa (☞ Dining, *above*).

JAZZ CLUBS

Bratislava hosts an annual jazz festival in the fall, but the city lacks a good venue for regular jazz gigs. That said, **Čierny Havran Club** (✉ Biela ul. 6, ☎ 07/5333159) occasionally presents local jazz acts.

ROCK CLUBS

Bratislava's live-music and club scene is expanding and venues are changing fast. Check the *Slovak Spectator* for the lowdown on the latest clubs. **Hysteria Pub** (✉ Odbojárov 9, ☎ 07/5254495) plays rock and dance tracks. **Harley-Davidson Club** (⊠ Rebarborova ul. 1, ☎ 07/ 5523585) is (surprise!) an American-style hard-rock joint. Take Bus 220 to the Ružinovský cintorín (Ružinov Cemetery) stop. If you prefer to stay downtown, you can try **Diskobar Centrum Pub** (⊠ Župné nám. 3, ☎ no phone).

The Arts

CONCERTS

The **Slovak Philharmonic Orchestra** plays a full program, featuring Czech and Slovak composers as well as European masters, at its home in the Reduta. You can get tickets at the box office, which is open weekends from 1 to 5 PM. ⊠ *Medená 3,* ☎ *07/5333351.*

FILM

Most new releases are shown in their original language with Slovak subtitles. **Charlie Centrum** regularly shows American classics, in English, in a friendly, artsy environment. ⊠ *Špitálska 4,* ☎ *07/363430.*

OPERA AND BALLET

The **Slovak National Theater** (☞ Exploring Bratislava, *above*) is the place for high-quality opera and ballet. Buy tickets at the theater office on the corner of Jesenského and Komenského streets weekdays between noon and 6 PM or 30 minutes before showtime. ⊠ *Hviezdoslavovo nám. 1,* ☎ *07/5333083.*

THEATER

Traditional theater is usually performed in Slovak. For non-Slovak speakers, the **Stoka Theater** blends nontraditional theater with performance art in a provocative and entertaining way. For details, contact the theater box office. ⊠ *Pribinova 1,* ☎ *07/324463.*

Shopping

Bratislava is an excellent place to find Slovak arts and crafts of all types. You will find plenty of folk-art and souvenir shops along **Obchodná ulica** (Shopping Street) as well as on **Námestie SNP.** Stores still come and go in this rapidly changing city, so don't be too surprised if some of the listed stores have vanished.

Antikvariát Steiner (⊠ Ventúrska ul. 20, ☎ 07/5333778) stocks beautiful old books, maps, graphics, and posters. **Dielo** (⊠ Námestie SNP 12, ☎ 07/368648; ⊠ Obchodná ul. 27, ☎ 07/5334568; ⊠ Obchodná 33, ☎ 07/5330566) has designer jewelry and clothing in addition to very unusual and fun ceramic pieces and other works of art.

For Slovak folk art, try **Folk, Folk** (⊠ Obchodná ul. 10, ☎ 07/5334292; ⊠ Rybárska brána 2, ☎ 07/5330176) for a wide-ranging choice, including pottery, handwoven tablecloths, wooden toys, and dolls with Slovak folk costumes. **ÚĽUV** (⊠ Námestie SNP 12, ☎ 07/323802) has a nice selection of hand-painted table pottery and vases, wooden figures, village folk clothing, and numerous types of small corn-husk figures, which are dirt cheap and can be very beautiful, though not easy to transport.

Bratislava A to Z

Arriving and Departing

BY BOAT

Hydrofoils travel the Danube between Vienna and Bratislava and Budapest and Bratislava from May to September. Boats depart in the morning from Bratislava, on the eastern bank of the Danube near the intersection of Mostová and Vajanského nábrežie, and return from Vienna or Budapest in the evening. Tickets cost $40–$80 per person and should be purchased in person at the dock. For reservations call Slovenská plavba dunajská (Slovak Danube Cruise; ☎ 07/363522 or 07/5362226).

BY BUS

There are numerous buses from Prague to Bratislava; the five-hour journey costs around 300 Sk. From Vienna, there are four buses a day from Autobusbahnhof Wien Mitte. The journey takes 1½–2 hours and costs about AS150. Bratislava's main bus terminal, Autobusová Stanica, is roughly 2 km (1 mi) from the city center; to get downtown, take Trolley 217 to Mierové námestie or 220 to the Tesco department store; or flag down a taxi.

BY CAR

There are good freeways from Prague to Bratislava via Brno (D1 and D2); the 315-km (203-mi) journey takes about 3½ hours. From Vienna, take the A4 and then Route 8 to Bratislava. The 60-km (37-mi) journey should take about 1½ hours. From Budapest, take route 10 to Komárno, then route 63 from Komárno to Bratislava; the trip takes roughly 2½ hours.

BY PLANE

Although few international airlines provide direct service to Bratislava, **ČSA** (☎ 07/361042 or 07/361045), the Czech national carrier, offers connections to Bratislava via Prague. You can also fly into Vienna's Schwechat Airport, about 60 km (37 mi) to the west, and proceed to Bratislava by either bus or train—a one-hour journey.

BY TRAIN

Reasonably efficient train service regularly connects Prague and Bratislava. Trains leave from Prague's Hlavní nádraží (main station) and from Holesovice station, and the journey takes five to six hours. The Intercity trains are slightly more expensive but faster. From Vienna, four trains daily make the one-hour trek to Bratislava. Bratislava's train station, **Hlavná Stanica**, is about 2 km (1 mi) from the city center; to travel downtown from the station, take Streetcar 1 or 13 to Poštová ulica or jump in a taxi.

Getting Around

Bratislava is compact, and most sights can be covered easily on foot. Taxis are reasonably priced and easy to hail; at night, they are the best option for returning home from wine cellars and clubs.

BY BUS AND TRAM

Buses and trams (*trolejbus*) in Bratislava run frequently and connect the city center with outlying sights. Stops are marked with signs picturing a bus or tram and listing the transportation lines served from the stop. Tickets cost 7 Sk and are available from large hotels, news agents, and tobacconists. You can't buy tickets on a bus or tram; you should also be leery of the orange vending machines at the major stops, since they're often out of order. Validate tickets on board (watch how the locals do it). The fine for riding without a validated ticket is 700 Sk, payable on the spot.

BY TAXI

Meters start at 20 Sk–30 Sk and jump 13 Sk–16 Sk per 1 km (½ mi). The number of dishonest cabbies, sadly, is on the rise; to avoid being ripped off, watch to see that the driver engages the meter. If the meter is broken, negotiate a price with the driver before even getting in the cab. Taxis are hailable on the street, or call 07/303111 or 301111.

Contacts and Resources

EMBASSIES

United States (✉ Hviezdoslavovo nám. 4, ☎ 07/5330861). **United Kingdom** (✉ Panská 16, ☎ 07/5317688). There are no Canadian or Australian embassies.

EMERGENCIES

Police (☎ 158). **Ambulance** (☎ 155). One **pharmacy** (✉ Palackého 10, ☎ 07/5319665) near the Old Town maintains 24-hour service; other pharmacies hold late hours on a rotating basis.

ENGLISH-LANGUAGE BOOKSTORES

Try **Big Ben Bookshop** (✉ Michalská 1, ☎ 07/5333632); there's also the beautiful secondhand bookstore **Antikvariát Steiner** (✉ Ventúrska ul. 20, ☎ 07/52834).

GUIDED TOURS

The best tours of Bratislava are offered by **BIS** (☞ Visitor Information, *below*), although tours during the off-season are conducted in German and only on weekends. Tours generally start at Primaciálne námestie. For an English-language tour, call ahead for an appointment; they prefer groups, but will accommodate various meeting places and times. Tours typically take two hours and cost 1,000 Sk per person. **Satur** (☞ Visitor Information, *below*) also offers tours of the capital from May through September; these also normally start at Primaciálne námestie. As with BIS, you'll need to make an appointment for an English-language tour, though you can arrange a meeting time and place.

TRAVEL AGENCIES

Tatratour (✉ Bajkalská 25, ☎ 07/5233252 or 07/5211219, FAX 07/5213624) is a large, dependable agency that can help arrange sightseeing tours throughout Slovakia. Its office in Dunaj Department Store (✉ Nám. SNP 30, ☎ 07/5335012) also acts as an official representative of American Express. **Satur** (☞ Visitor Information, *below*) can also provide basic travel-agency services, such as changing traveler's checks and booking bus and train tickets to outside destinations.

VISITOR INFORMATION

Bratislava's tourist information service, **Bratislavská Informačná Služba** (BIS; ✉ Klobučnícka 2, ☎ 07/5334370), can assist in finding a hotel or private accommodation. The office is also a good source for maps and basic information; it's open weekdays 8–4:30 (until 7 June–Sept.) and Saturday 8–1 (June–Sept. weekends 8 to 2). If you are arriving by train, the small BIS office in the station, open daily 8–8, can be very helpful.

The country's national travel agency, **Satur Tours and Travel** (formerly known as Čedok; ✉ Jesenského 5, ☎ 07/367645, FAX 07/323816), can help find accommodations in one of its hotels across the country and can book air, rail, and bus tickets. It's open weekdays from 9 to 6 and Saturday from 9 to noon.

THE HIGH TATRAS

Visiting the Vysoké Tatry (High Tatras) alone would make a trip to Slovakia worthwhile. Although the range is relatively compact as mountains go (just 32 km/20 mi from end to end), its peaks seem wilder and more starkly beautiful than even the Alps. Some 20 Tatras peaks exceed 8,000 ft, with the highest Gerlachovský Štít at 8,710 ft. The 35 mountain lakes are remote and clear, very cold, and sometimes eerily deep. Swimming is not permitted in the cold glacier lakes of the Tatras.

Most of the tourist facilities in the High Tatras are concentrated in three neighboring resort towns: Štrbské pleso, to the west; Smokovec, in the middle; and Tatranská Lomnica, to the east. Each town is pretty similar in terms of convenience and atmosphere, and all provide easy passage to the hills, so it makes little difference where you choose to begin your explorations of the mountains.

Hiking

The best way to see these beautiful mountains is on foot. Three of the best Tatras walks (three to five hours each) are outlined below, arranged according to difficulty (with the easiest and prettiest first), although a reasonably fit person of any age will have little trouble with any of the three. Yet even though the trails are well marked, it is very important to buy a walking map of the area—the detailed *Vysoké Tatry, Letná Turistická Mapa* is available for around 20 Sk at newspaper kiosks. If you're planning to take any of the higher-level walks, be sure to wear proper shoes with good ankle support. Also use extreme caution in early spring, when melting snow can turn the trails into icy rivers.

Skiing

The entire region is crisscrossed with paths ideal for cross-country skiing. You can buy a special ski map at newspaper kiosks. The season lasts from the end of December through April, though the best months are traditionally January and February. Renting ski equipment is not much of a problem, and it is reasonably priced. Ždiar, toward the Polish border, has a good ski area for beginners.

Numbers in the margin correspond to numbers on the Slovakia map.

Poprad

⑲ *329 km (204 mi) east of Bratislava along Highways E75 and E50.*

Poprad, the gateway to the Tatras, is a good place to begin exploring the region. But don't expect a beautiful mountain village. Poprad fell victim to some of the most insensitive Communist planning perpetrated in the country after the war. There's no need to linger here. Instead, drive or take the electric railroad to the superior sights and facilities of the more rugged resorts just over 30 km (20 mi) to the north.

Dining and Lodging

$ ✕ **Slovenská Reštaurácia.** If you have to spend a few hours in Poprad,
★ having a meal in this charming rustic restaurant is the best way of doing so. Try the *bryndzové halušky* (dumplings with goat cheese) or *strapačky s kapustou* (homemade noodles with sauerkraut). ⊠ *Ul. 1. mája 216,* ☎ *092/722870. No credit cards.*

$ ⊞ **Europa.** This cozy little hotel is next to the train station. From the reception area to the modest, old-fashioned rooms (with neither bathrooms nor TVs), the place exudes a faint elegance. ⊠ *Wolkerova ul.,* ☎ *092/721883. 40 rooms without bath. Bar. No credit cards.*

En Route A kilometer and a half (1 mile) northeast of Poprad is the medieval hamlet of **Spišská Sobota,** now a suburb of Poprad but formerly one of the main centers of the historic Spiš Empire. Sobota's lovely old square has a Romanesque church, rebuilt in Gothic style in the early 16th century, with an ornate altar carved by master Pavol of Levoča. But the most impressive of all is the setting, a 16th-century oasis amid the cultural desert of socialist realism.

Smokovec

⑳ *32 km (20 mi) north of Poprad.*

The High Tatras

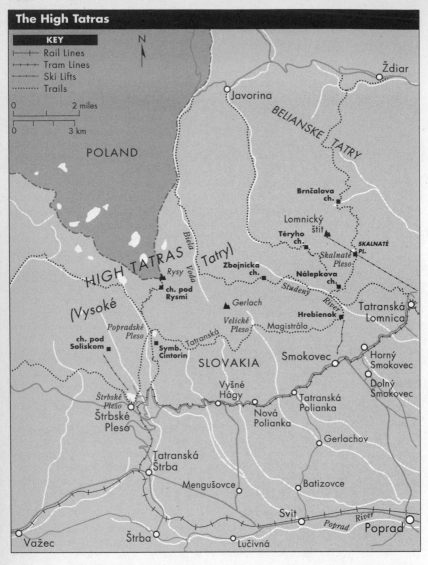

KEY
- ┼ Rail Lines
- ┼┼┼ Tram Lines
- ┼┼┼ Ski Lifts
- ······· Trails

N

0   2 miles
0   3 km

POLAND

Javorina

Ždiar

BELIANSKE TATRY

Biela Voda

Rysy

HIGH TATRAS

(Vysoké

Tatry)

Brnčalova ch.

Lomnický štít

Téryho ch.

SKALNATÉ PL.

Skalnaté Pleso

Zbojnícka ch.

ch. pod Rysmi

Nálepkova ch.

Gerlach

Studený River

Tatranská Lomnica

Velické Pleso

Hrebienok

Popradské Pleso

Tatranská

Magistrála

ch. pod Soliskom

Symb. Cintorin

SLOVAKIA

Smokovec

Horný Smokovec

Dolný Smokovec

Štrbské Pleso

Štrbské Pleso

Vyšné Hágy

Tatranská Polianka

Gerlachov

Tatranská Štrba

Nová Polianka

Mengušovce

Batizovce

Svit

Poprad River

Poprad

Važec

Štrba

Lučivná

The first town you'll reach by road or rail from Poprad is Smokovec, the undisputed center of the Slovak Tatras resorts and a good starting point for mountain excursions. Smokovec is divided into two principal areas, Starý Smokovec (Old Smokovec) and Nový Smokovec (New Smokovec), which are within a stone's throw of each other.

The Tatras are tailor-made for hikers of all levels. Starý Smokovec is a great starting point for a trek that parallels a cascading waterfall for much of its three-hour length. From Starý Smokovec, walk out along the main road in the direction of Tatranská Lomnica for roughly 1 km (½ mi). In Tatranská Lesná, follow the yellow-marked path that winds gently uphill through the pines.

Farther along there are red markers leading to the funicular at Hrebienok, which brings you back to the relative comforts of Starý Smokovec. However, if you're in good physical shape and there is plenty of daylight left, consider extending your hike by four hours. (The extension is striking, but avoid it during winter, when you may find yourself neck-deep in snow.) Just before the Bilková chata, turn right along the green path and then follow the blue, red, and then green trails in the direction of windswept **Tery chata,** a turn-of-the-century chalet perched amid five lonely alpine lakes. The scenery is a few notches above dazzling. Once you reach the chalet after two strenuous hours of hiking, backtrack to Bilková chata and follow the signs to the funicular at Hrebienok.

Dining and Lodging

$$ ✕ **Restaurant Koliba.** This charming restaurant with rustic decor and
★ an open-face grill serves up tasty local fare. Try *kapustová polievka,* sauerkraut soup with mushrooms and sausage. ✉ *Starý Smokovec,* ☎ *0969/422204. No credit cards. Closed Sun.*

$$ ✕🏨 **Villa Dr. Szontagh.** Away from the action in Nový Smokovec,
★ this steepled little chalet offers mostly peace and quiet. The darkly furnished rooms and public areas are well maintained, and the courtly staff goes out of its way to please. The decent restaurant has an extensive wine cellar. ✉ *Nový Smokovec,* ☎ *0969/422061. 9 rooms with bath, 4 apartments, 1 suite. Restaurant, cafeteria. AE, MC, V. Closed Nov.–mid-Dec.*

$$$ 🏨 **Grand Hotel.** Along with its sister hotel in Tatranská Lomnica
★ (Grandhotel Praha; ☞ *below*), this hotel epitomizes Tatra luxury at its turn-of-the-century best. The hotel's golden Tudor facade rises majestically over the town, with the peaks of the Tatras looming in the background. In season, skiers and hikers crowd the reception area and hallways, but the rooms themselves are quiet. Breakfast is included. ✉ *Starý Smokovec,* ☎ *0969/422154,* FAX *0969/422157. 78 rooms, 52 with bath; 5 apartments. Restaurant, bar, café, pool, sauna. AE, DC, MC, V.*

Outdoor Activities and Sports

PARAGLIDING

Local sports shops provide equipment for many sports, including paragliding and paraskiing. The rates, surprisingly, are very reasonable. For information, consult the sporting-goods store **Športcentrum** (✉ Starý Smokovec V/5, ☎ 0969/422425). It's a 10-minute walk along the highway, to the east of Starý Smokovec.

SKIING

For buying or renting equipment, try the Športcentrum (☎ 0969/422425) in Starý Smokovec; there's also the **Ski Service** in the Švajčiarsky Dom, next to the Grand Hotel (☞ *above*). Arrive early (it opens at 8)—the equipment rents quickly when there is snow.

Štrbské Pleso

㉑ *18 km (11 mi) west of Smokovec.*

Štrbské pleso is the main center in the Tatras for active sports. The best ski slopes are not far away, and many excellent hiking trails are within easy reach. The town not only has the most modern hotels (and the most jarringly modern hotel architecture), but it also commands the finest panoramas in the Tatras.

Lodging

$$$ 🏨 **Patria.** This modern, slanting pyramid on the shores of a mountain
★ lake has two obvious advantages: location and view. Ask for a room on a higher floor; those overlooking the lake have balconies, and the other side opens onto the mountains. ✉ *Štrbské pleso,* ☎ *0969/ 492591,* FAX *0969/492590. 140 rooms, 10 apartments. 3 restaurants, bar, café, pool, barbershop, convention center. AE, DC, MC, V.*

$$ ⛄ **Fis.** Right next to the ski jump and within easy reach of several slopes, this hotel is for young, athletic types. It makes no pretense to elegance, preferring a busy jumble of track suits, families with young children, and teenagers on the make. The rooms, each with a balcony, are pleasant, if a little institutional. ⊠ *Štrbské pleso,* ☎ *0969/492221,* FAX *0969/492422. 70 rooms. 3 restaurants, pool, sauna, exercise room. AE, DC, MC, V.*

Outdoor Activities and Sports

SKIING

You can buy skis and equipment, plus a thousand other things, in the department store **Javor** (⊠ Near train station, ☎ 0969/492835). The Patria and Fis hotels (☞ *above*) rent skis; the Patria also has a ski school.

Tatranská Lomnica

㉒ *16 km (10 mi) southwest of Štrbské pleso.*

Tatranská Lomnica, on the eastern end of the electric rail line, offers a near-perfect combination of peace, convenience, and atmosphere. Moreover, the lift behind the Grandhotel Praha brings some of the best walks in the Tatras to within 10 minutes or so of your hotel door.

The Magistrale, a 24-km (15-mi) walking trail that skirts the peaks just above the tree line, offers some of the best views for the least amount of exertion. A particularly stunning stretch of the route—which is marked by red signposts—begins in Tatranská Lomnica and ends 5 km (3 mi) away in Starý Smokovec. The total walking time is three or four hours.

To start the walk, take the funicular behind the Grandhotel Praha in Tatranská Lomnica to Skalnaté pleso—a 10-minute proposition. From here you can access the trail immediately; or if you are really adventurous, consider a 30-minute detour via cable car (25 Sk) to the top of Lomnický Štít (8,635 ft), the second-highest peak in the range. Because of the harsh temperatures (be sure to dress warmly even in summer), you're permitted to linger at the top for only 30 minutes, after which you take the cable car back down.

Return to the cable-car station at Skalnaté pleso and follow the red markers of the Magistrale Trail to the right (as you stand facing Tatranská Lomnica below). The first section of the trail cuts sharply across the face of the Lomnický Mountain just above the tree line. The trail then bends through a series of small valleys, each view more outstanding than the last. Finally, you'll begin a small descent into the woods. Continue by following the signs to Hrebienok.

NEED A BREAK?
Don't pass up the chance to take a break at the rustic **Bilíkova Chata** (☎ 0969/422439) in a little clearing just before you reach Hrebienok. This cozy cabin is a veritable oasis after the long walk. It's open 7:30 AM to 9 PM from December to March and 7 AM to 10 PM between July and mid-September.

From Hrebienok, take the funicular down to Starý Smokovec. It runs at 45-minute intervals beginning at 6:30 AM and ending at 7:45 PM, but check the schedule posted at the Bilíková Chata for any schedule changes.

Dining and Lodging

$$ ✕ **Zbojnícka Koliba.** This stylish cottage restaurant serves up savory shish kebab made on an open-face grill in a romantic setting, though the portions are snack-size. ⊠ *Tatranská Lomnica,* ☎ *0969/467267. No credit cards. Closed Sun. No lunch.*

$$$ ✕🏨 **Grandhotel Praha.** This large, multiturreted mansion, dating from
★ the turn of the century and resting in the foothills of the Lomnický Štít,
is one of the wonders of the Tatras. Although it is no longer filled with
the rich and famous, the hotel has managed to retain an air of relaxed
elegance. Rooms are large and nicely decorated—ask for a large cor-
ner room with a view of the mountains. Since the hotel is far from the
action, the price remains reasonable for what's offered. ✉ *Tatranská
Lomnica,* ☎ *0969/467941,* ℻ *0969/467891. 90 rooms. Restaurant,
sauna, aerobics, nightclub. AE, DC, MC, V.*

Outdoor Activities and Sports
SKIING
Skalnaté pleso, above Tatranská Lomnica, has moderately challeng-
ing slopes. You can rent skis at the Metalurg and Slovan hotels.

The High Tatras A to Z

Arriving and Departing
BY BUS
Daily bus service connects Prague and Bratislava with Poprad, but on
this run trains tend to be quicker and more comfortable. From Bratislava
the trip takes about six and a half hours; from Prague the journey will
take 10 hours or longer, depending on the route.

BY CAR
Poprad, the gateway to the Tatras, is 328 km (205 mi) from Bratislava,
with a four-lane stretch between the capital and Trenčín and a well-
marked, two-lane highway thereafter; the drive takes about four and
a half hours. The drive to Poprad from Prague takes the main east–
west highway about 560 km (350 mi) from the Czech capital in the
direction of Hradec Králové. The eight-hour drive from Prague is rel-
atively comfortable, very scenic, and can be broken up easily with an
overnight stay in Olomouc, in the Czech Republic province of Moravia.
The road is well marked, with some four-lane stretches.

BY PLANE
Tatra Air (☞ Getting Around *in* Slovakia A to Z, *below*) offers service
from Bratislava to Košice. From Košice, it's easiest to take a train to
Poprad.

BY TRAIN
Regular rail service connects both Prague and Bratislava with Poprad,
but book ahead: The trains are often impossibly crowded, especially
in August and during the skiing season. A trip from Bratislava's Hlavná
Stanica to Poprad's station, **Železničná stanica Poprad** (✉ Wolkerova
ul. 479, ☎ 092/721139), takes four hours on an Intercity train. Trains
leave Bratislava every two or three hours; the most convenient are often
the overnight trains. The journey from Prague to Poprad takes about
10 hours; several night trains depart from Prague's Hlavní nádraží (main
station) and from Holešovice station.

Getting Around
BY BUS
The **SAD** bus network links all the towns in the High Tatras, but un-
less you are traveling to a town not directly on an electric rail route,
the train service is faster, and often a little bit cheaper.

BY CAR
Having a car is more of a hindrance than a help if you're just going to
the High Tatras. Traveling the electric railway is much quicker than
taking the winding roads that connect the resorts, and hotel parking
fees can add up quickly. However, if you plan to tour the region's smaller

towns and villages, or if you are continuing on to eastern Slovakia, a car will prove nearly indispensable. Drives between towns can be quite short; going between Poprad and Smokovec, for instance, takes roughly 15 minutes, while the drive from Poprad to Štrbské Pleso lasts under an hour.

BY TRAIN

An efficient electric railway (which shares the regular train stations) connects Poprad with the High Tatras resorts, and the resorts with one another. Trains run every 30 to 60 minutes; there is a schedule information contact (☎ 092/62509), but it's only in Slovak. If you're going only to the Tatras, you won't need any other form of transportation.

Contacts and Resources

EMERGENCIES

Police (☎ 158). **Medical emergencies** (☎ 155). **Car repair** (☎ 0969/422571).

GUIDED TOURS

From Poprad airport, **TLS Air** offers a novel biplane flight over the Tatras region; contact the Satur office in Poprad (☞ Visitor Information, *below*). The Satur office in Starý Smokovec (☞ Visitor Information, *below*) is also helpful in arranging tours of the Tatras and surrounding area. From May to October, Satur offers a bargain tour of Levoča, Kežmarok, and Markušovce for groups of eight or more, with English and German commentary.

LATE-NIGHT PHARMACIES

Pharmacies (*lekáreň*) are in all three major resorts and in the neighboring town of Ždiar. Only pharmacies in Poprad maintain late hours on a rotating basis.

VISITOR INFORMATION

There are tourist information centers in all the resort towns listed above. **Starý Smokovec** (✉ Dom Služieb—House of Services, ☎ 0969/186); **Štrbské pleso** (✉ Hotel Toliar, ☎ 0969/492690); **Tatranská Lomnica** (✉ Múzeum, ☎ 0969/467289). **Slovakoturist** (☎ 0969/422031), in Horný Smokovec, can arrange private accommodations, including stays in mountain cottages.

You'll find Satur offices in **Poprad** (✉ Námestie sv. Egídia 3006/116, ☎ 092/721353, FAX 092/63619) and **Starý Smokovec** (☎ 0969/422710), where you can change money, get hiking and driving maps, and find assistance in booking hotels (but not private rooms).

For more in-depth information on routes, mountain chalets, and weather conditions, contact the **Horská služba** (Mountain Rescue Service; ☎ 0969/422820) in Starý Smokovec. **Asociácia horských vodcov** (Mountain Guides Association; ☎ 0969/422066) can also provide guides for the more difficult routes for 2,500 Sk to 4,000 Sk per day.

CENTRAL SLOVAKIA

Though generally overlooked by tourists, central Slovakia is the country's heart and soul. This is where the nation was born and where Slovak folklore and deep-rooted traditions continue to flourish.

Formerly a medieval mining town, Banská Bystrica lies at the heart of the region and is the ideal base from which to explore the towns and villages surrounding it. The region's two other historical mining towns, Banská Štavnica and Kremnica, have remained more or less frozen in time since their glory days in the Middle Ages.

The beauty of central Slovakia, however, lies not so much in its architecture as in its inspiring natural landscapes. The region is not only home to the High Tatras (☞ *above*) but also contains the Low Tatras, the second-highest mountain range in Slovakia and largest by area. In winter, some of the best skiing slopes in the country can be found in the Low Tatras, which are mostly free from the hordes of tourists migrating to the High Tatras. In summer, the area offers wonderful hiking trails, caves, and scenic valleys.

Unfortunately, in central Slovakia you will also find some of the worst crimes against nature. In an effort to enrich the region in the 1950s, the Communist regime built many large steel- and tank-producing factories, which litter some of the most beautiful valleys in the country. Many of the worst can be seen while heading east from Banská Bystrica in the direction of Brezno; to call them an eyesore would be an understatement.

Numbers in the margin correspond to numbers on the Slovakia map.

Banská Bystrica

㉓ *124 km (77 mi) southwest of Poprad, 205 km (128 mi) east of Bratislava.*

Surrounded by three mountain ranges—the Low Tatras, the Fatras, and the Slovak Rudohorie—Banská Bystrica is in an ideal starting point for exploring the beauty of the region. (The outlying areas are plagued with concrete apartment buildings, but you can't have everything.)

Banská Bystrica has been around since the 13th century, acquiring its wealth from the nearby mines. Following the Tartar invasion in 1241, the Hungarian king Belo IV granted special privileges to encourage the immigration of German settlers, who together with the natives developed the prosperous mining of copper and precious metals. During the 19th century, the town was a major focus of Slovak national life, and it was from a school here that the teaching of the Slovak language originated and spread to the rest of the country.

The city is also famous as the center of the Slovak National Uprising during World War II. It was here that the underground Slovak National Council initiated the revolt on August 29, 1944. For some two months, thousands of Slovaks valiantly rose up against the Slovak puppet regime and their Nazi oppressors, forcing the Germans to divert critically needed troops and equipment from the front lines. Though the Germans eventually quashed the uprising on October 27, the costly operation is credited with accelerating the Allied victory and gaining Slovakia the short-lived appellation of ally.

You'll find reminders of the uprising (known in Slovak by the initials SNP) just about everywhere. One of the main sights is the **Múzeum Slovenského Národného Povstania** (Museum of the Slovak National Uprising), which stands in a large field just outside the center of town, between Horná ulica and Ulica Dukelských Hrdinov. It's difficult to miss the monument's massive concrete wings—the effect is particularly striking at night. The museum's focus has been shifting from communism to more recent national events. ⊠ *Kapitulská ul. 23,* ☎ *088/723258.* ⊡ *10 Sk.* ⊙ *May–Sept. Tues.–Sun. 9–6, Oct.–Apr. Tues.–Sun. 9–4.*

If you're partial to less recent history, head for the main square, the Námestie SNP, with its cheery collection of Renaissance and Baroque houses. The most impressive is the **Thurzo House**, an amalgamation of two late-Gothic structures built in 1495 by the wealthy Thurzo family. The genuine Renaissance sgraffiti on the outside were added during the 16th century, when the family's wealth was at its height. Today the building houses the Stredoslovenské múzeum (Central Slovak Museum) which is more interesting for the chance to see inside the house than for its artifacts. ⊠ *Námestie SNP 4,* ☎ *088/725897.* 🎟 *10 Sk.* ☉ *Weekdays 8–noon and 1–4, Sun. 9–noon and 1–4 (mid-June–mid-Sept. until 5).*

En Route   South of Banská Bystrica in the direction of Zvolen is the tiny village of Hronsek. This hamlet certainly warrants a stop—it has a wooden church built without a single piece of metal. The builders of this Protestant church, which was constructed at the time of the Counter-Reformation, abided by strict guidelines stipulating that wood was the only material to be used for building a church—even nails had to be made of wood.

Dining and Lodging

$$ ✗ **Starobystrická Pivnica.** Grilled food is the house specialty at this clas-
★   sic wine cellar, which serves a spicy version of Slovak cuisine—such as the spicy pepper steak. ⊠ *Námestie SNP 9,* ☎ *088/754326. MC, V.*

$$$ ✗🏨 **Arcade Hotel.** This 16th-century building on the main square is
★   an ideal place to stay; the rooms and apartments vary in size, comfort, and cost, but all are equipped with the basic creature comforts, including a refrigerator and satellite TV. ⊠ *Námestie SNP 5,* ☎ *088/702111,* FAX *088/723126. 9 rooms, 2 suites, 3 apartments. Restaurant, bar, café, dance club, meeting room. AE, DC, MC, V.*

$$ 🏨 **Lux.** This is one of the few successful high-rise hotels in Slovakia, managing to combine modernity with some semblance of style. Rooms (especially on the upper floors facing town) have a magnificent view over the mountains. ⊠ *Nám. slobody 2,* ☎ *088/7402318,* FAX *088/ 743853. 112 rooms with bath, 1 suite, 7 apartments. Restaurant, bar, café. MC, V.*

Outdoor Activities and Sports

The mountainous region surrounding Banská Bystrica is ideal for all sorts of outdoor activities, from walking to skiing. The most attractive hiking trails are to the north of Banská Bystrica and in the area between Banská Bystrica and Kremnica. There is a hiking map of the Low Tatras, which includes routes for cyclists, available at tourist information (you can inquire here about bike rentals, too, since not many places rent them).

Nightlife and the Arts

The best bet for entertainment is seeing an opera or a ballet at the **Štátna Opera** (⊠ Národná 11, ☎ 088/724418); or there are puppet shows at the **Bábkové Divadlo na Rázcestí** (⊠ Kollárova 18, ☎ 088/753023). Another option is spending an evening in one of the city's wine cellars, listening to Gypsy music.

Kremnica

❷   *50 km (31 mi) southwest of Banská Bystrica.*

Kremnica, known as the Golden City, was one of the most famous mining towns in Slovakia and one of the richest gold mines in medieval Europe. What you'll find today is a beautifully preserved medieval town, surrounded by sturdy walls and gates that guarded the gold once stored in Kremnica's vaults. You can enter the town through the impressive **Dolná Brána** (Lower Gate), dating from 1441. Beyond, you'll see some of the best-kept merchant houses in Slovakia.

You can learn about the town's 650-year history as a mining and minting center at the **Kremnické múzeum** (Kremnica Museum). For coin enthusiasts, the second floor has fascinating exhibits of coins in use in Central Europe from Celtic and Roman times to the modern day. English commentary is available. ⊠ *Štefánikovo nám. 10,* ☎ *0857/ 742696.* ⛶ *16 Sk.* ⊙ *Oct.–Apr. Tues.–Sat. 8:30–4:30, May–Sept. Tues.–Sun. 9–5.*

Dining

$ ✕ **Jeleň.** For a delicious lunch or dinner, try this unassuming restaurant in the new part of town, outside the walls. Start out with the delicious lentil soup, and then try the roast beef with paprika sauce and dumplings. ⊠ *Dolná ul. 22,* ☎ *0857/744105. No credit cards.*

Banská Štiavnica

㉕ *42 km (26 mi) south of Kremnica, 45 km (28 mi) south of Banská Bystrica.*

Since the 11th century, this little town has earned its wealth from mining, and today it is essentially one large mining museum. German miners arrived here to exploit rich gold and silver deposits, and their success is apparent in some of the town's remaining monuments, such as the golden Trinity column and the impressive Lutheran church.

Built on the rocks above town, the **Starý zámok**(Old Castle) dates back to the early 13th century (with additions in practically every subsequent building style). It served as a fortress to protect the wealth of the local bigwigs against the Turkish invaders. ⊠ *Starozámocká 11,* ☎ *0859/ 23113.* ⛶ *15 Sk.* ⊙ *Tues.–Sun. 9–4.*

The **Nový zámok** (New Castle) was built between 1564 and 1571 as part of an effort to strengthen fortification of the town against invasions from the Turks. The six-story Renaissance building was used as a watchtower and later became the town's live clock—the exact time was announced every quarter hour by a trumpet. Inside you'll find historical exhibits of the Turkish invasions in the 16th and 17th centuries. ⊠ *Novozámocká 22,* ☎ *0859/21543.* ⛶ *20 Sk.* ⊙ *May–Sept., Tues.– Sun. 8–4; Oct.–Apr., weekdays 8–3.*

You can view some of the town's original mining buildings and machinery dating back to the early 13th century at the **Banské múzeum** (Open Air Mining Museum). The museum is about 2 km (1 mi) from town. ⊠ *Štiavnické Bane,* ☎ *0859/22971.* ⛶ *20 Sk.* ⊙ *July–Aug. Tues.–Sun. 9–5, Sept.–June weekdays 8–3.*

OFF THE **MANSION SAINT ANTON –** Don't miss this charming late-Baroque
BEATEN PATH château in the small village of Antol, just outside Banská Štavnica. The château displays its original furnishings and has an exhibition on hunting arms and game. ⊠ *Svätý Anton,* ☎ *0859/23932.* ⛶ *50 Sk.* ⊙ *May–Sept., Tues.–Sun. 8–4; Oct.–Apr., Tues.–Sat. 8–3.*

Dining and Lodging

$$ ✕▥ **Salamander.** This brand-new hotel, in a beautifully renovated
★ 16th-century building, has everything you would expect from a first-class establishment. The rooms are large and bright, and the public areas are decorated with antiques. ⊠ *Palárikova 1,* ☎ *0859/23992,* ▥ *0859/621262. Restaurant, ice cream parlor, outdoor café. AE, DC, MC, V.*

$ ✕▥ **Antolský Mlyn.** This family-run pension is in a tiny village just outside Banská Štavnica near the château at Antol. Though small, the rooms are modern and have new, clean bathrooms. ✉ *Svätý Anton*, ☎ *0859/ 621011. 7 rooms with shower, 1 apartment. Restaurant. No credit cards.*

Central Slovakia A to Z

Arriving and Departing

BY CAR

It's most convenient to get to Banská Bystrica by car. From Bratislava, take the E571 to Zvolen via Nitra, and then follow the E66 to Banská Bystrica; the trip should take roughly 2½ hours. Driving from either Vienna or Prague takes about four hours. The E58 leads from Vienna to Bratislava. From Prague, take the E65 to Brno, then the E50 to Zvolen, and continue on the E66 to Banská Bystrica.

BY TRAIN

Unless you have a car, the best means of arriving in Banská Bystrica is by rail. There are daily trains from Bratislava, and the journey takes almost three hours. The trip from Košice to Banská Bystrica, one of the most scenic railway routes in the country (take the northern, not the southern, route), lasts about five hours.

Getting Around

BY BUS AND TRAIN

For those without a car, Banská Bystrica is the most convenient base, since it serves as a hub for the complex rail and bus system.

BY CAR

Driving through this region is relatively quick and hassle-free. The drive between Banská Bystrica and Kremnica along Routes 66 and 65, for instance, can be done in under an hour. In some cases, such as the drive to Banská Štiavnica, the roads are small but well marked.

Contacts and Resources

EMERGENCIES

Police (☎ 158). **Ambulance** (☎ 155).

GUIDED TOURS

The **Satur** office in Banská Bystrica (✉ Nám. Slobody 4, ☎ 088/ 742575) can book hotels and arrange English-language tours at a reasonable cost.

VISITOR INFORMATION

Banská Bystrica (✉ Nám. Štefana Moyzesa 26, ☎ 088/186). **Kremnica** (✉ Štefánikovo nám. 35/44, ☎ 0857/742856). **Banská Štiavnica** (✉ Radničné nám. 1, ☎ 0859/21859).

EASTERN SLOVAKIA

To the east of the High Tatras lies an expanse of Slovakia that seldom appears on tourist itineraries. However, eastern Slovakia is a veritable hiker's paradise. In addition to the offerings at Slovenský Raj, trails fan out in all directions in the area known as Spišská Magura, to the north and east of Kežmarok. Good outdoor swimming can be found in the lakes in Slovenský Raj and in Michalovce, east of Košice.

For 1,000 years, eastern Slovakia was isolated from the West; much of the region was regarded simply as the hinterland of Greater Hungary. Isolation has its advantages, however, and therein may lie the charm of this area. The Baroque and Renaissance facades that dominate the towns of Bohemia and Moravia make an appearance in eastern Slovakia as well, but they're often done in local wood instead of stone; look especially for the wooden altars in Levoča and other towns.

The relative isolation also fostered the development of an entire civilization in medieval times, the Spiš, with no counterpart in the Czech Republic or even elsewhere in Slovakia. The territory of the kingdom, which spreads out to the east and south of the High Tatras, was originally settled by Slavonic and later by German immigrants who came here in medieval times to work the mines and defend the western kingdoms against invasion. Some 24 towns eventually came to join the Spiš group, functioning as a miniprincipality within the Hungarian monarchy. The group had its own hierarchies and laws, which were quite different from those brought in by Magyar or Saxon settlers.

Although the last Spiš town lost its independence 100 years ago, much of the group's architectural legacy remains—another fortuitous by-product of isolation, namely economic stagnation. Spiš towns are predominantly Gothic beneath their graceful Renaissance overlays. Their steep shingled roofs, high timber-framed gables, and brick-arched doorways have survived in a remarkable state of preservation. Needless to say, Spiš towns are worth seeking out when you see them on a map; look for the prefix "Spišsky" preceding a town name.

Farther to the northeast, the influences of Byzantium are strongly felt, most noticeably in the form of the simple wooden churches that dominate the villages along the frontier with Poland and Ukraine. This area marks a border in Europe that has stood for a thousand years: the ancient line between Rome and Constantinople, between Western Christianity and the Byzantine Empire. The busy industrial cities of Prešov and Košice, with their belching factories and rows of housing projects, quickly bring you back to the 20th century.

When visiting the region, keep in mind that more expensive does not necessarily mean better when it comes to food. Stay clear of the large hotels and instead look to innovative, privately owned restaurants. Eastern Slovakia has successfully borrowed the best dishes and techniques from the Hungarians, the Ukrainians, and the Poles to create an original and delicious cuisine.

Numbers in the margin correspond to numbers on the Slovakia map.

Bardejov

26 *88 km (55 mi) east of Kežmarok.*

Bardejov is a great surprise, tucked away in this remote corner of Slovakia yet possessing one of the nation's most enchanting squares. Indeed, Bardejov owes its splendors precisely to its location astride the ancient trade routes to Poland and Russia. It's hard to put your finger on exactly why the square is so captivating—it could be the lack of arcades in front of the houses or the pointed roofs of the houses, which have a lighter, almost comic effect.

The exterior of the Gothic **Kostol svätého Egídia** (St. Egidius Church), built in stages in the 15th century, is undeniably handsome, but take a walk inside for the real treasure. The nave is lined with 11 priceless, purely Gothic side altars, all carved between 1460 and 1510 and perfectly preserved. The most famous of the altars is to the left of the main altar (look for the number 1 on the side). The intricate work of Stefan Tarner, it depicts the birth of Christ and dates from the 1480s. ⊠ *Radničné nám.*

The modest building with late-Gothic portals and Renaissance detailing in the center of the town square is the **Radnice** (town hall). ⊠ *Radničné nám. 17.*

★ You may want to visit the pink **Šariš** (Icon Museum) to view its collection of 16th-century icons and paintings, taken from the area's numerous Russian Orthodox churches. Many of the icons depict the story of St. George slaying the dragon (for the key to the princess's chastity belt!). The legend of St. George, which probably originated in pre-Christian mythology, was often used to attract the peasants of the area to the more abstemious myths of Christianity. Pick up the short but interesting commentary in English when you buy your ticket. ⊠ *Radničné nám. 13,* ☎ *0935/722009.* ⊠ *25 Sk.* ☉ *May–Sept. Tues.– Sun. 9–noon and 12:30–5:30, Oct.–Apr. 8–noon and 12:30–4.*

Lodging

$$ 🏨 **Roland.** This pension is right on the main square, but it's still a quiet place at night. Rooms are filled with plain-Jane wooden furniture, but there are nice views of a neighboring park and church. ⊠ *Radničné nám. 22,* ☎ *0935/186. 3 suites. Restaurant. No credit cards.*

Jedlinka

13 km (8 mi) north of Bardejov along the road to Svidník.

The area's great delights are unquestionably the old wooden churches still in use in their original village settings. Like most others, the one in Jedlinka dates from the 18th and 19th centuries and combines Byzantine and Baroque architectural elements. Its three onion-domed towers rise above the west front. Inside, the north, east, and south walls are painted with biblical scenes; the west wall was reserved for icons (many of which now hang in the icon museum in Bardejov). The churches are usually locked, but if you happen across a villager, ask him or her (with appropriate key-turning gestures) to let you in. More often than not, someone will turn up with a key, and you'll have your own guided tour.

Medzilaborce

㉗ *40 km (25 mi) east of Svidník, 70 km (43 mi) east of Bardejov.*

The sleepy border town of Medzilaborce is quickly becoming the unlikely mecca for fans of pop-art guru Andy Warhol. It was here in 1991, near the birthplace of Warhol's parents, that the country's cultural authorities, in conjunction with the Andy Warhol Foundation for Visual
★ Arts in New York, opened the **Múzeum moderného umenia rodiny Warholovcov** (Warhol Family Museum of Modern Art). In all, the museum holds 17 original Warhol silk screens, including two from the famous Campbell's Soup series, and portraits of Lenin and singer Billie Holiday. The Russian Orthodox church across the street lends a suitably surreal element to the setting. ⊠ *ul. Andyho Warhola,* ☎ *0939/ 21059.* ⊠ *15 Sk.* ☉ *Tues.–Sun. 10–6.*

Košice

㉘ *30 km (19 mi) south of Prešov, 418 km (259 mi) east of Bratislava.*

In Košice you'll leave rural Slovakia behind. Though rich historically, Košice is a sprawling, modern city, the second largest in Slovakia after Bratislava. Positioned along the main trade route between Hungary and Poland, the city was the second largest in the Hungarian Empire (after Buda) during the Middle Ages. With the Turkish occupation of the Hungarian homeland in the 16th and 17th centuries, the town became a safe haven for the Hungarian nobility.

In this century the city has been shuttled between Hungary, Czechoslovakia, and now Slovakia. Sadly, Slovak efforts to eliminate Hungarian influence in Košice after World War II were remarkably successful. As you walk around, you'll be hard-pressed to find evidence that this was once a great Hungarian city—even with the Hungarian frontier just 20 km (12 mi) away. The city remains home to a popular Hungarian theater, as well as a successful Romany (Gypsy) theater, the only one of its kind in the world.

You won't see many Westerners strolling Košice's enormous medieval square, the **Hlavná ulica**; most of the tourists here are Hungarians on a day trip to shop and sightsee. The town square is dominated on its
★ southern flank by the huge tower of the Gothic **Dóm svätej Alžbety** (Cathedral of St. Elizabeth). Built in the 15th century and finally completed in 1508, the cathedral is the largest in Slovakia. First walk over to the north side (facing the square) to look at the famed Golden Door. Inside the church is one of Europe's largest Gothic altarpieces, a 35-ft-tall medieval wood carving attributed to the master Erhard of Ulm. You can also pay a visit to the great Hungarian leader Francis Rakóczi II, most of whose remains (he left his heart in Paris) were placed in a crypt under the north transept of the cathedral. Although generally open to worshipers, the church is under renovation, and you may not be able to wander at will. ⊠ *Hlavná ul.* ◷ *Daily services at 7* PM.

On the east side of the town square is the **Dom Košického vládneho programu** (House of the Košice Government Program), where the Košice Program was proclaimed on April 5, 1945, announcing the reunion of the Czech lands and Slovakia into one national state. ⊠ *Hlavná ul.*

The **Štátne divadlo** (State Theater), a mishmash of neo-Renaissance and neo-Baroque elements built at the end of the last century, dominates the center of the town square. For a town this size, the quality of theater, ballet, and opera productions is very impressive. Tickets are reasonably priced and can be bought at the theater box office. ⊠ *Hlavná ul. 58,* ☎ *095/6221231.* ◷ *Weekdays 1–6, or 1 hr before performances.*

On the main street between the theater and the cathedral is the **Hudobná fontána** (Music Fountain). Water from this elaborate fountain springs in harmony with music (generally classical), accompanied by colored lights. It's worth a visit in the evening just to see all the pairs of lovers huddled around it. ⊠ *Hlavná ul.*

NEED A
BREAK?
To feel like you've really stepped into turn-of-the-century Vienna, have a cup of coffee and dessert in the elegant art-nouveau confines of the **Café Slavia** (⊠ Hlavná ul. 63, ☎ 095/6233190).

The **Miklušova väznica** (Nicholas Prison), an old Gothic building used as a prison and torture chamber until 1909, now houses a museum with exhibits on Košice's history. You can even visit the underground premises of the former torture chamber to see replicas of the torture instruments. ⊠ *Pri Miklušovej väznici 10,* ☎ *095/6222856.* ▱ *20 Sk.* ◷ *Tues.–Sat. 9–5, Sun. 9–1.*

OFF THE
BEATEN PATH
KRÁSNA HÔRKA – Sitting on top of a hill, this fairy-tale castle can be seen from miles around. It is one of the best-preserved fortifications from the Middle Ages in Slovakia. The museum houses a valuable collection of paintings and a wide assortment of furniture and weapons from the 15th through 17th centuries. To get here, head west on E57 in the direction of Rožnava and turn right at Krásnohradské Podhradie, from where you can follow signs up to the castle; it takes about an hour from Košice. ⊠ *Krásnohradské Podhradie,* ☎ *no phone.* ◷ *Tues.–Sun. 8–5:30.*

Dining and Lodging

$ ✕ **Sedliacky Dvor.** This tiny restaurant, decorated as an old country
★   cottage complete with wooden tables, a pitchfork, and a picket fence,
     serves mouthwatering local specialties. You'll receive an enormous
     plate piled high with various meats and either rice, mushrooms, and
     cheese or dumplings and red and white cabbage. ⊠ *Biela 3,* ☎ *095/
     6220402. No credit cards.*

$$$ ✕🏠 **Penzión pri Radnici.** This small pension is ideal for business trav-
★   elers—modern apartments come with studies and fax machines. The
     upstairs restaurant is a bit upscale. If you want a quick lunch, try the
     buffet downstairs, which serves tasty local food at dirt-cheap prices.
     ⊠ *Bačíkova 18,* ☎ *095/6228601,* 𝐅𝐀𝐗 *095/6227824. 1 suite, 2 apart-
     ments. Restaurant, beer garden, café, cafeteria. AE, MC, V.*

$$$ 🏠 **Hotel Cobra.** This hotel is a breath of fresh air when compared to
★   the concrete-block hotels that still plague much of Slovakia. The rooms
     are bright and the bathrooms pleasant. The hotel is a few minutes' walk
     outside the city center in a quiet residential area. ⊠ *Jiskrova 3,* ☎ *095/
     622903,* 𝐅𝐀𝐗 *095/6225918. 10 rooms, 3 apartments. Restaurant, bar,
     beer garden. AE, DC, MC, V.*

Nightlife

If you're looking for a lively evening, **Jazz Club** (⊠ Kováčska 39, ☎
095/6230467), a cozy basement bar, is a popular local hangout. The
name is a bit misleading though, as the club has not only live and taped
jazz music but disco, country, and rap music as well.

Levoča

★ ㉙ *358 km (224 mi) northeast of Bratislava, 90 km (56 mi) west of
     Košice.*

You'll enter Levoča, the center of the Spiš kingdom and the quintessential Spiš town, through the medieval Košice Gate. This medieval capital of the Spiš region was founded around 1245 and flourished between
the 14th and 17th centuries, when it was an important trade center
for art and crafts.

The main sights in the town are lined along and in the middle of the
main square, **Námestie Majstra Pavla.** Take a closer look at the sgraf-
fiti-decorated **Thurzov dom** (Thurzo House, No. 7), named for the powerful mining family. The wonderfully ornate gables are from the 17th
century, though the sgraffiti were added in the 19th century. (It is open
to the public.) At the top of the square is the **Malý župný dom** (Small
County House, No. 60), the former administrative center of the Spiš
region, now used as an archive. Above the doorway, in sgraffito, is the
coat of arms of the Spiš alliance. The monumental classical building
next door, the **Veľký župný dom** (Large County House), was built in
the early 19th century by Anton Povolný, who was also responsible
for the Evangelical Church at the bottom of the square. It's now under
renovation and will then be used as a local government office.

★   The most impressive sight in town is the **Kostol svätého Jakuba** (St.
     Jacob Church), a huge Gothic structure begun in the early 14th cen-
     tury but not completed in its present form until a century later. The
     interior is a breathtaking concentration of Gothic religious art. It was
     here in the early 16th century that the greatest Spiš artist, Pavol of Levoča,
     created his most unforgettable pieces. The carved-wood high altar, said
     to be the world's largest and incorporating a truly magnificent carv-
     ing of the Last Supper in limewood, is his most famous work. The 12
     disciples are in fact portraits of Levoča merchants. For 2 Sk, a tape
     recording in an iron post at the back of the church gives you detailed

information in English. ⊠ *Nám. Majstra Pavla,* ☎ *no phone.* ◨ *20 Sk.* ⏱ *Tues.–Sun. 8:30–4.*

The **Mestská radnica** (town hall), with its fine example of whitewashed Renaissance arcades, gables, and clock tower, was built in 1551 after the great fire of 1550 destroyed the old Gothic building along with much of the town. The clock tower now houses an excellent museum, with exhibits of guild flags and a good collection of paintings and wood carvings. Here you can also look at the 18th-century Lady in White, painted on a doorway through which, as legend has it, she let in the enemy for a promise of wealth and a title. For this act of treason, the 24-year-old beauty's head was chopped off. ⊠ *Nám. Majstra Pavla,* ☎ *0966/ 512449.* ◨ *15 Sk.* ⏱ *Tues.–Sun. 9–11:30, noon–5.*

OFF THE
BEATEN PATH

SPIŠSKÝ HRAD (Spiš Castle) – A former administrative center of the kingdom, this is the largest castle in Slovakia (and one of the largest in Europe). Spiš overlords occupied this site starting in 1209. The museum has a good collection of torture devices, and the castle has a beautiful view of the surrounding hills and town. From Levoča, it's worth taking the short 16-km (10-mi) detour east along Route 18 to this magnificent spot. ⊠ *Spišský hrad,* ☎ *0966/512786.* ◨ *30 Sk.* ⏱ *May and Sept.– Oct., Tues.–Sun. 9–6, June–Aug., daily 9–6.*

En Route From Levoča, head south on Route 533 through Spišská Nová Ves, continuing along the twisting roads to the junction with Route 535. Turn right onto Route 535, following the signs to Mlynky and beyond, through the tiny villages and breathtaking countryside of the national park known as **Slovenský Raj** (Slovak Paradise). It is a wild and romantic area of cliffs and gorges, caves and waterfalls, perfect for adventurous hikers. The gorges are accessible by narrow but secure iron ladders. The main tourist centers are Čingov in the north and Dedinky in the south.

Dining and Lodging

$ ✕ **U Janusa.** This family-owned restaurant is the perfect place to get a taste of Slovak culture as well as cuisine. Try one of the local specialties, such as homemade sausage or dumplings with goat cheese. ⊠ *Kláštorská 22,* ☎ *0966/514592. No credit cards.*

$$ ✕⊞ **Arkada Hotel.** The large, bright rooms and historic ambience
★ make this one of the few near-perfect hotels in the country. This hotel is housed in a 13th-century building that in the 17th century became the first printing shop in the Austro-Hungarian Empire. ⊠ *Nám. Majstra Pavla 26,* ☎ FAX *0966/512255. 23 rooms, 3 apartments. Restaurant, café. AE, MC, V.*

$$$ ⊞ **Hotel Satel.** Levoča should win an award for having two of the best
★ hotels in the country. This beautiful 18th-century mansion is built around a picturesque courtyard. The rooms are large and bright, though some of the furniture, especially the peach-colored sofa chairs, is a bit gaudy. ⊠ *Nám. Majstra Pavla 55,* ☎ *0966/512943,* FAX *0966/ 514486. 21 rooms, 2 suites. Restaurant, bar. AE, DC, MC, V.*

Eastern Slovakia A to Z

Arriving and Departing

BY BUS

Daily bus service connects Prague and Bratislava with Košice, but on this run, trains tend to be quicker and more comfortable, if a bit more expensive. (Intercity trains have air-conditioning, while buses do not.) The ride from Bratislava takes about five hours; from Prague, the trip lasts about nine hours.

BY CAR

Poprad, a good starting point for a tour of eastern Slovakia, lies on Slovakia's main east–west highway about 560 km (350 mi) from Prague in the direction of Hradec Králové. The seven- to eight-hour drive from Prague can be broken up easily with an overnight in Olomouc. The drive from Bratislava to Poprad is 328 km (205 mi), with a four-lane stretch from Bratislava to Trenčín and a well-marked two-lane highway thereafter. The drive from Bratislava to Košice takes roughly seven hours; it's best to take the E571 via Nitra, Zvolen, and Rožňava.

BY PLANE

Tatra Air (☞ Getting Around *in* Slovakia A to Z, *below*) offers regular flights from Bratislava to Košice at reasonable prices.

BY TRAIN

Trains regularly connect Košice with Prague (12 hours) and Bratislava (six hours), but book in advance to ensure a seat on these sometimes crowded routes. Several night trains make the run between Košice and Prague's main stations, Hlavní nádraží and Holešovice.

Getting Around

BY BUS

Most of the region is reachable via the extensive SAD bus network. The only exceptions are some of the smaller towns in northeastern Slovakia. Most buses run only on weekdays; plan carefully or you may end up getting stuck in a small town that is ill equipped for visitors.

BY CAR

A car is essential for reaching some of the smaller towns such as Medzilaborce, Ladomirová, and Dukelský priesmyk. Roads are of variable quality. Try to avoid driving at night, as routes are not well marked. Still, some sections give you beautiful panoramas, such as Route 547 between Košice and Levoča. A good four-lane highway links Prešov with Košice.

BY TRAIN

Regular trains link Poprad with the Košice station, **Železničná stanica Košice** (✉ Železničná ul. 1, ☎ 095/6223700), and some of the other larger towns, but you'll have to resort to the bus to reach smaller villages. Train stations tend to be in the town centers.

Contacts and Resources

EMERGENCIES

Police (☎ 158). **Ambulance** (☎ 155). **Pharmacies** (*lekárne*) in larger towns take turns staying open late and on Sunday. Look for the list posted on the front door of each pharmacy. For after-hours service, ring the bell; you will be served through a little hatch door.

TRAVEL AGENCIES

The **Satur** offices in eastern Slovakia are the best—and sometimes the only—places providing basic assistance and information. They offer tours of the region and can book you a room at one of their hotels. **Košice** (✉ Hlavná ul. 1, ☎ 095/6223122 or 095/6223847); **Prešov** (✉ Hlavná ul. 1, ☎ 091/724041); **Kežmarok** (✉ Hlavné nám. 64, ☎ 0968/523121).

VISITOR INFORMATION

The following towns have offices: **Bardejov** (✉ Radničné nám. 21, ☎ 0935/186). **Kežmarok** (✉ Hlavné nám. 46, 0968/4047); **Košice** (✉ Hlavná ul. 8, ☎ 095/186); **Levoča** (✉ Nám. Majstra Pavla 58, ☎ 0966/513763 or 0966/186); and **Prešov** (✉ Hlavná ul. 67, ☎ 091/186).

SLOVAKIA A TO Z

Arriving and Departing

By Boat

Hydrofoils travel the Danube between Vienna and Bratislava, and Budapest and Bratislava from May to September. Boats depart in the morning from Bratislava, on the eastern bank of the Danube at the intersection of Mostová and Vajanského nábrežie, and return from Vienna or Budapest in the evening. Tickets cost $40–$80 per person and should be purchased in person at the dock. For reservations call **Slovenská plavba dunajská** (Slovak Danube Cruise; ☎ 07/363522 or 07/5362226).

By Bus

There is no direct bus service from the United Kingdom to Slovakia; the closest you can get is Vienna. **National Express** (✉ Coach Travel Center, 13 Lower Regent St., London SW1Y 4LR, ☎ 0171/833-4472) operates daily in summer.

By Car

For highway and driving time information between Prague and Bratislava, Budapest and Bratislava, and Vienna and Bratislava *see* Arriving and Departing by Car in Bratislava A to Z, *above*.

By Plane

The best airports for traveling to Slovakia are **Prague's Ruzyně Airport** and **Vienna's Schwechat Airport.** ČSA, the Czech national carrier (☎ 212/765-6545 in the U.S.), offers regular service to Prague from Newark and Montréal. These flights generally have direct connections from Prague to Bratislava ($60–$75 each way); the trip takes about an hour. Vienna's Schwechat Airport is a mere 60 km (37 mi) west of Bratislava. Four buses a day stop at Schwechat en route to Bratislava; the journey takes just over an hour. Numerous trains and buses also run daily between Vienna and Bratislava. From New York, a flight to Bratislava (with a stopover in Prague) takes 11–12 hours. From Montréal it is 8½ hours; from Los Angeles, 17 hours.

British Airways (☎ 0181/759-5511 in the U.K.) has daily nonstop service to Prague from London; **ČSA** (☎ 0171/255-1898 in the U.K.) flies twice daily nonstop from London. Numerous airlines offer service between London and Vienna.

By Train

Bratislava is the country's largest international train hub. There are no direct trains from London. You can take a direct train from Paris via Frankfurt to Vienna (and connect to another train or bus), or from Berlin via Dresden and Prague (en route to Budapest). Vienna is a good starting point for Bratislava. There are several trains that make the 70-minute run daily from Vienna's Südbahnhof.

Getting Around

By Bicycle

A special bike trail links Bratislava and Vienna, paralleling the Danube for much of its 40-km (25-mi) length. For the more adventurous bikers, the Low Tatras (Nízke Tatry) have scenic biking trails. Not many places rent bikes, however; inquire at tourist information centers or at your hotel for rental information.

By Bus

SAD (Slovenská autobusová doprava; ☎ 07/5267231), the national bus carrier for Slovakia, maintains a comprehensive network in Slovakia.

Buses are usually much quicker than the normal trains and more frequent than express trains, though prices are comparable with train fares. Buy your tickets (*cestovné lístky*) from the ticket window at the bus station or directly from the driver on the bus. Long-distance buses can be full, so you might want to book a seat in advance; any Satur office will help you do this. The only drawback to traveling by bus is figuring out the timetables. They are easy to read, but beware of the small letters denoting exceptions to the times given.

By Car

PARKING

Downtown parking lots are limited in all major cities, particularly Bratislava; the fees vary. In larger cities, you should get a parking card (*parkovacia karta*) for streetside parking; the cards are available at newspaper kiosks and cost 5 Sk for an hour's parking time.

ROAD CONDITIONS

Slovakia has few multilane highways, but the secondary road network is in reasonably good shape, and traffic is usually light. Roads are poorly marked, however, so an essential purchase is the *Auto Atlas SR,* which is inexpensive and available at bookstores throughout Slovakia.

RULES OF THE ROAD

Slovakia follows the usual Continental rules of the road. A right turn on red is permitted only when indicated by a green arrow. Signposts with yellow diamonds indicate a main road where drivers have the right of way. The speed limit is 130 kph (80 mph) on four-lane highways; 90 kph (55 mph) on open roads; and 60 kph (37 mph) in built-up areas. The fine for speeding is roughly 300 Sk, payable on the spot. To use the highways you'll need a special label (*dialničná známka*) to display on your car window. Labels cost between 200 Sk and 400 Sk, depending on the size of the vehicle; they're available at post offices or gas stations. If you rent a car, this label should be provided. Seat belts are compulsory, and drinking before driving is prohibited.

To report an accident, call the emergency number (☎ 155 for ambulance, 158 for police); in case of car failure call the rescue service (☎ 154).

By Plane

Tatra Air maintains internal air service within Slovakia, linking Bratislava with Košice. Reservations can be made through Tatra Air's Bratislava office (☎ 07/292306).

By Train

Slovakia's state-run rail system, **Železnice Slovenskej republiky,** is quite extensive, although buses are still the best way to reach small towns. Trains vary in speed, but it's not really worth taking anything less than an "express" train, marked in red on the timetable. Tickets are relatively cheap; first class is considerably more spacious and comfortable and on full trains well worth the 50% increase over the price of standard tickets. If you don't specify "express" when you buy your ticket, you may have to pay a supplement on the train. If you haven't bought a ticket in advance at the station, it's easy to buy one on the train for a small extra charge. On timetables, departures appear on a yellow background; arrivals are on white. It is possible to book couchettes (sleepers) on most overnight trains, but don't expect much in the way of comfort. The European East Pass and InterRail Pass are valid for all rail travel within Slovakia.

Contacts and Resources

B&B Reservation Agencies

Satur Tours and Travel Agency (☞ Visitor Information, *below,* or regional A to Z sections, *above*) throughout the country can make B&B reservations.

Car Rentals

There are no special requirements for renting a car in Slovakia, but be sure to shop around, as prices can differ greatly. Hertz offers Western makes for as much as $1,000 per week. Smaller, local companies, on the other hand, may rent local cars for as little as $130 per week for a manual transmission, economy car without air conditioning but with unlimited mileage. You may buy general accident and theft insurance, which costs an additional $25 and $7 respectively. Prices are comparable whether or not you arrange for a rental before arriving in Slovakia. There is a 6% tax on car rentals.

The following agencies are in Bratislava: **Auto Danubius** (⊠ Trnavská 9, ☎ 07/273754); **Hertz** (⊠ Hotel Forum, Hodžovo nám. 2, ☎ 07/5334441); **Recar** (⊠ Svätoplukova 1, ☎ 07/5266436).

Europcar InterRent (⊠ Štefánik Airport, ☎ 07/5220285; ⊠ Hotel Danube, Rybné nám. 1, ☎ 07/5340841 or 07/5340847).

Customs and Duties

ON ARRIVAL

You may import duty-free into Slovakia 250 cigarettes or the equivalent in tobacco, 1 liter of spirits, 2 liters of wine, ½ liter of perfume, and up to 1,000 Sk worth of gifts and souvenirs.

As with the Czech Republic, if you take into Slovakia any valuables or foreign-made equipment from home, such as cameras, it's wise to carry the original receipts with you or register the items with U.S. Customs before you leave (Form 4457). Otherwise you could end up paying duty upon your return.

ON DEPARTURE

There is no limit on the amount of goods purchased for noncommercial use, but to be on the safe side, hang on to all receipts. Only antiques bought at specially designated shops may be exported; permission from a committee of the National Heritage and Environment Center (☎ 07/374444) is required.

Emergencies

Ambulance (☎ 155). **Car rescue service** (☎ 154). **Police** (☎ 158). **Pharmacies** (*lekárne*) in cities take turns staying open late or on Sunday. Look for the list posted on the front door of each pharmacy. For after-hours service, ring the bell; you will be served through a little hatch door.

Guided Tours

Satur (☞ Visitor Information, *below,* or regional A to Z sections, *above*) is helpful in arranging tours of cities and sites.

Language

Slovak, a western-Slavic tongue closely related to both Czech and Polish, is the official language of Slovakia. English is popular among young people, but German is still the most useful language for tourists.

Mail

POSTAL RATES

Postcards to the United States and Canada cost 10 Sk; letters, 16 Sk. Postcards to Great Britain cost 7 Sk; letters, 12 Sk.

If you don't know where you'll be staying, you can have mail held *poste restante* (general delivery) at post offices in major towns, but the letters should be marked Pošta 1 to designate a city's main post office. You will be asked for identification when you collect mail. The poste restante window in Bratislava is at Námestie SNP 5.

Money and Expenses

COSTS

Bratislava is easily the most expensive area in Slovakia; as a rule, small country towns are extremely reasonable. While overcharging foreigners is not a widespread practice, you may find that state-subsidized theaters do charge visitors higher prices.

CURRENCY

The unit of currency in Slovakia is the crown, or koruna, written as Sk, and divided into 100 halierov. There are bills of 20, 50, 100, 200, 500, 1,000, and 5,000 Sk, and coins of 10, 20, and 50 halierov and 1, 2, 5, and 10 Sk.

At press time, the rate of exchange was around 34 Sk to the American dollar, 24 Sk to the Canadian dollar, and 56 Sk to the pound sterling.

SAMPLE PRICES

A cup of coffee, 15 Sk; museum entrance, 10 Sk–50 Sk; a good theater seat, from 60 to 750 Sk (some theaters, including the Slovak National Theater, charge foreigners a hefty fee and locals pay only a margin of this price); a half liter (pint) of beer, 15 Sk; a 2-km (1-mi) taxi ride, 150 Sk; a bottle of Slovak wine in a good restaurant, 100 Sk–150 Sk; a glass (2 deciliters, or 7 ounces) of wine, 25 Sk.

National Holidays

January 1 (Day of founding of the Slovak Republic); January 6 (Twelfth Night); April 2 and 5, 1999, April 21 and 23, 2000 (Good Friday and Easter Monday); May 1 (Labor Day); May 8 (Liberation of the Republic); July 5 (Sts. Cyril and Methodius); August 29 (anniversary of the Slovak National Uprising); September 1 (Constitution Day); September 15 (Our Lady of Sorrows); November 1 (All Saints' Day); and December 24–26.

Opening and Closing Times

Banks are open weekdays 8–3; they remain open through the general lunch hour. Museums are usually open Tuesday–Sunday 10–5. Shops are generally open weekdays 9–6 and stay open slightly later on Thursdays; some close between noon and 2. Many are also open Saturday 9–noon (department stores, 9–4).

Outdoor Activities and Sports

Slovakia's stretches of beautiful countryside make perfect backdrops for hiking, biking, simmering in thermal pools, mountain climbing, paragliding, or downhill and cross-country skiing. Several daylong boating trips or kayaking with camping opportunities can be undertaken on a dozen of Slovakia's rivers, particularly the Dunajec, Hron, Orava, and Váh. For more information, *see* Bicycling, Fishing, *and* Hiking *in* Pleasures and Pastimes, *above*.

Passports and Visas

American and British citizens do not need a visa to enter Slovakia. A valid passport is sufficient for stays of up to 30 days. Questions should be directed to the Slovakian Embassy (✉ 3900 Linnean Ave. NW, Washington, DC, ☎ 202/363–6315). Canadian citizens must obtain a visa (C$50) before entering the country; for applications and information contact the Slovak Embassy (✉ 50 Rideau Terr., Ottawa, Ontario K1M 2A1, ☎ 613/749–4442).

Rail Passes

Train tickets within Slovakia are still quite cheap; a rail pass often does not give significant savings. The **European East Pass** is good for unlimited first-class travel on the national railroads of Austria, the Czech Republic, Slovakia, Hungary, and Poland. The pass allows five days of travel within a 15-day period ($169) or 10 days of travel within a 30-day period ($275). Apply through your travel agent or through **Rail Europe** (✉ 226–230 Westchester Ave., White Plains, NY 10604, ☎ 914/682–2999 or 800/848–7245).The **InterRail Pass,** available only to European citizens at Satur offices, is valid for 22 days of unlimited train travel in the Czech Republic, Slovakia, Poland, Hungary, and Croatia. The Eurail pass is not valid in Slovakia. For more information, *see* Train Travel *in* the Gold Guide

Student and Youth Travel

In summer, student dormitories in main cities are turned into hostels providing accommodation at reasonable prices. Satur (☞ Visitor Information, *below*) is the best place to arrange dormitory stays or obtain other student-oriented information; it also offers special youth tours in the country. Student discounts are common for museums and other sights. For general information about student identity cards and youth hostels, *see* Students *in* the Gold Guide.

Telephones

COUNTRY CODE

The country code for Slovakia is 421. When dialing from outside the country, drop the initial zero from the area code.

INTERNATIONAL CALLS

Dial **AT&T** (00–421–00101) or **MCI** (001–881–422–0042) to reach an English-speaking operator who can connect your direct, collect, or credit-card call to the United States. Otherwise, you can make a more time-consuming and expensive international call from Bratislava's main telecommunications office (✉ Kolárska 12) or, for an even larger fee, at major hotels throughout the country. For international directory inquiries call 0149; call 0139 for information on international services and rates.

LOCAL CALLS

Public pay phones are easily found in town centers. Most public phones accept prepaid phone cards, which are available at post offices and some newsstands. A local call costs at least 1.80 Sk. For local directory assistance call 120. Call 121 for directory inquiries in Slovakia that are outside the city from which you're calling. Not all operators speak English so you may have to ask a hotel clerk for help.

Tipping

Gratuities are not automatically added to restaurant bills; to reward good service, round up the bill to the nearest multiple of 10 (if the bill comes to 86 Sk, for example, give the waiter 90 Sk). A tip of 10% is considered appropriate inexpensive restaurants or on group tabs. A 20 Sk tip for porters is usually sufficient. For room service, a 20-Sk tip is sufficient. In taxis, round up the bill to the nearest multiple of 10. Give tour guides and helpful concierges 20 Sk–30 Sk.

Travel Agencies

Tatratour (✉ Bajkalská 25, Bratislava, ☎ 07/5233252 or 07/5211219, FAX 07/5213624) is a large, dependable agency that can help arrange sightseeing tours throughout Slovakia. Its Bratislava office in Dunaj

Department Store (☎ 07/5335012) also acts as an official representative of American Express in Slovakia. Satur (☞ Visitor Information, *below*) can also provide basic travel-agency services, such as changing traveler's checks and booking bus and train tickets to outside destinations.

Visitor Information

Satur Tours and Travel Agency (formerly known as Čedok) has remained the official travel bureau for Slovakia. With offices in almost every city throughout the country, it will supply you with hotel and tour information and book air, rail, and bus tickets, but do not expect much in the way of general information. For Satur addresses and telephone numbers, *see* Visitor Information *in* regional A to Z sections, *above*. For in-depth information on local events, call the Information Centre (☎ 186 preceded by specific regional area code). English speakers are generally available.

4 Hungary

Freed from the iron fist of Soviet rule, newly democratic Hungary is in the midst of full-swing revitalization. Budapest offers breathtaking Old World grandeur and thriving cultural life—a must-stop on any trip to Central Europe. In distinctive smaller cities like Pécs, Szeged, Debrecen, and Kecskemét, cobblestone streets wind among lovely Baroque buildings. In the countryside, gleaming sunflower fields blanket gently swelling hills, and sleepy villages of thatched-roof cottages cluster around carefully tended vineyards. Hearty meals spiced with rich red paprika, the generosity and warmth of the Magyar soul: These and more sustain visitors to this land of vital spirit and beauty.

By Alan Levy
and Julie
Tomasz

H

UNGARY SITS AT THE CROSSROADS of Central
Europe, having retained its own identity by absorbing countless invasions and foreign occupa-
tions. Its industrious, resilient people have a history of brave but
unfortunate uprisings: against the Turks in the 17th century, the Hapsburgs in 1848, and the Soviet Union in 1956. Each has resulted in a
period of readjustment, a return to politics as the art of the possible.

The 1960s and '70s saw matters improve politically and materially for
the majority of Hungarians. Communist Party leader János Kádár remained relatively popular at home and abroad, allowing Hungary to
expand and improve trade and relations with the West. The bubble began
to burst during the 1980s, however, when the economy stagnated and
inflation escalated. The peaceful transition to democracy began when
young reformers in the party shunted aside the aging Kádár in 1988
and began speaking openly about multiparty democracy, a market
economy, and a break from Moscow—daring ideas at the time.

Events quickly gathered pace, and by spring 1990, as the Iron Curtain
fell, Hungarians went to the polls in the first free elections in 40 years.
A center-right government led by Prime Minister József Antal took office, sweeping away the Communists and their renamed successor
party, the Socialists, who finished fourth. Ironically, four years later,
in the nation's next elections, Hungarians voted out the ailing center-
right party in favor of none other than the Hungarian Socialist Party,
which ruled in coalition with the Free Democrats until it was ousted
again in the 1998 elections. Voting the center-right FIDESZ party, led
by 35-year-old Viktor Orbán, into power, the nation has chosen an entirely new generation to take it into the new millennium.

Because Hungary is a small, agriculturally oriented country, visitors
are often surprised by its grandeur and Old World charm, especially
in the capital, Budapest, which bustles with life as never before. Hungarians like to complain about their economic problems, but they
spare visitors bureaucratic hassles at the border and airport. Entry is
easy and quick for Westerners, most of whom no longer need visas.
Gone are the days when visitors were forced to make daily currency
exchanges and register with local police on arrival.

Two rivers cross the country: The famous Duna (Danube) flows from
the west through Budapest on its way to the southern frontier, and the
smaller Tisza flows from the northeast across the Nagyalföld (Great
Plain). What Hungary lacks in size it makes up for in beauty and
charm. Western Hungary is dominated by the largest lake in Central
Europe, Lake Balaton. Although some overdevelopment has blighted
its splendor, its shores are still lined with Baroque villages, relaxing spas,
magnificent vineyards, and shaded garden restaurants serving the catch
of the day. In eastern Hungary, the Nagyalföld offers visitors a chance
to explore the folklore and customs of the Magyars (the Hungarians'
name for themselves and their language). It is an area of spicy food,
strong wine, and the proud *csikós* (horsemen).

Hungarians are known for their hospitality and love talking to foreigners,
although their unusual language can be a problem. Today, however,
everyone seems to be learning English, especially young people. But
what all Hungarians share is a deep love of music, and the calendar is
studded with it, from Budapest's famous opera to its annual spring music
festival. And everywhere Gypsy violinists are likely to serenade you during your evening meal.

Hungary (Magyarország)

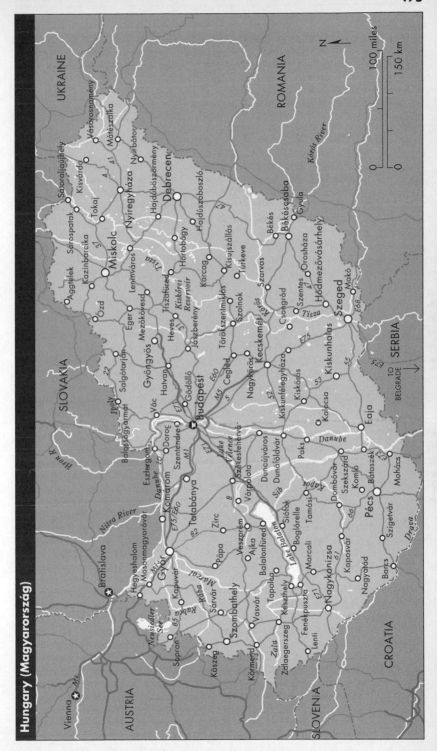

Pleasures and Pastimes

Beaches and Water Sports

Lake Balaton, the largest lake in Central Europe, is the most popular playground of this landlocked nation. If you're looking to relax in the sun and do a little windsurfing, swimming, or boating, settle in here for several days, basing yourself in either the northern shore's main town, Balatonfüred, or picturesque Tihany.

Dining

Through the lean postwar years the Hungarian kitchen lost none of its spice and sparkle. Meats, rich sauces, and creamy desserts predominate, but the more health-conscious will also find salads, even out of season. (Strict vegetarians should note, however, that even meatless dishes are usually cooked with lard [*zsír*].) In addition to the ubiquitous dishes with which most foreigners are familiar, such as chunky beef *gulyás* (goulash) and *paprikás csirke* (chicken paprika) served with *galuska* (little pinched dumplings), traditional Hungarian classics include fiery *halászlé* (fish soup), scarlet with hot paprika; *fogas* (pike perch) from Lake Balaton; and goose liver, duck, and veal specialties. Lake Balaton is the major source of fish in Hungary, particularly for *süllő*, a kind of perch. Hungarians are also very fond of carp (*ponty*), catfish (*harcsa*), and eel (*angolna*), which are usually stewed in a garlic-and-tomato sauce.

Portions are large, so don't plan to eat more than one main Hungarian meal a day. Desserts are lavish, and every inn seems to have its house *torta* (cake), though *rétes* (strudels), *Somlói galuska* (a steamed sponge cake soaked in chocolate sauce and whipped cream), and *palacsinta* (stuffed crepes) are ubiquitous. Traditional *rétes* fillings are *mák* (sugary poppy seeds), *meggy* (sour cherry), and *túró* (sweetened cottage cheese); palacsintas always come rolled with *dió* (sweet ground walnuts), túró, or *lekvár* (jam)—usually *barack* (apricot).

In major cities, there is a good selection of restaurants, from the grander establishments that echo the imperial past of the Hapsburg era to the less expensive, rustic spots favored by locals. In addition to trying out the standard *vendéglő* or *étterem* (restaurants), you can eat at an *önkiszolgáló étterem* (self-service restaurant), a *bistró étel bár* (sit-down snack bar), a *büfé* (snack counter), an *eszpresszó* (café), or a *söröző* (pub). And no matter how strict your diet, don't pass up a visit to at least one *cukrászda* (pastry shop). Our dining choices focus primarily on Hungarian and Continental cuisine; if you find yourself longing for something farther afield, you should be able to find it in the larger cities.

Although prices are steadily increasing, there are plenty of good, affordable restaurants offering a variety of Hungarian dishes. Even in Budapest, eating out can provide you with some of the best value for the money of any European capital. In almost all restaurants, an inexpensive prix-fixe lunch called a *menü* is available, usually for as little as 350 Ft. It includes soup or salad, an entrée, and a dessert. One caveat: Some of the more touristy restaurants sometimes follow the international practice of embellishing tourists' bills; it doesn't hurt to check the prices discreetly before ordering and the total before paying. Budapest made international news last year for a flagrant overcharging incident; authorities have since cracked down on the guilty establishments. Also note that many restaurants have a fine-print policy of charging for each slice of bread consumed from the bread basket.

Hungarians eat early—you risk offhand service and cold food after 9 PM. Lunch, the main meal for many, is served from noon to 2. At most moderately priced and inexpensive restaurants, casual but neat dress is acceptable.

CATEGORY	BUDAPEST*
$$$$	over 3,200 Ft.
$$$	2,300 Ft.–3,200 Ft.
$$	1,400 Ft.–2,300 Ft.
$	under 1,400 Ft.

per person for a three-course meal, excluding wine and tip

Folk Art

Hungary's centuries-old traditions of handmade, often regionally specific folk art are still beautifully alive. Intricately carved wooden boxes, vibrantly colorful embroidered tablecloths and shirts, matte-black pottery pitchers, delicately woven lace collars, ceramic plates splashed with painted flowers and birds, and decorative heavy leather whips are among the favorite handcrafted pieces a visitor can purchase. You'll find them in folk-art stores around the country but can purchase them directly from the artisans at crafts fairs and from peddlers on the streets. Dolls dressed in national costume are also popular souvenirs.

Hiking

Northern Hungary offers great opportunities for hikers and nature seekers. Base yourself in Eger—for lovely sightseeing, excellent wine, and good lodging—and make day trips north to Szilvásvárad for hiking or biking in the hills of the Bükk range and south for the same in the Mátra range, near Gyöngyös. Moving slightly farther north, you can spend a night or two in the magical palace hotel in Lillafüred, making excursions to the magnificent caves at Aggtelek, near the Slovak border, and to Tokaj, farther east, for some less athletic wine tasting.

Lodging

Outside Budapest there are few very expensive hotels, so you will improve your chances of having a memorable lodging experience by arranging a stay in one of the options noted below. For specific recommendations or information about how to book lodging in these accommodations, see the lodging and information sections throughout the chapter.

Bought back from the government over the last several years, more and more of Hungary's magnificent, centuries-old castles and mansions are being restored and opened as country resorts; a night or two in one of these majestic old places makes for an unusual and romantic (but not always luxurious) lodging experience. Northern Hungary has some of the best. At press time, reconstruction and renovations were under way on what was soon to be the Kastélyhotel Sasvár (Sasvár Castle Hotel) in the tiny mountain village of Parádsasvár, about 25 km (15 mi) north of Gyöngyös. The 19th-century mansion was expanded in German Rennaissance style by virtuoso architect Miklós Ybl. Now, after years of neglect, the castle will be transformed into a four-star luxury hotel with 56 rooms and four suites; it is slated to open by late 1998.

Guest houses, also called *panziók* (pensions), provide simple accommodations—well suited to people on a budget. Like B&Bs, most are run by couples or families and offer simple breakfast facilities and usually have private bathrooms; they're generally outside the city or town center. Arrangements can be made directly with the panzió or through local tourist offices and travel agents abroad. Another good budget option is renting a room in a private home. In the provinces it is safe to accept rooms offered to you directly; they will almost always be clean and in a relatively good neighborhood, and the prospective landlord will probably not cheat you. Look for signs reading SZOBA KIADÓ (or the German ZIMMER FREI). Reservations and referrals can also be made by any tourist office, and if you go that route, you have someone to complain to if things don't work out.

Village tourism is a growing trend in Hungary, affording visitors a chance to sink into life in tiny, typical villages around the country. The Hungarian Tourist Board's *Village Tourism* publication provides descriptions and color photos of many of the village homes now open to guests, either by renting a home or as an overnight guest. Apartments in Budapest and cottages at Lake Balaton are available for short- and long-term rental and can make the most economic lodging for families—particularly for those who prefer to cook their own meals. Rates and reservations can be obtained from tourist offices in Hungary and abroad. Also consult the free annual accommodations directory published by **Tourinform** (☞ Visitor Information *in* Hungary A to Z, *below*); published in five languages, it lists basic information about hotels, pensions, bungalows, and tourist hostels throughout the country. A separate brochure lists the country's campgrounds.

For single rooms with bath, count on paying about 80% of the double-room rate. During the off-season (in Budapest, September through March; at Lake Balaton, May and September), rates can drop considerably. Prices at Lake Balaton tend to be significantly higher than those in the rest of the countryside. Note that most large hotels require payment in hard currency (either U.S. dollars or Deutschemarks).

CATEGORY	BUDAPEST*	OTHER AREAS*
$$$$	over $200	over $70
$$$	$140–$200	$50–$70
$$	$80–$140	$30–$50
$	under $80	under $30

All prices are for a standard double room with bath and breakfast during peak season (June through August).

Porcelain

Among the most sought-after items in Hungary are the exquisite hand-painted Herend and Zsolnay porcelain. Unfortunately, the prices on all makes of porcelain have risen considerably in the last few years. For guaranteed authenticity, make your purchases at the specific Herend and Zsolnay stores in major cities, or at the factories themselves in Herend and Pécs, respectively.

Spas and Thermal Baths

Several thousand years ago, the first settlers of the area that is now Budapest chose their home because of its abundance of hot springs. Centuries later, the Romans and the Turks built baths and developed cultures based on medicinal bathing. Now there are more than 1,000 medicinal hot springs bubbling up around the country. Budapest alone has some 14 historic working baths, which attract ailing patients with medical prescriptions for specific water cures as well as "recreational" bathers—locals and tourists alike—wanting to soak in the relaxing waters, try some of the many massages and treatments, and experience the architectural beauty of the bathhouses themselves.

For most, a visit to a bath involves soaking in several thermal pools of varying temperatures and curative contents—perhaps throwing in a game of aquatic chess—relaxing in a steam room or sauna, and getting a brisk, if not brutal, massage (average cost: 200 Ft. for a half hour). Many bath facilities are single-sex or have certain days set aside for men or women only, and most people walk around nude or with miniature loincloths, provided at the door. Men should be aware that some men-only baths have a strong gay clientele.

In addition to the ancient beauties there are newer, modern baths open to the public at many spa hotels. They lack the charm and aesthetic appeal of their older peers but provide the latest treatments in sparkling facilities. Of the areas outside Budapest covered in this guidebook, Debrecen, Hévíz, and Eger are famous spa towns with popular bath facilities. For more information, page through the "Hungary: Land of Spas" brochure published by the Hungarian Tourist Board, available free from most tourist offices.

Wine, Beer, and Spirits

Hungary tempts wine connoisseurs with its important wine regions, especially Villány, near Pécs, in the south; Eger and Tokaj in the north; and the northern shore of Lake Balaton. Kéknyelű, Szürkebarát, and especially Olaszrizling are all common white table wines; Tokay, one of the great wines of the world (☞ Tokaj, *below*), can be heavy, dark, and sweet, and is generally drunk as an aperitif or a dessert wine. It's expensive, especially by Hungarian standards, so it's usually reserved for special occasions.

The gourmet red table wine of Hungary, Egri Bikavér (Bull's Blood of Eger, usually with *el toro* himself on the label), is the best buy and the safest bet with all foods. Other good reds and the best rosés come from Villanyi; the most adventurous reds—with sometimes successful links to both Austrian and Californian wine making and viticulture—are from the Sopron area.

Before- and after-dinner drinks tend toward schnapps, most notably *Barack-pálinka,* an apricot brandy. A plum brandy called *Kosher szilva-pálinka,* bottled under rabbinical supervision, is very chic. Unicum, Hungary's national liqueur, is a dark, thick, vaguely minty, and quite potent drink that could be likened to Germany's Jägermeister. Its chubby green bottle makes it a good souvenir to take home.

Major Hungarian beers are Köbányai, Dreher, Aranyhordó, Balaton Világos, and Aszok.

Exploring Hungary

Hungary's main geographical regions begin with the capital city and thriving urban heart of **Budapest.** Just north of Budapest, the Danube River forms a gentle heart-shape curve along which lie the romantic and historic towns of the region called the **Danube Bend.** Southwest of Budapest are the vineyards, quaint villages, and popular, developed summer resorts around **Lake Balaton.** The more rural and gently mountainous stretch of **northern Hungary** also includes the handsome, vibrant town of Eger and the famous wine village of Tokaj; the contrastingly flat and dry expanses of the **Great Plain,** in the east, are spiced with legendary traditions of horsemanship and agriculture and anchored by the interesting and lively cities of Kecskemét and Debrecen. The verdant, rolling countryside of **Transdanubia** stretches west of the Danube to the borders of Austria, Slovenia, and Croatia; in the northern hills nestle the gemlike, beautifully restored towns of Sopron and Kőszeg, and in the south, the culturally rich, dynamically beautiful city of Pécs. Given Hungary's relatively small size, most of these points are less than a few hours away from Budapest by car.

Great Itineraries

Numbers in the text correspond to numbers in the margin and on the Exploring Budapest, The Danube Bend, Lake Balaton and Transdanubia, and Northern Hungary and the Great Plain maps.

IF YOU HAVE 3 DAYS

⚁ **Budapest** ①–㊲ alone offers a full vacation's worth of things to see and experience, but in one day an efficient and motivated visitor can pack in some of the don't-misses: exploration of **Castle Hill** ①–⑭, a stroll on the **Danube korzo,** a glimpse of **Országház** ㉘, a look at **Hősök tere** ㊿, followed by a dip in the **Széchenyi Fürdő,** a hearty meal, and a night at the **Operaház** ㊼. After a night's rest in Budapest, hop on an early boat to explore the charming artists' village of **Szentendre** ㊽ and the majestic fortress of **Visegrád** ㊾, upriver in the Danube Bend. You can spend another night in Budapest; the next morning, drive down to **Badacsony** ㊿ on Lake Balaton's northern shore. Follow a refreshing swim with a lunch of fresh Balaton fish and some wine tasting in the cool cellars on Mount Badacsony's vineyard-covered slopes. On your way back to Budapest, stop for a stroll on **Tihany**'s ㊽ cobblestone streets and drink in the views from its lovely hilltop abbey.

IF YOU HAVE 6 DAYS

Spend two full days exploring ⚁ **Budapest** ①–㊲; on your third day visit the Danube Bend's crown jewels, the villages of **Szentendre** ㊽ and **Visegrád** ㊾, making the trip by scenic boat or by car. Return to Budapest for the night and head out the next morning for a day on the Great Plain, strolling among the sights of lovely ⚁ **Kecskemét** ㊱ before venturing out to the *puszta* (prairie) in the **Bugac National Park** ㊵ or **Kerekegyháza** to experience the unique horsemanship stunts and demonstrations of Hungary's legendary cowboys, the *csikós.* Depending on how much you want to drive and how much of Budapest's nightlife you want to take in, you can either go back to Budapest (85 km/53 mi from Kecskemét) for the night or spend it here in Kecskemét. On day five, drive down to ⚁ **Pécs** ㊲ to see its beautiful town square, cathedral, and excellent museums. After a night's rest, make your way on scenic secondary roads through southern Transdanubia to **Keszthely** ㊼ on the northwestern tip of Lake Balaton, visiting the spectacular Festetics mansion before moving east along the northern shore to ⚁ **Badacsony** ㊿. On the way, make a stop in picturesque **Szigliget** ㊼ and scale its castle hill to gaze at the sweeping Lake Balaton view. In Badacsony, spend the rest of the afternoon hiking up the vineyard-carpeted slopes of Mount Badacsony, rewarded by generous wine tastings in the local cellars and a big fish dinner with live Gypsy music. Depending on your traveling speed (and the amount of wine you've tasted), instead of sleeping in Badacsony, you may prefer to move on along the northern shore and spend the fifth night in ⚁ **Tihany** ㊽ or ⚁ **Balatonfüred** ㊻, both of which have good lodging possibilities with more facilities and amenities. Either way, you can spend your sixth day exploring Tihany and Balatonfüred, cooling off with a swim in the lake before heading back to Budapest.

When to Tour

The ideal times to visit Hungary are in the spring (May through June) and end of summer and early fall (late August through September). The months of July and August, peak vacation season for Hungarians as well as foreign tourists, can be extremely hot and humid; Budapest is stuffy and crowded, and the entire Lake Balaton region is overrun with vacationers. Many of Hungary's major fairs and festivals take place during the spring and fall, including the late-March to early April Spring Festival (in many cities and towns) and the myriad wine-harvest festivals in late summer and early fall. Lake Balaton is the only area that really closes down and gets boarded up during the low season, generally from mid- or late September until at least Easter, if not mid-May. Summer holds the unforgettable and quintessentially Hungarian sights of sweeping fields of swaying golden sunflowers and giant white storks summering in their bushy nests built on chimney tops.

BUDAPEST

Situated on both banks of the Danube, Budapest unites the colorful hills of Buda and the wide, businesslike boulevards of Pest. Though it was the site of a Roman outpost during the 1st century, the city was not officially created until 1873, when the towns of Óbuda, Pest, and Buda were joined. Since then, Budapest has been the cultural, political, intellectual, and commercial heart of Hungary; for the 20% of the nation's population who live in the capital, anywhere else is simply *vidék* ("the country").

Budapest has suffered many ravages in the course of its long history. It was totally destroyed by the Mongols in 1241, captured by the Turks in 1541, and nearly destroyed again by Soviet troops in 1945. But this bustling industrial and cultural center survived as the capital of the People's Republic of Hungary after the war—and then, as the 1980s drew to a close, it became one of the Eastern Bloc's few thriving bastions of capitalism. Today, judging by the city's flourishing cafés and restaurants, markets and bars, the stagnation enforced by the Communists seems a thing of the very distant past.

Much of the charm of a visit to Budapest lies in unexpected glimpses into shadowy courtyards and in long vistas down sunlit cobbled streets. Although some 30,000 buildings were destroyed during World War II and in 1956, the past lingers on in the often crumbling architectural details of the antique structures that remain.

The principal sights of the city fall roughly into three areas, each of which can be comfortably covered on foot. The Budapest hills are best explored by public transportation. Note that street names have been changed in the past several years to purge all reminders of the Communist regime. Underneath the new names, the old ones remain, canceled out by a big red slash. Also note that a Roman-numeral prefix listed before an address refers to one of Budapest's 22 districts.

Exploring Budapest

Várhegy (Castle Hill)

Most of the major sights of Buda are on Várhegy (Castle Hill), a long, narrow plateau laced with cobblestone streets, clustered with beautifully preserved Baroque, Gothic, and Renaissance houses, and crowned by the magnificent Royal Palace. The area is theoretically banned to private cars (except for those of neighborhood residents and Hilton Hotel guests), but the streets manage to be lined bumper to bumper with Trabants and Mercedes all the same—sometimes the only visual element to verify you're not in a fairy tale. As in all of Budapest, thriving urban new has taken up residence in historic old; international corporate offices, diplomatic residences, restaurants, and boutiques occupy many of its landmark buildings. But these are still the exceptions, as most flats and homes are lived in by private families. The most striking example, perhaps, is the Hilton Hotel on Hess András tér, which has ingeniously incorporated remains of Castle Hill's oldest church (a tower and one wall), built by Dominican friars in the 13th century.

Numbers in the text correspond to numbers in the margin and on the Castle Hill (Várhegy) map.

A GOOD WALK

Castle Hill's cobblestone streets and numerous museums are made to be explored on foot: Plan to spend about a day here. Most of the transportation options for getting to Castle Hill deposit you on Szent György tér or Dísz tér. It's impossible not to find Castle Hill, but it is possible to be confused about how to get on top of it. If you're already on the Buda side of the river, you can take the Castle bus—*Várbusz*—from the Moszkva tér metro station, northwest of Castle Hill. If you're starting out from Pest, you can take a taxi or Bus 16 from Erzsébet tér or, the most scenic alternative, cross the Széchenyi Lánchíd (Chain Bridge) on foot to Clark Ádám tér and ride the *Sikló* (funicular rail) up Castle Hill (☞ Clark Ádám tér, *below*).

Begin your exploration by walking slightly farther south to visit the **Királyi Palota** at the southern end of the hill. Of the palace's several major museums, the **Magyar Nemzeti Galéria** ② and the **Budapesti Történeti Múzeum** ③ are particularly interesting. From here, you can cover the rest of the area by walking north along its handful of charming streets. From Dísz tér, start with Tárnok utca, whose houses and usually open courtyards offer glimpses of how Hungarians have integrated contemporary life into Gothic, Renaissance, and Baroque settings; of particular interest are the houses at No. 16, now the Arany Hordo restaurant, and at No. 18, the 15th-century Arany Sas Patika (Golden Eagle Pharmacy Museum), with a naïf Madonna and child in an overhead niche. This tiny museum displays instruments, prescriptions, books, and other artifacts from 16th- and 17th-century pharmacies. Modern commerce is also integrated into Tárnok utca's historic homes; you'll encounter numerous folk souvenir shops and tiny boutiques lining the street. Tárnok utca funnels into Szentháromság tér, home of **Mátyás templom** ⑦ and, just behind it, the **Halászbástya** ⑧.

After exploring them, double back to Dísz tér and set out northward again on Úri utca, which runs parallel to Tárnok utca; this long street is lined with beautiful, genteel homes. The funny little Telefónia Museum, at No. 49, is worth a stop, as is the **Budavári Labirintus** ⑥, at No. 9. At the end of Úri utca you'll reach **Kapisztrán tér** ⑬. From here, you can walk south again on a parallel street, Országház utca (Parliament Street), the main thoroughfare of 18th-century Buda; it takes its name from the building at No. 28, which was the seat of Parliament from 1790 to 1807. You'll end up back at Szentháromság tér, with just two streets remaining to explore.

You can stroll down charming little Fortuna utca, named for the 18th-century Fortuna Inn, which now houses the **Magyar Kereskedelmi és Vendéglátóipari Múzeum** ⑨. At the end of Fortuna utca you'll reach **Bécsi kapu tér** ⑫, opening to Moszkva tér just below. Go back south on the last of the district's streets, Táncsics Mihály utca, stopping at the **Középkori Zsidó Imaház** ⑪ and the **Zenetörténeti Múzeum** ⑩. Next door, at No. 9, is the Baroque house (formerly the Royal Mint) where rebel writer Tancsics Mihály was imprisoned in the dungeons and freed by the people on the Day of Revolution, March 15, 1848. You'll find yourself in front of the Hilton Hotel, back at Hess András tér, bordering Szentháromság tér. Those whose feet haven't protested yet can finish off their tour of Castle Hill by doubling back to the northern end and strolling south back to Dísz tér on **Tóth Árpád sétány,** the romantic, tree-lined promenade along the Buda side of the hill.

TIMING

Castle Hill is small enough to cover in one day, but perusing its major museums and several tiny exhibits will require more time.

SIGHTS TO SEE

⑫ **Bécsi kapu tér** (Vienna Gate Square). Marking the northern entrance to Castle Hill, the stone gateway (rebuilt in 1936) called Vienna Gate opens toward Vienna—or, closer at hand, Moszkva tér just below. The square named after it has some fine Baroque and rococo houses but is

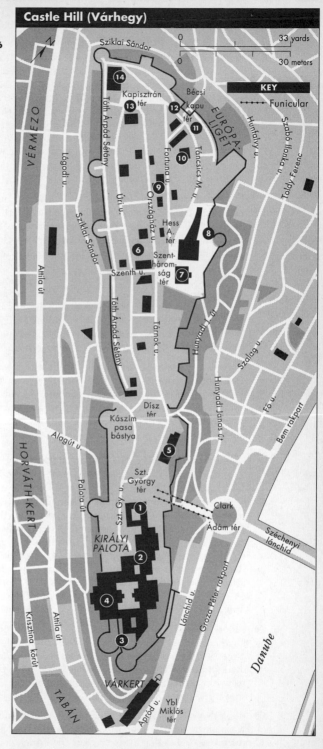

Bécsi kapu tér, **12**
Budapesti Történeti
Múzeum, **3**
Budavári Labirintus, **6**
Hadtörténeti
Múzeum, **14**
Halászbástya, **8**
Kapisztrán tér, **13**
Középkori Zsidó
Imaház, **11**
Ludwig Múzeum, **1**
Magyar Kereskedelmi
és Vendéglátóipari
Múzeum, **9**
Magyar Nemzeti
Galéria, **2**
Mátyás templom, **7**
Országos Széchenyi
Könyvtár, **4**
Várszínház, **5**
Zenetörténeti
Múzeum, **10**

Castle Hill (Várhegy)

KEY

Funicular

dominated by the enormous neo-Romanesque (1913–1917) head-quarters of the **Országos Levéltár** (Hungarian National Archives), which resembles a cathedral-like shrine to paperwork.

③ Budapesti Történeti Múzeum (Budapest History Museum). The palace's Baroque southern wing (E) contains the Budapest History Museum, displaying a fascinating permanent exhibit of modern Budapest history from Buda's liberation from the Turks in 1686 through the 1970s. Viewing the vintage 19th- and 20th-century photos and videos of the castle, the Széchenyi Lánchíd, and other Budapest monuments—and seeing them as the backdrop to the horrors of World War II and the 1956 Revolution—helps to put your later sightseeing in context; while you're browsing, peek out one of the windows overlooking the Danube and Pest and let it start seeping in.

Through historical documents, objects, and art, other permanent exhibits depict the medieval history of the Buda fortress and the capital as a whole. This is the best place to view remains of the medieval Royal Palace and other archaeological excavations. Some of the artifacts unearthed during excavations are in the vestibule in the basement; others are still among the remains of medieval structures. Down in the cellars are the original medieval vaults of the palace; portraits of King Matthias and his second wife, Beatrice of Aragon; and many late-14th-century statues that probably adorned the Renaissance palace. ⊠ *Royal Palace (Wing E), Szt. György tér 2,* ☎ *1/375–7533.* ▣ *270 Ft.* ☉ *Mar.–mid-May and mid-Sept.–Oct., Wed.–Mon. 10–6; mid-May–mid-Sept., daily 10–6; Nov.–Feb., Wed.–Mon. 10–4.*

⑥ Budavári Labirintus (Labyrinth of Buda Castle). Used as a wine cellar during the 16th and 17th centuries and then as an air-raid shelter during World War II, the labyrinth—entered at Úri utca 9 below an early 18th-century house—can be explored with a tour or, if you dare, on your own. There are some English-language brochures available. ⊠ *Úri utca 9,* ☎ *1/375–6858.* ▣ *750 Ft.* ☉ *Daily 9:30–7:30.*

| NEED A BREAK? | For a light snack, pastry, and coffee, **Café Miro** (⊠ Úri u. 30, ☎ 1/375–5458) is a fresh, hip alternative to the Old World Budapest cafés. |

⑭ Hadtörténeti Múzeum (Museum of Military History). Fittingly, this museum is lodged in a former barracks, on the northwestern corner of Kapisztrán tér. The exhibits, which include collections of uniforms and military regalia, trace the military history of Hungary from the original Magyar conquest in the 9th century through the period of Ottoman rule to the middle of this century. You can arrange an English-language tour in advance for around 1,000 forints. ⊠ *I, Tóth Árpád sétány 40,* ☎ *1/356–9522.* ▣ *270 Ft.* ☉ *Apr.–Sept., Tues.–Sun. 10–6; Oct.–Mar., Tues.–Sun. 10–4.*

★ **⑧ Halászbástya** (Fishermen's Bastion). The wondrous porch overlooking the Danube and Pest is the neo-Romanesque Fishermen's Bastion, a merry cluster of white stone towers, arches, and columns above a modern bronze statue of St. Stephen, Hungary's first king. Medieval fishwives once peddled their wares here, but the site is now home to souvenirs, crafts, and music.

⑬ Kapisztrán tér (Capistrano Square). Castle Hill's northernmost square was named after St. John of Capistrano, an Italian friar who in 1456 recruited a crusading army to fight the Turks who were threatening Hungary. There's a statue of this honored Franciscan on the northwest corner; also here are the **Museum of Military History** (☞ *above*) and the remains of the 12th-century Gothic **Mária Magdolna templom**

(Church of St. Mary Magdalene). Its *torony* (tower), completed in 1496, is the only part left standing; the rest of the church was destroyed by air raids during World War II.

★ **Királyi Palota** (Royal Palace, commonly called Buda Castle). During a seven-week siege at the end of 1944, the entire Castle Hill district of palaces, mansions, and churches was turned into one vast ruin. The final German stand was in the Royal Palace, which was utterly gutted by fire; by the end of the siege its walls were reduced to rubble, and just a few scarred pillars and blackened statues protruded from the wreckage. The destruction was incalculable, yet it gave archaeologists and art historians an opportunity to discover the medieval buildings that once stood on the site of this Baroque and neo-Baroque palace. Fortunately, details of the edifices of the kings of the Árpád and Anjou dynasties, of the Holy Roman Emperor Sigismund, and of the great 15th-century king Mátthiás Corvinus had been preserved in some 80 medieval reports, travelogues, books, and itineraries that were subsequently used to reconstruct the complex.

The postwar rebuilding was slow and painstaking. In some places debris more than 20 ft deep had to be removed; the remains found on the medieval levels were restored to their original planes. Freed from mounds of rubble, the foundation walls and medieval castle walls were completed, and the ramparts surrounding the medieval royal residence were re-created as close to their original shape and size as possible. Out of this herculean labor emerged the Royal Palace of today, a vast cultural center and museum complex (☞ Budapesti Történeti Múzeum, *above, and* Ludwig Muzeum, Magyar Nemzeti Galéria, *and* Országos Széchenyi Könyvtár, *below*).

⑪ **Középkori Zsidó Imaház** (Medieval Synagogue). The excavated one-room Medieval Synagogue is now used as a museum. On display are objects relating to the Jewish community, including religious inscriptions, frescoes, and tombstones dating to the 15th century. ✉ *Táncsics Mihály u. 26,* ☎ *1/355–8849.* 💺 *120 Ft.* ☉ *May–Oct., Tues.–Fri. 10–2, weekends 10–6.*

❶ **Ludwig Múzeum** This collection of more than 200 pieces of Hungarian and contemporary international art, including works by Picasso and Lichtenstein, occupies the castle's northern wing. ✉ *Royal Palace (Wing A), Dísz tér 17,* ☎ *1/375–7533.* 💺 *120 Ft., free Tues.* ☉ *Tues.– Sun. 10–6.*

❾ **Magyar Kereskedelmi és Vendéglátóipari Múzeum** (Hungarian Museum of Commerce and Catering). The 18th-century Fortuna Inn now serves visitors in a different way—as the Catering Museum. Displays in a permanent exhibit show the city as a tourist destination from 1870 to the 1930s; you can see, for example, what a room at the Gellért Hotel, still operating today, would have looked like in 1918. The Commerce Museum, just across the courtyard, chronicles the history of Hungarian commerce from the late 19th century to 1947, when the new Communist regime "liberated" the economy into socialism. The four-room exhibit includes everything from an antique chocolate-and-caramel vending machine to early shoe-polish advertisements. You can rent an English-language recorded tour for 200 Ft. ✉ *Fortuna utca 4,* ☎ *1/375–6249.* 💺 *120 Ft., free Fri.* ☉ *Wed.–Fri. 10–5, weekends 10–6.*

❷ **Magyar Nemzeti Galéria** (Hungarian National Gallery). The immense center block of the Royal Palace (made up of Wings B, C, and D) exhibits a wide range of Hungarian fine art, from medieval ecclesiastical paintings and statues, through Gothic, Renaissance, and Baroque art, to a rich collection of 19th- and 20th-century works. Especially notable are the works of the romantic painter Mihály Munkácsy, the impressionist Pál Szinyei Merse, and the surrealist Kosztka Csontváry, whom Picasso much admired. There is also a large collection of modern Hungarian sculpture. There are labels and commentary in English for both permanent and temporary exhibits. If you contact the museum in advance, you can book a tour for up to five people with an English-speaking guide. ⊠ *Royal Palace (entrance in Wing C), Dísz tér 17,* ☎ *1/375–7533.* ▣ *Gallery 220 Ft., tour 1,000 Ft.* ⊙ *Mid-Mar.–Oct., Tues.–Sun. 10–6; Nov.–mid-Mar., Tues.–Sun. 10–4. (Note: Mid-Jan.–mid-Mar. hrs. may be reduced to Fri.–Sun. only, 10–4).*

★ ❼ **Mátyás templom** (Matthias Church). The Gothic Matthias Church is officially the Buda Church of Our Lady but better known by the name of the 15th century's "just king" of Hungary, who was married here twice. It is sometimes called the Coronation Church, because the last two kings of Hungary were crowned here: the Hapsburg emperor Franz Joseph in 1867 and his grandnephew Karl IV in 1916. Originally built for the city's German population in the mid-13th century, the church has endured many alterations and assaults. For almost 150 years it was the main mosque of the Turkish overlords—and the predominant impact of its festive pillars is decidedly Byzantine. Badly damaged during the recapture of Buda in 1686, it was completely rebuilt between 1873 and 1896 by Frigyes Schulek, who gave it an asymmetrical western front, with one high and one low spire, and a fine rose window; the south porch is from the 14th century.

The **Szentháromság Kápolna** (Trinity Chapel) holds an *encolpion,* an enameled casket containing a miniature copy of the Gospel to be worn on the chest; it belonged to the 12th-century king Béla III and his wife, Anne of Chatillon. Their burial crowns and a cross, scepter, and rings found in their excavated graves are also displayed here. The church's **treasury** contains Renaissance and Baroque chalices, monstrances, and vestments. High Mass is celebrated every Sunday at 10 AM with full orchestra and choir—and often with major soloists; get here early if you want a seat. During the summer there are usually organ recitals on Friday at 8 PM. Tourists are asked to remain at the back of the church during weddings and services (it's least intrusive to come after 9:30 AM weekdays and between 1 and 5 PM Sundays and holidays). ⊠ *I, Szentháromság tér 2,* ☎ *1/355–5657.* ⊙ *Daily 7 AM–8 PM.* ▣ *Church free, except during concerts; treasury 100 Ft.* ⊙ *Treasury daily 9:30–5:30.*

❹ **Országos Széchenyi Könyvtár** (Széchenyi National Library). The western wing (F) of the Royal Palace is home to the National Library, which houses more than 2 million volumes. Its archives include well-preserved medieval codices, manuscripts, and historic correspondence. This is not a lending library, but the reading rooms are open to the public (though you must show a passport), and even the most valuable materials can be viewed on microfilm. Small, temporary exhibits on rare books and documents are usually on display; the hours and admission fees for these are quite variable. Note that the entire library closes for one month every summer, usually in July or August. ⊠ *Royal Palace (Wing F). To arrange a tour with an English-speaking guide,* ☎ *1/375–7533.* ▣ *300 Ft.* ⊙ *Reading rooms Mon. 1–9, Tues.–Sat. 9–9; exhibits Mon. 1–6, Tues.–Sat. 10–6.*

Statue of Prince Eugene of Savoy. In front of the Royal Palace, facing the Danube by the entrance to Wing C, stands an equestrian statue of Prince Eugene of Savoy, a commander of the army that liberated Hungary from the Turks at the end of the 17th century. From here there is a superb view across the river to Pest.

Szentháromság tér (Holy Trinity Square). This square is named for its Baroque **Trinity Column,** erected in 1712–1713 as a gesture of thanksgiving by survivors of a plague. The column stands in front of the famous Gothic Matthias Church (☞ *above*), its large pedestal a perfect seat from which to watch the wedding spectacles that take over the church on spring and summer weekends: From morning till night, frilly engaged pairs flow in one after the other and, after a brief transformation inside, back out onto the square.

★ **Tóth Árpád sétány.** This romantic, tree-lined promenade along the Buda side of the hill is often mistakenly overlooked by sightseers. Beginning at the Museum of Military History (☞ *above*) the promenade takes you "behind the scenes" along the back sides of the matte-pastel Baroque houses you saw on Úri utca, with their regal arched windows and wrought-iron gates. On a late spring afternoon, the fragrance of the cherry trees may be enough to revive even the most weary.

Úri utca. Running parallel to Tárnok utca, Úri utca has been less commercialized by boutiques and other shops; the longest and oldest street in the castle district, it is lined with many stately houses, all worth special attention for their delicately carved details. Both gateways of the Baroque palace at **Nos. 48–50** are articulated by Gothic niches. The **Telefónia Múzeum** (Telephone Museum), at No. 49, is an endearing little museum entered through a central courtyard shared with the local district police station. Although vintage telephone systems are still in use all over the country, both the oldest and most recent products of telecommunication—from the 1882 wooden box with hose attachment to the latest, slickest fax machines—can be observed and tested here. *Telefónia Múzeum:* ⊠ *Úri utca 49,* ☎ *1/201–8188.* ▱ *60 Ft.* ✆ *Nov.–Apr., Tues.–Sun. 10–4; May–Oct., Tues.–Sun. 10–6.*

⑤ Várszínház (Castle Theater). Once a Franciscan church, this was transformed into a more secular royal venue in 1787 under the supervision of courtier Farkas Kempelen. The first theatrical performance in Hungarian was held here in 1790. Heavily damaged during World War II, the theater was rebuilt and reopened in 1978. While the building retains its original late-Baroque-style facade, the interior was renovated with marble and concrete. It is now used as the studio theater of the National Theater and occasionally for classical recitals, and there is usually a historical exhibition in its foyer—usually theater-related, such as a display of costumes. ⊠ *Színház utca 1–3,* ☎ *1/375–8011.*

⑩ Zenetörténeti Múzeum (Museum of Music History). This handsome gray-and-pearl-stone 18th-century palace is where Beethoven allegedly stayed in 1800 when he came to Buda to conduct his works. Now a museum, it displays rare manuscripts and old instruments downstairs in its permanent collection and temporary exhibits upstairs in a small, sunlit hall. The museum also often hosts intimate classical recitals. ⊠ *Táncsics Mihály u. 7,* ☎ *1/214–6770.* ▱ *170 Ft.* ✆ *Mid-Nov.–late-Dec. and first 2 wks of Mar., Tues.–Sun. 10–5; mid-Mar.–mid-Nov., Tues.–Sun. 10–6.*

Tabán and Gellért-hegy (Tabán and Gellért Hill)

Spreading below Castle Hill is the old quarter called the Tabán (from the Turkish word for "armory"). A onetime suburb of Buda, it was known at the end of the 17th century as Little Serbia (*Rác*) because so many Serbian refugees settled here after fleeing from the Turks. It later became a district of vineyards and small taverns. Though most of the small houses characteristic of this district have been demolished—mainly in the interest of easing traffic—a few picturesque buildings remain.

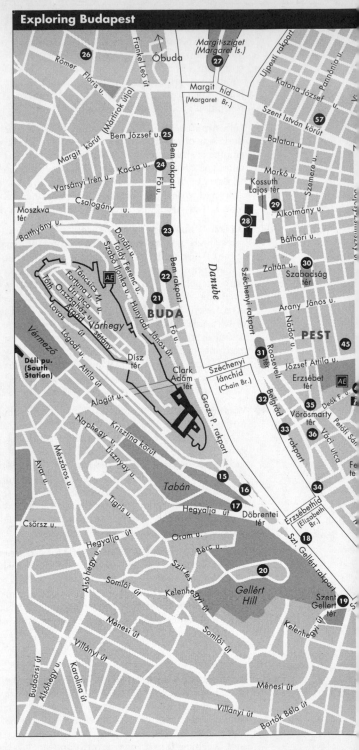

Exploring Budapest

Lehel tér

Rippl-Rónai u.

53

Dózsa György út

51

Hősök tere

52

Városliget

Olof Palme sétány

Nyugati pu. (West Station)

Nyugati tér

Podmaniczky utca

Szinyei Merse u.

Bajza u.

Benczúr u.

Ajtósi Dürer sor

Kodály Körönd

Rózsa u.

Felső erdősor

Városligeti fasor

Dózsa György út

Teréz körút

Szondi u.

Aradi út

Damjanich u.

Jókai u.

Andrássy út

50

Dembinszky u.

Oktogon

Vörösmarty u.

Rottenbiller utca

István u.

49

Liszt Ferenc tér

Erzsébet körút

Thököly út

Verseny u.

48

Hársfa u.

Keleti pu. (East Station)

Lázár u.

47

Paulay Ede u.

Baross tér

45

46

Király u.

Dob utca

Rákóczi út

Kerepesi út

Deák tér

44

Károly krt.

Wesselényi utca

Klauzál u.

Köztársaság tér

Kerepesi temető (Cemetery)

Dohány utca

56

43

42

Rákóczi út

Népszínház u.

Teleki László tér

Kossuth L. u.

Szentkirályi u.

Puskin u.

55

Bérkocsis u.

Luzsa u.

Ferenciek tere

37

Múzeum krt.

Bródy Sándor u.

József körút

Somogyi Béla u.

Déri Miksa u.

Mátyás tér

Dankó u.

Veres Pálné u.

38

Múzeum u.

Krúdy u.

József u.

41

Baross utca

Baross utca

Kálvin tér

40

Üllői út

Nap u.

Práter u.

Szigony u.

Diószeghy Sámuel u.

Vámház krt.

Rádoy u.

54

Tömő u.

Korányi S. u.

39

Lónyai u.

Ferenc körút

Üllői út

19

Szabadsághíd (Liberty Br.)

Fővám tér

Közraktár u.

Thaly Kálmán u.

KEY

Danube

Műegyetem rakpart

Boráros tér

Mester u.

AE American Express Office

Rail Lines

i Tourist Information

Petőfihíd (Petőfi Br.)

Márton u.

0   550 yards

0   500 meters

N

Gellért-hegy (Gellért Hill), 761 ft high, is the most beautiful natural formation on the Buda bank. It takes its name from St. Gellért (Gerard) of Csanad, a Venetian bishop who came to Hungary in the 11th century and was supposedly flung to his death from the top of the hill by pagans. The walk up can be tough, but take solace from the cluster of hot springs at the foot of the hill, which soothe and cure bathers at the Rác, Rudas, and Gellért baths.

Numbers in the text correspond to numbers in the margin and on the Exploring Budapest map.

A GOOD WALK

From the **Semmelweis Orvostörténeti Múzeum** ⑮, walk around the corner to Szarvas tér and a few yards toward the river to the **Tabán plébánia-templom** ⑯. Walking south on Attila út and crossing to the other side of Hegyalja út, you'll be at the foot of Gellért Hill. From here, take a deep breath and climb the paths and stairs to the **Citadella** ⑳ fortress at the top of the hill (about 30 minutes). After taking in the views and exploring the area, you can descend and treat yourself to a soak or a swim at the **Gellért Szálloda és Thermál Fürdő** ⑲ at the southeastern foot of the hill. On foot, take the paths down the southeastern side of the hill. You can also take Bus 27 down the back of the hill to Móricz Zsigmond körtér and walk back toward the Gellért on busy Bartók Béla út, or take Tram 47, 49, 18, or 19 a couple of stops to Szent Gellért tér.

TIMING

The Citadella and Szabadság Szobor are lit in golden lights every night, but the entire Gellért-hegy is at its scenic best every year on August 20, when it forms the backdrop to the spectacular St. Stephen's Day fireworks display.

SIGHTS TO SEE

★ ⑳ **Citadella.** The fortress atop the hill was a much-hated sight for Hungarians. They called it the Gellért Bastille, for it was erected, on the site of an earlier wooden observatory, by the Austrian army as a lookout after the 1848–1849 War of Independence. But no matter what its history may be, the views here are breathtaking. Its transformation into a tourist site during the 1960s improved its image, with the addition of cafés, a beer garden, wine cellars, and a hostel. In its inner wall is a small graphic exhibition (with some relics) of Budapest's 2,000-year history. ☎ *No phone.* ☞ *Free.* ☉ *Accessible at all times.*

Erzsébethíd (Elizabeth Bridge). This bridge was named for Empress Elizabeth (1837–1898), called Sissi, of whom the Hungarians were particularly fond. The original bridge was built between 1897 and 1903; at the time, it was the longest single-span suspension bridge in Europe. It was destroyed by the Germans in 1945 and its modern replacement dates from 1964.

★ ⑲ **Gellért Szálloda és Thermál Fürdő** (Gellért Hotel and Thermal Baths). At the foot of the Gellért Hill are these beautiful art-nouveau establishments. The Danubius Hotel Gellért (☞ Lodging, *below*) is the oldest spa hotel in Hungary, with hot springs that have supplied curative baths for nearly 2,000 years. It is the most popular among tourists, as you don't need reservations, it's quite easy to communicate, and there's a wealth of treatments—including chamomile steam baths, salt-vapor inhalations, and hot mud packs. Many of these treatments require a doctor's prescription; they will accept prescriptions from foreign doctors. Men and women have separate steam and sauna rooms; both the indoor pool and the outdoor wave pool (☞ Outdoor Activities and Sports, *below*) are coed. ✉ *XI, Gellért tér 1,* ☎ *1/385–3555 (baths).* ☞ *Indoor baths and steam rooms 500 Ft. per 1½ hrs; indoors and pool*

1,300 Ft. per day. ⊙ *Baths weekdays 6 AM–6 PM, weekends 6:30 AM–1 (May–Sept. until 4 PM). May–Sept. weekend massage only until 1 PM. Wave pool May–Sept., daily 6 AM–6 PM.*

⑰ **Rác Fürdő** (Rác Baths). The bright-yellow building tucked away at the foot of Gellért Hill near the Elizabeth Bridge houses these baths, built during the reign of King Zsigmond in the early 15th century and rebuilt by Miklós Ybl in the mid-19th century. Its waters contain alkaline salts and other minerals; you can also get a massage. Women can bathe on Monday, Wednesday, and Friday; men on Tuesday, Thursday, and Saturday (☞ Outdoor Activities and Sports, *below*). These baths are particularly popular with the gay community. ⊠ *I, Hadnagy utca 8–10,* ☎ *1/356–1322.* ☒ *450 Ft.* ⊙ *Mon.–Sat. 6:30 AM–6 PM.*

⑱ **Rudas Fürdő** (Rudas Baths). This bath is on the riverbank, the original Turkish pool making its interior possibly the most dramatically beautiful of Budapest's baths. A high, domed roof admits pinpricks of bluish-green light into the dark, circular stone hall with its austere columns and arches. Fed by eight springs with a year-round temperature of 44°C (111°F), the Rudas's highly fluoridated waters have been known for 1,000 years. The facility is open to men only (though it does not have a large gay following); a less interesting outer swimming pool is open to both sexes (☞ Outdoor Activities and Sports, *below*). Massages are available. ⊠ *I, Döbrentei tér 9,* ☎ *1/356–1322.* ☒ *400 Ft.* ⊙ *Weekdays 6 AM–6 PM, weekends 6 AM–noon.*

⑮ **Semmelweis Orvostörténeti Múzeum** (Semmelweis Museum of Medical History). This splendid Baroque house was the birthplace of Ignác Semmelweis (1818–1865), the Hungarian physician who proved the contagiousness of puerperal (childbed) fever. It's now a museum that traces the history of healing. Semmelweis's grave is in the garden. ⊠ *Apród utca 1–3,* ☎ *1/375–3533.* ☒ *100 Ft.* ⊙ *Tues.–Sun. 10:30–5:30.*

Szabadság Szobor (Liberation Memorial). Visible from many parts of the city, this 130-ft-high 1947 memorial, which starts just below the southern edge of the Citadella and towers above it, honors the 1944–1945 siege of Budapest and the Russian soldiers who fell in the battle. It is the work of noted Hungarian sculptor Zsigmond Kisfaludi-Stróbl, and from the distance it looks light, airy, and even liberating. A sturdy young girl, her hair and robe swirling in the wind, holds a palm branch high above her head. Until recently, she was further embellished with sculptures of giants slaying dragons, Red Army soldiers, and peasants rejoicing at the freedom that Soviet liberation promised (but failed) to bring to Hungary. Since 1992, her mood has lightened: In the Budapest city government's systematic purging of Communist symbols, the Red Combat infantrymen who had flanked the Liberation statue for decades were hacked off and carted away. A few are now on display among the other evicted statues in the Szobor Park in the city's 22nd district (☞ Off the Beaten Path, *below*). ⊠ *Gellért-hegy.*

OFF THE BEATEN PATH

SZOBOR PARK (Statue Park) – For a look at Budapest's too-recent Iron Curtain past, make the 30-minute trip out to this open-air exhibit, cleverly nicknamed "Tons of Socialism," where 42 of the Communist statues and memorials that once dominated the city's streets and squares have been put out to pasture since the political changes in 1989. Here you can wander among mammoth Lenin and Marx statues and buy socialist-nostalgia souvenirs while songs from the Hungarian and Russian workers' movement play bombastically in the background. ⊠ *XXII, Balatoni út, corner of Szabadkai út,* ☎ FAX *1/227–7446.* ☒ *250 Ft.* ⊙ *Mid-Apr.–Oct., daily 8–8; Nov.–mid-Apr., weekends 10–dusk.*

Szarvas-ház (Stag House). This Louis XVI–style building is named for the former Szarvas Café or, more accurately, for its extant trade sign, with an emblem of a stag not quite at bay, which can be seen above the triangular arched entryway. For years, the structure housed the Arany Szarvas restaurant, which preserved some of the mood of the old Tabán, but at press time it was closed for renovations and seemed likely to change hands and reopen as something else. ⊠ *Szarvas tér 1.*

⑯ Tabán plébánia-templom (Tabán Parish Church). In 1736, this church was built on the site of a Turkish mosque and subsequently renovated and reconstructed several times. Its present form—mustard-color stone with a rotund, green clock tower—could be described as restrained Baroque. ⊠ *I, Attila u. 1.*

North Buda

Most of these sights are along Fő utca (Main Street), a long, straight thoroughfare that starts at the Chain Bridge and runs parallel to the Danube. It is lined on both sides with multistory late-18th-century houses—many darkened by soot and showing their age more than those you've seen in sparklingly restored areas like Castle Hill. This north-bound exploration can be done with the help of Bus 86, which covers the waterfront, or on foot, although distances are fairly great.

Numbers in the text correspond to numbers in the margin and on the Exploring Budapest map.

A GOOD WALK

Beginning at **Batthyány tér** ㉓, with its head-on view of Parliament across the Danube, continue north on Fő utca, passing (or stopping to bathe at) the famous Turkish **Király-fürdő** ㉔. From **Bem József tér** ㉕, one block north, turn left (away from the river) up Fekete Sas utca, crossing busy Margit körút and turning right, one block past, up Mecset utca. This will take you up the hill to **Gül Baba türbéje** ㉖.

TIMING

The tour can fit easily into a few hours, including a good hour-and-a-half soak at the baths; expect the walk from Bem József tér up the hill to Gül Baba türbéje to take about 25 minutes. Fő utca and Bem József tér can get congested during rush hours (from around 7:30 to 8:30 AM and 4:30 to 6 PM). Remember that museums are closed Mondays and that the Király Baths are open to men and women on different days of the week.

SIGHTS TO SEE

㉓ Batthyány tér. This lovely square, open on its river side, affords a grand view of Parliament, directly across the Danube. The M2 subway, the HÉV electric railway from Szentendre, and various suburban and local buses converge on the square, as do peddlers hawking everything from freshly picked flowers to mismatched pairs of shoes. At No. 7 Batthyány tér is the beautiful, Baroque twin-towered **Szent Anna-templom** (Church of St. Anne), dating from 1740–1762, its oval cupola adorned with frescoes and statuary.

NEED A BREAK? | The **Angelika** café (⊠ Batthyány tér 7, ☎ 1/212–3784), housed in the Church of St. Anne building, serves swirled meringues, chestnut-filled layer cakes, and a plethora of other heavenly pastries, all baked on the premises from family recipes. You can sit inside on small velvet chairs at marble-topped tables or at one of the umbrella-shaded tables outdoors. It's open daily 10 AM–10 PM.

㉕ Bem József tér. This square near the river is not particularly pic-turesque and can get heavy with traffic, but it houses the statue of its important namesake, Polish general József Bem, who offered his services to the 1848 revolutionaries in Vienna and then Hungary. Reorganizing the rebel forces in Transylvania, he was the war's most successful general. It was at this statue on October 23, 1956, that a great student demonstration in sympathy with the Poles' striving for liberal reforms exploded into the brave and tragic Hungarian uprising suppressed by the Red Army.

㉑ **Corvin tér.** This charming, small, shady square on Fő utca is the site of the turn-of-the-century Folk Art Institute administration building and the concert hall Budai Vigadó (☞ Nightlife and the Arts, *below*) at No. 8.

㉖ **Gül Baba türbéje** (Tomb of Gül Baba). Gül Baba, a 16th-century dervish and poet whose name means "father of roses" in Turkish, was buried in a tomb built of carved stone blocks with four oval windows. He fought in several wars waged by the Turks and fell during the siege of Buda in 1541. The tomb remains a place of pilgrimage; it is considered Europe's northernmost Muslim shrine and marks the spot where he was slain. Set at an elevation on Rózsadomb (Rose Hill), the tomb is near a good lookout for city views. ⊠ *Mecset utca 14,* ☎ *1/355–8764.* 🎫 *100 Ft.* ☉ *May–Oct., Tues.–Sun. 10–4.*

Ⓒ **Gyermek vasút** (Children's Railway). The 12-km (7-mi) Children's Railway runs from Széchenyihegy to Hűvösvölgy. The sweeping views make the trip well worthwhile for children and adults alike. Departures are from Széchenyihegy, which you can reach by taking a cogwheel railway. ⊠ *Cogwheel railway station: intersection of Szilágyi Erzsébet fasor and Pasaréti út.* 🎫 *140 Ft. each way.* ☉ *Trains run mid-Jan.–late Mar. and mid-Sept.–Dec., Wed.–Sun. 8–4; mid-Jan. and Apr.–mid-Sept., Tues.–Sun. 8–5.*

OFF THE
BEATEN PATH

JÁNOSHEGY (Janos Hill) – A *libegő* (chairlift) will take you to Janos Hill—at 1,729 ft, the highest point in Budapest—where you can climb a lookout tower for the best view of the city. ⊠ *Take Bus 158 from Moszkva tér to the last stop, Zugligeti út,* ☎ *1/395–6494 or 1/376–3764.* 🎫 *One-way 200 Ft., round-trip 300 Ft.* ☉ *Mid-May–mid-Sept., daily 9–5; mid-Sept.–mid-May (depending on weather), daily 9:30–4; closed every other Mon.*

Kapucinus templom (Capuchin Church). This church was converted from a Turkish mosque at the end of the 17th century. Damaged during the revolution in 1849, it acquired its current romantic-style exterior when it was rebuilt a few years later. ⊠ *Fő utca.*

㉔ **Király-fürdő** (King Baths). The royal gem of Turkish baths in Budapest was built in the 16th century by the Turkish pasha of Buda. Its stone cupola, crowned by a golden moon and crescent, arches over the steamy, dark pools indoors. It is open to men on Monday, Wednesday, and Friday; to women on Tuesday, Thursday, and Saturday (☞ Outdoor Activities and Sports, *below*). These baths are very popular with the gay community. ⊠ *II, Fő utca 84,* ☎ *1/202–3688.* 🎫 *400 Ft.* ☉ *Weekdays 6:30 AM–6 PM, Sat. 6:30 AM–noon.*

㉒ **Szilágyi Dezső tér.** This is another of the charming little squares punctuating Fő utca; here you'll find the composer Béla Bartók's house, at No. 4.

Margit-sziget (Margaret Island)

More than 2½ km (1½ mi) long and covering nearly 200 acres, **Margit-sziget** ㉗ is ideal for strolling, jogging, sunbathing, or just loafing. In good weather, the island draws a multitudinous cross section of the city's population out to its gardens and sporting facilities. The outdoor pool complex of the Palatinus Baths (toward the Buda side), built in 1921, can attract tens of thousands of people on a summer day. Nearby are a tennis stadium, a youth athletic center, boathouses, sports grounds, and, most impressive of all, the Nemzeti Sportuszoda (National Sports Swimming Pool), designed by the architect Alfred Hajós (while still in his teens, Hajós won two gold medals in swimming at the first modern Olympic Games, held in Athens in 1896). In addition, walkers, joggers, bicyclists, and rollerbladers do laps around the island's perimeter and up and down the main road, closed to traffic except for Bus 26 (and a few official vehicles), which travels up and down the island and across the Margaret Bridge to and from Pest.

The island's natural curative hot springs have given rise to the Danubius Grand and Thermal hotels on the northern end of the island (☞ Lodging, *below*) and are piped in to two spa hotels on the mainland, the Aquincum on the Buda bank and the Hélia on the Pest side.

A GOOD WALK

Entering the island from its southern end at the **Margit-híd,** stroll (or rent a bicycle and pedal) north along any of the several tree-shaded paths, including the **Müvész sétány,** pausing for a picnic on an open lawn, and eventually ending up at the rock garden at the northern end. From here, you can wander back to the southern end or take Bus 26 on the island's only road.

TIMING

A leisurely walk simply from one end to the other would take about 40 minutes, but it's nice to spend extra time wandering. To experience Margaret Island's role in Budapest life fully, go on a Saturday or Sunday afternoon to join and/or watch people whiling away the day. Sunday is a particularly good choice for strategic sightseers, who can utilize the rest of the week to cover those city sights and areas that are closed on Sundays. On weekdays, you'll share the island only with joggers and kids playing hooky from school.

SIGHTS TO SEE

Margit-híd (Margaret Bridge). At the southern end of the island, the Margaret Bridge is the closer of the two entrances for those coming from downtown Buda or Pest. Just north of the Chain Bridge, the bridge walkway provides gorgeous midriver views of Castle Hill and Parliament. Toward the end of 1944, the bridge was blown up by the retreating Nazis while it was crowded with rush-hour traffic. It was rebuilt in the same unusual shape—forming an obtuse angle in midstream, with a short leg leading down to the island. The original bridge was built during the 1840s by French engineer Ernest Gouin in collaboration with Gustave Eiffel.

㉗ Margit-sziget (Margaret Island). The island was first mentioned almost 2,000 years ago as the summer residence of the commander of the Roman garrison at nearby Aquincum. Later known as Rabbit Island (Insula Leporum), it was a royal hunting ground during the Árpád dynasty. King Imre, who reigned from 1196 to 1204, held court here, and several convents and monasteries were built here during the Middle Ages. (During a walk round the island, you'll see the ruins of a few of these buildings.) It takes its current name from St. Margaret, the pious daughter of King Béla IV, who at the ripe old age of 10 retired to a Dominican nunnery here.

☾ Margit-sziget Vadaspark (Margaret Island Game Park). Just east of the rose garden is a small would-be petting zoo, if the animals were allowed to be petted. A fenced-in compound houses a menagerie of goats, rabbits, donkeys, assorted fowl and ducks, and gargantuan peacocks that sit heavily on straining tree branches. ▨ *Free.*

Marosvásárhelyi zenélő kút (Marosvásárhely Musical Fountain). At the northern end of the island is a copy of the water-powered Marosvásárhely Musical Fountain, which plays songs and chimes. The original was designed more than 150 years ago by a Transylvanian named Péter Bodor. It stands near a picturesque, artificial **rock garden** with Japanese dwarf trees and lily ponds. The stream coursing through it never freezes, for it comes from a natural hot spring causing it instead to give off thick steam in winter that enshrouds the garden in a mystical cloud.

Művész sétány (Artists' Promenade). Through the center of the island runs the Artists' Promenade, lined with busts of Hungarian artists, writers, and musicians. Shaded by giant plane trees, it's a perfect place to stroll. The promenade passes close to the **rose garden** (in the center of the island), a large grassy lawn surrounded by blooming flower beds planted with hundreds of kinds of flowers. It's a great spot to picnic or to watch a game of soccer or Ultimate Frisbee, both of which are regularly played here on weekend afternoons.

Downtown Pest and the Kis Körút (Little Ring Road)

Budapest's urban heart is full of bona fide sights plus innumerable tiny streets and grand avenues where you can wander for hours admiring the city's stately old buildings—some freshly sparkling after their first painting in decades, others silently but still elegantly crumbling.

Dominated by the Parliament building, the district surrounding Kossuth tér is the legislative, diplomatic, and administrative nexus of Budapest; most of the ministries are here, as are the National Bank and Courts of Justice. Downriver, the romantic Danube promenade, the Duna Korzó, extends along the stretch of riverfront across from Castle Hill. With Vörösmarty tér and pedestrian shopping street Váci utca just inland, this area forms Pest's tourist core. Going south, the Korzó ends at Március 15 tér. One block in from the river, Ferenciek tere marks the beginning of the university area, spreading south of Kossuth Lajos utca. Here, the streets are narrower and the echoes of your footsteps echo off of the elegantly aging stone buildings.

Pest is laid out in broad circular *körúts* ("ring roads" or boulevards). Vámház körút is the first sector of the 2½-km (1½-mi) Kis körút (Little Ring Road), which traces the route of the Old Town wall from Szabadsághíd (Liberty Bridge) to Deák tér. Construction of the inner körút began in 1872 and was completed in 1880. Changing names as it curves, after Kálvin tér it becomes Múzeum körút (passing by the National Museum), and then Károly körút for its final stretch ending at Deák tér. Deák tér, the only place where all three subway lines converge, could be called the dead-center of downtown. East of the körút are the weathered streets of Budapest's former ghetto.

A GOOD WALK

Starting at Kossuth tér to see the **Országház** ㉘ and the **Néprajzi Múzeum,** it's worth walking a few blocks southeast to take in stately **Szabadság tér** ㉚ before heading back to the Danube and south to the foot of the **Széchenyi Lánchíd** at **Roosevelt tér** ㉛. As this tour involves quite a bit of walking, you may want to take Tram 2 from Kossuth tér a few stops downriver to Roosevelt tér to save your energy. While time and/or energy may not allow it just now, at some point during your visit, a walk across the Chain Bridge is a must. From Roosevelt tér go south, across the street, and join the **korzó** ㉜ along the river, strolling past the **Vigadó** ㉝ at Vigadó tér, all the way to the **Belvárosi plébánia**

templom ㉞ at Március 15 tér, just under the Elizabeth Bridge. Double back up the korzó to Vigadó tér and walk in from the river on Vigadó utca to **Vörösmarty tér** ㉟.

Follow the crowds down pedestrian-only **Váci utca** ㊱, crossing busy Kossuth Lajos utca near Ferenciek tere and continuing along Váci utca's southern stretch to the **Vásárcsarnok** ㊴. Doubling back a few blocks on Váci utca, turn right onto Szerb utca and stroll past the **Szerb Ortodox templom** to the street's end at **Egyetem tér** ㊳. Here, you are going through the darker, narrower streets of this student-filled, increasingly trendy area. A detour into any of the other side streets will give you a good flavor of the area. Walking south on Kecskeméti utca, you will reach **Kálvin tér** ㊵. To save time and energy, you can also take Tram 47 or 49 from Fővám tér, in front of the Vásárcsarnok, one stop away from the Danube to Kálvin tér. Just north of Kálvin tér on Múzeum körút is the **Magyar Nemzeti Múzeum** ㊶. The **Nagy Zsinagóga** ㊷ is about ¾ km (⅓ mi) farther north along the Kis körút (Small Ring Road)—a longish walk or a short tram ride. From here, more walking along the körút, or a tram ride to the last stop, brings you to Pest's main hub, Deák tér. The **Szent István Bazilika** ㊺ is an extra but rewarding 500-yard walk north on Bajcsy-Zsilinszky út.

TIMING

This is a particularly rich part of the city; the suggested walk will take the better part of a day, including time to visit the museums, stroll on the korzó, and browse on Vaci utca—not to mention time for lunch. Keep in mind that the museums are closed on Monday.

SIGHTS TO SEE

㉞ **Belvárosi plébánia templom** (Inner City Parish Church). Dating to the 12th century, this is the oldest ecclesiastical building in Pest. It's actually built on something even older—the remains of the Contra Aquincum, a 3rd-century Roman fortress and tower, parts of which are visible next to the church. There is hardly any architectural style that cannot be found in some part or another, starting with a single Romanesque arch in its south tower. The single nave still has its original Gothic chancel and some 15th-century Gothic frescoes. Two side chapels contain beautifully carved Renaissance altarpieces and tabernacles of red marble from the early 16th century. During Budapest's years of Turkish occupation, the church served as a mosque—and this is remembered by a *mihrab,* a Muslim prayer niche. During the 18th century, the church was given two Baroque towers and its present facade. In 1808 it was enriched with a rococo pulpit, and still later a superb winged triptych was added to the main altar. From 1867 to 1875, Franz Liszt lived only a few steps away from the church, in a town house where he held regular "musical Sundays" at which Richard and Cosima Wagner were frequent guests and participants. Liszt's own musical Sunday mornings often began in this church. An admirer of its acoustics and organ, he conducted many masses here, including the first Budapest performance of his *Missa Choralis,* in 1872. ⊠ *V, Március 15 tér 2,* ☎ *1/317–3322.*

㊳ **Egyetem tér** (University Square). Budapest's University of Law sits here in the heart of the city's university neighborhood. On one corner is the cool gray-and-green marble **Egyetemi Templom** (University Church), one of Hungary's most beautiful Baroque buildings. Built between 1725 and 1742, it has an especially splendid pulpit.

㊹ **Evangélikus Templom and Evangélikus Múzeum** (Lutheran Church and Lutheran Museum). The neoclassical Lutheran Church sits in the center of it all on busy Deák tér. Classical concerts are regularly held here. The church's interior designer, János Krausz, flouted then-traditional church architecture by placing a single large interior beneath the huge vaulted roof structure. The adjoining school is now the Lutheran Museum, which traces the role of Protestantism in Hungarian history and contains Martin Luther's original will. ⊠ *Deák Ferenc tér 4,* ☎ *1/317–4173.* 🖃 *Museum 200 Ft.; church free (except during concerts).* ☉ *Museum Tues.–Sun. 10–6.*

㊲ Ferenciek Templom (Franciscan church). This pale-yellow church was built in 1743. On the wall facing Kossuth Lajos utca is a bronze relief showing a scene from the devastating flood of 1838; the detail is so vivid that it almost makes you seasick. A faded arrow below the relief indicates the high-water mark of almost 4 ft. Next to it is the **Nereids Fountain,** a popular meeting place for students from the nearby Eötvös Loránd University. ⊠ *V, Ferenciek tere.*

Görög Ortodox templom (Greek Orthodox Church). Built at the end of the 18th century in late-Baroque style, the Greek Orthodox Church was remodeled a century later by Miklós Ybl, who designed the Opera House and many other important Budapest landmarks. The church retains some fine wood carvings and a dazzling array of icons by a late-18th-century Serbian master Miklós Jankovich. ⊠ *V, Petőfi tér 2/b.*

㊵ Kálvin tér (Calvin Square). Calvin Square takes its name from the neoclassical Protestant church that tries to dominate this busy traffic hub; more glaringly noticeable, however, is the billboard of a giant Pepsi advertisement. The Kecskeméti Kapu, a main gate of Pest, once stood here, as well as a cattle market that was a notorious den of thieves. At the beginning of the 19th century, this was where Pest ended and the prairie began.

NEED A BREAK? The Hotel Korona's popular café, **Korona Passage** (⊠ Kecskeméti utca 14, ☎ 1/317–4111), has a *palacsinta* (crepe) bar where you can watch the cooks prepare giant Hungarian crepes brimming with such fillings as apple, chocolate, and *túró* (sweetened cottage cheese). The café also serves soups and sandwiches and has a salad bar.

★ ㉜ Korzó. The neighborhood to the south of Roosevelt tér has regained much of its past elegance—if not its architectural grandeur—with the erection of the Atrium Hyatt, Inter-Continental, and Budapest Marriott luxury hotels. Traversing all three and continuing well beyond them is the riverside Korzó, a pedestrian promenade lined with park benches and appealing outdoor cafés from which one can enjoy postcard-perfect views of Gellért Hill and Castle Hill directly across the Danube. Try to take a stroll in the evening, when the views are lit up in shimmering gold.

NEED A BREAK? The **Bécsi Kávéház** (Viennese Café; ⊠ V, Apáczai Csere János u. 12–14, ☎ 1/327–6333), in the Hotel Inter-Continental, serves mouthwatering *isler* (giant chocolate-covered cookies filled with apricot or raspberry jam) and cream pastries.

Közgazdasági Egyetem (University of Economics). Just below the Liberty Bridge on the waterfront, the monumental neo-Renaissance building was once the Customs House. Built in 1871–1874 by Miklós Ybl, it is now also known as *közgáz,* after a stint during the Communist era as Karl Marx University. ⊠ *Fővám tér.*

㊶ Magyar Nemzeti Múzeum (Hungarian National Museum). Built between 1837 and 1847, the museum is a fine example of 19th-century classicism—simple, well proportioned, and surrounded by a large garden. In front of this building on March 15, 1848, Sándor Petőfi recited his revolutionary poem, the "National Song" ("Nemzeti dal"), and the "12 Points," a list of political demands by young Hungarians calling on the people to rise up against the Hapsburgs. Celebrations of the national holiday commemorating the failed revolution are held on these steps every year on March 15.

The museum's most sacred treasure, the **Szent Korona** (Holy Crown), reposes with other royal relics in a domed Hall of Honor off the main lobby. The crown sits like a golden soufflé above a Byzantine band of holy scenes in enamel and pearls and other gems. It seems to date from the 12th century, so it could not be the crown that Pope Sylvester II presented to St. Stephen in the year 1000, when he was crowned the first king of Hungary. Nevertheless, it is known as the Crown of St. Stephen and has been regarded—even by Communist governments—as the legal symbol of Hungarian sovereignty and unbroken statehood. In 1945 the fleeing Hungarian army handed over the crown and its accompanying regalia to the Americans rather than have them fall into Soviet hands. They were restored to Hungary in 1978.

Other rarities include a completely furnished Turkish tent; masterworks of cabinet making and wood carving, including pews from churches in Nyírbátor and Transylvania; a piano that belonged to both Beethoven and Liszt; and, in the treasury, masterpieces of goldsmithing, among them the 11th-century Constantions Monomachos crown from Byzantium and the richly pictorial 16th-century chalice of Miklós Pálffy. Looking at it is like reading the "Prince Valiant" comic strip in gold. The epic Hungarian history exhibit has exhibits chronicling the end of communism and the much-celebrated exodus of the Russian troops. ⌧ *IX, Múzeum körút 14–16,* ☎ *1/338–2122.* ⌼ *270 Ft.* ☉ *Mid-Mar.–mid-Oct., Wed.–Sun. 10–6; mid-Oct.–mid-Mar., Wed.–Sun. 10–5. Museum may open Tues. also, depending on demand; call ahead to check.*

★ ㊷ **Nagy Zsinagóga** (Great Synagogue). Seating 3,000, Europe's largest synagogue was designed by Ludwig Förs and built between 1844 and 1859 in a Byzantine-Moorish style described as "consciously archaic Romantic-Eastern." Desecrated by German and Hungarian Nazis, it was painstakingly reconstructed with donations from all over the world; its doors reopened in fall 1996. While it is used for regular services during much of the year, it is generally not used in midwinter as the space is too large to heat; between December and February, visiting hours are erratic. In the courtyard behind the synagogue, a weeping willow made of metal honors the victims of the Holocaust. Liszt and Saint-Saëns are among the great musicians who have played its grand organ. ⌧ *Dohány u. 2–8,* ☎ *1/342–1335.* ⌼ *Free.* ☉ *Weekdays 10–3, Sun. 10–1. Closed Jewish holidays and Dec.*

★ ㉙ **Néprajzi Múzeum** (Museum of Ethnography). The 1890s neoclassical temple formerly housed the Supreme Court. Now an impressive permanent exhibition, "The Folk Culture of the Hungarian People," explains all aspects of peasant life from the end of the 18th century until World War I; explanatory texts are provided in both English and Hungarian. Besides embroideries, pottery, and carvings—the authentic pieces you can't see at touristy folk shops—there are farming tools, furniture, and traditional costumes. The central room of the building alone is worth the entrance fee: a majestic hall with ornate marble staircases and pillars, and towering stained-glass windows. ⌧ *V, Kossuth tér 12,* ☎ *1/332–6340.* ⌼ *250 Ft., Tues. free.* ☉ *Mid-Mar.–mid-Oct., Tues.–Sun. 10–6; mid-Oct.–mid-Mar., Tues.–Sun. 10–4.*

★ ㉘ **Országház** (Parliament). The most visible, though not highly accessible, symbol of Budapest's left bank is the huge neo-Gothic Parliament. Mirrored in the Danube much the way Britain's Parliament is reflected by the Thames, it lies midway between the Margaret and Chain bridges and can be reached by the M2 subway (Kossuth tér station) and waterfront Tram 2. A fine example of historicizing, eclectic fin-de-siècle architecture, it was designed by the Hungarian architect Ímre Steindl and built by a thousand workers between 1885 and 1902. The grace and dignity of its long facade and 24 slender towers, with spacious arcades and high windows balancing its vast central dome, lend this living landmark a refreshingly Baroque spatial effect. The exterior is lined with 90 statues of great figures in Hungarian history; the corbels are ornamented by 242 allegorical statues. Inside are 691 rooms, 10 courtyards, and 29 staircases; some 88 pounds of gold were used for the staircases and halls. These halls are also a gallery of late-19th-century Hungarian art, with frescoes and canvases depicting Hungarian history, starting with Mihály Munkácsy's large painting of the Magyar Conquest of 896. Unfortunately, because Parliament is a workplace for legislators, the building is not open to individual visitors and must be toured in groups at certain hours on specific city tours organized by IBUSZ Travel (☞ Visitor Information *in* Budapest A to Z, *below*). ✉ *V, Kossuth tér.*

㉛ **Roosevelt tér** (Roosevelt Square). This square opening onto the Danube is less closely connected with the U.S. president than with the progressive Hungarian statesman Count István Széchenyi, dubbed "the greatest Hungarian" even by his adversary, Kossuth. The neo-Renaissance palace of the **Magyar Tudományos Akadémia** (Academy of Sciences) on the north side was built between 1862 and 1864, after Széchenyi's suicide. It is a fitting memorial, for in 1825, the statesman donated a year's income from all his estates to establish the academy. Another Széchenyi project, the Széchenyi Lánchíd (☞ *below*), leads into the square; there stands a statue of Széchenyi near one of another statesman, Ferenc Deák, whose negotiations led to the establishment of the dual monarchy after Kossuth's 1848–1849 revolution failed. Both men lived on this square.

★ ㉚ **Szabadság tér** (Liberty Square). This is the site of the **Magyar Televízió** (Hungarian Television Headquarters), a former stock exchange with what look like four temples and two castles on its roof, and a solemn-looking neoclassical shrine, the **Nemzeti Bank** (National Bank). The bank's Postal Savings Bank branch, adjacent to the main building but visible from behind Szabadság tér on Hold utca, is another exuberant Art Nouveau masterpiece of architect Ödön Lechner, built in 1901 with colorful majolica mosaics, characteristically curvaceous windows, and pointed towers ending in swirling gold flourishes. In the square's center remains one of the few monuments to the Russian "liberation" that were spared the recent cleansing of symbols of the past regime. The decision to retain this obelisk—because it represents liberation from the Nazis during World War II—caused outrage among many groups, prompting some to vow to haul it away themselves (though for the moment it remains). With the Stars and Stripes flying out in front, the **American Embassy** is at Szabadság tér 12.

Széchenyi Lánchíd (Chain Bridge). This is the oldest and most beautiful of the Danube's eight bridges. Before it was built, the river could be crossed only by ferry or by a pontoon bridge that had to be removed when ice blocks began floating downstream in winter. It was constructed at the initiative of the great Hungarian reformer and philanthropist Count István Széchenyi, using an 1839 design by the French civil engineer

William Tierney Clark. This classical, almost poetically graceful and symmetrical suspension bridge was finished by his Scottish namesake, Adam Clark, who also built the 383-yard tunnel under Castle Hill, thus connecting the Danube quay with the rest of Buda. After it was destroyed by the Nazis, the bridge was rebuilt in its original form (though slightly widened for traffic) and was reopened in 1949, on the centenary of its inauguration. At the Buda end of the bridge is **Clark Ádám tér** (Adam Clark Square), where you can zip up to Castle Hill on the sometimes crowded Sikló funicular rail. ⊠ *250 Ft.* ✆ *Funicular daily 7:30 AM–10 PM; closed every other Mon.*

★ ㊺ **Szent István Bazilika** (St. Stephen's Basilica). Dark and massive, this is one of the chief landmarks of Pest and the city's largest church—it can hold 8,500 people. Its very Holy Roman front porch greets you with a tympanum bustling with statuary. The basilica's dome and the dome of Parliament are by far the most visible in the Pest skyline, and this is no accident: With the Magyar Millennium of 1896 in mind, both domes were planned to be 315 ft high.

The millennium was not yet in sight when architect József Hild began building the basilica in neoclassical style in 1851, two years after the revolution was suppressed. After Hild's death, the project was taken over in 1867 by Miklós Ybl, the architect who did the most to transform modern Pest into a monumental metropolis. Wherever he could, Ybl shifted Hild's motifs toward the neo-Renaissance mode that Ybl favored. When the dome collapsed, partly damaging the walls, he made even more drastic changes. Ybl died in 1891, five years before the 1,000-year celebration, and the basilica was completed in neo-Renaissance style by József Kauser—but not until 1905.

Below the cupola is a rich collection of late-19th-century Hungarian art: mosaics, altarpieces, and statuary (what heady days the millennium must have meant for local talents!). There are 150 kinds of marble, all from Hungary except for the Carrara in the sanctuary's centerpiece: a white statue of King (St.) Stephen I, Hungary's first king and patron saint. Stephen's mummified right hand is preserved as a relic in the **Szent Jobb Kápolna** (Holy Right Chapel); the guard will illuminate it for you for two minutes for a minimal charge. Visitors can also climb the 364 stairs (or take the elevator) to the top of the cupola for a spectacular view of the city. Extensive restorations have been under way at the aging basilica for years, with a target completion date of 2010, and some part of the structure is likely to be under scaffolding when you visit. ⊠ *V, Szt. István tér,* ✆ *1/317–2859.* ⊠ *Church free, Szt. Jobb chapel 100 Ft., cupola 350 Ft.* ✆ *Church Mon.–Sat. 7–7, Sun. 1–7; Szt. Jobb Chapel Apr.–Sept., Mon.–Sat. 9–5, Sun. 1–5; Oct.–Mar., Mon.–Sat. 10–4, Sun. 1–4; Cupola Apr. and Sept.–Oct., daily 10–5; May–Aug., daily 9–6.*

Szerb Ortodox templom (Serbian Orthodox Church). Built in 1688, this lovely burnt-orange church, one of Budapest's oldest buildings, sits in a shaded garden surrounded by thick stone walls of the same color detailed with large-tile mosaics and wrought-iron gates. ⊠ *V, Szerb utca.*

㉟ **Váci utca.** Immediately north of Elizabeth Bridge is Budapest's best-known shopping street and most unabashed tourist zone, Váci utca, a pedestrian precinct with electrified 19th-century lampposts and smart shops with credit-card emblems on ornate doorways. No bargain basement, Váci utca gets its special flavor from the mix of native furriers, tailors, designers, shoemakers, and folk artists, as well as an increasing number of internationally known boutiques. There are also bookstores and china and crystal shops, as well as gourmet food stores redolent of paprika. Váci utca's second half, south of Kossuth Lajos utca, was transformed into another pedestrian-only zone a few years ago and has a different character from its northern side. The street is a clash of past and future: A tiny button shop and a knife and scissor sharpening store struggle alongside tacky souvenir vendors and flashy boutiques. Watch your purses and wallets—against inflated prices *and* active pickpockets.

㊸ Városház. The monumental former city council building, which used to be a hospital for wounded soldiers and then a resort for the elderly ("home" would be too cozy for so vast a hulk), is now Budapest's city hall. It's enormous enough to loom over the row of shops and businesses lining Károly körút in front of it but can only be entered through courtyards or side streets (Gerlóczy utca is the most accessible). The Tuscan columns at the main entrance and the allegorical statuary of *Atlas, War,* and *Peace* are especially splendid. There was once a chapel in the center of the main facade, but now only its spire remains. ⊠ *V, Városház u. 9–12,* ☎ *1/318–6066.*

㊴ Vásárcsarnok (Central Market Hall). The magnificent hall, a 19th-century iron-frame construction, was reopened in late 1994 after years of renovation (and disputes over who would foot the bill). Even during the leanest years of Communist shortages, the abundance of food came as a revelation to shoppers from East and West. Today, the cavernous, three-story hall once again teems with people browsing among stalls packed with salamis and red-paprika chains. Upstairs you can buy folk embroideries and souvenirs. ⊠ *IX, Vámhaz körút 1–3.* ☉ *Mon. 6 AM–5 PM, Tues.–Fri. 6 AM–6 PM, Sat. 6 AM–2 PM.*

㉝ Vigadó (Concert Hall). Designed in a striking romantic style by Frigyes Feszl and inaugurated in 1865 with Franz Liszt conducting his own *St. Elizabeth Oratorio,* the concert hall is a curious mixture of Byzantine, Moorish, Romanesque, and Hungarian motifs, punctuated by dancing statues and sturdy pillars. Brahms, Debussy, and Casals are among the other phenomenal musicians who have graced its stage. Mahler's *Symphony No. 1* and many works by Bartók were first performed here. While you can go into the lobby on your own, the hall is open only for concerts. ⊠ *V, Vigadó tér 2.*

★ **㉟ Vörösmarty tér** (Vörösmarty Square). This large, handsome square at the northern end of Váci utca is the heart of Pest's tourist life. Street musicians and sidewalk cafés make it one of the liveliest places in Budapest and a good spot to sit and relax—if you can ward off the aggressive caricature sketchers. Grouped around a white-marble statue of the 19th-century poet and dramatist Mihály Vörösmarty are luxury shops, airline offices, and an elegant former pissoir. Now a lovely kiosk, it displays gold-painted historic scenes of the square's golden days.

NEED A BREAK?
The best-known, tastiest, and most tasteful address on Vörösmarty Square belongs to the **Gerbeaud** pastry shop (⊠ Vörösmarty tér 7, ☎ 1/318–1311), founded in 1858 by a French confectioner and later taken over by the Swiss family Gerbeaud. Filling most of a square block, it offers dozens of sweets (as well as sandwiches, coffee, and other not so sugary snacks), served in a salon with green-marble tables and Regency-style marble fireplaces or at tables outside in summer. A mildly hostile staff is an integral part of the Gerbeaud tradition.

Zsidó Múzeum (Jewish Museum). The four-room museum, around the corner from the Great Synagogue (☞ *above*) has displays explaining the effect of the Holocaust on Hungarian and Transylvanian Jews. (There are labels in English.) In late 1993, burglars ransacked the mu-

seum and got away with approximately 80% of its priceless collection; several months later, the stolen objects were found in Romania
and returned to their home. ✉ *Dohány utca 2*, ☎ *1/342–8949.* ▣
150 Ft. suggested donation. ☉ *Mon.–Thurs. 10–6, Fri. 10–3, Sun.
10–2.*

Andrássy Út

Behind St. Stephen's Basilica, at the crossroad along Bajcsy-Zsilinszky
út, begins Budapest's grandest avenue, **Andrássy út.** For too many years,
this broad boulevard bore the tongue-twisting name of Népköztársaság
útja (Avenue of the People's Republic) and, for a while before that, Stalin
Avenue. In 1990, however, it reverted to its old name honoring Count
Gyula Andrássy, a statesman who in 1867 became the first constitu-
tional premier of Hungary. The boulevard that would eventually bear
his name was begun in 1872, as Buda and Pest (and Óbuda) were about
to be unified. Most of the mansions that line it were completed by 1884.
It took another dozen years before the first **underground railway** on
the Continent was completed for—you guessed it—the Magyar Millennium in 1896. Though preceded by London's Underground (1863),
Budapest's was the world's first electrified subway. Only slightly modernized but refurbished for the 1996 millecentenary, this "Little Metro"
is still running a 4-km (2½-mi) stretch from Vörösmarty tér to the far
end of City Park. Using tiny yellow trains with tanklike treads, and
stopping at antique stations marked FÖLDALATTI (Underground) on their
wrought-iron entranceways, Line 1 is a tourist attraction in itself. Six
of its 10 stations are along Andrássy út.

A GOOD WALK

A walking tour of Andrássy út's sights is straightforward: Begin at its
downtown end, near Deák tér, and stroll its length (about 2 km/1¼
mi) all the way to **Hősök tere** ㊿. The first third of the avenue, from
Bajcsy-Zsilinszky út to the eight-sided intersection called Oktogon, boasts
a row of eclectic city palaces with balconies held up by stone giants.
Pause at the **Operaház** ㊼ and other points along the way. One block
past the Operaház, Andrássy út intersects Budapest's Broadway:
Nagymező utca contains several theaters, cabarets, and nightclubs. Andrássy út alters when it crosses the Nagy körút (Outer Ring Road), at
the Oktogon crossing. Four rows of trees and scores of flower beds
make the thoroughfare look more like a garden promenade, but its cultural character lingers. Farther up, past **Kodály körönd,** the rest of Andrássy út is dominated by widely spaced mansions surrounded by
private gardens. At Hősök tere, browse through the **Műcsarnok** ㊾
and/or the **Szépművészeti Múzeum** ㊾, and finish off with a stroll into
the Városliget (City Park; ☞ *below*). You can return to Deák tér on
the subway, the Millenniumi Földalatti (Millennial Underground).

TIMING

As most museums are closed Mondays, it's best to explore Andrássy
út on other days, preferably weekdays or early Saturday, when stores
are also open for browsing. During opera season, you can time your
exploration to land you at the Operaház stairs just before 7 PM to watch
the spectacle of opera goers flowing in for the evening's performance.

SIGHTS TO SEE

☾ **Budapest Bábszínház** (Budapest Puppet Theater). In this templelike,
eclectic building, you'll find colorful shows that both children and adults
deem enjoyable even if they don't understand Hungarian. Watch for
showings of *Cinderella* (*Hamupipőke*) and *Snow White and the Seven
Dwarfs* (*Hófehérke*), part of the theater's regular repertoire. ✉ *VI, Andrássy út 69,* ☎ *1/322–5200.*

Drechsler Kastély (Drechsler Palace). Across the street from the Operaház is the French Renaissance–style Drechsler Palace. An early work by Ödön Lechner, Hungary's master of Art Nouveau, it is now the home of the National Ballet School. ⊠ *VI, Andrássy út 25.*

Hopp Ferenc Kelet-Ázsiai Művészeti Múzeum (Ferenc Hopp Museum of Eastern Asiatic Arts). Stop in here to see the rich collection of exotica from the Indian subcontinent and Far Eastern ceramics. ⊠ *Andrássy út 103,* ☎ *1/322–8476.* 🎟 *80 Ft.* ⊙ *Oct.–mid-Apr., Tues.–Sun. 10–4; mid-Apr.–Sept., Tues.–Sun. 10–6.*

★ ⑤ **Hősök tere** (Heroes' Square). Andrássy út ends in grandeur at Heroes' Square, with Budapest's answer to Berlin's Brandenburg Gate. Cleaned and refurbished in 1996 for the millecentenary, the **Millenniumi Emlékmű** (Millennial Monument) is a semicircular twin colonnade with statues of Hungary's kings and leaders between its pillars. Set back in its open center, a 118-ft stone column is crowned by a dynamic statue of the archangel Gabriel, his outstretched arms bearing the ancient emblems of Hungary. At its base ride seven bronze horsemen: the Magyar chieftains, led by Árpád, whose tribes conquered the land in 896. Before the column lies a simple marble slab, the Nemzeti Háborús Emlék Tábla (National War Memorial), the nation's altar, at which every visiting foreign dignitary lays a ceremonial wreath. England's Queen Elizabeth upheld the tradition during her royal visit in May of 1992. In 1991 Pope John Paul II conducted a mass here. Just a few months earlier, half a million Hungarians had convened to recall the memory of Imre Nagy, the reform-minded Communist prime minister who partially inspired the 1956 revolution. Heroes' Square is flanked by the **Műcsarnok** and the **Szépművészeti Múzeum** (☞ *below*).

Kodály Körönd. A handsome traffic circle with imposing statues of three Hungarian warriors—leavened by a fourth one of a poet—the Kodály Körönd is surrounded by plane and chestnut trees. Look carefully at the towered mansions on the north side of the circle—behind the soot you'll see the fading colors of ornate frescoes peeking through. The circle takes its name from the composer Zoltán Kodály, who lived just beyond it at Andrássy út 89.

⑤ **Liszt Ferenc Emlékmúzeum** (Franz Liszt Memorial Museum). Andrássy út No. 67 was the original location of the old Academy of Music and Franz Liszt's last home; entered around the corner, it now houses a museum. Several rooms display the original furniture and instruments from Liszt's time there; another room shows temporary exhibits. The museum hosts excellent, free classical concerts year round, except in August. ⊠ *Vörösmarty u. 35,* ☎ *1/342–7320.* 🎟 *100 Ft.* ⊙ *Weekdays 10–6, Sat. 9–5. Classical concerts (free with admission) Sept.–July, Sat. 11 AM. Closed Aug. 1–20.*

⑭ **Liszt Ferenc Zeneakadémia** (Franz Liszt Academy of Music). Along with the **Vigadó** (☞ Downtown Pest and the Kis körút [Little Ring Road], *above*), this is one of the city's main concert halls. The academy in fact has two auditoriums: a green-and-gold 1,200-seat main hall and a smaller hall for chamber music and solo recitals. Outside this exuberant Art Nouveau building, a statue of Liszt oversees the square. The academy has been operating as a highly revered teaching institute since 1907; Liszt was its first chairman and Erkel its first director. The pianist Ernő (formerly Ernst) Dohnányi and composers Béla Bartók and Zoltán Kodály were teachers here. ⊠ *Liszt Ferenc tér 8,* ☎ *1/342–0179.*

Lukács (⊠ VI, Andrássy út 70, ☎ 1/332–7942) shares its entrance with
an international bank, but its upstairs salon is steeped in classic café elegance. The room is anchored at one end by an ornate fireplace; you
can recharge with an espresso at one of the marble-topped tables clustered under a sparkling chandelier. The Lukács was built in 1912, during Budapest's café-culture glory days, but in the repressive 1950s it
was taken over by the secret police to serve as a meeting spot. To many
locals, it still evokes those dark times.

48 **Mai Manó Fotógaléria** (Mai Manó Photo Gallery). This weathered yet
ornate turn-of-the-century building was built as a photography studio,
where the wealthy bourgeoisie would come to be photographed by imperial and royal court photographer Manó Mai. Inside, ironwork and
frescoes ornament the curving staircase leading up to the tiny gallery,
the only one in Budapest which is exclusively devoted to photography.
Restorations are under way to rejuvenate the tired old building and to
expand the facilities. ⊠ *V, Nagymező u. 20,* ☎ *1/302–4398.* ☞ *Free.*
☉ *Weekdays 2–6.*

52 **Műcsarnok** (Palace of Exhibitions). The city's largest hall for special
exhibitions is a striking 1895 temple of culture with a colorful tympanum. After four years of exhaustive renovations, the Palace of Exhibitions reopened its doors during the 1995 Budapest Spring Festival.
Its program of events includes exhibitions of contemporary Hungarian and international art and a rich series of films, plays, and concerts.
⊠ *XIV, Dózsa György út 37,* ☎ *1/343–7401.* ☞ *250 Ft., Tues. free.*
☉ *Tues.–Sun. 10–6.*

★ **47** **Operaház** (Opera House). Miklós Ybl's crowning achievement is the
neo-Renaissance Opera House, built between 1875 and 1884. Badly
damaged during the siege of 1944–1945, it was restored for its 1984
centenary. Two buxom marble sphinxes guard the driveway; the main
entrance is flanked by Alajos Strobl's "romantic-realist" limestone
statues of Liszt and of another 19th-century Hungarian composer,
Ferenc Erkel, the father of Hungarian opera (his patriotic opera *Bánk
bán* is still performed for national celebrations).

Inside, the spectacle begins even before the performance does. You glide
up grand staircases and through wood-paneled corridors and gilt lime-
green salons into a glittering jewel box of an auditorium. Its four tiers
of boxes are held up by helmeted sphinxes beneath a frescoed ceiling
by Károly Lotz. Lower down there are frescoes everywhere, with in-
tertwined motifs of Apollo and Dionysus. In its early years, the Budapest Opera was conducted by Gustav Mahler (from 1888 to 1891)
and, after World War II, by Otto Klemperer.

The best way to experience the Opera House's interior is to see a ballet or opera; and while performance quality varies, tickets are relatively
cheap and easy to come by, at least by tourist standards. And descending from *La Bohème* into the Földalatti station beneath the Opera
House was described by travel writer Stephen Brook in *The Double
Eagle* as stepping "out of one period piece and into another." There
are no performances in summer, except for the weeklong BudaFest international opera and ballet festival in mid-August. Fifty-minute tours
(in English) are usually conducted daily at 3 PM and 4 PM; meet by the
sphinx at the Dálszínház utca entrance. (Call ahead to confirm that
one is being given). The cost is about 900 Ft. ⊠ *VI, Andrássy út 22,*
☎ *1/331–2550 (ext. 156 for tours).*

46 **Postamúzeum** (Postal Museum). The best of Andrássy út's many marvelous stone mansions is luckily visitable, for the Postal Museum oc-

cupies an apartment with frescoes by Károly Lotz (whose work adorns St. Stephen's Basilica and the Opera House). Among the displays is an exhibition on the history of Hungarian mail, radio, and telecommunications. There are English-language pamphlets available. Even if the exhibits don't thrill you, the venue is worth the visit. ☒ *Andrássy út 3*, ☏ *1/269–6838.* ☒ *70 Ft.* ☉ *Tues.–Sun. 10–6.*

★ ㊾ **Szépművészeti Múzeum** (Museum of Fine Arts). Across Heroes' Square from the Palace of Exhibitions and built by the same team of Albert Schickedanz and Fülöp Herzog, the Museum of Fine Arts houses Hungary's finest collection, rich in Flemish and Dutch old masters. With seven fine El Grecos and five beautiful Goyas as well as paintings by Velázquez and Murillo, the collection of Spanish old masters is one of the best outside Spain. The Italian school is represented by Giorgione, Bellini, Correggio, Tintoretto, and Titian masterpieces and, above all, two superb Raphael paintings: *Eszterházy Madonna* and his immortal *Portrait of a Youth*, rescued after a world-famous art heist. Nineteenth-century French art includes works by Delacroix, Pissarro, Cézanne, Toulouse-Lautrec, Gauguin, Renoir, and Monet. There are also more than 100,000 drawings (including five by Rembrandt and three studies by Leonardo), Egyptian and Greco-Roman exhibitions, late-Gothic winged altars from northern Hungary and Transylvania, and works by all the leading figures of Hungarian art up to the present. A 20th-century collection was added to the museum's permanent exhibits in 1994, comprising an interesting series of statues, paintings, and drawings by Chagall, Le Corbusier, and others. Labels are in both Hungarian and English; there's also an English-language booklet on the permanent collection for sale. ☒ *XIV, Dózsa György út 41*, ☏ *1/ 343–9759.* ☒ *250 Ft.* ☉ *Tues.–Sun. 10–5:30.*

Városliget (City Park)

A GOOD WALK

Heroes' Square is the gateway to the **Városliget** (City Park): a square km (almost half a square mi) of recreation, entertainment, beauty, and culture. A bridge behind the Millennial Monument leads across a boating basin that becomes an artificial ice-skating rink in winter; to the south of this lake stands a statue of George Washington, erected in 1906 with donations by Hungarian emigrants to the United States. Next to the lake stands **Vajdahunyad Vár,** built in myriad architectural styles. Visitors can soak or swim at the turn-of-the-century Széchenyi Fürdő, jog along the park paths, or careen on Vidám Park's roller coaster. There's also the Petőfi Csarnok, a leisure-time youth center and major concert hall on the site of an old industrial exhibition.

TIMING

Fair-weather weekends, when the children's attractions are teeming with kids and parents and the Széchenyi Fürdő brimming with bathers, are the best time for people-watchers to visit City Park; if you go on a weekday, the main sights are rarely crowded.

SIGHTS TO SEE

☚ **Budapesti Állatkert** (Budapest Zoo). This fairly depressing urban zoo is brightened—for humans, anyway—by an elephant pavilion decorated with Zsolnay majolica and glazed ceramic animals. ☒ *XIV, Állatkerti körút 6–12*, ☏ *1/343–6073.* ☒ *400 Ft.* ☉ *Mar. and Oct., daily 9–5; Apr. and Sept., daily 9–6; May, daily 9–6:30; June–Aug., daily 9–7; Nov.–Feb., daily 9–4 (last tickets sold 1 hr before closing).*

☚ **Fővárosi Nagycirkusz** (Municipal Grand Circus). This puts on colorful performances by local acrobats, clowns, and animal trainers, as well as by international guests, in its small ring. The performance schedule varies from November to June; you'll need to call ahead. ⊠ *XIV, Állatkerti körút 7,* ☎ *1/343–8300.* ⊡ *Weekdays 350–650 Ft., weekends 400–750 Ft.* ⊙ *July–Aug., Wed.–Sat. 3 PM and 7 PM, Sun. 10 AM and 3 PM; closed Sept.–Oct.*

Széchenyi Fürdő (Széchenyi Baths). Dating from 1876, these vast baths are in a beautiful neo-Baroque building in the middle of City Park; they comprise one of the biggest spas in Europe. There are several thermal pools indoors as well as two outdoors, which remain open even in winter, when dense steam hangs thick over the hot water's surface—you can just barely make out the figures of elderly men, submerged shoulder deep, crowded around waterproof chessboards (☞ Outdoor Activities and Sports, *below*). ⊠ *XIV, Állatkerti körút 11,* ☎ *1/321–0310.* ⊡ *450 Ft.* ⊙ *May–Sept., daily 6–6; Oct.–Apr., daily 6–5.*

★ **Vajdahunyad Vár** (Vajdahunyad Castle). Beside the City Park's lake stands this castle, an art historian's Disneyland. The fantastic medley borrows from all of Hungary's historic and architectural past, starting with the Romanesque gateway of the cloister of Jak in western Hungary. A Gothic castle, Transylvanian turrets, Renaissance loggia, Baroque portico, and Byzantine decoration are all guarded by a spooky modern (1903) bronze statue of the anonymous medieval chronicler who was the first recorder of Hungarian history. Designed for the millennial celebration in 1896 but not completed until 1908, this hodgepodge houses the surprisingly interesting **Mezőgazdasági Múzeum** (Agricultural Museum), with intriguingly arranged sections on animal husbandry, forestry, horticulture, hunting, and fishing. ⊠ *XIV, Városliget, Széchenyi Island,* ☎ *1/343–3198.* ⊡ *Museum 170 Ft.* ⊙ *Mid-Feb.–Nov., Tues.–Sat. 10–5, Sun. 10–6; Dec.–mid-Feb., Tues.–Fri. 10–4, weekends 10–5.*

☕ **Vidám Park.** Budapest's somewhat weary amusement park is next to the zoo and is crawling with happy children with their parents or grandparents in tow. Rides cost around $1 (some are for preschoolers). There are also game rooms and a scenic railway. Next to the main park is a separate, smaller section for toddlers. In winter, only a few rides operate. ⊠ *Városliget, Állatkerti krt. 14–16,* ☎ *1/343–0996.* ⊡ *100 Ft.* ⊙ *Mid-Mar.–Aug., daily 10–7; Sept.–mid-Mar., daily 10–late afternoon.*

Eastern Pest and the Nagy Körút (Great Ring Road)

This section covers primarily Kossuth Lajos–Rákóczi út and the Nagykörút (Great Ring Road)—busy, less-touristy urban thoroughfares full of people, cars, shops, and Budapest's unique urban flavor.

Beginning a few blocks from the Elizabeth Bridge, Kossuth Lajos utca is Budapest's busiest shopping street. Try to look above and beyond the store windows to the architecture and activity along Kossuth Lajos utca and its continuation, Rákóczi út, which begins when it crosses the Kis körút (Little Ring Road) at the busy intersection called Astoria. Most of Rákóczi út is lined with hotels, shops, and department stores and it ends at the grandiose Keleti (Eastern) Railway Station.

Pest's Great Ring Road, the Nagy körút, was laid out at the end of the 19th century in a wide semicircle anchored to the Danube at both ends; an arm of the river was covered over to create this 114-ft-wide thoroughfare. The large apartment buildings on both sides also date from this era. Along with theaters, stores, and cafés, they form a boulevard unique in Europe for its "unified eclecticism," which blends a variety of historic styles into a harmonious whole. Its entire length of almost 4½ km (2¾ mi) from Margaret Bridge to Petőfi Bridge is traversed by Trams 4 and 6, but strolling it in stretches is also a good way to experience the hustle and bustle of downtown Budapest.

Like its smaller counterpart, the Kis Körút (Small Ring Road), the Great Ring Road comprises sectors of various names. Beginning with Ferenc körút at the Petőfi Bridge, it changes to József körút at the intersection marked by the Museum of Applied Arts, then to Erzsébet körút at Blaha Lujza Square. Teréz körút begins at the busy Oktogon crossing with Andrássy út and ends at the Nyugati (West) Railway Station, where Szent István takes over for the final stretch to the Margaret Bridge.

A GOOD WALK

Beginning with a visit to the **Iparművészeti Múzeum** ⑤, near the southern end of the boulevard, walk or take Tram 4 or 6 north (away from the Petőfi Bridge) to the New York Kávéház on Erzsébet körút, just past Blaha Lujza tér—all in all about 1¾ km (1 mi) from the museum. The neo-Rennaissance **Keleti pályaudvar** is a one-metro-stop detour away from Blaha Lujza tér. Continuing in the same direction on the körút, go several stops on the tram to **Nyugati pályaudvar** and walk the remaining sector, Szent István körút, past the **Vígszínház** ⑤ to Margaret Bridge. From the bridge, views of Margaret Island, to the north, and Parliament, Castle Hill, the Chain Bridge, and Gellért Hill, to the south, are gorgeous.

TIMING

As this area is packed with stores, it's best to explore during store hours—weekdays until around 5 PM and Saturdays until 1 PM; Saturdays will be most crowded. Keep in mind that the Iparművészeti Múzeum is closed Mondays.

SIGHTS TO SEE

★ ⑤ **Iparművészeti Múzeum** (Museum of Applied and Decorative Arts). The templelike structure housing this museum is indeed a shrine to Hungarian Art Nouveau, and in front of it, drawing pen in hand, sits a statue of its creator, Hungarian architect Ödön Lechner. Opened in the millennial year of 1896, it was only the third museum of its kind in Europe. Its dome of tiles is crowned by a majolica lantern from the same source: the Zsolnay ceramic works in Pécs. Inside its central hall are playfully swirling whitewashed, double-decker, Moorish-style galleries and arcades. The museum, which collects and studies objects of interior decoration and use, has five departments: furniture, textiles, goldsmithing, ceramics, and everyday objects. ⊠ *Üllői út 33–37,* ☎ *1/ 217–5222.* ☞ *170 Ft.* ⊙ *Tues.–Sun. 10–6.*

⑤ **Kapel Szent Roch** (St. Roch Chapel). The impact of this charming, yellow, 18th-century chapel is rendered even more colorful by peasant women peddling lace and embroidery on its small square. The chapel is the oldest remnant of Pest's former outer district. It was built beside a hospice where doomed victims of the great plague of 1711 were sent to die as far away as possible from residential areas. ⊠ *Corner of Rákóczi út and Gyulai Pál utca.*

NEED A BREAK?

Once the haunt of famous writers and intellectuals, whose caricatures decorate the walls, the **New York Kávéház** (⊠ VII, Erzsébet krt. 9–11, ☎ 1/322–1648) is an eclectic, neo-Baroque café and restaurant in the ornate 1894 New York Palace building.

Keleti pályaudvar (Eastern Railway Station). The grandiose, imperial-looking Eastern Railway Station was built in 1884 and considered Europe's most modern until well into this century. Its neo-Renaissance facade, which resembles a gateway, is flanked by statues of two British inventors and railway pioneers, James Watt and George Stephenson. ⊠ *VII, Rákóczi út.*

⑤⑥ **Köztársaság tér** (Square of the Republic). Surrounded by faceless concrete buildings, this square is not particularly alluring aesthetically but is significant because it was where the Communist Party of Budapest had its headquarters, and it was also the scene of heavy fighting in 1956. Here also is the city's second opera house, and Budapest's largest, the **Erkel Ferenc színház** (Ferenc Erkel Theatre).

Nyugati pályaudvar (Western Railway Station). The iron-laced glass hall of the Western Railway Station is in complete contrast to—and much more modern than—the newer Eastern Railway Station. Built in the 1870s, it was designed by a team of architects from Gustav Eiffel's office in Paris. ⊠ *VI, Teréz krt.*

Párizsi Udvar (Paris Court). This glass-roofed arcade was built in 1914 in richly ornamental neo-Gothic and eclectic styles—it's one of the most attractive sights of Pest. Nowadays it's filled with touristy boutiques. ⊠ *Corner of Petőfi Sándor utca and Kossuth Lajos utca.*

★ ⑤⑦ **Vígszínház** (Comedy Theater). This neo-Baroque, late-19th-century, gem-like theater twinkles with just a tiny, playful anticipation of Art Nouveau and sparkles inside and out since its 1994 refurbishment. The theater hosts primarily musicals, such as Hungarian adaptations of *Cats,* as well as dance performances and classical concerts. ⊠ *XIII, Pannónia u. 1,* ☎ *1/329–2340.*

Óbuda

Until its unification with Buda and Pest in 1872 to form the city of Budapest, Óbuda (the name means Old Buda) was a separate town that used to be the main settlement; now it is usually thought of as a suburb. Although the vast new apartment blocks of Budapest's biggest housing project and busy roadways are what first strike the eye, the historic core of Óbuda has been preserved in its entirety.

A GOOD WALK

Óbuda is easily reached by car, bus, or streetcar via the Árpád Bridge from Pest or by the HÉV suburban railway from Batthyány tér to the Árpád Bridge. Once you're there, covering all the sights on foot involves large but manageable distances along major exhaust-permeated roadways. One way to tackle it is to take Tram 17 from its southern terminus at the Buda side of the Margaret Bridge to Kiscelli utca and walk uphill to the **Kiscelli Múzeum.** Then walk back down the same street all the way past **Flórián tér,** continuing toward the Danube and making a left onto Hídfő utca or Szentlélek tér to enter **Fő tér.** After exploring the square and taking in the museums in the **Zichy Kúria,** walk a block or two southeast to the HÉV suburban railway stop and take the train just north to the museum complex at **Aquincum.**

TIMING

It's best to begin touring Óbuda during the cooler, early hours of the day, as the heat on the area's busy roads can get overbearing. Avoid Mondays, when museums are closed.

SIGHTS TO SEE

Aquincum. This complex comprises the reconstructed remains of a Roman settlement dating from the 1st century AD and the capital of the Roman province of Pannonia. Careful excavations have unearthed a varied selection of artifacts and mosaics, giving a tantalizing inkling of what life was like in the provinces of the Roman Empire. A gymnasium and a central heating system have been unearthed, along with the ruins of two baths and a shrine to Mithras, the Persian god of light, truth, and the sun. The **Aquincum múzeum** (Aquincum Museum) displays the dig's most notable finds: ceramics; a red-marble sarcophagus showing a triton and flying Eros on one side and on the other, Telesphorus, the angel of death, depicted as a hooded dwarf; and jewelry from a Roman lady's tomb. ⊠ *III, Szentendrei út 139,* ☎ *1/250–1650.* ☒ *350 Ft.* ⊘ *Mid-Apr.–end of Apr. and Oct., Tues.–Sun. 10–5; May–Sept., Tues.–Sun. 10–6. Grounds open at 9.*

Flórián tér. The center of today's Óbuda is Flórián tér, where Roman ruins were first discovered when the foundations of a house were dug in 1778. Two centuries later, careful excavations were carried out during the reconstruction of the square, and today the restored ancient ruins lie in the center of the square in boggling contrast to the racing traffic and cement-block housing projects.

Fő tér. Óbuda's charming old main square is its most picturesque part. The square has been spruced up in recent years, and there are now several good restaurants and interesting museums in and around the Baroque **Zichy Kúria** (☞ *below*), which has become a neighborhood cultural center. Among the most popular offerings are the summer concerts in the courtyard and the evening jazz concerts.

Hercules Villa. A fine 3rd-century Roman dwelling, it takes its name from the myth depicted on its beautiful mosaic floor. The ruin was unearthed between 1958 and 1967 and is now only open by request (inquire at Aquincum). ⊠ *III, Meggyfa u. 19–21.*

Kiscelli Múzeum (Kiscelli Museum). A strenuous climb up the steep, dilapidated sidewalks of Remethegy (Hermit's Hill) will deposit you at this elegant, mustard-yellow Baroque mansion. Built between 1744 and 1760 as a Trinitarian monastery, today it holds an eclectic mix of paintings, sculptures, engravings, and sundry items related to the history of Budapest. Included here is the printing press on which poet and revolutionary Sándor Petőfi printed his famous "Nemzeti Dal" ("National Song"), in 1848, inciting the Hungarian people to rise up against the Hapsburgs. ⊠ *III, Kiscelli u. 108,* ☎ *1/250–0304.* ☒ *170 Ft.* ⊘ *Nov.–Mar., Tues.–Sun. 10–4; Apr.–Oct., Tues.–Sun. 10–6.*

Római amfiteátrum (Roman Amphitheater). Probably dating back to the 2nd century, Óbuda's Roman military amphitheater once held some 16,000 people and, at 144 yards in diameter, was one of Europe's largest. A block of dwellings called the Round House was later built by the Romans above the amphitheater; massive stone walls found in the Round House's cellar were actually parts of the amphitheater. Below the amphitheater are the cells where prisoners and lions were held while awaiting confrontation. ⊠ *Pacsirtamező u. at the junction where it meets Bécsi út.*

Zichy Kúria (Zichy Mansion). One wing of the Zichy Mansion is taken up by the **Óbudai Múzeum** (Óbuda Museum); permanent exhibitions here include traditional rooms from typical homes in the district of Békásmegyer and a popular exhibit covering the history of toys from 1860 to 1960. Another wing houses the **Kassák Múzeum**, which honors the literary and artistic works of a pioneer of the Hungarian avant-garde, Lajos Kassák. ⊠ *Zichy Mansion, Fő tér 1. Óbuda Museum:* ☎ *1/250–1020.* ☒ *100 Ft.* ⊘ *Mid-Mar.–mid-Oct., Tues.–Fri. 2–6, weekends 10–6; mid-Oct.–mid-Mar. Tues.–Fri. 2–5, weekends 10–5. Kassák Museum:* ☎ *1/368–7021.* ☒ *50 Ft.* ⊘ *Oct.–Feb., Tues.–Sun. 10–4; Mar.–Sept., Tues.–Sun. 10–6.*

Dining

In Budapest, numerous new ethnic restaurants—from Chinese to Mexican to Hare Krishna Indian—are springing up all the time. The pulse of the city's increasingly vibrant restaurant scene is in downtown Pest; restaurants on Castle Hill tend to be more touristy and expensive. Our choice of restaurants is primarily Hungarian and Continental, but if you get a craving for sushi or tortellini, consult the restaurant listings in the English-language publications for the latest information on what's cooking where. Remember that some restaurants, particularly the tourist-oriented ones, occasionally fall into the international practice of embellishing tourists' bills. Authorities in Budapest, however, have been cracking down on establishments reported for overcharging. Don't order from menus without prices, and don't accept dining or drinking invitations from women hired to lure people into shady situations.

Addresses below are preceded by the district number (in Roman numerals) and include the Hungarian postal code. Districts V, VI, and VII are in downtown Pest; I includes Castle Hill, the main tourist district of Buda. For price range information, *see* Dining *in* Pleasures and Pastimes, *above.*

Castle Hill

$$$$ ✕ **Alabárdos.** As medieval as its name, the Halberdier (the wielder of that ancient weapon, the halberd), this vaulted wooden room in a 400-year-old Gothic house sits across from the Matthias Church. It has only a handful of tables, set with exquisite Herend and Zsolnay porcelain, though in summer a courtyard garden doubles its capacity. The impeccable service, flowery decor, quiet music, and overriding discretion make this an excellent place for a serious business meal. For extra flare, order the popular flambéed mixed grill: waiters turn the room's lights off before delivering it to your table. Late lunchers and early diners should note that Alabárdos is closed between 4 and 7 PM. ⊠ *I, Országház u. 2,* ☎ *1/356–0851. Reservations essential. Jacket and tie. AE, DC, MC, V. Closed Sun. No lunch mid-Oct.–mid-Apr.*

Downtown Pest and the Small Ring Road

$$$–$$$$ ✕ **Múzeum.** The gustatory anticipation sparked by this elegant, candlelit salon with mirrors, mosaics, and swift-moving waiters is matched by wholly satisfying, wonderful food. The salads are generous, the Hungarian wines excellent, and the chef dares to be creative. ⊠ *VIII, Múzeum körút 12,* ☎ *1/267–0375. Jacket and tie. AE. Closed Sun.*

$$$ ✕ **Lou Lou.** This glowing bistro tucked onto a side street near the Danube
★ has been the hottest restaurant in Budapest for years. Blending local and Continental cuisines, the menu includes a succulent fresh salmon with lemongrass; the venison fillet with wild berry sauce is another mouthwatering choice. At press time, Lou Lou was planning to relocate to a larger space in fall 1998; check with Tourinform (☞ Visitor Information *in* Budapest A to Z, *below*) for the latest information. The restaurant closes between 3 PM and 7 PM. ⊠ *V, Vigyázó Ferenc u. 4,* ☎ *1/312–4505. Reservations essential. AE. Closed Sat. lunch and Sun.*

$$$ ✕ **Művészinas.** Walls hung with framed vintage prints and photos, an-
★ tique vitrines filled with old books, and tall, slender candles on the tables create a romantic haze here. Dozens of Hungarian specialties fill the long menu; beef, veal, and poultry are each prepared a half dozen ways, from sirloin "Budapest style" (smothered in a goose-liver, mushrooms, and sweet-pepper ragout) to spinach-stuffed turkey breast in garlic sauce. Poppy-seed palacsinta with plum sauce are a sublime dessert. ⊠ *VI, Bajcsy-Zsilinszky út 9,* ☎ *1/268–1439. Reservations essential. AE, MC, V.*

$$ ✕ **Amstel River Café.** Just steps from the tourist-filled Váci utca, you'll find this welcoming, low-key Dutch pub. The menu has something for everyone—from rabbit to Caesar salad to grilled chicken. Besides the

Amstel beers (of course), there's a weekly changing wine list. The breakfast menu—a rarity in Budapest—has everything from corn flakes to omelets to cold goose liver. ☒ *V, Párizsi u. 6,* ☎ *1/266–4334. No credit cards.*

$$ ✕ Cyrano. This smooth young bistro just off Vörösmarty tér has an
★ arty, contemporary bent, with wrought-iron chairs, green-marble floors, and long-stemmed azure glasses. The creative kitchen sends out elegantly presented Hungarian and Continental dishes, from standards such as goulash and chicken *paprikás* to more eclectic tastes like tender fried Camembert cheese with blueberry jam. ☒ *V, Kristóf tér 7–8,* ☎ *1/266–3096. Reservations essential. AE, DC, MC.*

$$ ✕ Duna-Corso. Having stood on this riverfront square for nearly two decades, this restaurant continues to offer good, solid food at reasonable prices right in the center of Pest's luxury-hotel belt. The bean-and-cabbage soup (laced with smoked pork), roast duck with sauerkraut, and goose cracklings with potatoes are as simple and hearty as ever, and the service is still pokey and friendly. For views of the castle and Chain Bridge, a table on the vast outdoor terrace is the best seat in town. ☒ *V, Vigadó tér 3,* ☎ *1/318–6362. No credit cards.*

$ ✕ Fészek. Hidden away inside the nearly 100-year-old Fészek Artists' Club is this large, neoclassical dining room. Inside it has high ceilings and mustard-color walls trimmed with ornate moldings, but if you come on a warm day, you can eat in a beautiful Venetian-style courtyard, originally monks' cloisters, with colorful majolica decorations and chestnut trees. The extensive menu features all the heavy Hungarian classics, with such specialties as turkey stuffed with goose liver and a variety of game dishes. You'll have to pay a 150-Ft. Artists' Club cover charge upon entering the building; if you've reserved a table in advance, it will be charged to your bill instead. ☒ *VII, Kertész u. 36 (corner of Dob u.),* ☎ *1/322–6043. AE, DC, MC, V.*

$ ✕ Kispipa. Under the same management as Fészek (☞ *above*), this tiny, well-known restaurant with arched yellow-glass windows and piano bar features a similar, expansive menu of first-rate Hungarian food; the venison ragout soup with tarragon is excellent. ☒ *VII, Akácfa u. 38,* ☎ *1/342–2587. Reservations essential. AE, MC. Closed Sun. and July–Aug.*

$ ✕ Tüköry Söröző. Hearty, decidedly nonvegetarian Hungarian fare comes in big portions at this popular spot close to Parliament. Best bets include pork cutlets stuffed with savory liver or apples and cheese, paired with a big mug of inexpensive beer. Courageous carnivores can sample the beefsteak tartare, topped with a raw egg. ☒ *V, Hold u. 15,* ☎ *1/269–5027. MC, V. Closed weekends.*

North Buda

$$$$ ✕ Vadrózsa. The "Wild Rose" always has fresh ones on the table; the restaurant is in a romantic old villa perched on a hilltop in the exclusive Rózsadomb district of Buda. It's elegant to the last detail, with white-glove service, and the garden is delightful in summer. Try the venison or grilled fish; the house specialty, grilled goose liver, is succulent perfection. ☒ *II. Pentelei Molnár u. 15,* ☎ *1/326–5817. Reservations essential. AE, DC, MC, V.*

$$$–$$$$ ✕ Udvarház. The views from this Buda hilltop restaurant are unsurpassed. As you dine indoors at tables set with white linens or outdoors on the open terrace, your meals are accompanied by vistas of the Danube bridges and Parliament far below. Excellent fresh fish is prepared tableside; you could also try veal and goose liver in paprika sauce, served with salty cottage cheese dumplings. Catering to the predominantly tourist crowd, folklore shows and live Gypsy music frequently enliven the scene. The buses up here are infrequent; it's easier to take

Dining
Alabárdos, **13**
Amstel River Café, **21**
Bagolyvár, **38**
Cyrano, **22**
Duna-Corso, **24**
Fészek, **33**
Gundel, **37**
Kehli, **1**
Kisbuda Gyöngye, **2**
Kispipa, **32**
Lou Lou, **28**
Marxim, **7**
Művészinas, **30**
Múzeum, **19**
Náncsi Néni, **8**
Robinson Restaurant, **36**
Tabáni Kakas, **14**
Tüköry Söröző, **29**
Udvarház, **6**
Vadrózsa, **5**

Lodging
Alba Hotel, **10**
Astoria, **20**
Atrium Hyatt, **26**
Budapest Hilton, **11**
Budapest Marriott, **23**
Citadella, **15**
Danubius Grand Hotel Margitsziget, **3**
Danubius Hotel Gellért, **18**
Danubius Thermal Hotel Helia, **4**
Flamenco, **17**
Hotel Centrál, **35**
Hotel Inter-Continental Budapest, **25**
Kempinski Hotel Corvinus Budapest, **27**
Kulturinov, **12**
Molnár Panzió, **16**
Nemzeti, **31**
Radisson SAS Béke, **34**
Victoria, **9**

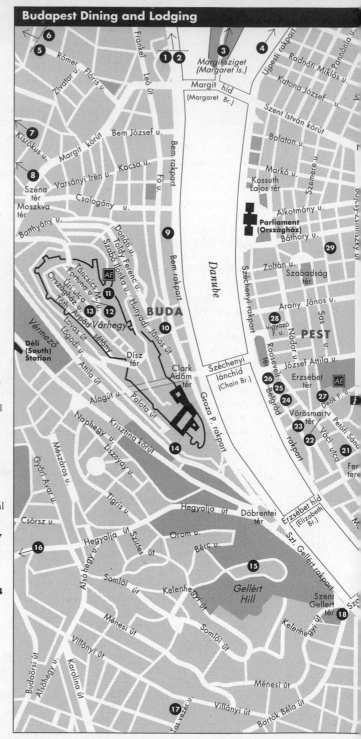

Budapest Dining and Lodging

Lehel
tér

Pannónia u.

Visegrádi u.

Váci út

Ferdinánd híd

Rippl-Rónai u.

Dózsa György út

Hősök
tere

Városliget

Olof Palme sétány

Szinyei Merse u.

Bajza u.

**Nyugati
(West)
Station**

Benczúr u.

Városligeti fasor

Aftósi Dürer sor

Nyugati
tér

Podmaniczky utca

Szondi u.

Rózsa u.

Felső erdősor

Damjanich u.

Dózsa György út

Bajcsy-Zsilinszky út

Teréz körút

Jókai u.

34

Eötvös u.

Aradi u.

35

Dembinszky u.

István u.

Nagymező u.

Mozsár u.

Andrássy út

Oktogon
(Square)

Vörösmarty u.

Dob u.

Rottenbiller utca

Versenly u.

Hajós u.

Liszt
Ferenc
tér

Thököly út

**Keleti (East)
Station**

Lázár u.

Paulay Ede u.

Hársfa u.

Baross
tér

Kerepesi út

Király u.

33

Kertész u.

Erzsébet körút

Dob utca

32

Akácfa u.

Klauzál u.

Rákóczi út

Fiumei út

30

Deák
tér

Károly krt.

Wesselényi utca

Nagy Diófa u.

Dohány utca

Rákóczi út

31

Népszínház u.

Köztársaság
tér

*Kerepesi
temető
(Cemetery)*

Károly krt.

Szentkirályi u.

József körút

Bérkocsis u.

Luza u.

Teleki
László
tér

21

Petőfi Sándor u.

Kossuth L. u.

20

Magyar u.

Puskin u.

Somogyi Béla u.

Déri Miksa u.

Dankó u.

Mátyás
tér

Ferenciek
tere

Kecskeméti u.

Múzeum krt.

19

Bródy Sándor u.

József u.

Veres Pálné u.

Múzeum u.

Krúdy u.

Baross utca

Molnár u.

Váci utca

Kálvin
tér

Baross utca

Szigony u.

Diószeghy Sámuel u.

Fővám
tér

Vámház krt.

Lónyay u.

Üllői út

Nap u.

Práter u.

Tömő u.

Koranyi S. u.

18

Szabadság híd
(Liberty Br.)

Ráday u.

Kinizsi u.

Knézits u.

Üllői út

Tömő u.

Danube

Műegyetem rakpart

Közraktár u.

Ferenc körút

Mester u.

Thaly Kálmán u.

KEY

Borárós
tér

Márton u.

N

AE American Express Office
— Rail Lines
i Tourist Information

Petőfi híd
(Petőfi Br.)

0   550 yards
0   500 meters

a car or taxi. ⊠ *III, Hármashatárhegyi út 2,* ☎ *1/388–6921. AE, DC, MC, V. Closed Mon. Nov.–Mar. No lunch weekdays Nov.–Mar.*

$$ ✕ **Náncsi Néni.** Aunt Nancy's restaurant is a perennial favorite, de-
★ spite its out-of-the-way location. Irresistibly cozy, the dining room
feels like Grandma's country kitchen: Chains of paprika and garlic dan-
gle from the low wooden ceiling above tables set with red-and-white
gingham tablecloths and fresh bread tucked into tiny baskets. Shelves
along the walls are crammed with jars of home-pickled vegetables, which
you can purchase to take home. On the home-style Hungarian menu
(large portions!) turkey dishes feature a creative flair, such as breast
fillets stuffed with apples, peaches, mushrooms, cheese, and sour
cream. Special touches include a popular outdoor garden in summer
and free champagne for all couples in love. ⊠ *II, Ördögárok út 80,*
☎ *1/397–2742. Reservations essential July–Aug. AE, MC, V.*

$ ✕ **Marxim.** Two years after the death of socialism in Hungary, this sim-
ple pizza-and-pasta restaurant opened up to mock the old regime—
and milk it for all it's worth. From the flashing red star above the door
outside to the photos of decorated hard-liners on the walls, the theme
is "Communist nostalgia." Crowds of teenagers and blaring rock
music make Marxim best suited for a lunch or snack. ⊠ *II, Kisrókus
u. 23,* ☎ *1/212–4183. AE, DC, MC, V. No lunch Sun.*

Óbuda

$$$ ✕ **Kehli.** This pricey but laid-back, sepia-toned neighborhood tavern
is on a hard-to-find street near the Óbuda end of the Árpád Bridge.
The food is hearty and heavy, just the way legendary Hungarian writer
and voracious eater Gyula Krúdy (to whom the restaurant is dedicated)
liked it when he lived in the neighborhood. Select from appetizers, such
as hot bone marrow with garlic toast, before moving on to fried goose
livers with mashed potatoes or turkey breast stuffed with cheese and
goose liver. ⊠ *III, Mókus utca 22,* ☎ *1/250–4241 or 1/368–0613.
AE, MC, V. No lunch weekdays.*

$$$ ✕ **Kisbuda Gyöngye.** Considered one of the city's finest restaurants,
★ this intimate Óbuda restaurant is filled with antique furniture, and its
walls are creatively decorated with an eclectic but elegant patchwork
of carved wooden cupboard doors and panels. Try the venison with
Transylvanian mushrooms or the popular *liba lakodalmas* (goose wed-
ding feast), a roast goose leg, goose liver, and goose cracklings. ⊠ *III,
Kenyeres u. 34,* ☎ *1/368–6402 or 1/368–9246. Reservations essen-
tial. AE, DC, MC, V. Closed Sun.*

Tabán and Gellért Hill

$$ ✕ **Tabáni Kakas.** This popular restaurant just below Castle Hill has a
distinctly friendly atmosphere and specializes in large helpings of poul-
try dishes, particularly goose. Try the catfish *paprikás* or the roast duck
with steamed cabbage. ⊠ *I, Attila út 27,* ☎ *1/375–7165. AE, MC, V.*

City Park

$$$$ ✕ **Gundel.** George Lang, Hungary's best-known restaurateur, show-
★ cases his native country's cuisine at this turn-of-the-century palazzo.
Dark-wood paneling, a dozen oil paintings by exemplary Hungarian
artists, and tables set with Zsolnay porcelain make this the city's plush-
est, most handsome dining room. Violinist György Lakatos, of the legendary Lakatos Gypsy musician dynasty, strolls from table to table
playing folk music, as waiters in black tie serve traditional favorites
such as tender veal in a paprika-and-sour-cream sauce and carp
Dorozsma (panfried with mushrooms). ⊠ *XIV, Állatkerti út 2,* ☎ *1/
321–3550. Reservations essential. Jacket and tie. AE, DC, MC, V.*

$$$$ ✕ **Robinson Restaurant.** At this intimate dining room on the park's small
lake, service is doting and the menu creative, with dishes such as crisp

roast suckling pig with champagne-drenched cabbage or fresh *fogas* (pike-perch) stuffed with spinach. Finish it off with a flaming cup of coffee *Diablo,* fueled with Grand Marnier. Padded pastel decor and low lighting wash the room in pleasant, if not Hungarian, elegance. ⊠ *XIV, Városliget,* ☎ *1/343–0955. Reservations essential. Jacket and tie. AE, DC, MC, V. Closed daily 4–6 PM.*

$$ ✕ **Bagolyvár.** George Lang opened this restaurant next door to his gas-
★ tronomic palace, Gundel (☞ *above*), in 1993. The informal yet pol-
ished dining room has a soaring wooden-beam ceiling, and the kitchen produces first-rate daily menus of home-style Hungarian specialties. Soups, served in shiny silver tureens, are particularly good. Musicians entertain with cimbalom music nightly from 7 PM. In warm weather there is outdoor dining in a lovely back garden. ⊠ *XIV, Állatkerti út 2,* ☎ *1/343–0217. AE, DC, MC, V.*

Lodging

Budapest is well equipped with hotels and hostels, but the increase in tourism since 1989 has put a strain on the city's often crowded lodg-ings. Advance reservations are strongly advised, especially at the lower-price hotels. Many of the major luxury and business-class hotel chains are represented in Budapest; however, all of them are Hungarian-run franchise operations with native touches that you won't find in any other Hilton or Marriott.

In winter it's not difficult to find a hotel room, even at the last minute, and prices are usually reduced by 20%–30%. By far the cheapest and most accessible beds in the city are rooms ($20–$25 for a double room) in private homes. Although most tourist offices book private rooms, the supply is limited, so try to arrive in Budapest early in the morning.

Addresses below are preceded by the district number (in Roman nu-merals) and include the Hungarian postal code. Districts V, VI, and VII are in downtown Pest; I includes Castle Hill, the main tourist dis-trict of Buda. For price range information, *see* Lodging *in* Pleasures and Pastimes, *above.*

$$$$ 🏨 **Atrium Hyatt.** The spectacular 10-story interior—a mix of glass capsule elevators, cascading tropical greenery, an open bar, and café— is surpassed only by the views across the Danube to the castle (rooms with a river view cost substantially more). After major renovations, rooms have been tastefully redesigned with classy, unobtrusive decor in muted blues and light woods, and sparkling bathrooms. ⊠ *V, Roo-sevelt tér 2, H-1051,* ☎ *1/266–1234,* 𝖥𝖠𝖷 *1/266–9101. 328 rooms, 27 suites. 3 restaurants, 2 bars, air-conditioning, in-room modem lines, no-smoking rooms, indoor pool, beauty salon, sauna, solarium, exer-cise room, casino, business services, meeting rooms, travel services, park-ing (fee). AE, DC, MC, V.*

$$$$ 🏨 **Budapest Hilton.** Built in 1977 around a 13th-century monastery
★ adjacent to the Matthias Church, this perfectly integrated architectural wonder overlooks the Danube from the choicest site on Castle Hill. Every contemporary room has a remarkable view; Danube vistas cost more. Complete renovations during 1999 promise a welcome update in room decor. Children, regardless of age, get free accommodation when sharing a room with their parents. Note: Breakfast is not included in room rates. ⊠ *I, Hess András tér 1–3, H-1014,* ☎ *1/214–3000, 800/ 445–8667 in the U.S. and Canada,* 𝖥𝖠𝖷 *1/356–0285. 295 rooms, 27 suites. 3 restaurants, 2 bars, café, wine cellar, air-conditioning, in-room modem lines, beauty salon, sauna, exercise room, casino, laun-dry services and dry cleaning, business services, meeting rooms, travel services, parking (free and fee). AE, DC, MC, V.*

$$$$ 🏨 **Budapest Marriott.** In this sophisticated yet friendly hotel on the
★   Danube in downtown Pest, attention to detail is evident, from the impeccable buffet of colorfully glazed pastries to the feather-light ring of
the front-desk bell. Guest rooms have lushly patterned carpets, floral
bedspreads, and etched glass. The layout takes full advantage of the
hotel's prime Danube location, offering breathtaking views of Gellért
Hill, the Chain and Elizabeth bridges, and Castle Hill from the lobby,
ballroom, every guest room, and even the impressive health club—which
is unquestionably the best hotel fitness center in the city. ⊠ *V, Apáczai
Csere János u. 4, H-1364,* ☎ *1/266–7000; 800/831–4004 in the U.S.
and Canada,* 📠 *1/266–5000. 362 rooms, 20 suites. 3 restaurants, bar,
air-conditioning, in-room modem lines, no-smoking rooms, health
club, squash, shops, baby-sitting, laundry service and dry cleaning, business services, meeting rooms, travel services, parking (fee). AE, DC,
MC, V.*

$$$$ 🏨 **Danubius Hotel Gellért.** The double-deck rotunda of this grand
Hungarian spa hotel leads you to expect a string orchestra playing "The
Emperor Waltz." Built in 1918, the Jugendstil Gellért was favored by
Otto von Habsburg, son of the last emperor. Rooms come in all shapes
and sizes—from palatial suites to awkward, tiny spaces. Now part of
the Danubius hotel chain, the Gellért began an ambitious three- to four-
year overhaul in 1998—including the addition of air-conditioning and
refurnishing of all rooms in the mood of the original Jugendstil style.
The best views—across the Danube or up Gellért Hill—are more expensive; avoid those that face the building's inner core. Though the hotel's
service can be a bit inconsistent, its famous pièce de résistance will make
up for it: the monumental, ornate thermal baths. Admission to the spa
is free to hotel guests (medical treatments cost extra); corridors and
an elevator lead directly to the baths from the second, third, and fourth
floors. ⊠ *XI, Gellért tér 1, H-1111,* ☎ *1/385–2200,* 📠 *1/466–6631.
199 rooms, 13 suites. Restaurant, bar, brasserie, café, no-smoking
rooms, indoor pool, beauty salon, spa, thermal baths, baby-sitting, business services, meeting rooms, parking (fee). AE, DC, MC, V.*

$$$$ 🏨 **Hotel Inter-Continental Budapest.** Formerly the Fórum Hotel, this
★   boxy, modern, riverside hotel consistently wins applause for its gracious appointments, excellent service, and gorgeous views across the
Danube to Castle Hill. Sixty percent of the rooms have river views (these
are more expensive); rooms on higher floors ensure the least noise. The
hotel café, Bécsi Kávéház, is locally known for its pastries. The central location and efficient business services makes the Intercontinen-
tal popular with businesspeople. Note: Breakfast is not included in the
room rates. ⊠ *V, Apáczai Csere János u. 12–14, Box 231, H-1368,*
☎ *1/327–6333,* 📠 *1/327–6357. 392 rooms, 16 suites. 2 restaurants,
bar, café, air-conditioning, in-room modem lines, no-smoking floors,
pool, health club, business center, meeting rooms, car rental, parking
(fee). AE, DC, MC, V.*

$$$$ 🏨 **Kempinski Hotel Corvinus Budapest.** Opened in August 1992, this
★   sleek luxury hotel is the favored lodging of visiting VIPs—from rock
superstars to business moguls. From overnight shoe-shine service to
afternoon chamber music in the lobby, the Kempinski exudes solici-
tousness. Unlike those of other nearby hotels, rooms are spacious, with
blond and black Swedish geometric inlaid woods and an emphasis on
functional touches, such as three phones in every room. Large, sparkling
bathrooms, most with tubs and separate shower stalls and stocked with
every toiletry, are the best in Budapest. The hotel's business services
also stand out as the city's best. An automatic current in the smallish
pool allows you to swim long distances without getting anywhere. Breakfast is not included in the room rates. ⊠ *V, Erzsébet tér 7–8, H-1051,*
☎ *1/266–1000, 800/426–3135 in the U.S. and Canada,* 📠 *1/266–*

2000. *337 rooms, 28 suites. 2 restaurants, bar, lobby lounge, pub, air-conditioning, in-room modem lines, no-smoking rooms, indoor pool, barbershop, beauty salon, massage, health club, shops, laundry service and dry cleaning, business services, meeting rooms, travel services, parking (fee). AE, DC, MC, V.*

$$$ ▣ **Danubius Grand Hotel Margitsziget.** Built in 1873 and long in disrepair, this venerable hotel reopened in 1987 as a Ramada Inn and was recently taken over by the Danubius hotel chain. Room rates may have increased since the 1870s, but the high ceilings haven't been lowered. Nor have the old-fashioned room trimmings—down comforters, ornate chandeliers—been lost in the streamlining. Choose between views across the Danube onto a less attractive, industrial section of Pest or out onto the verdant lawns and trees of a tranquil park. Because it's connected to a bubbling thermal spa next door and is located on car-free Margaret Island in the Danube right between Buda and Pest, the Danubius Grand feels removed from the city but is still only a short taxi or bus ride away. ✉ *XIII, Margit-sziget, H-1138,* ☎ *1/329–2300 or 1/349–2769 (reservations),* FAX *1/353–3029. 164 rooms, 10 suites. 2 restaurants, no-smoking rooms, indoor pool, beauty salon, massage, spa, sauna, thermal baths, exercise room, bicycles, meeting rooms, travel services, free parking. AE, DC, MC, V.*

$$$ ▣ **Danubius Thermal Hotel Helia.** A sleek Scandinavian design and less hectic location upriver from downtown make this spa hotel on the Danube a change of pace from its Pest peers. Its neighborhood is nondescript, but guests can be in town in minutes or take advantage of the thermal baths and special health packages—including everything from Turkish baths to electrotherapy and fitness tests. The staff is friendly and helpful, and most of the comfortable rooms have Danube views. ✉ *XIII, Kárpát u. 62–64, H-1133,* ☎ *1/270–3277,* FAX *1/270–2262. 254 rooms, 8 suites. Restaurant, bar, café, indoor pool, beauty salon, hot tub, massage, sauna, spa, steam room, thermal baths, tennis courts, exercise room, business services, meeting rooms, free parking. AE, DC, MC, V.*

$$$ ▣ **Flamenco.** Classy though sometimes overlooked, this hotel in the Buda foothills is a welcome addition to this side of the river. A wall of windows in the low-ceilinged lobby opens out onto views of a park. Service is professional, and the well-kept contemporary rooms are priced at the lowest end of this category. ✉ *XI, Tas Vezér utca 7, H–1113,* ☎ *1/372–2068 or* ☎ *1/372–2000,* FAX *1/372–2100. 352 rooms, 8 suites. 2 restaurants, indoor pool, beauty salon, sauna, solarium, business services, meeting rooms, travel services, parking (fee). AE, DC, MC, V.*

$$$ ▣ **Radisson SAS Béke.** The well-situated Béke (on a main boulevard near the Nyugati [West] Railroad Station) is a budget family inn turned luxury hotel—it now has a glittering turn-of-the-century facade, a lobby lined with mosaics and statuary, and bellmen bowing before the grand marble staircase. Guest rooms resemble solidly modern living rooms, with two-tone wood furnishings and pastel decor. ✉ *VI, Teréz krt. 43, H-1067,* ☎ *1/301–1600,* FAX *1/301–1615. 238 rooms, 8 suites. 2 restaurants, 2 bars, café, air-conditioning, in-room modem lines, no-smoking rooms, pool, beauty salon, sauna, solarium, casino, business center, meeting rooms, travel agency, parking (fee). AE, DC, MC, V.*

$$ ▣ **Alba Hotel.** Tucked behind an alleyway at the foot of Castle Hill, this spotless, modern hotel is a short walk via the Chain Bridge from lively business and shopping districts. Rooms are snug and quiet, with clean white-and-pale-gray contemporary decor and charmingly typical Budapest views over a kaleidoscope of rooftops and chimneys. Half have bathtubs. ✉ *I, Apor Péter u. 3, H-1011,* ☎ *1/375–9244,* FAX *1/375–9899. 95 rooms. Bar, breakfast room, air-conditioning, no-smoking rooms, meeting room, parking (fee). AE, DC, MC, V.*

$$ ▣ **Astoria.** At a busy intersection in downtown Pest stands a revitalized turn-of-the-century hotel that remains an oasis of quiet in hectic surroundings. Staff members are always—but unobtrusively—on hand. Rooms are genteel, spacious, and comfortable, and renovations have remained faithful to the original decor: rather like Grandma's sitting room, in Empire style with an occasional antique. The Astoria's opulent café is a popular meeting place. ⊠ *V, Kossuth Lajos u. 19–21, H-1053,* ☎ *1/317–3411,* 𝖥𝖠𝖷 *1/318–6798. 125 rooms, 5 suites. Restaurant, bar, café, no-smoking rooms, nightclub, business services, meeting rooms, free parking. AE, DC, MC, V.*

$$ ▣ **Hotel Centrál.** Relive history—stay in this hotel, well situated in a leafy diplomatic quarter just one block from Heroes' Square, as visiting Communist dignitaries once did. The architecture and furnishings are straight out of the 1950s, but rooms are comfortable and most have unusually large bathrooms. Suites, however, as well as six of the standard rooms, are classically elegant, with turn-of-the-century Hungarian furnishings; ask for the suite that was Rudolf Nureyev's favorite. ⊠ *VI, Munkácsy Mihály u. 5–7, H-1063,* ☎ *1/321–2000,* 𝖥𝖠𝖷 *1/322–9445. 36 rooms, 6 suites. Restaurant, free parking. AE, MC, V.*

$$ ▣ **Nemzeti.** With a lovely, baby-blue Baroque facade, the Nemzeti reflects the grand mood of the turn of the century. The high-ceiling lobby and public areas—with pillars, arches, and wrought-iron railings—are elaborately elegant. A timely renovation begun in late 1997 is transforming the once small, dark, unexceptional guest rooms with pretty, new furnishings and air-conditioning; be sure to ask for one of these rooms (20 DM extra) for optimal comfort. The hotel is located at bustling Blaha Lujza tér in the center of Pest, which tends toward the seedy after dark; although windows are double-paned, to ensure a quiet night, ask for a room facing the inner courtyard. ⊠ *VIII, József körút 4, H-1088,* ☎ *1/303–9310,* 𝖥𝖠𝖷 *1/314–0019,* ☎ 𝖥𝖠𝖷 *1/303–9162. 75 rooms, 1 suite. Restaurant, air-conditioning, piano bar, meeting room, travel services. AE, DC, MC, V.*

$$ ▣ **Victoria.** The Parliament building and city lights twinkling over the
★   river can be seen from the picture windows of every room at this young establishment right on the Danube. The tiny hotel mixes the charm of a small inn with the modern comforts and efficiency of a business hotel. The location—an easy walk from Castle Hill sights and downtown Pest—couldn't be better. ⊠ *I, Bem rakpart 11, H-1011,* ☎ *1/457–8080,* 𝖥𝖠𝖷 *1/457–8088. 27 rooms, 1 suite. Bar, air-conditioning, sauna, meeting room, travel services, parking (fee). AE, DC, MC, V.*

$ ▣ **Citadella.** Comparatively basic, the Citadella is nevertheless very popular for its price and for its stunning location—right inside the fortress. Half of the rooms compose a youth hostel, giving the hotel a lively communal atmosphere. None of the rooms have bathrooms, but half have showers. Breakfast is not included in the rates. ⊠ *XI, Citadella sétány, Gellérthegy, H–1118,* ☎ *1/366–5794,* 𝖥𝖠𝖷 *1/386–0505. 20 rooms, none with bath. Breakfast room. No credit cards.*

$ ▣ **Kulturinov.** One wing of a magnificent 1902 neo-Baroque castle now
★   houses basic budget accommodations. Rooms come with two or three beds and are clean and delightfully peaceful; they have showers but no tubs. The neighborhood—one of Budapest's most famous squares in the luxurious castle district—is magical. ⊠ *I, Szentháromság tér 6, H-1014,* ☎ *1/355–0122 or 1/375–1651,* 𝖥𝖠𝖷 *1/375–1886. 16 rooms. Snack bar, library, meeting rooms. AE, DC, MC, V.*

$ ▣ **Molnár Panzió.** Fresh air and peace and quiet could lure you to this immaculate guest house nestled high above Buda on Széchenyi Hill. Rooms in the octagonal main house are polyhedric, clean, and bright, with pleasant wood paneling and pastel-color modern furnishings; most have distant views of Castle Hill and Gellért Hill, and some have balconies. Eight rooms in a new (1997) addition next door are more private and have superior bathrooms. Breakfast here is more appealing than usual—with scrambled eggs in addition to the standard breads and jams. ⊠ *XII, Fodor u. 143, H-1124,* ☎ *1/395–1873,* ☎ FAX *1/395–1872. 23 rooms. Restaurant, bar, sauna, exercise room, playground, travel services, free parking. AE, DC, MC, V.*

Nightlife and the Arts

Nightlife

Budapest's nightlife is vibrant and diverse. For basic beer and wine drinking, *söröző́s* (beer bars) and *borozó́s* (wine bars) abound, although the latter tend to serve the early-morning-spritzer-before-work types rather than nighttime revelers. For quiet conversation there are *drink-bárs* in most hotels and all over town, but beware of the inflated prices and steep cover charges. Cafés are preferable for unescorted women.

Most nightspots and clubs have bars, pool tables, and dance floors. Although some places do accept credit cards, it's best to expect to pay cash for your night on the town. As is the case in most other cities, the life of a club or disco in Budapest can be somewhat ephemeral. Those listed below are quite popular and seem to be here to stay. But for the very latest on the more transient "in" spots, consult the nightlife sections of the *Budapest Sun* and *Budapest Week.*

Budapest also has its share of seedy go-go clubs and so-called "cabarets," some of which are known for scandalously excessive billing and physical intimidation. Be wary if you are "invited" in by women lingering nearby, and don't order anything without first seeing the price.

A word of warning to the smoke-sensitive: Budapest is a city of smokers. No matter where you spend your night out, chances are you'll come home smelling of cigarette smoke.

BARS AND CLUBS

Angel Bar and Disco (⊠ VII, Szövetség u. 33, ☎ 1/351–6490) is one of Budapest's enduring and most popular gay bars (though all persuasions are welcome), with a rollicking dance floor. It's closed Monday–Wednesday.

Bahnhof (⊠ VI, Váci út 1, at Nyugati pu.) is, appropriately, in the Nyugati (Western) train station and attracts swarms of young people to its large, crowded dance floor to live bands and DJ'd music. It's closed Sunday–Tuesday.

The most popular of Budapest's Irish pubs and a favorite expat watering hole is **Becketts** (⊠ V, Bajcsy-Zsilinszky út 72, ☎ 1/311–1035), where Guinness flows freely and excellent Irish fare is served amid the gleams of polished wood and brass.

One of the city's hottest spots is **Café Capella** (⊠ V, Belgrád rakpart 23, ☎ 1/318–6231), where a welcoming, gay-friendly crowd flocks to the glittery drag shows (held a few times a week) and revels to DJ'd club music until dawn.

A hip, mellow crowd mingles at the stylish **Cafe Incognito** (⊠ VI, Liszt Ferenc tér 3, ☎ 1/351–9428), with low lighting and funky music kept at a conversation-friendly volume. Couches and armchairs in the back are comfy and private. It closes relatively early—at midnight.

Café Pierrot (⊠ I, Fortuna u. 14, ☎ 1/375–6971), an elegant café and piano bar on a small street on Castle Hill, is well suited to a secret rendezvous.

The look is sophisticated and stylish but the mood low-key and unpretentious at the **Fél 10 Jazz Club** (⊠ VIII, Baross u. 30, cellular ☎ 06–60/318-467), near Kálvin tér. Three open levels with balconylike sitting areas, a dance floor, and two bars are impeccably decorated with wrought-iron tables and maroon-cushioned chairs.

Established Hungarian jazz headliners and young up-and-comers play nightly at the **Long Jazz Club** (⊠ VII, Dohány u. 22–24, ☎ 1/322–0066). It's closed Sunday.

Housed in an old stone mansion near Heroes' Square, the conceptually schizophrenic **Made Inn** (⊠ VI, Andrássy út 112, ☎ 1/311–3437) has an elaborate decor modeled on an underground mine shaft, a kitchen specializing in Mediterranean foods, a large outdoor bar, and a disco dance floor packed with local and international Beautiful People with cell phones and fake-bake tans. Live bands play most nights.

Cool (and trendily dark) **Underground** (⊠ VI, Teréz krt. 30, ☎ 1/311–1481) is below the artsy Művész movie theater. Exposed metal beams and girders and wackily shaped scrap-metal chairs and tables give this bar the requisite industrial look; the DJ spins progressive popular music. Weekends are packed with younger, sometimes rowdy, hipsters.

CASINOS

Most casinos are open daily from 2 PM until 4 or 5 AM and offer gambling in hard currency—usually dollars—only.

The **Gresham Casino** (⊠ V, Roosevelt tér 5, ☎ 1/317–2407) is in the famous Gresham Palace at the Pest end of the Chain Bridge. Sylvester Stallone is alleged to be an owner of the popular **Las Vegas Casino** (⊠ V, Roosevelt tér 2, ☎ 1/317–6022), in the Atrium Hyatt Hotel. In an 1879 building designed by prolific architect Miklós Ybl, who also designed the State Opera House, the **Várkert Casino** (⊠ I, Miklós Ybl tér 9, ☎ 1/202–4244) is the most attractive of the city's casinos.

The Arts

For the latest on arts events, consult the entertainment listings of the English-language newspapers (☞ Contacts and Resources *in* Budapest A to Z, *below*). Their weekly entertainment calendars map out all that's happening in Budapest's arts and culture world—from thrash bands in wild clubs to performances at the Opera House. Another option is to stop in at the **National Philharmonic ticket office** (⊠ Vörösmarty tér 1, ☎ 1/318–0281) and browse through the scores of free programs and fliers and scan the walls coated with upcoming concert posters. Hotels and tourist offices will also provide you with a copy of the monthly publication *Programme,* which contains details of all cultural events.

Tickets can be bought at the venues themselves, but many ticket offices sell them without extra charge. Prices are still very low, so markups of even 30% shouldn't dent your wallet if you book through your hotel. Inquire at Tourinform if you're not sure where to go. Ticket availability depends on the performance and season—it's usually possible to get tickets a few days before a show, but performances by major international artists sell out early. Tickets to Budapest Festival Orchestra concerts and other festival events also go particularly quickly.

Theater and opera tickets are sold at the **Central Theater Booking Office** (Pest: ⊠ VI, Andrassy út 18, ☎ 1/312–0000). For classical concert, ballet, and opera tickets, as well as tickets for major pop and rock shows, go to the **National Philharmonic Ticket Office** (☞ *above*). **Music Mix Ticket Service** (⊠ V, Váci utca 33, ☎ 1/338–2237 or 1/317–7736) specializes in popular music but handles other genres as well.

In case you want to see the world.

At American Express, we're here to make your journey a smooth one. So we have over 1,700 travel service locations in over 120 countries ready to help. What else would you expect from the world's largest travel agency?

do more

In case you want to be welcomed there.

We're here to see that you're always welcomed at establishments everywhere. That's why millions of people carry the American Express® Card – for peace of mind, confidence, and security, around the world or just around the corner.

do more

Cards

In case you're running low.

We're here to help with more than 118,000 Express Cash locations around the world. In order to enroll, just call American Express before you start your vacation.

do more

Express Cash

And just in case.

We're here with American Express® Travelers Cheques and Cheques *for Two.* They're the safest way to carry money on your vacation and the surest way to get a refund, practically anywhere, anytime.

Another way we help you...

do more®

Travelers Cheques

CLASSICAL MUSIC AND OPERA

The tiny recital room of the **Bartók Béla Emlékház** (Bartók Béla Memorial House; ⊠ II, Csalán út 29, ☎ 1/376–2100) hosts intimate Friday evening chamber music recitals by well-known ensembles from mid-March to June and September to mid-December.

The **Budapest Kongresszusi Központ** (Budapest Convention Center; ⊠ XII, Jagelló út 1–3, ☎ 1/209–1990) is the city's largest-capacity (but least atmospheric) classical concert venue and usually hosts the largest-selling events of the Spring Festival.

The homely little sister of the Opera House, the **Erkel Színház** (Erkel Theater; ⊠ VII, Köztársaság tér 30, ☎ 1/333–0540) is Budapest's other main opera and ballet venue. There are no regular performances in the summer.

Liszt Ferenc Zeneakadémia (Franz Liszt Academy of Music; ⊠ VI, Liszt Ferenc tér 8, ☎ 1/342–0179), usually referred to as the Music Academy, is Budapest's premier classical concert venue, hosting orchestra and chamber music concerts in its splendid main hall. It's sometimes possible to grab a standing-room ticket just before a performance here.

The glittering **Magyar Állami Operaház** (Hungarian State Opera House; ⊠ VI, Andrassy út 22, ☎ 1/331–2550), Budapest's main venue for operas and classical ballet, presents an international repertoire of classical and modern works as well as such Hungarian favorites as Kodály's *Háry János*. Except during the one-week BudaFest international opera and ballet festival in mid-August, the Opera House is closed during the summer.

Colorful operettas like those by Lehár and Kalman are staged at their main Budapest venue, the **Operetta Theater** (⊠ VI, Nagymező u. 19, ☎ 1/332–0535); also look for modern dance productions and Hungarian renditions of popular Broadway classics.

Classical concerts are held regularly at the **Pesti Vigadó** (Pest Concert Hall; ⊠ V, Vigadó tér 2, ☎ 1/318–9167).

ENGLISH-LANGUAGE MOVIES

Many of the English-language movies that come to Budapest are subtitled in Hungarian rather than dubbed. There are more than 30 cinemas that regularly show films in English, and tickets are very inexpensive by Western standards (about 800 Ft.). Consult the movie matrix in the *Budapest Sun* or *Budapest Week* for a weekly list of what's showing.

FOLK DANCING

Many of Budapest's district cultural centers regularly hold traditional regional folk-dancing evenings, or dance houses (*táncház*), often with general instruction at the beginning. These sessions provide a less touristy way to taste Hungarian culture.

Almássy Recreation Center (⊠ VII, Almássy tér 6, ☎ 1/352–1572) holds numerous folk-dancing evenings, representing Hungarian as well as Greek and other ethnic cultures. Traditionally the wildest táncház is held Saturday nights at the **Inner City Youth and Cultural Center** (⊠ V, Molnár u. 9, ☎ 1/317–5928), where the stomping and whirling go on way into the night. Hungary's best-known folk ensemble, Muzsikás, hosts a weekly dance house at the **Marczibányi téri Művelődési ház** (Marczibányi tér Cultural Center; ⊠ II, Marczibányi tér 5/a, ☎ 1/212–5789), usually on Thursday nights. Muzsikás lead singer, Márta Sebestyén, appears less and less frequently with the group since her singing was featured in the movie *The English Patient,* launching her into international recognition; call ahead to find out when she'll perform next.

FOLKLORE PERFORMANCES

The **Hungarian State Folk Ensemble** performs regularly at the **Budai Vigadó** (⊠ I, Corvin tér 8, ☎ 1/201–5846); shows incorporate music, dancing, and singing.

The **Folklór Centrum** (⊠ XI, Fehérvári út 47, ☎ 1/203–3868) has been a major venue for folklore performances for more than 30 years. It hosts regular traditional folk concerts and dance performances from spring through fall.

THEATERS

The **Madách Theater** (⊠ VII, Erzsébet körút 31–33, ☎ 1/322–2015) produces colorful musicals in Hungarian, including a popular adaptation of *Cats*. English-language dramas are not common in Budapest, but when there are any, they are usually staged at the **Merlin Theater** (⊠ V, Gerlóczy utca 4, ☎ 1/317–9338). In summer, the Merlin usually hosts an English-language theater series. Another musical theater is the **Thália Theater** (⊠ VI, Nagymező u. 22–24, ☎ 1/331–0500). The sparkling **Vígszínház** (Comedy Theater; ⊠ XIII, Pannónia út 1, ☎ 1/269–5340) hosts classical concerts and dance performances but is primarily a venue for musicals, such as the Hungarian adaptation of *West Side Story*.

Outdoor Activities and Sports

Bicycling

Because of constant thefts, bicycle rentals are difficult to find in Hungary. **Bringóhintó,** a rental outfit on Margaret Island (⊠ Hajós Alfréd sétány 1, across from Thermal Hotel, ☎ 1/329–2072), offers popular four-wheel pedaled contraptions called *Bringóhintók,* as well as traditional two-wheelers; standard bikes cost about 450 Ft. per hour, 600 to 1,000 Ft. for 24 hours. For more information about renting in Budapest, contact **Tourinform** (⊠ V, Sütő u. 2, ☎ 1/317–9800). For brochures and general information on bicycling conditions and suggested routes, try Tourinform or contact the **Magyar Kerékpáros Túrázók Szövetsége** (Bicycle Touring Association of Hungary; ⊠ V, Bajcsy-Zsilinszky út 31, 2nd floor, Apt. 3, ☎ 1/332–7177).

Golf

Golf is still a new sport in Hungary, one that many Hungarians can't afford. The closest place to putt is 35 km (22 mi) north of the city at the **Budapest Golfpark** (☎ 1/317–6025, 1/317–2749, or 06–26/392–463) in Kisoroszi. The park has an 18-hole, 72-par course and a driving range. Greens fees range from 5,000 Ft. to 6,000 Ft. Carts and equipment can be rented. The park is closed November–February.

Health and Fitness Clubs

Andi Stúdió (⊠ V, Hold u. 29, ☎ 1/311–0740) is a trendy fitness club with adequate but sometimes overcrowded facilities. For about 550 Ft. you can work out on the weight machines (no real cardiovascular equipment to speak of) and sit in the sauna, or take an aerobics class, held every hour. **Gold's Gym** (⊠ VIII, Szentkirályi u. 26, ☎ 1/267–4334) stands out as being the least cramped gyms, with good weight-training and cardiovascular equipment and hourly aerobics classes in larger-than-usual spaces. A one-visit pass costs around 750 Ft.

Horseback Riding

Experienced riders can ride at the **Nemzeti Lovarda** (National Horse Academy; ⊠ VIII, Kerepesi út 7, ☎ 1/313–5210) for about 800 Ft. per hour. Call ahead to assure yourself a horse. In the verdant outskirts

of Buda, the **Petneházy Club** (✉ 1029 Feketefej út 2, Adyliget, ☎ 1/
376–5992) is a fully equipped resort with horseback-riding lessons and
trail rides for around 1,500 Ft. per hour.

Jogging

The path around the perimeter of **Margaret Island**, as well as the numerous pathways in the center, is level and inviting for a good run.
Városliget (City Park) in flat Pest has paths good for jogging.

Spas and Thermal Baths

In addition to those listed below, newer, modern baths are open to the
public at hotels, such as the **Danubius Grand Hotel Margitsziget** (✉
XIII, Margitsziget, ☎ 1/329–2300) and the **Thermal Hotel Helia** (✉
XIII, Kárpát u. 62, ☎ 1/270–3277). They lack the charm of their older
peers but provide the latest treatments.

Gellért Thermal Baths (☞ Tabán and Gellért Hill *in* Exploring Budapest,
above); **Király Baths** (☞ North Buda *in* Exploring Budapest, *above*);
Rác Baths. (☞ Tabán and Gellért Hill *in* Exploring Budapest, *above*);
Rudas Baths. (☞ Tabán and Gellért Hill *in* Exploring Budapest, *above*);
Széchenyi Baths (☞ Városliget *in* Exploring Budapest, *above*).

The **Lukács Baths** (✉ II, Frankel Leó u. 25–29, ☎ 1/326–1695) were
built in the 19th century but modeled on the Turkish originals and fed
with waters from a source dating from the Bronze Age and Roman times.
It's open Monday–Saturday 6:30–6, Sunday 6:30–4; the facilities are
coed. Admission to the baths costs 450 Ft.

Tennis and Squash

On Margaret Island, **Euro-Gym Fitness Club** (✉ XIII, Europa House,
Margitsziget, ☎ 1/339–8672) charges 500 Ft.–700 Ft. per hour to play
on one of its eight clay courts; it's open from mid-April to mid-October, and you'll need to reserve a day or two in advance. **On-line Squash
Club** (✉ Budaörs, Forrás u. 8, ☎ 23/416–945), on the near outskirts
of town, is a trendy full-facility fitness club with five squash courts.
Hourly rates run around 1,900 Ft.–2,700 Ft., depending on when you
play. The club rents equipment and stays open until 11 PM. **Városmajor Tennis Academy** (✉ XII, Városmajor u. 63–69, ☎ 1/202–5337)
has five outdoor courts (clay and hexapet) available daily 7 AM–9 PM.
They are lit for night play and covered by a tent in winter. Court fees
run around 1,200 Ft. per hour in summer, 1,800 Ft.–2,800 Ft. in winter. Racket rentals and lessons are also offered. The Marriott Hotel's
World Class Fitness Center (✉ V, Apáczai Csere János u. 4, ☎ 1/266–
4290) has one excellent squash court available for 3,000 Ft. an hour;
be sure to reserve it a day or two in advance.

Shopping

Shopping Districts

You'll find plenty of expensive boutiques, folk-art and souvenir shops,
foreign-language bookstores, and classical-record shops on or around
touristy **Váci utca,** Budapest's famous, upscale pedestrian-only promenade. While a stroll along Váci utca is integral to a Budapest visit,
browsing among some of the smaller, less touristy, more typically Hungarian shops in Pest—on the **Kis körút** (Small Ring Road) and **Nagy
körút** (Great Ring Road)—may prove more interesting and less pricey.
Lots of arty boutiques are springing up in the section of District V **south
of Ferenciek tere and toward the Danube,** and around **Kálvin tér.**
Charming **Falk Miksa utca,** also in the fifth district, running south from
Szent István körút, is one of the city's best antiques districts, lined on
both sides with atmospheric little shops and galleries.

Department Stores

Skála Metro (⊠ VI, Nyugati tér 1–2, ☎ 1/353–2222), opposite the Nyugati (Western) Railroad Station, is one of the largest and best-known department stores, selling a little bit of not entirely everything. **Fontana,** on Váci utca, has several floors of cosmetics, clothing, and other goods, all with price tags reflecting the store's expensive address.

Markets

For true bargains and possibly an adventure, make an early morning trip to the vast **Ecseri Piac** (⊠ IX, Nagykőrösi út; take Bus 54 from Boráros tér), on the outskirts of the city. A colorful, chaotic market that shoppers have flocked to for decades, it is an arsenal of second-hand goods, where you can find everything from frayed Russian army fatigues to Herend and Zsolnay porcelain vases to antique silver chalices. Goods are sold at permanent tables set up in rows, from trunks of cars parked on the perimeter, and by lone, shady characters clutching just one or two items. As a foreigner, you may be overcharged, so prepare to haggle—it's part of the flea-market experience. Also, watch out for pickpockets. Ecseri is open weekdays 8–4, Saturday 8–3, but the best selection is on Saturday mornings.

A colorful outdoor flea market is held weekend mornings from 7 to 2 at **Petőfi Csarnok** (⊠ XIV, Városliget, Zichy Mihály út 14, ☎ 1/251–7266), in City Park. The quantity and selection are smaller than at Ecseri Piac, but it offers a fun flea-market experience closer to the city center. Many visitors buy red-star medals, Russian military watches, and other memorabilia from Communist days here. One other option is **Vásárcsarnok** (☞ Downtown Pest and the Kis körút [Little Ring Road] *in* Exploring Budapest, *above*).

Specialty Stores

ANTIQUES

Falk Miksa utca (☞ Shopping Districts, *above*), lined with antiques stores, is a delightful street for multiple-shop browsing.

The shelves and tables at tiny **Anna Antikvitás** (⊠ V, Falk Miksa u. 18–20, ☎ 1/302–5461) are stacked with exquisite antique textiles—from heavily embroidered wall hangings to dainty lace gloves. Exquisite cloth and lace parasols line the ceiling, but these, unfortunately, are not for sale; similar ones are, however, sometimes available. The store also carries assorted antique objets d'art. **BÁV Műtárgy** (⊠ V, Ferenciek tere 12, ☎ 1/318–3381; ⊠ V, Kossuth Lajos u. 3, ☎ 1/318–4403; ⊠ V, Szent István krt. 3, ☎ 1/331–4534), the State Commission Trading House, has antiques of all shapes, sizes, kinds, and prices at its several branches around the city. While they all have a variety of objects, porcelain is the specialty at the branch on Kossuth Lajos utca, and paintings at the Szent István körút store. **Polgár Galéria és Aukciósház** (⊠ V, Kossuth Lajos u. 3, ☎ 1/318–6954) sells everything from jewelry to furniture and also holds several auctions a year. **Qualitás** (⊠ V, Falk Miksa u. 32; ⊠ V, Kígyó u. 5; ⊠ VII, Dohány u. 1) sells paintings, furniture, and decorative objects at its branches around town.

ART GALLERIES

Budapest has dozens of art galleries showing and selling old works as well as the very latest. **Dovin Gallery** (⊠ V, Galamb u. 6, ☎ 1/318–3673) specializes in Hungarian contemporary paintings. New York celebrity Yoko Ono opened **Gallery 56** (⊠ V, Falk Miksa u. 7, ☎ 1/269–2529) to show art by internationally famed artists, such as Keith Haring, as well as works by up-and-coming Hungarian artists. You can also visit **Mai Manó Fotógaléria** (☞ Andrássy út *in* Exploring Budapest, *above*).

BOOKS

You'll encounter bookselling stands throughout the streets and metro stations of the city, many of which sell English-language souvenir picturebooks at discount prices. **Váci utca** is lined with bookstores that sell glossy coffee-table books about Budapest and Hungary.

Atlantisz (✉ V, Váci u. 31–33) has a selection of English classics, as well as academic texts. **Bestsellers** (✉ V, Október 6 u. 11, ☎ 1/312–1295) sells exclusively English-language books and publications, including best-selling paperbacks and a variety of travel guides about Hungary and beyond. The **Central European University Bookshop** (✉ V, Nádor u. 9, ☎ 1/327–3096), in the Central European University, is a more academically focused branch of Bestsellers bookstore. If you're interested in reading up on this part of the world, this is the store for you. You'll also find a good selection of books in English at **Idegennyelvű Könyvesbolt** (✉ V, Petőfi Sándor u. 2 [in Párisi udvar]), which specializes in foreign-language books. **Írók boltja** (Writers' Bookshop; ✉ VI, Andrássy út 45, ☎ 1/322–1645), one of Budapest's main literary bookstores, has a small but choice selection of Hungarian fiction and poetry translated into English. The hushed, literary atmosphere is tangible, and small tables are set out for reading and enjoying a cup of self-serve tea and instant coffee.

CHINA, CRYSTAL, AND PORCELAIN

Hungary is famous for its age-old Herend porcelain, which is hand-painted in the village of Herend near Lake Balaton. For the Herend name and quality without the steep price tag, visit **Herend Village Pottery** (✉ II, Bem rakpart 37, ☎ 1/356–7899), where you can choose from Herend's practical line of durable ceramic cups, dishes, and table settings. The brand's Budapest store, **Herendi Porcelán Márkabolt** (✉ V, József Nádor tér 11, ☎ 1/317–2622), sells a variety of the delicate (and pricey) pieces, from figurines to dinner sets. Hungary's exquisite Zsolnay porcelain, created and hand-painted in Pécs, is sold at the **Zsolnay Márkabolt** (✉ V, Kígyó u. 4, ☎ 1/318–3712).

Hungarian and Czech crystal is considerably less expensive here than in the United States. **Goda Kristály** (✉ V, Váci u. 9, ☎ 1/318–4630) has beautiful colored and clear pieces. **Haas & Czjzek** (✉ VI, Bajcsy-Zsilinszky út 23, ☎ 1/311–4094) has been in the business for more than 100 years, selling a variety of porcelain, glass, and ceramic pieces in traditional and contemporary styles. Crystal and porcelain dealers also sell their wares at the Ecseri Piac flea market (☞ Markets, *above*), often at discount prices, but those looking for authentic Herend and Zsolnay should beware of imitations.

CLOTHING

Fidji Boutique (✉ V, Váci u. 30, ☎ 1/266–7113) has racks of snazzy men's clothes by international designers like Christian Dior. The **Hugo Boss Shop** (✉ V, Erzsébet tér 7–8, ☎ 1/266–7867), in the Kempinski Hotel, has a good selection of men's suits. High-fashion women's outfits by top Hungarian designers are for sale at **Monarchia** (✉ V, Szabadsajtó út 6, ☎ 1/318–3146), a tiny boutique with rich burgundy velvet draperies and ceilings higher than its floor space. **Manier** (✉ V, Váci u. 48 [entrance at Nyári Pál u. 4], ☎ 1/318–1812) is a popular haute couture salon run by talented Hungarian designer Anikó Németh offering women's pieces ranging from quirky to totally outrageous. The store's second branch is across the street at Váci utca 53.

FOLK ART

Handmade articles, such as embroidered tablecloths and painted plates, are sold all over the city by Transylvanian women wearing traditional scarves and colorful skirts. You can usually find them standing at **Moszkva tér, Jászai Mari tér,** outside the **Kossuth tér** metro, around **Váci utca,** and in the larger metro stations.

Éva Dolls (✉ V, Kecskeméti u. 10, ☎ 1/266–5373), a small store near Kálvin tér, has pricey but beautiful crafts. All types of folk art—pottery, blouses, jewelry boxes, wood carvings, embroidery—can be purchased at one of the many branches of Népművészet Háziipar, also called **Folkart Centrum** (✉ V, Váci u. 14, ☎ 1/318–5840), a large cooperative chain. Prices are reasonable, and selection and quality are good. **Holló Műhely** (✉ V, Vitkovics Mihály u. 12, ☎ 1/317–8103) sells the work of László Holló, a master wood craftsman who has resurrected traditional motifs and styles of earlier centuries. There are lovely hope chests, chairs, jewelry boxes, candlesticks, and more, all hand-carved and hand-painted with cheery folk motifs—a predominance of birds and flowers in reds, blues, and greens.

HOME DECOR AND GIFTS

Bon-Bon (✉ VIII, Baross u. 4, ☎ no phone) is a cramped little boutique near Kálvin tér packed with bohemian beads and necklaces, handpressed paper and cards, colorful ceramic mugs, and various assorted knickknacks—all at very reasonable prices. **Hephaistos Háza** (✉ VI, Zichy Jenő u. 20, ☎ 1/332–6329) is one of Budapest's hottest interior design stores, selling tastefully eclectic wrought-iron furniture and accessories with its signature curlicue flourishes. You can commission an entire room's decor (many local restaurants and bars do) or, more realistically, take home a creative candleholder or two.

MUSIC

Recordings of Hungarian folk music or of pieces played by Hungarian artists are increasingly available on compact discs, though cassettes and records are much cheaper and are sold throughout the city. CDs are normally quite expensive—about 4,000 Ft.

Amadeus (✉ V, Szende Pál u. 1, ☎ 1/318–6691), just off of the Duna korzó, has an extensive selection of classical CDs. **Hungaroton Hanglemez Szalon** (✉ V, Vörösmarty tér 1, ☎ 1/338–2810) has a large selection of all types of music and is centrally located. Its separate, extensive section on Hungarian artists is great for gift- or souvenir-browsing. The **Rózsavölgyi Zenebolt** (✉ V, Szervita tér 5, ☎ 1/318–3500) is an old, established music store crowded with sheet music and largely classical recordings, but with other selections as well.

TOYS

For a step back into the world before Tickle Me Elmo and action figures, stop in at the tiny **Játékszerek Anno** (Toys Anno; ✉ VI, Teréz krt. 54, ☎ 1/302–6234) store, where fabulous repros of antique European toys are sold. From simple paper puzzles to lovely stone building blocks to the 1940s wind-up metal monkeys on bicycles, these "nostalgia toys" are beautifully simple and exceptionally clever. Even if you're not a collector, it's worth a stop just to browse.

WINE

Stores specializing in Hungarian wines have become a trend in Budapest over the past few years. The best of them is the store run by the **Budapest Bortársaság** (Budapest Wine Society; ✉ I, Batthyány u. 59, ☎ 1/212–0262, ☎ FAX 1/212–2569). The cellar shop at the base of Castle Hill always has an excellent selection of Hungary's finest wines, chosen by the wine society's discerning staff, who will happily help you with your purchases. Tastings are held Saturdays from 2 to 5 PM.

Budapest A to Z

Arriving and Departing

BY BOAT

From early July through August, two swift hydrofoils leave Vienna daily at 8 AM and 1 PM (once-a-day trips are scheduled mid-April–early July and September–early November). After a 5½-hour journey downriver, with a stop in the Slovak capital, Bratislava, and views of Hungary's largest church, the cathedral in Esztergom, the boats head into Budapest via its main artery, the Danube. The upriver journey takes about an hour longer. For reservations and information in Budapest, call **MA-HART Tours** (☎ 1/318–1704 or 1/318–1586; 43–1/729–2161 or 43–1/729–2162 in Vienna). The cost is 750 AS one-way.

BY CAR

The main routes into Budapest are the M1 from Vienna (via Győr), the M3 from near Gyöngyös, the M5 from Kecskemét, and the M7 from the Balaton; the M3 and M5 are being upgraded over the next few years and extended to Hungary's borders with Slovakia and Serbia.

BY PLANE

Ferihegy (☎ 1/296–9696), Hungary's only commercial airport, is about 22 km (14 mi) southeast of Budapest. All Lufthansa and Malév flights operate from the newer Terminal 2, 4 km (2½ mi) farther from the city; other airlines use Terminal 1. For same-day **flight information,** call 1/296–7155; operators theoretically speak some English.

The most convenient way to fly between Hungary and the United States is with **Malév Hungarian Airlines** (06/80–212–121 toll free; 1/235–3804 [ticketing]; 1/296–9696 [after-hours flight information]) non-stop direct service between JFK International Airport in New York and Budapest's Ferihegy Airport—the only nonstop flight that exists. All are on roomy Boeing 767-200s and take approximately nine hours. The service runs daily most of the year

Malév and other national airlines fly nonstop from most European capitals. **British Airways** (☎ 1/266–7790 or 1/318–3299) and Malév offer daily nonstop service between Budapest and London.

Between the Airport and Downtown: Many hotels offer their guests car or minibus transportation to and from Ferihegy, but all of them charge for the service. You should arrange for a pickup in advance. If you're taking a taxi, allow 40 minutes during nonpeak hours and at least an hour during rush hours (7 AM–9 AM from the airport, 4 PM–6 PM from the city). Official **Airport Taxis** (☎ 1/282–2222) are queued at the exit and overseen by a taxi monitor; rates are fixed according to the zone of your final destination. A taxi ride to the center of Budapest will cost around 3,500 Ft. There's also a special 1,990-Ft. rate to the airport if you call one day in advance to arrange for a pickup. Avoid taxi drivers who approach before you are out of the arrivals lounge.

LRI Centrum-Airport-Centrum (☎ 1/296–8555 or 1/296–6283) minibuses run every half hour from 5:30 AM to 9:30 PM to and from the Erzsébet tér bus station (Platform 1) in downtown Budapest. It takes almost the same time as taxis but costs only 700 Ft. from either airport terminal. The **LRI Airport Shuttle** provides convenient door-to-door service between the airport and any address in the city. To get to the airport, call to arrange a pickup (☎ 1/296–8555 or 1/296–6283); to get to the city, make arrangements at LRI's airport desk. Service to or from either terminal costs around 1,400 Ft. per person; since it nor-

mally shuttles several people at once, remember to allow time for a few
other pickups or dropoffs.

There are three main *pályaudvar* (train stations) in Budapest: **Keleti**
(Eastern; ✉ VII, Rákóczi út, ☎ 1/313–6835); **Nyugati** (Western; ✉
V, Nyugati tér, ☎ 1/331–5346), and **Déli** (Southern; ✉ XII, Alkotás
u., ☎ 1/375–6593). Trains from Vienna usually operate from the
Keleti Station, while those to Balaton depart from the Déli.

Getting Around

Trams (*villamos*) and buses (*autóbusz*) are abundant and convenient.
One fare ticket (80 Ft.; valid on all forms of public transportation) is
valid for only one ride in one direction. Tickets cannot be bought on
board; they are widely available in metro stations and newsstands and
must be canceled on board—watch how other passengers do it—unless you've purchased a *napijegy* (day ticket, 600 Ft.; a three-day
"tourist ticket" costs 1,200 Ft.), which allows unlimited travel on all
services within the city limits. Hold on to whatever ticket you have;
spot-checks by aggressive undercover checkers (look for the red arm-
bands) are numerous and often targeted at tourists. Trolley-bus stops
are marked with red, rectangular signs that list the route stops; regular bus stops are marked with similar light blue signs. (The trolley-buses
and regular buses themselves are red and blue, respectively.) Tram
stops are marked by light blue or yellow signs. Most lines run from 5
AM and stop operating at 11 PM, but there is all-night service on certain key lines. Consult the separate night-bus map posted in most
metro stations for all-night routes.

Budapest, like any Western city, is plagued by traffic jams during the
day, but motorists should have no problem later in the evening. Parking, however, is a problem—prepare to learn new parking techniques
such as curb balancing and sidewalk straddling. Free parking is a thing
of the past on most central city streets; hourly fees are paid either to
automats or attendants. Motorists not accustomed to sharing the city
streets with trams should pay extra attention. You should be prepared
to be flagged down numerous times by police conducting routine
checks for drunk driving and stolen cars. Be sure all of your papers
are in order and readily accessible; unfortunately, the police have been
known to give foreigners a hard time.

Service on Budapest's subways is cheap, fast, frequent, and comfortable; stations are easily located on maps and streets by the big letter
M (for metro). Tickets—80 Ft.; valid on all forms of mass transportation—can be bought at hotels, metro stations, newsstands, and
kiosks. They are valid for one ride only; you can't change lines or direction. Tickets must be canceled in the time-clock machines in station
entrances and should be kept until the end of the journey, as there are
frequent checks by undercover inspectors; a fine for traveling without
a validated ticket is about 1,000 Ft. A *napijegy* (day ticket) costs 600
Ft. (a three-day "tourist ticket," 1,200 Ft.) and allows unlimited travel
on all services within the city limits.

Line 1 (marked FÖLDALATTI), which starts downtown at Vörösmarty
tér and follows Andrássy út out past Gundel restaurant and City Park,
is an antique tourist attraction in itself, built in the 1890s for the Magyar Millennium; its yellow trains with tank treads still work. Lines 2
and 3 were built 90 years later. Line 2 (red) runs from the eastern sub-

urbs, past the Keleti (Eastern) Station, through the Inner City area, and under the Danube to the Déli (Southern) Station. (One of the stations, Moszkva tér, is where the *Várbusz* [Castle Bus] can be boarded.) Line 3 (blue) runs from the southern suburbs to Deák tér, through the Inner City, and northward to the Nyugati (West) Station and the northern suburbs. On all three lines, fare tickets are canceled in machines at the station entrance. All three metro lines meet at the Deák tér station and run from 4:30 AM to shortly after 11 PM.

BY TAXI

Taxis are plentiful and a good value, but make sure they have a working meter. The average initial charge is 50 Ft.–75 Ft., plus about 110 Ft. per km (½ mi) and 30 Ft. per minute of waiting time. Many drivers try to charge outrageous prices, especially if they sense that their passenger is a tourist. Avoid unmarked "freelance" taxis; stick with those affiliated with an established company. Your safest and most reliable bet is to do what the locals do: Order a taxi by phone; it will arrive in about five to 10 minutes. The best rates are with **Citytaxi** (☎ 1/211–1111) and **Fő taxi** (☎ 1/222–2222).

Contacts and Resources

APARTMENT RENTALS

Apartments, available for short- and long-term rental, can be the most economic lodging for families or groups. A short-term rental in Budapest may cost anywhere from $30 to $60 a day.

Amadeus Apartments (✉ IX, Üllői út 197, H-1091, ☎ 06–30/422–893, FAX 1/302–8268) oversees five well-kept apartments in downtown Budapest, each consisting of two rooms plus a fully equipped kitchen and bathroom. Free transportation from the train station or airport is included; guarded parking areas are provided for a fee for those with cars. The two-person, high-season rate is approximately $40 a night.

IBUSZ Welcome Hotel Service (✉ Apáczai Csere János u. 1, ☎ 1/318–3925 or 1/318–5776, FAX 1/317–9099), open 24 hours a day, books private apartments, arranges rooms in private homes, and reserves rooms in inns and hotels. **Cooptourist** (✉ I, Attila u. 107, ☎ 1/375–2846 or 1/375–2937) arranges private apartments and rooms and makes reservations in its affiliated inns and hotels.

B&B RESERVATION AGENCIES

The rate per night for a double room in Budapest is around $23 (which usually includes the use of a bathroom but not breakfast). Two reliable resources are: **IBUSZ Welcome Hotel Service** (☞ *above*) and **Cooptourist** (☞ *above*)

CAR RENTALS

Avis (main office, ✉ V, Szervita tér 8, ☎ 1/318–4240; Terminal 1, ☎ 1/296–6421; Terminal 2, ☎ 1/296–7265), **Budget-Pannonia** (main office, ✉ Hotel Mercure Buda, I, Krisztina körút 41–43, ☎ 1/356–6333; Terminal 1, ☎ 1/296–8197; Terminal 2, ☎ 1/296–8481), and **Hertz** (also known in Hungary as Mercure Rent-a-Car; ✉ V, Marriott Hotel, Apáczai Csere János u. 4, ☎ 1/266–4361; Terminal 1, ☎ 1/296–7171; Terminal 2, ☎ 1/296–6988) are all here. Rates are high: Daily rates for automatics begin around $55–$60 plus 60¢ per km (½ mi); personal, theft, and accident insurance (not required but recommended) runs an additional $25–$30 per day. Rates tend to be significantly lower if you arrange your rental *from home* through the American offices. Ask your travel agent for help.

Local companies offer lower rates. Inquire at **Americana Rent-a-Car** (✉ Ibis Hotel Volga, XIII, Dózsa György út 65, ☎ 1/270–2542; 1/

320–8287) about unlimited mileage weekend specials. Rates include free delivery and pickup of the car anywhere in the city. **Fötaxi** (main office, ⊠ VII, Kertész u. 24–28, ☎ 1/322–1471; Terminal 1, ☎ 1/296–8629; Terminal 2, ☎ 1/296–8606) has special rates on smaller and non-Western makes, including inexpensive Russian Ladas (not a luxury make).

EMBASSIES AND CONSULATES
Canada (⊠ XII, Zugligeti út 51–53, ☎ 1/275–1200). **U.K.** (⊠ V, Harmincad u. 6, ☎ 1/266–2888, FAX 1/266–0907). **U.S.** (⊠ V, Szabadság tér 12, ☎ 1/267–4400).

EMERGENCIES
Ambulance (☎ 104), or call **Falck–SOS** (⊠ II, Kapy u. 49/b, ☎ 1/200–0100 or 1/200–0122), a 24-hour private ambulance service with English-speaking personnel. **Doctor:** Ask your hotel or embassy for recommendations or visit the **R-Clinic** (⊠ II, Felsőzöldmáli út 13, ☎ 1/325–9999), a private clinic staffed by English-speaking doctors offering 24-hour medical and ambulance service. The clinic accepts major credit cards and prepares full reports for your insurance company. U.S. and Canadian visitors are advised to take out full medical insurance. U.K. visitors are covered for emergencies and essential treatment. **Dentist: Professional Dental Associates** (⊠ II, Sobrás u. 9, ☎ 1/200–4447 or 1/200–4448) is a private, English-speaking dental practice consisting of Western-trained dentists and hygienists; service is available 24 hours a day. **Police** (☎ 107).

ENGLISH-LANGUAGE BOOKSTORES
See Books *in* Shopping, *above.*

ENGLISH-LANGUAGE PERIODICALS
Several English-language weekly newspapers have sprouted up to placate Budapest's large expatriate community. The *Budapest Sun, Budapest Week,* and the *Budapest Business Journal* are sold at major newsstands, hotels, and tourist points.

GUIDED TOURS
Orientation Tours: IBUSZ Travel (⊠ Rubin Aktiv Hotel, XI, Dajka Gábor u. 3, ☎ 1/319–7520, 1/319–7519) conducts three-hour bus tours of the city that operate all year and cost about 4,000 Ft. Starting from Erzsébet tér, they take in parts of both Buda and Pest. **Gray Line Cityrama** (⊠ V, Báthori u. 22, ☎ 1/302–4382) also offers a three-hour city bus tour (about 4,000 Ft. per person). Both have commentary in English.

Special-Interest Tours: IBUSZ, Gray Line Cityrama, and **Budapest Tourist** organize a number of unusual tours, with trips to the Buda Hills, goulash parties, and visits to such traditional sites as the National Gallery and Parliament. These companies will provide English-speaking personal guides on request. Also check at your hotel.

Boat Tours: From late March through October boats leave from the dock at Vigadó tér on 1½-hour cruises between the railroad bridges north and south of the Árpád and Petőfi bridges, respectively. The trip, organized by **MAHART Tours** (☎ 1/318–1704), runs only on weekends and holidays (once a day, at noon) from March until May, then twice daily from May to October (at noon and 7 PM); the cost is about 800 Ft. From mid-June through August, the evening cruise leaves at 7:45 PM and features live music and dancing for 100 Ft. more.

Hour-long evening sightseeing cruises on the *Danube Legend* depart nightly at 8:15 in April and October, and three times nightly (at 8:15, 9, and 10) from May through September. Guests receive headphones and listen to a recorded explanation of the sights in the language of their choice. Drinks are also served. Boats depart from Pier 6–7 at Vigadó tér (☎ 1/317–2203 for reservations and information).

The *Duna-Bella* takes guests on two-hour tours on the Danube, including a one-hour walk on Margaret Island and shipboard cocktails. Recorded commentary is provided through earphones. The tour is offered July through August, six times a day; September, three times a day; and October and November, once a day. Boats depart from Pier 6–7 at Vigadó tér (☎ 1/317–2203 for reservations and information).

Jewish-Heritage Tours: Chosen Tours (⊠ XII, Zolyomi lépcső 27, ☎ 1/319–3427, ☎ FAX 1/319–6800) offers a three-hour combination bus and walking tour ($17) called "Budapest Through Jewish Eyes," highlighting the sights and cultural life of the city's Jewish history. Tours run daily except Saturday and often include pick-up service from central hotels. Arrangements can also be made for off-season tours, as well as custom-designed tours.

Personal Guides: The major travel agencies—**IBUSZ Travel** and **Budapest Tourist** (☞ Visitor Information, *below*)—will arrange for guides.

LATE-NIGHT PHARMACIES

The state-run pharmacies close between 6 and 8 PM, but several pharmacies stay open at night and on the weekend, offering 24-hour service, with a small surcharge for items that aren't officially stamped as urgent by a physician. You must ring the buzzer next to the night window and someone will respond over the intercom. Staff is unlikely to speak English; ask for help from someone who speaks Hungarian. Central ones in Pest include those at **Teréz körút 41** (☎ 1/311–4439) in the sixth district, near the Nyugati Train Station; and the one at **Rákóczi út 39** (☎ 1/314–3695) in the 8th district, near the Keleti Train Station. In Buda, there is one across the street from the Déli train station at **Alkotás utca 1/b** (☎ 1/355–4691), in the 12th district.

TRAVEL AGENCIES

American Express (⊠ V, Déak Ferenc u. 10, ☎ 1/266–8680, FAX 1/267–2028). **Getz International** (⊠ V, Falk Miksa u. 5, ☎ 1/312–0645 or 1/312–0649, FAX 1/312–1014). **Vista Travel Center** (⊠ VI, Andrássy út 1, ☎ 1/269–6032 or 1/269–6033, FAX 1/269–6031).

VISITOR INFORMATION

Budapest Tourist (⊠ V, Roosevelt tér 5, ☎ 1/317–3555). **IBUSZ** (central branch: ⊠ V, Ferenciek tere 10, ☎ 1/318–6866). **IBUSZ Welcome Hotel Service** (⊠ Apáczai Csere János u. 1, ☎ 1/318–3925 or 1/318–5776, FAX 1/317–9099), open 24 hours. **Tourinform** (⊠ V, Sütő u. 2, ☎ 1/317–9800). **Tourism Office of Budapest** (⊠ V, Március 15 tér 7, ☎ 1/266–0479; ⊠ VI, Nyugati pályaudvar, ☎ 1/302–8580).The Tourism Office of Budapest (☞ *above*) has developed the **Budapest Card,** which entitles holders to unlimited travel on public transportation; free admission to many museums and sights; and discounts on various services from participating businesses. The cost (at press time) is 2,000 Ft. for two days, 2,500 Ft. for three days; one card is valid for an adult plus one child under 14.

THE DANUBE BEND

About 40 km (25 mi) north of Budapest, the Danube abandons its eastward course and turns abruptly south toward the capital, cutting through the Börzsöny and Visegrád hills. This area is called the Danube Bend and includes the Baroque town of Szentendre, the hilltop castle ruins and town of Visegrád, and the cathedral town of Esztergom. The most scenically varied part of Hungary, the region is home to a chain of riverside spas and beaches, bare volcanic mountains, and limestone hills. Here, in the heartland, are the traces of the country's history— the remains of the Roman Empire's frontier, the battlefields of the Middle Ages, and the relics of the Hungarian Renaissance.

The west bank of the Danube is the more interesting side, with three charming and picturesque towns—Szentendre, Visegrád, and Esztergom. The district can be covered by car in one day, the total round-trip no more than 112 km (70 mi), although this affords only a cursory look. A day trip to Szentendre while based in Budapest plus two days for Visegrád and Esztergom, with a night in either (both have lovely small hotels), would be best.

On the Danube's eastern bank, Vác is the only larger town of any real interest. The Danube is not crossed by any bridges, but there are numerous ferries (between Visegrád and Nagymaros, Basaharc and Szob, Szentendre Island and Vác), making it possible to combine a visit to both sides of the Danube on the same excursion.

Though the Danube Bend's west bank contains the bulk of historical sights, the less-traveled east bank has the excellent hiking trails of the Börzsöny mountain range, which extends along the Danube from Vác to Zebegény before curving toward the Slovak border. The Pilis and Visegrád hills on the Danube's western side and the Börzsöny Hills on the east are popular nature escapes.

Work had started on a hydroelectric dam near Nagymaros, across from Visegrád, in the mid-1980s. The project was proposed by Austria and what was then Czechoslovakia, and reluctantly agreed to by Hungary, but protests from the Blues (Hungary's equivalent of Germany's Greens), coupled with rapid democratization, succeeded in halting the project and rescuing a region of great natural beauty. But it didn't last: The International Court at the Hague ruled in September 1998 that the original agreement between what is now Slovakia and Hungary was still valid and the two countries signed a preliminary agreement to start building the dam either at Nagymaros or Pilismarot, nearby, over the next eight years. Protests were continuing at press time.

Numbers in the margin correspond to numbers on the Danube Bend map.

Szentendre

★ ❺❽ *21 km (13 mi) north of Budapest.*

A romantic little town with a lively atmosphere and a flourishing artists' colony, this is the highlight of the Danube Bend. With its profusion of enchanting church steeples, colorful Baroque houses, and winding, narrow cobblestone streets, it's no wonder Szentendre attracts swarms of visitors, tripling its population in peak season.

Szentendre was first settled by Serbs and Greeks fleeing the advancing Turks in the 16th and 17th centuries. They built houses and churches in their own style—rich in reds and blues seldom seen elsewhere in Hungary. To truly savor Szentendre, duck into any and every cobblestone side street that appeals to you. Baroque houses with shingle roofs (often with an arched eye-of-God upstairs window) and colorful stone walls will enchant your eye and pique your curiosity.

Fő tér is Szentendre's picturesque main square, the centerpiece of which is an ornate **Memorial Cross** erected by Serbs in gratitude because the town was spared from a plague. The cross has a crucifix-

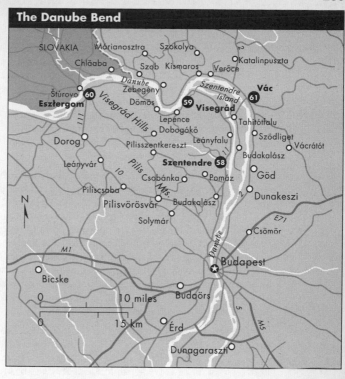

The Danube Bend

ion painted on it and stands atop a triangular pillar adorned with a dozen icon paintings.

Every house on Fő tér is a designated landmark, and three of them are open to the public: the **Ferenczy Múzeum** (Ferenczy Museum) at No. 6, with paintings of Szentendre landscapes; the **Kmetty Múzeum** (Kmetty Museum) at No. 21, with works by János Kmetty, a pioneer of Hungarian avant-garde painting; and the **Szentendrei Képtár** (Municipal Gallery) at Nos. 2–5, with an excellent collection of local contemporary art and international changing exhibits. ✉ *Each museum 100 Ft. ⊙ Mid-Mar.–Oct., Tues.–Sun. 10–4; Nov.–mid-Mar., Fri.–Sun. 10–4.*

Gracing the corner of Görög utca (Greek Street) and Szentendre's main square, Fő tér, the so-called **Görög templom** (Greek Church, also known as Blagovestenska Church) is actually a Serbian Orthodox church that takes its name from the Greek inscription on a red-marble gravestone set in its wall. This elegant edifice was built between 1752 and 1754 by a rococo master, Andreas Mayerhoffer, on the site of a wooden church dating to the Great Serbian Migration (around 690). Its greatest glory—a symmetrical floor-to-ceiling panoply of stunning icons—was painted between 1802 and 1804 by Mihailo Zivkovic, a Serbian painter from Buda. ⊠ *Görög u. at Fő tér.* ✉ *70 Ft. ⊙ Mar.–Oct., Tues.–Sun. 10–5.*

★ If you have time for only one of Szentendre's myriad museums, don't miss the **Margit Kovács Museum,** which displays the collected works of Budapest ceramics artist Margit Kovács, who died in 1977. She left behind a wealth of richly textured work that ranges from ceramics to life-size sculptures. Admission to the museum is limited to 15 persons at a time, so it is wise to line up early or at lunchtime, when the herds of tour groups are occupied elsewhere. ⊠ *Vastagh György u. 1 (off*

Görög u.), ☎ *26/310–244.* 🎫 *250 Ft.* ☉ *Mid-Mar.–early Oct., daily 10–6; early Oct.–mid-Mar., Tues.–Sun. 10–4.*

Perched atop Vár-domb (Castle Hill) is Szentendre's oldest surviving monument, the **Katolikus plébánia templom** (Catholic Parish Church), dating to the 13th century. After many reconstructions, its oldest visible part is a 15th-century sundial in the doorway. The church's small cobblestone yard hosts an arts-and-crafts market and, often on weekends in summer, street entertainment. From here, views over Szentendre's angular tile rooftops and steeples and of the Danube beyond are superb. ⊠ *Vár-domb.* 🎫 *Free.* ☉ *Erratically; check with Tourinform (☞ Visitor Information, below).*

★ The **Szerb Ortodox Egyházi Gyüjtemény** (Serbian Orthodox Collection of Religious Art) displays exquisite artifacts relating to the history of the Serbian Orthodox Church in Hungary. Icons, altars, robes, 16th-century prayer books, and a 17th-century cross with (legend has it) a bullet hole through it were collected from all over the country, after being sold or stolen from Serbian churches that were abandoned when most Serbs returned to their homeland at the turn of the century and following World War I. The museum shares a tranquil yard with the imposing Serbian Orthodox Cathedral. ⊠ *Pátriárka u. 5,* ☎ *26/312–399.* 🎫 *70 Ft.* ☉ *May–Sept., daily 10–6; Oct.–Nov. and Mar.–Apr., Tues.–Sun. 10–4; Dec.–Feb., Fri.–Sun. 10–4.*

The crimson steeple of the handsome **Szerb Ortodox Bazilika** (Serbian Orthodox Cathedral) presides over a restful tree-shaded yard crowning the hill just north of Vár-domb (Castle Hill). It was built in the 1740s with a much more lavish but arguably less beautiful iconostasis than is found in the Greek Church below it. ⊠ *Pátriárka u.,* ☎ *26/312–399.* ☉ *Erratically; check with Tourinform (☞ Visitor Information, below) or Serbian Orthodox Collection of Religious Art museum officials.*

NEED A BREAK?	For a quick cholesterol boost, grab a floppy, freshly fried *lángos* (flat, salty fried dough) drizzled with sour cream or brushed with garlic at **Piknik Büfé** (⊠ Dumtsa Jenő u. 22), just next door to the Tourinform office.

Szentendre's farthest-flung museum is the **Szabadtéri Néprajzi Múzeum** (Open-Air Ethnographic Museum), the largest open-air museum in the country. It is a living re-creation of 18th- and 19th-century village life from different regions of Hungary—the sort of place where blacksmith shops and a horse-powered mill compete with wooden houses and folk handicrafts for your attention. During regular crafts demonstrations, visitors can sit back and watch or give it a try themselves. Five kilometers (3 miles) to the northwest, the museum is reachable by bus from the Szentendre terminus of the HÉV suburban railway. ⊠ *Szabadságforrás út,* ☎ *26/312–304.* 🎫 *250 Ft.* ☉ *Apr.–Oct., Tues.–Sun. 10–5.*

Dining and Lodging

$$ ★ ✕ **Aranysárkány.** On the road up to the Serbian Orthodox Cathedral, the Golden Dragon lies in wait with seven large tables, which you share with strangers on a busy night. The delicious food is prepared in a turbulent open kitchen, but all the activity is justified by the cold cherry soup with red wine or the hot *sárkány leves* (Dragon Soup) with quail eggs and vegetables. Try the grilled goose liver *Orosházi* style, wrapped in bacon and accompanied by a layered potato-and-cheese cake. The cheese dumplings with strawberry whipped cream are also recommended. ⊠ *Alkotmány u. 1/a,* ☎ *26/311–670. AE, MC, V.*

$$ ✕ **Rab Ráby.** Fish soup and fresh grilled trout are the specialties in this
★ extremely popular, friendly restaurant with rustic wood beams and myr-
iad old instruments, lanterns, cowbells, and other eclectic antiques. ⊠
Péter Pál u. 1, ☎ *26/310–819. Reservations essential in summer. No
credit cards.*

$$ ✕ **Régi Módi.** This attractive upstairs restaurant with fine wines and
game specialties is approached through a courtyard across from the
Margit Kovács Múzeum. Lace curtains and antique knickknacks give
the small dining room a homey intimacy. The summer terrace is a delightful place to dine alfresco and look out over the red-tile rooftops.
⊠ *Futó u. 3,* ☎ *26/311–105. AE, MC, V.*

$$ ✕ **Vidám Szerzetesek.** The Happy Monks opened as a family restau-
rant, though in recent years it has become something of a tourist
haunt; the reasonably priced menu, after all, is in 20 languages. The
atmosphere is casual and decidedly cheerful; the food is typically Hun-
garian: heavy, hearty, and delicious. Try the *Suhajda* (hat soup), topped
with a tasty dough cap baked over the bowl. ⊠ *Bogdányi út 3–5,* ☎
26/310–544. AE, MC, V. Closed Mon.

$$ ⊡ **Bükkös Panzió.** Just west of the main square and across the bridge
over tiny Bükkös Brook, this neat, well-run inn is one of the most con-
veniently located hotels in the village. The narrow staircase and small
rooms give it a homey feel. ⊠ *Bükkös part 16, H-2000,* ☎ *26/312–
021,* ☎ FAX *26/310–782. 16 rooms. Restaurant, laundry services.
MC, V.*

$$ ⊡ **Kentaur Ház.** This handsome, modern, chalet-style hotel is a two-
minute walk from Fő tér, on what may be Hungary's last surviving square
still to bear Marx's name. Rooms are clean and simple, with pale-gray
carpeting, blond unfinished-wood paneling, and pastel-pink walls
hung with original paintings by local artists. Upstairs rooms are sun-
niest and most spacious. ⊠ *Marx tér 3–5, H-2000,* ☎ FAX *26/312–
125. 16 rooms. Bar, breakfast room. No credit cards.*

$$ ⊡ **St. Andrea Panzió.** This remodeled *panzió* atop a grassy incline has
all the makings of a Swiss chalet. Attic space has been converted into
modernized rooms with clean tile showers. On a warm day you can
eat breakfast on the outside patio. The owners are very friendly; they've
even been known to specially cook meals for guests arriving late at night.
⊠ *Egres u. 22, H-2000,* ☎ FAX *26/311–989, cellular* ☎ *06–20/230–
198. 16 rooms, 2 suites. Restaurant. No credit cards.*

Outdoor Activities and Sports

BICYCLING

The waterfront and streets beyond Szentendre's main square are perfect for a bike ride—free of jostling cobblestones and relatively calm
and quiet. Check with Tourinform (☞ Visitor Information, *below*) for
local rental outfits. Rentals are available in Budapest (☞ Outdoor Activities and Sports *in* Budapest A to Z, *above*); bicycles are permitted
on the HÉV suburban railway. Many people make the trip between
Budapest and Szentendre on bicycle along the designated bike path,
which runs on busy roads in some places but is pleasant and separate
from the road for the stretch between Békásmegyer and Szentendre.

Nightlife and the Arts

Most of Szentendre's concerts and entertainment events occur during the spring and summer. For current schedules and ticket information, contact **Tourinform** (⊠ Dumtsa Jenő u. 22, ☎ 26/317–965
or 26/317–966).

The annual **Spring Festival,** usually held from mid-March through
early April, offers classical concerts in some of Szentendre's churches,
as well as jazz, folk, and rock performances in the cultural center and

other venues about town. In July, the **Szentendre Summer Days** festival brings open-air theater performances and jazz and classical concerts to Fő tér and the cobblestone courtyard fronting the town hall. Although the plays are usually in Hungarian, the setting alone can make it an enjoyable experience.

Shopping

Flooded with tourists in summer, Szentendre is saturated with the requisite **souvenir shops.** Among the attractive but overpriced goods sold in every store are dolls dressed in traditional folk costumes, wooden trinkets, pottery, and colorful hand-embroidered tablecloths, doilies, and blouses. The best bargains are the hand-embroidered blankets and bags sold by dozens of elderly women in traditional folk attire, who stand for hours on the town's crowded streets. (Because of high weekend traffic, most Szentendre stores stay open all day Saturday and Sunday, unlike those in Budapest. Galleries are closed Monday and accept major credit cards, although other stores may not.)

The one tiny room of **art-éria galéria** (⊠ Városház tér 1, ☎ 26/310–111) is crammed with paintings, graphics, and sculptures by 21 of Szentendre's best contemporary artists.

Topped with an abstract-statue trio of topless, pale-pink and baby-blue women in polka-dot bikini panties, the **Christoff Galéria** (⊠ Bartók Béla u. 8, ☎ 26/317–031) is hard to miss as you climb the steep hill to its door. The gallery sells works by local and Hungarian contemporary artists, including those of ef Zambo, creator of its crowning females. It's best to call ahead to check opening times.

The **Erdész Galéria** (⊠ Bercsényi u. 4, ☎ 26/317–925) displays an impressive selection of contemporary Hungarian art, as well as gifts such as leather bags, colored glass vases, and handmade paper—not to mention some unique, curvaceous silver pieces made by a famous local jeweler.

Beautiful stationery, booklets, and other handmade paper products are displayed and sold at the **László Vincze Paper Mill** (⊠ Angyal u. 5, ☎ 26/318–501). In this small workshop at the top of a broken cobblestone street, Mr. Vincze lovingly creates his thick, watermarked paper, using traditional, 2,000-year old bleaching methods.

The sophisticated **Műhely Galéria** (⊠ Fő tér 20, ☎ 26/310–139), on Szentendre's main square, displays paintings, statues, and other artworks by approximately 30 local artists.

Péter-Pál Galéria (⊠ Péter-Pál u. 1, ☎ 26/311–182) has a good selection of handmade textiles, wrought-iron work, glass, and ceramics.

Visegrád

59 *23 km (14 mi) north of Szentendre.*

Visegrád was the seat of the Hungarian kings during the 14th century, when a fortress built here by the Angevin kings became the royal residence. Today, the imposing fortress at the top of the hill towers over the peaceful little town of quiet, tree-lined streets and solid old houses. The forested hills rising just behind the town offer popular hiking possibilities. For a taste of Visegrád's best, climb to the Fellegvár, and wander and take in the views of the Danube curving through the countryside; but make time to stroll around the village center a bit—on Fő utca and other streets that pique your interest.

★ Crowning the top of a 1,148-ft hill, the dramatic **Fellegvár** (Citadel) was built in the 13th century and served as the seat of Hungarian kings in the early 14th century. In the Middle Ages, the citadel was where the Holy Crown and other royal regalia were kept, until they were stolen by a dishonorable maid of honor in 1440; 23 years later, King Matthias had to pay 80,000 Ft. to retrieve them from Austria. (Now the crown is safe in the Hungarian National Museum in Budapest.) A *panoptikum* (akin to slide projection) show portraying the era of the kings is included free with admission. The breathtaking views of the Danube Bend below are ample reward for the strenuous, 40-minute hike up. ☎ 26/398–101. ☞ 200 Ft. ☉ Mid-Mar.–mid-Nov., daily 9–5; mid-Nov.–mid-Mar., weekends 10 AM–dusk; closed in snowy conditions.

In the 13th–14th centuries, King Matthias Corvinus had a separate palace built on the banks of the Danube below the citadel. It was eventually razed by the Turks, and not until 1934 were the ruins finally excavated. Nowadays you can see the disheveled remnants of the **Királyi palota** (Royal Palace) and its **Salamon torony** (Salomon Tower), referred to together as the **Mátyás Király Múzeum** (King Matthias Museum). The Salomon Tower houses two small exhibits displaying ancient statues and well structures from the age of King Matthiás. Especially worth seeing is the red-marble well built by a 15th-century Italian architect. Above a ceremonial courtyard rise the palace's various halls; on the left you can still see a few fine original carvings, which give an idea of how magnificent the palace must once have been. Inside the palace is a small exhibit on its history, as well as a collection of gravestones dating from Roman times to the 19th century. Fridays in May, the museum hosts medieval-crafts demonstrations. ☒ *Fő u. 23,* ☎ *26/398–026.* ☞ *Royal Palace 250 Ft., Salomon Tower 150 Ft.* ☉ *Royal Palace Tues.–Sun. and holidays falling on Mon. 9–4:30; Salomon Tower: May–Sept., Tues.–Sun. and holidays falling on Mon. 9–4:30.*

OFF THE BEATEN PATH
MILLENNIAL CHAPEL – Like a tiny precious gem, the miniature chapel sits in a small clearing, tucked away on a corner down Fő utca, Visegrád's main street. The bite-size, powder-yellow church was built in 1896 to celebrate the Hungarian millennium and is open only on Pentecost and a few other holidays. ☒ *Fő u. 113.*

Dining and Lodging

$$ ✕ **Gulás Csárda.** This cozy little restaurant, decorated with antique folk
★ art and memorabilia, has only five tables inside, but additional tables are added outside during the summer. The cuisine is typical home-style Hungarian, with a limited selection of tasty traditional dishes. Try the *halászlé* (fish stew) served in a pot and kept warm on a small spirit burner. ☒ *Nagy Lajos király u.,* ☎ *no phone. No credit cards.*

$$ ✕ **Sirály Restaurant.** Right across from the ferry station, the airy Seagull Restaurant is justifiably well regarded for its rolled fillet of venison and its many vegetarian dishes, including fried soy steak with vegetables. In summer, when cooking is often done on the terrace overlooking the Danube, expect barbecued meats and stews, soups, and *gulyas* served in old-fashioned pots. ☒ *Rév u. 15,* ☎ *26/398–376. AE, MC, V. Closed Nov.–Feb.*

$ ✕ **Fekete Holló.** The popular "Black Raven" restaurant has an elegant yet comfortable atmosphere—a great place for a full meal or just a beer. Try the chef's creative specialties, such as coconut chicken leg with pineapples, or stick to regional staples like fresh, grilled fish; either way save room for the *palacsinta* (sweet pancakes with nuts and chocolate). ☒ *Rév út 12,* ☎ *26/397–289. No credit cards. Closed Nov.–Mar.*

$$$ ⌷ **Silvanus.** Set high up on Fekete Hill, this hotel is renowned for its spectacular views. Rooms are bright and clean, with simple furnishings, and offer a choice of forest or Danube (1,200 Ft more expensive) views. Since it's at the end of a steep, narrow road, the Silvanus is recommended for motorists (although a bus does stop nearby) and hikers or bikers—there are linking trails in the forest behind. ⊠ *Fekete-hegy, H-2025,* ☎ FAX *26/398–311 or 26/398–311. 88 rooms, 5 suites. Restaurant, bar, café, pub, bowling, mountain bikes. AE, MC, V.*

$ ⌷ **Haus Honti.** This intimate alpine-style pension is in a quiet residential area, a three-minute walk from the town center. Apple trees and a stream running close to the house create a peaceful, rustic ambience. Tiny, clean rooms are tucked under sloping ceilings and have balconies, some with lovely Danube views. Breakfast, served outdoors in nice weather, costs a couple of dollars more. ⊠ *Fő u. 66, H-2025,* ☎ *26/398–120. 7 rooms. No credit cards.*

Nightlife and the Arts

The **Visegrád International Palace Games,** held annually on the second weekend in July, take the castle complex back to its medieval heyday, with horseback jousting tournaments, archery games, a medieval music and crafts fair, and other festivities. Contact Visegrád Tours (☞ Visitor Information *in* Danube Bend A to Z, *below*) for specifics.

Outdoor Activities and Sports

HIKING

Visegrád makes a great base for exploring the trails of the Visegrád and Pilis hills. A hiking map is posted on the corner of Fő utca and Rév utca, just above the pale-green Roman Catholic Parish Church. A well-trodden, well-marked hiking trail (posted with red signs) leads from the edge of Visegrád to the town of Pilisszentlászló, a wonderful 8½-km (5⅓ mi; about three-hour) journey through the oak and beech forests of the Visegrád Hills into the Pilis conservation region. Bears, bison, deer, and wild boar roam freely here and there are fields of yellow-blooming spring pheasant's eye and black pulsatilla.

SWIMMING

The outdoor thermal pools at **Lepence,** 3 km (2 m) southwest of Visegrád on Route 11, combine good soaking with excellent Danube Bend views. ⊠ *Lepence-völgyi Termál és Strandfürdő, Lepence,* ☎ *26/398–208.* ▨ *350 Ft.* ☉ *Daily May–Sept. 9–6:30*

TOBOGGAN SLIDE

🏔 Winding through the trees on Nagy-Villám Hill is the **Wiegand Toboggan Run,** one of the longest slides you've ever seen. You ride on a small cart that is pulled uphill by trolley, then careen down the slope in a small, steel trough that resembles a bobsled run. ⊠ *Panoráma út, ½ km (¼ mi) from Fellegvár,* ☎ *26/397–397.* ▨ *170 Ft. weekdays, 200 Ft. weekends and holidays; 850 Ft. for six runs weekdays, 950 Ft. weekends and holidays.* ☉ *May–Aug., daily 10–7; Mar.–Apr. and Sept.–Oct., daily 10–5; Nov.–Feb. (weather permitting), weekends 11–4.*

Esztergom

60 *21 km (13 mi) north of Visegrád.*

Esztergom stands on the site of a Roman fortress, at the westernmost curve of the heart-shape Danube Bend, where the Danube marks the border between Hungary and Slovakia. (The bridge that once joined these two countries was destroyed by the Nazis near the end of World War II, though parts of the span can still be seen.) St. Stephen, the first Christian king of Hungary and founder of the nation, was crowned here in the year 1000, establishing Esztergom as Hungary's first capital, which it remained for the next 250 years. The majestic Bazilika, Hungary's largest, is Esztergom's main draw, followed by the fine art collection of the Primate's Palace. If you like strolling, leave yourself a little time to explore the narrow streets of Viziváros (Watertown) below the Bazilika, lined with brightly painted Baroque buildings.

★ Esztergom's **Bazilika** (cathedral), the largest in Hungary, stands on a hill overlooking the town; it is now the seat of the cardinal primate of Hungary. It was here, in the center of Hungarian Catholicism, that the famous anti-Communist cleric, Cardinal József Mindszenty, was finally reburied in 1991, ending an era of religious intolerance and prosecution and a sorrowful chapter in Hungarian history. Its most interesting features are the Bakócz Chapel (1506), named for a primate of Hungary who only narrowly missed becoming pope; and the sacristy, which contains a valuable collection of medieval ecclesiastical art. If your timing is lucky, you could attend a concert during one of the various classical music festivals held here in summer (☞ Nightlife and the Arts, *below*). ⊠ *Szent István tér,* ☎ *33/311–895.* ☜ *Free.* ☉ *Apr.– late Oct., daily 7–6; late Oct.–Mar., weekdays 7–4, weekends 7–5.*

Considered by many to be Hungary's finest art gallery, the **Keresztény Múzeum** (Museum of Christian Art), in the Primate's Palace, has a thorough collection of early Hungarian and Italian paintings (the 14th- and 15th-century Italian collection is unusually large for a museum outside Italy). Unique holdings include the *Coffin of Our Lord* from Garamszentbenedek; the wooden statues of the Apostles and of the Roman soldiers guarding the coffin are masterpieces of Hungarian Baroque sculpture. The building also holds the Primate's Archives, which contain 20,000 volumes, including several medieval codices. Permission to visit the archives must be obtained in advance. *Primate's Palace:* ⊠ *Mindszenty tér 2,* ☎ *33/413–880.* ☜ *150 Ft.* ☉ *Mid-Mar.–Sept., Tues.–Sun. 10–6; Oct.–Dec. and Mar.–mid-Mar., Tues.–Sun. 10–5.*

To the south of the cathedral, on **Szent Tamás Hill,** is a small church dedicated to St. Thomas à Becket of Canterbury. From here you can look down on the town and see how the Danube temporarily splits, forming an island, **Prímás-sziget,** that locals use as a base for water-skiing and swimming, in spite of the pollution. To reach it, cross the Kossuth Bridge.

Dining and Lodging

$$ ✕ **Kispipa.** Lively and not far from the town center, this place is especially memorable for its good choice of wines. The food menu includes soups, stews, and traditional Hungarian dishes such as fried goose with heavy cream. ⊠ *Kossuth Lajos utca 19,* ☎ *no phone. Reservations not accepted. No credit cards.*

$$ ✕ **Primáspince.** Arched ceilings and exposed brick walls make a charming setting for refined Hungarian fare at this touristy but good restaurant just below the cathedral. Try the tournedos Budapest style (tender beef with sautéed vegetables and paprika) or the thick turkey breast Fiaker style (stuffed with ham and melted cheese). ⊠ *Szent István tér 4,* ☎ *33/313–495. AE, DC, MC, V. No dinner Jan.–Feb.*

$–$$ ✕ **Halászcsárda.** The specialty at this friendly, informal restaurant is fish (the fish soup is especially good). The casual outdoor patio, shielded by a thatched roof, gives the place a backyard-barbecue feel. ⊠ *Prímás-sziget, Gesztenye fasor 14,* ☎ *33/311–052. No credit cards.*

$$ ▥ **Alabárdos Panzió.** Conveniently located downhill from the cathedral, this cozy, remodeled home provides excellent views from upstairs. Rooms (doubles and quads) are small but less cramped than at other small pensions. ⊠ *Bajcsy-Zsilinszky u. 49, H-2500,* ☎ FAX *33/312– 640. 21 rooms. Breakfast room. No credit cards.*

$$ 🔲 **Hotel Esztergom.** Simply furnished and sports-oriented, this hotel has a good location on Primás-szíget. Tennis, swimming, bowling, horseback riding, and watersports facilities are nearby. All rooms have balconies. ⊠ *Primás szíget, Nagy Duna Sétány, H-2500,* ☎ *33/312–883,* ℻ *33/312–853. 34 rooms, 2 suites. Restaurant, bar, café, meeting room. AE, MC, V.*

$$ 🔲 **Ria Panzio.** In this small, friendly guest house near the cathedral, all of the small, no-frills rooms face a garden courtyard. ⊠ *Batthyány u. 11–13, H-2500,* ☎ *33/313–115. 13 rooms. Breakfast room. No credit cards.*

Nightlife and the Arts

Every two years Esztergom hosts the **Nemzetközi Gitár Fesztivál** (International Guitar Festival) during which renowned classical guitarists from around the world hold master classes and workshops for participants. Recitals are held nearly every night in Esztergom's **Zöldház Művelődési Központ** (Green House Cultural Center) or the **Tanítóképző Főiskola** (Teaching University), where the festival is based, or elsewhere in Budapest and neighboring towns. The climax of it all is the glorious closing concert, held in the basilica, in which the hundreds of participants join together and perform as a guitar orchestra. The festival runs for two weeks, usually beginning in early August; the next one will be held in 1999. Tickets and information are available at the tourist offices.

Vác

61 *34 km (21 mi) north of Budapest; 20 km (12 mi) south of Nagymaros, which is accessed by ferry from Visegrád.*

With its lovely riverfront promenade, its cathedral, and less delightful Triumphal Arch, the small city of Vác, on the Danube's east bank, is well worth a short visit if only to watch the sun slowly set from the promenade. Vác's historic town center is full of pretty Baroque buildings in matte yellows and reds and offers many visual rewards and photo opportunities for those who wander onto a few of its narrow cobblestone side streets heading in toward the river.

Vác's 18th-century **Székesegyház** (cathedral) on Konstantin tér is an outstanding example of Hungarian neoclassicism. It was built in 1763–1777 by Archbishop Kristóf Migazzi to the designs of the Italian architect Isidor Carnevale; the most interesting features are the murals by the Austrian Franz Anton Maulbertsch, both on the dome and behind the altar. Exquisite frescoes decorate the walls inside. ⊠ *Konstantin tér,* ☎ *27/317–010.* 🖼 *20 Ft.* ☉ *Apr.–Sept. (weather permitting), daily 9–6; Oct.–Mar. with advance arrangements only.*

NEED A BREAK? It's hard to resist the aromas of fresh-baked breads and sweets wafting out onto the cobblestone street from **Vuk Pék** bakery (⊠ Kossuth u. 16, ☎ no phone). Nor is it easy to miss its aquamarine facade.

In 1764, when Archbishop Migazzi heard that Queen Maria Theresa planned to visit his humble town, he hurriedly arranged the construction of a **triumphal arch.** The queen came and left, but the awkward arch remains, at the edge of the city's historic core next to a cement-and-barbed-wire prison complex. ⊠ *Köztársaság út, just past Barabás utca.*

The **promenade** along the Danube is a wonderful place to stroll or picnic, looking out at the flashing river or back toward the pretty historic town. The main entrance to the riverfront area is from Petróczy utca, which begins at the cathedral on Konstantin tér and feeds straight into the promenade.

Vácrátóti Arborétum, 4 km (2½ mi) from Vác, is Hungary's biggest and best botanical garden, with more than 12,000 plant species. The arboretum's top priority is botanical research and collection under the auspices of the Hungarian Academy of Sciences, but you're welcome to stroll along the paths and sit on benches in the leafy shade. If you're driving from Vác, follow signs towards Gödöllő, then towards Vácrátót. ⊠ *Alkotmány u. 4–6,* ☎ *28/360–122 or 28/360–147.* 🔲 *120 Ft.* ☉ *Apr.–Sept., daily 8–6; Oct.–Mar., daily 8–4.*

Dining

$ ✕ **Halászkert Étterem.** The large terrace of this riverfront restaurant next to the ferry landing is a popular place for a hearty lunch or dinner of Hungarian fish specialties. ⊠ *Liszt Ferenc sétány 9,* ☎ *27/315–985. AE, MC, V.*

Nightlife and the Arts

In July and August, a series of outdoor classical concerts is held in the verdant **Vácrátóti Arborétum** (☞ *above*). The last weekend in July brings the **Váci Világi Vígalom** (Vác World Jamboree) festival, with folk dancing, music, crafts fairs, and other festivities throughout town.

Outdoor Activities and Sports

Vác is the gateway to hiking in the forests of the **Börzsöny Hills,** rich in natural springs, castle ruins, and splendid Danube Bend vistas. Consult the Börzsöny hiking map, available at Tourinform, for planning a walk on the well-marked trails. The **Börzsöny Természetjáró Kör** (Börzsöny Nature Walk Group) organizes free guided nature walks every other Sunday all year round. Naturally, Hungarian is the official language, but chances are good that younger group members will speak English—but even without understanding what is spoken, the trips afford a nice opportunity to be guided through the area. Contact Tourinform (☞ Visitor Information *in* Danube Bend A to Z, *below*) for details.

Danube Bend A to Z

Arriving and Departing

BY BOAT

If you have enough time, you can travel to the west-bank towns by boat from Budapest, a leisurely and pleasant journey, especially in summer and spring. Boating from Budapest to Esztergom takes about five hours, to Visegrád about three hours. Boats leave from the main Pest dock at Vigadó tér. The disadvantage of boat travel is that a round-trip by slow boat doesn't allow much time for sightseeing; the Esztergom route, for example, allows only under two hours before it's time to head back. Many people head upriver by boat in the morning and back down by bus or train as it's getting dark. There is daily service from Budapest to Visegrád, stopping in Szentendre. Less frequent boats go to Vác, on the east bank, as well. Contact **MAHART** in Budapest for complete schedule information (☎ 1/318–1704).

For faster river travel, on summer weekends (generally from June to early September) a **hydrofoil** service brings Visegrád within an hour and Esztergom within just over an hour of Budapest. One-way fares are 1,000 Ft.–1,100 Ft. Timetables are also on display at the docks, in major hotels, and at most travel agencies in Budapest, or contact MAHART (☞ *above*).

Buses run regularly between Budapest's Árpád híd bus station and most towns along both sides of the Danube. The ride to Szentendre is about half an hour.

BY CAR

Route 11 runs along the western shore of the Danube, connecting Budapest to Szentendre, Visegrád, and Esztergom. Route 2 runs along the eastern shore for driving between Budapest and Vác.

BY TRAIN

Vác and Esztergom have frequent daily express and local train service to and from Budapest's Nyugati (Western) Station. Trains do not run to Visegrád. The **HÉV** suburban railway runs between Batthyány tér (or Margaret Island, one stop north) in Budapest and Szentendre about every 10 to 20 minutes every day; the trip takes 40 minutes and costs around 180 Ft.

Getting Around

BY BICYCLE

The Danube Bend is a good place to explore by bike; most towns are relatively close together. Some routes have separate bike paths, while others run along the roads. Consult the "Danube Bend Cyclists' Map" (available at tourist offices) and Tourinform (☞ Visitor Information, *below*) for exact information.

BY BOAT

Boat travel along the river is slow and scenic. **MAHART**'s (☞ *above*) boats ply the river between Budapest and Esztergom, Szentendre, and Visegrád. You can plan your sightseeing to catch a boat connection from one town to the other (☞ Arriving and Departing, *above*).

BY BUS

Buses are cheap and relatively comfortable; they link all major towns along both banks. If you don't have a car, this is the best way to get around, since train service is spotty.

BY FERRY

As there are no bridges across the Danube in this region, there is regular daily passenger and car **ferry service** between several points on opposite sides of the Danube (except in winter when the river is too icy). The crossing generally takes about 10 minutes and costs roughly 400 Ft. per car and about 100 Ft. per passenger. The crossing between Nagymaros and Visegrád is recommended, as it affords gorgeous views of Visegrád's citadel and includes a beautiful drive through rolling hills on Route 12 south of Nagymaros. Contact the relevant tourist office (☞ Visitor Information, *below*) for schedule details.

BY TRAIN

Train travel in the region is difficult; Visegrád has no train service and there are no direct connections between Szentendre and Esztergom.

Contacts and Resources

EMERGENCIES

Ambulance (☎ 104). **Fire** (☎ 105). **Police** (☎ 107).

GUIDED TOURS

IBUSZ Travel (☎ 1/319–7520 or 1/319–7519) organizes daylong bus trips from Budapest along the Danube, stopping in Esztergom, Visegrád, and Szentendre on Tuesdays, Fridays, and Sundays from May through October, and Saturdays only from November through April. There's commentary in English; the cost, including lunch and admission fees, is about 13,000 Ft.

Gray Line Cityrama (in Budapest, ☎ 1/302–4382) runs its popular "Danube Tour" (approximately 13,000 Ft.) tours daily Wednesday– Sunday from May until September. The full day begins with sightseeing in Visegrád, then Esztergom. After lunch, the tour moves on to Szentendre for a guided walk and makes a scenic return to Budapest down the Danube. (The tour returns by bus when the water level is low and in winter, when the tour is offered once a week.)

VISITOR INFORMATION

Budapest: Tourinform (✉ V, Sütő u. 2, ☎ 1/317–9800). **Esztergom:** Grantours (✉ Széchenyi tér 25, ☎ FAX 33/413–756); IBUSZ (✉ Kossuth L. u. 5, ☎ 33/312–552); **Komtourist** (✉ Lőrinc u. 6, ☎ 33/312– 082). **Szentendre:** Tourinform (✉ Dumsta J. u. 22, ☎ FAX 26/317–965). **Vác:** Tourinform (✉ Dr. Csányi krt. 45, ☎ 27/316–160). **Visegrád:** Visegrád Tours (✉ Sirály Restaurant, Rév u. 15, ☎ FAX 26/398–160).

LAKE BALATON

Lake Balaton, the largest lake in Central Europe, stretches 80 km (50 mi) across Hungary. Its vast surface area is drastically contrasted with its modest depths—only 9.8 ft at the center, and just 52.5 ft at its deepest point at the Tihany Peninsula. The Balaton—the most popular playground of this landlocked nation—is just 90 km (56 mi) to the southwest of Budapest, so it is within easy reach of the capital by car, train, bus, and even bicycle. On a hot day in July or August, it'll seem the entire country and half of Germany are packed towel to towel on the lake's grassy public beaches, paddling about in the warm water and consuming fried meats and beer at the omnipresent snack bars.

On the lake's hilly northern shore, ideal for growing grapes, is Balatonfüred, Hungary's oldest spa town, famed for its natural springs that bubble out curative waters. The national park on the Tihany Peninsula is just to the south, and regular boat service links Tihany and Balatonfüred with Siófok on the southern shore. Flatter and more crowded with resorts, cottages, and trade-union rest houses, the southern shore (beginning with Balatonszentgyörgy) is not as attractive as the northern one (north-shore locals say the only redeeming quality of the southern shore is its views back across the lake to the north), nor are there as many sights. Families with small children prefer the southern shore for its shallower, warmer waters (you can walk for almost 2 km/1 mi before it deepens). The water warms up to 25°C (77°F) in summer.

Every town along both shores has at least one *strand* (beach). The typical Balaton strand is a complex of blocky wooden changing cabanas and snack bars, fronted by a grassy flat stretch along the water for sitting and sunbathing. Most have paddleboat and other simple boat rentals. A small entrance fee is usually charged.

Those interested in exploring beyond the beach can set out by car, bicycle, or foot, on beautiful village-to-village tours—stopping to view lovely old Baroque churches, photograph a stork family perched high in its chimney-top nest, or climb a vineyard-covered hill for sweeping vistas. Since most vacationers keep close to the shore, a small amount of exploring into the roads and countryside heading away from the lake will reward you with a break from the summer crowds.

Numbers in the margin correspond to numbers on the Lake Balaton and Transdanubia map.

Veszprém

⑫ *116 km (72 mi) southwest of Budapest, 18 km (11 mi) north of Bal-*
atonfüred.

Hilly Veszprém is the center of cultural life in the Balaton region.
★ **Várhegy** (Castle Hill) is the most attractive part of town, north of Szabadság tér. **Hősök Kapuja** (Heroes' Gate), at the entrance to the castle, houses a small exhibit on Hungary's history. Just past the gate and
down a little alley to the left is the **Tűztorony** (Fire Tower); note that
the lower level is medieval, while the upper stories are Baroque. There
is a good view of the town and surrounding area from the balcony.
Tower: ☎ *88/320–485.* ☉ *May–Oct., daily 10–6.*

Vár utca, the only street in the castle area, leads to a small square in
front of the **Bishop's Palace** and the **cathedral**; outdoor concerts are
held here in the summer. Vár utca continues past the square up to a
terrace erected on the north staircase of the castle. Stand beside the modern statues of St. Stephen and his queen, Gizella, for a far-reaching view
of the old quarter of town.

OFF THE   **HEREND** – Sixteen kilometers (10 miles) northwest of Veszprém on Road
BEATEN PATH 8, Herend is the home of Hungary's renowned hand-painted porcelain.
The factory, founded in 1839, displays many valuable pieces in its
Herend Porcelán Művészeti Múzeum (Herend Museum of Porcelain Arts).
⊠ *Kossuth Lajos u. 144,* ☎ *88/261–144.* ▣ *200 Ft.* ☉ *May–Oct.,*
Mon.–Sat. 8:30–4, Sun. 9–4:30; Nov.–mid-Dec. and Mar., weekdays
10–3; Apr., weekdays 8:30–4, Sat. 9–4:30.

Dining

$ ✕ **Club Skorpio.** This city-center eatery might look like an alpine hut,
but the menu is a cut above, with specialties such as pheasant soup
and steamed wild duck. ⊠ *Virág Benedek út 1,* ☎ *88/420–319. No*
credit cards.

$ ✕ **Diana.** The Diana is just a little southwest of the town center but
★ worth the trip if you want to experience the old-fashioned charm of a
small provincial Hungarian restaurant. The fish and game specialties
are perennial favorites. There is also a 10-room pension on the premises.
⊠ *József Attila u. 22,* ☎ *88/421–061. No credit cards.*

Balatonfüred

⑬ *115 km (71 mi) southwest of Budapest.*

Fed by 11 medicinal springs, Balatonfüred first gained popularity as
a health resort (the lake's oldest) where ailing people with heart conditions and fatigue would come to take or, more accurately, to drink
a cure. The waters, said to have stimulating and beneficial effects on
the heart and nerves, are still an integral part of the town's identity
and consumed voraciously, but only the internationally renowned car-
diac hospital has actual bathing facilities. Today Balatonfüred, also
known simply as Füred, is probably the Balaton's most popular destination, with every amenity to match. Above its busy boat landing,
beaches, and promenade lined with great plane and poplar trees, the
twisting streets of the Old Town climb hillsides thickly planted with
vines. The climate and landscape also make this one of the best wine-
growing districts in Hungary. Every year in July, the most elaborate of
Lake Balaton's debutante cotillions, the Anna Balls, is held here.

The center of town is **Gyógy tér** (Spa Square), where the bubbling
waters from five volcanic springs rise beneath a slim, colonnaded pavil-

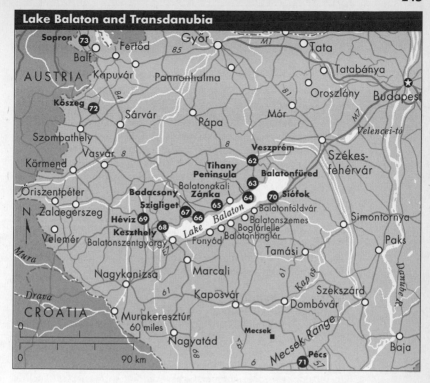

Lake Balaton and Transdanubia

ion. In the square's centerpiece, the neoclassical **Well House** of the Kossuth Spring, you can sample the water, which has a pleasant, surprisingly refreshing taste despite the sulfurous aroma; for those who can't get enough, a sign indicating a 30-liter-per-person limit is posted. All the buildings on the square are pillared like Greek temples. At No. 3 is the **Horváth Ház** (Horváth House), where the Szentgyörgyi-Horváth family arranged the first ball in 1825 in honor of their daughter Anna.

The Anna Ball, the event in Lake Balaton that most approximates a debutante cotillion, is now held every July in another colonnaded building on the square, the **former Trade Unions' Sanatorium** (1802); at press time, this was undergoing renovations and was due to reopen as a hotel. Under its arcades is the **Balatoni Pantheon** (Balaton Pantheon): aesthetically interesting tablets and reliefs honoring Hungarian and foreign notables who either worked for Lake Balaton or spread the word about it. Among them is Jaroslav Hašek, the Czech author of the *Good Soldier Schweik,* who also wrote tales about Balaton. On the eastern side of the square is the **Állami Kórház** (State Hospital), where hundreds of patients from all over the world are treated. Here, too, Rabindranath Tagore, the Indian author and Nobel Prize winner, recovered from a heart attack in 1926. The tree that he planted to commemorate his stay stands in a little grove at the western end of the paths leading from the square down to the lakeside. Tagore also wrote a poem for the planting, which is memorialized beneath the tree on a strikingly animated bust of Tagore: WHEN I AM NO LONGER ON EARTH, MY TREE,/LET THE EVER-RENEWED LEAVES OF THY SPRING/MURMUR TO THE WAYFARER:/THE POET DID LOVE WHILE HE LIVED. In the same grove are trees honoring visits by another Nobel laureate, the Italian poet Salvatore Quasi-modo, in 1961; and Indian prime minister Indira Gandhi, in 1972. An adjoining grove honors Soviet cosmonauts and their Hungarian part-ner-in-space, Bertalan Farkas.

Beginning near the boat landing, the **Tagore sétány** (Tagore Promenade) runs for nearly a kilometer (almost ½ mi) and is lined by trees, restau-rants, and shops.

A stroll up **Blaha Lujza utca** from Gyógy tér will take you past sev-eral landmarks, such as the **Blaha Lujza Ház** (Lujza Blaha House), a neoclassical villa built in 1867 and, later, the summer home of this famous turn-of-the-century actress, humanist, and singer (today it's a hotel); and the charming little **Kerek templom** (Round Church), con-secrated in 1846, built in a classical style and with a truly rounded interior.

NEED A   The plush **Kedves Café** (✉ Blaha Lujza u. 7, ☎ 87/343–229), built in
BREAK?   1795, was once the favorite summer haunt of well-known Hungarian
              writers and artists. Now more touristy than literary, it is still one of Lake
              Balaton's most popular and famous pastry shops.

Dining and Lodging

$$ ✕ **Baricska Csárda.** Perched on a hill overlooking wine and water—
★ its own vineyard and Lake Balaton—this rambling, reed-thatched inn is complete with wood-beamed rooms, vaulted cellars, and terraces. The food is hearty yet ambitious: roasted trout, fish *paprikás* with gnoc-chi to soak up the creamy sauce, and delicious desserts mixing pump-kin and poppy seed. In summer, Gypsy wedding shows are held nightly under the grape arbors. ✉ *Baricska dülő, off Rd. 71 (Széchenyi út) behind Shell station,* ☎ *87/343–105. Reservations essential. AE, V. Closed mid-Nov.–mid-Mar.*

$$ ✕ **Tölgyfa Csárda.** Perched high on a hilltop, the Oak Tree Tavern has breathtaking views over the steeples and rooftops of Balatonfüred and the Tihany Peninsula. Its decor and menu are worthy of a first-class Budapest restaurant, and nightly live Gypsy music keeps the atmosphere festive. ✉ *Meleghegy (up the hill at the end of Csárda utca),* ☎ *87/ 343–036. No credit cards. Closed late Oct.–mid-Apr.*

$$$$ ▦ **Annabella.** The cool, spacious guest quarters in this large, Miami-
★ style high-rise are especially pleasant in summer heat. Overlooking the lake and Tagore Promenade, it has access to excellent swimming and water-sports facilities. All rooms have balconies; for best vistas, re-quest a room on a high floor with a view of the Tihany peninsula. ✉ *Deák Ferenc u. 25, H-8231,* ☎ *87/342–222,* FAX *87/483–029. 383 rooms, 5 suites. Restaurant, bar, brasserie, café, 1 indoor pool, 1 out-door pool, barbershop, massage, sauna, solarium, bicycles, night-club, baby-sitting, laundry service, travel services. AE, DC, MC, V. Closed mid-Oct.–mid-Apr.*

$$$$ ▦ **Marina.** The Marina's central beachfront location is its main draw. Built in the mid-'80s, it is undergoing a major overhaul, which should cheer up its dated feel. Rooms in the homely 12-story "Marina" build-ing range from snug to small; suites have balconies but suffer from tiny bathrooms and extremely dark bedrooms. Your safest bet is to get a newly renovated, high-floor room with a lake view. Or better, stay in the "Lido" wing, which opens directly onto the water and where

rooms (suites only) get plenty of sun. ⊠ *Széchenyi út 26, H-8230,* ☎ *87/343–644,* FAX *87/343–052. 291 rooms, 58 suites. Restaurant, bar, pub, indoor pool, beauty salon, massage, sauna, solarium, bowling, beach, boating, water sports, nightclub, laundry service, travel services. AE, DC, MC, V. Closed Oct.–late Apr.*

$$$ ⊞ **Park.** Hidden on a side street in town but close to the lakeshore, this family-run spot is noticeably calmer than Füred's bustling main hotels. Rooms are large and bright, with high ceilings and tall windows. However, the decor is uninspired, Eastern Bloc-style, with low, narrow beds and plain green and brown upholstery. Suites have large, breezy balconies but small bathrooms. ⊠ *Jókai u. 24, H-8230,* ☎ FAX *87/343–203 or 87/342–005. 38 rooms, 3 suites. Restaurant, bar, fitness room, sauna, meeting room, parking. No credit cards. Closed late Oct.–late Mar.*

Outdoor Activities and Sports

Most hotels have their own private beaches, with water-sports facilities and equipment or special access to these nearby. Besides these, Balatonfüred has three public beaches, where you can rent sailboards, paddleboats, and other water toys; these are also available at Hungary's largest campground, **Füred Camping** (⊠ Széchenyi u. 24, next to the Hotel Marina, ☎ 87/343–823). Although motorboats are banned from the lake, those desperate to water-ski can try the campground's electric water-ski machine, which tows enthusiasts around a 1-km (½-mi) circle. A two-tow ticket runs around 600 Ft.

In season you can rent bicycles from temporary, private outfits set up in central locations around town and near the beaches; one is usually working at the entrance to Füred Camping. Inquire at the tourist office for other current locations. Average prices for mountain-bike rentals are 500 Ft. per hour or 2,500 Ft. per day. You can also usually rent mopeds in front of the Halászkert restaurant (⊠ Széchenyi út 2) for around 800 Ft. per hour and 3,500 Ft. per day.

Trail rides and horseback-riding lessons are available at the **Csikós Lovasudvar** (⊠ Klára-puszta, Pécshely, ☎ 87/445–308), about 10 km (6 mi) away in Pécshely. Half-hour lessons cost around 1,300 Ft., hour-long trail rides about 1,500 Ft. More passive horse enthusiasts can go on a carriage ride for about 900 Ft. per person per hour.

Tihany and the Tihany Félsziget (Tihany Peninsula)

64 *11 km (7 mi) southwest of Balatonfüred.*

The quaint town of Tihany, with its twisting, narrow cobblestone streets and hilltop abbey, is on the Tihany Félsziget (Tihany Peninsula), joined to the mainland by a narrow neck and jutting 5 km (3 mi) into the lake. Only 12 square km (less than 5 square mi), the peninsula is not only a major tourist resort but perhaps the most historic part of the Balaton area. In 1952 the entire peninsula was declared a national park, and because of its geological rarities, it became Hungary's first nature-conservation zone. On it are more than 110 geyser craters, remains of former hot springs, reminiscent of those found in Iceland, Siberia, and Wyoming's Yellowstone Park.

The smooth Belső Tó (Inner Lake), 82 ft higher than Lake Balaton, is one of the peninsula's own two lakes; around it are barren yellowish-white rocks and volcanic cones rising against the sky. Though the hills surrounding the lake are known for their white wines, this area produces a notable Hungarian red, Tihany cabernet.

★ Tihany's crowning glory is the **Bencés Apátság** (Benedictine Abbey), with foundations laid by King Andras I in 1055. The abbey's charter—containing some 100 Hungarian words in its Latin text, thus making it the oldest written source of the Hungarian language—is kept in Pannonhalma (☞ Transdanubia, *below*). Rebuilt in Baroque style between 1719 and 1784, the abbey's church towers above the village. Its gilt-silver high altar, abbot's throne, pulpit, organ case, choir parapet, and swirling crowd of saintly and angelic faces are all the work (between 1753 and 1765) of Sebestyén Stuhlhoff. A joiner from Augsburg, Stulhoff lived and worked in the monastery as a lay brother for 25 years after the death of his Hungarian sweetheart. Local tradition says he immortalized her features as the angel who is kneeling on the right-hand side of the altar to the Virgin Mary. The magnificent Baroque organ, adorned by stucco cherubs, can be heard during evening concerts in summer.

In a Baroque house adjoining and entered through the abbey is the **Bencés Apátsági Múzeum** (Benedictine Abbey Museum). The best exhibits are in the basement lapidarium: relics from Roman colonization, including mosaic floors; a relief of David from the 2nd or 3rd century; and 1,200-year-old carved stones—all labeled in English as well as Hungarian. Three of the upstairs rooms were lived in for five days in 1921 by the last emperor of the dissolved Austro-Hungarian monarchy, Karl IV, in a futile foray to regain the throne of Hungary. Banished to Madeira, he died of pneumonia there a year later. The rooms are preserved with nostalgic relish for Franz Joseph's doomed successor. ⊠ *Első András tér 1,* ☎ *87/448–405 abbey, 87/448–650 museum .* ⊡ *180 Ft.* ☾ *May–Sept., Mon.–Sat. 9–5:30, Sun. 11–5:30; Nov.–Mar., Mon.–Sat. 10–3, Sun. 11–3; Apr. and Oct., Mon.–Sat. 10–4:30, Sun. 11–4:30.*

The **Szabadtéri Múzeum** (Open-air Museum), Tihany's outdoor museum of ethnography, assembles a group of old structures, including a potter's shed (with a local artist-in-residence) and the former house of the Fishermen's Guild, with an ancient boat (used until 1934) parked inside. ⊠ *Along Batthyány utca and neighboring streets,* ☎ *no phone.* ☾ *May–Sept., Tues.–Sun. 10–6.*

Visszhang domb (Echo Hill), at the end of Piski István sétány, is where as many as 16 syllables can be bounced off the abbey wall. Nowadays, with the inroads of traffic and construction, you'll have to settle for a two-second echo.

NEED A BREAK?   You can practice projecting from the terraces of the **Echo Restaurant** (⊠ Visszhang út 23, ☎ 87/448–460), an inn atop Echo Hill. While you're at it, try some *fogas* (young pike perch), carp, and catfish specialties.

Dining and Lodging

$$ ✕ **Pál Csárda.** Two thatched cottages house this simple restaurant, where cold fruit soup and fish stew are the specialties. You can eat in the garden, which is decorated with gourds and strands of dried peppers. ⊠

Visszhang u. 19, ☏ *87/448–605. Reservations not accepted. AE, MC, V. Closed Apr.–Oct.*

$ ✕ **Halásztánya.** The relaxed atmosphere and local fish specialties—like fogas fillets with garlic—contribute to this restaurant's popularity. ⊠ *Visszhang u. 11,* ☏ *87/448–771. Reservations not accepted. AE, MC, V. Closed Nov.–Easter*

$$$$ ⊞ **Kastély Hotel.** Lush landscaped lawns surround this stately neo-
★ Baroque mansion on the water's edge, built in the 1920s for József Hapsburg and taken over by the Communist state in the '40s (it is still owned by the government). Inside, it's all understated elegance; rooms have soaring ceilings and crisp sheets. Rooms with lake-facing windows and/or balconies (slightly more expensive) are the best. Next door, a newer, unattractive concrete building houses the Kastely's sister, the Park Hotel, with 60 less expensive, though dated, rooms. ⊠ *Fürdötelepi út 1, H-8237,* ☏ *87/448–611,* FAX *87/448–409. 25 rooms, 1 suite. Restaurant, bar, café, sauna, miniature golf, 2 tennis courts, beach, water sports. AE, DC, MC, V. Closed mid-Oct.–mid-Apr.*

$$$–$$$$ ⊞ **Club Tihany.** This 32-acre holiday village is essentially a year-round resort of almost Club Med proportions at the tip of the Tihany Peninsula. The list of activities is formidable—from fishing to thermal bathing at the full-service spa. The best and largest rooms in the resort's six-floor main building, the Hotel Tihany, are in its newer wing. Less fancy but more convenient for families are the 160 bungalows in various architectural styles—suburban A-frame, modern atrium, or mini-farmhouse—but all with kitchen facilities. Note: Hotel building prices include mandatory breakfast and dinner. ⊠ *Rév u. 3, H-8237,* ☏ *87/ 448–088,* FAX *87/448–110. 330 rooms, 161 bungalows. 3 restaurants, 2 bars, wine bar, pool, beauty salon, spa, tennis, exercise room, beach, water sports, meeting rooms. AE, DC, MC, V.*

$$ ⊞ **Kolostor.** Cozy, wood-paneled rooms are built into an attic above a popular restaurant and brewery in the heart of Tihany village. Rates include breakfast. ⊠ *Kossuth u. 14, H-8237,* ☏ FAX *87/448–009. 5 rooms. Restaurant. MC, V. Closed Nov.–Mar.*

Nightlife and the Arts

The **Benedictino Abbey**'s popular summer organ-concert series runs from July to August 20 and features well-known musicians performing on the abbey's magnificent organ. Concerts are generally held weekends at 8:30 PM. Contact the abbey (☞ *above*) for information and tickets.

Outdoor Activities and Sports

BICYCLING

Bicycle rentals are available from **Tihany Tourist** (☞ Visitor Information *in* Lake Balaton A to Z, *below*); a mountain bike costs about 500 Ft. per hour.

FISHING

Belső-tó (Inner Lake) is a popular angling spot in which you can try your luck at hooking ponty, catfish, and other local fish. Fishing permits can be bought on site at the fishing warden's office (☏ 87/448–998), next door to the Tóvendéglő restaurant on the southwest side of the lake.

HIKING

Footpaths crisscross the entire peninsula, allowing visitors to climb the small hills on its west side for splendid views of the area or hike down Belső-tó (Inner Lake). If in midsummer you climb its highest hill, the **Csúcshegy** (761 ft—approximately a two-hour hike), you will find the land below carpeted with purple lavender. Introduced from France into Hungary, lavender thrives on the lime-rich soil and strong sunshine of Tihany. (The State Lavender and Medicinal Herb Farm here supplies the Hungarian pharmaceutical and cosmetics industries.)

HORSEBACK RIDING

Aszófő Lovasudvar (Aszófő Riding Center; ⊠ Aszófői út 1, ☎ 87/445–078) offers horseback-riding lessons, rides in the ring, and trail rides; longer tours include a stop at a local wine cellar. A two-hour trail ride costs around 1,600 Ft. The center has showers and changing rooms, as well as a snack bar.

En Route The miniature town of Örvényes, about 7 km (4½ mi) west of Tihany, has the only working **vizi malom** (water mill) in the Balaton region. Built in the 18th century, it still grinds grain into flour while also serving as a tiny museum. In the miller's room is a collection of folk art, wood carvings, pottery, furniture, and pipes. On a nearby hill are the ruins of a **Romanesque church**; only its chancel has survived. On Templom utca, a few steps from the bridge, is the Baroque **St. Imre templom** (St. Imre Church), built in the late 18th century. *Water mill:* ⊠ *Szent Imre u. 1,* ☎ *87/449–360.* ☞ *50 Ft.* ☉ *May, daily 9–4; June–Sept., daily 9–5.*

Another kilometer (½ mi) west of Örvényes, **Balatonudvari** is a pleasant beach resort famous for its cemetery, which was declared a national shrine because of its beautiful, unique heart-shape tombstones carved from white limestone at the turn of the 18th century. The cemetery is essentially on the highway, at the eastern end of town; it is easily visible from the road. Balatonudvari's beach itself is at **Kiliántelep,** 2 km (1 mi) to the west.

The thriving beach resort of **Balatonakali,** 3 km (2 mi) west of Kiliántelep, has ferry service and three large camping grounds. On the slopes of Fenye-hegy, above the town, are vineyards lined with whitewashed winepress houses with thatched roofs and stone cellars, similar to those at Örvényes, if not as ornate. A 4-km (2½-mi) excursion into the volcanic hills north of Balatonakali leads to **Dörgicse,** a sleepy, less-trafficked little village where elderly ladies will stop their yard work to watch your car go by. Here you can view ruins of a medieval double church dating from the 11th century or take a 10-minute walk to the strange rock formations of **Kő-völgy** (Stone Valley).

Zánka

 21 km west of Tihany.

Zánka is a popular, relatively low-key beach resort with a large, pleasant beach, as well as a small, older village section up the hill from the water. The iron-rich Vérkút (Blood Spring), named after the bright stains it left on the rocks near which it flowed, put Zánka on the map as a spa late in the 19th century but has since dried up. The town's **Református templom** (Reformed Church; ⊠ Petőfi Sándor u. 3) is of medieval origin, but it was rebuilt in 1786 and again a century later with various elements preserved—leaving a pulpit supported by Roman foundations and Romanesque columns. The church is open during services, Sundays at 11 AM; someone is usually around to let you in an hour or so before.

The town of Zánka is not to be confused with the neighboring Zánka Gyermeküdülő (Zánka Children's Resort), the vast, unattractive former Communist Pioneer Camp. Keep this in mind if you're taking the train, as the stops for the two places are consecutive.

Lodging

$$ 🔲 **Kővirág Panzió.** A 10-minute drive inland from Zánka's beach, this family-run pension is in the peaceful village of nearby Köveskál. Six two-story suites are in a lovely, restored turn-of-the-century building (converted from a bull stable), with whitewashed walls and arched eye-of-God windows peeking out from under a reed-thatched roof. Each unit has a rustic-village feel, furnished with original hand-painted peasant furniture and mix-and-match antique carved-wood pieces. On cool nights you can build a fire in typical stone beehive fireplaces, with animal skins (wild boar, woolly sheep, or spotted cow) sprawled on the stone floors before them. Those who don't miss TVs, telephones, and other amenities may enjoy the Kővirág as an escape from the Balaton shore's myriad standard, faceless hotels. With large downstairs living rooms and two bedrooms upstairs sleeping four, the apartments offer good value and comfort for families or couples traveling together. ⊠ *Fő út 9/A, H-8274 Köveskál,* ☎ *87/478–569. 6 suites. Restaurant. No credit cards. Closed Oct.–Apr.*

Outdoor Activities and Sports

Zánka is well situated for inland exploring in the beautiful hilly countryside of the Káli-medence (Káli Basin). You can hike, bike, drive, or use a combination of these to get to the peak of Hegyestő, a volcanic protrusion that is the area's highest hill (1,102 ft) and is supposed to possess mysterious "positive energy." (Access to Hegyestő is via the road to Monszló after leaving Zánka.)

Three kilometers (2 miles) inland, to the northwest, is **Kővágóörs,** one of the prettiest villages of the Balaton, with a fine array of cottages in the local peasant style. It makes a wonderful place to pedal or stroll.

Badacsony

★ ⑥⑥ *20 km (12 mi) southwest of Zánka.*

One of the northern shore's most treasured images is the slopes of Mt. Badacsony (1,437 ft high), simply called the Badacsony, rising from the lake. The mysterious, coffinlike basalt peak of the Balaton Highlands is actually an extinct volcano flanked by smaller cone-shape hills. The masses of lava that coagulated here created bizarre and beautiful rock formations. At the upper edge, salt columns tower 180–200 ft like organ pipes in a huge semicircle. In 1965 Hungarian conservationists won a major victory that ended the quarrying of basalt from Mt. Badacsony, which is now a protected nature-preservation area.

The land below has been tilled painfully and lovingly for centuries. There are vineyards everywhere and splendid wine in every inn and tavern. In descending order of dryness, the best-loved Badacsony white wines are Rizlingszilváni, Kéknyelű, and Szürkebarát. Their proud producers claim that "no vine will produce good wine unless it can see its own reflection in the Balaton." They believe it is not enough for the sun simply to shine on a vine; the undersides of the leaves also need light, which is reflected from the lake's mirrorlike surface. Others claim the wine draws its strength from the fire of old volcanoes.

Badacsony is really an administrative name for the entire area and includes not just the mountain but also five settlements at its foot.

A good starting point for Badacsony sightseeing is the **Egry József Múzeum** (József Egry Museum), formerly the home and studio of a famous painter of Balaton landscapes. His evocative paintings depict the lake's constantly changing hues, from its angry bright green during storms to its tranquil deep blues. ✉ *Egry sétány 12,* ☎ *87/431–140.* 🎫 *120 Ft.* ⊘ *May–Sept., Tues.–Sun. 10–6.*

Szegedy Róza út, the steep main street climbing the mountain, is flanked by vineyards and villas. This is the place to get acquainted with the writer Sándor Kisfaludy and his beloved bride from Badacsony, Róza Szegedy, to whom he dedicated his love poems. At the summit of her street is **Szegedy Róza Ház** (Róza Szegedy House), a Baroque winepress house built in 1790 on a grand scale—with thatched roof, gabled wall, six semicircular arcades, and an arched and pillared balcony running the length of the four raftered upstairs rooms (it was here that the hometown girl met the visiting bard from Budapest). The house is now a memorial museum to both of them, furnished much the way it was when he was doing his best work immortalizing his two true loves, the Badacsony and his wife. ✉ *Szegedy Róza út 87,* ☎ *no phone.* 🎫 *120 Ft.* ⊘ *Apr.–Sept., Tues.–Sun. 10–6.*

The steep climb to the **Kisfaludy kilátó** (Kisfaludy Lookout Tower) on Mt. Badacsony's summit is an integral part of the Badacsony experience and a rewarding bit of exercise. Serious summitry begins behind the Kisfaludy House at the **Rózsakő** (Rose Stone), a flat, smooth basalt slab with many carved inscriptions. Local legend has it that if a boy and a girl sit on it with their backs to Lake Balaton, they will marry within a year. From here, a trail marked in yellow leads upstairs to the foot of the columns that stretch to the top. Steep flights of stone steps take you through a narrow gap between rocks and basalt walls until you reach a tree-lined plateau. You are now at the 1,391-ft level. Follow the blue triangular markings along a path to the lookout tower. Even with time out for rests and views, the ascent from Rózsakő should take less than an hour.

Wine-tasting opportunities abound in Badacsony. Many restaurants and inns have their own tastings, as do the numerous smaller, private cellars dotting the hill. Look for signs saying *bor* or *Wein* (wine, in Hungarian and German, respectively) to point the way. Most places are open mid-May to mid-September daily from around noon until 9 or 10. Just outside of town, **Rizapuzta** (✉ Badacsonytomaj, Rizapuszta, ☎ 87/471–243) is a cellar and restaurant with regular tastings.

Dining and Lodging

$$ ✕ **Halászkert.** The festive Fish Garden has won numerous international awards for its tasty Hungarian cuisine. Inside are wooden rafters and tables draped with cheerful traditional blue-and-white *kékfestő* tablecloths; outside is a large terrace with umbrella-shaded tables. The extensive menu has such fresh-from-the-lake dishes as the house *halászlé* (fish stew), and *párolt harcsa* (steamed catfish) drenched with a paprika-caper sauce. ✉ *Park u. 5,* ☎ *87/431–054. MC, V. Closed Nov.–Mar.*

$$ ✕ **Kisfaludy-ház.** Perched above the Szegedy Róza House is this Badacsony institution, once a winepress house owned by the poet's family. Its wine cellar lies directly over a spring, but the main draw is a vast two-tiered terrace that affords a breathtaking panoramic view of virtually the entire lake. Naturally, the wines are excellent and are incorporated into some of the cooking, such as creamy wine soup. ✉ *Szegedy Róza u. 87,* ☎ *87/431–016. MC, V. Closed Nov.–Mar.*

BONUS MILES MAKE GREAT SOUVENIRS.

Earn Miles With Your MCI Card.

Take the MCI Card along on this trip and start earning miles for the next one. You'll earn frequent flyer miles on all your calls and save with the low rates you've come to expect from MCI. Before you know it, you'll be on your way to some other international destination.

Sign up for MCI by calling
1-800-FLY-FREE

Earn Frequent Flyer Miles.

Is this a great time, or what? :-)

Easy To Call Home.

1. To use your MCI Card, just dial the WorldPhone access number of the country you're calling from.
2. Dial or give the operator your MCI Card number.
3. Dial or give the number you're calling.

# Austria (CC) ♦	022-903-012
# Belarus (CC)	
From Brest, Vitebsk, Grodno, Minsk	8-800-103
From Gomel and Mogilev regions	8-10-800-103
# Belgium (CC) ♦	0800-10012
# Bulgaria	00800-0001
# Croatia (CC) ★	0800-22-0112
# Czech Republic (CC) ♦	00-42-000112
# Denmark (CC) ♦	8001-0022
# Finland (CC) ♦	08001-102-80
# France (CC) ♦	0-800-99-0019
# Germany (CC)	0800-888-8000
# Greece (CC) ♦	00-800-1211
# Hungary (CC) ♦	00▼800-01411
# Iceland (CC) ♦	800-9002
# Ireland (CC)	1-800-55-1001
# Italy (CC) ♦	172-1022
# Kazakhstan (CC)	8-800-131-4321
# Liechtenstein (CC) ♦	0800-89-0222
# Luxembourg	0800-0112
# Monaco (CC) ♦	800-90-019
# Netherlands (CC) ♦	0800-022-9122
# Norway (CC) ♦	800-19912
# Poland (CC) ÷	00-800-111-21-22
# Portugal (CC) ÷	05-017-1234
Romania (CC) ÷	01-800-1800
# Russia (CC) ÷ ♦	
To call using ROSTELCOM ■	747-3322
For a Russian-speaking operator	747-3320
To call using SOVINTEL ■	960-2222
# San Marino (CC) ♦	172-1022
# Slovak Republic (CC)	00-421-00112
# Slovenia	080-8808
# Spain (CC)	900-99-0014
# Sweden (CC) ♦	020-795-922
# Switzerland (CC) ♦	0800-89-0222
# Turkey (CC) ♦	00-8001-1177
# Ukraine (CC) ÷	8▼10-013
# United Kingdom (CC)	
To call using BT ■	0800-89-0222
To call using C&W ■	0500-89-0222
# Vatican City (CC)	172-1022

Flying to France on Friday? Get Francs from Chase on Thursday. Call Currency To Go at 935-9935 for overnight delivery.

CHASE CURRENCY TO GO 935-9935

$\mathcal{O}$r pounds for London. Or Deutschmarks for Düsseldorf. Or any of 75 foreign currencies. Call **Chase Currency To Go**^{SM} **at 935-9935** in area codes 212, 718, 914, 516 and Rochester, N.Y.; all other area codes call 1-800-935-9935. We'll deliver directly to your door.* Overnight. And there are no exchange fees. Let Chase make your trip an easier one.

CHASE. The right relationship is everything.^{SM}

$$–$$$ ⊞ **Club Tomaj.** On the shore of Lake Balaton in the Badacsonytomaj neighborhood, this is the largest hotel in the area. It's just a step away from the hotel to the Club's private beach. At press time it was going under new ownership, and there were plans for renovation. ✉ *Balatoni út 14, H-8258 Badacsonytomaj,* ☎ *87/471–040,* FAX *87/471–059. 46 rooms, 4 suites. Restaurant, café, sauna, tennis court, bowling, beach. MC, V. Closed mid-Oct.–Apr.*

$$–$$$ ⊞ **Hotel Volán.** This bright yellow, restored 19th-century mansion is a cheerful, family-oriented inn with a manicured yard for sunning and relaxing. Well-kept rooms are in the main house and in four modern additions behind it. ✉ *Római út 169, H-8261 Badacsony,* ☎ *87/430– 704 or 87/430–705,* ☎ FAX *87/431–013. 23 rooms. Restaurant, bar, pool, tennis court. No credit cards.*

Outdoor Activities and Sports

The upper paths and roads along the slopes of Mt. Badacsony are excellent for scenic walking. Well-marked trails lead up to the summit of Mt. Badacsony.

For beach activities, you can go to one of Badacsony's several beaches or head 6 km (4 mi) northeast, to those at Balatonrendes and Ábrahámhegy, combined communities forming quiet resorts.

Szigliget

★ ⑥⑦ *11 km (7 mi) west of Badacsony.*

The village of Szigliget was formerly an island in the Balaton. It's a tranquil, picturesque town with a fine array of thatched-roof winepress houses and a small, attractive beach. Towering over the town is the ruin of the 13th-century **Óvár** (Old Castle), a fortress so well protected that it was never taken by the Turks; it was demolished in the early 18th century by Hapsburgs fearful of rebellions. A steep path starting from Kisfaludy utca brings you to the top of the hill, where you can explore the ruins, under ongoing archaeological restoration (a sign maps out the restoration plan), and take in the breathtaking views.

Down in the village on Iharos út, at the intersection with the road to Badacsony, the Romanesque remains of the **Avas templon** (Avas Church), from the Arpad dynasty, still contain a 12th-century basalt tower with stone spire. The **Eszterházy Summer Mansion** in the main square, Fő tér, was built in the 18th century and rebuilt in neoclassical style in the 19th. Lately a holiday retreat for writers (and closed to the public), it has a 25-acre park with yews, willows, walnuts, pines, and more than 500 kinds of ornamental trees and shrubs.

Keszthely

⑥⑧ *18 km (10 mi) west of Szigliget.*

Keszthely, the largest town on the northern shore, lies at the westernmost end of Lake Balaton. With a beautifully preserved pedestrians-only avenue (Kossuth Lajos utca) in the historic center of town, the spectacular Baroque Festetics Kastély, and a relative absence of honky-tonk, Keszthely is far more classically attractive and sophisticated than other large Balaton towns. Continuing the cultural and arts tradition begun by Count György Festetics two centuries ago, Keszthely hosts numerous cultural events, including an annual summer arts festival. Just south of town is the vast swamp called Kis-Balaton (Little Balaton), formerly part of Lake Balaton and now a protected nature area filled with birds. Water flowing into Lake Balaton from its little sibling frequently churns up sediment, making the water around Keszthely's beaches disconcertingly cloudy.

The **Pethő Ház,** a striking town house of medieval origins, was rebuilt in Baroque style with a handsome arcaded gallery above its courtyard. Hidden through its courtyard you'll find the restored 18th-century **synagogue,** in front of which stands a small memorial honoring the 829 Jewish people from the neighborhood, turned into a ghetto in 1944, who were killed during the Holocaust. ⊠ *Kossuth Lajos u. 22.*

★ Keszthely's magnificent **Festetics Kastély** (Festetics Palace) is one of the finest Baroque complexes in Hungary. Begun around 1745, it was the seat of the enlightened and philanthropic Festetics dynasty, which had acquired Keszthely six years earlier. The palace's distinctive church-like tower and more than 100 rooms were added between 1883 and 1887; the interior is exceedingly lush. The **Helikon Könyvtár** (Helikon Library) in the south wing contains some 52,000 volumes, with precious codices and documents of Festetics family history. Chamber and orchestral concerts are held in the **Mirror Gallery** ballroom or, in summer, in the courtyard. The palace opens onto a splendid park lined with rare plants and fine sculptures. ⊠ *Kastély u. 1,* ☎ *83/312–191.* 🖙 *750 Ft.* ☉ *June, Tues.–Sun. 9–5; July–Aug., daily 9–6; Sept.–May, Tues.–Sun. 10–5.*

Dining and Lodging

$–$$ ✕ **Gösser Söröző.** This beer garden keeps long hours and plenty of beer on tap. The food is better than you might guess judging just from the touristy atmosphere. Aside from barroom snacks, the menu includes *gombás rostélyos* (stuffed pepper) and *töltöttpaprika* (grilled steak and mushrooms). ⊠ *Kossuth Lajos u. 35, just north of Fő tér,* ☎ *83/ 312–265. AE, MC, V.*

$$$$ 🏨 **Danubius Hotel Helikon.** This large and comfortable lakeside hotel has plenty of sports facilities, such as an indoor swimming pool, indoor tennis courts, sailing, surfing, rowing, fishing, and, in winter, skating. The comfortable, modern rooms are on the small side, but they have soothing, cream-and-blue bedspreads and curtains. ⊠ *Balaton part 5, H-8360,* ☎ *83/311–330,* 𝔽𝔸𝕏 *83/315–403. 224 rooms, 8 suites. Restaurant, bar, indoor pool, beauty salon, sauna, 2 indoor tennis courts, bowling, health club, beach, water sports. AE, DC, MC, V.*

$$$ 🏨 **Béta Hotel Hullám.** This attractive turn-of-the-century mansion with an elegant tower sits right on the Balaton shore. Rooms are clean and simply furnished with functional brown furniture; they have TVs and minibars but no telephones. Guests can use the pool and other recreational facilities at the nearby Danubius Hotel Helikon (🖙 *above*). ⊠ *Balatonpart 1, H-8360,* ☎ *83/312–644,* 𝔽𝔸𝕏 *83/315–950. 44 rooms, 6 suites. Restaurant, bar, beach. AE, DC, MC, V. Closed Nov.–Mar.*

Nightlife and the Arts

The **Balaton Festival,** held annually in May, features high-caliber classical concerts and other festivities in venues around town and outdoors on Kossuth Lajos utca. In summer, classical concerts and master classes are held almost daily in the Festetics Palace's Mirror Hall.

Outdoor Activities and Sports

BALLOONING

Hot-air balloon rides in the Keszthely region have become popular with those tourists who can afford it (about 17,000 Ft. per person). Dr. Bóka György (a practicing M.D. and balloon pilot) and his friendly team will take you up in his blue-and-yellow balloon for an hour-long tour—the trip includes a postlanding champagne ritual. Flights depend strongly on wind and air-pressure conditions; in summer, they can usually fly only in early morning and early evening. Transportation to and from the site is included. Contact **Med-Aer** (✉ Móricz Zsigmond u. 7, ☎ 83/312–421) at least one week in advance to reserve your spot.

BIRD-WATCHING

The largest river feeding Balaton, the Zala, enters the lake at its southwestern corner. On either side there is a vast swamp, formerly part of the lake. Known as **Kis-Balaton** (Little Balaton), its almost 3,500 acres of marshland were put under nature preservation in 1949. In 1953 a bird-watching station was opened nearby, and ornithologists have found some 80 species nesting among the reeds, many of them rare for this region. The white egret is the most treasured of them. Most of the area can be visited only by special permission. Contact Horváth Jenő at the **Kutató-ház** (Research Station; ✉ Fenékpuszta, ☎ 83/315–341) of the Közép Dunántúl Természetvédelmi Igazgatóság (Central Transdanubian Environmental Protection Directorate) to arrange a bird-watching tour (around 2,500 Ft.) The Kis-Balaton is entered near where Highway 71 ends its trip around the lake and yields to Highway 76 continuing south.

HORSEBACK RIDING

János Lovarda (János Stable; ✉ Sömögyedüllő, ☎ 83/314–533 or 83/312–534) offers lessons, rides in the ring, and carriage rides.

WATER SPORTS

You can rent paddleboats and other water toys at the public beach (next to the Béta Hotel Hullám) or from the Danubius Hotel Helikon (☞ Dining and Lodging, *above*).

Hévíz

⑥⑨ *6 km (4 mi) inland (northwest) from Keszthely.*

Hévíz is one Hungary's biggest and most famous spa resorts, with the largest natural curative thermal lake in Europe. Lake Hévíz covers nearly 60,000 square yards, with warm water that never grows cooler than 33°C–35°C (91.4°F–95°F) in summer and 30°C–32°C (86°F–89.6°F) in winter, thus allowing year-round bathing, particularly where the lake is covered by a roof and looks like a racetrack grandstand. Richly endowed with sulfur, alkali, calcium salts, and other curative components, the Hévíz water is recommended for spinal, rheumatic, gynecological, and articular disorders and is drunk to help digestive problems and receding gums. Fed by a spring producing 86 million liters of water a day, the lake cycles through a complete water change every 28 hours. Squeamish bathers, however, should be forewarned that along with its photogenic lily pads, the lake naturally contains assorted sludgy mud and plant material. It's all good for you, though—even the mud, which is full of iodine and estrogen.

The vast spa park is home to hospitals, sanatoriums, expensive hotels, and a casino. The public bath facilities are in the **Állami Gyógyfürdő Kórház** (State Medicinal Bath Hospital), a large, turreted complex on the lakeshore. Bathing for more than three hours at a time is not recommended. ✉ *Dr. Schülhof Vilmos sétány 1,* ☎ *83/340–455.* 💷 *500 Ft. (valid for 3 hrs).* ☉ *May–Sept., daily 9–5; Oct.–Apr., daily 9–4.*

OFF THE BEATEN PATH	**CSILLAGVÁR (Star Castle) –** It's worth stopping in Balatonszentgyörgy to see this castle, hidden away at the end of a dirt road past a gaping quarry. The house was built in the 1820s as a hunting lodge for László, the Festetics family's eccentric. Though it is not star-shape inside, wedge-shape projections on the ground floor give the outside this effect. Today

it is a museum of 16th- and 17th-century life in the border fortresses of the Balaton. ⊠ *Irtási dűlő,* ☎ *85/377–532.* 🎫 *100 Ft.* ☉ *May–Aug., daily 9–6.*

The beautifully furnished **Talpasház** (House on Soles) is another architecturally interesting stop, so named because its upright beams are encased in thick foundation boards. The house is filled not only with exquisite antique peasant furniture, textiles, and pottery but also with the work of contemporary local folk artists; some of their work is for sale on the premises, and visitors can also try to create their own works on a pottery wheel. ⊠ *Csillagvár u. 68,* ☎ *no phone.* 🎫 *70 Ft.* ☉ *Late May–Sept., daily 9–7.*

Lodging

$$$$ 🏨 **Danubius Thermal Hotel Aqua.** This large, luxurious spa-hotel has its own thermal baths and physiotherapy unit (plus a full dental service!). It has a convenient city-center location, but the rooms are smaller than average and therefore not suited to families who intend to share a single room. Numerous cure packages are available. ⊠ *Kossuth Lajos u. 13–15, H-8380,* ☎ *83/341–090,* 𝔽𝔸𝕏 *83/340–970. 229 rooms. Restaurant, bar, outdoor pool, indoor thermal pool, beauty salon, massage, sauna, solarium, spa. AE, DC, MC, V.*

$$$$ 🏨 **Danubius Thermal Hotel Hévíz.** Very similar in its offerings to those of its sibling and neighbor the Thermal Aqua (☞ *above*), this large spa-hotel edges it out with nicer (and larger) rooms, since the hotel was renovated in 1997. Suites have air-conditioning. ⊠ *Kossuth Lajos u. 9–11, H-8380,* ☎ *83/341–180,* 𝔽𝔸𝕏 *83/340–666. 203 rooms. Restaurant, bar, café, 1 indoor pool, 1 outdoor pool, sauna, solarium, thermal baths, casino. AE, DC, MC, V.*

Fonyód

20 km (12 mi) east of Balatonszentgyörgy, 45 km (28 mi) west of Siófok.

With seven beaches stretching 7 km (4½ mi) along the shore, Fonyód is second only to Siófok among the most-developed resorts on the southern shore of the lake. Fonyód sits at the base of a twin-peaked hill rising directly from the shore. Atop one of the peaks, **Sipos Hegy** (Sipos Hill; 764 ft), stood an important fortress during Turkish times. Only its trenches and the foundation walls of a Romanesque church still stand; the peak is worth climbing for the views of its crowning ruin from the disheveled courtyard: You look across the lake almost directly at Badacsony and, off in the distance to the left, Keszthely. Beginning at the train station, red markers indicate the path up the hill; allow a little over an hour for the uphill walk.

Dining

$$ ✕ **Présház Csárda.** A tiny road winds up the hill to the 150-year-old Winepress-House Inn—a whitewashed, thatched-roof structure—where you can order fresh fish dishes and local wines. ⊠ *Lenke u. 22,* ☎ *no phone. No credit cards. Closed Sept.–mid-May.*

OFF THE BEATEN PATH **BUZSÁK –** An interesting excursion from Fonyód is to the village of Buzsák, 16 km (10 mi) to the south. Buzsák is famous for its colorful folk art and unique peasant needlework. You can buy newly made crafts in local shops, but earlier masterworks are displayed in the museum of the **Buzsáki Népművészeti Tájház** (Buzsák Regional Folk Art House), three venerable, well-decorated rustic buildings. Inquire about the village Saints' Festival, known as the Buzsáki Búcsú, held for two or three days around August 20. ⊠ *Tanács tér 7,* ☎ *85/330–342.* ▣

50 Ft. ⊙ Mid-Apr.–mid-Oct., daily 9–5. Mid-Oct.–mid-Apr. by appointment only.

Siófok

⑦ *18 km (11 mi) east of Balatonföldvár, 105 km (65 mi) southwest of Budapest.*

Siófok is the largest city on the southern shore and one of Hungary's major tourist and holiday centers. It is also arguably the ugliest. In 1863 a railway station was built for the city, paving the way for its "golden age" at the turn of the century. During the closing stages of World War II the city sustained heavy damage; to boost tourism during the 1960s, the Pannonia Hotel Company built four of what many consider to be the ugliest hotels in the area. If, however, these were Siófok's *only* ugly buildings, there would still be hope for a ray of aesthetic redemption. But the sad truth is, the city is overrun by unsightly modern structures. Its shoreline is now a long, honky-tonk strip crammed with concrete-bunker hotels, discos, go-go bars, and tacky restaurants. So while Siófok is not for those seeking a peaceful lakeside getaway, it is exactly what hordes of action-seeking young people want—an all-in-one playground.

One worthwhile attraction is the **Kálmán Imre Múzeum** (Imre Kálmán Museum), housed in the birthplace of composer Kálmán (1882–1953), known internationally as the Prince of Operetta. Inside this small house-cum-museum are his first piano, original scores, his smoking jacket, and lots of old pictures. ⊠ *Kálmán Imre sétány 5,* ☎ *84/311–287.* ⊡ *120 Ft. ⊙ Apr.–Oct., Tues.–Sun. 9–5; Nov.–Mar., Tues.–Sun. 9–4.*

Dining and Lodging

$$ ✕ **Janus Étterem.** This elegant restaurant, once an old villa, was renovated in 1992 under the guidance of Imre Makovecz, one of Hungary's preeminent architects. The menu features fresh fish and excellent Hungarian specialties. ⊠ *Fő u. 93–95,* ☎ *84/312–546. AE, DC, MC, V.*

$ ✕ **Csárdás Étterem.** The oldest and one of the best restaurants in Sió-
★ fok, this has consistently won awards for its hearty, never-bland Hungarian cuisine. House specialties include a breaded and fried pork fillet stuffed with cheese, ham, and smoked bacon. ⊠ *Fő u. 105,* ☎ *84/310–642. AE, MC, V. Closed Nov.–Mar. 15.*

$$$–$$$$ 🛏 **Janus.** Every room in this bright luxury hotel, opened in 1993, is clean and comfortably contemporary and contains a minibar and a safe. The "relaxation center" downstairs has a swimming pool, sauna, and whirlpool. ⊠ *Fő u. 93–95, H-8600,* ☎ *84/312–546,* 𝔽𝔸𝕏 *84/312–432. 22 rooms, 7 suites. Restaurant, bar, café, indoor pool, sauna, exercise room, meeting rooms. AE, DC, MC, V.*

$$ 🛏 **Hotel Korona.** This three-story rectangular block has the advantage of being somewhat removed from the multilane traffic of the city's main street and about 100 yards from the lakeshore. All rooms have balconies; though no-frills, they're clean. ⊠ *Erkel Ferenc u. 53, H-8600,* ☎ *84/310–471. 34 rooms. Restaurant, tennis court. AE, MC, V.*

Nightlife and the Arts

Loyal to Siófok-born operetta composer Imre Kálmán, popular operetta concerts are held regularly in the summer at the **Kulturális Központ** (Cultural Center; ⊠ *Fő tér 2,* ☎ *84/311–855*).

Outdoor Activities and Sports

GO-CARTS

Speed demons can whiz around at the **Go Cart Track** (⊠ On Hwy. 70, by the railroad crossing, ☎ 06/209–229–984); a 10-minute drive is around 1,500 Ft.

MOPEDS

No resort is a bona fide tourist town without moped rentals, and in Siófok they're available from the rental outfit set up in the parking lot on Kinizsi utca, in front of the main stand of hotels. Bicycles are also for rent here. Prices fluctuate, so check with Tourinform (☞ Visitor Information *in* Lake Balaton A to Z, *below*).

TENNIS

The **Sport Centrum** (⊠ Küszhegyi út, ☎ 84/314–523) has eight tennis courts as well as a handball court, sauna, and, lest things are getting too athletic, a bar.

WATER SPORTS

Boating and other water-sports equipment is available for hire at the **Water Sports Center,** on the waterfront on Vitorlás utca 10 (☎ 84/311–161). Kayaks and canoes cost 500 Ft.–600 Ft. per hour, sailboats around 6,000 Ft. per hour.

Lake Balaton A to Z

Arriving and Departing

BY BUS

Buses headed for the Lake Balaton region depart from Budapest's Erzsebét tér station daily; contact **Volánbusz** (☎ 1/317–2318) for current schedules.

BY CAR

Highway E71 /M7 is the main artery between Budapest and Lake Balaton. M7 continues down the lake's southern shore to Siófok and towns farther west. E71 goes along the northern shore to Balatonfüred and lakeside towns southwest. The drive from Budapest to Siófok, for example, takes about an hour and a half, except on weekends, when traffic can be severe. From Budapest to Balatonfüred is about the same.

BY TRAIN

Daily express trains run from Budapest's Déli (South) Station to Siófok and Balatonfüred. The roughly two-hour trips cost about $5 each way.

Getting Around

BY BOAT

The slowest but most scenic way to travel between Lake Balaton's major resorts is by ferry. Schedules for **MAHART** (☎ 1/318–1704 in Budapest), the national ferry company, are available from most of the tourist offices listed below.

BY BUS

Buses frequently link Lake Balaton's major resorts, but book ahead to avoid long waits. Reservations can be made through the tourist offices or **Volánbusz** (☎ 1/317–2318 in Budapest).

BY CAR

Road 71 runs along the northern shore; M7 covers the southern shore. Driving is the most convenient way to explore the area, but remember that traffic can be heavy during summer weekends.

BY TRAIN

Trains from Budapest serve the resorts on the northern shore; a separate line links resorts on the southern shore. The **Siófok** station (⊠ Millenium tér, ☎ 84/310–061) is in the center of town; the **Balatonfüred** station (⊠ Castricum tér, ☎ 87/343–652) is very close to town center. **Veszprém**'s train station (⊠ Jutasi út 34, ☎ 88/324–583) is about 2 km (1 mi) outside of town. There is no train service to Tihany. While most towns are on a rail line, it's inconvenient to decipher the train schedules; trains don't run very frequently, so planning connections can be tricky. Since many towns are just a few km apart, getting stuck on a local train can feel like an endless stop-start cycle. Be sure to book tickets well in advance in high season.

Contacts and Resources

EMERGENCIES

Ambulance (☎ 104). **Fire** (☎ 105). **Police** (☎ 107).

GUIDED TOURS

IBUSZ Travel has several tours to Balaton from Budapest; inquire at the office in Budapest (✉ Rubin Aktiv Hotel, XI, Dajka Gábor u. 3, ☎ 1/319–7520, 1/319–7519). You can also arrange tours directly with the hotels in the Balaton area and with the help of Tourinform offices (see Visitor Information, *below*); these can include boat trips to vineyards, folk-music evenings, and overnight trips to local inns.

Gray Line Cityrama (in Budapest, ☎ 1/302–4382) takes groups twice a week from April to October from Budapest to Balatonfüred for a walk along the promenade and then over to Tihany for a tour of the abbey. After lunch, you'll take a ferry across the Balaton, and then head back to Budapest, with a wine-tasting stop on the way.

MAHART (☎ 84/310–050) offers several boating tours and cruises on Lake Balaton. The sailboat **"Panorama Tour"** leaves Siófok Saturday at 9:30 AM and stops for guided sightseeing in Balatonfüred and Tihany. The total trip takes seven hours and is offered early July through August. The **"Sunset Tour"** is a 1½-hour cruise on the lake during which guests can sip a glass of champagne while watching the sun sink. Departures are from Siófok early July through August, daily at 7:30 PM. From Balatonfüred, you can board a ship for an all-day tour of the wine-growing area of Badacsony, including wine tastings, sightseeing, and lunch. This **"Wine Tasting Tour"** runs early July through August, Thursday at 9:30 AM. The **"Badacsony Tour"** is also a trip to Badacsony but it departs at 10:30 AM from Keszthely, on the same days as the tour from Balatonfüred, and returns at 4:30 PM.

VISITOR INFORMATION

Badacsony: Tourinform (✉ Római út 55, Badacsonytomaj, ☎ FAX 87/472–023). **Balatonfüred:** Tourinform (✉ Petőfi u. 8, ☎ 87/342–237); Balatontourist (✉ Tagore sétány 1, ☎ 87/342–822 or 87/343–471). **Fonyód:** Siótours (✉ Ady Endre u. 2, ☎ 85/361–850 or 85/361–852). **Hévíz:** Hévíz Tourist (✉ Rákóczi u. 4, ☎ 83/341–348). **Keszthely:** Tourinform (✉ Kossuth u. 28, ☎ FAX 83/314–144). **Siófok:** Tourinform (✉ Víztorony, ☎ FAX 84/310–117); IBUSZ (✉ Fő u. 174, ☎ 84/311–066). **Tihany:** Tourinform (✉ Kossuth u. 20, ☎ FAX 87/448–804); Tihany Tourist (✉ Kossuth u. 11, ☎ 87/448–481). **Veszprém:** Tourinform (✉ Rákóczi út 3, ☎ 88/404–548).

NORTHERN HUNGARY

Northern Hungary stretches from the Danube Bend, north of Budapest, along the northeastern frontier with Slovakia as far west as Sátoraljaújhely. It is a clearly defined area, marked by several mountain ranges of no great height but of considerable scenic beauty. Most of the peaks reach 3,000 ft and are thickly wooded almost to their summit. Grottoes and caves abound, as well as thermal baths. In the state game reserves, herds of deer, wild boars, and eagles are not uncommon sights.

Historically, the valleys of northern Hungary have always been of considerable strategic importance, as they provided the only access to the Carpathian Mountains. **Eger,** renowned throughout Hungarian history as one of the guardians of these strategic routes, retains its splendor, with many ruins picturesquely dotting the surrounding hilltops. The **Mátra Mountains,** less than 90 km (55 mi) from Budapest, provide opportunities for year-round recreation and are the center for winter sports. Last but not least, this is one of the great wine-growing districts of Hungary, with Gyöngyös and Eger contributing the "Magyar nectar" and Tokaj producing the "wine of kings."

Numbers in the margin correspond to numbers on the Northern Hungary and the Great Plain map.

Hollókő

★ **㉔** *100 km (62 mi) northeast of Budapest.*

This tiny mountain village close to the Slovakian border was added to the UNESCO list of World Cultural Heritage Sites in 1988 to help preserve its unique medieval structure and age-old Palóc (ethnographic group indigenous to northern Hungary) cultural and handcrafting traditions still practiced today by the village's 400 inhabitants. The most famous of these traditions are those practiced during Easter, when the villagers dress in colorful embroidered costumes. UNESCO's distinction has brought arguably positive and negative elements to Hollókő. The small village has become a popular day-trip tourist destination and has adapted somewhat to that role; for example, the villagers agree to dress in traditional costume on days when bus tours come through.

But Hollókő is authentically enchanting: Old whitewashed houses with hand-carved wooden verandas and awnings cluster together on narrow cobblestone pathways; directly above them loom the hilltop ruins (now being restored) of a 13th-century castle. For information on Hollókő's Easter festivities and other events, contact the cultural foundation **Hollókőért közalapítvány** (⊠ Kossuth u. 68, Hollókő 3176, ☎ ⅢⅩ 32/379–266).

Dining

$ ✕ **Muskátli Vendéglő.** Named for the bright red and pink flowers lining its windowsills, the "Geranium Restaurant" is a cozy little eatery on Hollókő's main street. Specialties include *Palócgulyás,* a rich local goulash thick with chunks of pork and beans, and *Nógrádi palócpecsenye,* pork cutlets smothered in mustard-garlic sauce. ⊠ *Kossuth út 61,* ☎ *32/379–262. AE, DC, MC, V. Closed Mon., and Mon.–Wed. Jan.–Feb.*

OFF THE
BEATEN PATH
★

KASTÉLY SZIRÁK (Szirák Castle) – About 35 km (22 mi) along route 21 and then some lovely side roads from Hollókő's small cluster of homes is this stately, Baroque castle. Built in 1748 on the foundations of a 13th-century knights' hostel, it was the home of Count József Teleki, an arts patron who created a vast library and had the main hall covered with frescoes depicting Ovid's *Metamorphoses.* The castle was seized by the Russian military in 1944; most of the contents were destroyed as they turned it into a military hospital. Thirty-three years later, restoration began, and now this is one of the country's best castle hotels. Antiques (if not the originals) fill the rooms, and in Count Teleki's own three-room suite, you can see the door to his secret stairway into the backyard and gaze out the window at the centuries-old Japanese acacia tree. The "honeymoon room" is unfortunately situated directly off the lobby; it is not recommended for those seeking true privacy. A newer wing houses

Northern Hungary and the Great Plain

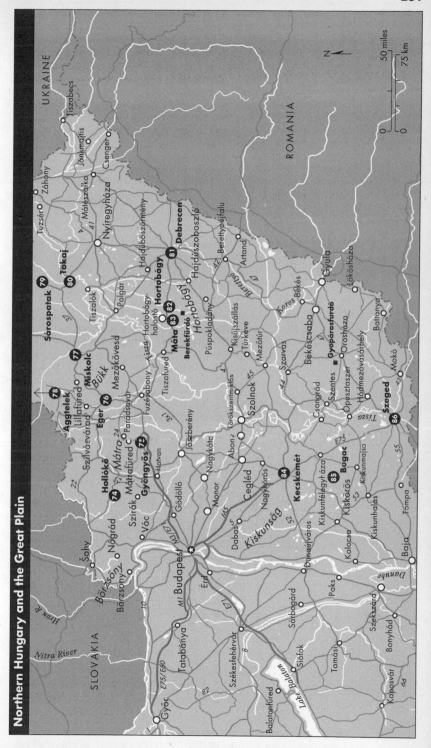

the "tourist hotel," comprising bland, dated units that share nothing of the castle's aura. Double rooms in the main castle building cost $68 per night (suites cost $84); doubles in the newer wing run $45 per night. All rates include breakfast. If you'd just like to peek at the castle's interior, a docent will (for a tip) show you the main hall, where the frescoes have been beautifully restored. You can also go horseback riding, even if you're not a guest. ⊠ *Pf: 3, H–3044 Szirák,* ☎ FAX *60/353–053. 21 rooms, 4 suites. Restaurant, sauna, tennis court, horseback riding, meeting rooms. AE, DC, MC, V.*

Gyöngyös

 40 km (25 mi) southeast of Hollókő, 75 km (46 mi) northeast of Budapest.

The city of Gyöngyös, famous for its excellent wines (don't pass up the chance to sample the *Debrői hárslevelű,* a magnificent white wine produced in a nearby village), lies at the base of the volcanic Mátra mountain range, Hungary's best-developed mountain vacation area. Early in the 1960s huge lignite deposits were discovered, and the large-scale mines and power stations established since then have changed the character of the entire region.

Although it doesn't have many reasons to linger in its own right, Gyöngyös serves as the gateway to the Mátras and is a good starting point for visiting the many beautiful resorts that lie just north of it. The best known is Mátrafüred, at 1,300 ft, which can be reached by narrow-gauge railway from Gyöngyös. Just a few miles from Mátrafüred is Kékestető, the highest point in Hungary (3,327 ft).

Among the chief sights of the town is the 15th-century **Szent Bertalan templom** (Church of St. Bartholomew), on Fő tér. It is one of Hungary's largest Gothic churches and was beautifully restored in the mid-1990s. Next to the altar is a 16th-century bronze baptismal font; there's also a newly uncovered fresco of King Károly IV's visit to Gyöngyös after a serious fire. ⊠ *Fő tér.* ⊠ *Church free, treasury 50 Ft.* ☉ *Church daily 9–noon and 2–4 or 5; treasury Tues.–Sun. 10–noon and 2–5.*

The **Mátra Múzeum** (Mátra Museum), in a handsome neoclassical mansion, provides a helpful preparation for excursions into the Mátras with its extensive exhibits on the flora and fauna of the region, as well as geological and historical displays. In addition to hearing recorded sounds of indigenous bird songs, you can examine deer, eagles, and other fauna you may encounter, as well as those you'll be luckier to avoid, like the sharp-tusked wild boar. Also on display is "Bruno," the hulking 1- to 2-million-year-old skeleton of a young mammoth found in the northern Mátra. Unless you're a fan of dank cellars filled with snakes and bugs (and their smell), avoid the "Mikro-varium" exhibit downstairs. ⊠ *Kossuth Lajos u. 40,* ☎ *37/311–447.* ⊠ *200 Ft.* ☉ *Mar.– Oct., Tues.–Sun. 9–5; Nov.–Feb., Tues.–Sun. 10–2.*

Outdoor Activities and Sports

Make a stop at the Eger tourist office (☞ Visitor Information *in* Northern Hungary A to Z, *below*) for maps, books, and advice about the area's rich outdoor offerings.

BICYCLING

Avar Túrakerékpár Klub (⊠ Béke út 4, Mátrafüred, ☎ 06–20/410– 102) is a good source for information and organizes custom-designed bicycle tours for all abilities. From mid-May through the end of the summer it also holds regular Saturday afternoon trips (meeting at

3 PM) open to all (though they don't provide bikes); call ahead to confirm details. Contact Tourinform (☞ Visitor Information *in* Northern Hungary A to Z, *below*) for bike-rental information.

Mátrafüred and Mátraháza are popular starting points for hikes up Kékestető, Hungary's highest peak. Views from the TV and lookout tower are phenomenal. Don't expect to find yourself alone with only the rushing wind at the top of the peak; it's actually somewhat developed, with a couple of hotels where you can spend a night dozing in the highest bed in Hungary.

The **Horus Riding Center** (⊠ Gyöngyvásár tér, ☎ 37/315–523) offers guided trail rides for groups of six or more, rides in outdoor and indoor rings, riding lessons, and carriage rides. It is closed Mondays.

En Route   Route 24 is the scenic route between Gyöngyös and Eger, climbing and twisting through the Mátras. You can pause in **Sirok** to snap a photo of its castle ruins, piled high on a hill looming over the village.

Eger

★ ⑦ *40 km (25 mi) east of Gyöngyös.*

With vineyard surroundings and more than 175 of Hungary's historic monuments—a figure surpassed only by Budapest and Sopron—the picturebook Baroque city of Eger is ripe for exploration. Lying in a fertile valley between the Mátra Mountains and their eastern neighbor, the Bükk range, Eger bears witness to much history, heartbreak, and glory. It was settled quite early in the Hungarian conquest of the land, and it was one of five bishoprics created by King Stephen I when he Christianized the country almost a millennium ago.

In 1552 the city was attacked by the Turks, but the commander, István Dobó, and fewer than 2,000 men and women held out for 38 days against 80,000 Turkish soldiers and drove them away. One of Hungary's great legends tells of the women of Eger pouring hot pitch onto the heads of the Turks as they attempted to scale the castle walls (the event is depicted in a famous painting now in the National Gallery in Budapest). Despite such heroism, however, Eger fell to the Turks in 1596 and became one of the most important northern outposts of Muslim power until its reconquest in 1687.

Today, Eger's cobblestone streets are ripe for strolling and sightseeing, lined with restored Baroque and rococo buildings. Wherever you wander, make a point of peeking into open courtyards, where you're likely to happen upon an otherwise hidden architectural gems.

The grand, neoclassical **Bazilika** (basilica), the second-largest cathedral in Hungary, was built in the center of town early in the 19th century. It is approached by a stunning stairway flanked by statues of saints Stephen, László, Peter, and Paul—the work of Italian sculptor Marco Casagrande, who also carved 22 biblical reliefs inside and outside the building. From June through August, organ recitals are given Monday through Saturday at 11:30 AM and Sunday at 12:45 PM. It's best to visit when no masses are being held—after 9 AM or before 7 PM. ⊠ *Eszterházy tér,* ☎ *36/316–592.* 🔄 *Free.* ☉ *Daily 6 AM–7 PM.*

The square block of a Baroque building opposite the basilica is a former **lyceum,** now the Eszterházy Teacher Training College. The handsome library has a fine trompe-l'oeil ceiling fresco that gives an intoxicating illusion of depth. High up in the structure's six-story observatory, now a museum, is a horizontal sundial with a tiny gold cannon, which, when filled with gunpowder, used to explode at exactly high noon. Also, the noonday sun, shining through a tiny aperture, makes a palm-size silvery spot on the meridian line on the marble floor. Climb higher to the "Specula Periscope" grand finale: In a darkened room a man manipulates three rods of a periscope—in operation since 1776—to project panoramic views of Eger onto a round table. Children squeal with delight as real people and cars hurry and scurry across the table like hyperactive Legos. ⊠ *Eszterházy tér 1,* ☎ *36/410–466.* ⊡ *170 Ft.* ☉ *Mid-Mar.–May, Tues.–Fri. 9:30–1:30, weekends 9:30–12:30; June–Sept., Tues.–Sat. 9:30–3:30, weekends 9:30–12:30.*

Eger's rococo **Cistercia templom** (Cistercian Church), closed for many years, has been reclaimed by the order and can be visited during mass on Sundays (held at 7, 8, and 10 AM and 7 PM); other times it can be viewed through a locked gate. The church was built during the first half of the 18th century. Its main altar (1770) is dominated by a splendid statue of St. Francis Borgia kneeling beneath Christ on the cross. ⊠ *Széchenyi u. 15,* ☎ *36/313–496.* ⊡ *Free.* ☉ *Mon.–Thurs. and Sat. 10–noon and 2:30–5:30, Sun. 11–noon and 2:30–5:30.*

NEED A BREAK?	On Eger's central pedestrian street, the **Dobos Cukrászda** (⊠ Széchenyi u. 6, ☎ 36/413–335) is a great spot to revive wearied sightseers with the house specialty, *Dobos Bomba* (chocolate-covered cake).

On a hilltop almost 1 km (½ mi) away from the end of Széchenyi utca is the light, lovely, dove-gray **Ráctemplom** (Serbian Orthodox Church), which contains more than 100 icon paintings on wood that look as if they were fashioned from gold and marble. ⊠ *Vitkovits u. 30,* ☎ *no phone.* ☉ *Tues.–Sun. 10–4.*

The **Nagypréposti palota** (Provost's House), on picturesque Kossuth Lajos utca, is a small rococo palace still considered one of Hungary's finest mansions despite abuse by the Red Army (soldiers ruined several frescoes by heating the building with oil). The Provost's House now serves as European headquarters of the International Committee of Historic Towns (ICOMOS) and is, alas, not open regularly to the public. ⊠ *Kossuth Lajos u. 4.*

During a brief stay in Eger (1758–1761), German artist Henrik Fazola graced many buildings with his work, but none so exquisitely as the multilevel, mirror-image twin gates to the **Megye Ház** (County Council Hall). Sent to Paris in 1889 for the international exposition, the gates won a gold medal 130 years after their creation. On the wall to the right of the entrance, note the sign that indicates the level of floodwaters during the flooding of the Eger stream on August 31, 1878. In fact, if you stay alert, you will see similar signs throughout this area of the city. Inside the Megye Ház is a museum with exhibits about Eger and Heves County in the 18th and 19th centuries. ⊠ *Kossuth Lajos u. 9,* ☎ *36/312–744.* ⊡ *100 Ft.* ☉ *Apr.–Oct., Tues.–Sun. 9–5.*

Eger Vár (Eger Castle), now a haunting ruin, was built after the devastating Tartar invasion of 1241–1242; when Béla IV returned from exile in Italy, he ordered the erection of mighty fortresses like those he had seen in the west. Within the castle walls, an imposing Romanesque cathedral was built and then, during the 15th century, rebuilt in Gothic style; today only its foundations remain. Inside the foundation area, a statue of Szent István (St. Stephen), erected in 1900, looks out benignly over the city. Nearby are catacombs that were built in the second half of the 16th century by Italian engineers. By racing back and forth through this labyrinth of underground tunnels and appearing at various ends of the castle, the hundreds of defenders tricked the attacking Turks into thinking there were thousands of them. The Gothic-style **Püspök Ház** (Bishop's House) contains the castle history museum and, in the basement, a numismatic museum where coins can be minted and certified (in English). There is also an art gallery, displaying Italian and Dutch Rennaissance works. A prison museum is near the main entrance. English-speaking guides are often available at the castle ticket booth, but it's best to call ahead and request one; tours cost roughly 250 Ft. ⊠ *Dózsa György tér,* ☎ *36/312–744.* ▨ *Castle 100 Ft., museums (including general castle admission) 280 Ft. Video and camera fees 500 Ft. and 200 Ft., respectively.* ☉ *Castle grounds Apr.–Oct., daily 6 AM– 8 PM; Nov.–Mar., daily 6 AM–5 PM. Exhibits Apr.–Oct., Tues.–Sun. 9–5; Nov.–Mar., Tues.–Sun. 9–3 (prison exhibit closed Nov. and Mar.; catacombs remain open on Mon.).*

Downtown, picturesque **Dobó tér** is marked by two intensely animated statues produced early in this century by a father-and-son team. *Dobó the Defender* is by Alajos Stróbl; the sculpture of a Magyar battling two Turks, by Stróbl's son, Zsigmond Kisfaludi-Stróbl. Their works flank the **Minorita templom** (Minorite church), which with its twin spires and finely carved pulpit, pews, and organ loft, is considered one of the best Baroque churches in Central Europe. *Church:* ▨ *Free.* ☉ *Daily 10–5.*

A bridge over the Eger stream—it's too small to be classified as a river— leads to an early 17th-century Turkish **minaret,** from the top of which Muslims were called to prayer; this is the northernmost surviving Turkish building in Europe. ⊠ *Torony u.* ▨ *80 Ft.* ☉ *Apr.– Sept., daily 9–6.*

Eger wine is renowned beyond Hungary. The best-known variety is *Egri Bikavér* (Bull's Blood of Eger), a full-bodied red wine. Other outstanding vintages are the *Medoc Noir,* a dark red dessert wine; *Leányka,* a delightful dry white; and the sweeter white *Muskotály.* The place to sample them is the **Szépasszony-völgy,** a vineyard area within Eger's city limits. Some 250 small wine cellars (some of them literally holes-in-the-wall and most of them now private) stand open and inviting in the warm weather, and a few are there in winter, too. You may be given a tour of the cellar, and wines will be tapped from the barrel into your glass by the vintner himself at the tiniest cost (but it's prudent to inquire politely how much it will cost before imbibing).

Dining and Lodging

$$ ✕ **Fehér Szarvas.** The name of this rustic cellar adjoining the Hotel Park (☞ *below*) means "white stag," and game is the uncontested specialty: venison fillet served in a pan sizzling with chicken liver, sausage, and herb butter; leg of wild boar in a red-wine sauce of mushrooms and bacon. The skulls and skins hanging from rafters and walls make the inn look like Archduke Franz Ferdinand's trophy room. ⊠ *Klapka György u. 8,* ☎ *36/411–129. AE, MC, V. No lunch.*

$–$$ ✕ **Talizmán.** In a rustic arched basement room a few doors away from
★ Eger's castle gate, this is one of the most popular restaurants in the region (many people make the trip from Budapest just to eat here). The menu, in English and German, features *legényfogó leves* (wedding soup or, literally, "catcher of young men"). Made with meat, vegetables, cream, and liver, this stew is one of the lures that Hungarian girls have used for centuries to attract potential husbands. ⊠ *Kossuth Lajos u. 19,* ☎ *36/410–883. Reservations essential. AE, V.*

$ ✕ **HBH Bajor Sörház.** Although designed to look like a Bavarian beer tavern, this place does not reek of hops or smoke. Instead, it's a lovely family restaurant decorated with sepia photos of old Eger. Specialties include a tart oxtail soup, served family style in a silver tureen, and the *sör ivó kedvence* (Beer Drinker's Delight)—a pork cutlet stuffed with brains and baked in a pastry crust. Both go well with the Munich Hofbräuhaus beer, brewed on the premises, which gives the house its initials. ⊠ *Bajcsy Zsilinszky u. 19 (on Dobó tér)*, ☏ *36/316–312. AE, MC, V.*

$$$ ⊡ **Hotel Eger-Park.** Two very different hotels share the same phone num-
★   ber and a connecting passageway but have separate addresses around the corner from each other. The Park is an old-fashioned grand hotel, very genteel, with spacious rooms, though it usually closes from November through March. The Eger, built in 1982, looks like a monstrous honeycomb from the outside, but is more tastefully and imaginatively modern inside; it's open year-round. Guests are free to use the facilities of both hotels. ⊠ *Park: Klapka György u. 8, H-3300,* ☏ *36/413–233,* ℻ *36/413–114.* ⊠ *Eger: Szálloda u. 1–3, H-3300,* ☏ *36/413–233,* ℻ *36/413–114. 159 rooms, 6 suites. 3 restaurants, 2 bars, pool, sauna, solarium, 2 tennis courts, bowling, health club, billiards, laundry services, meeting rooms. AE, DC, MC, V.*

$$$ ⊡ **Hotel Senator Ház.** This little inn sits on Eger's main square in a
★   lovely 18th-century town house. Rooms are bright and clean, decorated in pale tans and whites, and come equipped with large-hotel amenities, such as hair dryers and minibars. The miniature lobby, furnished with leather chairs and antiques, feels like a cozy, elegant study. ⊠ *Dobó tér 11, H-3300,* ☏ *36/411–711,* ☏ ℻ *36/320–466. 11 rooms. Restaurant, air-conditioning, free parking. AE, MC, V.*

$$ ⊡ **Minaret.** Although this modern hotel stands in contrast to the neighboring 17th-century Turkish tower, it manages to look as though it has been here forever. Rooms are nothing special, with dark-brown basic furnishings and brown-and-gray industrial carpeting, but the location and price (at the low end of this category) are excellent and the atmosphere friendly and informal. A tiny outdoor pool is an unusual touch for such a central hotel. ⊠ *Harangöntő u. 3–5, H-3300,* ☏ *36/410–233 or 36/410–020,* ☏ ℻ *36/410–473. 38 rooms with shower. Restaurant, outdoor pool. AE, MC, V.*

$–$$ ⊡ **Garten Panzió.** Named after its profusion of lilacs, geraniums, and acacias, this informal, family-run pension sits at the top of a quiet, rural hill, a 10-minute walk from Eger's main square. Rooms here are clean and brightened with fresh flowers and live plants; all have TVs but no telephones. The suites, with eat-in kitchens, are great for families. The smiling owners, Olga and Sanyi, can arrange tennis at the neighboring courts. You can request rates with or without breakfast. ⊠ *Legányi u. 6, H-3300,* ☏ *36/320–371. 7 rooms, 2 suites. Breakfast room. No credit cards.*

Nightlife and the Arts

Old Jack's Pub (⊠ Rákóczi út 28, ☏ 36/425–050) is a popular English-style pub just outside the center of town.

All summer long (June to mid-September), live **bands** play for free out on Kis Dobó tér, part of Eger's main square, nightly from 7 to 10 PM. The **Agria Fesztivál** (Agria Art Festival) runs June through July, featuring theater performances and concerts of musical genres from Renaissance to jazz to laser karaoke. Performances are held several times a week, usually in the lovely inner courtyard of the Franciscan Church. Every summer during the first two weeks of August, **Ünnepi Hetek a Barokk Egerben** (Festival Weeks in Baroque Eger) is held, a cultural festival offering classical concerts, dance programs, and more in Eger's

picturesque venues and streets and squares. In early September, the three-
to four-day **Szüreti Hetek Egerben** (Eger Harvest Festival) celebrates
the grape harvest with a traditional harvest parade through the town
center, ample wine tastings in the main squares, appearances by the
crowned Wine Queen, and an outdoor Harvest Ball on Dobó tér.

Outdoor Activities and Sports

BICYCLING

The forested hills of the Bükk National Park around the village of Szilvásvárad, north of Eger, comprise some of the country's most popular mountain-biking terrain. Rentals, maps, route advice, and tour guides
are available at Csaba Tarnai's **Mountain Bike Kölcsönző** (✉ Szalajka-
völgy út, at entrance to Bükk National Park in Szilvásvárad, Szalajka
Valley, ☎ 60/352–695).

HIKING

Bükk National Park, just north of Eger, has plenty of well-marked, well-
used trails. The most popular excursions begin in the village of Szilvásvárad. Tourinform (☞ Visitor Information *in* Northern Hungary
A to Z, *below*) can give you a hiking map and suggest routes according to the level of difficulty and duration.

HORSEBACK RIDING

A famous breeding center of the prized white Lipizzaner horses, the
village of Szilvásvárad (☞ Off the Beaten Path, *below*) is the center of
the region's horse culture. If you'd like to do some riding, contact **Kovács
Péter Lovardája** (Peter Kovács's Stable; ✉ Egri út 62, Szilvásvárad, ☎
36/355–343). In Eger, the stables at the **Mátyus Udvarház** (✉ Off Nosz-
vaji út, ☎ 36/312–804) can accommodate your every equestrian need.
Hourly rates in the area run around 1,800 Ft. for taking the reins into
your own hands outdoors. A one-hour carriage ride for up to three
people runs about 3,200 Ft.

SWIMMING

Eger's **Strandfürdo** (open-air baths; ✉ Petőfi Sándor tér 2, ☎ 36/
412–202) are set in a vast park in the center of town. You can pick
where to plunge from among six pools of varying sizes, temperatures,
and curative powers.

OFF THE
BEATEN PATH
SZILVÁSVÁRAD – About 25 km (16 mi) from Eger up into the Bükk
Mountains brings you to this picturesque village, one of Hungary's most
important equestrian centers. For more than 500 years, the white Lipizzaner horses have been bred here, and every year on a weekend in
early September they prance and pose in the Lipicai Lovasfesztivál, an
international carriage-driving competition held in the equestrian stadium.
At other times, you can see them grazing in the village fields and also
familiarize yourself with their proud history at the **Lipicai Múzeum** (Lipizzaner Museum). Szilvásvárad is also a popular base from which to take
advantage of the excellent hiking and biking opportunities through the
surrounding gentle green hills of Bükk National Park (☞ Outdoor Activities and Sports, *above*). *Lipicai Múzeum:* ✉ *Park u. 8,* ☎ *36/355–
155.* ▩ *60 Ft.* ☉ *Apr.–Oct. Tues.–Sun. 9–noon and 1–5.*

Miskolc

❼ *63 km (39 mi) northeast of Eger.*

East of the Bükk Mountains lies industrial Miskolc, the third-largest
city (population 200,000) in Hungary. A sprawling, dirty city cluttered
with factories and industrial plants (many of them now idle), Miskolc
is often maligned as one of the country's least desirable places to visit.

Yet it contains some interesting Baroque buildings, as well as the medieval castle of Diósgyőr, clashing yet coexisting with the housing projects and traffic that surround it. And one of Miskolc's prime, unexpected assets is the nearby beautiful countryside. As you travel west toward Lillafüred, past behemoth factories and plants, it's hard not to be wary of just what sort of countryside lies ahead; but almost immediately after passing the LEAVING MISKOLC sign and just before despair settles in, the scenery changes dramatically: The tree-covered hills of the Bükk range rise and crowd together as the road curves up and around them.

The regal, ruined stone body of **Diósgyőri Vár** (Diósgyőr Castle) stands exposed in the midst of Miskolc's urban clamor, as if trapped in a land that was long taken over by an entirely new reality. With four mighty towers, Diósgyőr is considered one of Hungary's most beautiful medieval castles. Built between the mid-13th and late 14th centuries, it was originally a retreat for King Louis I, of the Angevin dynasty, but was later adopted by the queens (the castle is also known as Queen's Castle). The opening hours can be erratic in winter; it's best to call ahead. ⊠ *Vár u. 24,* ☎ *46/370–735.* ☞ *250 Ft.* ☉ *Daily 9–6.*

Dining and Lodging

$$$ ✕⊞ **Hotel Palota.** As you round the bend on the road from Miskolc,
★   the fairy-tale spire of this hotel's tower rises majestically from a fold in the hills. Built in 1930, the Palota was a luxury hotel until World War II; in 1998, renovation brought it back to something like its old self. The lobby and other public rooms have soaring, ornately sculpted ceilings; rich woodwork; and epic frescoes. Some original furnishings are still here, including burgundy-velvet wallpaper, crystal chandeliers, and heavily carved wooden chairs. Guest rooms are fairly simple, with low-key wood furnishings and large windows, most looking out onto the surrounding greenery; they're equipped with minibars, TVs, and telephones. The striking Mátthiás Restaurant is in a round room with vaulted ceilings and original stained-glass windows depicting what were Hungary's most important cities. It specializes in game from the Bükk Mountains and trout from the nearby stocked lake; there's live traditional Hungarian music every evening. ⊠ *Erzsébet sétány 1, H-3517 Miskolc Lillafüred,* ☎ *46/331–411,* 𝔽𝔸𝕏 *46/379–273. 115 rooms, 18 suites. Restaurant, bar, indoor pool, sauna, solarium, fitness room, bowling, meeting rooms. AE, DC, MC, V.*

Aggtelek

🔞 *55 km (35 mi) north of Miskolc.*

One of the most extensive cave systems in Europe lies at Aggtelek, right on the Slovak border. Containing the largest stalactite system in Europe, the largest of the caves, the Baradla, is 24 km (15 mi) long, extending under Slovakia; its stalactite and stalagmite formations are of extraordinary size—some more than 49 ft high. In one of the chambers of the cave is a 600-seat concert hall, where classical concerts are held every summer. When the lights are left off for a brief period, you experience the purest darkness there is; try holding your hand up to your face—no matter how hard you strain, you won't see it.

Additional caves are being discovered and opened to the public. There are three entrances: in Aggtelek, at Vörös-tó (Red Lake), and in the village of Jósvafő. Guided tours vary in length and difficulty, from the short, one-hour walks beginning at Aggtelek or Jósvafő to the five- to eight-hour, 7-km (4½-mi) exploration. Of the shorter tours, the medium-length (2-hour) tour beginning at Vörös-tó is considered the best; the group congregates at Jósvafő and then takes a public bus (about 45

Ft.) to the Vörös-tó entrance, then makes its way back to Jósvafő underground. Although tours are conducted in Hungarian, written English translations are available at the ticket offices. Requests for the long tour must be sent in writing to the National Park headquarters at least one month ahead of time so the unmaintained sections can be rigged with proper lighting.

The caves are open year-round—they maintain a constant temperature, regardless of the weather. Keep in mind that it's chilly and damp underground—bring a sweater or light jacket and wear shoes with good traction. ⊠ *Directorate of Aggtelek National Park, Tengerszem oldal 1, H-3758 Jósvafő,* ☎ ℻ *48/350–006,* ℻ *48/343–073. 1-hr tours beginning at Aggtelek: Apr.–Sept., daily at 10, 1, 3, and 5, Oct.–Mar., daily at 10, 1, and 3;* ⊡ *450 Ft. 1-hr tours from Jósvafő: Apr.–Sept., daily at 10, noon, and 5, Oct.–mid-Mar daily at 10, noon, and 3;* ⊡ *350 Ft. 2-hr tours from Jósvafő: Apr.–Sept., daily at 8:45, 1:15, and 2:45, Oct.–Mar., daily at 8:45 and noon;* ⊡ *550 Ft. Long tour (with 1-month prior written request) from Aggtelek: 2,800 Ft. (minimum 5 adults or equivalent admission cost).*

Sárospatak

⑦⑨ *80 km (50 mi) northeast of Miskolc.*

For hundreds of years, this northern town at the foot of the Zemplén Mountains thrived as the region's elite cultural and intellectual center, its progressive Calvinist College (now a state-run school) educating such famous national thinkers as statesman Lajos Kossuth and writer Zsigmond Móricz. In 1616, Sárospatak's golden age began when its gorgeous castle became home to the famous Hungarian noble family, the Rákóczi, and was the scene of their unsuccessful plot to free Hungary from the Hapsburgs. Today, however, Sárospatak's reality is more that of an economically struggling eastern town. Its rich, historic aura, however, remains in its picturesque castle and many fine medieval houses.

The library of today's **Református kollégium** (Reformed College, formerly the Calvinist College) is treasured as one of the country's most beautiful. The main hall, designed by Mihály Pollack in 1817, is a grand yet refined open room with pillars stretching up to an ornately frescoed ceiling. Tours are given hourly; English-speaking guides are available. ⊠ *Rákóczi út 1,* ☎ *47/311–057.* ⊡ *170 Ft.* ⊙ *Mon.–Sat. 9–5.*

★ Poised on the bank of the Bodrog River, the part-Gothic, part-Renaissance, part-Baroque **Sárospatak vár** (Sárospatak Castle) is one of Hungary's most beautiful castles—now excellently restored. Begun in the 11th century, it was constructed and added to over several centuries. A six-lanced rose emblem, which signifies silence, marks the spot in the castle's northeast corner where the Rákóczi family conspired to incite a revolution against the Hapsburgs. The first, though unsuccessful, uprising was led by Ferenc Rákóczi I on April 9, 1670; in 1703, after his father's death, Ferenc Rákóczi II led a nine-year rebellion that was ultimately fruitless. The castle museum houses an excellent collection of antique furniture from the 16th to 19th centuries, portraits of the Rákóczi family, and various weapons and antique clothing. ⊠ *Szt. Erzsébet út 19,* ☎ *47/311–083.* ⊡ *200 Ft.* ⊙ *Mar.–Oct., Tues.–Sun. 10–6; Nov.–Feb., Tues.–Sun. 10–5.*

Dining and Lodging

$–$$ ✕⊞ **Hotel Bodrog.** Sárospatak's main hotel and restaurant is centrally located and adequately comfortable and clean but is trapped in its charmless, 1980s Communist institutionality. Inside the drab cement-block exterior are rooms with basic furnishings, though they do have televisions and minibars. One floor has air-conditioning. The restaurant has an extensive selection of wines from nearby Tokaj and serves standard Hungarian fare. Fresh grilled trout from the Bodrog River is a good bet. Breakfast is not included in the rates. ⊠ *Rákóczi u. 58, H-3950,* ☎ *47/311–744,* FAX *47/311–527. 50 rooms. Restaurant, sauna, meeting rooms. AE, MC, V.*

$ ✕⌂ **Hotel Borostyán.** This small hotel in a medieval building just steps from the castle was a monastery established by Ferenc Rákóczi II in the late 17th century. In true monastic style, rooms are on the small side, many with a small set of steps splitting them into two levels; furnishings are simple, with small beds and wood floors. The restaurant serves a good *Sárospataki cigánypecsenye,* garlicky pork cutlets topped with a sunny-side-up egg. ⊠ *Kádár Kata u. 28, H-3950,* ☎ *47/312–611,* FAX *47/311–551. 5 rooms with bath, 4 with shared toilet. Restaurant, sauna, solarium, exercise room. No credit cards.*

Nightlife and the Arts

In late July, the **Sárospatak Cultural Center** (⊠ Eötvös u. 6, ☎ 47/311–811) hosts a Dixieland and blues festival performed by Hungarian musicians. During the annual **Zempléni Művészeti Napok** (Zemplén County Arts Days) in mid- to late August, well-known musicians perform classical concerts in the castle's courtyard. For information, contact the Sárospatak Cultural Center (☞ *above*) or the IBUSZ office (☞ Visitor Information *in* Northern Hungary A to Z, *below*).

Tokaj

⑧⓪ *54 km (33 mi) east of Miskolc.*

This enchanting little village is the center of one of Hungary's most famous wine regions. It is home of the legendary Aszú wine, a dessert wine made from grapes allowed to shrivel on the vine. Aszú is produced to varying degrees of sweetness, based on how many bushels of sweet grape paste made from these grapes are added to the wine essence, the already highly sweet juice first pressed from them; the scale goes from two *puttonyos* (bushels) to nectar-rich six puttonyos.

The region's famed wines, dubbed (allegedly by Louis XV) the "wine of kings and king of wines," are typically golden yellow with slightly brownish tints and an almost oily texture and have been admired outside Hungary since Polish merchants first became hooked in the Middle Ages. In 1562, after a few sips of wine from the nearby village of Tállya, Pope Pius IV is said to have declared, *"Summum pontificem talia vina decent"* ("These wines are fit for a pope"). Other countries—France, Germany, and Russia included—have tried without success to produce the wine from Tokaj grapes; the secret apparently lies in the combination of volcanic soil and climate.

The surrounding countryside is beautiful, especially in October, when the grapes hang from the vines in thick clusters. Before or after descending into the wine cellars for some epic tasting, be sure to pause while the bells toll at the lovely Baroque Roman Catholic church (1770) on the main square and wend your way along some of the narrow side streets winding up into the vineyard-covered hills: Views of the red-tile roofs and sloping vineyards are like sweet Aszú for the eyes. If you can still focus after a round of wine tasting, be sure to look up at the top of lampposts and chimneys, where giant white storks preside over the village from their big bushy nests. They usually return to their nests in late April or May after wintering in warmer climes.

The third floor of **Tokaj Múzeum** (Tokaj Museum), housed in a late-18th-century building, displays objects connected with the history of the wine's production. The first and second floors contain exhibits of ecclesiastical art and the history of the county, respectively. ⊠ *Bethlen Gábor u. 7,* ☎ *47/352–636.* ▣ *180 Ft.* ☉ *Mar.–Oct., Tues.–Sun. 9–5; Nov.–Feb., Tues.–Sun. 9–4.*

Tokaj's most famous wine cellar, the nearly 700-year-old **Rákóczi-pince** (Rákóczi Cellar), is also Europe's largest, comprising some 1½ km (1 mi) of branching tunnels extending into the hills (today, about 1,312 ft are in use). Here you can sample Tokaj's famed wines and purchase bottles of your favorites for the road (all major credit cards are accepted). A standard cellar tour with a tasting of six different wines and some *pogácsa* (salty biscuits) costs around 1,200 Ft. (While these are not given in English, there are some English-language pamphlets available.) ⊠ *Kossuth tér 13,* ☎ *47/352–408.* ☉ *Mar.–Oct., daily 10–7 (July–Aug. until 8).*

The Várhelyi family offer wine tastings in the cool, damp cellar of their 16th-century house, called **Hímesudvar**. After the initial tasting, you can purchase bottles of your favorite wines and continue imbibing in their pleasant garden. A standard sampling of five different wines starts at around 500 Ft. If you don't see anyone on arriving, don't hesitate to ring the bell. ⊠ *Bem út 2,* ☎ *47/352–416.* ☉ *Daily 9–9.*

Dining and Lodging

Tokaj Tours (☞ Visitor Information *in* Northern Hungary A to Z, *below*) in can book you a room in a private home as well as in other hotels and pensions in the area.

$ ✕ **Róna Étterem.** In this simple dining room you can order excellent Hungarian dishes from goose liver to fresh carp. It's pleasantly decorated with original paintings by local artists. ⊠ *Bethlen Gábor u. 19,* ☎ *47/352–116. No credit cards. Closed Jan.–Feb.*

$ ✕▥ **Hotel Tokaj.** What is possibly the weirdest-looking building in the country houses Tokaj's main hotel. Giant red balls that look like clown's noses protrude from each boxy cement balcony under a rainbow-striped facade. There is talk every year of giving the building a makeover, but it may still be years away. Rooms are simply furnished and adequately comfortable, and most have balconies. The large, popular restaurant features excellent fish specialties, including spicy *halászlé* (fish soup) served with a swirl of sour cream. ⊠ *Rákóczi u. 5, H-3910,* ☎ *47/352–344,* ℻ *47/352–759. 42 rooms. Restaurant. AE, MC, V.*

$ ▥ **Makk Marci Panzió.** Rooms in this family-run pension in the center of town are clean and cozy. Reserve well ahead of time—the rooms fill up quickly. Breakfast is served in the pizzeria downstairs. ⊠ *Liget köz 1, H-3910,* ☎ ℻ *47/352–336. 7 rooms. Restaurant. AE, MC.*

Nightlife and the Arts

Classical concerts by well-known artists are performed here during the **Zemplén Művészeti Napok** (Zemplén Art Days), a countywide classical music festival held annually in mid-August. For information, contact Tourinform or Tokaj Tours (☞ Visitor Information *in* Northern Hungary A to Z, *below*).

Naturally, Tokaj's best festival is the annual **Szüreti Hét** (Harvest Week) in early October, celebrating the autumn grape harvest with a parade, a street ball, folk-art markets, and a plethora of wine-tasting opportunities from the local vintners' stands set up on and around the main square. For information, contact Tourinform or Tokaj Tours (☞ Visitor Information *in* Northern Hungary A to Z, *below*).

Northern Hungary A to Z

Arriving and Departing

BY BUS

Most buses to northern Hungary depart from Budapest's Népstadion station.

BY CAR

Highway M3 is the main link between Budapest and northern Hungary.

BY TRAIN

Trains between Eger and Budapest run several times daily from Keleti Station. Trains run frequently all day between Budapest and Miskolc.

Getting Around

BY CAR

The M3 is the main highway cutting north to Slovakia. Secondary roads through the Mátra and Bükk mountains are windy but in good shape and wonderfully scenic—this is the best way to see the region.

BY TRAIN

Several daily trains connect Miskolc with Sárospatak and Miskolc with Tokaj. Szilvásvárad and Eger are easily accessible from each other by frequent trains. The **Eger** train station (⊠ Állomás tér 1, ☏ 36/314–264) is about 1 km (½ mi) from center of town (a 20-minute walk). **Miskolc**'s station (⊠ Tiszai pályaudvar, ☏ 46/412–665) is about 15 minutes by bus or tram from the center of town.

Contacts and Resources

VISITOR INFORMATION

Eger: Tourinform (⊠ Dobó tér 2, ☏ 36/321–807, FAX 36/321–304). **Gyöngyös:** Tourinform (⊠ Fő tér 10, ☏ FAX 37/311–155). **Miskolc:** Tourinform (⊠ Minszent tér 1, ☏ FAX 46/348–921). **Sárospatak:** IBUSZ (⊠ Rákóczi u. 15, ☏ FAX 47/311–244). **Tokaj:** Tourinform (⊠ Serház u. 1, ☏ 47/353–390); Tokaj Tours (⊠ Serház u. 1, ☏ FAX 47/352–323).

THE GREAT PLAIN

Hungary's Great Plain—the Nagyalföld—stretches south from Budapest to the borders of Croatia and Serbia and as far east as Ukraine and Romania. It covers an area of 51,800 square km (20,000 square mi) and is what most people think of as the typical Hungarian landscape. Almost completely flat, it is the home of shepherds and their flocks and, above all, of splendid horses and the *csikós,* their riders. The plain has a wild, almost alien air; its sprawling villages consist mostly of one-story houses, though there are many large farms. The plain, which is divided into two almost equal parts by the Tisza River, also contains several of Hungary's most historic cities—it has much from medieval times (largely because it was never occupied by the Turks), and today it remains the least developed area of Hungary.

As you near the region, you will soon find yourself driving in a hypnotically straight line through the dream landscape of the Hortobágy, a grassy *puszta,* or prairie. Here, the land flattens out like a *palacsinta* (pancake), opening into vast stretches of dusty grassland interrupted only by stands of trees and distant thatched-roof *tanyák* (ranches), the only detectable movement the herds of *racka* sheep or cattle drifting lazily across the horizon guided by shepherds and their trusty *puli* herd dogs. Covering more than 250,000 acres, the Hortobágy became the first of Hungary's four national parks in 1973; its flora and fauna—including primeval breeds of longhorn cattle and *racka* sheep, prairie dogs, and *nóniusz* horses—are all under strict protection.

No matter how little time you have, you should make a point of taking in a traditional horse show, like the one offered by the Epona Riding Center in Máta. As touristy as the shows are, they are integral to the Great Plain experience, not to mention a lot of fun.

Debrecen

81 *226 km (140 mi) east of Budapest.*

With a population approaching a quarter of a million, Debrecen is Hungary's second-largest city. Though it has considerably less clout than Budapest, Debrecen was Hungary's capital twice, albeit only briefly. In 1849 Lajos Kossuth declared Hungarian independence from the Hapsburgs; in 1944, the Red Army liberated Debrecen from the Nazis and made the city the provisional capital until Budapest was taken.

Debrecen has been inhabited since the Stone Age. It was already a sizable village by the end of the 12th century and, by the 14th, an important market town. It takes its name from a Slavonic term for "good earth," and, indeed, much of the country's wheat, produce, meat, and poultry, has been produced in this area for centuries.

Today, Debrecen is a vibrant, friendly city, with a sizable population of young people attending its several esteemed universities. Debrecen has only one trolley line (appropriately numbered 1), but it runs fast and frequently in a nearly straight line from the railroad station along Piac utca and out to the Nagyerdő (Great Forest), a giant city park. All in all, it's a good place to spend a day exploring the sights before heading out for a puszta experience.

For almost 500 years, Debrecen has been the stronghold of Hungarian Protestantism—its inhabitants have called it "the Calvinist Rome." In 1536 Calvinism began to replace Roman Catholicism in Debrecen, and two years later the **Református Kollégium** (Reformed College) was founded on what is now Kálvin tér (Calvin Square). Early in the 19th century the college's medieval building was replaced by a pillared structure that offers a vivid lesson in Hungarian religious and political history: The facade's busts honor prominent students and educators as well as Calvin and Huldrych Zwingli. Inside, the main staircase is lined with frescoes of student life and significant moments in the college's history (all painted during the 1930s in honor of the school's 400th anniversary). At the top of the stairs is the **Oratory**, which has twice been the setting for provisional parliaments. In 1849 Lajos Kossuth first proclaimed Hungarian sovereignty here, and the new National Assembly's Chamber of Deputies met here during the last stages of the doomed revolution. Kossuth's pulpit and pew are marked, and two rare surviving flags of his revolution hang on the front wall. Some relics from 1944 line the back wall. Also worth seeing are the college's **library,** which rotates exhibitions of illuminated manuscripts and rare Bibles; and two **museums**—one of the school's history, the other of religious art. ⊠ *Kálvin tér 16,* ☎ *52/414–744.* ⊠ *70 Ft.* ⊙ *Tues.–Sat. 9–5, Sun. 9–1.*

Because the Oratory in the Reformed College was too small, Kossuth reread his declaration of independence by popular demand to a cheering public in 1849 in the twin-turreted **Nagytemplom** (Great Church). As befits the austerity of Calvinism, the Great Church is devoid of decoration, but, with all the Baroque architecture throughout Hungary, you may welcome the contrast. ⊠ *Kálvin tér 16,* ☎ *52/327–017.* ⊠

Church 50 Ft., tower 80 Ft. ⊙ *May–Oct., weekdays 9–4, Sat. 9–noon, Sun. 11–1; Nov.–Apr., Mon.–Sat. 10–noon, Sun. 11–1.*

The café in the majestic **Grand Hotel Arany Bika** (✉ Piac u. 11–15, ☎ 52/416–777) serves delicious, if somewhat expensive, coffees and pastries, daily 7 AM–midnight. Its intimate wood-paneled nooks are ideal for a private or romantic snack.

The **Déri Múzeum** (Déri Museum) was founded in the 1920s to house the art and antiquities of a wealthy Hungarian silk manufacturer living in Vienna. Its two exhibition floors are devoted to local history, archaeology, and weapons, as well as to Egyptian, Greek, Roman, Etruscan, and Far Eastern art. On the top floor are Hungarian and foreign fine art from the 15th to the 20th century, including the striking *Ecce Homo* by Mihály Munkácsy. ✉ *Déri tér 1, ☎ 52/417–560, ext. 577.* ▦ *90 Ft. (120 Ft. including Munkácsy exhibit).* ⊙ *Apr.–Oct., Tues.–Sun. 10–6; Nov.–Mar., Tues.–Sun. 10–4.*

Debrecen's main artery, **Piac utca** (Market Street), which has reverted to its old name after decades as Red Army Way, runs from the Great Church to the railroad station. At the corner of Széchenyi utca, the **Kistemplom** (Small Church)—Debrecen's oldest surviving church, built in 1720—looks like a rococo chess-piece castle. It is known to the locals as the "truncated church" because, early in this century, its onion dome was blown down in a gale. Across the street from the Kistemplom is the **Megyeház** (county hall), built in 1911–1912 in Transylvanian Art Nouveau, a darker and heavier version of the Paris, Munich, and Vienna versions. The ceramic ornaments on the facade are of Zsolnay majolica. Inside, stairs and halls are illuminated by brass chandeliers that spotlight the symmetry and delicate restraint of the decor. In the Council Hall upstairs, stained-glass windows by Károly Kernstock depict seven leaders of the tribes that conquered Hungary in 896. Note: The church is kept closed, except during mass, but the priests and caretakers next door at the church office are happy to open it for you during the hours listed below. *Kistemplom:* ✉ *Révész tér 2, ☎ 52/343–872.* ▦ *40 Ft.* ⊙ *Weekdays 9 AM–11:30 AM, Sun. 9:30–10 AM. Megyeház:* ✉ *Piac utca 54, ☎ 52/417–777.* ⊙ *Mon.–Thurs. 8–3:30, Fri. 8–1.*

★ The **Timárház** (Tanner House) opened in a restored 19th-century building in 1995 as the center for preserving and maintaining the ancient folk-arts-and-crafts traditions of Hajdú-Bihár county. In its delightful, small complex you can wander into the artisans' workshops and watch them creating exquisite pieces—from impossibly fine, intricately handmade lacework to colorful hand-loomed wool rugs. The artisans—among the best in the country—encourage visitors of all ages to try their hand at the crafts. The complex's showroom displays magnificent leather whips, heavy wool shepherd robes, and other examples of the county's traditional folk art; the embroidered textiles are some of the best you'll see anywhere. Although the displayed pieces are not for sale, the staff can help visitors contact the artists to custom-order something. A tiny gift shop, however, does sell a small selection of representative goods at great prices. ✉ *Nagy Gál István u. 6, ☎ 52/368–857.* ▦ *80 Ft.* ⊙ *Late Mar.–late Oct., Tues.–Fri. 10–6, Sat. 10–2; late Oct.–late Mar., Tues.–Fri. 10–5, Sat. 10–2.*

A 10-minute walk from the Megyeháza along Kossuth Lajos utca will take you to the 19th-century **Vörös templom** (Red Church), as remarkable a Calvinist church as you'll find anywhere in Europe. Outwardly an undistinguished redbrick house of worship, built with the usual unadorned interior, the church celebrated its 50th anniversary at the zenith of the applied-arts movement in Hungary. Its worshipers commissioned artist Jenő Haranghy to paint the walls with biblical allegories using no human bodies or faces (just an occasional limb) but rather plenty of grapes, trees, and symbols. Giant, gaudy frescoes covering the walls, ceilings, niches, and crannies represent, among other subjects, a stag in fresh water, the Martin Luther anthem "A Mighty Fortress Is Our God," and the 23rd Psalm (with a dozen sheep representing the 12 Tribes of Israel and the 12 Apostles). The Red Church is open only during religious services (10 AM on Sunday and religious holidays), but you might try for a private church visit from the deaconage (☎ 52/325–736) on Kossuth Lajos utca. ⊠ *Méliusz tér.*

Debrecen's one trolley line runs out to the **Nagyerdő** (Great Forest), a huge city park with a zoo, sports stadium, swimming pools, artificial rowing lake, a 20-acre thermal spa, amusement park, restaurants, open air theater, and the photogenic Kossuth Lajos University, its handsome neo-Baroque facade fronted by a large pool and fountain around which six bronze nudes pose in the sun. The university is one of the few in Central Europe with a real campus, and every summer, from mid-July to mid-August, it is the setting for a world-renowned Hungarian-language program.

Dining and Lodging

$$ ✕ **Csokonai.** Across the street from the Asian-style Csokonai Theater,
★ in a candlelit brick cellar, is Debrecen's best restaurant. It is a consistent winner of the gastronomic award *védnöki tábla*, a much-coveted honor. The restaurant is known for its shellfish, roasted-at-the-table skewered meats, frogs' legs, paprika crab, and many kinds of fish. One of the owner's innovations is to let guests cook their own meat *à la Willa-franca* (a hot old-fashioned iron that you press on the meat to cook it). ⊠ *Kossuth u. 21,* ☎ *52/410–802. No credit cards.*

$ ✕ **Sörpince a Flaskához.** When you walk into this completely unpretentious and very popular neighborhood pub, you may be surprised when you're presented with a nicely bound menu in four languages. The English section proclaims the virtues of "salty Hungarian pancake dishes," which include pancakes stuffed with fish and "Beer Cellar pancakes baked from salty batter stuffed with pork liver." They taste even better than they read. ⊠ *Miklós u. 4,* ☎ *52/414–582. AE, MC, V.*

$$$$ 🏨 **Grand Hotel Arany Bika.** The "Golden Bull" is an Art Nouveau clas-
★ sic erected in 1915; a wing was added to this downtown landmark in 1966. The guest rooms in the old ("grand") section are simple and attractive, with high ceilings, wood floors, and Oriental-style rugs; those in the newer, less-expensive "tourist" wing are clean but a bit institutional. The thermal spa facility comes complete with hydro-massage and in-house consultants. ⊠ *Piac u. 11–15, H-4025,* ☎ *52/416–777,* FAX *52/421–834. 230 rooms, 4 suites. Restaurant, café, indoor pool, sauna, spa, solarium, exercise room, casino, business services, meeting rooms. AE, DC, MC, V.*

$$$ 🏨 **Hotel Cívis.** Fronting on Debrecen's main square and backing onto a stylish shopping center of which it is a part, this hotel was originally built as an apartment house—hence the well-equipped kitchenettes in every room. The decor—inside and out—is uniformly brown; as if to reinforce the color scheme, there are plenty of sepia-toned photos of old Debrecen. Room rates include use of the neighboring Hotel Arany Bika's swimming and spa facilities. Try to get a room that's not facing the main street; those that do can be noisy. ⊠ *Kálvin tér 4, H-4026,* ☎ FAX *52/418–522. 60 rooms, 4 suites. Restaurant, 2 bars, sauna, business services, meeting room, parking (fee). AE, DC, MC, V.*

$ **⊞ Centrum Panzió.** This cheery little inn is just down the street from
★ the Great Church. Most guest rooms are in a charming, two-story yellow villa with a red-tile roof; casual, smaller rooms are in cozy, shel-
lacked log cabins. All rooms are immaculately neat, with contemporary
furnishings and satellite TVs with VCRs; suites also have well-stocked
kitchenettes (and one has a fireplace). Smoking is not permitted inside,
only in the garden. Rates do not include breakfast. ⊠ *Péterfia u. 37/
A, H-4026,* ☎ ℻ *52/416–193. 13 rooms, 7 suites. Breakfast room.
No credit cards.*

Nightlife and the Arts

One of Debrecen's main cultural venues is the **Csokonai Theater** (⊠
Kossuth u. 10, ☎ 52/417–811), which is devoted to theater productions (though none in English). The **Kölcsey Cultural Center** (⊠ Hunyadi u. 1–3, ☎ 52/419–647) is a full-fledged cultural center, with
everything from music, dance, and theater performances to aerobics
classes.

Debrecen summers are filled with annual cultural festivals. Preceding
the season, in mid- to late March, the **Debrecen Tavaszi Fesztivál** (Debrecen Spring Festival) packs two weeks full of concerts, dance and
theater performances, and special art exhibits. Main events are held
at the Csokonai Theater, the Bartók Hall, and the Kölcsey Cultural Center. Contact the Kölcsey Cultural Center (☞ *above*) or Tourinform for
information. The biannual **Bartók Béla Nemzetközi Kórusverseny**
(Béla Bartók International Choral Festival), held in 1998 and scheduled next for early July 2000, is a competition for choirs from around
the world and provides choral-music aficionados with numerous full-
scale concerts in the Bartók Hall. Jazz fans can hear local ensembles
as well as groups from around Hungary and abroad during the **Debreceni Jazz Napok** (Debrecen Jazz Festival) in mid-July. One of city's
favorite occasions is the **Debreceni Virágkarnevál** (Flower Carnival)
on St. Stephen's Day (August 20), when a festive parade of flower-encrusted floats and carriages makes their way down Debrecen's main
street along the tram line all the way to the Nagyerdő Stadium.

Outdoor Activities and Sports

The Great Forest is bubbling with thermal baths and pools. One complex, the **Nagyerdei Lido** (⊠ Nagyerdei Strand; ☎ 52/346–000), has
eight pools, including a large pool for active swimming (most people
soak idly in Hungary's public pools) and a wave pool.

A visit to the Great Plain is hardly complete without at least some contact with horses. There are several horseback-riding outfits outside Debrecen on the puszta; Tourinform (☞ Visitor Information *in* The Great
Plain A to Z, *below*) can help arrange excursions.

Hortobágy

㉒ *39 km (24 mi) west of Debrecen.*

The main visitor center for and gateway to the prairie is the little village of Hortobágy. Traveling from Debrecen, you'll reach this town
just before you would cross the Hortobágy River. Before heading out
to the prairie itself, you can take in Hortobágy's own sights: a prairie
museum, its famous stone bridge, and the historic Hortobágyi Csárda.

Crossing the Hortobágy River is one of the puszta's famous symbols:
the curving, white-stone **Kilenc-lyukú híd** (Nine-Arch Bridge). It was
built in the early 19th century and is the longest (548 ft) stone bridge
in Hungary. ⊠ *On Route 33, at Petőfi tér.*

Built in 1699, the **Hortobágyi Csárda** (Hortobágy Inn) has been a regional institution for most of the last three centuries. Its construction is typical of the Great Plain: a long, white stone structure with arching windows, brown-wood details, and a stork nest—and occasionally storks—on its chimney. Though it no longer has guest rooms, its restaurant and service facilities have expanded vastly in recent years (☞ Dining, *below*). ⊠ *Petőfi tér 2,* ☎ *52/369–139. Closed Jan.*

For a glimpse into traditional Hortobágy pastoral life, visit the **Pásztormúzeum** (Shepherd Museum), across the street from the Hortobágyi Inn. Exhibits focus on traditional costumes and tools, such as the shepherds' heavy, embroidered cloaks and carved sticks. The lot in front of the museum is the tourism center for the area, bustling with visitors and local touristic enterprises, including the helpful local Tourinform office. ⊠ *Petőfi tér 1,* ☎ *52/369–119.* 🎫 *250 Ft.* ☉ *Mid-May–Sept., daily 9–6; Oct. and Mar.–mid-May., daily 9–4; rest of the year with prior notice only).*

OFF THE
BEATEN PATH

HORTOBÁGYHALASTÓ – About 5 km (3 mi) west of Hortobágy, Hortobágyhalastó (Great Plain Fish Pond) is a tiny, sleepy hamlet at the end of a dirt road where chickens strut about and the center of town is essentially an old phone booth. However, it's not the village but the 5,000-acre-pond nature reserve of the same name at its edge that draws dedicated bird-watchers to look for some of the 150 species in residence. A nature walk around the entire reserve will take most of a day and requires advance permission from the Hortobágyi Nemzeti Park Igazgatóság (National Park's headquarters (⊠ Sumen u. 2, H-4024 Debrecen, ☎ 52/319–472 or 52/319–206, ℻ 52/310–645); contact Tourinform in Debrecen (☞ Visitor Information *in* the Great Plain A to Z, *below*) for assistance.

Dining

$ ✕ **Hortobágyi Csárda.** This historic roadside inn could get by on fame
★ and trappings alone—dried corn-and-paprika wreaths, flasks, saddles, and antlers hang from its rafters and walls—but the excellent food will grab your attention. This is the place to order the regional specialty: *Hortobágyi húsospalacsinta* (Hortobágy pancakes), which are filled with beef and braised with a tomato-and-sour-cream sauce. The portions are small, so follow the pancakes with *bográcsgulyás*—spicy goulash soup puszta style, with meat and dumplings. Veal *paprikás* and solid beef and lamb *pörkölt* (thick stews with paprika and sour cream) are also recommended, as are the cheese-curd or apricot-jam dessert pancakes. ⊠ *Petőfi tér 2,* ☎ *52/369–139. AE, DC, MC, V. Closed Jan.*

Nightlife and the Arts

The **Hortobágyi Lovas Napok** (Hortobágy Horseman Days) is held every year on the first weekend in July next to the Nine-Arch Bridge, offering three days of traditional horse stunts and demonstrations, colorful folklore shows, riding contests, and other horsey festivities. The festivities also take place in neighboring Máta.

The three-day **Hortobágyi híd vásár** (Hortobágy Bridge Fair), held annually around August 20, brings horse shows, a folk-art fair, ox roasts, and festive crowds to the plot beneath the famous Nine-Arch Bridge.

Máta

❽❸ *About 2 km (1 mi) southwest of Hortobágy.*

The hamlet of Máta is home to the **Epona Lovasfalu** (Epona Rider Village), with some 500 champion horses and award-winning riders, which over the last few years have made it the region's most important equestrian center. From around May through September there is a daily hour-and-a-half-long "Rangeman's Show." Groups of 16 can ride the prairie in covered wagons pulled by horses of the prize-winning *nóniusz* breed and driven by herders. You'll see herds of *racka* sheep with twisted horns, gray cattle, water buffalo, and wild boars, all tended by shepherds, cowherds, and swineherds dressed in distinctive costumes and aided by shaggy *puli* herd dogs and Komondor sheepdogs. At various stops along the route of this minirodeo, *csikós* (horsemen) do stunts with the animals; the best involves five horses piloted by one man who stands straddling the last two. Inspired guests can even try a little (less risky) riding themselves with help from the csikós. In winter and in bad weather, indoor shows are organized. Call ahead to inquire about arranging for an English-speaking guide. ✉ *Hortobágy-Máta,* ☎ *52/369–020.* ☞ *Riding shows and wagon tours 1,500 Ft.* ☉ *Departures at 10, noon, 2, and 4 (more frequently if demand warrants).*

Dining and Lodging

$$$$ ⊡ **Epona Rider Village.** This vast, luxury equestrian complex opened
★   in 1992 and has rapidly become one of Hungary's best and most imaginative resorts. The contemporary, puszta-style buildings house stables, family cottages, and special "rider houses," complete with private three-horse stables. The main building contains standard rooms, all with balconies and attractive contemporary furnishings. Tennis courts, a swimming pool, and myriad horse-related activities provide ample entertainment in an area otherwise considered to be the middle of nowhere. ✉ *H-4071 Hortobágy-Máta,* ☎ *52/369–020 or 52/369–092,* ℻ *52/369–027. 54 rooms, 4 suites. 2 restaurants, 2 bars, café, pool, massage, sauna, solarium, 2 tennis courts, exercise room, horseback riding, business services, meeting rooms. AE, DC, MC, V.*

Nightlife and the Arts

Equestrian fans will not want to miss the **Hortobágy International Horse Festival,** held here (and in neighboring Hortobágy) annually the first week of July, during which exciting show-jumping and carriage-driving competitions are held, as well as traditional horseback stunts by the csikós, folk-music and dance performances, and a folk-art fair.

Outdoor Activities and Sports

The **Epona Rider Village** (☞ *above*) offers horseback riding lessons (1,700 Ft. per half hour, beginner; 2,500 Ft. per hour, intermediate and advanced dressage) and guided rides out on the puszta (about 2,100 Ft. per hour) on its excellent horses.

Kecskemét

84   *191 km (119 mi) southwest of Debrecen.*

With a name roughly translating as "Goat Walk," this sprawling town smack in the middle of the country never fails to surprise unsuspecting first-time visitors with its elegant landmark buildings, interesting museums, and friendly, welcoming people. Its main square, Szabadság tér (Liberty Square), is marvelous, marred only by two faceless cement-block buildings, one of which houses the city's McDonald's (a true sign the city is not just a dusty prairie town anymore). Home of the elite Kodály Institute, where famous composer and pedagogue Zoltán Kodály's methods are taught, the city also maintains a fairly active cultural life.

The Kecskemét area, fruit center of the Great Plain, produces *barack pálinka,* a smooth yet tangy apricot brandy that can warm the heart and blur the mind in just one shot. Ask for home-brewed *házi pálinka,* which is much better than the commercial brews.

A short drive from town takes you into the expansive sandy grasslands of the Kiskunság National Park, the smaller of the two protected areas (the other is the Hortobágy National Park) of the Great Plain. You can watch a traditional horse show, do some riding, or immerse yourself in the experience by spending a night or two at one of the inns out on the prairie.

Until a small affiliated gallery opened recently in Budapest, the **Magyar Fotográfia Múzeum** (Hungarian Photography Museum) was the only museum in Hungary dedicated solely to photography. With a growing collection of more than 275,000 photos, documents, and equipment pieces, it continues to be the most important photography center in the country. The main exhibits are fine works by such pioneers of Hungarian photography as André Kertész, Brassaï, and Martin Munkácsi, all of whom moved and gained fame abroad. ⊠ *Katona József tér 12,* ☏ *76/483–221.* 🎟 *120 Ft.* ⊙ *Wed.–Sun. 10–5.*

The handsome Moorish-style **zsinagóga** (synagogue) anchoring one end of Liberty Square is beautifully restored but stripped of its original purpose. Today it is the headquarters of the House of Science and Technology, with offices and a convention center, but it also houses a small collection of Michelangelo sculpture reproductions from Budapest's Museum of Fine Arts. ⊠ *Rákóczi u. 2,* ☏ *76/487–611.* 🎟 *50 Ft..* ⊙ *Weekdays 8–4; closed during special events.*

Kecskemét's most famous building is the **Cifrapalota** (Ornamental Palace), a unique and remarkable Hungarian-style Art Nouveau building, built in 1902. A three-story cream-color structure studded with folksy lilac, blue, red, and yellow Zsolnay majolica flowers and hearts, it stands on Liberty Square's corner like a cheerful cream pastry. Once a residential building, it now houses the **Kecskeméti képtár** (Kecskemét Gallery), displaying artwork by Hungarian fine artists as well as occasional international exhibits. ⊠ *Rákóczi u. 1,* ☏ *76/480–776.* 🎟 *120 Ft.* ⊙ *Tues.–Sun. 10–5.*

NEED A BREAK?
You can treat yourself to fresh pastries or ice cream at the café that shares this book's name, the **Fodor Cukrászda** (Fodor Confectionery; ⊠ Szabadság tér 2, ☏ 76/497–545). It's right on the main square and is closed December 25–January 25.

★ Built in 1893–1896 by Ödön Lechner in the Hungarian Art Nouveau style that he created, the **Városház** (town hall) is one of the style's finest examples. Window frames are here arched, there pointed, and the roof, covered with tiny copper- and gold-color tiles, looks as if it has been rained on by coins from heaven. In typical Lechner style, the outlines of the central facade make a curvy line to a pointed top, under which 37 little bells add the finishing visual and auditory touch: Every hour from 7 AM to 8 PM, they flood the main square with ringing melodies from Kodaly, Beethoven, Mozart, and other major composers as well as traditional Hungarian folk songs. The building's **Dísz Terem** (Ceremonial Hall) is a spectacular palace of glimmering gold-painted vaulted ceilings, exquisitely carved wooden pews, colorful frescoes by Bertalan Székely (who also frescoed Budapest's Matthiás Church), and a gorgeously ornate chandelier that floats above the room like an ethereal bouquet of lights and shining brass. The hall is normally opened only to tour groups that have made prior arrangements. ⊠ *Kossuth tér 1,* ☏ *76/483–683.* 🎟 *Dísz terem 70 Ft.* ⊙ *Dísz Terem daily 8–9 AM.*

The oldest building on Kossuth tér is the **Szent Miklós templom** (Church of St. Nicholas), also known as the Barátság templom (Friendship Church) because of St. Nick's role as the saint of friendship. It was built in Gothic style in either the 13th or the 15th century (a subject of debate) but rebuilt in Baroque style during the 18th century. ⊠ *Kossuth tér 5.* ▣ *Free.*

The unusual, one-of-a-kind **Szórakoténusz Játékmúzeum és Műhely** (Szórakoténusz Toy Museum and Workshop) chronicles the history of Hungarian toys, beginning with archaeological pieces like stone figures and clay toys from medieval guilds; there are also changing international exhibits. In the workshop, artisans prepare traditional toys and invite visitors to try it themselves. Next door to the toy museum is the small **Magyar Naív Művészek Múzeuma** (Hungarian Naive Art Museum), where you can see a collection of this simple style of painting and sculpting created by Hungarian artists. ⊠ *Gáspár András u. 11,* ☎ *76/481–469.* ▣ *Museums 60 Ft., toy workshop 120 Ft.* ☉ *Toy Museum Tues.–Sun. 10–12:30 and 1–5; Naive Art Museum Tues.– Sun. 10–5; Toy Workshop alternate Sat. 10–noon and 2:30–5, Sun. 10–noon.*

OFF THE
BEATEN PATH

PIAC – As Kecskemét is Hungary's fruit capital, why not experience it firsthand by visiting the bustling *piac* (market), where—depending on the season—you can indulge in freshly plucked apples, cherries, and the famous Kecskemét apricots. Provided there is no sudden spring freeze, apricot season is around June through August. ⊠ *Budai u., near corner of Nagykörösi út.* ☉ *Tues.–Sun. 6–noon.*

Dining and Lodging

$$ ✕ **Liberté Kávéház.** This popular restaurant's location, right on Liberty Square, can't be beat. The seasonal menu features filling main dishes and meals-in-themselves soups. ⊠ *Szabadság tér 2,* ☎ *76/480–350. AE, MC, V.*

$–$$ ✕ **Kisbugaci Csárda.** Tucked away on a dark side street, this cozy eatery is warm and bright. The inner area has wood paneling and upholstered booths; the outer section has simple wooden tables covered with locally embroidered tablecloths and matching curtains. Food is heavy, ample, and tasty. Try the kitchen's goose specialties, like the *Bugaci libakóstoló*—a sampling of goose liver, thigh, and breast. Request a plate of dried paprikas if you really want to spice things up. ⊠ *Munkácsy u. 10,* ☎ *76/486–782. MC, V. No dinner Sun.*

$$ ✕▥ **Pongrácz Manor.** For total puszta immersion, spend a night or two
★ at this traditional Great Plain ranch, about 25 km (16 mi) from Kecskemét and 7 km (4½ mi) from the nearest little village. An attractive complex of whitewashed buildings with reed roofs, the manor has small, simple, and comfortable rooms with views onto the prairie. Those who dislike horses may not want to stay here, but horse lovers will be well occupied with riding opportunities (the stable houses some 70 horses), and there are plenty of chances to watch the resident champion csikósok do their daredevil stunts. Anglers can try their luck in the nearby lake; the restaurant's kitchen will cook to order whatever you catch (there's a limit of one fish per person, per day on what you can keep). Those without luck at the lake will not go hungry: The restaurant serves hearty regional dishes indoors or outside, many of which are baked in a traditional puszta wood-burning oven. The ranch is often booked up with tour groups, so reserve ahead. ⊠ *Kunpuszta 76, H-6041 Kerekegyháza,* ☎ ℻ *76/371–240. 26 rooms with bath, 5 rooms with shared bath, 4 suites. Restaurant, wine cellar, pool, sauna, 2 tennis courts,*

bowling, horseback riding, squash, fishing, billiards. No credit cards. Closed Jan.–Mar.

$$$ ⊞ **Arany Homok Hotel.** Kecskemét's biggest and best-known hotel has a prime location right on the picturesque main square—a delight for guests with windows facing the square but a shame for the square itself, which is marred by the hotel's heinous concrete-bunker design. Most rooms have pared-down blond-wood furnishings, generic gray wall-to-wall carpeting, and small bathrooms. All doubles have balconies. For quieter nights, avoid the rooms overlooking the bus station behind the hotel. Breakfast is not included in room rates. ⊠ *Kossuth tér 3, H-6000,* ☎ *76/486–286,* ℻ *76/481–195. 111 rooms, 4 suites. Restaurant, breakfast room, exercise room, casino, laundry service, meeting rooms, travel services. AE, DC, MC, V.*

$ ⊞ **Fábián Panzió.** It's hard to miss this very pink villa just off the main square. Inside, the pink (though muted) mixes with a white, turquoise, and lavender decor. The owners keep their pension immaculate: Floors in the tiny entranceway are polished until they look wet, and even the paths through the blooming back garden are spotless. Rooms—some in the main house and some in additional cottages in the garden—have extra amenities like air-conditioning (unusual outside of Budapest) and satellite TV. The largest and quietest rooms are in the back cottages. Breakfast is not included in room rates. ⊠ *Kápolna u. 14, H-6000,* ☎ *76/477–677,* ℻ *76/477–175. 10 rooms. Breakfast room, air-conditioning, laundry service. No credit cards.*

Nightlife and the Arts

The beautiful **Katona József Theater** (⊠ Katona József tér 5, ☎ 76/483–283) is known for its excellent dramatic productions (in Hungarian) and also hosts classical concerts, operas, and dance performances during the Spring Festival and other celebrations. The **Kodály Zoltán Zenepedagógiai Intézet** (Zoltán Kodály Music Pedagogy Institute; ⊠ Kéttemplom köz 1, ☎ 76/481–518) often holds student and faculty recitals, particularly during its biannual international music seminar in mid- to late July; the next one is scheduled for 1999.

Kecskemét's one- to two-week **Tavaszi Fesztivál** (Spring Festival) is held annually in mid-March and features concerts, dance performances, theater productions, art exhibits, and other cultural happenings by local and special guest artists from around the country and abroad. Every two years in early July, the city hosts a giant children's festival, **Európa Jövője Gyermektalálkozó** (Future of Europe Children's Convention), during which children's groups from some 25 countries put on colorful folk-dance and singing performances outside on the main square; the next one will be held in 2000.

For schedule and ticket information on all cultural events, contact Tourinform (☞ Visitor Information *in* The Great Plain A to Z, *below*).

Outdoor Activities and Sports

The nearby puszta is the setting for traditional horse-stunt shows, carriage rides, guided horseback rides, and other horsey activities. Full-length shows and daylong excursions are bus tour–centric (because of the costs involved), although essentially anything can be arranged if a smaller group or individuals are willing to pay for it. **Nyakvágó Kft.** (⊠ Kunszentmiklós, Bösztörpuszta-Nagyállás, ☎ ℻ 76/351–198 or ☎ 76/351–201) sometimes offers full- and half-day "Puszta Programs" for smaller groups of individuals who want to take part in the program on the same day. The program includes carriage rides, horse shows, a visit to a working farm, and folk dancing, all lubricated with wine and *pálinka* (brandy) and including typical puszta meals. A full-day program costs roughly 5,000 Ft., and a half day costs about 4,000 Ft. It's best to call a day or so in advance. Contact Tourinform or Bugac Tours (☞ Visitor Information *in* The Great Plain A to Z, *below, for both*) for other possibilities and for help making necessary arrangements.

Bugac

⑧⑤ *46 km (29 mi) south of Kecskemét.*

The Bugac puszta (Bugac Prairie) is the central and most-visited section of the 86,450-acre **Kiskunsági National Park**—the smaller sister of Hortobágy National Park (farther northeast); together they compose the entire Great Plain. Bugac puszta's expansive, sandy, impossibly flat grassland scenery has provided Hungarian poets and artists with inexhaustible material over the centuries. Although the dry, open stretches may seem numbingly uniform to the casual eye, the Bugac's fragile ecosystem is the most varied of the entire park; its primeval juniper trees, extremely rare in the region, are the area's most protected and treasured flora. Today, Bugac continues to inspire visitors with its strong equestrian traditions and the fun but touristy horse shows and tours offered in its boundaries. The park's half-hour traditional horse show is held daily at around 1 PM; its price is included in the entrance fee. You can also wander around the area and peek into the Kiskunság National Park Museum, which has exhibits about pastoral life on the prairie. *Park:* ⊠ *Bugac puszta.* ⊠ *1,500 Ft.* ☉ *Mid-Apr.–Oct., daily 9:30–5. Information:* ⊠ *Karikás Csárda,* ☎ *76/372–688; in Kecskemét,* ⊠ *Bugac Tours, Szabadság tér 5/a,* ☎ *76/481–643 or 76/482–500.*

Dining

$$ ✕ **Bugaci Csárda.** Bugac's most famous and popular restaurant is a tourbus magnet but is still considered a mandatory part of a puszta visit. It's at the end of a dirt road just past the park's main entrance, in a traditional whitewashed, thatched-roof house decorated inside with cheerful red-and-white folk embroideries. Here you can feast on all the Hungarian standards. ⊠ *Hwy. 54, next to park entrance,* ☎ *76/372–522. No credit cards. Closed Nov.–Mar.*

Outdoor Activities and Sports

The region specializes in equestrian sports. Possibilities for horseback-riding lessons, trail rides, and horse carriage rides abound. Contact **Bugaci Ménes** (☎ FAX 76/372–617) in Bugac; or **Bugac Tours** (⊠ Szabadság tér 5/a, Kecskemét, ☎ 76/482–500, ☎ FAX 76/481–643; ⊠ Karikás Csárda, Bugac, ☎ 76/372–688).

Szeged

⑧⑥ *87 km (54 mi) south of Kecskemét.*

The largest city in southern Hungary was almost completely rebuilt after a disastrous flood in 1879, using a concentric plan not unlike that of the Pest side of Budapest, with avenues connecting two boulevards like the spokes of a wheel.

Szeged is famous for two things: its open-air festival, held each year in July or August, and its paprika. But Szeged's paprikas are useful not only in goulash kettles but in test tubes as well: Local biochemist Albert Szentgyörgyi won the Nobel Prize in 1937 for his discoveries about vitamin C, extracted from his hometown vegetable. In late summer and early autumn, Szeged has a rich array of rack after rack of red peppers drying in the open air.

Although it lacks a large number of traditional sights, Szeged is a favorite place for young budget travelers who enjoy the dynamic atmosphere at its peak during the school year, when students from the city's schools and universities liven up the streets, cafés, and bars.

The heart of the inner city is the large **Széchenyi tér,** lined with trees and surrounded by imposing buildings. Most notable is the eclectic neo-Baroque **Városház** (town hall; ⊠ Széchenyi tér 10), built at the turn of the 19th century and after suffering major damage during the flood of 1879, reconstructed by well-known eclectic Art Nouveau architect Ödön Lechner. At the square's opposite end is the pale-green **Hotel Tisza** (⊠ Wesselényi u. 4), its guest rooms and lobby looking tired and worn but whose lovely and still active concert hall was the site of multiple performances by legendary composer Béla Bartók. Its restaurant was a favorite haunt of famous writer Mihály Babits.

NEED A BREAK?
Grab a hot strudel stuffed with apple, poppy seed, or peppery cabbage at the counter of **Hatos Rétes bakery** (⊠ Klauzal tér 6), a popular spot not only for a quick strudel but also palacsinta—salty (ham, cheese) or sweet (plum, raspberry, chestnut).

★ Szeged's most striking building is the **Fogadalmi Templom** (Votive Church), an imposing neo-Romanesque brick edifice built between 1912 and 1929 in fulfillment of a municipal promise made after the Great Flood. One of Hungary's largest churches, it seats 6,000 and has a splendid organ with 12,000 pipes. The church forms the backdrop to the annual Szegedi Szabadtéri Játékok (Szeged Open-air Festival), held in vast Dóm tér (Cathedral Square). Outstanding performances of Hungary's great national drama, Imre Madách's *Tragedy of Man*, are given each summer at the festival, as well as a rich variety of other theatrical pieces, operas, and concerts. A performance of a different sort is given here daily at 12:15 PM, when the mechanical figures on the church's clock put on their five-minute show to music. ⊠ *Dóm tér,* ☎ *62/312–157 or 62/323–955. Church:* ☞ *Free.* ☉ *Mon.–Wed. and Fri.–Sat. 8:30–5:30, Thurs. 12:30–5:30, Sun. 1–5:30. Crypt:* ☞ *50 Ft.* ☉ *Apr.–Sept., Tues–Sun. 10–2.*

Szeged's **Régi Zsinagóga** (Old Synagogue) was built in 1839 in neoclassical style. On its outside wall a marker written in Hungarian and Hebrew shows the height of the floodwaters in 1879. It is open only rarely for special events. ⊠ *Hajnóczi u. 12.* ☉ *Apr.–Sept., Sun.–Fri. 9–noon and 1–6*

★ Near the Old Synagogue, at the corner of Gutenberg utca and Jósika utca, is the larger **Új Zsinagóga** (New Synagogue), finished in 1905; it is Szeged's purest and finest representation of Art Nouveau. Its wood and stone carvings, wrought iron, and furnishings are all the work of local craftsmen. A memorial to Szeged's victims of Nazism is in the entrance hall. ⊠ *Gutenberg u. 20,* ☎ *62/423–849.* ☞ *150 Ft.* ☉ *Apr.–Oct., Sun.–Mon. 9–noon and 1–6; Nov.–Mar., Sun.–Mon. 9–1. Closed Jewish holidays.*

OFF THE BEATEN PATH
NEMZETI TÜRTÉNETI EMLÉKPARK – The ultimate in monuments to Hungarian history and pride is the enormous National Historic Memorial Park in Ópusztaszer, 29 km (18 mi) north of Szeged. It was built on the site of the first parliamentary congregation of the nomadic Magyar tribes, held in AD 895, in which they agreed to be ruled by mighty Árpád. Paths meander among an open-air museum of traditional village buildings. The main reason to come is the Feszty Körkép (Feszty Panorama), an astounding 5,249-ft 360-degree panoramic oil painting depicting the arrival of the Magyar tribes to the Carpathian Basin 1,100 years ago—effectively, the birth of Hungary. It was painted in 1892–1894 by Árpád Feszti and ex-

hibited in Budapest to celebrate the Magyar millennium. Sixty percent of it was destroyed during a World War II bombing, and it wasn't until 1991 that a group of art restorers brought it here and started a painstaking project to resurrect it in time for Hungary's millecentennial celebrations in 1996. Today, housed in its own giant rotunda, the painting is viewable as part of a multimedia experience: Groups of up to 100 at a time are let in every half hour for a 25-minute viewing of the painting, accompanied by a recorded explanation and, at the end, a special sound show in which different recordings are played near different parts of the painting—galloping horses, trumpeting horns, screaming virgins, rushing water—to the scene depicted. The attraction is so popular that on summer weekends it's a good idea to call ahead and reserve a spot in the slot of your choice (tickets are for a set showing). The explanation is in Hungarian, but English-language versions on CD, available at the entrance, can be listened to on headphones before or after the viewing. The panorama is the only park attraction open in winter. ⊠ *Szoborkert 68, Ópusztaszer,* ☎ *62/ 275–257 or 62/275–133.* 🎫 *Park 500 Ft., Feszty körkép and park 900 Ft.* ☉ *Apr.–Oct., daily 9–7; Nov.–Mar., daily 9–5.*

Dining and Lodging

$$ ✕ **Alabárdos Étterem.** This elegant eatery is housed in an 1810 landmark and its specialty is not just a meal but an experience: The lights are dimmed as waiters rush to your table with a flaming spear of skewered meats, which they then prepare in a spicy ragout at your table. ⊠ *Oskola u. 13,* ☎ *62/312–914. AE, MC, V. Closed Sun.*

$$ ✕ **Öreg Körössy Halászkert Vendéglő.** This traditional thatched-roof fisherman's inn on the Tisza River was first opened in 1930; decades later, the atmosphere is still rustic and festive, and the menu still features the original house staples like rich-red *Öreg Kőrössy halászlé* (fish soup), *Kőrössy* fish *paprikás,* and *sült hal* (whole roast fish)—all fresh from the Tisza. To appreciate the river's role further, take a look at the line on the wall marking the water's level during a flood in 1970. ⊠ *Felső-Tiszapart 1,* ☎ *62/327–410. No credit cards.*

$ ✕ **Botond Restaurant.** An 1810 neoclassical building that formerly housed Szeged's first printing press is now this popular restaurant. House specialties include *Tenkes-hegyi szűzérmek* (Tenkes Hill pork tenderloin), served with bacon, mushrooms, and paprika. Its outdoor terrace is a prime dining spot in good weather. ⊠ *Széchenyi tér 13,* ☎ *62/312– 435. AE, D, MC, V.*

$ 🛏 **Marika Panzió.** This friendly inn sits on a historic street in the Alsóváros (Lower Town), a five-minute drive from the city center. Cozy rooms have light-wood paneling and larger-hotel amenities like color TVs and minibars. The back garden has a small swimming pool. ⊠ *Nyíl u. 45, H-6725,* ☎ 🗚 *62/443–861. 9 rooms. Breakfast room, pool, free parking. No credit cards.*

Nightlife and the Arts

Szeged's own symphony orchestra, theater company, and famous contemporary dance troupe form the solid foundation for a rich cultural life. The **Szeged Nemzeti Színház** (Szeged National Theater; ⊠ Kárász u. 15, ☎ 62/476–555) stages Hungarian dramas, as well as classical concerts, operas, and ballets. Chamber-music concerts are often held in the conservatory and in the historic recital hall of the **Hotel Tisza** (⊠ Wesselényi u. 1). Szeged's most important event, drawing crowds from around the country, is the annual **Szegedi Szabadtéri Napok** (Szeged Open-Air Festival), a tradition established in the 1930s, held mid-July through most of August. The gala series of dramas, operas, operettas, classical concerts, and folk-dance performances by Hungarian and international artists is held outdoors on the vast cobblestone Dóm tér

(Cathedral Square). Tickets are always hot commodities; plan far ahead. For tickets and information, contact the ticket office (⊠ Deák u. 28–30, ☎ 62/471–411).

Shopping

You'll have no trouble finding packages of authentic **Szegedi paprika** in all sizes and degrees of spiciness in most of the city's shops. Szeged's other famous product is its excellent **salami** made by the local Pick Salami factory, which has been producing Hungary's most-famous, most-exported salamis since 1869. You'll find an extensive selection at the Pick factory outlet stores (⊠ Jókai u. 7, in Nagyáruház Passage, ☎ 62/421–860; ⊠ Maros u. 21, next to factory, ☎ 62/421–879).

The Great Plain A to Z

Arriving and Departing

BY BUS

Volánbusz operates service from Budapest's Népstadion and Erzsébet tér terminals to towns throughout the Great Plain.

BY CAR

From Budapest, the M4 goes straight to Debrecen, the M5 to Kecskemét and Szeged.

BY TRAIN

Service to the Great Plain from Budapest is quite good; daily service is available from the capital's Nyugati (West) and Keleti (East) stations. Express trains run between Budapest and Debrecen, Kecskemét, and Szeged. Trains also run from Romania into Debrecen.

Getting Around

BY BUS

Buses connect most towns in the region.

BY CAR

The flat expanses of this region make for easy, if eventually numbing, driving. Secondary-route 47 runs along the eastern edge of the country, connecting Debrecen and Szeged. Debrecen and Kecskemét are easily driven between as well via the M4 through Szolnok, then dropping south in Cegléd. The puszta regions of Bugac and Hortobágy are accessible from Kecskemét and Debrecen by well-marked roads.

BY TRAIN

The various parts of the region are connected via the rail junctions in Szolnok and Cegléd, in the geometric center of the Great Plain. The **Szeged** train station (⊠ Tisza pályaudvar, ☎ 62/421–821) is a 30-minute walk from town center; you can also take a tram. The trains for **Kecskemét** (⊠ Kodály Zoltán tér 7, ☎ 76/322–460) are on the Szeged line; the trip between the towns takes roughly an hour. The ride from Szolnok to **Debrecen** (⊠ Petőfi tér 12, ☎ 52/346–777) takes about an hour and a half.

Contacts and Resources

GUIDED TOURS

Gray Line Cityrama (in Budapest, ☎ 1/302–4382) runs day trips several times a week to the Great Plain from Budapest. They begin with a sightseeing walk through Kecskemet, then head out to the prairie town of Lajosmizse for drinking, dining, Gypsy music, carriage rides, and a traditional csikós horse show. The cost is approximately 14,000 Ft.

IBUSZ Travel (in Budapest, ☎ 1/318–6866) also operates full-day tours out to the Great Plain, to Lajosmizse as well as to Bugac, both first taking in Keckemét's sights. Costs run 14,000 Ft–15,000 Ft.

Bugac: Bugac Tours (✉ Karikás Csárda, Bugac, ☎ 76/372–688; ✉ Szabadság tér 5/a, Kecskemét, ☎ 76/482–500, FAX 76/481–643). **Debrecen:** Tourinform (✉ Piac u. 20, ☎ 52/412–250, FAX 52/314–139). **Hortobágy:** Tourinform (✉ Pásztormúzeum, ☎ 52/369–105). **Kecskemét:** Tourinform (✉ Kossuth tér 1, ☎ FAX 76/481–065). **Szeged:** Tourinform (✉ Victor Hugo u. 1, ☎ 62/311–711, FAX 62/312–509).

TRANSDANUBIA

Western Hungary, often referred to as Transdanubia (Dunántúl in Hungarian), is the area south and west of the Danube, stretching to the Slovak and Austrian borders in the west and north and to Slovenia and Croatia in the south. It presents a highly picturesque landscape, including several ranges of hills and small mountains. Most of its surface is covered with farmland, vineyards, and orchards—all nurtured and made verdant by a climate that is noticeably more humid than in the rest of the country.

The Romans called the region Pannonia (for centuries it was a frontier province; today it is far richer in Roman ruins than the rest of Hungary). Centuries later, the 150-year Turkish occupation left its mark on the region, particularly in the south, where it's not uncommon to see a former mosque serving as a Christian church. Austrian influence is clearly visible in the region's Baroque buildings, particularly in the magnificent Eszterházy Palace in Fertőd. Vienna, after all, is rarely more than a few hours' drive away.

En Route   Perched proudly above the countryside on top of a high hill on the way to Sopron—135 km (84 mi) west of Budapest, 100 km (62 mi) east of
★   Sopron—the vast, 1,000-year old Benedictine **Pannonhalma Apátság** (Pannonhalma Abbey) gleams like a gift from heaven. During the Middle Ages, it was an important ecclesiastical center and wielded considerable political influence. The abbey housed Hungary's first school and was allegedly the first place the Holy Scriptures were read on Hungarian soil. It's still a working monastery and school; 60 monks and 360 students live there. A late-Gothic cloister and a 180-ft neoclassical tower are the two stylistic exceptions to the predominantly Baroque architecture. The library of more than 300,000 volumes houses some priceless medieval documents, including the first to contain a large number of Hungarian words: the 11th-century deed to the abbey of Tihany. Visits are permitted only with a guide, which is included in the admission price. Tours begin every hour on the hour; last one of the day begins at the closing hour listed below. There are regularly scheduled English and other foreign-language tours at 11 and 1. Occasional organ recitals are held in the basilica in summer. ✉ *Pannonhalma, off Route 82 south of Győr,* ☎ *96/570–191,* FAX *96/570–162.* ⊡ *500 Ft. (750 Ft. for foreign-language guide).* ☉ *Late Mar.–May and Oct.–mid-Nov., daily 9–4; June–Sept., daily 9–5; mid-Nov.–late Mar., Tues.–Sun. 10–3; closed Sun. mornings and during mass.*

Numbers in the margin correspond to numbers on the Lake Balaton and Transdanubia map.

Sopron

★ ㊡   *211 km (131 mi) northwest of Budapest, 100 km (62 mi) west of Pannonhalma.*

Lying on the Austrian frontier, between Lake Fertő (in German, Neusiedlersee) and the Sopron Hills, Sopron is one of Hungary's most picturesque towns. Barely an hour away from Vienna by car, it is a bargain shopping center for many Austrians, who flock here for the day. The joke in Sopron is that every day at noon, "We play the Austrian national hymn so that the Austrians have to stand still for two minutes while we Hungarians shop." Dental work is also a bargain by Austrian standards; the town is chock-full of dentist advertisements in German, and nearly every hotel boasts an in-house dentist.

There is much more to Sopron, however, than conspicuous consumption by foreigners. Behind the narrow storefronts along the City Ring Várkerület (called Lenin Boulevard until 1989) and within the city walls (one set built by Romans, the other by medieval Magyars) lies a horseshoe-shape inner city that is a wondrous eclectic mix of Gothic, Baroque, and Renaissance, centered on Fő tér, the charming main square of perfectly proportioned Italianate architecture. Sopron's faithful and inspired restoration won a 1975 Europe Prize Gold Medal for Protection of Monuments, and the work continues slowly and carefully.

Today's city of 60,000 was a small Celtic settlement more than 2,300 years ago. During Roman times, under the name of Scarabantia, it stood on the main European north–south trade route, the Amber Road; it also happened to be near the junction with the east–west route used by Byzantine merchants. In 896 the Magyars conquered the Carpathian basin and later named the city Suprun for a medieval Hungarian warrior. After the Hapsburgs took over the territory during the Turkish wars of the 16th and 17th centuries, they renamed the city Ödenburg (Castle on the Ruins) and made it the capital of the rich and fertile Austrian Burgenland. Ferdinand III, later Holy Roman Emperor, was crowned king of Hungary here in 1625, and at a special session of the Hungarian Parliament in 1681, Prince Paul Esterházy was elected palatine (ruling deputy) of Hungary. And always, under any name or regime, Sopron was a fine and prosperous place in which to live.

A sightseeing note: For those who plan to visit as many museums as they can, one collective ticket covering most of Sopron's museums is available for 400 Ft.

The symbol of the town's endurance—and entranceway to the Old City—is the 200-ft-high **Tűztorony** (Fire Tower), with foundations dating to the days of the Árpád dynasty (9th–13th centuries) and perhaps back to the Romans. Remarkable for its uniquely harmonious blend of architectural styles, the tower has a Romanesque base rising to a circular balcony of Renaissance loggias topped by an octagonal clock tower that is itself capped by a brass Baroque onion dome and belfry. The upper portions were rebuilt after most of the earlier Fire Tower was, appropriately, destroyed by the Great Fire of 1676, started by students roasting chestnuts in a high wind. Throughout the centuries the tower bell tolled the alarm for fire or the death of a prominent citizen, and from the loggias live musicians trumpeted the approach of an enemy or serenaded the citizenry. Both warning concerts were accompanied by flags (red for fire, blue for enemy) pointing in the direction of danger. ⊠ Fő tér, ☏ 99/311–463. ⊞ 100 Ft. ☉ May–Sept., Tues.–Sun. 10–6; Oct.–Apr., Tues.–Sun. 10–2.

★ At No. 8 on Fő tér, Sopron's main square, is the city's finest Renaissance building: the turreted **Storno Ház** (Storno House). Inside its two-story loggia, a museum houses a remarkable family collection of furniture, porcelain, sculptures, and paintings. (There are tape-recorded tours available in English.) The Stornos were a rags-to-riches dynasty of chimney sweeps who over several generations bought or just relieved grateful owners of unwanted treasures and evolved into a family of painters and sculptors themselves. The dynasty died out in Switzerland and Germany a few years ago, but its heirs and the Hungarian state have agreed nothing will be removed from the Storno House. On an exterior wall of the house hangs a plaque commemorating visits by King Matthias Corvinus (1482–1483) and Franz Liszt (1840 and 1881). ⊠ *Fő tér 8,* ☎ *99/311–327.* ⊡ *100 Ft.* ☉ *May–Sept., Tues.–Sun. 10–6; Jan.–Apr. and Oct.–Dec., Tues.–Sun. 10–2. Upstairs museum can be visited by guided tour only, given every ½ hr (last one begins ½ hr before closing).*

A fine Renaissance courtyard leads to the **Rómaikori Kőtár** (Roman Archaeology Museum) in a churchlike vaulted medieval cellar—a perfect setting for the gigantic statues of Jupiter, Juno, and Minerva unearthed beneath the main square during the digging of foundations for the city hall a century ago. On the second floor a separate museum (with identical hours and admission prices) re-creates the living environment of 17th- and 18th-century apartments. ⊠ *Fő tér 6,* ☎ *99/311–327.* ⊡ *40 Ft.* ☉ *May–Aug., Tues.–Sun. 10–6; Sept., Tues.–Sun. 10–2.*

The 19th-century Angels' Drugstore is now the **Angyal Patika Múzeum** (Angel Pharmacy Museum), with old Viennese porcelain vessels and papers pertaining to Ignaz Philipp Semmelweis (1815–1865), the Hungarian physician whose pioneering work in antiseptics, while he was in Vienna, made childbirth safer. ⊠ *Fő tér 2,* ☎ *99/311–327.* ⊡ *40 Ft.* ☉ *Tues.–Sun. 9:30–noon and 12:30–2.*

The centerpiece of Fő tér, Sopron's exquisite main square, is a sparkling, spiraling three-tiered **Szentháromság szobor** (Holy Trinity Column), aswirl with gilded angels—the earliest (1701) and loveliest Baroque monument to a plague in all of Hungary.

Standing before Fő tér's Holy Trinity Column is the early Gothic (1280–1300) **Kecske templom** (Goat Church), named, legend has it, for a medieval billy goat that scratched up a treasure, enabling early-day Franciscans to build a church on the site (the Benedictines took over in 1802). More likely, however, the name comes from the figures of goats carved into its crests: the coat of arms of the Gutsch family, who financed the church. The Goat Church has a soaring, pointed, 14th-century steeple; three naves; its original Gothic choir (betraying French influence); and, after several rebuildings, a Hungarian Gothic-Baroque red-marble pulpit, a rococo main altar, Baroque altars, and a painting of St. Stephen by one of the Stornos. ⊠ *Fő tér at Templom utca.* ⊡ *Free.* ☉ *Daily 8–8.*

In the Gothic **Plébánia hivatal** (Chapter House) of the Goat Church, monks meditated, contemplating on the curved pillars the Seven Deadly Sins in sculptures similar to those atop Notre-Dame Cathedral in Paris. Avarice is a monkey; Lewdness, a bear; Incredulity, a griffin; Inconstancy, a crab crawling backward; and Vanity, a woman with a mirror in hand. ⊠ *Templom u. 1.* ⊡ *Free (donations accepted).* ☉ *Apr.–mid-Oct., daily 10–noon and 2–5.*

The medieval **zsinagóga** (synagogue), complete with a stone *mikva*, a ritual bath for women, is now a religious museum, with a plaque honoring the 1,587 Jews of Sopron who were murdered by the Nazis; only 274 survived, and today there are scarcely enough Jews to muster a *minyan* (quorum of 10), let alone a congregation. ⊠ *Új u. 22,* ☎ *99/311–327.* ⊡ *80 Ft.* ☉ *May–Aug., Wed.–Mon. 9–5; Sept., Wed.–Mon. 10–2.*

The **Cézár Ház** (Cézár House) has a wine cellar downstairs, but upstairs, in rooms where the Hungarian Parliament met in 1681, is a private **museum** created by the widow of József Soproni-Horváth (1891–1961), a remarkable artist who prefixed his hometown's name to his own so he wouldn't be just another Joe Croat. This Horváth nevertheless stands out for the wonders he worked with watercolors. He used that fragile medium to bring large surfaces alive in a density usually associated with oil paintings, while depicting realistic scenes, such as a girl grieving over her drowned sister's body. ⊠ *Hátsókapú u. 2,* ☎ *99/312–326.* 🎫 *100 Ft.* ⊙ *Thurs.–Sun. 10–1 (Sat. also 3–6).*

Along **Szent György utca** (St. George Street), numerous dragons of religion and architecture coexist in sightly harmony. The **Erdődy Vár** (Erdődy Palace) at No. 16 is Sopron's richest rococo building. Two doors down, at No. 12, is the **Eggenberg ház** (Eggenberg House), where the widow of Prince Johann Eggenberg held Protestant services during the harshest days of the Counter-Reformation and beyond. But the street takes its name from **Szent György templom** (St. George's Church), a 14th-century Catholic church so sensitively "baroqued" some 300 years later that its interior is still as soft as whipped cream. The church is generally open daily 9–5; the other buildings are not open to the public.

Mária szobor (St. Mary's Column), with its finely sculpted biblical reliefs, is a superb Baroque specimen. It was built in 1745 to mark the former site of the medieval Church of Our Lady, destroyed by Sopron citizens in 1632 because they feared the Turks would use it as a strategic firing tower. ⊠ *At the Előkapu (Outer Gate).*

....

NEED A
BREAK?
Tiny glass chandeliers and marble-topped tables grace the spacious **Várkapu Kávéház** (⊠ Hátsókapu u. 3, ☎ 99/311–523). Pick a fresh pastry to complement a potent espresso.

....

Strolling along **Várkerület,** the circular boulevard embracing Sopron's inner core, you'll experience a vibrant harmony of beautifully preserved Baroque and rococo architecture and the fashionable shops and cafés of Sopron's thriving downtown business district.

Dining and Lodging

$–$$ ✕ **Barokk Étterem.** The "Baroque Restaurant" opened in 1992, supplanting authentic Baroque designs with pastel colors and modern fixtures. Still, the entrance is through a lovely courtyard (though during the day it is crammed with racks of clothing from the neighboring boutiques), and the dining room has an arched ceiling. Specialties include meat fondue for two, trout, and beef Wellington with goose-liver stuffing. ⊠ *Várkerület 25,* ☎ *99/312–227. AE, MC, V. Closed Sun.*

$ ✕ **Corvinus.** The location, in the 700-year old Storno House on Sopron's delightful cobblestoned main square, couldn't be better. Sitting at the outdoor tables, you can practically do your sightseeing during lunch. Inside, the informal dining room has vaulted ceilings painted black with gold stars; downstairs is a cozy brick cellar lit by candles. The menu has an array of pizzas as well as Hungarian standards, such as roast goose liver. The special Hungarian soup comes in a small ceramic pot sealed with a baked-on pastry cap. ⊠ *Fő tér 7–8,* ☎ *99/ 314–841. AE, MC, V.*

$$$ ✕🏨 **Palatinus Hotel.** The location of this central hotel couldn't be better—it's within easy reach of every important sight. The interior shows its 1980s heritage; rooms are simply furnished with low wooden beds and generic carpeting. However, the staff is friendly and multilingual. Breakfast is served in the Palatinus's popular, informal restaurant, which prepares fresh, traditional Hungarian offerings all day. ⊠ *Új u.*

23, H-9400, ☎ ꜰᴀx 99/311–395. 25 rooms with shower, 4 suites. Restaurant, travel services. AE, DC, MC, V.

$$$$ 🖭 **Hotel Sopron.** On a hill just above the city core, this classy, mod-
★ ern hotel built in the early 1980s is blessed with gorgeous views of Sopron's steeples and rooftops. Rooms have contemporary furnishings;
those on the first two floors have balconies. Unless you prefer looking at the cemetery behind the hotel, request a room with a city view.
Only the suites have air-conditioning. ✉ Fövényverem u. 7, H-9400,
☎ 99/314–254, ꜰᴀx 99/311–090. 107 rooms, 6 suites. Restaurant, bar,
outdoor pool, sauna, solarium, 2 tennis courts, exercise room, bicycles, playground, meeting room. AE, DC, MC, V.

$$$$ 🖭 **Pannonia Med Hotel.** In the 17th century, the Golden Hind Inn stood
here, welcoming stagecoach travelers on their journeys between Vienna
and Budapest. Leveled by a fire, the inn was rebuilt in elegant neoclassical
style in 1893 to become the Pannonia Med Hotel. More than a century later, its public areas continue to shine, with soaring ceilings and
delicate chandeliers. Decor in standard guest rooms is disappointingly
less inspiring (as is the staff service), with comfortable but simple furnishings; at press time, however, plans were under way to refurnish all
rooms in period style. Several more expensive suites are decorated with
reproduction antiques. ✉ Várkerület 75, H-9400, ☎ 99/312–180, ꜰᴀx
99/340–766. 54 rooms, 12 suites. Restaurant, bar, air-conditioning,
beauty salon, pool, sauna, solarium, spa, meeting rooms, free parking. AE, DC, MC, V.

Nightlife and the Arts

From mid- to late March, Sopron's cultural life warms up during the
annual **Tavaszi Fesztivál** (Spring Festival), offering classical concerts,
folk-dance performances, and other events. Peak season for cultural
events is from mid-June through mid-July, when the **Sopron Ünnepi Hetek**
(Sopron Festival Weeks) brings music, dance, and theater performances
and art exhibits to churches and venues around town. Contact Tourinform (☞ Visitor Information *in* Transdanubia A to Z, *below*) or the
Theater and Festival Office (✉ Széchenyi tér 17–18, ☎ 99/511–730)
for details.

Outdoor Activities and Sports

The forested hills of the Fertő-Hanság National Park around Sopron
have many well-marked hiking trails. Ask for a map and advice at the
tourist office (☞ Visitor Information *in* Transdanubia A to Z, *below*).

Shopping

Várkerület is Sopron's main shopping street.

Herend Village Pottery (✉ Új u. 5, ☎ 99/338–668) sells high-quality
Herend ceramics hand-painted with tiny blue flowers and other cheerful, colorful patterns.

If you can't wait to shop at the less expensive factory outlet in Pécs
(☞ *below*), you can purchase exquisite Zsolnay porcelain at the **Zsolnay Márkabolt** (✉ Előkapu 11, ☎ 99/311–367), a tiny room lined
with glass cabinets displaying the delicate wares.

En Route   Twenty-seven kilometers (17 miles) southeast of Sopron in Fertőd, the
★ magnificent yellow Baroque **Eszterházy Palace,** built in 1720–1760 as
a residence for the Hungarian noble family, is prized as one of the country's most exquisite palaces. Though badly damaged in World War II,
it has been painstakingly restored, making it clear why in its day it was
referred to as the Hungarian Versailles. Its 126 rooms include a lavish
Hall of Mirrors and a three-story-high concert hall, where classical concerts are held in summer (usually Saturday at 6 ᴘᴍ). Joseph Haydn,

court conductor to the Eszterházy family here for 30 years, is the subject of a small museum inside. Slippers—mandatory, to preserve the palace floors—are provided at the entrance. ⊠ *Bartók Béla u. 2, Fertőd (just off Rte. 85),* ☎ *99/370–971.* ☜ *700 Ft.* ☉ *Mid-Apr.–mid-Oct., Tues.–Sun. 9–5; mid-Oct.–mid-Apr., Tues.–Sun. 9–4.*

Kőszeg

☎ *45 km (28 mi) south of Sopron.*

Clustered at an altitude of 886 ft in the forested hills near the Austrian border, Kőszeg is Hungary's highest and also one of its most enchanting little cities. Justly called the "jewel box of Hungary," Kőszeg is a living postcard of quiet cobblestone streets winding among Gothic and Baroque houses, with picturesque church steeples and a castle tower rising up in between.

Continually quarreled over by the Austrians and Hungarians, Kőszeg was designed with an eye for defense—a moat, a drawbridge, thick ramparts, and a 14th-century fortified castle were essential to its survival. It was from this castle in 1532 that a few hundred Hungarian peasant soldiers beat back a Turkish army of nearly 200,000 and forced Sultan Suleiman I to abandon his attempt to conquer Vienna. To celebrate Christianity's narrow escape, the bells of Kőszeg's churches and castle toll every day at 11 AM, the hour the Turks turned tail.

Music, too, reigned in Kőszeg: Haydn spent many of his creative years in Kőszeg as court composer to the Eszterházys; Franz Liszt gave a concert in 1846 in what is now just the shabby shell of Kőszeg's grandiose but beloved Ballhouse.

Jézus Szíve Plébánia Templom (Sacred Heart Church) is a creamy neo-Gothic concoction by Viennese architect Ludwig Schöne. Erected between 1892 and 1894, it is reminiscent both of Vienna's St. Stephen's Cathedral (for its mosaic roof and spires) and, inside, of Venice's San Marco (for the candy-stripe pillars supporting its three naves). If, after inspecting the church, you stand outside admiring its facade from Chernel utca at the right rear, you will see a wholly different church, with flying buttresses and wriggly little pinecone spires. While the church is generally open daily from 8 to 8, it is only accessible during mass. If you come to see the interior during a service, you must remain in the back of the church; there's usually a small window of opportunity (from about 8:30–9 AM) to explore the whole interior. A small admission may be charged. ⊠ *Fő tér at Várkör,* ☎ *94/360–195.*

The **Szent Jakab templom** (St. James Church) is the treasure of the city. St. James dates much further back than its 18th-century Baroque facade and even beyond its Gothic interior; in fact, St. James is the oldest church in Kőszeg. Inside are astonishingly well preserved 15th-century wall paintings, one of the Virgin Mary with mantle (painted, in fresco technique, on wet plaster) and one of a giant St. Christopher (painted *al secco,* on dry wall). ⊠ *Jurisics tér at Rajnis u.* ☜ *Free.* ☉ *Daily 9–5.*

Right next to St. James Church is the smaller **Szent Imre templom** (St. Emerich's Church). If you're wondering why two landmarks serving the same purpose were planted side by side, they symbolize Kőszeg's ethnic mix, formed over the centuries by Hungarian tribes moving west and by Germans expanding to the east. Not long after the Counter-Reformation, St. Emerich's Church converted to Catholicism and replaced many of its Protestant trappings with Baroque furnishings, most notably a high altar flanked by vivid statues of St. Stephen inviting and St. Ladislas defending the Virgin Mary. ⊠ *Jurisics tér at Chernel u.* ☒ *Free.* ☉ *Daily 9–5.*

Jurisics tér (Jurisics Square) was named after the Croatian captain Miklós Jurisics, who commanded Kőszeg's dramatic defense against the Turks in 1532. Like other fine squares in this part of Hungary, this one is not square but triangular.

On one side of Jurisics tér is a sprightly Gothic dowager of a **Városház** (city hall), dressed for a midsummer ball with red and yellow stripes skirting the ground floor; the upper level is decorated with fresco medallions of the Kőszeg, Hungarian, and Jurisics crests, painted in 1712. Inside the front door is a surprising courtyard with walls painted cool white and brown, reminiscent of a Hungarian *csárda* (inn). The interior is not open to the public. ⊠ *Jurisics tér 8.*

Jurisics Square converges on the handsome **Hősi kapu** (Heroes' Gate), whose imposing tower's Renaissance-Gothic facade belies its fairly recent construction, in 1932, to celebrate the 400th anniversary of the Turkish siege. This historic victory is commemorated in relief inside the portal, where another relief mourns Kőszeg's loss of life in World War I, a defeat that also cost the city two-thirds of its market for textiles and agriculture after the breakup of the Austro-Hungarian Empire. The observation tower affords fine views. ⊠ *Jurisics tér 6,* ☎ *94/ 360–240.* ☒ *120 Ft.* ☉ *Tues.–Sun. 10–5.*

The **Sgraffitóház** dates to the Renaissance, when sgraffito was still a respectable art form. It now houses a pizzeria. ⊠ *Jurisics tér 7.*

Beneath a loft for drying medicinal herbs, the **Apotéka az Arany Egyszarvúhoz** (Golden Unicorn Pharmacy) is now a pharmacy museum (Patika Múzeum) with antique furniture, equipment, and paintings related to the pharmacy's history. ⊠ *Jurisics tér 11,* ☎ *94/ 360–337.* ☒ *120 Ft.* ☉ *Apr.–Aug., Tues.–Sun. 10–5; Sept.–Mar., Tues.–Sun. 11–3.*

On the corner of Rájnis József utca and Várkör (City Ring), the street that girdles the inner town, you are welcomed into the old quarter by **statues of Sts. Leonard and Donatus.** The former carries a chain, for he is patron saint of prisoners and blacksmiths (as well as shepherds, animals, and sick people). The latter, the patron saint of wine, should hang his holy head a little. Kőszeg wine growers thrived until the turn of the 20th century, when phylloxera wiped out their industry. Now Kőszeg "imports" its wine from nearby Sopron. Rájnis utca nevertheless still has a few wine cellars, where the stuff is happily drunk with gusto.

NEED A
BREAK?

While you're in the town's historic wine district, it's only fitting to raise a glass or two at the **Kőszeg Szöllő Termelői Szövetkezete Borozója** (Kőszeg Vintners Association Winery; ⊠ Rajnis u. 16), in the cellar of a 15th-century Gothic house. It's usually closed on Mondays.

The **Jurisics Vár** (Jurisics Castle), which you enter by crossing two former moats, is named not for the nobility who have inhabited it over the years but for the Croatian captain Miklós Jurisics, who commanded its victorious defense against the Turks in 1532. In the first enclosure are a youth hostel, a bathhouse where the local brass band rehearses, and a modern (1963) statue of the heroic Jurisics. One of the most interesting exhibits in the **Jurisics Miklós Vármúzeum** (Jurisics Castle Museum), which has exhibits on the city's and the castle's histories, is the "Book of the Vine's Growth," a chronicle kept for more than a century and a half, starting in 1740, by a succession of town clerks whose duty was to trace the sizes and shapes of vine buds on April 24 of each year. The tradition is still played out the same time every year. ⊠ *Rájnis József u. 9,* ☎ *94/360–240.* 🖾 *120 Ft.* ☯ *Tues.–Sun. 10–5.*

Dining and Lodging

$ ✗ Ibrahim Kávézó. Named after a Turkish pasha, this small café has a strong Turkish theme, with a red canopy hanging above the tiny bar and bright-blue painted ceilings peppered with bronze studs. The larger back room has a kitschy fountain with a bronze cobra spitting water. Try the venison bourguignonne with potato dumplings. ⊠ *Fő tér 17,* ☎ *94/360–854. No credit cards.*

$ ✗ Kulacs Vendéglő. This informal eatery is popular for its central location near Fő tér, its home-style fare, and its low prices. If your arteries can handle it, try the *Kulacs pecsenye*: spareribs covered with fried onions and bacon and topped with a sunny-side-up egg. Typical Hungarian red-and-white embroidered tablecloths and curtains add a cheerful touch to the small dining room. ⊠ *Várkör 12,* ☎ *94/362–318. No credit cards.*

$$ 🏨 Írottkő. Centrally located on the town's main square, this modern hotel manages to blend in with the neighboring old houses. Its four-story atrium is sleek, and the guest rooms are functional but not so luxurious that you'd want to stay indoors when there's so much to see outside. The staff is friendly and multilingual. ⊠ *Fő tér 4, H-9730,* ☎ *94/360–373. 52 rooms with bath or shower. Pub. AE, DC, MC, V.*

$ 🏨 Alpokalja Pánzio. On the western edge of town along the highway to Austria, this cheerful, clean chalet-style pension is convenient if you're traveling by car. Clean, white-walled rooms are small and sunny. If views are important, be sure to avoid rooms that face the auto yard and train tracks out back. Breakfast is not included in room rates. ⊠ *Szombathelyi u. 8, H-9730,* ☎ 🖷 *94/360–056. 27 rooms with shower. Restaurant. AE, DC, MC, V.*

$ 🏨 Szálloda az Arany Strucchoz. This inn, built in 1718, is now one of the oldest hotels in Hungary. Although it is definitely showing its age, it has an excellent location: on the main square next to the Sacred Heart Church. The spacious rooms have wilting, bare-bones furnishings adequate for a decent night's sleep. Renovations are under way, however, and at press time the ground-floor café had been nicely revamped, while rooms were being outfitted with new bathrooms and color TVs. The corner room with 19th-century Biedermeier furnishings and a balcony looking onto the main square is the prize of the hotel—it's just a few dollars more than the standard rooms. ⊠ *Várkör 124, H-9730,* ☎ *94/360–323,* ☎ 🖷 *94/360–139. 18 rooms with bath or shower. Restaurant. No credit cards.*

Nightlife and the Arts

Kőszeg is anything but a night town. An evening's activity can usually center on dinner and a prebedtime stroll. For exact schedule and ticket information on cultural events, contact Savaria Tourist (☞ Visitor Information *in* Transdanubia A to Z, *below*).

Each year in late April, music and dance festivities are organized to celebrate the **szöllő rajzolás** (grape drawing), a tradition since 1740 in which the town clerks record the sizes and shapes of the year's vine buds in a special book on April 24. The town's biggest cultural event is the annual **Ost–West Fesztival** (East West Folk Festival) in mid-June— a weekend of open-air international folk music and dance performances on Fő tér, in the castle courtyard, and throughout the inner town. The grape **harvest** is usually celebrated in late September with a series of woodwind ensemble concerts and a harvest parade.

Pécs

71 *365 km (226 mi) southeast of Kőszeg, 197 km (122 mi) southwest of Budapest.*

The southwest's premier city and the fifth largest in Hungary, Pécs (pronounced *paytch*) is a vibrant, cultured, beautiful city that will leave you aesthetically and intellectually satiated. Pécs went through various incarnations in the course of its long history. The Franks called it Quinque Ecclesiae; the Slavs, Pet Cerkve; and the Hapsburgs, Fünfkirchen; all three names mean "five churches." Today there are many more churches, plus two mosques, and a handsome synagogue. In any language, however, Pécs could just as well be renamed City of Many Museums, for on one square block alone there are seven. Three of them—the Zsolnay, Vasarely, and Csontváry—justify a two- or three-day stay in this sparkling, eclectic city in the Mecsek Hills, just 30 km (19 mi) north of the Slovenian border.

At the foot of Széchenyi tér, the grand sloping monumental thoroughfare that is the pride of the city, stands the dainty **Zsolnay Fountain,** a petite Art Nouveau majolica temple guarded by shiny ox-head gargoyles made of green eosin porcelain that gush pure drinking water piped into Pécs via Roman aqueducts. The fountain was built in the early 19th century by the famous Zsolnay family, who pioneered and developed their unique porcelain art here in Pécs.

NEED A BREAK?	A short walk down pedestrians-only Király utca, opening from Széchenyi tér, is the **Caflisch Cukrászda** (✉ Király u. 32, ☎ 72/310–391), a small, informal café established in 1789 with tiny round tables and small chandeliers. Open until 10 PM, it is especially cozy in candlelight.

★ Széchenyi tér is crowned by a Turkish oddity that is a tourist's delight: a 16th-century mosque. Dating from the years of Turkish occupation (1543–1686), the mosque is now the Catholic **Belvárosi plébánia templom** (Inner City Parish Church), which you might infer from the cross surmounting a gilded crescent atop the dome. Despite the fierce religious war raging on its walls—Christian statuary and frescoes beneath Turkish arcades and mihrabs (prayer niches)—this church, also referred to as the Gazi Khassim Pasha Jammi, remains the largest and finest relic of Turkish architecture in Hungary. ✉ *Széchenyi tér.* ✆ *Free.* ☉ *Mid-Apr.–mid-Oct., weekdays 10–4, weekends 11:30–4; mid-Oct.–mid-Apr., weekdays 11–noon.*

★ Occupying the upper floor of the oldest surviving building in Pécs, the **Zsolnay Múzeum** (Zsolnay Museum) dates from 1324 and was built and rebuilt in Romanesque, Renaissance, and Baroque styles over its checkered history. A stroll through its rooms is a merry show-and-tell waltz through a revolution in pottery that started in 1851, when Miklós Zsolnay, a local merchant, bought the site of an old kiln and set up a stoneware factory for his son Ignác to run. Ignác's brother, Vilmos, a shopkeeper with an artistic bent, bought the factory from him in 1863, imported experts from Germany, and, with the help of a Pécs pharmacist for chemical experiments and his daughters for hand painting, created the distinctive, namesake porcelain.

Among the museums's exhibits are Vilmos's early efforts at Delft-blue handmade vases, cups, and saucers; his two-layer ceramics; examples of the gold-brocade rims that became a Zsolnay trademark; and table settings for royal families. Be sure to look up and notice the unusual Zsolnay chandeliers lighting your way. A new exhibit in the rooms across the hall re-creates a room in the family's home, to evoke a sense of the milieu in which they lived and worked. There is a Zsolnay store in the center of Pécs at Jokai tér 2 (☞ Shopping, *below*), where you can purchase a wide selection of ceramics. ⊠ *Káptalan u. 2,* ☎ *72/310–172.* 🎟 *180 Ft.* ☉ *Tues.–Sun. 10–6.*

If you haven't had enough Zsolnay after visiting the Zsolnay Museum, join the groups of tourists (usually German or Hungarian) braving heavily trafficked Zsolnay Vilmos utca to visit the **Zsolnay porcelán gyár** (Zsolnay Porcelain Factory), where gleaming monumental towers and statuary of seemingly pollution-proof porcelain hold their own among giant smokestacks. The factory can be visited by guided tour only with groups of 10–30. Call the factory or ask Tourinform to help find out when the next group is coming so that you can tag along.

On a hill behind the factory is the ultimate monument to the dynasty's founder, who died in 1900: the **Zsolnay Mausoleum,** with the bones of Vilmos and his wife in a blue ceramic well and, over the doorway, a relief of Vilmos, with disciples wearing the faces of his wife, daughters, and son kneeling before him. The mausoleum is open Tuesday–Sunday 10–6 and can be seen on approximately one-hour tours with a guide, provided on-site. For a tour in English, call ahead (☎ 06/30–297–803) to make sure it's available. Admission and tour fee for the mausoleum is 250 Ft. ⊠ *Zsolnay Vilmos u. 69, factory tour information* ☎ *72/325–266.* 🎟 *Free.*

The pioneer of Op Art (who later settled in France) was born Győző Vásárhelyi in 1908 in the funny house that is the **Vasarely Múzeum** (Vasarely Museum). The first hall is a corridor of visual tricks devised by his disciples, at the end of which hangs a hypnotic canvas of shifting cubes by Jean-Pierre Yvaral. Upstairs, the illusions grow profound: A zebra gallops by while chess pieces and blood cells seem to come at you. ⊠ *Káptalan u. 3,* ☎ *72/310–172.* 🎟 *180 Ft.* ☉ *Tues.–Sun. 10–6.*

Another museum on Káptalan Street is the **Endre Nemes Múzeum** (Endre Nemes Museum) with displays (accompanied by English texts) of the ceramics of Vilmos Zsolnay and his followers. Another section of the museum contains a street scene titled *Utca* (street), constructed entirely of white foam plastic by the sculptor Erzsébet Schaár. The people on the street are constructed of gypsum, simple in body structure but with finely drawn heads and faces—see if you can find Marx and Sándor Petőfi, the famous Hungarian poet. ⊠ *Káptalan u. 5,* ☎ *72/ 310–172.* 🎟 *120 Ft.* ☉ *Apr.–Oct., Tues.–Sun. 10–6.*

★ One of the three major galleries in Pécs, the **Csontváry Múzeum** (Csontváry Museum) is just around the corner from its peers; but if you've just left the Vasarely (☞ *above*) and you have the time, it's probably best to wait a day and bring a fresh eye to this next museum. Mihály Tivadar Csontváry Kosztka (1853–1919) was a pharmacist who worked, as he put it, to "catch up with, let alone surpass, the great masters." An early expressionist and forerunner of surrealism, Csontváry influenced Picasso; his work is to be found almost exclusively here and in a room of the Hungarian National Gallery in Budapest.

The paintings in the five rooms of the museum in Pécs are arranged to show Csontváry's progression from soulful portraits to seemingly conventional landscapes executed with decidedly unconventional colors to his 1904 *Temple of Zeus in Athens* (about which Csontváry said, "This is the first painting in which the canvas can no longer be seen"). After a 1905 tryout in Budapest, Csontváry was ready for a 1907 exhibition in Paris, which turned out to be a huge critical success. Not long after finishing his last great epic painting, *Mary at the Well in*

Nazareth (1908), megalomania gripped him. Though his canvases grew ever larger, Csontváry finished nothing that he started after 1909 except a patriotic drawing of Emperor Franz Joseph, completed at the start of World War I in 1914. The last room of the exhibit is filled only with sketches. After he died in Budapest in 1919, Csontváry's canvases were about to be reused as furniture covers when a collector from Pécs named Gedeon Gerlóczy rescued them with a ransom of 10,000 Ft. The collection in Pécs is now valued at more than $10 million. ⊠ *Janus Pannonius u. 11,* ☎ *72/310–172.* ▨ *180 Ft.* ☉ *Tues.–Sun. 10–6.*

★ One of Europe's most magnificent cathedrals is the famous **Pécs Bazilica** (Pécs Basilica), promoted from cathedral to basilica rank after Pope John Paul II's visit in 1991. At the beginning of the 19th century, Mihály Pollack directed the transformation of the exterior, changing it from Baroque to neoclassical; its interior remained Gothic. Near the end of the century, Bishop Nándor Dulánszky decided to restore the cathedral to its original Árpád-period style—the result is a four-spired monument that has an utterly breathtaking interior frescoed in shimmering golds, silvers, and blues. ⊠ *Szent István tér.* ▨ *180 Ft. (including treasury and crypt).* ☉ *Apr.–Oct., weekdays 9–5, Sat. 9–2, Sun. 1–5; Nov.–Mar., Mon.–Sat. 10–4, Sat. 10–1, Sun. 1–4.*

In front of Pécs Basilica is a small park, just beyond which is the 4th-century **Ókeresztény mauzóleum,** Hungary's largest and most important early Christian mausoleum. Some of the subterranean crypts and chapels date to its earliest days; the murals on the walls (Adam and Eve, Daniel in the lion's den, the Resurrection) are in remarkably good condition. ⊠ *Szent István tér,* ☎ *72/311–526.* ▨ *180 Ft.* ☉ *Tues.–Sun. 10–6.*

OFF THE
BEATEN PATH

VILLÁNY – Thirty kilometers (19 miles) south of Pécs, nestled in the low, verdant Villányi Hills, is the town of Villány, center of one of Hungary's most famous wine regions. Villány's exceptional and unique red wines are heralded here and abroad; its burgundies, cabernets, and ports are said to give the best of their French and Italian peers a run for the money. Many wine cellars offer regular wine tastings and sales. Tourinform in Pécs has an informative brochure and listing of cellars. Those who wish to educate themselves before imbibing can stop in the **Bor Múzeum** (Wine Museum; ⊠ Bem u. 8, ☎ 72/492–130) for a look at the history of the region's viticulture, which dates back some 2,000 years. The museum is open Tuesday through Sunday 9–5; admission is free.

Dining and Lodging

$$ ✕ **Iparos Kisvendéglő.** The very popular, informal Craftsman restaurant has a wide selection of pork, turkey, chicken, veal, and game dishes, as well as a small selection of fresh salads. ⊠ *Rákóczi út 24–26,* ☎ *72/333–400. AE, DC, MC, V.*

$–$$ ✕ **Cellárium.** Deep in an ancient cellar dating to Turkish times, this delightful restaurant has a cheerful, youthful atmosphere. The owner's creative touches include dressing the waiters in prison uniforms and putting the extensive, very reasonably priced menu into the form of a small newspaper titled *Cella News,* which guests can take home with them. Adventurous palates may try the "Hungarian stew with the comb and balls of cockerel," a rustic village dish rarely offered in restaurants. ⊠ *Hunyadi u. 2,* ☎ *72/314–453. MC, V.*

$–$$ ✕ **Dóm.** This small restaurant on Pécs's pedestrian shopping street is dominated by a giant wood-frame structure designed after the city's basilica. Dark wood pewlike booths and high frescoed ceilings further the theme. The menu includes Hungarian classics as well as the popular house specialty—a choice of meat on sizzling lava stones. ⊠ *Király u. 3,* ☎ *72/310–732. No credit cards.*

$$$ ⚏ **Palatinus.** This hotel maintains a good balance between old and new:
★ The building's facade has preserved its traditional look, while the rooms are modern in most every respect (equipped with TVs and telephones), though unexceptional in decor. Best views are from the fifth floor. The hotel's stunning ballroom, built in the Hungarian Secessionist style, is well suited for parties and conferences; in fact, the Hungarian composer Béla Bartók held a concert of his own here in 1923. You won't hear a roar of traffic; it's in the pedestrian zone. ⊠ *Király u. 5, H-7621,* ☎ *72/233–022,* FAX *72/232–261. 88 rooms, 6 suites. Restaurant, brasserie, massage, sauna, solarium. AE, DC, MC, V.*

$$ ⚏ **Toboz Panzió.** Nestled among the pines high up in the Mecsek Hills, the delightful Pinecone Pension offers forest tranquillity just a short drive or bus ride from downtown or 20–30 minutes by foot. Hiking trails into the hills begin just behind the house. Rooms are clean and bright, especially those with skylight windows. Room sizes vary, and some of the shower stalls in those without private bathrooms are awkwardly built right into the bedroom; for optimal comfort, request a large room with a private bath on the top floor. Breakfast is served for an additional charge. ⊠ *Fenyves sor 5, H-7635,* ☎ FAX *72/325–232 or 72/210–631. 12 rooms. Breakfast room. No credit cards.*

Nightlife and the Arts

NIGHTLIFE

British-style pubs are all the rage in Hungarian city nightlife, and the **John Bull Pub** (⊠ Széchenyi tér 1, ☎ 72/325–439), part of a successful chain around the country, plays the part well, done up with dark woods and polished brass and amply stocked with Guinness on tap. The **Fregatt Arizona Pub** (⊠ Király u. 21, ☎ 72/210–486), with pub-type decor and low vaulted ceilings, is another popular English-style bar with Guinness on tap.

THE ARTS

The **Pécsi Nemzeti Színház** (Pécs National Theater; ⊠ Színház tér 1, ☎ 72/211–965) is the main venue for regular performances by the Pécs Symphony Orchestra and the theater's opera and modern ballet companies. The theater is closed from late May until September, except for the **Nemzetközi Színházi Fesztivál** (International Theater Festival), held from late June into early July. **September** brings harvest-related festivities such as classical concerts, folk-music and -dance performances, and a parade or two to venues in and around Pécs. Inquire at Tourinform (☞ Visitor Information *in* Transdanubia A to Z, *below*) for specifics. Tourinform publishes a monthly arts and events calendar in English and can help with further schedule and ticket information.

Outdoor Activities and Sports

The **Mecsek Hills** rise up just behind Pécs, with abundant well-marked hiking trails through its forests and fresh air. Guided walks are often organized on Saturday or Sunday by local naturalist groups; contact Tourinform (☞ Visitor Information *in* Transdanubia A to Z, *below*) for dates and times.

Shopping

Kiraly utca, a vibrant, pedestrians-only street lined with beautifully preserved romantic and Baroque facades, is Pécs's main shopping zone, full of colorful boutiques and outdoor cafés.

The best place in the whole country to buy exquisite Zsolnay porcelain is at the **Zsolnay Márkabolt** (⊠ Jókai tér 2, ☎ 72/310–220). As the Zsolnay factory's own outlet, the store offers guaranteed authenticity and the best prices on the full spectrum of pieces—from tea sets profusely painted with colorful, gold-winged butterflies to white-and-night-blue dinner services.

Bookpoint (⊠ Mária u. 9, ☎ 72/312–010), in the International English Center, sells a variety of new and used English-language books and periodicals, as well as postcards and posters. It's closed Saturdays.

Pécs's **kirakodóvásár** (flea market; ⊠ Vásártér, ☎ 72/224–313) offers great browsing and bargain hunting among its eclectic mix of goods—from used clothing to handcrafted folk art to fresh vegetables. It's held every weekend (from 6 until noon or 1), but the first weekend of every month is always the best in quantity and variety.

Transdanubia A to Z

Arriving and Departing

BY CAR

From Budapest, you can get to Pannonhalma, Fertőd, and Sopron via the M1 through Győr, switching onto the appropriate secondary route there. Pécs and Budapest are directly connected by the M6. The M1 runs into Austria, the M6 to the border of Croatia.

BY TRAIN

There are good rail connections from Budapest to Sopron and Pécs; the trip takes roughly three hours. Trains to Sopron and Fertőd go north through Győr. There are direct connections between Vienna and Sopron and Bratislava and Győr.

Getting Around

BY BUS

If you're without a car, you'll need to rely on buses to get you to smaller towns like Pannonhalma, which are not on the rail lines. Regular buses link all of the towns in our coverage. Inquire at tourist offices (☞ Visitor Information, *below*).

BY CAR

Traveling around Transdanubia is done best by car: Except for Pécs, all the towns covered here are fairly short driving distances from one another. Significantly farther south and east, Pécs can be reached from Szombathely along connecting major secondary roads past the southern tip of the Balaton and through Kaposvár. It's a beautiful drive.

BY TRAIN

Trains connect most of the areas covered. The **Sopron** train station (⊠ Vasútállomás, ☎ 99/311–422) is a five-minute walk to center of town. The trip from Sopron to **Kőszeg** (⊠ Alsókörút 2, ☎ 94/360–053) is not direct; you'd have to change in Szombathely, south of Koszeg, which sends you a good 30 minutes out of your way. The trip from Sopron to **Pécs** (⊠ Indóhász tér, ☎ 72/212–734 or 72/212–003) is quite long—about an hour and a half from Sopron to Szombathely, where you transfer to the train to Pécs, which takes nearly four and a half hours.

Contacts and Resources

VISITOR INFORMATION

Kőszeg: Savaria Tourist (⊠ Várkör 69, ☎ FAX 94/360–238). **Pécs:** Tourinform (⊠ Széchenyi tér 9, ☎ 72/213–315, FAX 72/212–632). **Sopron:** Tourinform (⊠ Liszt Ferenc u. 1, ☎ 99/338–592, ☎ FAX 99//338–892).

HUNGARY A TO Z

Arriving and Departing

By Bus

There is regular bus service between Budapest and selected major cities in the region. From Budapest, buses to Bratislava and Prague depart from the Erzsébet tér station (☎ 1/317–2562 for international information). Buses to Krakow, Sofia, and Brasso operate from the Népstadion station (☎ 1/252–4496). Buses to the west and south, to Austria and the former Yugoslavia, leave from the main Volán bus station at Erzsébet tér in downtown Pest (☎ 1/317–2562 for international information). Though inexpensive, these buses tend to be crowded, so reserve your seat.

By Car

At press time, Hungary was continuing a massive upgrading and reconstruction of many of its motorways, gearing up for its role as the main bridge for trade between the Balkan countries and the former Soviet Union and Western Europe. Work is scheduled to continue beyond 2000. To help fund the project, tolls on major highways were introduced for the first time in 1996. Charging 1,400 Ft. per car for the section between Győr and the border, the much-heralded M1 from Budapest to Vienna continues to be the most expensive road to travel in Europe. M1 tolls can be paid in dollars and with major credit cards, as well. Other toll roads include the M5, from Budapest to just south of Kecskemét (and eventually through Szeged to Serbia), charging about 1,100 Ft., and the M3 (incomplete and still free at press time), from Budapest to Slovakia.

By Plane

See Arriving by Plane *in* Budapest A to Z, *above.*

Hungary's only commercial airport is **Ferihegy** (☎ 1/296–9696), about 22 km (14 mi) southeast of Budapest. All Lufthansa and Malév flights operate from the newer Terminal 2, 4 km (2½ mi) farther from the city; other airlines use Terminal 1. The only nonstop flight between Hungary and the United States is with **Malév Hungarian Airlines** (☎ 06/80–212–121 toll free, or 1/235–3804 [ticketing]), which flies between JFK International Airport in New York and Ferihegy. The flight lasts about nine hours.

Malév and other national airlines fly nonstop from most European capitals. **British Airways** (☎ 1/266–7790 or 1/318–3299) and Malév offer daily nonstop service between Budapest and London.

By Train

International trains are routed to two stations in Budapest (☞ Budapest A to Z, *above*). Keleti pályaudvar (Eastern Station) receives most international rail traffic coming in from the west. Nyugati pályaudvar (Western Station) handles a combination of international and domestic trains.

Getting Around

By Boat

Hungary is well equipped with nautical transport, and Budapest is situated on a major international waterway, the Danube. Vienna is five hours away by hydrofoil or boat. For information about excursions or pleasure cruises, contact **MAHART Tours** (✉ Belgrád rakpart, Budapest V, ☎ 1/318–1704 or 1/318–1586).

By Bus

Long-distance buses link Budapest with most cities in Hungary. Services to the eastern part of the country leave from the Népstadion station (☎ 1/252–4496). For the Danube Bend, buses leave from the bus terminal at Árpád Bridge (☎ 1/329–1450).

By Car

Getting around by car is the best way to see Hungary. It's a small country, so even driving across the whole territory is manageable. Speed traps are numerous, so it's best to keep at the speed limit; fines run around the equivalent of $25 and must be paid on the spot. Spot checks are frequent, as well, and police can occasionally try to take advantage of foreigners, so always have your papers at hand.

Gas stations have become plentiful in Hungary, and many on the main highways stay open all night, even on holidays. Major chains, such as MOL, Shell, and OMV, now have Western-style full-facility stations with rest rooms, brightly lit convenience stores, and 24-hour service. Lines are rarely long, and supplies are essentially stable. Unleaded gasoline (*bleifrei* or *ólommentes*) is generally available at most stations and is usually the 95-octane-level choice. If your car requires unleaded gasoline, be sure to double-check for leaded gas before you pump.

To drive in Hungary, U.S. and Canadian visitors need an International Driver's License—although their domestic licenses are usually accepted anyway—and U.K. visitors may use their own domestic licenses.

PARKING

Gone are the "anything goes" days of parking in Budapest, when cars parked for free practically anywhere in the city, straddling curbs or angled in the middle of sidewalks. Now most streets in Budapest's main districts have restricted, fee parking; there are either parking meters that accept coins or attendants who approach your car as you park and charge you according to how many hours you intend to stay. Hourly rates average 140 Ft. In most cases, overnight parking in these areas is free. Budapest also has a number of parking lots and a few garages; two central-Pest locations are: V, Szervita tér and V, Aranykéz u. 4–6.

Smaller towns usually have free parking on the street, and some hourly-fee lots near main tourist zones. Throughout the country, no-parking zones are marked with the international "No Parking" sign: a white circle with a diagonal line through it.

ROAD CONDITIONS

There are three classes of roads: highways or motorways (designated by the letter M and a single digit), secondary roads (designated by a two-digit number), and minor roads (designated by a three-digit number). Highways and secondary roads are generally in good condition. The conditions of minor roads vary considerably; keep in mind that tractors and horse-drawn carts may slow your route down in rural areas. In planning your driving route with a map, opt for the larger roadways whenever possible; you'll generally end up saving time even if there is a shorter but smaller road. It's not so much the condition of the smaller roads but the kind of traffic on them and the number of towns (where the speed limit is 50 kph [30 mph]) they pass through that will slow you down. If you're in no hurry, however, explore the smaller roads!

RULES OF THE ROAD

Hungarians drive on the right and observe the usual Continental rules of the road. Unless otherwise noted, the speed limit in developed areas is 50 kph (30 mph), on main roads 80–100 kph (50–62 mph), and on highways 120 kph (75 mph). Keep alert: Speed-limit signs are few and far between. Seat belts are compulsory, and drinking alcohol is totally prohibited—there is a zero-tolerance policy, and the penalties are very severe.

By Train
Travel by train from Budapest to other large cities or to Lake Balaton is cheap and efficient. Remember to take *gyorsvonat* (express trains) and not *személyvonat* (locals), which are extremely slow. On timetables, tracks (*vágány*) are abbreviated with a "v;" *indul* means departing, while *érkezik* means arriving. Trains get crowded during weekend travel in summer; you're more likely to have elbow room if you pay a little extra for first-class tickets. The Hungarian Railroad Inter-City express—which links the country's major cities—is comfortable, clean, fast, and almost always on time; a *helyjegy* (seat reservation), which costs about 300 Ft., is advisable.

Only Hungarian citizens are entitled to student discounts on train fares; non-Hungarian senior citizens (men over 60, women over 55), however, are eligible for a 20% discount. InterRail cards are available for those under 26, and the Rail Europe Senior Travel Pass entitles senior citizens to a 30% reduction on all train fares. Snacks and drinks are becoming less available on trains, so pack a lunch for the road; train picnics are a way of life. For more information about rail travel, contact or visit **MAV Passenger Service** (✉ Andrassy út 35, Budapest VI, ☎ 1/461–5500 international information, 1/461–5400 domestic information).

Contacts and Resources

B&B Reservation Agencies
See Apartment Rentals and B&B Reservation Agencies *in* Budapest A to Z, *above.*

Car Rentals
There are no special requirements for renting a car in Hungary, but be sure to shop around, as prices can differ greatly. **Avis** and **Hortz** offer Western makes for as much as $550 and more per week. Smaller local companies, on the other hand, can rent Hungarian cars for as low as $150 per week. Try to make rental arrangements before you get to Hungary; renting a car when you get there costs quite a bit more than an advance reservation. *See* Car Rentals *in* Budapest A to Z, *above,* for a list of agencies.

Foreign driver's licenses are generally acceptable by car rental agencies but are technically not valid legally; they are almost always accepted by the police, but it can get messy and expensive if you are stopped by a police officer who insists you need an International Driver's License (which, legally, you do).

Customs and Duties
ON ARRIVAL
Objects for personal use may be imported freely. If you are over 16, you may bring in 500 cigarettes or 100 cigars or 500 grams of tobacco, plus 1 liter of wine, 1 liter of spirits, 5 liters of beer, and 0.25 liters of perfume. A customs charge is made on gifts valued in Hungary at more than 21,000 Ft.

ON DEPARTURE
Take care when you leave Hungary that you have the right documentation for exporting goods. Keep receipts of any items bought from Konsumtourist, Intertourist, or Képcsarnok Vállalat. A special permit is

needed for works of art, antiques, or objects of museum value. Upon leaving, you are entitled to a value-added tax (VAT) refund on new goods (i.e., not works of art, antiques, or objects of museum value) valued at more than 25,000 Ft. (VAT inclusive). But applying for the refund may rack up more frustration than money: Cash refunds are given only in forints, and you may find yourself in the airport minutes before boarding with a handful of soft currency, of which no more than 10,000 Ft. may be taken out of the country. If you made your purchases by credit card you can file for a credit to your card or to your bank account (again in forints), but don't expect it to come through in a hurry. If you intend to apply for the credit, make sure you get customs to stamp the original purchase invoice before you leave the country. For more information, pick up a tax refund brochure from any tourist office or hotel, or contact **Intel Trade Rt.** (⊠ I, Csalogány u. 6-10, ☎ 1/201–8120 or 1/356–9800) in Budapest. For further Hungarian customs information, inquire at the **National Customs and Revenue Office** (⊠ IX, Mester u. 7, Budapest, ☎ 1/218–0017). If you have trouble communicating, ask Tourinform (☎ 1/317–9800) for help.

Emergencies
Ambulance (☎ 104). **Fire** (☎ 105). **Hungarian Automobile Club**'s Yellow Angels breakdown service (☎ 088). **Police** (☎ 107).

Guided Tours
BOAT TOURS
Contact **MAHART Tours** (⊠ Belgrád rakpart, Budapest V, ☎ 1/318–1704) for information about its roster of boat tours on Lake Balaton and on the Danube in and beyond Budapest.

GENERAL
IBUSZ Travel (☞ *below*) offers a variety of changing bus tours to places around the country, from cave visits in the Mátra Mountains to wine tasting in the Tokaj region to traditional pig roasts on the Great Plain.

Language
Hungarian (*Magyar*) tends to look and sound intimidating at first because it is not an Indo-European language. Generally, older people speak some German, and many younger people speak at least rudimentary English, which has become the most popular language to learn. It's a safe bet that anyone in the tourist trade will speak at least one of the two languages. Also note that when giving names, Hungarians put the family name before the Christian name.

Mail
Airmail letters and postcards generally take seven days to travel between Hungary and the United States, sometimes more than twice as long, however, during the Christmas season.

In Hungary, go to Budapest's main **downtown post office** branch (⊠ Magyar Posta 4. sz., Városház utca 18, H-1052 Budapest). The post offices near Budapest's **Keleti** (Eastern) (⊠ VII, Baross tér 11c) and **Nyugati** (Western) (⊠ VI, Teréz körút 51) train stations are open 24 hours. The **American Express** office in Hungary is in Budapest (⊠ Deák Ferenc u. 10 H-1052 Budapest, ☎ 1/266–8680); there are poste restante services.

POSTAL RATES
Postage for an airmail letter to the United States costs about 125 Ft.; an airmail letter to the United Kingdom and elsewhere in Western Europe costs about 115 Ft. Airmail postcards to the United States cost about 85 Ft. and to the United Kingdom and the rest of Western Europe, about 80 Ft.

RECEIVING MAIL

Although it's not recommended for urgent or valuable correspondences, a *poste restante* service, for general delivery, is available through any post office in Budapest. The envelope should have your name written on it, as well as "Posta Maradó" (*poste restante*) in big letters.

Money and Expenses

Eurocheque holders can cash personal checks in all banks and in most hotels. Many banks now also cash American Express and Visa traveler's checks. **American Express** has a full-service office in Budapest (⊠ V, Deák Ferenc u. 10, ☎ 1/267–2020, 1/267–2313, or 1/266–8680; FAX 1/267–2029), which also dispenses cash to its cardholders; two smaller branches on Castle Hill—in the Budapest Hilton Hotel (☎ 1/214–6446) and the Sisi Restaurant (☎ 1/264–0118)—have a currency exchange. Budapest also has a **Citibank** (⊠ V, Vörösmarty tér 4) offering full services to account holders, including a 24-hour cash machine.

Plastic has recently entered Hungary's financial scene: Most major credit cards are accepted, though don't rely on them in smaller towns or less expensive accommodations and restaurants. Twenty-four-hour cash machines have sprung up throughout Budapest and in major towns around the country. Some accept Plus network bank cards and Visa credit cards, others Cirrus and MasterCard. You can withdraw forints only (automatically converted at the bank's official exchange rate) directly from your account. Most levy a 1% or $3 service charge. Instructions are in English. For those without plastic, many cash-exchange machines, into which you feed paper currency for forints, have also sprung up. Most bank automats and cash-exchange machines are clustered around their respective bank branches throughout downtown Pest.

COSTS

The forint was significantly devalued over the last few years and continues its decline, but inflation has decreased to just under 20% from its previous annual rate of more than 25%. You'll receive more forints for your dollar but will find that prices have risen to keep up with inflation. More and more hotels now set their rates in hard currency to avoid the forint's instability. Still, even with inflation and the 25% value-added tax (VAT) in the service industry, enjoyable vacations with all the trimmings still remain less expensive than in nearby Western cities like Vienna.

CURRENCY

Hungary's unit of currency is the forint (Ft.), no longer divided into fillérs as it was a few years ago. There are bills of 50, 100, 200, 500, 1,000, 2,000, 5,000, and 10,000 forints; and coins of 1, 2, 5, 10, 20, 50, 100, and 200 forints. The exchange rate was approximately 205 Ft. to the U.S. dollar, 142 Ft. to the Canadian dollar, and 338 Ft. to the pound sterling at press time. Although cash card and Eurocheque facilities are becoming easier to find in big cities, it is probably still wise to bring traveler's checks, which can be cashed all over the country in banks and hotels. There is still a black market in hard currency, but changing money on the street is risky and illegal, and the bank rate almost always comes close. Stick with banks and official exchange offices.

SAMPLE COSTS

Cup of coffee, 100 Ft.; bottle of beer, 300 Ft.–400 Ft.; soft drinks, 100 Ft.; ham sandwich, 150 Ft.; 2-km (1-mi) taxi ride, 150 Ft.; museum admission, 100 Ft.–250 Ft.

National Holidays

January 1; March 15 (Anniversary of 1848 Revolution); April 4–5, 1999, April 22–23, 2000 (Easter and Easter Monday); May 1 (Labor

Day); May 23–24 (1999; Pentecost); August 20 (St. Stephen's and Constitution Day); October 23 (1956 Revolution Day); December 24–26.

Opening and Closing Times

Banks are generally open weekdays 8–2 or 3, often with a one-hour lunch break at around noon; most close at 1 on Fridays. Museums are generally open Tuesday through Sunday from 10 to 6 and are closed on Mondays; most stop admitting people 30 minutes before closing time. Many have a free-admission day; see individual listings in tours below, but double-check, as the days tend to change. Department stores are open weekdays 10–5 or 6, Saturdays until 1. Grocery stores are generally open weekdays from 7 AM to 6 or 7 PM, Saturdays until 1 PM; "nonstops," or *éjjeli-nappali,* are (theoretically) open 24 hours.

Outdoor Activities and Sports

BICYCLING

Tourinform (☞ *below*) in Budapest can provide you with the "Hungary by Bike" brochure and general information on current rental outfits. For specifics on bicycling conditions and suggested routes, contact the **Bicycle Touring Association of Hungary** (✉ V, Bajcsy-Zsilinszky út 31, 2nd floor, Apt. 3, ☎ 1/332–7177).

CAMPING

Most of the some 300 campsites in Hungary are open from May through September. Since rates are no longer state-regulated, prices vary. An average rate is 800 Ft. a day per site in Budapest and the Balaton region, slightly less elsewhere. There's usually a small charge for hot water, electricity, and parking, plus an accommodations fee—about 500 Ft. per person per night. Children under 14 frequently get a 50% reduction. Camping is forbidden except in appointed areas. Information, reservations, and an informative campsite listing and map can be obtained from travel agencies and Tourinform (☞ *below*) You may also contact the **Hungarian Camping and Caravanning Club** (✉ VIII, Üllői út 6, ☎ 1/333–6536).

GOLF

The **Hungarian Professional Golf Association** is based at Budapest Golfpark (☎ 1/317–6025, 1/317–2749, or 26/392–463) in Kisoroszi.

Passports and Visas

Only a valid passport is required of U.S., British, and Canadian citizens. For additional information contact the **Hungarian Embassy** in the United States (✉ 3910 Shoemaker St. NW, Washington, DC 20008, ☎ 202/362–6730), in Canada (✉ 299 Waverley St. Ottawa, Ontario K2P 0V9, ☎ 613/230–9614), in London (✉ 35b Eaton Pl., London SW1X 8BY, ☎ 0171/235–5218), or in Australia (✉ 17 Beale Crescent Deakin Act., Canberra 2600, ☎ 6126/282–3226).

Rail Passes

There are several passes valid in Hungary. You can use the **European East Pass** on the national rail networks of Hungary, Austria, the Czech Republic, Poland, and Slovakia. The pass covers five days of unlimited first-class travel within a one-month period for $199. Additional travel days may be purchased. For travel only within Hungary, there's a **Hungarian Flexipass,** which costs $55 for five days of unlimited first-class train travel within a 15-day period or $69 for 10 days within a one-month period. Hungary is also the rare Eastern European country which is covered by a **Eurailpass,** which provides unlimited first-class rail travel, in all of the participating countries, for the duration of the pass. These are available for 15 days ($538), 21 days ($698), one month ($864), two months ($1,224), and three months ($1,512). For further information, *see* Train Travel *in* the Gold Guide.

Student and Youth Travel

In Hungary, as a general rule, only Hungarian citizens and students at Hungarian institutions qualify for student discounts on domestic travel fares and admission fees. Travelers under 25, however, qualify for excellent youth rates on international airfares; those under 26 are eligible for youth rates on international train fares. The International Student Identity Card (ISIC) is accepted in Budapest and other large Hungarian cities, but not as widely as it is in Western countries. If you buy your Student Identity Card in Budapest at the **Express Youth and Travel Office** (⊠ V, Zoltán utca 10, ☎ 1/311–6418; ⊠ V, Szabadság tér 16, ☎ 1/311–7679; ⊠ VII, Keleti train station, ☎ 1/342–1772) which specializes in providing information on all aspects of student and youth travel throughout the country and abroad, it will cost about one-third the price of buying the card in the United States.

Telephones

Within Hungary, most towns can be dialed directly—dial 06 and wait for the buzzing tone; then dial the local number. Note that cellular phone numbers are treated like long-distance domestic calls: Dial 06 before the number (when giving their cellular phone numbers, most people include the 06 anyway).

Dial 198 for directory assistance for all of Hungary. Operators are unlikely to speak English. A safer bet is to consult *The Phone Book,* an English-language telephone directory full of important Budapest numbers as well as cultural and tourist information; it's provided in guest rooms of most major hotels, as well as at many restaurants and English-language bookstores.

Though continuously improving, the Hungarian telephone system is still antiquated, especially in the countryside. Be patient. With the slow improving of Hungary's telephone system comes the problem of numbers changing—sometimes without forewarning. Tens of thousands of phone numbers in Budapest alone will be changed over the next few years; if you're having trouble getting through, ask your concierge to check the number for you (or if the number begins with a 1, try dialing it starting with a 3 instead—many changes will be of this type).

COUNTRY CODE

The country code for Hungary is 36. When dialing from outside the country, drop the initial zero from the area code.

INTERNATIONAL CALLS

Direct calls to foreign countries can be made from Budapest and all major provincial towns by dialing 00 and waiting for the international dialing tone; on pay phones the initial charge is 60 Ft. To reach an **AT&T** long-distance operator, dial 00–800–01111; for **MCI** dial 00–800–01411; for **Sprint,** dial 00–800–01877.

LOCAL CALLS

Hungarian pay phones use 20 Ft. coins—the cost of a three-minute local call—and also accept 10-Ft. and 50-Ft.coins. Gray card-operated telephones outnumber coin-operated phones in Budapest and the Balaton region. The cards—available at post offices and most newsstands and kiosks—come in units of 50 (800 Ft.) and 120 (1,800 Ft.) calls. It is unnecessary to use the city code, 1, when dialing within Budapest. Don't be surprised if a flock of kids gathers around your pay phone while you talk—collecting and trading used phone cards is a raging fad.

Tipping

Four decades of socialism have not restrained the extended palm in Hungary—so tip when in doubt. Hairdressers and taxi drivers expect 10%

to 15% tips, while porters should get a dollar or two. Coatroom attendants receive 100 to 200 Ft., as do gas-pump attendants if they wash your windows or check your tires. Gratuities are not included automatically to restaurant bills; when the waiter arrives with the bill, you should immediately add a 10% to 15% tip to the amount, as it is not customary to leave the tip on the table. If a Gypsy band plays exclusively for your table, you can leave 200 Ft. in a plate discreetly provided for that purpose.

Travel Agencies

American Express (✉ V, Déak Ferenc u. 1, Budapest, ☎ 1/266–8680, FAX 1/267–2028). **Getz International** (✉ V, Falk Miksa u. 5, Budapest, ☎ 1/312–0645 or 1/312–0649, FAX 1/312–1014). **Vista Travel Center** (✉ VI, Andrássy út 1, Budapest, ☎ 1/269–6032 or 1/269–6033; FAX 1/269–6031).

Visitor Information

Tourinform (✉ V, Sütő u. 2, ☎ 1/317–9800). **Budapest Tourist** (✉ V, Roosevelt tér 5, ☎ 1/317–3555). **IBUSZ Travel** (✉ Central branch: V, Ferenciek tere 10, ☎ 1/318–6866; tours and programs: ✉ Rubin Aktiv Hotel, XI, Dajka Gábor u. 3, ☎ 1/319–7520, 1/319–7519). **IBUSZ Welcome Hotel Service** (✉ V, Apáczai Csere János u. 1, ☎ 1/318–3925 or 1/318–5776), open 24 hours.

5 Poland

A country of flowers and trees and sunshine, of outdoor cafés and Old World charm, Poland is at its best in late spring and summer. Not-to-be-missed locales include historic Kraków, a uniquely preserved Baroque city where one of Poland's most famous sons, Copernicus, studied; the wild lakelands of Mazuria, with nesting storks and other wildlife; the grand landscapes of the Tatra Mountains, with their local wooden-building styles, brown bears, and mountain pastures covered with wildflowers in spring and snow-covered slopes dotted with skiers in winter. The birthplace of Chopin, Poland also delights visitors with its musical and theatrical traditions.

Updated by
Eleanore H.
Boyse

POLES ARE FOND OF QUOTING, with a wry grimace, an old Chinese valediction: "May you live in interesting times." The times are certainly interesting in 1990s Poland—home of the Solidarity political-labor-social movement that sent shock waves through the Soviet bloc beginning in 1980, and the first Eastern European state to shake off Communist rule. But as the grimace implies, being on the firing line of history is a challenging place to be. There are constant reminders that the return to capitalism, after 45 years of sovietism, is an experiment on a vast and unprecedented scale, bringing hardships for many but also benefits for a growing percentage of the population. After the Berlin Wall came tumbling down in 1989, there was widespread rejoicing. Today, however, the country has a hangover, and the question everyone asks is whether Poland can afford an aspirin.

As it turns out—thanks to its NATO membership, healthy IMF ratings, and ever-increasing privatization of state companies—Poland probably can. This hopeful economic picture is one reason why Warsaw and Kraków are enjoying a cultural renaissance. Little wonder travelers are now flocking to Central Europe's largest country in ever greater numbers. They're coming to visit the beautifully preserved medieval city of Kraków, breathtaking mountains, the Hanseatic castles of Gdańsk, and the haunting Baltic seascapes, but most of all, they're coming to witness a nation in the process of rebirth.

With 39 million inhabitants living in a territory of 315,000 square km (121,000 square mi), Poland is still suspended between the old world and the new, and the contrasts are many. You will see bright, new, privately owned shops in shabby buildings that have not been renovated for decades. Billboards glowingly advertise goods that most Poles cannot afford. Many public services, such as education and health care, are woefully underfunded as local authorities strive valiantly to satisfy voters' quickly rising expectations. Still, the Poles are intent on focusing on the future, not looking back to the past. Step inside faded, Communist-era buildings and you can sometimes find stockpiles of the best foods and clothing the West has to offer—few natives are nostalgic for the cheap and chintzy stuff of the past.

The official trappings of the Communist state were quickly dismantled after the Solidarity victory in the 1989 elections. The nation's name was changed back to the Republic of Poland and the state emblem is now, as before the war, a crowned eagle. Statues of Communist leaders have disappeared from public places, most street names have been changed, and Communist Party buildings have been turned into government offices, companies, schools, universities, or banks.

Communism never sat easily with the Poles. It represented the most recent stage in their age-old struggle to retain their national identity in the face of pressure from more powerful neighbors to the west and east. Converted to Christianity, and founded as a unified state during the 10th century on the great north European plain, Poland lay for a thousand years at the heart of Europe, precisely at the halfway point between the Atlantic coast of Spain and the Ural Mountains. With no easily demarcated or defensible frontiers, this gave it an enviable geostrategic position. During the Middle Ages, Poland fought against German advances, uniting with its eastern neighbors in 1410 to roundly defeat the Teutonic Knights in the Battle of Grunwald. In the golden age of Polish history—during the 16th and 17th centuries, of which you will be reminded by the splendid Renaissance and Baroque buildings in many parts of the country—Poland pushed eastward against its Slavic neighbors, taking Kiev and envisioning a kingdom that stretched from the Baltic to the Black Sea. It saw itself then as the bastion of Christendom holding back the hordes from the east, a role best symbolized when Polish king Jan III Sobieski led the allied Christian forces to defeat the Turks at Vienna in 1683. This role is often referred to in the context of more recent Polish history.

By the end of the 18th century, powerful neighbors had united to obliterate Poland—with its outmoded tendency to practice democracy at the highest levels of state and elect foreigners to the throne— from the map of Europe; its territories were to remain divided among the Austrian, Prussian, and Russian empires until the end of World War I. This period of partition is often used to explain patterns of character or public behavior—the Polish tendency to subvert organized authority, for example, or Polish allegiance to the role of the Roman Catholic Church as guardian of the national identity, a devotion that would survive intense and, on occasion, brutal pressure by the Communist secret police and other authorities.

The period of partition has also left physical traces on the map of Poland, despite a tendency in the postwar years to impose uniformity. The formerly Prussian-ruled regions of western Poland, centered in Poznań, are still regarded as cleaner and better organized than the Russian-ruled central areas around the capital, Warsaw; the former Austrian zone in the south, particularly the city of Kraków, retains a reputation for formality and propriety reminiscent of the Hapsburg period. The architecture of the three regions also bears traces of distinct 19th-century imperial styles.

During the 20th century, after a brief period of revived independence in the interwar years, Poland once again fell victim to the old struggle between east and west. It was first crushed by Hitler's *Drang nach Osten* (drive toward the east), which killed 6 million Polish citizens, including 3 million of the Jews who had played such a major role in the nation's history. Then, in 1945, the Soviet Union imposed a Communist system in Poland. As a consequence, Poland's borders were territorially shifted 322 km (200 mi) westward (annexing formerly German-held lands in the process) and losing the "kresy," or eastern territories. These mid-century experiences are embedded deeply in the Polish psyche. Poles show an almost mystical reverence for these struggles by remembering dozens of wartime anniversaries each year, which they celebrate with speeches, color guards, and by placing candles before countless memorials and cemeteries. Since 1989, it has been possible to openly mourn those who died fighting Soviet power and the Polish Communist authorities during the 1940s and '50s.

Poland's historic cities—Kraków, Warsaw, Gdańsk—tell much of the tale of European history and culture. Its countryside offers unrivaled possibilities of escape from the 20th century to a simpler time, to unspoiled nature, and to the remnants of the grand Polish past scattered throughout the country. Paradoxically, the Communists—who after 1956 dropped attempts to collectivize agriculture and kept the Polish peasant on his small plot of land—left much of rural Poland in a romantic, almost preindustrial state. Cornflowers still bloom, storks perch atop untidy nests set near cottage chimneys, and horse carts lazily make their way along worn field tracks. Travelers should try to ignore the appalling legacy of communism—architecturally in ugly soviet-style buildings, environmentally in pockets of terrible pollution—and concentrate on Poland's attractions.

Poland (Polska)

Baltic
Sea

Wejherowo

Gdynia   *Zatoka
Gdańska*

Gdańsk

Słupsk

Elb

Sławno

Kołobrzeg   Koszalin

Kościerzyna   Tczew

Miastko

Malbork

Świnoujście

Karlin

Starogard
Gdański

Sztum

*Zalew
Szczeciński*

Kwidzyn

Nowogard

Szczecinek

Chojnice

Szczecin

Goleniów

Jastrowie

Grudziądz

Stargard
Szczeciński

Kalisz
Pom.

Bydgoszcz

Wisła R.

Toruń

52

Pyrzyce

Piła

Chodzież

Notec R.

Rogoźno

Inowrocław

Włocła

Odra R.

GERMANY

Gorzów
Wielkopolski

E261

25

10

Skwierzyna

Pnjewy

Gniezno

Września

Krośniewice

K

Świebodzin

Poznań

E30

Środa
Wielkopolski

Jarocin

25

Zielona
Góra

Leszno

Kalisz

Zgierz

Kożuchów

Krotoszyn

Zduńska

Szprotawa

Rawicz

Ostrów
Wielkopolski

Sieradz

Lubin

Odra R.

14

8

Bolesławiec

Kępno

Wieluń

Zgorzelec

Legnica

Oleśnica

Jelenia
Góra

Wrocław

Kluczbork

45

43

E75

Wałbrzych

Brzeg

Częs

Nysa

Opole

Lubliniec

Kudowa Zdrój   Kłodzko

Gliwice

Bytom

S

Chorzów   Jó

Katowice

Wodzisław

Oś

CZECH
REPUBLIC

E46

Bielsko
Biała

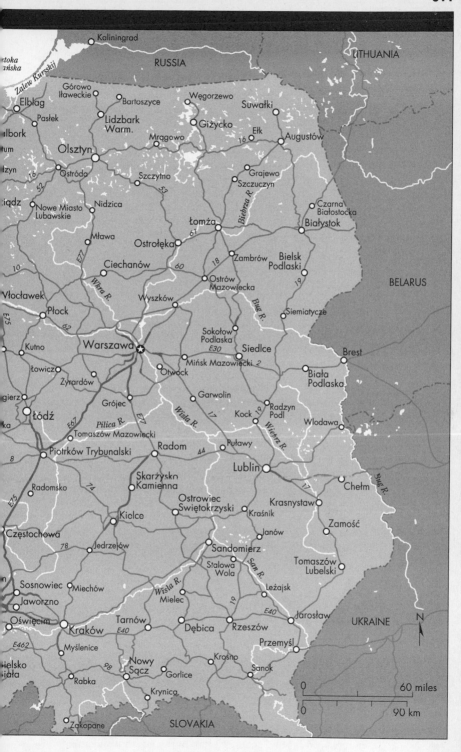

And, despite a certain wary reserve in public behavior, the Poles will win you over with their strong individualism, their sense of humor, and their capacity for fun. Today, more than ever, they are very politically aware of both local and international issues. Whether or not they are for or against free-fall capitalism, one thing remains certain: *Puppies* (Polish yuppies) want to get their MTV.

Pleasures and Pastimes

Dining

While even Poland's most ardent fans will admit that it does not have one of the world's great cuisines, the old traditions of Polish cuisine are being revived and the finer city restaurants are bringing a nouvelle flair to the tried-and-true favorites. Out in the countryside, however, you'll still find that after several days of eating like a Pole—salty smoked salmon, sausage, pork cutlets, cheese dumplings, milk shakes so thick they'll clog your straw—you'll probably be interested in a roughage fix of *ogórki kwaszone* (pickled cucumbers) salad. All in all, Polish food can be filling, tasty, and relatively cheap.

One of the joys of Polish cuisine is the soup, a fundamental part of the daily meal and potentially a meal in itself. Soups are invariably excellent, often thick and nourishing, with lots of peas and beans. Clear beet soup, *barszcz,* is regarded as the most traditional, but soured barley soup, *żurek,* should be tried at least once. Pickled or soused herring is also a favorite Polish entrée. The Polish chef's greatest love is pork in all its varieties, including suckling pig and wild boar. Traditional sausages, *kiełbasy,* usually dried and smoked, are delicious; *myśliwska* (hunter's sausage) is regarded as the greatest delicacy. Another popular hunter's dish, *bigos,* is made from soured and fresh cabbage, cooked (for several days or weeks) together with many different kinds of meat and sausage. *Kompot* (stewed fruit) is customarily served at an early stage in the meal, and you sip the juice rather than eat the fruit. Dessert remains a major institution in Polish life, and you'll see lots of people walking around in a whipped cream–induced haze at any time of the day or night. In Poland whipped cream is a basic food group.

The traditional waiter-service restaurant is still the main feature of the dining scene in Poland, across all price ranges. But if you are in a hurry there is more variety than ever. The old, low-cost, self-service *bar mleczny* (milk bars) and cheap cafeterias are disappearing, replaced by pizza parlors, burger joints, and other fast-food outlets. If you are really pressed for time, you will nearly always be able to find a street stall (usually housed in a small white caravan) that serves *zapiekanki:* French bread toasted with cheese and mushrooms. Street stalls selling spicy Vietnamese dishes are to be found in all Polish cities.

A selection of French, German, and Eastern European wines can usually be found in restaurants; the last often represent the best value for the money, especially the Hungarian reds such as *Egri Bikavér* (Bull's Blood of Eger) or one of the Bulgarian *Sofia* varieties. Note, however, that quality imported wines and spirits are highly taxed as luxury items, and the prices charged for them in restaurants can be astronomical.

Although upscale city restaurants have adapted to Western mealtimes, and some offer lunch starting at noon, Poles traditionally eat their main meal of the day (*obiad,* dinner) between 3 and 5. Many restaurants therefore open at 1 and do not get into full swing until mid-afternoon. Although in cities, there is a growing trend to stay open later ("to the last customer" is a popular new slogan), many restaurants still close relatively early, and it may be difficult to order a meal after 9. A few restaurants offer fixed-price meals between about 1 and 5; these do not always represent a savings over à la carte prices.

CATEGORY	WARSAW*	OTHER AREAS*
$$$$	over $50	over $30
$$$	$25–$50	$15–$30
$$	$10–$25	$7–$15
$	under $10	under $7

*per person for a three-course meal, including service but not drinks

Hiking, Walking, and Cycling

There are nearly endless possibilities for hiking in Poland. The most spectacular terrain is in the south in the Tatra Mountains and the Podhale region, and in the wild and deserted Bieszczady region in the southeast (on the Slovak and Ukrainian borders). All national parks have well-marked trails that traverse beautiful countryside, and have the additional advantage of providing overnight accommodations at regular intervals in walkers' huts and hostels; these can, however, be fairly primitive. Elsewhere in the country, it is more difficult to guarantee you'll find a bed at the right point on your route. For biking, the flat areas of the north are perhaps best for biking, but many parts of the country are provided with touring tracks and byroads.

Lodging

Lodging options are getting better and better, although travelers seeking elegant accommodations have far fewer options to choose from than in Western Europe or, say, Prague. Cheap and comfortable bed-and-breakfast accommodations in private homes or pensions are widely available only in the mountains or on the coast; look for signs in windows with the words POKOJE GOŚCINNE (guest rooms) or inquire at tourist information offices in resorts. In cities, private bed-and-breakfast accommodations are to be used only as a last resort; they are often run by disreputable proprietors who charge exorbitant prices.

The number of privately owned hotels and wayside motels has increased rapidly since 1989. Many of the more recent additions are smaller boutique-type hotels, and only a few—for example, the Marriott and Sheraton in Warsaw—are owned and managed by international chains. All other hotels bearing familiar names (Holiday Inn, Novotel) are run by Orbis, the state travel conglomerate, which at press time was in the process of privatization. Orbis hotels offer a good international standard of accommodation, usually at international prices. Standards at municipally owned hotels vary enormously; ask to see your room before checking in. Gromada, the peasant cooperative, runs excellent, inexpensive hotels. The Polish Tourist Association, PTTK, also has a network of very inexpensive hotels throughout Poland, but single and double rooms are limited in number, and most of the accommodations are in dormitories.

Prices and standards differ vastly. If you do your homework, you can find real bargains outside the major cities. Service charges are included in the room price, but value-added tax (VAT) of 7% is usually quoted as an additional charge. Breakfast is also often included, but this is not universal. Government star ratings (from five down to one) are outdated and refer to ownership category and size as much as to standards. They do, however, give an indication of price, which by no means always reflects the quality of the accommodations offered. Bathrooms may be fitted with either tubs or showers, and this is not necessarily reflected in the price. High-season prices on the coast (May to September) and in the southern mountain region (December to March and July through August) are up to 50% higher than off-season prices. Seasonal variations elsewhere in the country are less marked, apart from short-term high-season rates for special occasions, as in Poznań during the trade fair.

CATEGORY	COST*
$$$$	over $200
$$$	$100–$200
$$	$50–$100
$	under $50

All prices are for two people in a double room, with bath or shower and breakfast.

Music

Poland has a strong musical tradition, and in the big cities in season (which does not cover the main summer holiday period but rather runs from October to May), you will have opportunities to hear outstanding musicians and orchestras—still at very moderate prices. Café musical performances in the evenings are frequent, and many upmarket cafés have daytime pianists. Jazz is also popular; jazz clubs can be found for all tastes in most medium-size towns.

Shopping

Poland is not yet a shopper's paradise, although the range of shops and their offerings are increasing fast. Still, the country is well known for particular items. Leather products are well designed, of high quality, and cheaper than their Western counterparts. The best region for leather is the south, Kraków for more sophisticated products and the mountains for folk equivalents. Amber and silver jewelry are on sale all over Poland, but the best places to search for unusual pieces are on the Baltic coast. Wood, woven, and embroidered folk arts and crafts are found in Cepelia stores all over Poland; if possible, try to visit local folk artists' workshops. Glassware, including cut glass, is beautifully designed and relatively cheap. And, of course, anywhere in the country, you will find Polish vodka (*wódka*): *Polonez* or *Żytnia* are clear rye vodkas; *Żubrówka* is pale green and flavored with bison grass from the Białowieska forest; *Jarzębiak* is flavored with rowan berries.

Exploring Poland

Poles are still surprised to encounter travelers who come simply to visit; you may be asked frequently if you're visiting relatives. For many of the natives, Poland is not a place that steamrolls visitors with excessive natural beauty or great architecture. For the unwitting tourist, that may be true. But the savvy traveler will be enticed by a delightful and wide variety of scenery and architecture to enjoy. The silvery Baltic Sea coast and Mazurian Lakes of the north lie 650 km (400 mi) from the towering Tatra Mountains of the south—in between are historic cities and castles that deserve your attention. If you are using public transportation, Warsaw is the hub from which all fast trains radiate: It is usually wise to begin and end your travels through Poland here.

Great Itineraries

Numbers in the text correspond to numbers in the margin and on the Exploring Warsaw, Exploring Kraków, Southeastern Poland, Gdańsk and the Northeast, and Western Poland maps.

IF YOU HAVE 3 DAYS

Begin in ⊞ **Warsaw** ①–㊽, where you should take in the city's Old Town—destroyed during the Second World War and reconstructed during the 1950s—as well as the Baroque palace in Wilanów and the neoclassical palace on the water in the Łazienki Park. On your second day, rent a car so that en route to Kraków you can visit ⊞ **Kazimierz Dol-**

ny ⑧⑨, a charming Renaissance village on the Vistula River, and catch at least a glimpse of Poland's lush countryside. Alternatively, you can go to Kraków by public transportation via ⊞ **Częstochowa** ⑦⑨, where the 14th-century Pauline monastery contains Poland's holiest relic: the icon of the Black Madonna. No matter how you get there, leave at least a whole day for ⊞ **Kraków** ㊿–⑦⑩, once the nation's capital (before relinquishing the honor to Warsaw in 1611). Its uniquely intact Renaissance Old Town contains a wealth of works of art and is home to the university where Nicolaus Copernicus studied.

IF YOU HAVE 5 DAYS

Begin your stay in ⊞ **Gdańsk** ㊏ and explore the historic Old City, which was originally one of the main Hanseatic ports on the Baltic. By car, take the 1(E75) and Route 50 to ⊞ **Malbork** ㊐ and see the vast castle that was the headquarters of the Teutonic Knights (to do this properly, you need at least half a day). From Malbork, rejoin the 1(E75), and drop by another castle in Gniew before heading to ⊞ **Toruń** ㊗, a small walled town on the Vistula River and Copernicus's birthplace. From Toruń, take highways take 10 and 7(E77) to ⊞ **Warsaw** ①–㊾. This route can also be done easily by train, but if you wish to explore the Mazurian Lakes on your way to Warsaw, a car is essential. From Malbork, take the cross-country route via Dzierzgon to Ostróda, and then 16 to Olsztyn, before taking the 7(E77) to Warsaw. After a day exploring Warsaw, make your way to ⊞ **Kraków** ㊿–⑦⑩. From here take a day trip to **Zakopane** ⑦⑦, two hours away by bus, on the way admiring the foothills of the Podhale region and the High Tatra range in the distance. A day in Zakopane will allow you to try regional cooking and get a feel for life in the mountains.

When to Tour Poland

With its characteristically gray, cold weather and short daylight hours, the Polish winter may persuade you to spend your vacation in the Caribbean. So, unless you are a skier, spring—though sometimes late— is a good time for intense, energetic sightseeing. Summers can be hot and humid, especially in southern Poland, but this is still the busiest tourist season. If you are interested in the arts, remember that theaters and concert halls close completely for the months of July and August and often do not get going with the new season's programs until October. The fabled Polish Golden Autumn, when the leaves do their thing, lasts until November and can be a good time for touring. The winter sports season is from December to March, when high-season rates are once again in effect in the mountains. In general, central heating is universal and efficient in Poland, but air-conditioning is a rarity.

WARSAW

Your first view of Warsaw (Warszawa) is likely to produce an impression of monotonous gray concrete, broken suddenly by a curious, wedding-cake edifice towering over the city: This is the Palace of Culture and Science, Stalin's early 1950s gift to the city. In the early 1990s, an American businessman wanted to purchase it to cut off the elaborate pinnacle and crenellated outbuildings and develop the remaining skyscraper into a business center. Suddenly, Warsovians, after decades of mocking this symbol of Russian imperialism, grudgingly admitted to a sentimental attachment to it. The entrepreneur's scheme fell through, and the Palace of Culture will still be there in the year 2000 to act as a useful orientation point to visitors.

Central Warsaw's predominating bleakness is a legacy of the tragedy that befell what had been, prior to World War II, a marvelous Central

European city. Seventy-five percent of it was destroyed during a heroic uprising against the Nazis in 1944. Warsaw was rebuilt in the 1950s and '60s in postwar "functional" styles and then, as economic times grew harder, largely left to decay. But as you start to explore, your initial reservations will fade away. Fragments of the Warsaw that survived the war acquire a special poignancy in their isolation: odd rows of Art Nouveau tenements, such as those on the south side of the great square around the Palace of Culture and Science, or on ulica Wilcza; the elegant Aleje Ujazdowskie, now the diplomatic quarter, leading to the Belvedere Palace and the Łazienki Palace and Park. The reconstructed areas of the city—the historic Old Town area, rebuilt brick by brick in the 1950s; the Royal Castle; the Ujazdowski Palace—are moving tributes to the Poles' ability to survive and preserve their history.

Moreover, Warsaw is at last getting a face-lift, and the pace of change is so fast that even the locals can't keep up. The butcher shop where customers have faithfully lined up over the past 25 years closes down of an evening, to be replaced the next day by a sleek, white-tiled computer outlet. The local grocery turns overnight into a well-lighted boutique selling imported fashions at prices that former clients cannot afford. All of this is brightening the face of the city; gleaming paint and tiles in strong primary colors, clean windows, and fierce strip lighting are still a novelty in Warsaw. While some may live to regret the disappearance of the local shoemaker or tailor—those picturesque survivors whom communism froze in a time warp—the new arrivals create a vibrant image. Visitors in search of Old World charm may be disappointed, but they can console themselves with the thought that the range of facilities available in many areas—most especially dining out—is markedly improved. Future forward, the city is now intent on resurrecting long-suppressed cultural activities, which can now be appreciated in an atmosphere of experimentation and possibility.

Exploring Warsaw

The geographical core and political center of Poland since 1611, when King Zygmunt III moved the capital here from Kraków, Warsaw will doubtless shock the first-time visitor with its bleak postwar architecture. When one learns, however, of the history of this city, dismay is sure to turn first to amazement and then to deep admiration for the surviving one-third of its inhabitants who so energetically rebuilt their city—literally from the ashes—starting in 1945. Warsaw was in the worst possible location during World War II, and perhaps nowhere else in Europe are there so many reminders of that time; numerous plaques can be found describing multiple massacres of Poles by the Nazis. (The city's darkest hours came in April 1943, when the inhabitants of the Jewish ghetto rose up in arms against the Nazis and were brutally put down, and in the summer of 1944, when the Warsaw Uprising was ultimately defeated.)

Amid the drabness you will find a few architectural attractions. Although many of the buildings in central Warsaw were built in an austere, quasi-Gothic, Stalinist style, a large number of prewar buildings were carefully restored or, in many cases, completely reconstructed following clues in old prints and paintings. A case in point is the beautiful **Rynek Starego Miasta** (Old Town Square). The Royal Palace, which houses a museum, is the greatest of the rebuilt monuments.

Apart from the embankment carved out by the Vistula River, which runs through the city north to south, Warsaw is entirely flat. Most sights, attractions, and hotels lie to the west of the river. Major thoroughfares include **Aleje Jerozolimskie,** which runs east–west, and **Nowy Świat,** which runs north–south through a main shopping district, passes the university, and ends at the entrance to the **Stare Miasto** (Old Town). Be careful about Nowy Świat: Its name changes six times between its starting point in Wilanów (where it's called Aleja Wilanowska) and its terminus (where it's named Krakowskie Przedmieście). To orient yourself, start at the central train station, the Marriott Hotel, or the Palace of Culture, all of which sit within a block of one another on Aleje Jerozolimskie (the Marriott, a glass skyscraper, and the Palace of Culture, the brick monstrosity that looks like a wedding cake, are the two most visible buildings in town). Walk west toward the river on Aleje Jerozolimskie two blocks to Nowy Świat. Heading north, this street is a main shopping district, closed to all traffic except buses; in about 20 minutes the street (now called **Krakowskie Przedmieście**) will terminate at **plac Zamkowy,** the plaza that marks the entrance to the Old Town. North of this point is **Nowe Miasto** (New Town), primarily a residential area, and to the west lie **Muranów** and **Mirów,** former Jewish districts. **Praga,** a poorer quarter of workers and artisans that emerged from the war fairly intact, and the enormous **Zoological Park** are situated east of the Wisła river.

Numbers in the text correspond to numbers in the margin and on the Exploring Warsaw map.

Stare Miasto (Old Town) and Nowe Miasto (New Town)

The rebuilding of the historic Old Town, situated on an escarpment on the left bank of the Vistula, is a real phoenix-risen-from-the-ashes story. Postwar architects, determined to get it absolutely as it was before, turned to old prints, photographs in family albums, and paintings, in particular the detailed views of the 18th-century Bernardo Bellotto (the nephew of Canaletto). This actually resulted in a curious back-to-front situation, since some of Bellotto's views were painted not from real life but from sketches of projects that were never realized. Whatever your feelings about reproduction architecture—and there's a lot of it in Warsaw—it seems to have worked. It is closed to traffic, and in its narrow streets you can leave the 20th century behind and relax for a while. Everything here is within easy walking distance. Just a short stroll beyond the Barbakan gate is the Nowe Miasto, or New Town, which also has sights well worth seeing.

A GOOD WALK

Begin at **plac Zamkowy** ①, first visiting the **Zamek Królewski** ②. Make your way next along the narrow ulica Kanonia, where you'll find the great cracked Zygmunt bell in the middle of a quiet, cobbled square—exactly where it fell from the cathedral tower during the bombardment of 1939. Continue along ulica Jezuicka, where you might turn through one of the archways and admire the view over the Vistula from the terrace that runs along the back of the houses. The **Rynek Starego Miasta** ③ is a place to relax and to take in buildings like the Klucznikowska Mansion at Rynek Starego Miasta 21. Now housing an elegant restaurant, this fine structure has the original, 15th century, Gothic brick portal and cellars. Be sure to visit the **Muzeum Historyczne Warszawy** ④—do not miss its 20-minute film in English on the history of the city—or the **Muzeum im. Adama Mickiewicza** ⑤. Continue north from the Rynek along Krzywe Koło and the ramparts of the Old Town's walls to reach the **Barbakan** ⑥, marking the boundary between the Old and New Towns.

On ulica Freta, you will find the **Kościół Dominkanów** ⑦ and the house where Marie Skłodowska-Curie was born, now the **Muzeum Marii Skłodowskiej-Curie** ⑧. Ulica Freta takes you to the **Rynek Nowego Miasta** ⑩, near which there are fine churches from different architectural periods, built from the 15th to 17th centuries, including **Kościół**

Archikatedralna Bazylika św. Jana, **15**
Barbakan, **6**
Botanical Gardens, **38**
Femina Cinema, **46**
Former Headquarters of the Polish Communist Party, **29**
Fragment of Ghetto Wall, **43**
Galeria Zachęta, **25**
Gestapo Headquarters, **37**
Grób Nieznanego Żołnierza, **24**
Jewish Cemetery, **49**
Jewish Historical Institute and Museum, **45**
Kościół Dominkanów, **7**
Kościół Jezuitów, **16**
Kościół Karmelitów, **18**
Kościół Najświętszej Marii Panny, **11**
Kościół Sakramentek, **12**
Kościół św. Aleksandra, **32**
Kościół św. Anny, **17**
Kościół św. Krzyża, **20**
Kościół Wizytek, **19**
Muzeum Etnograficzne, **26**
Muzeum im. Adama Mickiewicza, **5**
Muzeum Marii Skłodowskiej–Curie, **8**
Muzeum Narodowe, **30**
Muzeum Wojska Polskiego, **31**
Pałac Belweder, **41**
Pałac Czapskich, **22**
Pałac Kazanowskich, **21**
Pałac Krasińskich, **14**
Pałac Kultury i Nauki, **33**
Pałac Łazienkowski, **40**
Pałac Namiestnikowski, **23**
Pałac Ostrogskich, **28**
Park Łazienkowski, **39**
Park Ujazdowski, **35**
Pałac Wilanowski, **42**
Plac Zamkowy, **1**
Pomnik Bohaterów Getta, **47**
Pomnik Bohaterów Warszawy 1939–1945, **13**

Exploring Warsaw
NOWE MIASTO (NEW TOWN)
STARE MIASTO (OLD TOWN)
MURANÓW
Rynek Nowego Miasto
Stawki
ul. Dzika
a Dubois
Generała Władysława Andersa
Bonifraterska
Franciszkańska
Wałowa
Rybaki
Wybrzeże Gdańskie
Bugaj
Świętojerska
ul. Świętojańska
ul. Dziekania
ul. Piwna
Miodowa
Długa
ul. Lewartowskiego
M. Anielewicza
ul. Zamenhofa
Nowolipki
Karmelicka
Plac Bankowy
pl. Teatralny
Senatorska
Wierzbowe
Krakowska
al. Solidarności
Ogród Saski
Elektoralna
Al. Jana Pawła II
Królewska
Mazowiecka
Marszałkowska
Zielna
Plac Grzybowski
Żelazna
Twarda
Świętokrzyska
Pereca
Pańska
pl. Defilad
Chmielna
Prosta
Emilii Plater
Sienna
Złota
Central Station
al. Jerozolimskie
Poznańska
Wspólna
Towarowa
Hoża
Wilcza
Koszykowa
KEY
American Express Office
Tourist Information
Rail Lines
0
750 yards
750 meters
al. Niepodległości
Nowowiejska
Filtrowa
Raszyńska
Wawelska
al. Arm

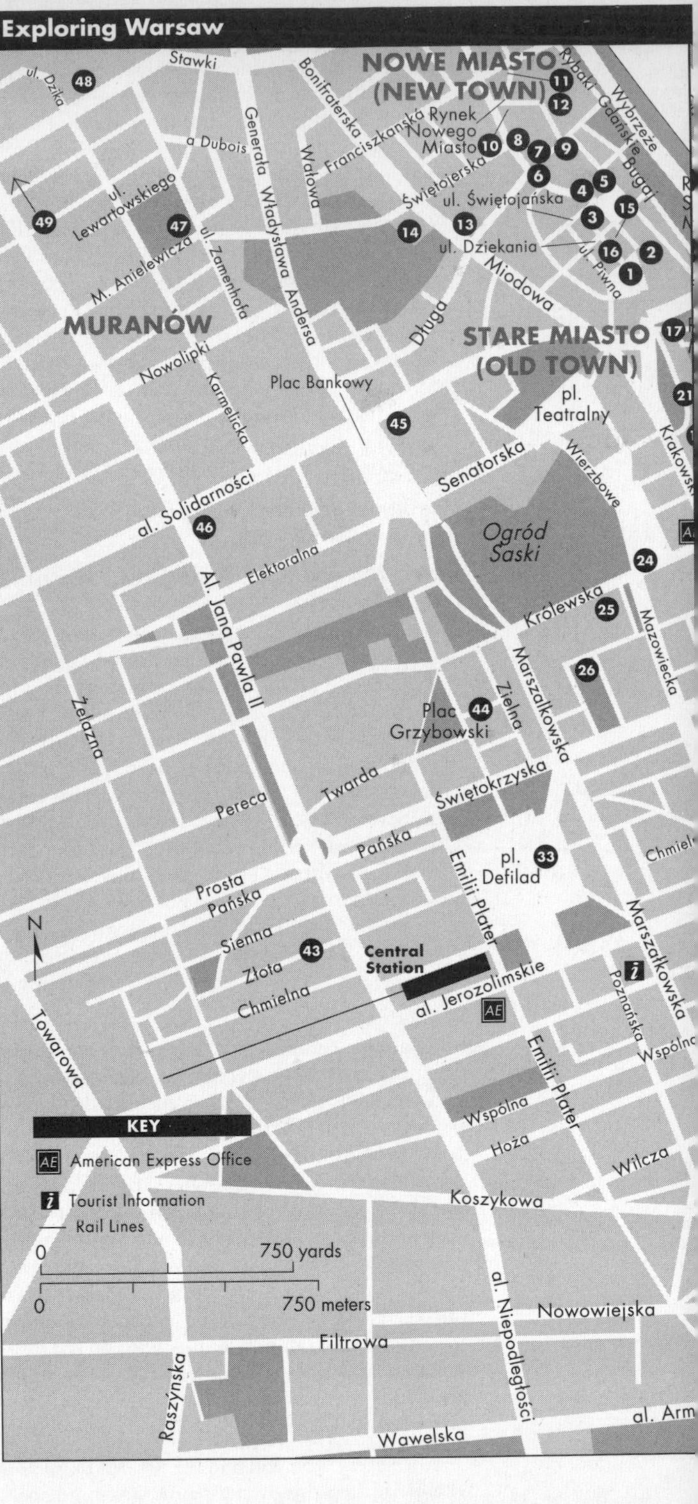

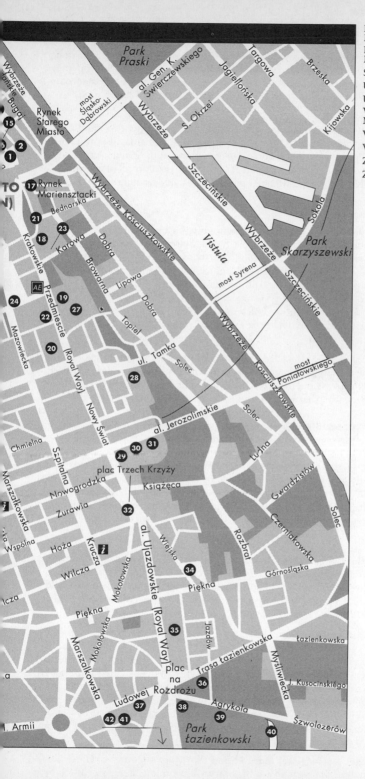

Najświętszej Marii Panny ⑪ and **Kościół Sakramentek** ⑫. Returning from the New Town, take ulica Świętojerska to plac Krasińskich, with its **Pomnik Bohaterów Warszawy 1939–1945** ⑬, and go back along ulica Długa to the Barbakan. Ulica Nowomiejska will take you back to the Rynek and then go by ulica Świętojańska, with **Archikatedralna Bazylika świętego Jana** ⑮ on your left, to return to plac Zamkowy.

TIMING

The Old Town is not large in area. If you are content to admire the exteriors of buildings, you can easily see it in half a day. But to take it in fully, you will need a whole day to explore. At the Zamek Królewski, give yourself about three hours if you want to explore all of its exhibits. The Rynek Starego Miasta, with its cafés and restaurants, is a good place to relax in the evening.

SIGHTS TO SEE

⑮ **Archikatedralna Bazylika świętego Jana** (Cathedral of St. John). Ulica Świętojańska, leading from the Rynek Starego Miasta to the Zamek Królewski, takes its name from Warsaw's Cathedral of St. John, which was built at the turn of the 14th century; coronations of the Polish kings took place here from the 16th to the 18th century. The crypts contain the tombs of the last two princes of Mazovia, the archbishops of Warsaw, and such famous Poles as the 19th-century novelist Henryk Sienkiewicz, the Nobel Prize–winning author of *Quo Vadis?* ⊠ *Ul. Świętojańska 8.*

⑥ **Barbakan.** The pinnacled Barbakan, the mid-16th-century stronghold in the old city wall on ulica Freta, now marks the boundary between the Old Town and the New Town. From here you can see the partially restored wall that was built to enclose the Old Town. ⊠ *Ul. Freta.*

OFF THE
BEATEN PATH

KOŚCIÓŁ ŚW. STANISŁAWA KOSTKI – In October 1984, Polish secret police officers murdered the popular parish priest Jerzy Popiełuszko because of his sermons, which the Communist regime considered gravely threatening. Thereafter, the martyred Popiełuszko's church became the site of huge and very moving Solidarity meetings. You can visit his grave on the grounds of this church in the district of Żoliborz, north of the New Town. Take a taxi or Bus A or J from ulica Bonifraterska to plac Komuny Paryskiej; then walk two blocks west along ulica Zygmunta Krasinskiego. ⊠ *Ul. Stanisława Hozjusza 2.*

⑦ **Kościół Dominkanów** (Dominican Church). The Baroque Dominican Church in Warsaw's New Town was badly damaged in the aftermath of the 1943 uprising, when the adjoining monastery served as a field hospital for wounded insurrectionists. It was reconstructed in the 1950s. ⊠ *Ul. Freta 8–10.*

⑯ **Kościół Jezuitów** (Jesuit Church). On the left-hand side of the entrance to St. John's Cathedral is the early 17th-century Jesuit Church, founded by King Jan Sobieski, the victor at Vienna. Throughout the postwar years, a visit to this church at Eastertime was considered a must by Warsovians: Its Gethsemane decorations always contained a hidden political message (in 1985, the risen Christ had the face of Father Jerzy Popiełuszko, the Warsaw priest murdered the previous year by Polish secret police officers). ⊠ *On the north side of ul. Świętojańska, 1 block up from pl. Zamkowy.*

⑪ **Kościół Najświętszej Marii Panny** (St. Mary's Church). The oldest church in the New Town, St. Mary's was built as a parish church by the princes of Mazovia in the early 15th century. It has been destroyed and rebuilt many times throughout its history. ⊠ *Przyrynek 2.*

⑫ **Kościół Sakramentek** (Church of the Sisters of the Blessed Sacrament). Built as a thanksgiving offering by King John Sobieski's queen, Marysieńka, after his victory against the Turks at Vienna in 1683, the cool, white Kościół Sakramentek stands on the east side of New Town Square. ⊠ *Rynek Nowego Miasta 2.*

④ **Muzeum Historyczne Warszawy** (Warsaw Historical Museum). Four fine examples of **Renaissance mansions** can be found on the northern side of the Old Town Square (note the sculpture of a black slave on the facade of No. 34, the **Negro House.**) These historical homes, some of which contain Renaissance ceiling paintings, now house this museum, which offers a daily screening (at noon in English) of a short documentary film on the history of Warsaw. ⊠ *Rynek Starego Miasta 28–42,* ☏ *022/635–16–25.* 🎫 *Zł 3.* ⊙ *Tues. and Thurs. 12–5; Wed. and Fri. 10–3; weekends 10:30–4:30.*

⑤ **Muzeum im. Adama Mickiewicza** (Adam Mickiewicz Museum of Literature). Mickiewicz was Poland's greatest Romantic poet, and this museum, which contains manuscripts, mementos, and portraits, focuses on him and many other Polish writers. ⊠ *Rynek Starego Miasta 20,* ☏ *022/831–40–61.* 🎫 *Zł 3.* ⊙ *Mon.–Tues. and Fri. 10–3, Wed.–Thurs. and Sat. 11–6, Sun. 11–5.*

⑧ **Muzeum Marii Skłodowskiej-Curie** (Marie Curie Museum). The house in which Marie Curie was born is on ulica Freta; a small museum inside is dedicated to the great physicist, chemist, winner of two Nobel Prizes, and discoverer of radium. ⊠ *Ul. Freta 16,* ☏ *022/831–80–92.* 🎫 *Zł 2.* ⊙ *Tues.–Sat. 10–4, Sun. 10–2.*

⑭ **Pałac Krasińskich** (Krasinski Palace). The late-17th-century, Baroque Krasinski Palace currently houses the historic prints collection of Poland's National Library. It can be visited only by appointment. ⊠ *Pl. Krasińskich 5,* ☏ *022/831–3241 for tours.*

① **Plac Zamkowy** (Castle Square). Many visitors enter the Old Town through Castle Square, the plaza area on the southern border of the district. You can't miss the **Zygmunt Column,** which honors King Zygmunt III Wasa, king of Poland and Sweden, who in the early 17th century moved the capital to Warsaw from Kraków.

⑬ **Pomnik Bohaterów Warszawy 1939–1945** (Monument to the Heroes of Warsaw). Unveiled in 1989, this monument constitutes a poignant reminder of what World War II meant for the citizens of Warsaw. Massive bronze figures raise defiant fists above the sewer openings used by Polish resistance fighters in Warsaw's Old Town to escape the Nazis in 1944. ⊠ *Corner of pl. Krasińskich and ul. Długa.*

⑩ **Rynek Nowego Miasta** (New Town Square). Warsaw's New Town was actually founded at the turn of the 14th and 15th centuries. This part of the city, however, was rebuilt after the war in 18th- and 19th-century style so has a more elegant and spacious feel about it than the Old Town. The centerpiece of the district is the leafy New Town Square, slightly more irregular and relaxed than its Old Town counterpart. The houses on the square, and in nearby streets like ulica Kościelna, have curiously stark and formalized wall paintings.

★ ③ **Rynek Starego Miasta** (Old Town Square). This is the hub of life in Warsaw's Old Town. The earliest settlers arrived at this spot during the 10th and 11th centuries. Legend has it that a peasant named Wars was directed to the site by a mermaid named Sawa—hence the name of the city in Polish, Warszawa (Sawa has been immortalized in Warsaw's official emblem). In the 14th century Warsaw was already a walled city, and in 1413 its citizens obtained a borough charter from the princes of Mazovia. The present layout of the Old Town dates from that time, and traces of the original Gothic buildings still surround the Old Town Square. The appearance of today's square, however, largely dates from the 16th and early 17th centuries, when Warsaw's wealth and importance grew rapidly as a result of the 1569 Polish-Lithuanian union and Warsaw's new status as capital city.

The Old Town Square is usually very active, even though no traffic is allowed and there is no longer a formal market. Artists and craftspeople of all kinds still sell their wares here in the summer, but don't expect many bargains—tourists are their prime targets. Musical performances are often held here on weekends on a stage erected at the north end. Horse-drawn cabs await visitors. To explore some of the square's beautiful and historic houses, visit the Adam Mickiewicz Museum of Literature (☞ *above*) on the east side of the square and the Warsaw Historical Museum (☞ *above*) on the north side. After being almost completely annihilated during World War II, these mansions were meticulously reconstructed using old prints, plans, and paintings. For some of the best Gothic details, look for No. 31, traditionally known as the House of the Mazovian Dukes. At night the square is romantically floodlit, and if you're after good food and atmosphere, this is one of Warsaw's best bets.

NEED A BREAK?   **Hortex** (⊠ Rynek Starego Miasta 3–9) has a large open-air café in summer; at the same address on the ground floor is a quick-service lunch bar.

❾ Warszawska Syrenka (Warsaw Mermaid). Krzywe Koło (Crooked Wheel Street) runs from the Old Town Square to the reconstructed ramparts of the city wall. From this corner, which is graced by a towering stone mermaid known as the Warszawska Syrenka, you can again look out over the Vistula and also over the Nowe Miasto (New Town), stretching to the north beyond the city walls. As you look out over the town walls and down the Vistula embankment, you will see the **Stara Prochownia** (Old Powder Tower) on ulica Boleść, just past the intersection with ulica Bugaj; this has now been turned into an interesting theater, a popular venue for poetry readings, music, and drama.

★ **❷ Zamek Królewski** (Royal Castle). Warsaw's Royal Castle stands on the east side of Castle Square (☞ *above*). The princes of Mazovia first built a residence on this spot overlooking the Vistula in the 14th century; its present Renaissance form dates from the reign of King Sigismund III, who needed a magnificent palace for his new capital. Reconstructed later than the Old Town, in the 1970s, it now gleams as it did in its earliest years, with gilt, marble, and wall paintings; it houses impressive art collections—including the famous views of Warsaw by Canaletto's nephew Bernardo Bellotto (also known, like his uncle, as Canaletto), which were used to rebuild the city after the war. Tours in English are available. ⊠ *Pl. Zamkowy 4,* ☎ *022/657–21–70.* 🖾 *Zł 10, Sun. zł 3.* ☉ *Tues.–Sun. 10–3.*

NEED A BREAK?   **Kawiarnia Literacka** (⊠ Krakowskie Przedmieście 87/89, ☎ 022/826–57–84), on the ground floor of the PEN club premises, is an airy café offering classic jazz on weekend evenings.

The Royal Route

All towns with kings had their "Royal Routes," and in Warsaw it stretches south from Castle Square for 4 km (2½ mi), running through busy Krakowskie Przedmiéscie, along Nowy Świat, and on to the Belvedere Palace and the Park Łazienkowski. The route is lined with some of Warsaw's finest churches and palaces, but there are also landmarks of some of Warsaw's most famous folk, including Frédéric Chopin. As a child Fryderyk (to use the Polish spelling) played in the

Casimir Palace gardens, gave his first concert in the Radziwiłł Palace (now Governor's Palace), then moved with his family to the building that once housed the city's Academy of Fine Arts. Today, the Chopin Society is headquartered in the Ostrogski Palace.

A GOOD WALK

Krakowskie Przedmieście and **Nowy Świat** form the first part of the Royal Route, or King's Road, which led from the Royal Castle to the summer palace at Wilanów, a distance of about 7½ km (4½ mi). The first stage of the route, from plac Zamkowy to Aleje Jerozolimskie, is about 3 km (2 mi). Krakowskie Przedmieście is a wide thoroughfare lined with fine churches—**Kościół świętej Anny** ⑰, **Kościół Karmelitów** ⑱, **Kościół Wizytek** ⑲, **Kościół świętego Krzyża** ⑳—and elegant mansions and palaces, including **Pałac Kazanowskich** ㉑, **Pałac Czapskich** ㉒, **Pałac Namiestnikowski** ㉓, and **Pałac Potockich.**

You can detour from the route down the hill via ulica Bednarska to the leafy 18th-century Rynek Mariensztacki, a 10-minute walk. Another detour—this one to the west along Bagińskiego—will bring you in two minutes to the wide-open spaces of the plac Piłsudskiego, site of the **Grób Nieznanego Żołnierza** ㉔ and the **Teatr Wielki.** Take ulica Mazowiecka from the southwest corner, passing the **Galeria Zachęta** ㉕ on your right, and turn west onto ulica Kredytowa. On your right is the 18th-century neoclassical Kościół Ewangelicko-Augsburski, which like Kościół świętego Aleksandra in plac Trzech Krzyży was modeled on Rome's Pantheon. Go a block farther to find the **Muzeum Etnograficzne** ㉖; return to Krakowskie Przedmieście via ulica Traugutta. Beyond the campus of **Warsaw University** ㉗, beside the statue of Nicolaus Copernicus, the road narrows and becomes ulica Nowy Świat, a pedestrian precinct with elegant shops and cafés housed in 18th-century houses. From here, you can detour down the hill to the east—a 10-minute walk—to the **Pałac Ostrogskich** ㉘. At the south end of ulica Nowy Świat you will find the massive **former headquarters of the Polish Communist Party** ㉙ and, immediately east of this building, the **Muzeum Narodowe** ㉚—in which you can easily spend half a day—and the **Muzeum Wojska Polskiego** ㉛. At the south end of plac Trzech Krzyży is **Kościół świętego Aleksandra** ㉜, built in the early 19th century as a copy of the Roman Pantheon. If you have time, from the tram stop at the corner of Nowy Świat make the two-stop trip west along Aleje Jerozolimskie to the **Pałac Kultury i Nauki** ㉝.

TIMING

Walking at a brisk pace, you can cover this route in an hour, but to soak in the sights along the way, allow a whole morning or afternoon.

SIGHTS TO SEE

㉙ **Former Headquarters of the Polish Communist Party.** Anti-Communists love the irony of this solid structure and once despised symbol of oppression being the seat of the Warsaw Stock Exchange. ⊠ *Cnr. of Al. Jerozolimskie and Nowy Świat.*

㉕ **Galeria Zachęta** (Zachęta Gallery). Built at the end of the 19th century by the Society for the Encouragement of the Fine Arts, this gallery has no permanent collection but organizes thought-provoking special exhibitions (primarily modern art) in high-ceilinged, well-lighted halls. It was in this building in 1922 that the first president of the post–World War I Polish Republic, Gabriel Narutowicz, was assassinated by a right-wing fanatic. Admission costs to the exhibits vary. ⊠ *Pl. Małachowskiego 3,* ☏ *022827–69–09.* ⊙ *Tues.–Sun. 10–6.*

㉔ **Grób Nieznanego Żołnierza** (Tomb of the Unknown Soldier). Built as a memorial after World War I, the Tomb of the Unknown Soldier contains the body of a Polish soldier brought from the eastern battlefields of the Polish-Soviet war of 1919–1920—a fact not much mentioned in the 45 years of Communist rule after World War II. Ceremonial changes of the guard take place at 10 AM Sundays; visitors may be surprised to see the Polish Army still using the goose step on such occasions. The memorial is a surviving fragment of the early 18th-century **Saxon Palace,** which used to stand here on the west side of plac Piłsudskiego. Behind the fragment are the delightful **Ogród Saski** (Saxon Gardens), which were once the palace's park and were designed by French and Saxon landscape gardeners. ✉ *Between pl. Piłsudskiego and ul. Marszałkowska.*

⑱ **Kościół Karmelitów** (Church of the Discalced Carmelites). This late-17th-century Baroque church sits at the back of a square off the main line of the street. ✉ *Krakowskie Przedmieście 52.*

㉜ **Kościół świętego Aleksandra** (St. Alexander's Church). Built in the early 19th century as a copy of the Roman Pantheon, St. Alexander's stands on an island in the middle of **plac Trzech Krzyży,** a name that is notoriously difficult for foreigners to pronounce and means "Three Crosses Square." One of the crosses in question is on the church itself.

⑳ **Kościół świętego Krzyża** (Holy Cross Church). The heart of Poland's most famous composer, Fryderyk Chopin, is immured in a pillar inside this Baroque church. Atop the church steps is a massive sculpted crucifix. Across from the church is the **statue of Nicolaus Copernicus,** which, like many other notable Warsaw monuments, is the work of the 19th-century Danish sculptor Bertel Thorvaldsen (the statue stands in front of the neoclassical Staszic Palace, the headquarters of the Polish Academy of Sciences). ✉ *Krakowskie Przedmieście 3.*

⑰ **Kościół świętej Anny** (St. Anne's Church). Built in 1454 by Anne, princess of Mazovia, St. Anne's Church stands on the south corner of plac Zamkowy. It was rebuilt in High Baroque style after destruction during the Swedish invasions in the 17th century; thanks to 1990s redecoration and regilding it glows once again. A plaque on the wall outside marks the spot where Pope John Paul II celebrated mass in 1980, during his first visit to Poland after his election to the papacy. ✉ *Krakowskie Przedmieście 68.*

⑲ **Kościół Wizytek** (Church of the Visitation Sisters). In front of this late-Baroque church stands a statue of Cardinal Stefan Wyszyński, primate of Poland from 1948 to 1981. Wyszyński was imprisoned during the 1950s but lived to see a Polish pope and the birth of Solidarity; the fresh flowers always lying at the foot of the statue are evidence of the warmth with which he is remembered. ✉ *Krakowskie Przedmieście 30.*

㉖ **Muzeum Etnograficzne** (Ethnographic Museum). An interesting collection of Polish folk art, crafts, and costumes from all parts of the country resides on display here. ✉ *Ul. Kredytowa 1,* ☎ *022/827–76–41.* 🎫 *Zł 2.* ⏲ *Tues. and Thurs.–Fri. 9–4, Wed. 11–6, weekends 10–5.*

★ ㉚ **Muzeum Narodowe** (National Museum of Warsaw). In a functional 1930s building, the National Museum has an impressive collection of contemporary Polish and European paintings, Gothic icons, and works from antiquity. ✉ *Al. Jerozolimskie 3,* ☎ *022/621–10–31.* 🎫 *Zł 3.5, free Wed.* ⏲ *Tues.–Wed. 10–3, Thurs. noon–4, Fri.–Sun. 10–4; closed day after holidays.*

㉛ **Muzeum Wojska Polskiego** (Polish Army Museum). If you're interested in military matters, you might want to visit this museum's exhibits of weaponry, armor, and uniforms, which trace Polish military history for the past 10 centuries. Heavy armaments are displayed outside. ✉ *Al.*

Jerozolimskie 3, ☎ *022/629–52–71.* 🖭 *Zł 2, free Wed..* � *Wed.–Sun. 10–4; closed day after holidays.*

NEED A
BREAK?
Blikle (✉ Nowy Świat 35), Warsaw's oldest cake shop, has a black-and-white-tile café that offers savory snacks as well as Blikle's famous doughnuts.

㉒ **Pałac Czapskich** (Czapski Palace). Now the home of the Academy of Fine Arts, the Czapski Palace dates from the late 17th century but was rebuilt in 1740 in the rococo style. Zygmunt Krasiński, the Polish romantic poet, was born here in 1812, and Chopin once lived in the palace mews. ✉ *Krakowskie Przedmieście 5.*

㉑ **Pałac Kazanowskich** (Kazanowski Palace). On the corner of Krakowskie Przedmieście and ulica Bednarska is this 17th century palace. It was given a neoclassical front elevation in the 19th century, but the courtyard at the rear still contains massive late-Renaissance buttresses and is worth a visit because of its plaque commemorating the episode of Zagloba's fight with the monkeys, from Sienkiewicz's historical novel *The Deluge.* In a small garden in front of the palace stands a **monument to Adam Mickiewicz,** the great Polish romantic poet. It was here that Warsaw University students gathered in March 1968, after a performance of Mickiewicz's hitherto banned play *Forefathers' Eve,* which set in motion the events that led to the fall of Poland's Communist leader Władysław Gomułka, a wave of student protests, and a regime-sponsored anti-Semitic campaign. ✉ *Krakowskie Przedmieście 62.*

㉝ **Pałac Kultury i Nauki** (Palace of Culture and Science). This massive wedding-cake Stalinist-Gothic structure is the main landmark in the city, and from the 30th floor you can get a panoramic view. The old joke runs that this is Warsaw's best view because it is the only place where you can't see the palace. To view all of urban Warsaw from 234 yards up, buy tickets (for zł 7) at the booth near the east entrance. The building houses a number of facilities, including a swimming pool and the **Museum of Science and Technology.** Also in the Palace of Culture and Science is the **Teatr Lalek**—a good puppet theater, an art form at which the Poles excel (entrance on north side, ☎ 022/620–49–50). ✉ *Pl. Defilad,* ☎ *022/620–02–11.*

㉓ **Pałac Namiestnikowski** (Governor's Palace). This palace was built in the 17th century by the Radziwiłł family (into which Jackie Kennedy's sister Lee later married). In the 19th century it functioned as the administrative office of the czarist occupiers—hence its present name. In 1955 the Warsaw Pact was signed here; later the palace served as the headquarters for the Presidium of the Council of Ministers, and since 1995 it has been the official residence of Poland's president. In the forecourt is an **equestrian statue of Prince Józef Poniatowski,** a nephew of the last king of Poland and one of Napoléon's marshals. He was wounded and drowned in the Elster River during the Battle of the Nations at Leipzig in 1813, following the disastrous retreat of Napoléon's Grande Armée from Russia. ✉ *Krakowskie Przedmieście 46–48.*

㉘ **Pałac Ostrogskich** (Ostrogski Palace). The headquarters of the **Towarzystwo im. Fryderyka Chopina** (Chopin Society) is in the 17th-century Ostrogski Palace, which towers above ulica Tamka. The best approach is via the steps from ulica Tamka. In the 19th century the Warsaw Conservatory was housed here (Paderewski was one of its students); now a venue for Chopin concerts, it is also home to the **Muzeum Fryderyka Chopina** (Frédéric Chopin Museum), a small collection of mementos, including the last piano played by him. The works of Chopin (1810–1849), Poland's greatest composer, took their roots from folk rhythms and melodies of exclusively Polish invention. Thanks to Chopin, Poland could fairly claim to have been the fountainhead of popular music in Europe, since the composer's polonaises and mazurkas whirled their way around the continent in the mid-19th century. ✉ *Ul. Okólnik 1,* ☎ *022/827–54–71.* ⌖ *Free.* ☉ *Wed.–Mon. 10–2.*

NEED A
BREAK?
Nowy Świat (✉ Nowy Świat 63), on the corner of Nowy Świat and ulica Świętokrzyska, is a spacious, traditional café, with plenty of foreign-language newspapers for those who want to linger over coffee.

Teatr Wielki (Opera House). The massive, neoclassical Opera House, built in the 1820s and reconstructed after the war, has an auditorium with more than 2,000 seats. There is also a **Muzeum Teatralne** (Museum of Theater; ☎ 022/826–52–13), open daily 10–2, on the first floor of the building. ✉ *Pl. Teatralny.*

㉗ **Warsaw University.** The high, wrought-iron gates of Warsaw University lead into a leafy campus; the **Pałac Kazimierzowski** (Kazimierzowski Palace), which currently houses the university administration, was, in the 18th century, the Military Cadet School where Tadeusz Kościuszko studied. ✉ *Krakowskie Przedmieście 26–28.*

Park Łazienkowski (Łazienki Park) and the Diplomatic Quarter

Aleje Ujazdowskie, Warsaw's fashionable Corso, which in the 19th century was thronged with smart carriages and riders eager to be "seen," is now a favorite with Sunday strollers, leading to beautiful Park Łazienkowski and the white wedding-cake Pałac Łazienkowski, the private residence of the last king of Poland.

A GOOD WALK

The Park Łazienkowski and the diplomatic quarter lie along the Royal Route leading from the Old Town to Wilanów, at the point beyond plac Trzech Krzÿy. From here it is about 3 km (2 mi) to the southern edge of the Park Łazienkowski. Enter Aleje Ujazdowskie, a fashionable avenue where the rich built residences during the 19th century. Many of their mansions now house foreign embassies. A five-minute walk down ulica Wiejska, on your left, brings you to the **Sejm** ㉞. Parallel to Aleje Ujazdowskie after ulica Piękna you may choose to stroll under the trees of the **Park Ujazdowski** ㉟, keeping farther away from the traffic. At plac Na Rozdrożu you'll leave the diplomatic quarter and enter Warsaw's "Whitehall." If you are interested in modern art, the **Zamek Ujazdowski** ㊱, the home of the Center for Contemporary Art, is 200 yards east from plac na Rozdrożu, down a path through the park parallel to the Trasa Łazienkowska. The wartime **Gestapo headquarters** ㊲ is 200 yards in the opposite direction from the square, on Aleje Szucha. The rest of this part of the Royal Route is lined with government buildings, among them the office of the Council of Ministers. On your left are the **Botanical Gardens** ㊳ and **Park Łazienkowski** ㊴. To reach the **Pałac Łazienkowski** ㊵, enter by the gates opposite ulica Bagatela, beside the **Pałac Belweder** ㊶.

At the top of the hill of the Vistula embankment, you enter ulica Belwederska, where you should board Bus 122 for **Pałac Wilanowski** ㊷, since the rest of the Royal Route, which until the 1980s ran through open countryside, is now lined with housing developments.

TIMING

Take a morning or afternoon to explore this route. If, however, you wish to linger at some of the sights, make it a whole day: The Park

Łazienkowski and Pałac Łazienkowski deserve three or four hours at the least. This tree-lined walk is good for a hot summer day.

SIGHTS TO SEE

③⑧ Botanical Gardens. These gardens, covering an area of roughly 3 acres, were laid out in 1818. At the entrance stands the neoclassical **observatory**, now part of Warsaw University. ⊠ *Al. Ujazdowskie 4.*

③⑦ Gestapo headquarters. The building that currently houses the Ministry of Education was Gestapo headquarters during World War II; a small museum details the horrors that took place behind its peaceful facade. ⊠ *Al. Szucha 25,* ☎ *022/629–49–19.* ⊠ *Free.* ☉ *Wed.–Sun. 10–4.*

④① Pałac Belweder (Belvedere Palace). Built in the early 18th century, the palace was reconstructed in 1818 in neoclassical style by the Russian governor of Poland, the Grand Duke Constantine. Until 1994 it was the official residence of Poland's president. The Pałac Belweder stands just south of the main gates to the Park Łazienkowski. Across the street and a block farther south stands the **Russian Embassy** (⊠ Belwederska 49) a reminder of Poland's long and tangled relationship with Russia. This massive, colonial-style former Soviet Embassy channeled directives from Moscow to a more or less compliant Polish Communist government. ⊠ *Ul. Belwederska 2.*

★ **④⓪ Pałac Łazienkowski** (Palace on the Water). The magnificent palace is the focal point of the Park Łazienkowski. This Neoclassical summer residence was so faithfully reconstructed after the war that there is still no electricity—be sure to visit when it's sunny, or you won't see anything of the interior. The palace holds some splendid 18th-century furniture as well as part of Stanisław August's art collection. ⊠ *Ul. Agrykola 1,* ☎ *022/621–62–41.* ⊠ *Zł 5.* ☉ *Tues.–Sun. 9:30–3.*

★ **④② Pałac Wilanowski** (Wilanów Palace). A Baroque gateway and false moat lead to the wide courtyard that stretches along the front of Wilanów Palace, built between 1681 and 1696 by King Jan III Sobieski. After his death, the palace passed through various hands before being bought at the end of the 18th century by Stanisław Kostka Potocki, who amassed a major art collection, laid out the gardens, and opened the first public museum here in 1805. Potocki's neo-Gothic tomb can be seen to the left of the driveway as you approach the palace. The palace interiors still hold much of the original furniture; there's also a striking display of 16th- to 18th-century Polish portraits on the first floor. English-speaking guides are available.

Outside, to the left of the main entrance, is a romantic park with pagodas, summerhouses, and bridges overlooking a lake. Behind the palace is a formal Italian garden from which you can admire the magnificent gilt decoration on the palace walls. There's also a **gallery** of contemporary Polish art in the grounds, and stables to the right of the entrance now house a poster gallery, the **Muzeum Plakatu Wilanó**. The latter is well worth visiting, for this is a branch of art in which Poles have historically excelled. ⊠ *Ul. Wiertnicza 1,* ☎ *022/42–07–95.* ⊠ *Palace zł 8, park zł 2.* ☉ *Wed.–Mon. 9:30–2:30.*

③⑨ Park Łazienkowski (Łazienki Park). The 180 acres of the Łazienki Park, commissioned during the late 18th century by King Stanisław August Poniatowski, run along the Vistula escarpment, parallel to and east of the Royal Route. The **Muzeum łowiectwa i Jezdziectwa** (Museum of Hunting) in the old coach houses on the east side of the park contains a fascinating collection of stuffed birds and animals native to Poland. If you prefer live fauna, look out for the peacocks that wander through the park and the delicate red squirrels that in Poland answer to the name

Basia, a diminutive of Barbara. One of the most beloved sights in the park is the **Pomnik Fryderika Chopina** (Chopin Memorial), a sculpture under a streaming willow tree that shows the composer in a typical romantic pose. In summer, outdoor concerts of Chopin's piano music are held here every Sunday afternoon. ⊠ *Between pl. na Rozdrożu and ul. Bagatela. Museum:* ☎ *022/621–6241.* 🎟 *Zł 5.* ⊙ *Weekdays 10– 4, weekends 9–4.*

👆 ③⑤ **Park Ujazdowski** (Ujazdów Park). At the entrance to the formal gardens of the Park Ujazdowski on the corner of Aleje Ujazdowskie and ulica Piękna, there is a **19th-century weighing booth** just inside the gate, still in operation. There is also a well-equipped **playground** for small children, with sand, swings, and slides.

③④ **Sejm.** The Polish Houses of the Sejm (parliament) are housed in a round, white debating chamber that was built during the 1920s, after the rebirth of an independent Polish state. ⊠ *Ul. Wiejska 6.*

<table>
<tr><td>NEED A
BREAK?</td><td>**Słodki Fukier** (⊠ Ul. Mokotowska 45) This tiny café, near the American Embassy, serves delicious pastries and a wonderful array of teas.</td></tr>
</table>

③⑥ **Zamek Ujazdowski.** If you are interested in modern art, you will find it in the somewhat unlikely setting of the 18th-century Zamek Ujazdowski, reconstructed in the 1980s. This is now the home of the Center for Contemporary Art, which hosts a variety of exhibitions by Polish, European, and North American artists. ⊠ *Al. Ujazdowskie 6 (walk down through the park from pl. na Rozdrożu),* ☎ *022/628–12–71.* 🎟 *Zł 3.* ⊙ *Tues.–Sun. 11–5.*

Jewish Warsaw

The quiet streets of Mirów and Muranów, which now contain mostly apartment buildings, once housed the largest Jewish population in Europe: about 380,000 people in 1939. The Nazis sealed off this area from the rest of the city on November 15, 1940, and the congested area became rapidly less populated as people died from starvation and disease. Between July and September 1942, the Nazis deported about 300,000 ghetto residents to the death camp at Treblinka. On April 19, 1943, remaining inhabitants instigated the Warsaw Ghetto Uprising. Children threw homemade bombs at tanks, and men and women fought soldiers hand to hand. In the end, almost all of the remaining inhabitants died in the uprising or fled through the sewers to the "Aryan side." Although this tour of a ghost world is overshadowed by the specter of the Holocaust, it is one that many still must make.

A GOOD WALK

The wartime ghetto area is northwest of Warsaw's Old Town. Begin on ulica Złota to see the **fragment of the Ghetto Wall** ㊸; then walk north along ulica Jana Pawła II until you reach ulica Twarda, and go west, past a synagogue and across plac Grybowski to **ulica Próżna** ㊹. Go west through a small market area to ulica Marzałkowska and go left to plac Bankowy and the **Jewish Historical Institute and Museum** ㊺. From there, walk west along Aleje Solidarności toward ulica Jana Pawła II, passing the **Femina cinema** ㊻ on your left. Turn north along ulica Jana Pawła II to ulica Mordechaja Anielewicza; here turn east to reach the monument **Pomnik Bohaterów Getta** ㊼. From here, take ulica Karmelicka north to ulica Stawki, where you will find the **Umschlagplatz** ㊽. Trams run along ulica Jana Pawła II to help you on your route; from the corner of ulica Dzika and ulica Okopowa you can take any tram south along ulica Okopowa to reach the **Jewish Cemetery** ㊾.

TIMING

It is possible to see all of the sights described in a few hours, although this would involve some energetic walking. Better to allow a whole day, to give time for reflection and to explore the cemetery fully.

SIGHTS TO SEE

46 Femina cinema. Before the war this area was the heart of Warsaw's Jewish quarter, which was walled off by the Nazis in November 1940 to isolate the Jewish community from "Aryan" Warsaw. The cinema is one of the few buildings in this district that survived the war. It was here that the ghetto orchestra organized concerts in 1941 and 1942; many outstanding musicians found themselves behind the ghetto walls and continued to make music despite the dangers. ✉ *Al. Solidarności 115.*

43 Fragment of Ghetto Wall. In the courtyard of this building, through the archway on the right, stands a 10-ft-tall fragment of the infamous Ghetto wall that existed for one year from November 1940. ✉ *Ul. złota 60.*

49 Jewish Cemetery. Behind a high brick wall on ulica Okopowa you will find Warsaw's Jewish Cemetery, an island of continuity amid so much destruction of the city's Jewish heritage. The cemetery, which is still in use, survived the war, and although allowed to become badly overgrown and neglected during the postwar period, it is gradually being restored. Here you will find fine 19th-century headstones and much that testifies to the Jewish community's role in Polish history and culture. Ludwik Zamenhof, the creator of Esperanto, is buried here, as are Henryk Wohl, minister of the treasury in the national government during the 1864 uprising against Russian rule; Szymon Askenazy, the historian and diplomat; Hipolit Wawelberg, the cofounder of Warsaw Polytechnic; and poet Bolesław Leśmian. ✉ *Okopowa 49–51 (take Bus 170 from pl. Bankowy).*

OFF THE
BEATEN PATH

POWĄZKI CEMETERY – Dating from 1790, Warsaw's oldest cemetery is well worth a visit if you are in the reflective mood. Many well-known Polish names appear on the often elaborate headstones and tombs; there is a recent memorial to the victims of the Katyn massacre. Enter from ulica Powązkowska. ✉ *Ul. Powązkowska 43–45 (next to the Jewish cemetery).* ☉ *Sun.–Thurs. 9–3, Fri. 9–1.*

45 Jewish Historical Institute and Museum. You will find this behind a glittering new office block on the southeast corner of plac Bankowy—the site of what had been the largest temple in Warsaw, the Tłomackie Synagogue. For those seeking to investigate their family history, the Institute houses the **Ronald S. Lauder Foundation Genealogy Project**, which acts as a clearinghouse of information on available archival resources and on the history of towns and villages in which Polish Jews resided. English-speaking staff members are available weekdays after 10. The Institute also houses a museum that displays a permanent collection of mementos and artifacts and periodically organizes special exhibitions. At press time (summer 1998), the museum was closed for an extensive renovation, so call to check on the reopening date. ✉ *Ul. tłomackie 3,* ☎ *022/827–92–21.* ✉ *Free.*

47 Pomnik Bohaterów Getta (Monument to the Heroes of the Warsaw Ghetto). On April 19, 1943, the Jewish Fighting Organization began an uprising in a desperate attempt to resist the mass transports to Treblinka that had been taking place since the beginning of that year. Though doomed from the start, the brave ghetto fighters managed to keep up their struggle for a whole month. But by May 16, General Jürgen Stroop could report to his superior officer that "the former Jewish district in Warsaw had ceased to exist." The ghetto had become a smoldering ruin, razed by Nazi flamethrowers. A monument marks the location of the house at nearby **ulica Miła 18**, the site of the uprising's command bunker and where its leader, Mordechai Anielewicz, was killed. ⊠ *Ul. Zamenhofa, between ul. Anielewicza and ul. Lewartowskiego.*

㊹ Ulica Próżna This is the only street in Jewish Warsaw where tenement buildings have been preserved on both sides of the street. The Lauder Foundation has instigated a plan to restore the street to its original state. No. 9 belonged to Zelman Nożyk, founder of the ghetto synagogue.

㊽ Umschlagplatz. This plaza was the rail terminus from which tens of thousands of the Warsaw ghetto's inhabitants were shipped in cattle cars to the extermination camp of Treblinka, about 100 km (60 mi) northeast of Warsaw. The school building to the right of the square was used to detain those who had to wait overnight for transport; the beginning of the rail tracks survives on the right. At the entrance to the square is a memorial gateway, erected in 1988 on the 45th anniversary of the uprising. ⊠ *Corner of ul. Stawki and ul. Dzika.*

OFF THE
BEATEN PATH

CHOPIN AND RADZIWIŁŁ ESTATES – If you have an extra day in Warsaw a trip to the **Puszcza Kampinoska** (Kampinoski National Park), located about an hour west of the city, is highly recommended, for two of Warsaw's loveliest abodes are situated here: the birthplace of Chopin and the Radziwiłł country estate. There are many tours available to these two sights (☞ Guided Tours *in* Warsaw A to Z, *below*), and this is by far the best way to view them quickly. Both places can also be reached by bus from Dworzec PKS (⊠ Al. Jerozolimskie 144, ☎ 022/9433). Żelazowa **Wola** is a mecca for all Chopin lovers. The composer's birthplace, a small 19th-century manor house, is filled with original furnishings and is devoted to Chopin's life; on summer Sundays, concerts are held on the terrace at 11 AM and 3 PM. The house is located 58 km (36 mi) from Warsaw. If driving, go 30 km (18½ mi) north of Warsaw, and then turn southwest from the 2(E30) at Sochaczew on Route 580. Not too far away is **Nieborów**, the stunning country estate of the Radziwiłł family, centered on a Baroque palace designed by Tilman van Gameren in the late 17th century. In 1945, the estate was taken over by the National Museum of Warsaw and still contains its historic furnishings. The palace contains a charming small hotel (book ahead; no children allowed). Also worth a visit is the nearby 1780 park **Arkadia**, located 5 km (3 mi) away in the direction of Łowicz. If driving, go 30 km (18½ mi) north of Warsaw on the 2(E30), and then turn north at Sochaczew on Route 705 and at Bolimów take a left. ⊠ *Żelazowa Wola:* ☎ *046/863-33-00.* 🎟 *Zł 6.* ☉ *Tues.–Sun. 9–4. Nieborów:* ☎ *046/838-56-20.* 🎟 *Zł 6.* ☉ *Tues.–Fri. 10–4.*

Dining

Like everything else in Warsaw, the dining scene is changing rapidly. New restaurants offer ethnic cuisine (Korean, Japanese, Chinese, and Italian are particularly popular), while others spin such hip variations as "Peasant Chic" and "light Old Polish." Gone are the old, seedy bars, often replaced by clean and brightly tiled pizza parlors. Prices have also risen spectacularly, and eating out in Warsaw is now much more expensive than in other Polish towns. Check the price of the wine before ordering, as restaurants can charge astronomical prices for an ordinary bottle. For the higher-priced dining spots, it is essential to make reservations. Almost all restaurants are closed on public holidays.

$$$$ ✕ **Belvedere.** You could not find a more romantic setting for lunch or
★ dinner than this elegant restaurant in the New Orangery at Łazienki

Park. The lamp-lighted park spreads out beyond the windows, and candles glitter below the high ceilings. Polish cuisine is a specialty, and many dishes are prepared with a variety of fresh mushrooms; try the mushroom soup. Also recommended is the roast boar, served with an assortment of vegetables. ⊠ *Park Łazienki; enter from Agrykola or ul. Gargarina,* ☎ *022/41–48–06. Jacket and tie. AE, DC, MC, V.*

$$$$ ✕ **Dom Restauracyjny Gessler.** You come here partly for the atmospheric setting: a warren of candlelit bare-brick cellars and ground-floor rooms in one of the historic houses on the Old Town Square. Start with *łosoś książąt polskich* (salmon, Polish princes–style, cooked in cream), or *bulion z kołdunami* (broth with dumplings); this could be followed by duck in a marjoram-based sauce, served with noodles. ⊠ *Rynek Starego Miasta 19–21,* ☎ *022/831–16–61. AE, DC, MC, V.*

$$$$ ✕ **Fukier.** This long-established wine bar on the Old Town Square has now become a fascinating network of elaborately decorated dining rooms: There is a talking parrot in a cage, and candles adorn all available shelf space (sometimes set dangerously close to clients' elbows). The food is "light Old Polish": Steak, served on a grill, is a specialty and might be followed by one of a range of rich cream gâteaux. ⊠ *Rynek Starego Miasta 27,* ☎ *022/31–10–13. Reservations essential. AE, DC, MC, V.*

$$$ ✕ **Bazyliszek.** As a second-floor restaurant in a 17th-century merchant's house on the Old Town Square, this place has long received top marks for atmosphere. Dine here under high ceilings of carved wood, if possible in the Knight's Room, where suits of armor and crossed swords decorate the walls. The mainstay of the menu is traditional Polish fare, with an emphasis on game dishes—try the stewed hare in cream sauce, served with beets and noodles. There is a good café downstairs that offers cheaper food. ⊠ *Rynek Starego Miasta 3/9,* ☎ *022/831–18–41. AE, DC, MC, V.*

$$$ ✕ **Flik.** Set on a corner overlooking the Morskie Oko Park, this restaurant in Mokotów has a lovely, geranium-frilled terrace. Inside, the dining room has well-spaced tables, light cane furniture, and lots of greenery. The fresh salmon starter is delicious and could be followed by *zrazy* (rolled beef fillet stuffed with mushrooms). There is a self-service salad bar, and downstairs is a small, casual café. ⊠ *Ul. Puławska 43,* ☎ *022/49–44–06. AE, DC, MC, V.*

$$$ ✕ **Opus One.** For a change from Polish food, try this popular Austrian restaurant for hot pretzels, huge Wiener schnitzel, and homemade potato salad. These, along with a pianist and occasional live jazz, attract loads of Polish yuppies. ⊠ *Pl. Młynarskiego 2,* ☎ *022/827–51–00. AE, DC, MC, V.*

$$$ ✕ **Restauracja Polska.** With a stylish room and some of the best food
★ to be found in the city, this basement restaurant is the place to be seen in Warsaw these days. The tasteful main salon has antique furnishings and large bouquets of flowers. You can't go wrong here with the food, but do try the homemade pierogi or the bigos. For dessert, the chocolate-nut torte is outstanding. ⊠ *Nowy Świat 21,* ☎ *022/826–38–77. AE, DC, MC, V.*

$$$ ✕ **Wilanów.** Historic decor is one plus of this restaurant, housed in an old stable building opposite the Wilanów Palace, 13 km (8 mi) from the city center. The dimly lighted main dining room on the ground floor, known as Hunters' Hall, is decorated with stuffed trophies, and diners make themselves at home in wood-paneled half-booths of an odd kidney shape. The restaurant offers a unique variety of Polish and Continental dishes. Among these are *Wawelska* steak, larded with prunes and cooked in a bacon wrap, and the *Sobieski* pork cutlet in a sweetish fruit-base sauce. ⊠ *Ul. Wiertnicza 27,* ☎ *022/42–13–63. AE, DC, MC, V.*

Dining

Lodging

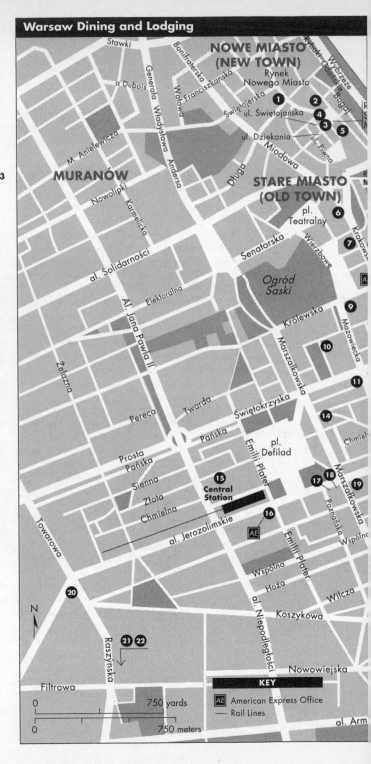

Warsaw Dining and Lodging

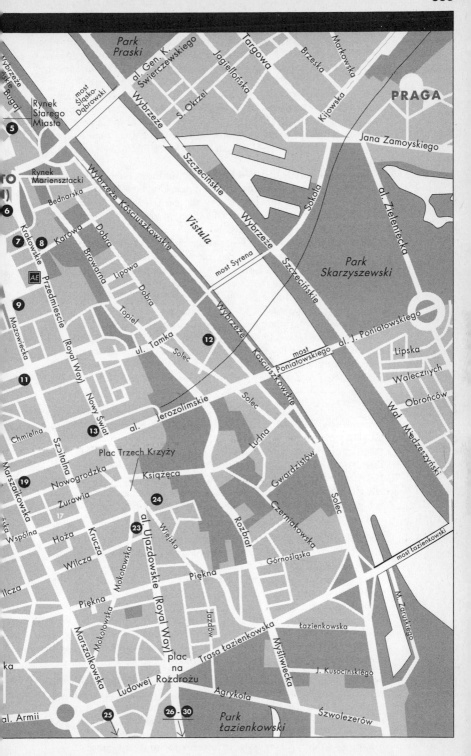

PRAGA

Park
Praski

al. Gen. K.
Swierczewskiego

Targowa

Brzeska

Markowska

Jagiellońska

S. Okrzei

Kijowska

Jana Zamoyskiego

Wybrzeże

most
Śląsko-
Dąbrowski

Rynek
Starego
Miasto

5

Szczecińskie

Wybrzeże

Sokola

al. Zielieniecka

Rynek
Mariensztacki

Wybrzeże Kościuszkowskie

Bednarska

6

Vistula

Park
Skarzyszewski

Karowa

Dobra

Krakowskie

7 **8**

Browarna

Lipowa

Dobra

most Syrena

Szczecińskie

AE

Przedmieście (Royal Way)

Topiel

9

Mazowiecka

ul. Tamka

Solec

12

Wybrzeże Kościuszkowskie

al. J. Poniatowskiego

Lipska

most
Poniatowskiego

11

Nowy Świat

al. Jerozolimskie

Solec

Solec

Waleczrych

Obrońców

Chmielna

Szpitalna

13

Ludna

Wał Miedeszyński

Plac Trzech Krzyży

Gwardzistów

Nowogrodzka

Książęca

19

Marszałkowska

Zurawia

24

Czerniakowska

Solec

17

Wspólna

Hoża

Krucza

23

Wiejska

Rozbrat

most Łazienkowski

Wilcza

Mokotowska

al. Ujazdowskie (Royal Way)

Piękna

Górnośląska

Piękna

Mokotowska

Jazdów

Łazienkowska

Marszałkowska

Trasa Łazienkowska

M. Zaruskiego

al. Armii

plac
na
Rozdrożu

Agrykola

Myśliwiecka

J. Kusocinskiego

Ludowej

25

26 - 30

Park
Łazienkowski

Szwolezerów

$$ ✕ **Kamienne Schodki.** This vaulted restaurant, in a 16th-century house on the corner of the Old Town Square, is famous for its roast duck served with apples (actually, for a long time, it was the only dish offered). The chicken or pork *à la polonaise* with garlic stuffing is also quite good. Save room for the light and creamy pastries. ✉ *Rynek Starego Miasta 26*, ☎ *022/831–08–22. AE, DC, MC, V.*

$$ ✕ **Klub Aktora.** An "in" place for expats and hip Warsavians, the Aktora thrives under the watchful eye of Stanisław Pruszyński, who escaped from Poland in 1955 to become a restaurateur in Canada, only to return to Poland after communism fell. The chicest time to come may be afternoon tea. ✉ *Al. Ujazdowskie 45*, ☎ *022/628–93–66. AE, DC, MC, V.*

$$ ✕ **Menora.** The only certified kosher restaurant in Poland, this is situated on the dilapidated prewar side of plac Grzybowski, opposite the Jewish Theater and synagogue. Try the carp Jewish style (*karp po żydowsku*) or the crepes with meat filling (*kreplach*). ✉ *Plac Grzybowski 2*, ☎ *022/620–37–54. AE, DC, MC, V.*

$ ✕ **Pod Barbicanem** This milk bar situated "under the Barbican gate" is the best deal in town if you can tolerate the grouchy cashier. Enjoy the enormous bowls of homemade soups, the chicken cutlets with mashed potatoes and fresh seasonal vegetables, and the *naleśniki* (crepes with fresh cheese filling). ✉ *Ul. Mostowka 28*, ☎ *022/831–47–37. No credit cards.*

$ ✕ **U Hopfera.** This small and busy restaurant on the Royal Way has brightly checked tablecloths, fresh flowers, and a friendly and efficient staff. It specializes in Polish dishes, ranging from *schab ze śliwkami* (pork baked with plums) to homemade pierogi with beef stuffing. ✉ *Ul. Krakowskie Przedmieście 53*, ☎ *022/635–73–52. AE, DC, MC, V.*

Lodging

Warsaw's overall shortage of hotel beds is likely to continue through the dawn of the millennium. Happily, the situation at the top end of the price range is improving as more and more luxe hotels steadily open. Lower down the price scale, options remain restricted. Bed-and-breakfast accommodations are difficult to find. In summer there are generally more options with student hostels renting out their spaces. Demand is high, so book well in advance. Breakfast is included in hotel rates unless otherwise noted.

Warsaw is a small city, and the location of your hotel is not of crucial importance in terms of travel time to major sights or night spots. Many hotels are clustered in the downtown area near the intersection of ulica Marszałkowska and Aleje Jerozolimskie. This is not an especially scenic area; nevertheless, the neighborhood doesn't exactly become a "concrete desert" after business hours, since there are still many residential properties as well as restaurants and nightspots. Note: With a rising crime rate in the city, it is best to be cautious when strolling downtown at night, although the greatest hazards more usually turn out to be uneven pavements and inadequate lighting.

The hotels on plac Piłsudskiego, which is close to parks and within easy walking distance of the Old Town, offer more pleasant surroundings. Most of the suburban hotels have no particular scenic advantage, though they do provide immediate access to larger tracts of open space and fresh air. *See* B&B Reservation Agencies *in* Warsaw A to Z, *below,* for agencies that provide lodging information and reservations.

$$$$ 🏨 **Bristol.** Built in 1901 by a consortium headed by Ignacy Paderewski, ★ the concert pianist who served as Poland's prime minister in 1919–1920, the Bristol was long at the center of Warsaw's social life. Impressively situated on the Royal Way, next to the Radziwiłł Palace, the Bristol survived World War II more or less intact. The Bristol continues to maintain its long tradition of luxury and elegance under the new ownership of Le Meridien. It has one of the best cafés in town—no one can resist its pastries. ⊠ *Krakowskie Przedmieście 42–44, 00–325,* ☎ *022/625–25–25,* FAX *022/625–25–77. 163 rooms, 43 suites. 2 restaurants, bar, café, pool, sauna, solarium. AE, DC, MC, V.*

$$$$ 🏨 **Holiday Inn.** Designed, and later franchised, by Holiday Inn, this gleaming six-story complex opposite Warsaw's Central Station avoids some of the standard chain-hotel impersonality. It's softly carpeted and furnished throughout in shades of gray and blue; a tree-filled, steel-and-glass conservatory fronts the building up to the third floor. The generously proportioned guest rooms have projecting bay windows that overlook the very center of the city. ⊠ *Ul. Złota 48, 00–120,* ☎ *022/697–39–99,* FAX *022/697–38–99. 365 rooms, 8 suites. 3 restaurants, 2 bars, café. AE, DC, MC, V.*

$$$$ 🏨 **Jan III Sobieski.** Since it opened in 1991, this hotel's bright pink, blue, and yellow illusionist facade has startled more than a few Warsovians. Inside, however, the decor is more conventional, and service is impeccable. The rooms are reasonably sized and warmly furnished in soft rosewood and flowered prints. ⊠ *Pl. Zawiszy 1, 02–025,* ☎ *022/658–44–44,* FAX *022/659–88–28. 377 rooms, 27 suites. 2 restaurants, bar, café. AE, DC, MC, V.*

$$$$ 🏨 **Marriott.** Located in the high-rise Lim Center opposite the Central Station, the Marriott currently offers one of the city's best accommodations; it was the first hotel in Poland to be under direct American management. The staff is well trained and helpful; everyone speaks some English. The views from every room—of central Warsaw and far beyond—are spectacular on a clear day. The fitness facilities are most satisfactory. The Lila Veneda restaurant on the second floor runs a special Sunday brunch, complete with Dixieland band. ⊠ *Al. Jerozolimskie 65–79, 00–697,* ☎ *022/630–63–06,* FAX *022/830–00–50 489 rooms, 31 suites. 3 restaurants, 3 bars, pool, health club, casino, nightclub, business center, parking. AE, DC, MC, V.*

$$$$ 🏨 **Sheraton.** Halfway along the Royal Route from the Old Town to
★ the Łazienki Palace, this modern, six-story, curved building overlooks plac Trzech Krzyży, and behind it are the parks that run along the Vistula embankment. The interiors are bright, the rooms generously sized, and the well-trained staff succeeds in making the Sheraton the friendliest hotel in Warsaw. ⊠ *Ul. Bolesława Prusa 2, 00–504,* ☎ *022/657–61–00,* FAX *022/657–62–00. 350 rooms, 20 suites. 3 restaurants, cafés, sauna, health club. AE, DC, MC, V.*

$$$$ 🏨 **Victoria Inter-Continental.** Overlooking plac Piłsudskiego, the Victoria, opened in the late 1970s, was until 1989 Warsaw's only luxury hotel, hosting a stream of official visitors and state delegations. The large and comfortably furnished guest rooms are decorated in tones of brown and gold. Health facilities include an attractive basement swimming pool and three exercise rooms, and the hotel is just across the street from the jogging (or walking) paths of the Saxon Gardens. ⊠ *Ul. Królewska 11, 00–065,* ☎ *022/657–80–11,* FAX *022/657–80–57. 347 rooms, 13 suites. 3 restaurants, bar, pool, health clubs, casino, nightclub, parking (fee). AE, DC, MC, V.*

$$$ 🏨 **Europejski.** Although it retains traces of its earlier grandeur, this hotel is now clearly struggling to maintain standards. The 19th-century building was reopened in 1962 after postwar reconstruction; the renovators managed to retain some original features, including two grand marble staircases. The rooms, with somewhat shabby furnishings, are very diverse in size and shape; almost all have views overlooking historic Warsaw—on one side, the Royal Route, on the other, plac Piłsudskiego. Guests are allowed, for an extra fee, to use the pool and health club facilities of the nearby Victoria Hotel, which is under the same management. The hotel is not air-conditioned. ⊠ *Krakowskie Przedmieście 13, 00–065,* ☎ *022/826–50–51,* FAX *022/826–11–11. 233 rooms, 5 suites. Restaurant, bar. AE, DC, MC, V.*

$$$ 🏨 **Forum.** This dun-colored, 30-story, Swedish-designed metal cube has been a fixture on the Warsaw skyline since 1974. Guest rooms are of average size, and those on the east side of the building offer good views—but don't choose the Forum if you're counting on cheerful surroundings. Depressing tones of brown and green predominate, and the furnishings seem to have been chosen for function rather than comfort. The staff, used to dealing with rapid-turnover group tours, can be offhand. The hotel is not air-conditioned, and it's in the middle of a heavily built-up district. On the plus side, it is within easy reach of the entertainment districts. ⊠ *Ul. Nowogrodzka 24/26, 00–511,* ☎ *022/621–02–71,* FAX *022/625–04–76. 750 rooms, 13 suites. 2 restaurants, bar. AE, DC, MC, V.*

$$ 🏨 **Gromada.** Opened in 1995 and just under 1 km (½ mi) to Warsaw's airport and about 7 km (4½ mi) from the city center, the Gromada is run by a peasants' cooperative; the dining room is one of its attractions, and breakfast is particularly recommended. The rooms are comfortable, if standardized. The hotel stands well back from the busy main road and has wooded grounds. There is good bus service into town. ⊠ *Ul. 17 Stycznia 32, 02–148,* ☎ *022/846–54–01,* FAX *022/846–15–80. 140 rooms. Restaurant, bar, sauna. AE, DC, MC, V.*

$$ 🏨 **Gromada Dom Chłopa.** With an excellent location in the center of Warsaw, this white, five-story hotel was built during the late 1950s by the Gromada peasants' cooperative and originally had a plant-and-seed store on the ground floor. Times have changed: The store now sells TVs. The hotel, which has just undergone renovation, offers clean and reasonably priced accommodations; rooms are rather small, but the colors are lively, and the bathrooms have been updated. The downtown location is excellent. There is no air-conditioning. ⊠ *Pl. Powstańców Warszawy 2, 00–030,* ☎ *022/625–15–45,* FAX *022/625–21–40. 282 rooms. Restaurant, bar. AE, DC, MC, V.*

$$ 🏨 **Metropol.** This 1960s hotel is right on Warsaw's main downtown intersection. The single rooms (which form the majority) are large enough to contain a bed, armchairs, and desk without feeling crowded; bathrooms, though small, are attractively tiled and fitted. Each room, however, has a balcony overlooking busy ulica Marszałkowska, and traffic noise can be very intrusive when the windows are open. There is no air-conditioning. ⊠ *Ul. Marszałkowska 99, 00–693,* ☎ *022/629–40–01,* FAX *022/625–30–14. 175 rooms, 16 suites. Restaurant. AE, DC, MC, V.*

$$ 🏨 **Novotel.** The Novotel can be recommended for a good night's sleep, as it is some distance away from the hustle and bustle of the city center. It's only five minutes from Okęcie Airport (fortunately, *not* under any flight paths) and it's right across the road from a major area of gardens and parks. Though removed from the heart of the city, the hotel is on the main bus routes; Bus 175 will take you downtown in 10–15 minutes. The atmosphere is friendly, and the rooms are light, clean, and comfortable. ⊠ *Ul. 1 Sierpnia 1, 02–134,* ☎ *022/846–40–51,* FAX *022/846–36–86. 150 rooms. Restaurant, bar, parking (fee). AE, DC, MC, V.*

$$ 🏨 **Parkowa.** This 1970s hotel, reserved for official government dele-
★ gations, frequently has rooms available to the general public. It is just south of the Belvedere Palace in a landscaped area adjacent to the Łazienki Park. The hotel has recently been renovated and now offers attractive, Western-style accommodations (including air-condition-

ing). ⊠ *Ul. Belwederska 46/50, 00–594,* ☎ *022/694–80–00,* FAX *022/ 41–60–29. 44 rooms. Restaurant, bar, sauna. AE, DC, MC, V.*

$$ 🏨 **Polonia.** The Art Nouveau Polonia was the only Warsaw hotel to survive World War II intact. Much of the hotel's period splendor was lost in a major renovation completed in 1974, when the rooms were standardized (it was also renovated in the mid-1990s). The high-ceiling rooms are, however, still reasonably spacious and comfortable; quite a few of the doubles and suites retain their stylish bay windows and balconies, and many of the bathrooms are large. The restaurant is a marvelous set piece of fin-de-siècle elegance. There is no air-conditioning; note that single rooms do not have baths. ⊠ *Al. Jerozolimskie 45, 00– 692,* ☎ *022/628–72–41,* FAX *022/628–66–22. 210 rooms, 28 suites. Restaurant, bar, café. AE, DC, MC, V.*

$ 🏨 **Belfer.** This hotel is situated in Powiśle, across the road from the Vistula River and 10 minutes by foot (admittedly all uphill) from the Royal Route. Traffic noise can be a big problem in front-facing rooms, but courtyard-facing rooms are peaceful. The decor throughout is dull, with plenty of dark-wood paneling and chocolate-brown paint, and there is no air-conditioning, though the rooms are spacious and comfortable, and everything is clean. ⊠ *Wybrzeże Kościuszkowskie 31/33, 00–379,* ☎ *022/625–05–71,* FAX *022/625–26–00. 360 rooms, 10 doubles with bath. Restaurant, café. AE, DC, MC, V.*

$ 🏨 **Hera.** This three-story socialist-realist building on the edge of Łazienki Park was taken over from the Communist Central Committee in 1990 by Warsaw University. It is used mainly for university guests, but overflow rooms are rented throughout the year. The spartanly decorated rooms are of good size and many overlook the beautiful Łazienki park. It is probably the best-located hotel in the price range. ⊠ *Ul. Belwederska 26/30, 00–594,* ☎ *022/41–02–54,* FAX *022/41–08–05. 40 rooms. Restaurant. AE, DC, MC, V.*

$ 🏨 **Stegny Sports Hotel and Camping.** A stone's throw from downtown Warsaw on the road to Wilanow Palace, this hotel is situated next to an outdoor speed skating rink and was the host of the 1997 World Speed Skating Championships. It offers a cheap and quiet place to stay, with extremely simple rooms (with bathrooms down the hall). There is also a year-round campsite on the premises. ⊠ *Ul. Idzikowskiego 4, 00– 594,* ☎ *022/42–27–00. 25 rooms. Restaurant, sauna, 2 indoor-outdoor tennis courts, skating rink. No credit cards.*

Nightlife and the Arts

Warsaw has much to offer those interested in the arts. Find out what's on from the English-language *Warsaw Insider,* available at most major hotels. If you read Polish, the monthly *IKS (Informator Kulturalny Stolicy),* and the daily *Gazeta Wyborcza* have the best listings—or go to Warsaw's only major ticket agency, **ZASP,** at Aleje Jerozolimskie 25 (☎ 022/621–94–54). If you speak Polish, you can call **Telefoniczny Informator Kulturalny** (☎ 022/629–84–89); it's open daily 10 AM–6 PM. The tickets for most performances are still inexpensive, but if you want to spend even less, most theaters sell general-admission entrance tickets—*wejściówki*—for a few złoty, immediately before the performance. These do not entitle you to an exact reserved seat number but allow you to take an unoccupied seat. Wejściówki are often available for performances for which all standard tickets have been sold.

As throughout Central Europe, people tend to meet for a drink in the evenings in *kawiarnie* (cafés)—where you can linger for as long as you like over a serving of coffee or brandy—rather than in bars (most cafés are open until 10). But Western-style bars have become more popular and there is also a growing fashion for pubs. Discos and rock clubs are mushrooming; jazz clubs have a wide audience. Casinos are mainly the haunt of foreign visitors and the new, rich business class of Poles.

Nightlife

BARS AND LOUNGES

If you've got to know the score, **Champions** sports bar and restaurant (⊠ Lim Center, Al. Jerozolimskie 65/79, ☎ 022/630–40–33) is a great place to watch American basketball and football games. **Harenda** (⊠ Krakowskie Przedmieście 4/6, entrance from ul. Obożna, ☎ 022/826–29–00) occasionally offers some good jazz and has an outdoor terrace that gets crowded in summer. The **John Bull Pub** (⊠ Zielna 37, ☎ 022/620–06–56) is open till midnight and serves English draught beers. **Morgan's** (⊠ Ul. Okólnik 1, entrance from ul. Tamka, ☎ 022/826–81–38) is the latest Irish pub in town.

CASINOS

The **Casino Warsaw** (⊠ Al. Jerozolimskie 65/79, ☎ 022/830–01–78), on the second floor of the Marriott hotel, is Warsaw's plushest and most sedate casino; the clients are often international businessmen or Polish jet-setters. It's open daily 11 AM–7 AM. The **Queen's Casino** (⊠ Pałac Kultury i Nauki, entrance from ul. Emilii Plater, ☎ 022/620–85–23) is in a splendid room in the basement of the Congress Hall of the Palace of Culture. It's open daily 4 PM–6 AM. The **Victoria Casino** (⊠ Ul. Królewska 11, ☎ 022/657–80–11) is also popular and open daily 1 PM–5 AM.

DISCOS

Ground Zero (⊠ Ul. Wspólna 62, ☎ 022/625–43–80), a former bomb shelter, is a large and crowded bi-level disco. **Hades** (⊠ Al. Niepodległości 162, ☎ 022/49–12–51) is a popular disco in the cellars of the Central School of Economics, with plenty of seating space. **Orpheus,** in the Marriott (⊠ Al. Jerozolimskie 65/79, ☎ 022/630–54–16), has an elegant air and is very expensive. There is a well-established disco at the student club **Stodoła** (⊠ Batorego 10, ☎ 022/25–86–25). **Tango** (⊠ Al. Jerozolimskie 4, ☎ 022/622–19–19) is a pricey disco; on Thursdays there is a cabaret show for zł 105, which includes a buffet supper.

JAZZ CLUBS

Akwarium (⊠ Ul. Emilii Plater 49, ☎ 022/620–50–72), the Polish Jazz Association's club, runs a regular evening program of modern jazz; top Polish musicians and foreign groups perform here. **Blue Velvet** (⊠ Krakowskie Przedmieście 5, ☎ 022/828–11–03) has regular modern jazz evenings. **Kawiarnia Literacka** (⊠ Krakowskie Przedmieście 87/89, ☎ 022/826–57–84) has classic jazz on weekends.

The Arts

FILM

Since 1989 it seems every cinema in Warsaw has been showing foreign films—mainly U.S. box-office hits—nonstop. These are generally shown in their original version, with added subtitles. **Relax** (⊠ Ul. Złota 8, ☎ 022/827–77–62) is a popular large cinema in the center of town. **Skarpa** (⊠ Ul. Kopernika 7–9, ☎ 022/826–48–96), off ulica Nowy Świat, is large and modern.

Don't count on seeing many Polish films while visiting Warsaw; only one cinema specializes in Polish features, **Iluzjon Filmoteki Narodowej** (⊠ Ul. Narbutta 55a, ☎ 022/48–33–33). **Wars** (⊠ Rynek Starego Miasta 5–7, ☎ 022/831–44–88), a cinema on the New Town Square, occasionally forgets about box-office success and shows an old Polish classic; it has a good program of foreign films.

MUSIC

The **Filharmonia Narodowa** (National Philharmonic; ⊠ Ul. Sienkiewicza 10, ☎ 022/826–57–12) offers an excellent season of concerts, with visits from world-renowned performers and orchestras as well as Polish musicians. Very popular concerts of classical music for children— run for years by Jadwiga Mackiewicz, who is herself almost a national institution—are held here on Sundays at 2; admission is from zł 5. **Studio Koncertowe Polskiego Radia** (Polish Radio Concert Studio; ⊠ Ul. Woronicza 17, ☎ 022/645–50–00), open since 1992, has excellent acoustics and popular programs. The **Royal Castle** (⊠ Plac Zamkowy 4, ☎ 022/65–72–170) has regular concerts in its stunning Great Assembly Hall. **Towarzystwo im. Fryderyka Chopina** (Chopin Society; ⊠ Ul. Okólnik 1, ☎ 022/827–54–71) organizes recitals and chamber concerts in the Pałac Ostrogskich. In summer, free Chopin concerts are held at the Chopin monument in **Łazienki Park** on Sundays and at Chopin's birthplace, **Żelazowa Wola,** 58 km (36 mi) outside of Warsaw (☞ Exploring, *above*).

OPERA AND DANCE

Teatr Wielki (⊠ Pl. Teatralny, ☎ 022/826–32–88), Warsaw's grand opera, stages spectacular productions of the classic international opera and ballet repertoire, as well as Polish operas and ballets. Stanisław Moniuszko's 1865 opera *Straszny Dwór* (*Haunted Manor*), a lively piece with folk costumes and dancing, is a good starting point if you want to explore Polish music: The visual aspects will entertain you, even if the music is unfamiliar. Plot summaries in English are available at most performances. **Warszawska Opera Kameralna** (⊠ Al. Solidarności 76, ☎ 022/831–22–40), the Warsaw chamber opera, which is housed in a beautifully restored 19th-century theater building in the Muranów district, has a very ambitious program and a growing reputation for quality performances.

THEATER

The **Globe Theater Group** (☎ 022/620–44–29) performs American and British plays. **"Gulliver" Teatr Lalek** (⊠ Ul. Różana 16, ☎ 022/45–16–76) is one of Warsaw's excellent puppet theaters. **Teatr Narodowy** (⊠ Pl. Teatralny, ☎ 022/26–32–87), adjoining the opera house and under the same management, stages Polish classics. **Teatr Żydowski** (⊠ Plac Grzybowski 12/16, ☎ 022/620–70–25), Warsaw's Jewish theater, performs in Yiddish, but most of its productions are colorful costume dramas in which the action speaks as loudly as the words. Translation into English is provided through headphones.

Outdoor Activities and Sports

Health Clubs

The best health-club facility in Warsaw is the **Fitness Center** at the Sheraton Hotel (⊠ Ul. B. Prusa 2, ☎ 022/657–61–00). The center has the latest equipment, aerobics and other classes, and child care; it's open to nonmembers.

Hiking

In Warsaw the local branch of **PTTK** (Ramblers' Association) organizes daylong hikes in the nearby countryside on weekends: Watch the local papers for advertisements of meeting points and routes.

Horse Racing

You can reach Warsaw's beautiful but seedy **racecourse** by taking Tram 14 or 36 or one of the special buses marked WYŚCIGI, which run from the east side of the Palace of Culture and Science on Saturdays in season (May–October). Betting is on a tote system. ⊠ *Ul. Puławska 266,* ☎ *022/843–14–41.* 🖼 *Stands zł 10.*

Jogging

Along with dogs and bicycles, joggers are banned from Warsaw's largest and most beautiful park, the Łazienki. The 9½-km (6-mi) trail through parkland and over footbridges from the **Ujazdowski Park** to Mariensztat (parallel to the Royal Route) is a good route. The **Vistula embankment** (the paved surface runs for about 12 km/8 mi) makes for a good straight run. The **Pilsudski Park** has a circular route of about 4½ km (3 mi). The somewhat restricted pathways of the **Ogród Saski** offer the possibility of jogging in the center of town.

Soccer

Warsaw's soccer team, **Legia,** plays at the field at ulica Łazienkowska 3. ☎ *022/621–08–96.* 🖼 *From zł 15.*

Swimming

Your best bet is the **Bristol Hotel** indoor pool (⊠ Krakowskie Przedmieśie 42/44, ☎ 022/625–25–25). Warsaw's indoor pools tend to be overcrowded, and some restrict admission to those with season tickets; it's best to check first. At the **Spartańska** (⊠ Ul. Spartańska 1, ☎ 022/48–67–46) you can usually persuade them to let you swim on a special one-day pass.

Shopping

Warsaw's shopping scene is booming, with more and more international chains (Marks & Spencer, London's noted department store, will open its doors by late 1999) and boutiques setting up shop. As a result, locally produced items are sometimes harder to find than ridiculously expensive imported ones. Shopping hours are usually from 11 AM to 7 PM on weekdays and 10 AM to 1 PM on Saturdays. **RUCH** kiosks, which sell bus and train tickets, newspapers, and cosmetics, are usually open from 7 to 7.

Shopping Districts

Warsaw's four main shopping streets are **ulica Marszałkowska** (from ul. Królewska to pl. Zbawiciela), **Aleje Jerozolimskie** (from the Central Station to pl. Generala de Gaulle), **ulica Nowy Świat,** and **ulica Chmielna.** Ulica Marszałkowska and Aleje Jerozolimskie offer mainly larger stores. Nowy Świat and ulica Chmielna have smaller stores and more specialized boutiques.

Department Stores

Warsaw's oldest department store, **Braci Jabłkowskich,** at the corner of ulica Krucza and ulica Chmielna, with a monumental staircase and Art Nouveau stained-glass windows, has a range of separate stores selling clothing, jewelry, and household items. The **Central Department Stores** (⊠ Ul. Marszałkowska 104–122), divided into the **Wars, Sawa,** and **Junior** sections, have changed their image. The old empty halls, through which people dashed searching for a rare special find, are gone; instead, the stores have rent out space to private boutiques selling mainly imported fashion items.

Specialty Stores

ANTIQUES

Desa stores (⊠ Ul. Marszałkowska 34, ☎ 022/621–66–15; ⊠ Ul. Nowy Świat 51, ☎ 022/827–47–60; ⊠ Rynek Starego Miasta 4/6, ☎ 022/831–16–81) have a fine range of antique furniture, art, and china. Remember, however, that most antiques cannot be exported.

ART GALLERIES

Galeria Nowy Świat (✉ Nowy Świat 23, ☎ 022/826–35–01) has painting, ceramics, and designer furniture. **Galeria Sztuki** (✉ Ul. Świętokrzyska 32, ☎ 022/652–11–77) has one of the finest selections of contemporary Polish art.

FOLK ART AND CRAFTS

Arex (✉ Ul. Chopina 5B, ☎ 022/629–66–24) is the best place to go for traditional Polish wood carvings. The **Cepelia** stores (✉ Pl. Konstytucji 5, ☎ 022/621–26–18; ✉ Rynek Starego Miasta 10, ☎ 022/831–18–05) sell a variety of folk art, including wood carvings, and silver and amber jewelry.

GLASS AND CRYSTAL

A. Jabłonski (✉ Ul. Nowy Świat 52) offers unique pieces of handblown glass and crystal. **Szlifierna skła** (✉ Ul. Nowomeijska 1/3, ☎ 022/831–46–43), next to the Old Town Square, custom engraves all kinds of crystal goods.

JEWELRY

There are many jewelry (*Jubiler*) stores clustered around the old town and ulica Nowy Świat. The **Art Gallery** (✉ Rynek Starego Miasto 13) has a great selection of silver and amber, although much of it is somewhat overpriced. One of the oldest and best-established stores in Poland is **W. Kruk** (✉ Pl. Konstytucji 6, ☎ 022/628–75–34).

LEATHER

JKM (✉ Krakowskie Przedmieście 65, ☎ 022/827–22–62) is a small shop crammed with well-designed bags, suitcases, and gloves from the best Polish producers. **Pekar** (✉ Al. Jerozolimskie 29, ☎ 022/621–90–82) carries a wide range of bags, gloves, and jackets.

Street Markets

The largest Warsaw market, known as the Russian market and composed largely of private sellers hawking everything from antiques to blue jeans, is at the **Tysiąclecie Sports Stadium,** on the other side of the river at Rondo Waszyngtona. If you go, watch out for pickpockets.

Warsaw A to Z

Arriving and Departing

BY BUS

The private long-distance bus service **Polski Express** (☎ 022/620–03–30 for information and reservations; English spoken) arrives and departs from Jana Pawła II between the Central Train Station and the Holiday Inn. Polski Express also has a stop at the airport.

Warsaw's main bus station, **Dworzec PKS** (✉ Al. Jerozolimskie 144, ☎ 022/94–33), 10 minutes on bus 172 from Warzawa Centralna, serves most long-distance express routes and cities to the west of the city (such as Chopin's birthplace, at Żelazowa Wola; ☞ Exploring Warsaw, *above*). Local services for points north of the city run from **Dworzec PKS Marymont** in the northern district of Żoliborz (✉ Corner of ul. Marymoncka and ul. Żeromskiego, ☎ 022/834–74–44); buses headed east leave from **Dworzec PKS Stadion** (✉ Intersection of ul. Targowa, ul. Zamoyskiego, and al. Zieleniecka, on the east bank of the Vistula, ☎ 022/94–33). Tickets for all destinations can be purchased at the main bus station.

BY CAR

Within the city, a car can be more a problem than a convenience. Warsaw currently has too many cars for its road network, and there can be major snarls. Parking can be very difficult. There is a real threat of theft—of contents, parts, or the entire car—if you leave a Western model unattended, and it is not easy to get quick service or repairs. If you do bring your car, park it overnight in a guarded parking garage.

BY PLANE

Warsaw's **Okęcie Airport** (☎ 022/650–42–20) is 7 km (4½ mi) south of the city center. **LOT,** the Polish airline (✉ Al. Jerozolimskie 65/79, ☎ 022/630–50–07; 952 for reservations), takes the lion's share of flights to and from Warsaw. Other airlines flying to Warsaw include **Air France** (☎ 022/628–12–81); **American Airlines** (☎ 022/625–30–02); **British Airways** (☎ 022/628–94–31); **Delta** (☎ 022/827–84–61); and **Lufthansa** (☎ 022/630–25–55).

Between the Airport and Downtown: The direct route to downtown, where almost all the hotels are, is along Aleje Żwirki i Wigury and ulica Raszyńska. **By Bus:** The AIRPORT–CITY bus leaves from Platform 4 outside Terminal 1 every 20 minutes and stops at all the major hotels and the Central Station. Tickets cost zł 6, and the trip takes about 25 minutes. Alternatively, Bus 175 leaves Okęcie about every 10 minutes. It also runs past most major downtown hotels and is reliable and cheap. Purchase tickets for zł 1.40 at the airport RUCH kiosks. If your immediate destination is not Warsaw, **Polski Express** now runs direct services from Okęcie to major Polish cities (☎ 022/630–03–30 for information and reservations). **By Taxi:** Avoid at all costs the taxi hawkers and unmarked vehicles (no number at the top) outside the arrivals hall—not only are these cabs expensive but they can also be dangerous. Your best bet is to call a **Radio Taxi** service (☎ 919, 9622, or 9623) from one of the hotel desks in the arrivals area or call your hotel in advance and have them pick you up. A cab ride into the city should cost about zł 50.

BY TRAIN

Warsaw's **Dworzec Centralny** (Central Station; ☎ 022/25–50–00; 022/620–45–12 for international rail information; 022/620–03–61 for domestic rail information), as the name implies, is right in the heart of the city, at Aleje Jerozolimskie 54, between the Marriott and Holiday Inn hotels. Beware of pickpockets and muggers who prey on passengers as they board or leave trains. Local trains run from **Warszawa Śródmieście,** next to Central Station, on Aleje Jerozolimskie (☎ 022/628–47–41), or from **Dworzec Wileński** (✉ Ul. Targowa, ☎ 022/18–35–21). You can purchase train tickets at the train station or at Orbis and other travel agents.

Getting Around

Although Warsaw stretches more than 32 km (20 mi) in each direction, the sights of greatest interest to most tourists are concentrated primarily in two areas: Śródmieście, Warsaw's downtown, along ulica Marszałkowska; and Stare Miasto, the Old Town, just over 2 km (1 mi) away and centered on Rynek Starego Miasta. Both areas are best explored on foot; public transportation, though cheap and efficient, can be uncomfortably crowded. Taxis are readily available and are often the most convenient option for covering longer distances.

BY BUS

A trip on a city bus costs zł 1.40; you have to purchase tickets at a RUCH kiosk and cancel one in the machine on the bus for each ride. Buses, which halt at all stops along their route, are numbered 100 and up. Express buses are numbered from E-1 upward: Buses numbered 500–599 stop at selected stops. Check details on the information board at the bus stop. Night buses (numbered 600 and up) operate between 11 PM and 5 AM; the fare is zł 4, and for these trips you can buy tickets directly from the driver.

BY TAXI

In Warsaw, it is always best to use the **Radio Taxi** services (☎ 919 or 9622) as these are the most reliable and the operators usually speak English. The standard charge for the first kilometer is about zł 4 and zł 1.4 for each kilometer thereafter. It is not customary to tip taxi drivers, although you can round up the fare to the nearest złoty. Avoid unmarked Mercedes cabs as well as taxis that do not have a number on the top (9622, 9623, etc.), as they are likely to charge far more than the going rate.

BY TRAM

Trams are the fastest means of public transport, since they are not affected by traffic hold-ups. Purchase tickets from RUCH kiosks and cancel one ticket in the machine on the tram for each ride. Trams run on a north–south and east–west grid system along most of the main city routes, pulling up automatically at all stops. Each tram has a diagram of the system.

BY UNDERGROUND

Warsaw's underground opened in spring 1995. Although as yet it has only one line, running from the southern suburbs to the city center (Natolin to Pl. Politechniki), it is clean and fast and costs the same as tram and bus travel—use the same tickets, canceling them at the entrance to the station.

Contacts and Resources

B&B RESERVATION AGENCIES

Syrena (⊠ Ul. Krucza 17, ☎ 022/628–75–40) has a wide selection of accommodations in the city center although none include breakfast. The staff is helpful and speaks English.

DOCTORS AND DENTISTS

The **American Medical Center** (⊠ Ul. Wilcza 23, 35, ☎ 022/622–0497, 24 hrs) is run by an American doctor and has contacts with outside specialists. For dental care: **Austria-Dent Center** (⊠ Ul. Zelazna 54, ☎ 022/821–31–84), open weekdays 9–9, Saturdays 9–3.

EMBASSIES AND CONSULATE

All three embassies listed below are on or just off of Aleje Ujazdowskie; the British Consulate is closer to the center of town.

U.S. Embassy (⊠ Al. Ujazdowskie 29–31, ☎ 022/628–30–41). **Canadian Embassy** (⊠ Ul. Matejki 1–5, ☎ 022/629–80–51). **British Embassy** (⊠ Al. Roż 1, ☎ 022/628–10–01). **British Consulate** (⊠ Ul. Emilii Plater 28, ☎ 022/625–30–30).

EMERGENCIES

Police (☎ 997). **Ambulance** (☎ 999). Do not expect anyone at these numbers to speak English. Major embassies have someone on duty 24 hours a day to help their country's citizens in an emergency.

ENGLISH-LANGUAGE BOOKSTORES

Most major bookstores now have well-stocked English sections. Some of the best selections can be found at the following bookstores: **Empik** (⊠ Ul. Nowy Świat 15/17, ☎ 022/627–06–50); **Bookland—Longman** (⊠ Al. Jerozolimskie 61, ☎ 022/625–41–46).

GUIDED TOURS

Marzurkas Travel (⊠ Ul. Długa 8/14, ☎ 022/656–66–33) and **Local Rent a Car Poland LTD** (⊠ Europejski hotel, ul. Krakowskie Przedmieście 13, ☎ 022/657–81–81) offer a wide selection of daily tours of Warsaw as well as tours of Poland. These can be booked at major hotels or through the agencies directly. For tours that focus on Jewish Warsaw (or Jewish Poland) call **Our Roots—Jewish Information and Tourist Bureau** (⊠ Ul. Twarda 6, ☎ 022/620–05–56).

LATE-NIGHT PHARMACIES

The following pharmacies (*apteka*) are open 24 hours a day: **Apteka Grabowskiego,** on the first floor in ⊠ Dworzec Centralny, Al. Jerozolimskie 54, ☎ 022/25–69–86; plus branch stores on Freta Street (⊠ Ul. Freta 13, ☎ 022/831–50–91) and Widok Street (⊠ Ul. Widok 19, ☎ 022/827–35–93).

MONEY AND CURRENCY

To change money, head to the **Kantor Wymiany Walut** at ulica Marszałkowska 66, on the corner of ulica Wilcza; it has swift, friendly service and usually offers slightly better rates than hotels and banks. It is open weekdays 11–7 and Saturdays 9–2. Another option is the **Kantor** in the General Post Office at ulica Święto krzyska 31, open 24 hours a day. **TEBOS,** at the Central Railway Station on Aleje Jerozolimskie, at the foot of the staircase leading from the main hall to the access passage to platforms, is also open 24 hours a day; exercise caution, however—the Central Station is a haunt of pickpockets.

TRAVEL AGENCIES

American Express (⊠ Krakowskie Przedmieście 11, ☎ 022/635–20–02; 022/630–69–52, 24 hrs). **Getz International Travel Ltd.** (⊠ Al. Jerozolimskie 56C, ☎ 022/630–27–60) is an efficient agency with friendly service. **Carlson Wagonlit Travel** (⊠ Ul. Nowy Świat 64, ☎ 022/826–04–31) is a centrally located travel agency. **Orbis** (⊠ Ul. Bracka 16, ☎ 022/826–02–71) is especially good for train tickets.

VISITOR INFORMATION

The **Center for Tourist Information** (⊠ Pl. Zamkowy 1, ☎ 022/635–18–81), on Castle Square, is open 9–6 weekdays, 11–6 weekends. The **Warsaw Tourist Information Office** has several offices in Warsaw, including in the Hotel Dom Chłopa (⊠ Plac Powstańców, ☎ 022/94–31) and in the arrivals hall of the airport. Their offices are open weekdays 8–7 and weekends 9–3.

KRAKÓW

Renaissance arcades, enchanting onion domes, Baroque spires, storybook streets, and Leonardo da Vinci's sublime painting of *Cecilia Gallerani*—little wonder the stunning beauty of this 1,000-year-old city and its sights attracts hundreds of thousands of visitors annually. Kraków (Cracow), seat of Poland's oldest university and once the nation's capital (before finally relinquishing the honor to Warsaw in 1611), is one of the few Polish cities that escaped devastation by Hitler's armies during World War II. Today Kraków's fine towers, facades, and churches, reflecting seven centuries of Polish architecture, continue to make it the shop window of Poland. Its location, about 270 km (170 mi) south of Warsaw, also makes it a good starting point for hiking and skiing trips in the mountains of southern Poland.

North of Kraków, the industrial town of **Częstochowa,** where Poland's holiest icon, the Black Madonna, is housed in the Pauline monastery, can be visited as a lengthy day trip from Kraków.

Exploring Kraków

290 km (180 mi) south of Warsaw, 270 km (170 mi) southwest of Lublin, 260 km (161 mi) east of Wrocław.

Listed by UNESCO in 1978 as one of the world's 12 great historic cities and the seat of one of Europe's oldest universities, Kraków should be a priority destination in the region. Despite problems caused by pollution from nearby industrial Śląsk (Silesia), it is a uniquely preserved medieval city. Starting as a market town in the 10th century, Kraków became Poland's capital in 1037. The original walls are now gone, pulled down in the early 19th century and replaced by a ring of parkland known as the **Planty,** which encloses the Old Town.

To the southeast of the Old Town is a neighborhood—Kazimierz, chartered in 1335 and named for its founder, Kazimierz the Great—that was once a town in its own right. After 1495, when they were expelled from Kraków by King John Albert, this became the home of Kraków's Jewish community. The Jewish community of Kazimierz came to an abrupt and tragic end during World War II: A ghetto was established here in March 1941, and its inhabitants were transported to their deaths in the concentration camp of Auschwitz-Birkenau (☞ Małopolska, *below*).

Numbers in the text correspond to numbers in the margin and on the Exploring Kraków map.

Stare Miasto (Old Town)

With many of Kraków's streets a vast and lovely living museum, the Stare Miasto (Old Town), in particular, is a historical gold mine. Its ancient houses, churches, and palaces can overwhelm visitors with only a few days to see the sights. The heart of it all is Kraków's "drawing room"—the Rynek Główny, or Main Market Square.

A GOOD WALK

The Old Town is best explored on foot, beginning at the **Barbakan** ⑤⓪ and city gate on **ulica Floriańska** ⑤①. Here, you should visit both the Czartoryski Collection in the **Arsenal Miejski** ⑤② (which contains Leonardo da Vinci's legendary *Cecilia Gallerani*) and **Dom Jana Matejki** ⑤③, and admire the medieval mansions, as well. Ulica Floriańska will take you to the **Rynek Główny** ⑤④ at the center of the town, where you will find the **Kościół Mariacki** ⑤⑤, the Renaissance **Sukiennice** ⑤⑥, and a collection of magnificent Renaissance town houses.

The historic early buildings of the Jagiellonian University, the **Collegium Maïus** ⑤⑦ and **Collegium Juridicum** ⑤⑧, lie in streets leading off to the southwest and south of the square: Take ulica świelej. Anny to reach ulica Jagiellońska, and then go via ulica Gołębia (where you might visit **Robert Jahoda's Printing Press** ⑤⑨) to Plac Wszystkich Świętych, with the 13th-century **Franciscan church and monastery** ⑥⓪. From here take ulica Grodzka south to the 11th-century **Kościół świelej Andrzeja** ⑥①, before cutting through to Kraków's oldest street, ulica Kanonicza, where the canons of the cathedral once lived; their Chapter House now houses the Archdiocesan Museum. **Ulica Kanonicza** ⑥② leads to the Wawel hill, with its **cathedral** ⑥③ and the Renaissance **Zamek Królewski** ⑥④, which can easily take a half day to explore, if you have time. From the Wawel, you can stroll south down the Vistula embankment to visit the **Kościół na Skałce** ⑥⑤ and the fine 14th-century redbrick Gothic **Kościół świętej Katarzyny,** at ulica Skałeczna at the corner of ulica Augustyniańka.

TIMING

The Wawel Cathedral alone requires a whole morning or afternoon; the rest of the Old City, at least a day.

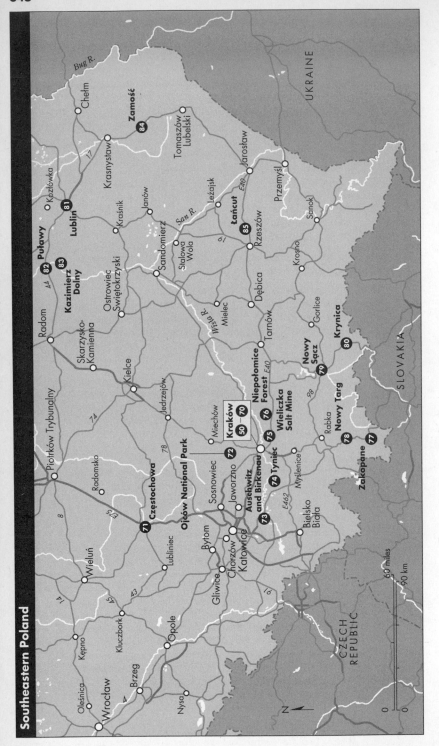

Southeastern Poland

Exploring Kraków

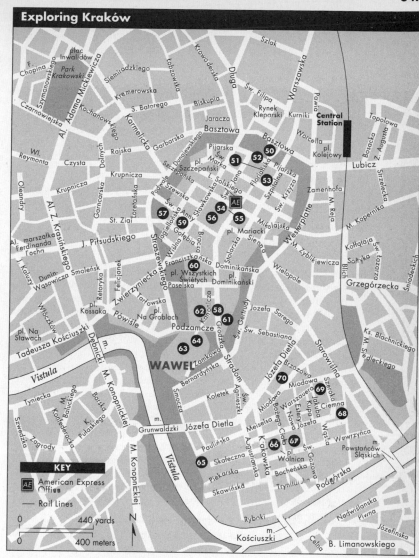

Arsenal Miejski, **52**
Barbakan, **50**
Collegium
Juridicum, **58**
Collegium Maïus, **57**
Dom Jana Matejki, **53**
Franciscan church
and monastery, **60**
Kościół Bożego
Ciała, **67**
Kościół Mariacki, **55**

Kościół na Skałce, **65**
Kościół
św. Andrzeja, **61**
Robert Jahoda's
Printing Press, **59**
Rynek Główny, **54**
Stara Synagoga, **68**
Sukiennice, **56**
Synagoga Remuh, **69**
Synagoga Tempel, **70**

Town Hall of
Kazimierz, **66**
Ulica Floriańska, **51**
Ulica Kanonicza, **62**
Wawel Cathedral, **63**
Zamek Królewski, **64**

SIGHTS TO SEE

★ ⑤ **Arsenal Miejski** (Municipal Arsenal). The surviving fragment of Kraków's city wall opposite the Barbakan, where students and amateur artists hang their paintings for sale in the summer, contains the Renaissance-period Municipal Arsenal, which now houses part of the National Museum's **Czartoryski Collection,** including several celebrated paintings, such as Raphael's *Portrait of a Young Man* and Rembrandt's *Landscape with the Good Samaritan.* The prize of the collection and, to many observers, the most beautiful portrait ever painted, is Leonardo da Vinci's *Cecilia Gallerani,* also known as the *Lady with an Ermine.* ⊠ *Ul. św. Jana 19,* ☎ *012/422–55–66.* 🎫 *Zł 3.* ⊙ *Wed.– Sun. 10–3:30, Fri. 10–6.*

⑤ **Barbakan.** Only one small section of Kraków's city wall still stands, centered on the 15th-century Barbakan, one of the largest strongholds of its kind in Europe. ⊠ *Ul. Basztowa, opposite ul. Floriańska.*

⑤ **Collegium Juridicum.** On one of Kraków's oldest streets is this magnificent Gothic building, raised in the early 15th century to house the university's law students. ⊠ *Ul. Grodzka 53.*

★ ⑤ **Collegium Maïus.** This is the earliest existing building of the Jagiellonian University, which was founded by Kazimierz the Great in 1364 as the first university in Poland. By 1400 the original buildings had become overcrowded and were replaced with the Collegium Maïus, the oldest university building in the country. The Jagiellonian's most famous student, Nicolaus Copernicus, studied here from 1491 to 1495. The first visual delight is the Italian-styled arcaded courtyard adorned with crystal vaulting. On the second floor, the museum and rooms, which can only be visited on a guided tour (call in advance for an appointment and an English guide), is a must for all visitors to Kraków. On the tour you will be shown the historic and stunningly beautiful reception rooms, still used for major University functions. The museum also includes the Copernicus globe, the first globe ever which delineated the American continents. Two other Jagiellonian university buildings worth noting, constructed later, are on ulica Gołębia: the **Collegium Physicum** at No. 13 and the **Collegium Slavisticum** at No. 20. ⊠ *Collegium Maius, ul. Jagiellońska 15,* ☎ *012/422–05–49.* 🎫 *Courtyard free, museum zł 5.* ⊙ *Museum weekdays 11–2:30, Sat. 11–1:30 (by appointment only).*

⑤ **Dom Jana Matejki.** The family house of 19th-century painter Jan Matejko now serves as a museum for his work. While you examine his romantic paintings, you can also admire the well-preserved interior of this 16th-century building. ⊠ *Ul. Floriańska 41,* ☎ *012/22–59–26.* 🎫 *Zł 3.* ⊙ *Tues.–Sun. 10–3:30, Fri. 10–6.*

⑥ **Franciscan church and monastery.** The mid-13th-century Franciscan church and monastery are among the earliest brick buildings in Kraków. It also has Art Nouveau stained-glass windows by Stanisław Wyspiański. ⊠ *Pl. Wszystkich Świętych 1.*

OFF THE
BEATEN PATH

KOPIEC KOŚCIUSZKI – This mound on the outskirts of Kraków was built in tribute to the memory of Tadeusz Kościuszko in 1820, three years after his death. The earth came from battlefields on which he had fought; soil from the United States was added in 1926. This is the best place from which to get a panoramic view of the city. Take Tram 1, 2, or 6 from plac Dominikański to the terminus at Salwator and then walk up Aleje Waszyngtona to the mound. ⊙ *Daily 10–dusk.*

★ ⑤ **Kościół Mariacki** (Church of Our Lady). Dominating the northeast corner of Kraków's Rynek Głowny is the twin-towered Church of Our

Lady. The first church was built on this site before the town plan of 1257, which is why it stands slightly askew from the main square; the present church, completed in 1397, was built on the foundations of its predecessor. You'll note that the two towers, added in the early 15th century, are of different heights. Legend has it that they were built by two brothers, one of whom grew jealous of the other's work and slew him with a bloody sword, a symbol of Magdeburg law, which still hangs in the Sukiennice (☞ *below*). From the higher tower, a strange bugle call—known as the "Hejnal Mariacki"—rings out to mark each hour. It breaks off on an abrupt sobbing note to commemorate an unknown bugler struck in the throat by a Tartar arrow as he was playing his call to warn the city of imminent attack, a tale celebrated through stories and novels as "the trumpeter of Kraków." The church's main show-piece is the magnificent wooden altarpiece with more than 200 carved figures, the work of the 15th-century artist Wit Stwosz (Veit Stoss). The panels offer a detailed picture of medieval life, and the figure in the bottom right-hand corner of the Crucifixion panel is believed to represent Stwosz himself. ⊠ *Rynek Główny at the corner of ul. Mikołajska.*

㉕ Kościół na Skałce (Church on the Rock). Standing on the Vistula em-bankment to the south of the Wawel Hill is the Pauline Church on the Rock. This is the center of the cult of St. Stanisław, bishop and mar-tyr, who is believed to have been beheaded, by order of the king, in the church that stood on this spot in 1079—a tale of rivalry similar to that of Henry II and Thomas à Becket. Beginning in the 19th century, this also became the last resting place for well-known Polish writers and artists; among those buried here are the composer Karol Szy-manowski and the poet and painter Stanisław Wyspiański. ⊠ *Between ul. Paulińska and ul. Skałeczna on the Vistula embankment.*

㉑ Kościół świelej Andrzeja (Church of St. Andrew). The 11th-century for-tified Church of St. Andrew is one of Kraków's few well-preserved Ro-manesque structures (the interior, however, is Baroque); it was here that the inhabitants of the district took refuge during Tartar raids. ⊠ *At the midpoint on the east side of ul. Grodzka.*

Pałac pod Baranami (Palace at the Sign of the Rams). On the corner of ulica świętej Anny, opposite the Town Hall Tower, several Gothic houses were converted into a Renaissance palace by Jost Decjusz, sec-retary to King Sigismund the Old. Confiscated during World War II from the Potocki family, which had owned it since the 19th century, it was home after the war to the famed satirical cabaret *Piwnica pod Baranami*. Returned to the Potocki family in 1990, today the build-ing contains shops, a café, and galleries.

㉙ Robert Jahoda's Printing Press. This small museum in a quiet back street shows the history of printing and bookbinding in Kraków. ⊠ *Ul. Gołębia 4,* ☎ *012/422–99–22.* ☞ *Zł 1.* ☉ *Daily 10–2.*

★ **㉔ Rynek Główny** (Main Market Square). Kraków's magnificent Main Mar-ket Square, which is Europe's largest medieval marketplace, measures 220 square yards and is on a par in size and grandeur with St. Mark's Square in Venice. It even has the same plague of pigeons—although legend tells us the ones here are no ordinary birds; they are allegedly the spirits of the knights of Duke Henry IV Probus, who in the 13th century were cursed and turned into birds.

The great square was not always so spacious. In an earlier period it also contained—in addition to the present buildings—a Gothic town hall, a Renaissance granary, a large weighing house, a foundry, a pil-lory, and hundreds of traders' stalls. A few flower sellers under colorful umbrellas are all that remain of this bustling commercial activity. A pageant of history has passed through this square. From 1320 on, Polish kings came here on the day after their coronation to meet the city's burghers and receive homage and tribute in the name of all the towns of Poland. Albert Hohenzollern, the grand master of the Teutonic Knights, came here in 1525 to pay homage to Sigismund the Old, king of Poland. And in 1794 Tadeusz Kościuszko took a solemn vow to overthrow czarist Russia.

The **Dom pod Jeleniami** (House at the Sign of the Stag) at No. 36 was once an inn where both Goethe (1790) and Czar Nicholas I (1849) found shelter. At No. 45 is the **Dom pod Orłem** (House at the Sign of the Eagle), where Tadeusz Kościuszko lived as a young officer in 1777; a little farther down the square, at No. 6, is the **Szary Dom** (Gray House), where he made his staff headquarters in 1794. In 1605, in the house at No. 9, the young Polish noblewoman Maryna Mniszchówna married the False Dymitri, the pretender to the Russian throne (these events are portrayed in Pushkin's play *Boris Godunov* and in Mussorgsky's operatic adaptation of it). At No. 16, in a **14th-century house** that belonged to the Wierzynek merchant family, is a famous restaurant named for them. In 1364, during a "summit" meeting attended by the Holy Roman Emperor, one of the Wierzyneks gave an elaborate feast for the visiting royal dignitaries; this was the beginning of the house's tradition for haute cuisine.

★ ⑤⑥ **Sukiennice** (Cloth Hall). A **statue of Adam Mickiewicz** is in front of the eastern entrance to the Renaissance Cloth Hall, which now stands in splendid near-isolation in the middle of the Main Market Square. The Gothic arches date from the 14th century, but after a fire in 1555 the upper part was rebuilt in Renaissance style. The inner arcades on the ground floor still hold traders' booths, now mainly selling local crafts. On the first floor, in a branch of the **National Museum,** you can view a collection of 19th-century Polish paintings. ✉ *Rynek Główny 1–3,* ☎ *012/422–11–66.* 🎫 *Zł 3.* ☉ *Tues.–Sun. 10–3:30, Thurs. 10–6.*

NEED A BREAK? | The **Kawiarnia Noworolski** (✉ Rynek Główny 1), next to the entrance to the National Museum in the Cloth Hall, is a wonderful place to sit and watch the goings-on in the square, as well as to observe the hourly trumpet call from the tower of the Church of Our Lady.

⑤① **Ulica Floriańska.** The beautiful **Brama Floriańska** (Florian Gate) was built around 1300 and leads through Kraków's old city walls into ulica Floriańska, one of the streets laid out according to the town plan of 1257. The Gothic houses of the 13th-century burghers still remain, although they were rebuilt and given Renaissance or neoclassical facades. The **house at ulica Floriańska 24,** decorated with an emblem of three bells, was once the workshop of a bell founder. The chains hanging on the walls of the **house at No. 17** barred the streets to invaders when the city was under siege. At No. 14 you will find the **Hotel pod Różą,** one of the city's oldest, where both Franz Liszt and Russian czar Alexander I stayed. And finally, at the left-hand corner where ulica Floriańska enters the market square, stands the **Dom pod Murzynami** (Negroes' House), a 16th-century tenement decorated with two black faces—testimony to the fascination with Africa entertained by Europeans in the Age of Discovery.

NEED A BREAK? | In the Art Nouveau café **Jama Michalikowa** (✉ Ul. Floriańska 45, ☎ 012/422–15–61), the walls are hung with drawings by late-19th-century customers, who sometimes paid their bills in kind.

★ ⑫ **Ulica Kanonicza.** One of Kraków's oldest streets, named for the canons of the cathedral who once lived here, leads from the center of town to the foot of the Wawel Hill. Most of the houses date from the 14th and 15th centuries, although they were "modernized" in Renaissance or later styles. During his Polish ministry, Pope John Paul II lived here in the **Chapter House** at No. 19 and later in the late-16th-century **Dean's House**, at No. 21. The Chapter House now houses the Archdiocesan Museum, with a small collection of manuscripts. ⊠ *Ul. Kanonicza 19.* ☎ *Zł 3.* ☉ *Wed.–Sun. 10–3.*

★ ⑬ **Wawel Cathedral.** The **Wawel Hill**, a rocky limestone outcrop on the banks of the Vistula, dominates the old part of the city and is an impressive complex of Gothic and Renaissance buildings—none more so than Wawel Cathedral and the Zamek Królewski (☞ *below*). The hill is a raised area of about 15 acres that formed a natural point for fortification on the flat Vistula Plain. During the 8th century it was topped with a tribal stronghold, and from the 10th century the elevation held a royal residence and served as the seat of the bishops of Kraków. Construction on Wawel Cathedral was begun in 1320, and the structure was consecrated in 1364. Lack of space for expansion on the hill has meant the preservation of the original austere structure, although a few Renaissance and Baroque chapels have been crowded around it. The most notable of these is the **Kaplica Zygmuntowska** (Sigismund Chapel), built in the 1520s by the Florentine architect Bartolomeo Bertecci and widely considered to be the finest Renaissance chapel north of the Alps.

From 1037, when Kraków became the capital of Poland, Polish kings were crowned and buried in the Wawel Cathedral. This tradition continued up to the time of the partitions, even after the capital had been moved to Warsaw. During the 19th century, only great national heroes were honored by a Wawel entombment: Tadeusz Kościuszko was buried here in 1817; Adam Mickiewicz and Juliusz Słowacki, the great romantic poets, were also brought back from exile to the Wawel after their deaths; and Marshal Józef Piłsudski, the hero of independent interwar Poland, was interred in the cathedral crypt in 1935.

You may also visit the cathedral treasury, archives, library, and museum. Among the showpieces in the library, one of the earliest in Poland, is the 12th-century *Emmeram Gospel* from Regensburg. After touring at ground level, you can climb the wooden staircase of the **Sigismund Tower**, entering through the sacristy. The tower holds the famous **Sigismund Bell**, which was commissioned in 1520 by King Sigismund the Old and is still tolled on all solemn state and church occasions. ☎ *Cathedral museum Zł 4.* ☉ *Tues.–Sun. 10–3.*

Wież Ratuszowa (Town Hall Tower). This tower at the southwest corner of the Main Market Square is all that remains of the 16th-century town hall, which was demolished in the early 19th century. The tower now houses a branch of the **Kraków History Museum** and offers a panoramic view of the old city. ☎ *Zł 3.* ☉ *June–Sept., Fri.–Wed. 9–3, Thurs. noon–5.*

★ ⑭ **Zamek Królewski** (Royal Castle). The castle that now stands on Kraków's Wawel Hill dates from the early 16th century, when the Romanesque residence that stood on this site was destroyed by fire. King Sigismund the Old brought artists and craftsmen from all over Europe to create his castle, and despite Baroque reconstruction after another fire in the late 16th century, several parts of the Renaissance castle remain, including the beautiful arcaded courtyard. After the transfer of the capital to Warsaw at the beginning of the 17th century, Wawel was stripped of its fine furnishings, and later in the century it was devastated by the Swedish wars. Under the Austrians in the 19th century, Wawel was turned into an army barracks. In 1911, a voluntary Polish society purchased the castle from the Austrian authorities and began restoration. Today you can visit the royal chambers, furnished in the style of the 16th and 17th centuries and hung with the 16th-century Belgian arras that during World War II was kept in Canada. The Royal Treasury on the ground floor contains a somewhat depleted collection of Polish crown jewels; the most fascinating item displayed here is the *Szczerbiec,* the jagged sword used from the early 14th century onward at the coronation of Polish kings. The Royal Armory houses a collection of Polish and Eastern arms and armor; in the west wing is an imposing collection of Turkish embroidered tents.

On your way out of the castle, note the smoke and flames rising every 10 minutes from the bottom of the hill. Every Polish child knows the legend of the fire-breathing dragon that once terrorized local residents from his **Smocza Jama** (Dragon's Den), a cave at the foot of Wawel Hill. The dragon threatened to destroy the town unless he was fed a damsel a week. In desperation the king promised half his kingdom and his daughter's hand in marriage to any man who could slay the dragon. The usual quota of knights tried and failed. But finally a crafty cobbler named Krak tricked the dragon into eating a lambskin filled with salt and sulfur. The dragon went wild with thirst, rushed into the Wisła River, and drank until it exploded. Krak the cobbler was made a prince, and the town was named (or renamed) for him. The Dragon's Den is still there, however, and every 15 minutes smoke and flame belch out of it to thrill young visitors. A bronze statue of the dragon itself stands guard at the entrance. Note that you should purchase your tickets early in the day for the Castle and the Dragon's Den as the number of tickets are limited and usually sell out quickly. ✉ *Ul. Grodzka,* ☎ *012/422–16–17. Castle:* 🎫 *Zł 10.* ☉ *Tues–Sun. 10–2:30; Dragon's Den: follow signs to Smocza Jama, below Thief's Tower on Wawel Hill near Vistula River.* 🎫 *Zł 3.* ☉ *May–Sept., Mon.–Thurs. and weekends 10–3.*

Kazimierz

A separate city in the Middle Ages, Kazimierz was an old Jewish district, settled at a time when industrious and enterprising Jews were welcomed by the Polish kings to escape persecution in Europe. Here they thrived until World War II.

A GOOD WALK

Southeast of the Wawel, you can take a tram from the corner of Bernadyńska and Starowiślna streets to the Kazimierz district (or on a pleasant day you can walk). The second tram stop on ulica Krakowska will take you to plac Wolnica, site of the **Town Hall** 66, now the Ethnographic Museum. To visit the synagogues of Kazimierz, make your way from plac Wolnica along ulica Bożego Ciała, passing the **Kościół Bożego Ciała** 67 from which the street takes its name, to ulica Józefa, where you will pass the **Synagoga Wysoka** (High Synagogue), turning left into ulica Jakuba to see the **Synagoga Ajzyk ,** which dates from 1638 and is now the Lauder Foundation Education Center. Then continue down ulica Józefa to ulica Szeroka, on the corner of which is the **Stara Synagoga** (Old Synagogue) 68, now the Jewish Historical Museum. Farther north along ulica Szeroka are the **Synagoga Remuh** 69 and **Jewish cemetery.** Across the street, at Ulica Dajwór 26, is the **Synagoga Poper or Bocian,** dating from 1620.

Take ulica Warschauera, noting the **Synagoga Kupa,** built by subscription in 1590, to ulica Estery, where you must turn north to reach ulica Miodowa. Here walk west to see the **Synagoga Tempel** 70 on the corner of ulica Podbrzezie. From here you can continue west along ulica Miodowa until you rejoin the tram route.

TIMING

The main sights of Kazimierz can be visited in a morning or afternoon, since there are only two museums that may be time-consuming.

SIGHTS TO SEE

67 **Kościół Bożego Ciała** (Corpus Christi Church). The 15th-century Corpus Christi Church was used by King Charles Gustavus of Sweden as his headquarters during the Siege of Kraków in 1655. ⊠ *Northeast corner of pl. Wolnica.*

68 **Stara Synagoga** (Old Synagogue). Standing at the corner of ulica Józefa and ulica Szeroka, this synagogue was built in the 15th century and reconstructed in Renaissance style following a fire in 1557. It was here in 1775 that Tadeusz Kościuszko successfully appealed to the Jewish community to join in the national insurrection. Looted and partly destroyed during the Nazi occupation, it has now been rebuilt and houses the **Museum of the History and Culture of Kraków Jews.** ⊠ *Ul. Szeroka 24,* ☎ *012/422–09–62.* ☒ *Zł 5.* ☉ *Wed.–Thurs. and weekends 9–3, Fri. 11–6; closed 1st weekend of month.*

NEED A
BREAK?

Ariel Café (⊠ Ul. Szeroka 17, ☎ 012/421–38–70). This "Jewish artistic café" is always full; musical and other performances are often given.

69 **Synagoga Remuh.** This 16th-century synagogue is still used for worship and is associated with the name of the son of its founder, Rabbi Moses Isserles, who is buried in the **cemetery** attached to the synagogue. Used by the Jewish community from 1533 to 1799, this is the only well-preserved Renaissance Jewish cemetery in Europe. (The so-called **new cemetery** on ulica Miodowa, which contains many old headstones, was established in the 19th century.) ⊠ *Ul. Szeroka 40.*

70 **Synagoga Tempel.** The 19th-century Reformed Tempel Synagogue is one of only two synagogues in Kraków still used for worship. ⊠ *Corner of ul. Miodowa and ul. Podbrzezie.*

00 **Town Hall of Kazimierz.** The 15th-century town hall, which stands in the middle of plac Wolnica, is now the Ethnographic Museum, displaying a well-mounted collection of regional folk art. ⊠ *Pl. Wolnica 1,* ☎ *012/656–28–63.* ☒ *Zł 5.* ☉ *Mon. 10–6, Wed.–Fri. 10–3, weekends 10–2.*

Dining

$$$$ ✕ **Hawełka.** Established in 1876, this second-floor restaurant sparkles
★ with crystal and gleaming cutlery. Attentive waiters will advise in English on a range of traditional Polish dishes. Try the fried eel in cream-and-dill sauce or one of the excellent veal dishes. The Hawełka also has a less-pricey restaurant on the ground floor, where mushroom soup served in a bread loaf is a great local favorite. ⊠ *Rynek Główny 34,* ☎ *012/422–47–53. Reservations essential. AE, DC, MC, V.*

$$$$ ✕ **Wierzynek.** Poland's most famous restaurant is in a fine 18th-cen-
★ tury upper room on the Rynek, glittering with chandeliers and silver. It was here after a historic meeting in 1364 that the king of Poland wined and dined the Holy Roman Emperor Charles IV, five kings, and a score of princes. Wierzynek is perhaps resting a little on its laurels these days, and the food may not really be any better than in other restaurants of its class, but the traditional Polish dishes—impressively served by armies of red-jacketed waiters—are very good. The kitchen excels in soups and game: Try the *żurek* (sour barley soup) followed by *zrazy,*

Kraków Dining and Lodging

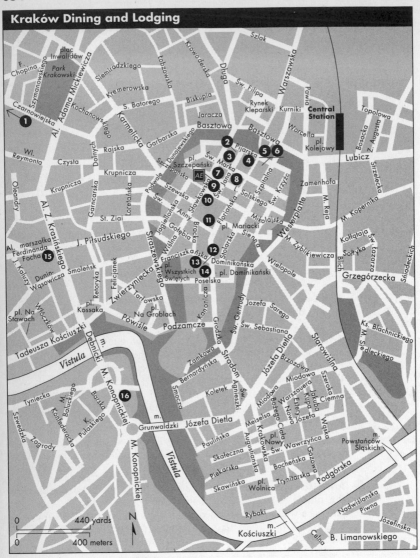

Dining
Balaton, **14**
Hawełka, **10**
Kurza Stopka, **13**
Pod Aniołami, **12**
U Pollera, **5**
Wierzynek, **11**
Wyrwigrosz, **3**

Lodging
Cracovia, **15**
Continental, **1**
Elektor, **6**
Forum, **16**
Francuski, **2**
Grand, **7**
Hotel Pollera, **5**
Pod Różą, **8**
Polski Pod Białym
Ortem, **4**
Saski, **9**

small beef rolls filled with mushrooms and served with buckwheat. ✉ *Rynek Główny 15, ☎ 012/422–10–35. Reservations essential. AE, DC, MC, V.*

$$$ ✗ **Pod Aniołami.** In summer, the restaurant is in a courtyard; in win-
★ ter it moves into a cozy cellar. A favorite place for Krakow's consular corps, it's staffed by waiters who are mostly young university students and all delightfully attentive. Recommendations include the trout dishes as well as the filet mignon. ✉ *Ul. Grodzka 35, ☎ 012/421–39–99. Reservations essential. No credit cards.*

$$ ✗ **U Pollera.** The large, balconied fin-de-siècle dining room has a look of decaying grandeur. The cuisine is eclectic but has a good choice of traditional Polish dishes. Chicken roasted with garlic and served with crispy potatoes is an excellent main course, and the chocolate gâteau for dessert is wonderfully light and creamy. ✉ *Ul. Szpitalna 30, ☎ 0124/22–16–21. AE, DC, MC, V.*

$$ ✗ **Wyrwigrosz.** This simple restaurant serves delicious Polish fare, such as a winning *Barszcz* (beet soup) and the *Kotlet schabowy* (pork cutlet) accompanied with potatoes and salad. The bar in the cellar frequently has outstanding jazz concerts as well as cabarets. ✉ *Ul. św. Jana 30, ☎ 012/421–29–94. No credit cards.*

$ ✗ **Balaton.** Kraków's Hungarian restaurant has dark-wood paneling and trestle tables with benches, relieved by bright folk-weave rugs and embroideries on the walls. *Zupa gulaszowa* (hot spiced fish soup) is good as a starter; follow it up with *placek ziemniaczany* (potato pancakes with pork stuffing). Good Hungarian wine is available. ✉ *Ul. Grodzka 37, ☎ 012/422–04–69.*

$ ✗ **Kurza Stopka.** This small and rather dark restaurant specializes in chicken dishes, as its name (Chicken's Claw) suggests. An unusual crisp and spicy risotto *paprykarz* (paprika) served with a cool cucumber salad is one of the kitchen's specialties. ✉ *Pl. Wszystkich Świętych 10, ☎ 021/433–55–38.*

Lodging

There is a serious shortage of rooms in Kraków, and it is essential to book well in advance, even in the slow winter months (during this time, the city is often used for large conferences). Kraków, unfortunately, lacks centrally located hotels of any refinement, and those that exist are often overpriced. Beware: Rooms facing the street in the Old Town can be noisy at night, so always request a quiet room.

$$$$ ⊟ **Elektor.** Probably a better option for businesspeople than for tourists, this recently opened hotel is eager to capture the top end of the market. Many foreign dignitaries have stayed here and its restaurant has even served Queen Elizabeth II. The rooms are spacious and have all the amenities of a first class hotel. The hotel is somewhat overpriced for what it offers, but no one can carp about the outstanding service. ✉ *Ul. Szpitalna 28, 31-024, ☎ 012/421–80–25, FAX 012/421–86–89. 9 rooms, 12 suites. Restaurant, bar. AE, DC, MC, V.*

$$$ ⊟ **Cracovia.** Opened in 1964, this mammoth five-story hotel opposite the Błonie (Kraków Common) long provided the city's only luxury accommodations. Now, after 30 years of catering to tourist groups, it is beginning to show signs of strain and has become somewhat downscale. But the rooms, although rather small and standardized, are well appointed with dark, heavy furniture, and the staff members do their best to make you feel at home. It's one of the few hotels to have consistent space during the summer season. ✉ *Al. F. Focha 1, 30–111, ☎ 012/422–86–66, FAX 012/421–95–86. 415 rooms, 10 suites. Restaurant, bar. AE, DC, MC, V.*

$$$ 🏨 **Forum.** Opened in 1988, this modern hotel has proven to be something of a disappointment. Although it commands spectacular views over the castle on Wawel Hill, it is on the right bank of the Vistula, adding 10 minutes' travel time to the Old City, while its immediate surroundings are slightly squalid. On the upside, rooms are spacious, with light and solidly comfortable furnishings; the bathrooms are particularly well appointed. The hotel also has the city's best health and sports facilities. ⊠ *Ul. Marii Konopnickiej 28, 30–302,* ☎ *012/266–95–00,* 🖷 *012/266–58–27. 265 rooms, 15 suites. Restaurant, 2 bars, indoor pool, sauna, tennis courts. AE, DC, MC, V.*

$$$ 🏨 **Francuski.** Perhaps Kraków's best hotel option now, this turn-of-
★ the-century hotel is just inside the only remaining fragment of the town walls, within five minutes' walk of the main square. The rooms are comfortable and furnished in updated period style. ⊠ *Ul. Pijarska 13, 31–015,* ☎ *012/422–51–22,* 🖷 *012/422–52–70. 27 rooms, 15 suites. Restaurant, café. AE, DC, MC, V.*

$$$ 🏨 **Grand.** This early 19th-century hotel on the corner of ulica Solskiego in the Old Town was completely renovated—the work took 12 years—before reopening in 1990. An air of Regency elegance predominates, but the whole is now showing slight signs of wear. The bedrooms are decorated with Regency-style striped wallpaper and bedspreads; most of the furniture is period reproduction. The corridors are agreeably unpredictable, with little alcoves and potted plants. ⊠ *Ul. Sławkowska 5–7, 31–016,* ☎ *012/421–72–55,* 🖷 *012/421–83–60. 50 rooms, 6 suites. Restaurant, bar. AE, DC, MC, V.*

$$ 🏨 **Continental.** This high-rise hotel, the first Holiday Inn built in Central Europe, is 3 km (2 mi) to the west of the city center in pleasant suburban surroundings on the far side of the Kraków Common. It provides standardized but comfortable and cheerfully decorated accommodations and has good parking facilities. Since it's close to open parkland and sports facilities, this is a good choice for those who want to combine sightseeing with a little exercise. ⊠ *Al. Armii Krajowej 11, 30–150,* ☎ *012/637–50–44,* 🖷 *012/637–59–38. 310 rooms. Restaurant, indoor pool, sauna, casino. AE, DC, MC, V.*

$$ 🏨 **Hotel Pollera.** In 1990 Pollera was returned to the Kraków lawyer who had been forced to sell it to the state in 1950. He is a descendant of the Poller for whom the hotel is named: an Austrian army officer who married a local girl and settled in Kraków in the early 19th century. The building's exterior has already had a face-lift, and the guest rooms are also gradually being renovated and upgraded with private bathrooms. The fine Art Nouveau entrance hall, dominated by an imposing grand staircase and stained-glass window, is as elegant as ever. ⊠ *Ul. Szpitalna 30, 31–024,* ☎ *012/22–10–44,* 🖷 *012/22–13–89. 42 rooms, 35 with bath. Restaurant. AE, DC, MC, V.*

$$ 🏨 **Pod Różą.** One of Kraków's oldest hotels, the Pod Róża has seen
★ many distinguished guests, including Czar Alexander I. After renovations in the mid-1990s, the large, high-ceiling guest rooms were perked up with bright furnishings. There is no elevator, though the hotel has only four stories. One of the hotel's best aspects is its location on beautiful ulica Floriańska. ⊠ *Ul. Floriańska 14, 31–021,* ☎ *012/422–12–44,* 🖷 *012/421–75–13. 30 rooms, 1 suite. Restaurant, casino. AE, DC, MC, V.*

$$ 🏨 **Polski Pod Białym Orłem.** Located across the street from the Florianska Gate and a few minutes' walk from the main square, this hotel has large, modestly furnished rooms—those that face Florianska Street tend to be noisy at night. ⊠ *Ul. Pijarska 17, 31–015,* ☎ *012/422–11–44,* 🖷 *012/422–14–26. 40 rooms. AE, DC, MC, V.*

$$ ▦ **Saski.** Opened by a Hungarian dissident in 1809, this hotel was returned to the original family in 1991 after having been confiscated by the state after World War II. A stupendous prewar elevator promises other glories, but the guest rooms are simple with sparse furnishings; bathrooms are modern with pale green towels and white fixtures. ⊠ Ul. Sławkowska 3, 31–014, ☎ 012/421–42–22, FAX 012/421–48–30. 63 rooms. AE, DC, MC, V.

Nightlife and the Arts

Kraków has a lively tradition in theater and music, and you will find many interesting programs. Pick up a copy of either *Karnet*, which offers detailed cultural information in English, or the monthly *Miesiąc w Kraków* (This Month in Kraków). The *Kraków Insider* also has details about what's going on.

Nightlife

BARS

The **"Bacchus" Drinks Bar** (⊠ Ul. Solskiego 21), a refurbished bar in the Old Town, is popular with the younger crowd. The **Grand Hotel Café** (⊠ Ul. Sławkowska 5–7, entrance from ul. Solskiego) is a good place for a quiet evening drink. **Pod Ratuszem** (⊠ Rynek Główny 1), underneath the Town Hall Tower, is a large bar in a labyrinth of small cellar rooms and is usually crowded.

CABARET AND JAZZ

The cabaret at **Jama Michalika** (⊠ Ul. Floriańska 45) has popular satirical and musical shows. The **Jazz Club "U Muniaka"** (⊠ Ul. Floriańska 3) is a large cellar club with daily sessions from 8 PM. **Loch Camelot** (⊠ Ul. św. Tomasza 17) is a wonderfully cozy place to get a drink or even an early morning coffee. There are also frequent cabarets in the basement. Regular jazz sessions are held at the **Piwnica pod Hubą** (⊠ Rynek Glóny 12). The journalists' club, **Pod Gruszką** (⊠ Ul. Szczepańska 1), has a programs of light musical floor shows.

The Arts

FILM

Kino pod Baranami (⊠ Rynek Glóny 27, ☎ 012/423–07–68) has a varied program and occasionally shows Polish films. There is also a popular disco and nightclub in the same building

MUSIC

☺ In Kraków the local philharmonic—**Filharmonia im. Karola Szymanowskiego** (⊠ Ul. Zwierzyniecka 1, ☎ 012/422–94–77)—has frequent concerts. Badly damaged by fire in 1991, the Philharmonic Hall was given a face-lift while being rebuilt. Special Saturday-matinée concerts for children are offered. Chamber-music concerts, occasionally given in the great hall in the Royal Castle on Wawel Hill (☞ Sights to See, *above*), are well worth looking out for.

OPERA AND DANCE

The **Teatr im. Juliusza Słowackiego** (⊠ Pl. św. Ducha 1, ☎ 012/422–40–22) provides a regular program of traditional opera and ballet favorites as well as dramatic performances in a stunningly beautiful hall.

THEATER

Scena pod Ratuszem (⊠ Wieża Ratuszowa, ☎ 012/421–16–57), a tiny theater in the cellar of the old Town Hall Tower, stages small-scale dramas in front of a bare-brick backdrop. The **Stary Teatr im. Heleny Modrzejewskiej** (⊠ Ul. Jagiellońska 1, ☎ 012/422–85–66), a 19th-century theater, stages some of the best productions in Poland; the famed film director Andrzej Wajda still directs here when his schedule permits.

Outdoor Activities and Sports

Hiking

The **Niepołomice Forest** (☞ Małowpolska, *below*) has extensive routes marked over flat and sandy terrain. **Ojców National Park** (☞ Małopolska, *below*) has marked trails for hikers, some of which are steeply uphill and fairly rough.

Jogging

If you want to jog in Kraków, the **Planty,** a ring of gardens around the Old Town, makes an excellent 5-km (3-mi) route and is easily accessible from most hotels. The **pathways along the Vistula** also provide a good jogging route: West of the Dębiński Bridge, take the path on the right bank; east of the bridge, the one on the left bank.

Shopping

Kraków has always been an interesting place for shopping, but here, as everywhere else in Poland, things are changing rapidly. Many of the craftspeople whose tiny shops made the Old Town such a fascinating place have been driven out of business by high rents and taxes. But the streets off the Rynek have a few new shops selling the leather products and wooden handicrafts that are specialties of this region. Most shops in Kraków are open weekdays 10–6, Saturdays 9–2.

In Kraków the **Sukiennice booths** on the main square are still a good place to look for tooled leather goods, local crystal and glass, wood carvings, and the embroidered felt slippers made in the Podhale region. Rabbit-skin slippers are also a local specialty. **Cepelia** on the west side of the Sukiennice (✉ Rynek Główny 1–3) has a broad selection of regional specialties. A small boutique inside the restaurant Wierzynek (✉ Rynek Głowny 15) sells the world-famous **Christopher Radko** Christmas ornaments.

Kraków A to Z

Arriving and Departing

BY BUS

Express bus service to Kraków runs regularly from most Polish cities. From the **PKS bus** station in Warsaw (✉ Al. Jerozolimskie), the journey takes three hours. Buses arrive at the main PKS station on plac Kolejowy (☎ 012/936), where you can change for buses to other destinations in the region. The bus station is just across the square from the train station.

BY CAR

A car will not be of much use to you in Kraków, since most of the Old Town is closed to traffic and distances between major sights are short. A car will be invaluable, however, if you set out to explore the rest of the region. You can approach Kraków either by the E7 highway (from Warsaw and north), or via the E40 (from the area around Katowice). There is a high incidence of car theft in most cities, so make sure your car is locked securely before you set out to explore. Use the parking facilities at your hotel or one of the attended **municipal garage parking lots** (try ✉ Pl. Szczepański or ✉ Pl. św. Ducha).

BY PLANE

Kraków can be reached by direct flight from most major European cities. The **Balice Airport** (☎ 012/411–19–55), 11 km (7 mi) west of the city, is the region's only airport. In spring and fall problems with fog can cause frustrating delays. Take Bus 208 from the Central Railway Station or Bus 152 from the Cracovia Hotel.

There are **LOT** flights daily to Balice Airport from Warsaw (flying time: 40 minutes). LOT's office in Kraków is at ulica Basztowa 15 (☎ 012/952); it's open weekdays 8–6.

Nonstop express trains from Warsaw take 2½ hours and arrive at **Kraków Główny** station on the edge of the Old Town (✉ Pl. Kolejowy, ☎ 012/933); they run throughout the day.

Getting Around
Most of Kraków's sights are best seen on foot; the Old Town area is relatively compact, and much of it is closed to traffic.

Contacts and Resources
Police (☎ 997). **Ambulance** (☎ 999). **Late-night pharmacy: Nonstop** (✉ Ul. Duwajewskiego 2, ☎ 012/422–65–04) is a centrally located pharmacy open 24 hours a day.

U.S. Consulate (✉ Ul. Stolarska 9, ☎ 012/429–66–55).

All major hotels will arrange tours of the city as well as the surrounding attractions. **Orbis** (✉ Rynek Główny 41, ☎ 012/422–40–35), through its subsidiary, **Cracow Tours,** offers a wide range of tours either by bus, minibus, or limousine, at prices ranging from $30 for a half-day coach tour to $140 for a full-day tour in a chauffeur-driven car. Half-day visits to the Nazi concentration camp at **Oświęcim** (Auschwitz) or to the **Wieliczka** salt mine are offered throughout the year, and they offer a standard half-day tour of Kraków, as well as junkets to Pieskowa Skała and Ojców. A day trip to the Dunajec River gorge (including a journey down the river by raft) is available in the summer. Orbis also organizes day trips to the pope's birthplace at **Wadowice,** to the Bernadine Monastery at **Kalwaria Zebrzydowska,** and to the Pauline Monastery at **Częstochowa.**

For tours of Jewish Kraków and its surroundings go to **Jarden Tours** (✉ Ul. Szeroka 2, ☎ 012/421–71–66).

Tourist Information Center (✉ Ul. Pawia 8, ☎ 012/422–60–91) is open weekdays 9–5, Saturday 9–2. **Orbis** (✉ Hotel Cracovia, Al. Focha 1, ☎ 012/421–98–80; ✉ Rynek Główny 41, ☎ 012/422–46–32), open weekdays 9–5, Saturday 9–2, is the place to change money as well as purchase train tickets.

MAŁOPOLSKA

Just to the south of Kraków, Poland's great plains give way to the gently folding foothills of the Carpathians, building to the High Tatras on the Slovak border. The fine medieval architecture of many towns in Małopolska (Little Poland) comes from a period when the area prospered as the intersection of thriving trade routes. In the countryside, wooden homesteads and strip-farmed tracts tell another story: of the hardships and poverty the peasantry endured before the 20th century brought tourists to the mountains. During the 19th century, when this part of Poland was under Austrian rule as the province of Western Galicia, hundreds of thousands of peasants fled from the grinding toil on poor soil to seek their fortune in the United States; it sometimes seems as if every family hereabouts has a cousin in America.

A visit to Kraków and Małopolska is incomplete without trips to at least two nearby destinations: the Wieliczka Salt Mine, declared one of the 12 wonders of the world by the United Nations, and Auschwitz and Birkenau, sites of the Nazis' most gruesome and brutal concentration camps. Farther afield are Ojców National Park and Zakopane, both of which offer first-rate hiking in unadulterated natural surroundings. If you've been looking for insight into the devout Catholicism of the Poles, head to Częstochowa, where 5 million people a year come to pray before a painting of the Virgin Mary and baby Jesus known as the Black Madonna.

Małopolska remains intensely Catholic and conservative, and the traditional way of life in the countryside is relatively intact. Folk crafts and customs are still very much alive, both in mountainous and foothill (*podhale*) areas: You may see carved-wood beehives in mountain gardens, and worshipers setting out for Sunday church in embroidered white-felt trousers.

This is Poland's main winter sports area: Zakopane currently aspires to host the Winter Olympics in 2006. The spa towns of Szczawnica, Krościenko, and Krynica are good bases for cross-country skiing.

This is one of the few regions in Poland that offer extensive options for inexpensive bed-and-breakfast accommodations in private pensions. Pensions (generally small hotels), as opposed to B & Bs, usually offer full board and hearty meals.

Numbers in the margin correspond to numbers on the Southeastern Poland map.

Częstochowa

❼ *120 km (74 mi) northwest of Kraków, 220 km (136 mi) southwest of Warsaw.*

The pilgrims' town of Częstochowa has only one attraction for tourists:
★ the 14th-century **Klasztor Paulinów** (Pauline Monastery) at Jasna Góra (Hill of Light); the remainder of the town is now grimly industrial. Inside the monastery, however, is Poland's holiest shrine, the famous *Black Madonna of Częstochowa,* an early 15th-century painting of a dark-skinned Madonna and child, the origins of which are uncertain (legend attributes the work to St. Luke). Pilgrims from all over Poland, many on foot, make their way to the shrine each August to participate in Marian devotions. The church and monastery were fortified in the 16th century, and 100 years later Jasna Góra held out against a Swedish siege for 40 days. It was here that the invading Swedish army was halted and finally driven out of the country. The Black Madonna's designation as savior of Poland dates from those turbulent days. The monastery was rebuilt in Baroque style during the 17th and 18th centuries, as was the interior of the Gothic church. The **Monastery Treasury** holds an important collection of manuscripts and works of art. ⊠ *Al. Najświętszej Marii Panny 1.* ☉ *Treasury daily 11–1 and 3–5.*

Dining and Lodging

$$ ✕ **Stacherczak.** Claiming to have the best Chinese chef in Poland, this small restaurant has gathered a loyal following since it opened in 1994. Try the soups, especially clear mushroom with soya noodles. The Polish food is also good. ⊠ *Ul. Dąbrowskiego 5,* ☎ *034/24–45–46. AE, DC, MC, V.*

$ ✕ **Wiking.** This crowded restaurant provides an emphatic touch of local color. Try the herrings in cream as a starter, followed by chicken with potatoes. ⊠ *Ul. Nowowiejska,* ☎ *034/24–57–68. No credit cards.*

$$ ⊞ **Orbis Patria Hotel.** This six-story 1980s hotel provides a predictable Orbis standard of cuisine and accommodations. Rooms are brightly furnished and comfortable, the staff cheerful and friendly. ⊠ *Ul. Popiełuszki 2, 42–200,* ☎ *034/24–70–01,* FAX *034/24–63–32. 96 rooms, 6 suites. AE, DC, MC, V.*

$ ⊞ **Hotel Polonia.** This comfortable hotel catered to well-to-do business travelers when it opened at the turn of the century. The mahogany double doors to the bedrooms remain, along with potted palms in the windows and velvet drapes. The high ceilings and windows make for drafts, but the hotel is clean and the beds comfortable. ⊠ *Ul. Piłsudskiego 9, 42–200,* ☎ *034/24–40–67,* FAX *034/65–11–05. 62 rooms, 40 with bath or shower. AE, DC, MC, V.*

Ojców National Park

72 *48 km (30 mi) northwest of Kraków.*

This national park covers the limestone gorge of the Prudnik River. The ridge above the gorge is topped by a series of ruined castles—the "eagles' nests"—that once guarded the trade route from Kraków to Silesia. The best preserved of these is at **Pieskowa Skała,** which now houses a branch of the Wawel Museum Art Collection. Caves in the limestone rock are linked with many stories and legends. In one, Władysław the Short, a medieval Polish king, is supposed to have escaped his German pursuers with the help of a spider that spun a web over the mouth of the cave in which he was hiding. The gorge is at its best in autumn, when shades of gold and red stand out against the white limestone. ⊠ *Take the E40 northwest and turn off at Jerzmanowice for Pieskowa Skała. PKS buses leave regularly from the bus station on pl. Kolejowy in Kraków. Władysław the Short's cave:* ☞ *Zł 45.* ☉ *May–Sept., daily 8–7. Pieskowa Skała Museum:* ☞ *Zł 4.* ☉ *Tues.–Sun. 10–3:30.*

Auschwitz and Birkenau

★ **73** *50 km (31 mi) southwest of Ojców National Park, 55 km (35 mi) west of Kraków.*

Between 1940 and 1945, more than 1.5 million people, 90% of them Jews from Poland and throughout Europe, died here in the Nazis' largest death-camp complex. In the small town of **Oświęcim** (better known by its German name, Auschwitz), the camp has come to be seen as the epicenter of the moral collapse of the West, proof of the human capacity for tremendous evil. The gas chambers at nearby **Brzezinka** (Birkenau) could exterminate thousands in a single day. The first inmates were Polish political prisoners, and the first gas victims were Russian POWs; the dead eventually included Jews, Romani (Gypsies), homosexuals, Jehovah's Witnesses, and so-called criminals.

The *Konzentrationslager* (concentration camp) had three parts: Auschwitz, Birkenau, and Monowitz (where a chemical plant was run by prison labor). The barracks at Auschwitz have been completely restored and made into a museum that one survivor, the author Primo Levi, described as "something static, rearranged, contrived." With that in mind, begin with the heart-rending **movie** filmed by Soviet troops on January 27, 1945, the day they liberated the few prisoners left behind by the retreating Germans. The English version runs a few times a day, although narration isn't really necessary. Purchase a guidebook in English (most exhibits are in Polish or German) and walk through the notorious gate marked ARBEIT MACHT FREI (Work will make you free). The most provocative exhibits are the huge piles of belongings confiscated from victims, as well as the 2 tons of human hair intended for use in the German textile industry. The execution wall, prison block, and the reconstructed crematorium at the end of the tour are harshly sobering. Although most of the victims were sent here simply for being Jewish, exhibits on Jewish prisoners have been allotted only one barrack (just like other nationalities). ⊠ *Ul. Więźniów Oświęcimia 20 (you can reach Oświęcim by train or bus from pl. Kolejowy in Kraków or by car on the E22a),* ☎ *033/432–227.* ▦ *Free.* ☉ *Museum June– Aug., daily 8–7; Sept.–May, daily 8–3.*

Far more affecting than Auschwitz are the unaltered barracks, electric fences, and blown-up gas chambers at the enormous **Birkenau** camp 3 km (2 mi) away. The greatest number of prisoners lived and died here, including hundreds of thousands who went directly to the gas chambers from boxcars in which they had been locked up for days. The camp has been preserved to look much the way it did after the Nazis abandoned it. A walk to the back area brings you to the **Monument to the Glory of the Victims,** designed by Polish and Italian artists and erected in 1967. Behind the trees to the right of the monument lies a farm pond, its banks still murky with human ashes and bone fragments. To hear the tape on the camp's history in English, ask the reception staff in the main guardhouse. ▦ *Free.* ☉ *Daily 9–4.*

Tyniec

㉔ *43 km (27 mi) east of Oświęcim, 12 km (8 mi) southwest of Kraków.*

The **Benedictine Abbey** at Tyniec is perched high on a cliff above the Vistula River. From this fortified cloister, the Confederates of Bar set off in 1772 to raid Kraków; as a result, later that year the abbey was destroyed by the Russian army. In 1817 the Benedictine order was banned, and the monks disbanded. It was not until 1939 that the order recovered the land, and not until the late 1960s that it again became an abbey and the work of reconstruction began in earnest. From May to September recitals of organ music are held in the abbey church. ⊠ *By car, take 7(E77) south of Kraków to A4 . Take A4 about 4 km (2½ mi) to Tyniec. By bus, take Bus 112 from Kraków's Dębniki PKS bus station.* ☉ *Daily 9–4.*

Wieliczka Salt Mine

★ **㉕** *12 km (7½ mi) southeast of Kraków on the E40.*

In this mine, which is on the UNESCO World Cultural Heritage List, salt has been mined for a thousand years. During the 11th century, Wieliczka was owned by the Benedictines of Tyniec abbey, who drew a large part of their income from its revenues. By the 14th century the salt was so prized that King Kazimierz the Great built city walls with 11 defense towers at Wieliczka to protect the mines from Tartar raids. There are historic galleries and chambers 150 yards below ground level, including underground lakes and underground chapels carved by medieval miners, the most magnificent of which is the **Chapel of the Blessed Kinga** (Queen Kinga was a 14th-century Polish queen, later beatified). Serious flooding in 1992 brought commercial salt production to a halt, but the historic part of the mine is open to visitors. ⊠ *Ul. Daniłowicza 10 (take a minibus from right outside the Kraków train station),* ☎ *012/278–32–66.* ▦ *Zł 10.* ☉ *Daily 8–4.*

Niepołomice

㉖ *12 km (7½ mi) east of Wieliczka, 25 km (15 mi) east of Kraków.*

The town of Niepołomice is on the western edge of the **forest** and has a 14th-century **hunting lodge** and **church** built by Kazimierz the Great.

The animals—including bison—remain, and you may be lucky enough to see some of them as you stroll under the ancient oak trees. ⊠ *By car, take the E40 east from Kraków and turn north at Wieliczka, or take a PKS bus or train from pl. Kolejowy in Kraków; on summer weekends Kraków city transport also runs special buses to Niepołomice from pl. Kolejowy.* ☺ *Church dawn–dusk.*

Zakopane

★ **77** *100 km (62 mi) south of Kraków.*

Nestled at the foot of the Tatra Mountains, 3,281 ft above sea level, Zakopane is the highest town in Poland (and the southernmost, as well). Until the 19th-century romantic movement started a fashion for mountain scenery, Zakopane was a poor and remote village. During the 1870s, when the Tatra Association was founded, people began coming to the mountains for their health and recreation, and Zakopane developed into Poland's leading mountain resort. At the turn of the century it was home to many writers, painters, and musicians. Stanisław Wyspiański based his best-known drama, *Wesele* (*Wedding*, 1901), on his experiences here. Stanisław Witkiewicz (Witkacy), the artist and playwright, lived here and was responsible for creating the elaborate carved-wood architecture that he called the Zakopane style.

The town is small, and its sights can easily be covered on foot. Ulica Krupówki, the main thoroughfare, runs downhill through the town from northwest to southeast; if you begin at the northwest end, you will pass many fine examples of the Zakopane style of wooden building as well as the town's museum, just beyond ulica Kościuszki, which links the town with the railway and bus stations and runs east to west across Krupówki. At the bottom of the hill, at the southeast end of ulica Krupówki is ulica Kościeliska, with an open-air museum of reconstructed farmsteads built in the traditional folk style, wooden St. Clement's Church, and Witkiewicz's Willa Koliba; the Atma Villa is just around the corner.

A cable railway can take you from the center of town up to the high ridge of **Gubałówka,** where on a clear day you will have a fine view of the Tatras and of the town. An alternative to riding the cable car back into town is to take the path along the ridge to Pałkówka and from there back down into town, about 9 km (5½ mi). Kids can have their photograph taken on the Gubałówka terrace in a carriage drawn by four white mountain sheepdogs and driven by a man dressed in a white bearskin. The cable railway station is down from the corner of ulica Krupówki and ulica Kościeliska.

At the foot of the hill in Zakopane is the mid-19th-century wooden church of **Kościół świelej Klemensa** (Church of St. Clement), the first church built in the town. The adjoining cemetery has a number of striking carved-wood memorials; Witkiewicz is buried here. ⊠ *Ul. Kościeliska opposite ul. Kasprusie.*

The **Muzeum Tatrzańskie** (Tatra Museum) on Zakopane's main street is worth a visit; it has splendid collections of the flora and fauna of the Tatras and a section with mountain crafts. ⊠ *Ul. Krupówki 10,* ☎ *018/201–52–05.* ⊠ *Zł 3.* ☺ *Tues.–Sun. 9–4.*

The **Willa Atma,** a wooden villa in Zakopane style, was home to the Polish composer Karol Szymanowski in the 1920s; it is now a museum with mementos of his life and work. ⊠ *Ul. Kasprusie 19,* ☎ *018/206–31–50.* ⊠ *Zł1.* ☺ *Tues.–Wed. and Fri.–Sun. 10–4, Thurs. 2–8.*

Stanisław Witkiewicz designed several villas in the Zakopane style. The elaborate **Willa pod Jedlami** (⊠ Ul. Koziniec 1) is considered one of his most ambitious works. Witkiewicz's very first project in the Zakopane style was the **Willa Koliba,** which is now a museum. ⊠ *Muzeum Stylu Zakopańskiego im. Stanisława Witkiewicza, ul. Kościeliska 18,* ☎ *018/201–36–02.* 🎫 *Zł 3.* ☉ *Wed.–Sun. 10–4.*

Dining and Lodging

$$$ ✕ **Giewont.** The dining room in the Giewont Hotel is high and galleried, decorated with crystal chandeliers and crisp white tablecloths on well-spaced tables. Service is elegant and discreet. The game dishes are the best items on the menu; try the roast pheasant when it's in season. ⊠ *Ul. Kościuszki 1,* ☎ *018/201–20–11. AE, DC, MC, V.*

$$ ✕ **Gazda.** As befits a hotel run by the peasants' cooperative Gromada,
★ the Gazda has excellent food. The large, light dining room, outfitted with linen tablecloths and napkins, is usually full; the service is friendly and prompt. Recommended dishes include roast lamb and, in season, the bilberry dessert pancakes. ⊠ *Ul. Zaruskiego 2,* ☎ *018/201–50– 11. AE, DC, MC, V.*

$$ ✕ **U Wnuka.** This is the best-known and longest-established regional
★ restaurant in Zakopane, with a great variety of local dishes: mountain robber's roast (*pieczeń po zbójnicku*), Zakopane pancakes, and shepherd's soup (*zupa juhaska*). It is usually crowded, service is slow, and portions are enormous. On weekends there is regional folk music. ⊠ *Ul. Kościeliska 8,* ☎ *018/206–61–47. AE, DC, MC, V.*

$$$ 🏨 **Kasprowy.** On the side of Gubałówka, this is convenient only if you have your own means of transportation; it's several miles outside town and a 15-minute walk from bus routes. However, the Kasprowy is a good option for skiers: The lift to Butory Wierch is nearby, as are beginners' slopes. The four-story hotel fits snugly into the hillside and has panoramic views of Mt. Giewont and beyond. The rooms are comfortable and well furnished (those overlooking Giewont have a 25% markup), but the public areas have become a little shabby since the hotel first opened in 1974. ⊠ *Ul. Polana Szymoszkowa 1, 34–500,* ☎ *018/201–40–11,* 𝖥𝖠𝖷 *018/201–57–00. 276 rooms, 12 suites. Restaurant, indoor pool. AE, DC, MC, V.*

$$ 🏨 **Gazda.** Opened in 1975 opposite the post office in the center of town, this hotel is in a pleasantly solid, low-rise building. Outside, the stone figure of a farmer in full folk costume reinforces the local theme (*gazda* means farmer). The rooms are comfortably furnished in stripped pine and decorated in light, bright colors. ⊠ *Gromada, ul. Zaruskiego 2, 34–500,* ☎ *018/201–50–11,* 𝖥𝖠𝖷 *018/201–53–30. 64 rooms, 54 with bath. Restaurant. AE, DC, MC, V.*

$$ 🏨 **Giewont.** If you can, pick a room with a view of the peak after which this late-19th-century hotel is named: Mt. Giewont. The rooms are reasonably well furnished in traditional style but vary greatly in size; it's a good idea to see the room before moving in. This hotel is right in the center of town. ⊠ *Ul. Kościuszki 1,* ☎ *018/201–20–11, 34–500,* 𝖥𝖠𝖷 *018/201–20–15 (reservations through the Kasprowy). 44 rooms. Restaurant. AE, DC, MC, V.*

Nightlife and the Arts

Zakopane offers theatrical and musical performances mainly connected with the artists and writers who made the town their home, particularly Witkacy and Karol Szymanowski; watch for posters on kiosks for announcements. There are also plenty of opportunities to hear traditional local folk orchestras. As for nightlife, Zakopane still goes to bed relatively early, but new nightspots are appearing all the time.

BARS

Morskie Oko, in the cellars of Morskie Oko (✉ Ul. Krupówki 30), has stone walls, a huge roaring fire in winter, and an unobtrusive traditional folk ensemble playing in the background. **U Ratowników** (✉ TOPR, ul. Piłsudskiego 63a) is in the headquarters of the mountain rescue organization: You can sit among a smoky throng on wooden benches, surrounded by portraits of past heroes of the association, and listen to the tales of its current members.

MUSIC

Occasional concerts are given in Zakopane at the **Willa Atma** (✉ Ul. Kasprusie 19, ☎ 018/206–31–50). There is a festival of Szymanowski's music in July, when concerts are held at various points in the town, and an autumn music festival (September–October). The **Kulczycki Gallery** (✉ Ul. Koziniec 8, ☎ 018/201–29–36) offers occasional concerts and other events.

THEATER

The **Teatr im. Stanisława Ignacego Witkiewicza** (✉ Ul. Chramcówki 15, ☎ 018/206–82–97) has two stages and often brings in well-known actors for the season.

Outdoor Activities and Sports

BIKING

Mountain biking has become increasingly popular. You can hire a bike at **Sport & Fun Company Ltd** (✉ Rondo 1, ☎ 018/201–56–03) for zł 50 per day. **Rent a bike** (✉ Ul. Sienkiewicza 37, ☎ 018/ 201–42–66) has a small selection of mountain bikes available.

HIKING

The **Gorczański, Pieniński,** and **Tatrzański national parks** all offer excellent hiking territory. The routes are well marked, and all national parks have maps at entrance points explaining distances, times, and degrees of difficulty of the trails. On the lower reaches of trails out of major tourist points (for example, Zakopane, Szczawnica, Krynica), walkers crowd the paths, but they thin out as you go higher up.

JOGGING

In Zakopane, the **Droga pod Reglami,** which runs along the foot of the Tatra National Park, makes an excellent, relatively flat jogging route; it can be approached from various points in the town.

SKIING

Zakopane acquired snow-making facilities in 1990 and is still the region's major center for downhill skiing, although Krynica and Krościenko also have facilities. You'll find the most advanced runs at **Kasprowy Wierch** mountain, accessed via a cable lift from Łozienice (☎ 018/201–45–10 lower station; 018/201–44–05 upper station). Chairlifts also bring skiers to the peaks of **Butory Wierch** (✉ Lift at ul. Powstańców Śląskich, ☎ 018/201–39–41) and **Nosal** (✉ Ul. Balzera, ☎ 018/201–31–81). Tickets can be hard to come by in season; it may be easier to get them in **Orbis** (✉ Ul. Krupówki 22), although you pay a surcharge of 30%.

Shopping

Leather and sheepskin products are local specialties, along with hand-knit socks, sweaters, and caps in white, gray, and black patterns made from rough, undyed wool. The best places to look are at the **Zakopane market,** held at the foot of ulica Krupówki, on the way to the Gubałówka cable railway. Wednesday is the main market day, but some stalls will be found here all week. Street vendors, who work here daily, as they do throughout the region, charge higher prices. **Limba** (✉ Ul. Kościeliska

1) has a fine assortment of handmade local costumes; there are also smaller items like belts and walking sticks.

DOLINA KOŚCIELISKA (Kościeliska Valley) – Nine kilometers (5 miles) southwest of Zakopane on the road to Kiry and Witów, this valley falls within the **Tatrzański Park Narodowy** (Tatra National Park), which covers the entire mountain range in both Poland and Slovakia. Remember that you are not allowed to pick flowers here—a strongly tempting pastime in spring, when the lower valley is covered with crocuses. The first part of the valley runs for roughly a mile through flat, open pasture, before the stream that gave the Kościeliska its name begins its descent through steep, rocky gorges. You finally emerge at **Ornak**, 5½ km (3½ mi) from the road, where there are splendid views. Horse-drawn carriages (sleighs in winter) wait at the entrance to take visitors halfway up the valley (for about zł 30), but if you want to reach Ornak, you must cover the last stage on foot. **Harnaś** is a bar at the entrance to the valley, where locals come to drink beer and where dishes like *fasolka po bretońsku* (Breton baked beans) or bigos are available from 8 AM to 10 PM. ⊠ *Take a bus from the PKS bus station in Zakopane on ul. Kościuszki to Kiry.*

BUKOWINA TATRZAŃSKA – Thirteen kilometers (8 miles) northeast of Zakopane, Bukowina Tatrzańska is an attractive, largely wood-built village set high on a ridge, once famed for its number of beekeepers and its honey. The path at the top of the ridge, parallel to the main road to Łysa Polana, affords spectacular views of the Tatra range and is a favored spot for winter sunbathing. ⊠ *Bukowina can easily be reached by PKS bus from the Zakopane bus station on ul. Kościuszki. By car, take E95 (the main road to Kraków) north from Zakopane, and 5 km (3 mi) out of town turn east onto Hwy. 961, which leads to the border crossing point at Polana. The left-hand turn into the village of Bukowina is clearly signposted.*

Morskie Oko

30 km (20 mi) southeast of Zakopane. Orbis in Zakopane runs a regular bus service to within 10 minutes' walk of the lake. If you feel more energetic, you can take a PKS bus from the bus station to Łysa Polana and follow the marked trail for 8 km (5 mi).

Morskie Oko is the largest and loveliest of the lakes in the High Tatras, 4,570 ft above sea level. The name means "Eye of the Sea," and an old legend claims it has a secret underground passage connecting it to the ocean. The **Mięguszowiecki** and **Mnich** peaks appear to rise straight up from the water, and the depth of the lake permanently shades it an intense blue.

Dining and Lodging

$ ✕🏠 **Schronisko im. Stanisława Staszica.** A climbers' and hikers' hostel, this establishment has a restaurant that serves large portions of basic fare like *fasolka po bretońsku* (buckwheat with mushrooms), or pancakes with whipped cream. You can also obtain a bed in a spartan, clean, three-, four-, five-, or six-person room for as little as $5. ⊠ *Box 201, Zakopane, 34–500,* ☎ *018/207–76–09. No credit cards.*

Nowy Targ

🟢 *24 km (15 mi) north of Zakopane, 90 km (56 mi) south of Kraków. Nowy Targ is on the main road from Zakopane to Kraków; buses run from Zakopane every hour.*

The unofficial capital of the Podhale region, Nowy Targ has been a chartered borough since the 14th century, when it stood at an intersection of international trade routes, and it remains an important market center for the entire mountain region. It is worth visiting on Thursday, market day, when farmers bring their livestock in for sale and a range of local products, including rough wool sweaters and sheepskin coats, are on sale. The White and Black Dunajec streams meet in Nowy Targ to form the Dunajec River, which then runs on through steep limestone gorges to Nowy Sącz.

En Route On the road to Szczawnica, 12 km (8 mi) east of Nowy Targ, is
★ **Dębno.** This village in the valley of the Dunajec River has a tiny wooden church dating from the 15th century (it's believed to be the oldest wooden building in the Podhale region); inside are medieval wall paintings and wooden sculptures. *Buses run from the marketplace in Nowy Targ.*

Krościenko, 25 km (15 mi) east of Nowy Targ and 35 km (22 mi) southwest of Nowy Sącz, is one of the villages that became a holiday resort during the late 19th century and is still popular today as a center for walking vacations. It has many interesting Zakopane-style wooden structures. *Best access by PKS bus from the train station in Nowy Sącz.*

The small spa of **Szczawnica,** 28 km (17½ mi) east of Nowy Targ, 35 km (22 mi) southwest of Nowy Sącz, dates from the late 19th century; you can stroll around in the high-vaulted pump rooms and sip the foul-tasting mineral waters. *Best access by PKS bus from the marketplace in Nowy Targ or outside the train station in Nowy Sącz.*

Nowy Sącz

⑦ *100 km (64 mi) southeast of Kraków, 80 km (50 mi) northeast of Zakopane.*

Nowy Sącz has existed as a market town since the 13th century; a ruined 14th-century castle remains from this early period, as do the church on the northeast side of the market square and the 15th-century church and chapter house on the east side.

Dining and Lodging

$$ ✕ **Zajazd Sądecki.** This restaurant emphasizes regional cuisine, such as pancakes highland-style, stuffed with pork and onions. The dining room is cozy, with pine furniture and crisp, white tablecloths. ⊠ *Ul. Królowej Jadwigi 67,* ☎ *018/442–67–17. No credit cards.*

$$ ⌂ **Beskid.** This standard, cube-shape Orbis hotel is a typical product of the mid-1960s. It commands good views while being conveniently located near the rail and bus stations in the town center. The rooms are rather small and drab but comfortable, brightened with Podhale folk elements. Breakfasts are delicious. ⊠ *Ul. Limanowskiego 1, 33–330,* ☎ *018/443–57–70,* ℻ *018/443–51–44. 63 rooms, 10 suites. Restaurant, bar. AE, DC, MC, V.*

Krynica

⑧ *32 km (20 mi) south of Nowy Sącz on Highway 99.*

Krynica is a spa and winter-sports center in a high valley. The salutary properties of the mineral waters were recognized during the 18th century, and the first **bathhouse** (⊠ Ul. Kraszewskiego 9) was built in 1807. Krynica was developed further in classic spa style in the late 19th century: It has a tree-lined promenade, a pump room, and concert halls. The waters here are not appetizing to the unaccustomed palate; they are the most concentrated mineral waters in Europe.

Lodging

$ ▣ **Hotel Meran.** This is a small, friendly, three-story hotel, with wooden balconies and good parking facilities. ✉ *Ul. Kościelna 9, 33–380,* ☎ *018/471–21–09. 30 rooms.*

Consult **Pensjonat Wisła** (✉ Bulwary Dietla 1, ☎ 018/471–55–12), a pension that also runs an information service on vacancies elsewhere. You can also look for signs in windows advertising POKOJE (rooms).

Małopolska A to Z

Arriving and Departing

BY BUS

Zakopane is most easily accessible by bus from Kraków, which takes two hours. There are also through services from Warsaw to Zakopane (travel time: five hours). Zakopane's **PKS bus** station is at the corner of ulica Kościuszki and ulica Chramcówki (☎ 018/201–46–03).

BY CAR

The 7(E77) highway—which takes you roughly halfway to Zakopane from Kraków—is now entirely four-lane, while Highway 95 has been substantially improved and widened. Side roads in the region can be very narrow and badly surfaced. In Zakopane and other towns in the region, it would be wise to leave your car at a guarded parking lot.

BY TRAIN

Zakopane's train station is on ulica Chramcówki (☎ 018/201–45–04). From Kraków, the trip to Zakopane takes six hours because of the rugged nature of the terrain. Unless you take the overnight sleeper from Warsaw, which arrives in Zakopane at 6 AM, it's better to change to a bus in Kraków.

Getting Around

BY BUS

Almost all villages in the region, however isolated, can be reached by PKS bus. The buses themselves can be ancient and slow—take an express service if it operates to your destination. An express bus—for which seats can be reserved in advance—runs from Kraków to Zakopane and back every two hours.

BY CAR

It is not strictly necessary to have a car to explore the southern region. Public transport will take you to even the most remote and inaccessible places. But it will take time and can be uncomfortably crowded. On the other hand, the narrow mountain roads can be trying and dangerous for drivers. Although the Kraków–Zakopane highway has recently been much improved, some stretches are still single lane, and horse-drawn carts can cause major delays.

BY TRAIN

Trains move slowly in the hilly region south of Kraków, but most towns are accessible by train, and the routes can be very picturesque. In **Zakopane** you can get more information from the station on ulica Chramcówki (☎ 01820/145–04).

Contacts and Resources

EMERGENCIES

Ambulance (☎ 999). **Nowy Sącz** hospital (✉ Ul. Młyńska 5, ☎ 018/443–88–77).

Krynica: Vita (✉ Ul. Kraszewskiego 61, ☎ 018/471–39–47). **Nowy Sącz** (✉ Rynek 27, ☎ 018/443–82–92). **Zakopane:** Apteka Pharbita (✉ Ul. Chramcówki 34, ☎ 018/206–82–21).

PRIVATE ACCOMMODATIONS
For information in Zakopane contact **BIT** (✉ Ul. Kościuszki 17, ☎ 018/201–22–11) for a full range of options, or **Centralne Biuro Zakwaterowania FWP** (✉ Ul. Kościuszki 19, ☎ 018/201–27–63) for places in pensions where prices range from zł 35 to zł 50 a day.

VISITOR INFORMATION
Częstochowa (✉ IT, Al. Najświętejszej Marii Panny 65, ☎ 034/241–360). **Krynica** (✉ Ul. Piłsudskiego 8, ☎ 018/471–57–46). **Nowy Sącz** (✉ Ul. Piotra Skargi 2, ☎ 018/443–55–97). **Zakopane** (✉ BIT, Ul. Kościuszki 17, ☎ 018/201–22–11; ✉ Orbis, Ul. Krupówki 22, ☎ 018/201–22–38).

LUBLIN AND EASTERN POLAND

Lublin's location in eastern Poland has "protected" it somewhat from the influences that have swept the country since it opened to the West in 1989. Visitors here can get a peek at the old Poland—less prosperous, more traditional. Historically, Lublin lay in the heart of Poland and served as a crossroads between east and west. It was in Lublin in 1569 that the eastern duchy of Lithuania joined the kingdom of Poland by signing the Union of Lublin, thus creating the largest empire in Europe at the time. Following World War II, when Poland's borders shifted westward, Lublin found itself near the Soviet border. This has led to considerable contact with the East, largely in the form of Russian and Ukrainian traders who flock to the city's marketplace to peddle their goods—everything from old auto parts to caviar and champagne—and, increasingly, make purchases in Poland for resale in their own countries.

This is not, however, to imply that the changes sweeping through Poland have bypassed Lublin. One of the most important current projects is the restoration of Lublin's chief monument, its walled Stare Miasto (Old Town). At the western end of Krakowskie Przedmieście, many of the buildings in the quaint cobblestone streets of this district have been beautifully restored, and the area is looking up. And despite its graying exterior and mild urban decay, Lublin is rich in parks, offering wild, lush greens in summer and golden yellows in autumn.

Lublin is also a good hub for exploring the villages and countryside of the eastern parts of the country. Less than one hour away from the city, visitors can enjoy a picnic in the palace grounds in Puławy or a walk along the banks of the Vistula River in the picturesque village of Kazimierz Dolny. Like Kazimierz, Zamość and Łańcut are accessible as a day trip from Lublin, but all these centers are also attractive places for longer stopovers if you have time.

Numbers in the margin correspond to numbers on the Southeastern Poland map.

Lublin

❽❶ *160 km (100 mi) southeast of Warsaw, 270 km (170 mi) northeast of Kraków.*

The tourist attractions of Lublin are in three distinct regions of the city. **Stare Miasto** (Old Town), a medieval walled city, is at the eastern end of Krakowskie Przedmieście, the main street. The castle and nearby Jewish cemetery are just outside the old city wall, to the northeast. The Catholic and Marie Skłodowska-Curie **universities** and the adjacent Saxon Gardens are on the western edge of the city, off Aleja Racław-ickie; take a bus west from Krakowskie Przedmieście. **Majdanek,** once the second-largest Nazi concentration camp in Europe, lies 5 km (3 mi) southeast of central Lublin and can be reached by Bus 153 or 156 from Krakowskie Przedmieście.

Situated at the eastern end of Lublin's main shopping street, Krakowskie Przedmieście, is the **Brama Krakowska** (Kraków Gate), a Gothic and Baroque structure that served as the main entrance to the medieval city. Today it separates modern Lublin from the Stare Miasto. It houses the **Muzeum Lubelskie** (Lublin History Museum), which offers an overview of the area's history. ☒ *Pl. Łokietka 3,* ☏ *081/532–60–01.* ☒ *Zł 2.* ☉ *Wed.–Sat. 9–4.*

Part of Lublin's tremendous success as a medieval trading center stemmed from a royal decree exempting the city from all customs du-ties. As a result, huge fortunes were made and kept, and the town's merchants were able to build the beautiful 14th- and 15th-century houses—complete with colorful frescoed facades—that surround the
★ **Rynek** (market square). The Rynek's unusual trapezoidal shape is the result of medieval builders adapting the construction of the town to the outline of the protective walls surrounding Lublin.

Filling the center of Lublin's Rynek is the reconstructed **Stary Ratusz** (Old Town Hall), built in the 16th century and rebuilt in neoclassical style in the 1780s by the Italian architect Domenico Merlini. Here a royal tribunal served as the seat of the Crown Court of Justice for Małopolska beginning in 1578; records of its activities can be seen in the museum. On Saturdays the hall fills with young couples waiting to be married. ☒ *Rynek 1,* ☏ *081/532–68–66.* ☒ *Zł 2.* ☉ *Wed.–Sun. 9–4.*

NEED A
BREAK?

At ulica Grodzka 5A, in one of the recently reconstructed medieval tene-ments, you can visit the small ground-floor **Apteka–Muzeum** (Museum of Pharmacy), which is a reconstruction of an early chemist's shop, and then drink a cup of coffee in the café behind it.

★ The **Dominican Church and Monastery,** dating from 1342, is the jewel of Lublin's Old Town; the interior was renovated in rococo style in the 17th century. Two of its 11 chapels are particularly noteworthy: the **Kaplica Firlej,** (Firlej Chapel) with its late-Renaissance architecture, and the **Kaplica Tyszkiewski,** (Tyszkiewski Chapel) with its early Baroque decoration. Circling the walls above the chapels are paintings depicting the bringing of a piece of the True Cross—the cross on which on which Jesus was crucified—to Lublin, and the protection the relic has given the city through the ages. Unfortunately, this protection did not extend to the relic itself, which was stolen from the Dominican Church in 1991. The church is often closed now, but try knocking on the monastery door to the right of the entrance to alert someone to admit you. ☒ *Ul. Złota.* ☒ *Free.* ☉ *Weekdays 9–noon and 3–6, weekends 3–6.*

Outside the old city wall, just around the corner from Kraków Gate, stands **Lublin Cathedral,** begun in 1625. The exterior of this Jesuit church is an example of Lublin Renaissance style—steep-pitched roofs, highly decorated gables, and elaborate patterned vaulting. Inside to the left of the Baroque high altar, a reproduction of the *Black Madonna of Częstochowa* is on display. You can reach the **Kaplica Akustyczna** (Whispering Chapel) by a passage to the right of the high altar. Watch what you say here—the acoustics are so astounding that a whisper in one corner can be heard perfectly in another. Next to the chapel is the **treasury,** holding what remains of the original illusionistic frescoes that decorated the church interior: The images were painted so skillfully that they appear almost three dimensional. ⊠ *Ul. Królewska.* ☎ *Whispering Chapel and treasury zł 2.*

During the late 14th century King Kazimierz the Great ordered the construction of **Lublin Castle,** as well as the defensive walls surrounding the city, to protect the wealthy trading center from invasion. Most of the castle was rebuilt in Mock Gothic during the 19th century, when it was converted to a prison. Run at various times by the Russian czar, the German Gestapo, and the Communist secret police, the castle prison witnessed the largest number of deaths during World War II, when the Nazis murdered more than 10,000 political prisoners. The ★ newly opened **Kaplica Trójcy Świętej** (Chapel of the Holy Trinity), which has been under restoration for decades, is the most outstanding attraction in Lublin. The 14th-century chapel is covered with Byzantium-style murals. Note the ancient graffiti on the walls. The **Castle Museum** houses historical exhibits and an art **gallery** known for Jan Matejko's *Unia Lubelska* (1869), which depicts the signing of the Lublin Union by the king of Poland and Grand Duke of Lithuania exactly three centuries earlier. ⊠ *Ul. Zamkowa 9,* ☎ *081/532–50–01.* ☎ *Zł 6.* ⊙ *Wed.–Sat. 9–4, Sun. 9–5.*

Lublin was a center of Jewish culture in the 16th century; the hill behind Lublin Castle is the site of the **Stary Cmentarz Żydowski** (Old Jewish Cemetery) destroyed during World War II by the German SS, which used the rubble from the headstones to pave the entranceway to Majdanek concentration camp. The park at the base of the castle hill was the site of the Jewish ghetto, in which Nazis imprisoned the Jewish population of Lublin until April 1943, when they sent them to Majdanek.

OFF THE
BEATEN PATH

MAJDANEK CONCENTRATION CAMP – Reminders of the horrors of World War II are never far away in Poland, and several miles southeast of Lublin's city center lie the remnants of the Majdanek concentration camp, second in scope only to Auschwitz. Established in July 1941, it grew to 1,235 acres, although the original plan was to make it five times as large. Majdanek originally housed 5,000 Polish, Russian, and Ukrainian prisoners of war, who were later followed by citizens of 29 other countries, most of them Jewish. From 1941 to 1944, more than 360,000 people lost their lives here, either by direct extermination or through illness and disease.

Standing at the camp entrance is one of two monuments designed for the 25th anniversary of the liberation of Majdanek. The **Monument of Struggle and Martyrdom** symbolizes the inmates' faith and hope; the **mausoleum** at the rear of the camp marks the death of that hope. Of the five fields constituting the original camp, only the gas chambers, watchtowers, and crematoria, as well as some barracks on Field Three, remain. The **visitor center,** to the left of the entrance monument, shows a movie about the camp (in English; last showing at 2 PM) and has a bookstore as well as a restaurant. ⊠ *Droga Męczenników Majdanka 67,* ☎ *081/7442–647.* ☎ *Free.* ⊙ *Tues.–Sun. 8–6.*

Dining and Lodging

$$ ✕ **Club Hades.** This local favorite is considered the best place to dine in Lublin. Specialties include onion soup and all kinds of meat dishes. ⊠ *Al. Peowiaków 12,* ☎ *081/532–56–41. No credit cards.*

$$ ✕ **Piwnica.** This popular restaurant features traditional Polish fare. The
★ pickled herring makes an excellent appetizer; recommended main
courses include typical meat entrées such as roast pork, veal cutlet, and
beef medallions with mashed potatoes. ⊠ *Ul. Skłodowska 12,* ☎ *081/
534–39–19. AE, DC, MC, V.*

$$$ ⊞ **Unia Hotel.** This six-story hotel is just off the main road, outside
★ the Old Town. Most of the public spaces are fairly cramped, but the
rooms are reasonably spacious and comfortably furnished. ⊠ *Al.
Racławickie 12, 20–037,* ☎ *081/533–20–61,* ℻ *081/533–30–21.
Restaurant, bar, casino. AE, DC, MC, V.*

$ ⊞ **Dom Nauczyciela.** This hotel, which was formerly reserved for
members of the Communist teachers union, is clean, comfortable, and
efficiently run, if lacking in elegance. The rooms are small but adequate.
⊠ *Ul. Akademicka 4, 20–033,* ☎ *081/533–03–66,* ℻ *081/533–
37–45. 80 rooms, 45 with bath. No credit cards.*

$ ⊞ **Victoria Hotel.** This venerable hotel is large and well situated within
walking distance of all the Old Town's landmarks. The rooms are on
the small side, but the service is efficient and friendly. Rooms over the
street, which is on a hill, can be noisy. ⊠ *Ul. Narutowicza 58–60, 20–
401,* ☎ ℻ *081/532–90–26. 190 rooms, 63 rooms with bath. Restaurant. AE, DC, MC, V.*

Nightlife and the Arts

For up-to-date information about movies, theater, and concerts in
Lublin, consult the local papers, *Kurier Lubelski* and *Dziennik Lubelski*. **Philharmonic** tickets can be purchased at ulica Kapuczyńska 7, Tuesday–Sunday noon–7. Theater tickets are available at **Centrum Kultury**
(⊠ *Ul. Peowiaków 12*), the home of all theater groups in Lublin. The
Teatr Muzyczny is at ulica Kunickiego 35 (☎ 081/532–76–13) and
has a repertoire of musicals and light operetta. Student nightlife centers on Marie Skłodowska-Curie University's **Chatka Żaka Club** (⊠ Ul.
I. Radziszewskiego 16, ☎ 081/533–32–01). The club offers a cafeteria, a bar, a popular disco, and a cinema that often shows American
movies.

Outdoor Activities and Sports

On hot summer days Lublin residents head for **Zalew Zemborzycki,** a
man-made lake that offers sailing and canoe rentals located about 4
km (2½ mi) south of central Lublin. *Take Bus 25 or 42 from Lublin
Cathedral.*

OFF THE ★ **KOZŁÓWKA** – Set in a beautiful and well-tended park, this 18th-century
BEATEN PATH palace (41 km/25 mi north of Lublin) was built for the Zamoyski family
and is one of a handful of palaces in Poland whose interiors have remained intact. Housed in the palace annex is a fascinating relic of the
Stalinist era, the **Museum of the Art of Socialist Realism.** The palace and
museum are reachable by bus from Lublin. If you are driving, take Route
19 north of Lublin to Lubartów (29 km/18 mi); then head west for 12 km
(7 mi). ☎ *081/855–29–88.* ▭ *Zł 7.* ☉ *Mar. 1–Dec. 1, Tues.–Sun. 10–4.*

Puławy

82 *40 km (25 mi) northwest of Lublin, 130 km (70 mi) southeast of Warsaw.*

The 18th-century **Puławy Palace** in the town of Puławy is worth a brief
stop. The palace was originally the residence of the Czartoryski family, a patriotic, politically powerful clan. Prince Adam Czartoryski
was one of the most educated men of his day and a great patron of the
arts and culture. He attracted so many prominent Poles to Puławy that

by the late 18th century it was said to rival Warsaw as a cultural and political capital. Today the yellow-and-white neoclassical building houses an agricultural institute.

Set in a building modeled on the Vesta Temple in Tivoli, Świątynia Sybilli (Sybil's Temple), completed in 1809, was Poland's first museum. The **Palace Chapel**, built in 1803, is based on the Pantheon in Rome. It's at ulica Aiguera, outside the palace grounds (from the palace front, walk two blocks north on ulica Czartoryskich to ulica Aiguera, and then left for two blocks). ⊠ *Ul. Czartoryskich 6A,* ☎ *0831/87–86–74.* ⊡ *Palace grounds free; Sybil's Temple zł 2.* ⊙ *Tues.–Sun. 10–2.*

Kazimierz Dolny

★ ⑧⑨ *12 km (7 mi) south of Puławy, 40 km (25 mi) west of Lublin, 130 km (80 mi) southeast of Warsaw.*

The visual effect of this small town is so pleasing that it has thrived for over a century as an artists' colony and vacation spot. Pitched on a steep, hilly bank of the placid Vistula River, it has an assortment of whitewashed facades and steeply pitched red-tile roofs peeking out over the treetops. Often referred to as the Pearl of the Polish Renaissance, Kazimierz Dolny prospered as a port town during the 16th and 17th centuries, but the partitioning of Poland left it cut off from the grain markets of Gdańsk. Thereafter the town fell into decline until it was rediscovered by painters and writers during the 19th century. Today nonartistic visitors can still enjoy the Renaissance architecture along the village's dusty cobblestone streets, or hike through the nearby hills and gorges.

One of the most powerful families in Kazimierz Dolny, the Przybyłas, left behind an ornate house, built in 1615. Adorning the facades of the **Przybyła Brothers' House,** on the southeast corner of the town's **Rynek** (market square), are the two-story bas-relief figures of St. Nicholas (left) and St. Christopher (right), the brothers' patron saints. The **Celej House,** seat of another powerful Kazimierz clan, stands one block toward the river from the square; it's embellished with griffins, dragons, and salamanders. The former residence now houses the **Town Museum of Kazimierz Dolny,** which has many paintings depicting local life of past eras. ⊠ *Ul. Senatorska 11,* ☎ *081/81–01–04.* ⊡ *Zł 2.* ⊙ *Tues.–Sun. 10–3.*

A covered passageway off ulica Senatorska leads up to the walled courtyard of the **Church and Monastery of the Reformati Order,** which stands on the southern hill overlooking the town's market square. In the late 18th century an encircling wall was built to protect the monastery's buildings. A plaque inside the passageway memorializes the Nazis' use of the site as a house of torture during World War II. The climb up to the courtyard is worthwhile just for the spectacular view it affords of the town. The ruins of the 14th-century **Kazimierz Castle,** which served as a watchtower to protect the Vistula trade route, stand on a steep hill to the northeast of the town's market square; from here there is a grand view over the town and the Vistula Valley. The **Góra Trzech Krzyży** (Three Crosses Hill) lies to the east of the Kazimierz Dolny market square; the crosses were constructed in 1708 to commemorate the victims of a plague that ravaged the town.

Lodging

$ ⌷ **SARP.** This ideally located hotel on the corner of the picturesque town square belongs and caters to the Architects' Association but will take other guests on a commercial basis. The rooms are large and irregular in shape, with simple but adequate furnishings. The restaurant is usually packed with intellectuals. ⊠ *Rynek 20, 24–120*, ☎ *081/81–05–44. 35 rooms, 15 with bath. Dining room. No credit cards.*

Outdoor Activities and Sports

BOATING

Boat rides on the Vistula leave from ulica Puławska 6. The half-hour ride takes you south to **Janowiec** with its Firlej Castle ruins.

HIKING

Take one of the numerous marked trails, ranging in length from 2 to 6 km (1 to 4 mi), and explore the hilly landscape around Kazimierz. All trails converge on the market square. Tourist tracks lead north (marked red) and south (marked green) along the river from the Rynek, along streets and cart paths, through orchards and quarries.

Zamość

84 *87 km (54 mi) to the southeast of Lublin, 318 km (198 mi) northeast of Kraków.*

The fortified town of Zamość was placed on the UNESCO list of World Natural and Cultural Heritage in 1992 for its wonderfully preserved, grand Renaissance-era central square, wide boulevards, and neat rows of colorful houses with brightly painted facades.

Zamość was conceived in the late 16th century by Hetman Jan Zamoyski as an outpost along the thriving trade route between Lublin and Lwów. The town thrived, and its strong fortifications spared it from destruction during the Swedish onslaught of the 17th century. The Polish victory over Lenin's Red Army near Zamość in 1920 kept the way clear for the country's restored independence. World War II saw the town renamed Himmlerstadt, with thousands of its residents (45% of the town was Jewish) deported or exterminated to make way for German settlers. The buildings are unscathed, but you may see some deeper meaning in the eyes of the village elders.

★ Zamość's **Rynek** (market square) is a breathtaking arcaded plaza surrounded by the decorative facades of homes built by local merchants during the 16th and 17th centuries. Dominating the square is the impressive, Baroque **town hall,** topped by a 164-ft spire. The **Muzeum Regionalne w Zamościu** (Zamość Regional Museum), which is housed in a charming town house next door to the town hall, has paintings of the Zamoyski clan, the town's founding family, and a scale model of Zamość. ⊠ *Ul. Ormiańska 24,* ☎ *084/638–64–94.* 🎫 *Zł 2.* ⊘ *Tues.–Sun. 10–4.*

Kolegiata Św. Tomasza (St. Thomas Collegiate Church), one of Poland's most beautiful Renaissance churches, stands near the southwest corner of the market square. In the presbytery are four 17th-century paintings ascribed to Domenico Robusti, Tintoretto's son. The church is also the final resting place of Jan Zamoyski, buried in the **Zamoyski Chapel,** to the right of the high altar.

The **Pałac Zamojskich** (Zamoski Palace), home of the founding family of Zamość, lies near the market square, beyond St. Thomas Collegiate Church. The palace lost much of its decorative detail in renovation and restoration and now serves as a courthouse. The Zamość **Arsenał** (Arsenal Museum) behind the Zamoyski Palace, houses a collection of Turkish armaments and rugs, as well as a model of the original town plan. ⊠ *Ul. Zamkowa 2,* ☎ *084/638–40–76.* 🎫 *Zł 4.* ⊘ *Tues.–Sun. 10–4.*

Near the northwest corner of the main square, behind the town hall, is the **Akademia** (Old Academy), a distinguished center of learning during the 17th and 18th centuries and once the third-largest university after those in Kraków and Vilnius (it is now a high school). The oldest entrance to Zamość, the **Brama Lubelska** (Lubin Gate) is to the northwest of the marketplace, across the road from the Old Academy. In 1588, Jan Zamoyski triumphantly led the Austrian archduke Maximilian into town through this gate after defeating him in his attempt to seize the Polish throne from Sigismund III. He then bricked up the gate to commemorate his victory.

What's left of Zamość's **fortifications** are found at the bottom of ulica Staszica: This is the **Brama Lwowska Bastion** (Lwów Gate and Bastion). With defenses like these, three stories high and 20 ft thick, it is easy to understand why Zamość was one of the few places to escape ruin in the Swedish attack. ▧ *Gate and bastion zł 1.* ☉ *Tues.–Sun. 10–4.*

South of the town's marketplace, on ulica Moranda, is the **rotunda,** a monument to a tragic era in Zamość's history. From 1939 to 1944 this fortified emplacement served as an extermination camp where tens of thousands of Poles, Jews, and Russians were brutally killed, some even burned alive. Now it serves as a memorial to the victims of Nazi brutality in the region. ▧ *Zł 7.* ☉ *Daily 10–5.*

Dining and Lodging

$ ✕ **Restauracja Ratuszowa.** This restaurant on the magnificent main square is housed in a redecorated Renaissance tenement. In summer, the menu can be quite extensive and includes an excellent *chłodnik* (cold beet soup). ✉ *Rynek Wielki 13,* ☎ *084/647–02. AE, DC, MC, V.*

$$ ▦ **Hotel Jubilat.** Built in the 1970s, this hotel offers comfortable rooms on the edge of the Old Town. The decor is dark, but everything is clean. ✉ *Ul. Wyszyńskiego 52, 22–400,* ☎ *084/638–64–01. 62 rooms. Restaurant. AE, DC, MC, V.*

$$ ▦ **Hotel Renesans.** This small hotel is located within a few blocks of the main square. The newly renovated lodging offers cheerful rooms as well as modern bathrooms. ✉ *Ul. Grecka 6, 22–400,* ☎ FAX *084/ 639–20–01. 20 rooms. Restaurant. AE, DC, MC, V.*

Łańcut

★ ⑧⑤ *17 km (10½ mi) northeast of Rzeszów, 130 km (81 mi) southwest of Zamość on highway 4(E40).*

The neo-Baroque **Łańcut Palace,** situated within a 76-acre natural reserve, is the main attraction in the town of Łańcut. Built during the 16th century, the palace is one of the most grandiose aristocratic residences in Eastern Europe. In the 19th century it was willed to the Potocki family, who amassed an impressive art collection here. Count Alfred Potocki, the last owner, emigrated to Liechtenstein in 1944 as Russian troops approached, escaping with 11 train cars full of art objects and paintings. Much was left behind, however, and after the war a museum was established in the palace (which had survived intact). Today you can see the family collection of art and interior decorations, including Biedermeier, neoclassical, and rococo furnishings. Of particular interest are the intricate wood-inlay floors, the tiny theater off the dining hall, and the hall of sculpture painted to resemble a trellis of grapevines. More than 40 rooms are open to the public, including the Turkish and Chinese apartments, which reflect the 18th-century fascination with the Near and Far East. Outside, a moat and a system of bastions laid out like a five-pointed star separate the inner Italian and rose gardens from the rest of the park. The **Carriage Museum,** in the old coach house outside the main gates, contains more than 50 vehicles and is one of the largest museums of its kind in Europe. ☎ *017/225–20–08.* ▧ *Both* *museums zł 8. ☉ Park daily until sunset; museums Tues.–Sat. 8–2:30, Sun. 9–4.*

Lodging

$ ⊞ **Hotel Zamkowy.** Although the accommodations in this 18th-cen-
★ tury palace seem anomalous by virtue of their 1970s decor, they are
cozy and overlook the palace courtyard. There are only 50 beds, so
reservations are imperative. ⊠ *Ul. Zamkowa 1, 37–100,* ☎ *017/
225–26–71. 23 rooms, 15 with bath. Restaurant. AE, DC, MC, V.*

OFF THE **LEŻAJSK –** This basilica and monastery of the Bernadine Fathers dates
BEATEN PATH back to the 17th century and is a major pilgrimage site. Frequent musical performances are given on the stupendous 17th-century organ.
There is also a museum attached to the monastery with exhibits of beautiful wood carvings. *Leżajsk is located 29 km (13 mi) north of Łańut, 46
km (25 mi) east of Rzeszów on Route 877.*

Lublin and Eastern Poland A to Z

Arriving and Departing

BY BUS

Lublin is the gateway to the region. **Dworzec PKS Główny** (⊠ Al.
Tysiąclecia 4, ☎ 081/747–89–22), just north of Stare Miasto near the
castle, connects Lublin with cities to the west and south. Buses run regularly to Puławy (1 hour), Kazimierz Dolny (1½ hours), Rzeszów (3
hours), and Warsaw (3 hours). Buses 5, 10, 35, 38, 154, and 161 connect the station with ulica Krakowskie Przedmieście.

Located about 4 km (2½ mi) southeast of the town center, **Dworzec
PKS Północny** (⊠ Ul. Gospodarcza) connects Lublin with points east.
Buses run frequently to Zamość (1¾ hours). You can reach the town
center on Bus 155 or 159.

BY TRAIN

Lublin Główny (⊠ Pl. Dworcowy, ☎ 081/531–56–42), the town's main
station, is about 4 km (2½ mi) south of the city center. Frequent train
service connects Lublin with Warsaw (2½ hours), Kraków (4½ hours),
and Zamość (3 hours). Buses 13 and 158 connect the train station with
the town center.

Getting Around

Most of Lublin's restaurants and hotels lie on or around ulica Krakowskie
Przedmieście and its continuation to the west, Aleje Racławickie. This
route is anchored by the Stare Miasto in the east and the Catholic University in the west. The Majdanek concentration camp is a few miles
southeast. You can easily explore the entire city on foot.

BY BUS

Lublin's bus system is convenient for traveling in from the train station and out to Majdanek. Buy a ticket at any RUCH kiosk and make
sure to cancel your tickets on the bus.

Contacts and Resources

EMERGENCIES

Police (☎ 997). **Ambulance** (☎ 999). **Late-night pharmacies:** Two
pharmacies (*apteki*) in **Lublin** (⊠ Ul. Bramowa 8, ☎ 081/532–05–21;
⊠ Krakowskie Przedmieście 49, ☎ 081/532–24–25) are open 24
hours.

VISITOR INFORMATION

Lublin's main source of tourist information—**Centrum Informacji Turystycznej**—is in the Old Town (⊠ Krakowskie Przedmieście 78, ☎

081/532–44–12). **Orbis** (⌧ Ul. Narutowicza 31/33, ☎ 081/532–22–56 or 081/532–22–59) books train tickets and exchanges money. In Zamość tourist information is provided by **Zamojski Ośrodek Informacji Turystycznej** (⌧ Rynek Wielki 13, ☎ 084/39–22–92) and **Orbis** (⌧ Ul. Grodzka 18, ☎ 084/639–30–01).

GDANSK AND THE NORTHEAST

With Gdańsk (the bustling city that was the birthplace of Solidarity), Riviera-like resorts, and Poland's Castle Country, this region of Poland can be particularly rewarding for the visitor. Until World War II, most of this area was included in Prussia and was referred to as "the sand box of the Holy Roman Empire." It is indeed sandy, but it contains some startlingly beautiful landscapes and magnificent historic sites, like the fortress of the Teutonic Knights at **Malbork** (close to and easily accessible by train from Gdańsk). In the northeast are 1,000 lakes and 1,000-year-old forests (and the attendant mosquitoes during the summer): The Mazurian and Augustów-Suwałki lake area forms a labyrinth of interconnecting rivers and canals, against a backdrop of ancient forests. **Olsztyn** is the best starting point for exploring this area, but you need a car to experience its delights fully.

Gdańsk, the third-largest city in Poland and the capital of this region, is linked with two smaller neighboring towns, **Gdynia** and **Sopot,** in an urban conglomeration called the **Trójmiasto** (Tri-City), on the western bank of the Bay of Gdańsk; these cities operate as a single organism and constitute one of Poland's most exciting and vibrant places.

Numbers in the margin correspond to numbers on the Gdańsk and the Northeast map.

Gdańsk

86 *350 km (219 mi) north of Warsaw, 340 km (215 mi) east of Szczecin.*

Maybe it's the sea air, or maybe it's the city's history of political tumult. Whatever the reason, Gdańsk is special to Poles, as well as Scandinavians and Germans, who visit the region in great numbers. Between 1308 and 1945 under the name Danzig, this Baltic port was an independent city-state, a majority of whose residents were ethnic Germans. When the Nazis fired the first shots of World War II here on September 1, 1939, they began a process of systematic destruction of Poland that would last for six years and leave millions dead. In 1997 Gdańsk celebrated its 1,000-year anniversary as a Baltic city. The city fathers made many improvements in the region's infrastructure, which now benefits visitors who missed the almost nonstop festivities of that year.

Today, the city remains famous as the cradle of the workers movement that came to be known as Solidarity. Food price increases in 1970 led to the first workers' strikes at the (former) Lenin Shipyards in Gdańsk. The Communist authorities brutally put down the protest, killing 40 workers in December of that year. Throughout the 1970s, small groups of anti-Communist workers and intellectuals based in Gdansk continued to organize. By August 1980, they had gained sufficient critical mass to form Solidarność (Solidarity), which the government was forced to recognize as the first independent trade union in the former Soviet bloc. Although the government attempted to destroy Solidarity after declaring martial law in December 1981, Solidarity activists continued to keep the objectives of democracy and independence from the U.S.S.R. alive. After the collapse of communism in 1989, Solidarity leader Lech Wałęsa became president of Poland in the nation's first free elections

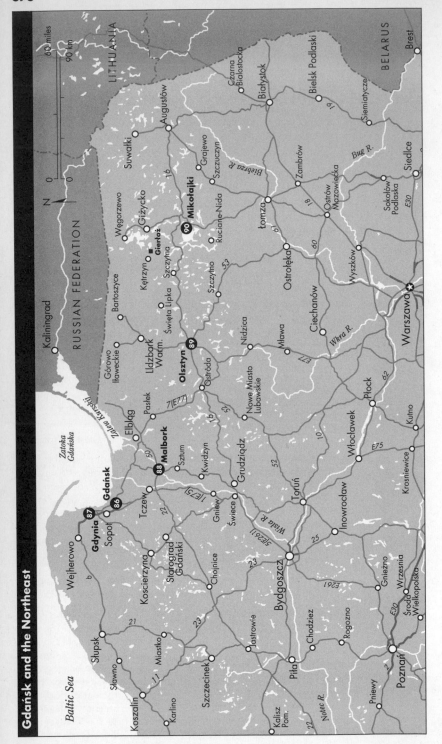

Gdańsk and the Northeast

Baltic Sea

LITHUANIA

RUSSIAN FEDERATION

Kaliningrad

BELARUS

Brest

Zatoka Gdańska

Zalew Kurońsk

60 miles
90 km

N

Wejherowo
Gdynia **87**
Sopot
86 **Gdańsk**
Tczew
88 **Malbork**
Elbląg
Paslęk
Sztum
Kwidzyn
Gniew
Świecie
Chojnice
Kościerzyna
Starogard Gdański
Słupsk
Sławno
Koszalin
Karlino
Miastko
Szczecinek
Kalisz Pom.
Jastrowie
Piła
Chodzież
Bydgoszcz
Grudziądz
Toruń
Inowrocław
Gniezno
Września
Środa Wielkopolska
Poznań
Pniewy
Rogoźno

Wejherowo
Górowo Iławeckie
Lidzbark Warm.
Bartoszyce
Świeta Lipka
Kętrzyn
Gierłoż
Szczytno
Węgorzewo
Giżycko
90 **Mikołajki**
Ruciane-Nida
Szczytno
Nidzica
89 **Olsztyn**
Ostróda
Nowe Miasto Lubawskie
Mława
Działdowo
Ciechanów
Płock
Włocławek
Kutno
Krośniewice
Suwałki
Augustów
Grajewo
Szczuczyn
Ełk
Łomża
Ostrołęka
Wyszków
Ostrów Mazowiecka
Zambrów
Sokołów Podlaski
Siedlce
Czarna Białostocka
Białystok
Bielsk Podlaski
Siemiatycze
Warszawa

Bug R.
Biebrza R.
Wkra R.
Wisła R.
Notec R.

16
53
7(E77)
50
22
23
21
11
23
6
60
19
8
61
E77
E75
52
10
25
2
E30

since World War II. As Gdańsk enters the 21st century, the carefully restored city streets hum with activity; economic reforms have introduced many new cultural events, galleries, and shops. Gdańsk University's presence keeps the city young and dynamic.

Gdańsk was almost entirely destroyed during World War II, but the streets of its **Główne Miasto** (Main Town) have been lovingly restored and still retain their historical and cultural richness. Like that of most other medieval cities, the historic core of Gdańsk can readily be explored on foot. North of Main Town, **Stare Miasto** (Old Town) contains many new hotels and shops, but several churches and the beautifully preserved Old Town Hall earn it its name. At the north end of the Old Town sit the Gdańsk Shipyards, St. Brigitte's Church (Kościół świętej Brygidy), and the monument to Solidarity. This site, which captivated world attention during the many clashes between workers and militarized police units during the 1970s and 1980s, has now settled back into its daily grind and the shipyard struggles to make the adjustment to the free market. The National Museum is just south of the old walls of the Main Town.

★ Built in the 15th through the 17th centuries, the **Dwór Artusa** (Artus Mansion), behind the Fontanna Neptuna (☞ *below*) on Gdańsk's Długi Targ, was named for King Arthur, who otherwise has no affiliation with the place (alas, there are no traces of Excalibur or Merlin). This and the other stately mansions on the Długi Targ are reminders of the traders and aristocrats who once resided in this posh district. The mansion's collection includes Renaissance furnishings, paintings, holy figures, and the world's largest Renaissance stove. ⊠ *Długi Targ 43,* ☎ *058/346–33–58.* 🎟 *Zł 8.* ۝ *Tues.–Sat. 10–4, Sun. 11–4.*

The largest brick church in the world and the largest church in Poland, ★ the **Kościół Najświętszej Marii Panny** (Church of Our Lady), on the north side of ulica Piwna in Gdańsk's Main Town, can accommodate 25,000 people. Also referred to in abbreviated form as Kościół Mariacki, this enormous 14th-century church underwent major restoration after World War II, and 15 of its 22 altars have been relocated to museums in Gdańsk and Warsaw. The highlight of a visit is climbing the hundreds of steps up the church tower. It costs zł 3 to make the climb, which makes it cheaper and more inspirational than an aerobics class—and the view is sensational. The church also contains a 500-year-old, 25-ft-high astronomical clock that has only recently been restored to working order after years of neglect. It keeps track of solar and lunar progressions, and it features the signs of the zodiac—something of an anomaly in a Catholic church.

Two blocks west of the Kościół Mariacki on ulica Piwna, the **Wielka Zbrojownia** (Great Armory) is a good example of 17th-century Dutch Renaissance architecture. The ground floor is now a trade center, and the upper floors house an art school.

Three huge and somber crosses perpetually draped with flowers stand outside the gates of the **Stocznia Gdańska** (Gdansk Shipyards; ⊠ Ul. Jana z Kolna). Formerly called the Lenin Shipyards, this place gave birth to the Solidarity movement, which later became the first independent trade union under a Communist government. The shipyards and the entire city also witnessed the long, violent struggle for autonomy that began as a series of impromptu street demonstrations in the early 1970s and blossomed into a political movement that swept the country's first free elections in 1989. The crosses are only one part of the monument to Solidarity; other parts include plaques commemorating the struggle and a moving quotation by Pope John Paul II upon visiting the monument in 1987: "The Grace of God could not have created anything better; in this place, silence is a scream."

The shipyard monument clearly symbolizes the fundamental link in the Polish consciousness between Catholicism and political dissent; another example is the **Kościół świelej Brygidy** (St. Brigitte's Church), a few blocks north of the shipyard monument on ulica Profesorska near Old Town Hall. After the government declared martial law in 1981 in an attempt to force Solidarity to disband, members began meeting here secretly during celebrations of mass. There is a statue of Pope John Paul II in the front. More recently, in 1995, the parish priest, who had done so much to support Solidarity, attracted hostile comment for his anti-Semitic pronouncements.

The **Żuraw Gdański** (Harbor Crane), built in 1444, was medieval Europe's largest and oldest crane. Today it houses the **Muzeum Morskie** (Maritime Museum), with a collection of models of the ships constructed in the Gdańsk Shipyards since 1945. At the museum ticket office, inquire about tickets for tours of the *Sołdek,* a World War II battleship moored nearby on the canal. ⊠ *Ul. Szeroka 67–68,* ☎ *058/301–86–11.* 🎫 *Zł 8.* ☉ *Oct.–June, Tues–Sun. 10–4, July–Sept., daily 10–4.*

The worthwhile **Muzeum Narodowe w Gdańsku** (National Museum in Gdańsk) is housed in the former Franciscan Monastery. Exhibits include 14th- to 20th-century art and ethnographic collections. ⊠ *Ul. Toruńska 1, off ul. Okopowa,* ☎ *058/301–70–61.* 🎫 *Zł 5.* ☉ *Daily 10–3.*

The small **Museum Archeologiczne Gdańska** (Gdańsk Archaeological Museum) features displays of Slavic tribal artifacts, including jewelry, pottery, boats, and bones. ⊠ *Ul. Mariacka 25–26,* ☎ *058/301–50–31.* 🎫 *Zł 3.* ☉ *Tues.–Sun. 10–4.*

★ The historic entrance to the Old City of Gdańsk is marked by the **Brama Wyżynna** (High Gate), off ulica Wały Jagiellońskie at the entrance to ulica Długa. This magnificent Renaissance gate, built in 1576, is adorned with the flags of Poland, Gdańsk, and the Prussian kingdom. As the king entered the city on his annual visit, he'd pass this gate first, then the **Brama Złota** (Golden Gate), which is just behind it and dates from 1614, combining characteristics of the Italian and Dutch Renaissance. Continuing east along ulica Długa reveals one of the city's most distinctive landmarks, the elaborately gilded **Fontanna Neptuna** (Neptune Fountain), at the western end of Długi Targ. Every day after dusk, this 17th-century fountain is illuminated, adding a romantic glow to the entire area. Around the fountain, vendors selling amber jewelry and souvenirs maintain a centuries-old tradition of trade at this point. At the water's edge is the eastern entrance to the medieval city of Gdańsk: the **Brama Zielona** (Green Gate). This 16th-century gate killed two birds with one stone; it doubled as a royal residence. Unfortunately, the name no longer fits: The gate is now painted brown. ⊠ *At the eastern end Długi Targ.*

The former parish church of Gdańsk's Old Town, **Kościół świelej Katarzyny** (St. Catherine's Church), at the corner of ulica Podmłyńska and ulica Katarzynki, is supposedly the oldest church in the city. Parts of it date to the 12th century, the tower was constructed in the 1480s, and the carillon of 37 bells was added in 1634. The 17th-century astronomer Jan Hevelius was buried in the presbytery of the church, below which lies what's left of the town's oldest Christian cemetery (10th century). On a small island in the canal, just north of the church, stands the **Wielki Młyn** (Great Mill). The largest mill in medieval Europe, it operated from the time of its completion in 1350 until 1945. ⊠ *Corner of ul. Podmłyńska and Na Piaskach.*

★ Although Gdańsk's original **Ratusz Główny** (town hall) was completely destroyed during World War II, a careful reconstruction of the exterior and interior now re-creates the glory of Gdańsk's medieval past. Inside the town hall, the **Muzeum Historii Miasta Gdańska** (Gdańsk Historical Museum) covers more than five centuries of Gdańsk's history in exhibits that include paintings, sculptures, and weapons. ✉ *Ul. Długa 47,* ☎ *058/301–48–72.* ☞ *Zł 4.* ⊙ *Tues.–Sun. 11–4.*

The district of Oliwa, north of the city center, is worth visiting for its
★ magnificent **cathedral.** Originally part of a Cistercian monastery, the church was erected during the 13th century. Like most other structures in Poland, it has been rebuilt many times, resulting in a hodgepodge of styles from Gothic to Renaissance to rococo. The cathedral houses one of the most amazing rococo organs you're ever likely to hear—and see. It has more than 6,000 pipes, and when a special mechanism is activated, wooden angels ring bells and a wooden star climbs up a wooden sky. Demonstrations of the organ and a brief narrated church history are given almost hourly on weekdays in summer, less frequently on weekends and the rest of the year. ✉ *Ul. Cystersów.*

In a beautiful park surrounding the cathedral in Oliwa are the **Muzeum Sztuki Współczesnej** (Modern Art Museum), with a large collection by Polish artists, from the interwar period onward, and the **Muzeum Etnograficzne** (Ethnographic Museum), which has fine examples of local crafts from the 19th century and an interesting display of amber folk jewelry. The cathedral and museums are best approached by train; get off at Gdańsk-Oliwa and walk west up ulica Piastowska to ulica Opacka; or take Tram 2 or 6 toward Sopot. *Muzeum Etnograficzne:* ✉ *Ul. Opacka 12; Muzeum Sztuki Współczesnej:* ✉ *Cystersw 15A, Pałac Opatów.* ☎ *058/552–12–71. For both:* ☞ *Zł 4, free Wed.,* ⊙ *Tues.–Sun. 9–4, Sun. 10–4.*

OFF THE
BEATEN PATH

WESTERPLATTE – Ten kilometers (6½ miles) north of the Old Town, Westerplatte is home to a branch of the National Museum. World War II broke out here, at the entrance to the northern port. On September 1, 1939, a German warship, the *Schleswig Holstein*, began a bombardment of the Polish army positions here. A monument to the men who attempted to defend the Westerplatte for seven days against impossible odds was erected in the 1960s. The Westerplatte can be reached by Bus 106 or 158 from ulica Okopowa, just outside the main town wall, or by water bus from the Dworzec Wodny at the end of ulica Długi Targ. ✉ *Ul. Majora Sucharskiego 1,* ☎ *058/343-69-72.* ☞ *Zł 5.* ⊙ *May–Oct., daily 9–4.*

Dining and Lodging

$$$ ✕ **Major.** Very well located on the main thoroughfare, the Major has
★ large tables and secluded booths set in a decor of glowing colors, enhanced by fresh flowers and oversize dinner plates. Try the game soup, followed by duck roasted with apples and buckwheat grits (*kasza gryczana*). During warm weather, enjoy watching people from the outside café. ✉ *Ul. Długa 18,* ☎ *058/301–10–69. AE, DC, MC, V.*

$$$ ✕ **Pod Łososiem.** "The Salmon," a historic Old Town inn that dates
★ to 1598, is the best restaurant in Gdańsk. As its name suggests, fish is the specialty here: Salmon or smoked eel makes a fine appetizer, and flounder and grilled trout are highly recommended entrées. The menu also extends to roast duck, pheasant, and goose. The dining area is warmly decorated with antique furniture, dark-wood paneling, and huge brass chandeliers; paintings of old Gdańsk adorn the walls. ✉ *Ul. Szeroka 54,* ☎ *058/301–76–52. AE, DC, MC, V.*

$$$ ✗ **Pod Wieżą.** This elegant restaurant has a reputation for good meat dishes and generous portions. If they're on the menu when you visit, try the *zupa rybna* (fish soup), veal steak with mushroom sauce, or roast duck with apples and brown rice. The waiters generally speak English and German. ✉ *Ul. Piwna 51,* ☎ *058/301–39–24. AE, DC, MC, V.*

$$$ ✗ **Tawerna.** This well-established (and well-touristed) restaurant over-
★ looking the river specializes in seafood. The restaurant is decorated with wood paneling and ship models. Particularly recommended is the fresh trout with almonds. ✉ *Ul. Powroźnicza 19–20, off Długi Targ,* ☎ *58/ 301–41–14. AE, DC, MC, V.*

$$ ✗ **Retman.** A clientele of mostly Germans and Danes lingers over plates of schnitzel and chateaubriand or freshwater fish in a candlelit, wood-paneled room on the water. ✉ *Ul. Stagiewna 1,* ☎ *058/301– 92–48. AE, DC, MC, V.*

$ ✗ **Pod Żurawiem.** This is a traditional restaurant (with a crowd that smokes up a storm), serving such Gdańsk favorites as *golonka* (pig's knuckle) and *gołąbki* (cabbage leaf stuffed with meat and rice in tomato sauce). ✉ *Ul. Wawrzywnicza 10,* ☎ *058/301–34–17. AE, DC, V, MC.*

$$$ 🏨 **Hotel Hanza.** This joint Polish-German venture opened in 1997 and
★ overlooks the canal. Its excellent location, attractively decorated rooms, and superb service have made it Gdańsk's premier hotel. It even has air-conditioning for the few weeks in the summer when cooling is really necessary. With all these pluses, it's wise to book well in advance for summer stays. ✉ *Ul. Tokarska 6, 80–888,* ☎ *058/305–34–27,* 𝖥𝖠𝖷 *058/305–33–86. 53 rooms, 7 suites. Restaurant, bar, exercise room, sauna, parking. AE, MC, DC, V.*

$$ 🏨 **Hewelius.** This large, modern high-rise hotel is within walking dis-
tance of the Old Town. Most rooms are spacious, if blandly furnished, with all modern conveniences. The top floors have impressive suites. ✉ *Ul. Heweliusza 22, 80–861,* ☎ *058/301–56–31,* 𝖥𝖠𝖷 *058/301–19– 22. 286 room, 10 suites. Restaurant, nightclub. AE, DC, MC, V.*

$$ 🏨 **Marina.** If you're having trouble getting a room in high season, this is a good place to try; the high-rise is just outside of town, but its upper floors have splendid views of the Old Town and the bay. ✉ *Ul. Jelitkowska 20, 80–341,* ☎ *058/53–20–79,* 𝖥𝖠𝖷 *058/53–04–60. 193 rooms with bath or shower. Restaurant, indoor pool, 2 tennis courts, bowling alley, nightclub. AE, DC, MC, V.*

Nightlife and the Arts

As elsewhere in Poland, finding fun nightlife in Gdańsk is no longer a problem. During the summer months, the Old Town teems with street musicians, families, and young people until the wee hours of the morning. The **Nadbałtyckie Centrum Kultury** (✉ Ul. Korzenna 33/35) is sit-
uated in the former Old Town Hall and has a wonderful café complete with English- and German-language newspapers. There's an **Irish Pub** in the basement next door. **U Szkota** (✉ Chlebnicka 9/10), opposite the Kościół Mariacki, is hard to miss, with brightly colored tartans hanging from the second-story windows. The Highland atmosphere is com-
plemented by waiters clad in Scottish kilts.

Recommended are the performances at Gdańsk's **Opera i Filharmonia Bałtycka** (Baltic Opera and Philharmonic; ✉ Al. Zwyciestwa 15, ☎ 058/341–05–63). Gdańsk also has a well-known theater company, **Teatr Wybrzeże** (✉ Ul. Świętego Ducha 2, ☎ 058/301–70–21).

Sopot

12 km (7½ mi) north of Gdańsk, 12 km (7½ mi) south of Gdynia.

Sopot is one of Poland's leading seaside holiday resorts, with miles of sandy beaches—in theory, now safe for bathing, as the Baltic's chronic pollution problems improve. Sopot enjoyed its heyday in the 1920s and '30s, when the wealthy flocked here to gamble and enjoy the town's demure, quiet atmosphere. Much of Sopot's life takes place close to the Grand Hotel, once *the* place to stay in Gdańsk. There is a marvelous 19th-century pier, which is the longest on the Baltic. Once the most elegant seaside resort in Poland, Sopot got a little too popular for its own good in the 1980s, when it began to look down-at-heel. Today, it is restoring its Riviera-like atmosphere.

Lodging

$$$ ⊡ **Grand Hotel.** This legendary late-19th-century hotel is located di-
★ rectly on the Bay of Gdańsk and offers spectacular views, especially from the dining room. For now, the rooms are standard Polish Orbis, but a major renovation is planned. ⊠ *Ul. Powstańców Warszawy 8– 12, 81–718,* ☎ *058/551–00–41,* FAX *058/551–61–24. 112 rooms. Restaurant, nightclub. AE, DC, MC, V.*

$$$ ⊡ **Villa Hestia.** In a villa built in 1894 by a shipping magnate, this tiny boutique hotel is one of Poland's finest, offering outstanding accommodations. Set in a garden landscaped with palms, it is in the center of Sopot and a 10-minute walk from the beach. ⊠ *Ul. Władysława IV 3/5, 81–703,* ☎ *058/551–21–00,* FAX *058/551–46–36. 2 rooms, 3 suites. Restaurant, pub. AE, DC, MC, V.*

Nightlife and the Arts

In Sopot, stroll down Ulica Bohatcrṕw Monte Cassino to find the café or pub of your choice. The **Kawiaret** (⊠ Ul. Bohatcŕw Monte Cassino 57/59) and the **Błekitny Pudel** (⊠ Ul. Bohatcrṕw Monte Cassino 44) are two of the most popular Sopot pubs.

Sopot is home to a branch of Gdańsk's Teatr Wybrzeże (☞ Nightlife and the Arts *in* Gdańsk, *above*), the **Scena Kameralna** (Chamber Theater; ⊠ Ul. Bohatcrów Monte Cassino 55/57, ☎ 058/551–58–12). **Opera Leśna** (Forest Opera; ⊠ Ul. Moniuszki 12, ☎ 058/551–18– 12) gives performances during the summer at its open-air opera house, situated in the forest to the west of town. The **Miedzynadodowy Festiwal Piosenki** (International Song Festival) is held in August in the open-air concert hall (Muszla Koncertowa) in Skwer Kuracyjny in the center of town near the pier.

Gdynia

87 *24 km (14 mi) north of Gdańsk, 12 km (7½ mi) north of Sopot.*

The northernmost of the three cities that make up the tricity area, Gdynia has less to offer the visitor than its southern neighbors. In 1922 it was only a tiny fishing village, but by 1939 it had grown into one of the Baltic's biggest ports. In addition to housing the shipyards and docks that dominate this industrial area, Gdynia boasts a beautifully landscaped **promenade.**

The **Muzeum Oceanograficzne-Akwarium Morskie** (Oceanographic Museum and Aquarium), near the harbor in Gdynia, has tanks holding more than a thousand species of fish. ⊠ *Al. Zjednoczenia 1,* ☎ *058/621–70–21.* ⊡ *Zł 4.* ☉ *Tues.–Sun. 10–5.*

Opposite the aquarium, a **Dar Pomorza** (Ship Museum) is housed in a World War II battleship, the *Błyskawica*; the museum is open May– mid-October, Tuesday–Sunday 10–1 and 2–4. In keeping with the nautical tradition of the town, Gdynia's **Muzeum Marynarki Wojennej** (Naval Museum), south of the pier on Bulwar Nadmorski, traces the history of Polish sea life from Slavic times to the present. ⊠ *Skwer Kościuszki 15,* ☎ *058/626–35–65.* ⊡ *Zł 3.* ☉ *Tues.–Sun. 10–4.*

Malbork

88 *45 km (28 mi) southeast of Gdańsk, on Route 50.*

One of the most impressive strongholds of the Middle Ages, the huge
★ **Zamek w Malborku** (Malbork Castle) is the central feature of the
quiet town of Malbork (the former German city of Marienburg). In
1230 the Teutonic Knights arrived on the banks of the Vistula River
and settled here, aiming to establish their own state on these conquered
Prussian lands. The castle passed into Polish hands after the second
Toruń Treaty in 1466 concluded the 13-year war between the Poles
and the Order of Teutonic Knights. For the next three centuries, Malbork served as the royal residence for Polish kings during their annual
visit to Pomerania. The castle was half destroyed during World War
II, after which the building underwent a major renovation. The two-
hour tours are the best way to see the castle; tours are available in English, and there's an English-language guidebook in the gift shop. ☎
055/272–33–64. 🎫 *Zł10.* ☉ *May–Sept., Tues.–Sun. 9–5; Oct.–
Apr., Tues.–Sun. 9–3.*

Located 67 km (42 mi) south of Gdańsk on Route 1(E75), the restored
castle of **Gniew** specializes in medieval-style festivals. Staff stage realistic reenactments of jousting tournaments and sword fights, followed
by wild boar roasts, all held in the town square—lined with arcaded
Gothic houses—and in the castle. The castle includes a museum, which
is open May to September, Tuesday through Sunday, 9 to 5, plus a hotel.
✉ *Plac Zamkowy 2, 83–140,* ☎ *069/135–21–62.* 🎫 *Zł 10.*

Olsztyn

89 *130 km (81 mi) southeast of Malbork, 150 km (93 mi) southeast of
Gdańsk, 215 km (133 mi) north of Warsaw.*

Since World War II, Olsztyn has served as the region's primary industrial center. The city is large with a good number of hotels and restaurants and serves as a jumping-off point for the Mazurian Lakes.

The Gothic **Brama Wysoka** (High Gate) marks the entrance to the old
town of Olsztyn and the main square. Southeast of the square is the
15th-century **Katedra Św. Jakuba** (St. James Cathedral). The **castle,**
with its ethnographic and historical **museum,** stands just to the west
of the town's square. Once again, Copernicus, that Renaissance man
who really got around in northern Poland, is featured in an exhibit.
He successfully directed the defense of the castle from 1516 to 1521
against the Teutonic Knights while serving as an administrator of
Warmia province. *Muzeum Warmii i Mazur:* ✉ *Ul. Zamkowa 1,* ☎
089/527–95–96. 🎫 *Zł 4.* ☉ *Tues.–Sun. 9–3.*

Lodging

$$ 🏨 **Orbis Novotel.** This standard 1970s hotel is the most comfortable
lodging in the area, set in beautiful surroundings on the shores of
Lake Ukiel. ✉ *Ul. Sielska 4A, 10–802,* ☎ *089/527–40–81,* 📠 *089/
527–54–03. 97 rooms. Restaurant, bar. AE, DC, MC, V.*

OFF THE   **LIDZBARK WARMIŃSKI** – (46 km [28½ mi] north of Olsztyn). In this town
BEATEN PATH   is the well-preserved 14th-century castle of the Teutonic Knights, which
               survived World War II only because the local population refused to help
               the Germans demolish it. Buses run to Lidzbark from Olsztyn. ✉ *Pl.
               Zamkowy,* ☎ *089/767-32-11.* 🎫 *Zł 1.* ☉ *Tues.–Sun. 9-2.*

Mikołajki

⑨ *85 km (53 mi) east of Olsztyn, 22 km (13½ mi) east of Mrągowo.*

One of the most popular Mazury resorts, Mikołajki is situated on the shores of Lake Tałty and Lake Mikołajskie. Boating is popular on nearby **Lake Śniardwy.** There is a nature preserve surrounding **Lake Łukajno,** 4 km (2½ mi) east of Mikołajki.

Lodging

$$$ **Hotel Gołębiewski.** This enormous hotel has just about everything you might want, including an indoor pool with massive water slides. Set right on a lake, it is a popular resort spot. ⊠ *Ul. Mrągowska 34, 11–730,* ☎ *087/216–517,* **FAX** *087/216–10. 378 rooms, 33 suites. 3 restaurants, bar, indoor pool, 4 tennis courts, horseback riding. AE, DC, MC, V.*

OFF THE
BEATEN PATH

"WOLF'S LAIR" – Just a few miles east of Ketrzyn lies Hitler's onetime bunker at Gierłoż. Built during World War II as his East Prussian military command post, its massively fortified concrete bunkers were blown up, but you can still climb in and among the remains and get a feel for his megalomania. Wolf's Lair was also where a small group of German patriots tried—and failed—to assassinate Hitler on July 20, 1944. *28 km (19 mi) north of Mrągowo at Gierłoż near Kętrzyn.*

ŚWIĘTA LIPKA – This 17th-century Baroque church is a major pilgrimage sight for Catholics. Of note is the elaborate organ. *15 km (9 mi) north of Mrągowo on the way to Ketrzyn.*

Gdańsk and the Northeast A to Z

Arriving and Departing

BY BUS

Gdańsk is a major gateway for the Baltic Coast and northeastern Poland. Right next to the train station, Gdańsk's **PKS** bus station (⊠ Ul. 3 Maja, ☎ 058302–15–32) may be useful to those who want to venture to small towns off the track; otherwise, train service is more frequent and more comfortable.

BY CAR

From Warsaw, the 7(E77), a two-lane road for part of its length, goes directly to Gdańsk. From the west, the quickest route to the coast from the border crossing at Frankfurt/Oder is to take the 2(E30) to Poznań, and then the 5(E261) via Gniezno and Bydgoszcz to Świecie, where it becomes the 1(E75) and continues via Tczew to the coast.

BY FERRY

Ferries travel daily from Gdańsk to Karlskrona and to Oxelösund, Sweden. You can book tickets at the **Orbis** office in the Hotel Hewelius (⊠ Ul. Heweliusa 22, ☎ 058/301–34–56) or at **Polferries** (Polish Baltic Shipping Company; ⊠ Ul. Przemysłowa 1, Gdynia, ☎ 058/343–18–87) or **Lion Ferry** (⊠ Ul. Kwiatowskiego 60, Gydnia, ☎ 058/665–14–14).

BY PLANE

There are several daily flights to Gdańsk from Warsaw, Hamburg and Copenhagen. The brand-new airport is located 16 km (10 mi) out of town in **Rębiechwo** (☎ 058/413–141) and can be reached by Bus 162 or by taxi. **LOT** (☎ 058/952) and **SAS** ☎ (058/341–31–11) are the main carriers.

BY TRAIN

The main rail station is **Gdańsk Główny** (⊠ Podwale Grodzkie 1, ☎ 058/301–00–51). Many daily trains leave here for Warsaw (4 hours), Kraków (8 hours), Poznań (4 hours), and Malbork (make sure to get on a train to Warsaw, which stops in Malbork—local trains can take ages).

Getting Around

BY CAR

The road network in this part of Poland is relatively well developed and there are plenty of gas stations. Although Gdańsk's Old Town and Main Town areas are easily walkable, a car is useful if you wish to visit other parts of the Trójmiasto (Sopot and the museums and cathedral at Oliwa), as well as sights farther afield.

BY BUS, TRAM, AND TROLLEY

A regular service runs through the Trójmiasto, taking you from Gdańsk through Oliwa and Sopot to Gdynia. The whole trip takes about 1¾ hours. The buses run from 5 AM to 11 PM; after 11 PM there is an hourly night-bus service. PKS buses link all the small towns and villages of the region.

BY TRAIN

All the towns of the region can be reached by train. Within the Trójmiasto area, a fast electric-train service runs every 15 minutes from Gdańsk Główny via Oliwa, Sopot, and Gdynia to Wejherowo. The service operates from 4 AM to 1 AM.

BY WATER BUS

In summer, an hourly service links Gdańsk with Sopot and Gdynia, via Westerplatte and Hel. In Gdańsk, the **station** is on the Długie Pobrzeż by the Zielona Brama (☎ 058/301–49–26); in Sopot, at the pier; in Gdynia at Aleje Zjednoczenia 2 (☎ 058/20–21–54).

Contacts and Resources

EMERGENCIES

Police: Gdańsk and Sopot (☎ 997). **Ambulance:** Gdańsk and Sopot (☎ 999). **Emergency room:** Gdańsk (⊠ Aleje Zwycięstwa 49, ☎ 058/302–29–29); Sopot (⊠ Ul. Chrobrego 6/8, ☎ 058/551–24–55).

LATE-NIGHT PHARMACIES

Gdańsk: The **Apteka Dworcowa** at the main rail station (⊠ Ul. Podwale Grodzkie 1, ☎ 058/301–28–41) provides 24-hour service. **Gdynia:** Pod Gryfem (⊠ Ul. Starowiejska 34, ☎ 058/620–19–82). **Sopot:** There is 24-hour service at **Apteka Kuracyjna** (⊠ Al. Niepodległości 861, ☎ 058/551–31–58).

VISITOR INFORMATION

Gdańsk: Agencja Infomacji Turystycznej (⊠ Ul. długa 45, ☎ 058/301–93–27) is centrally located. **Orbis** (⊠ Heweliusza 22, ☎ 058/301–45–44) has a good selection of maps and brochures. **Sopot: Orbis** (⊠ Ul. Bohatcrw Monte Cassino 49, ☎ 058/55–41–42).

WESTERN POLAND

Comprising the provinces of **Wielkopolska** (Great Poland) and **Dolny Śląsk** (Lower Silesia), western Poland has always been the traditional heartland of the Polish state—despite spending much of the past half-millennium under German, Prussian, and Austro-Hungarian control. Great Poland is part of the flat, vast plain that extends north through Europe and is characterized by smooth farmland, pockets of forest, and numerous lakes. There are many opportunities here for walking, swimming, fishing, and hunting. The hills of Lower Silesia rise gently to the

Karkonosze Mountains, where you'll find trails for energetic walkers and resorts that lure skiers during winter. Wrocław and Poznań, two of western Poland's primary cities, attract crowds year-round for theater, music, and other cultural diversions.

Although the early Polish state had its origins in the west, the region has fallen (more than once) under German influence. The Poles of Greater Poland are affectionately mocked by their countrymen for having absorbed the archetypal German habits of cleanliness, order, and thrift. Lower Silesia and Pomerania were integrated with Poland only in 1945, so don't be surprised if the west feels sober, restrained, and altogether more Germanic than anything you'll find elsewhere in Poland.

Gniezno, the first capital of Poland, is worth visiting for its cathedral and, together with a visit to the nearby early lake settlement at Biskupin, could be a day trip from Poznań. Toruń, the birthplace of Nicolaus Copernicus, is also a good base from which to explore the northern part of this region.

Numbers in the margin correspond to numbers on the Western Poland map.

Wrocław

(91) *350 km (220 mi) southwest of Warsaw, 260 km (165 mi) northwest of Kraków, 170 km (105 mi) south of Poznań.*

Midway between Kraków and Poznań on the Odra River, Wrocław, the capital of **Dolny Śląsk** (Lower Silesia), dates to the 10th century, when the Ostrów Tumski islet on the Odra became a fortified Slav settlement. There are now some 100 bridges spanning the city's 90-km (56-mi) network of slow-moving canals and tributaries, giving Wrocław its particular charm. Wrocław's population is also notable: Almost half the residents of Poland's fourth-largest city are less than 30 years old; most are students at one of the city's many institutions of higher learning.

Following the destruction that ravaged Wrocław during World War II, many of the city's historic buildings were restored. Wrocław's architectural attractions are its many brick Gothic churches, the majority of which lie in or around **Stare Miasto** (Old Town) and **Ostrów Tumski.** This area is small enough to explore easily on foot.

The **Rynek** (market square) together with the adjoining **plac Solny** (Salt Square) form the heart of Stare Miasto, which stretches between the Fosa Miejska moat and the Odra River. Wrocław's Rynek is almost as grand as Kraków's and bustles with activity. Many of the houses were restored for the Pope's visit in 1997. Note the little **Jaś i Małgosia** (Hansel and Gretel) houses, just off the square to the northwest, which are holding hands, so to speak, as they are charmingly linked by a Baroque arcade. ✉ *Intersection of ul. Odrzańska and ul. Wita Stwosza.*

★ The magnificently ornate **Ratusz** (town hall) is the highlight of the Rynek. Mostly Gothic in style, with a dash of Renaissance and Baroque, the Ratusz was under continuous construction from the 13th to the 16th century as Wrocław grew and prospered. In the center of the spired, pinnacled, and gabled **east facade** is a Renaissance **astronomical clock** from 1580. The **Gothic portal** was the main entrance of the Ratusz until 1616. The lavish **south facade,** dating from the 15th to 16th centuries, swarms with delicately wrought sculptures, friezes, reliefs, and oriels. Today the Ratusz houses the **Historical Museum of Wrocław.** ✉ *Rynek–Ratusz,* ☎ *071/44–36–38.* 🎟 *Zł 4.* ⏲ *Wed.–Fri. 10–4, weekends 10–5.*

Western Poland

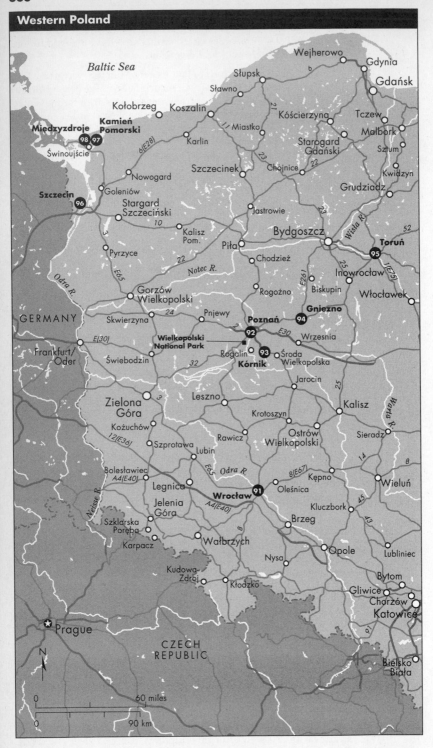

Baltic Sea

Wejherowo

Gdynia

Słupsk

Sławno

Gdańsk

Kołobrzeg Koszalin Kościerzyna Tczew

Kamień Pomorski Miastko Malbork

Miedzyzdroje 98 97 Karlin Starogard Gdański Sztum

Świnoujście Chojnice Kwidzyn

Nowogard Szczecinek Grudziadz

Szczecin 96 Goleniów

Stargard Szczeciński Jastrowie

Kalisz Pom. Piła Bydgoszcz **Toruń** 95

Pyrzyce Chodzież Inowrocław Włocławek

Gorzów Wielkopolski Rogoźno Biskupin

GERMANY Skwierzyna Pnjewy **Gniezno** 94

Wielkopolski National Park **Poznań** 92 Wrzesnia

Frankfurt/Oder Świebodzin Rogalin 93 Środa Wielkopolska

Kórnik

Jarocin

Zielona Góra Leszno Kalisz

Kożuchów Krotoszyn Sieradz

Szprotawa Rawicz Ostrów Wielkopolski

Lubin

Bolesławiec Odra R. Kępno Wieluń

Legnica **Wrocław** 91 Oleśnica

Jelenia Góra Kluczbork

Szklarska Poręba Brzeg

Karpacz Wałbrzych Opole Lubliniec

Nysa Bytom

Kudowa-Zdroj Kłodzko Gliwice

Chorzów

Katowice

★ Prague

N

CZECH REPUBLIC

Bielsko Biała

0   60 miles

0   90 km

★ The massive Gothic, 14th-century **Kościół świelej Marii Magdaleny** (St. Mary Magdalene's Church) has a 12th-century **Romanesque** portal on the south wall that is considered the finest example of Romanesque architecture in Poland. ⊠ *1 block east of the Rynek at the corner of ul. Szewska and ul. św. Marii Kaznodziejska.*

The 14th-century brick **Kościół świelej Elżbiety** (Church of St. Elizabeth) has been under reconstruction since fires ravaged it in 1975 and 1976. If the church is open, you can brave the 302-step climb to the top of the **tower** and look inside at its magnificent organ. ⊠ *Ul. Kiełbaśnicza; it can also be reached through the arcade linking the Jaś and Małgosia houses at the intersection of ul. Odrzańska and ul. Wita Stwosza.*

Wrocław's university district lies between ulica Uniwersytecka and the river. The vast 18th-century **Uniwersytet Wrocławski** (Wrocław University) was built between 1728 and 1741 by Emperor Leopold I on the site of the west wing of the former prince's castle. Behind the fountain and up the staircase is the magnificent assembly hall, **Aula Leopoldina.** The Aula is decorated with illusionist frescoes and life-size sculptures of great philosophers and patrons of learning. ⊠ *Aula, pl. Universytecki 1.* 🎫 *Zł 4 suggested donation.* ☉ *Daily 9–3:30.*

NEED A BREAK?

Café Uni (⊠ Pl. Uniwersytecki 11), with its outdoor patio and frequent recitals, is a good place to sip coffee and admire the 565-ft facade of the university.

★ **Ostrów Tumski** (Cathedral Island), to the north of the river—although no longer an island—is one of the city's oldest and most charming quarters. Its winding streets, beautiful bridges, and wonderful churches are nine blocks northwest of the Rynek. The **Most Piaskowy** (Sand Bridge), which connects the left bank of the Odra with the Wyspa Piasek (Sand Island), halfway to Ostrów Tumski, was once part of the amber route, an ancient trade route that led from the Baltic down to the Adriatic. On the other side of Wyspa Piaskowa, the **Most Tumski** (Cathedral Bridge) and **Most Młyński** (Mill Bridge), two gracefully designed and painted bridges, lead to Ostrów Tumski.

On the **Wyspa Piasek,** directly opposite the Most Piaskowy, is a former Augustinian monastery used as Nazi headquarters during the war; the building is now the **University Library.** The 14th-century **Kościół Najświętszej Marii Panny** (St. Mary's Church) is in the middle of the island. The church's Gothic interior was restored after World War II, with a lofty vaulted ceiling and brilliant stained-glass windows.

A cluster of churches stand on Ostrów Tumski, including the **Kościół świelej Piotra i świelej Pawła** (Sts. Peter and Paul Church), which has no aisles. The early 14th-century **Kościół świelej Krzyża** (Holy Cross Church), just beyond the **statue of Pope John XXIII** (1968) on Ostrów Tumski, is housed on the upper level of a rigid and forbidding building erected by Duke Henryk as his own mausoleum (the duke's Gothic sarcophagus has been moved to the Wrocław Historical Museum). On the lower level of Duke Henryk's mausoleum lies the 13th-century **Kościół świelej Bartłomieja** (St. Bartholomew's Church).

The 13th-century **Katedra świelej Jana Chrzciciela** (Cathedral of St. John the Baptist; ⊠ Pl. Katedralny), with its two truncated towers, is the focal point of Ostrów Tumski. Its chancel is the earliest example of Gothic architecture in Poland. The cathedral houses the largest organ in the country, with 10,000 pipes. On the southern side of the cathedral is **St. Elizabeth's Chapel;** the bust of Cardinal Frederick above the entrance, along with numerous other sculptures and frescoes, came from the studio of Bernini. The **Elector's Chapel,** in the northwestern corner of the cathedral, dates from the early 18th century and was designed by the Baroque architect Johann Fischer von Erlach of Vienna. As these chapels are often closed, check at the sacristy for an update as well as for admission fees. The **Muzeum Archidiecezjalne** (Archdiocesan Museum) lies north of St. John's Cathedral on Otrów Tumski; it has a collection of medieval Silesian art. ⊠ *Ul. Kanonia 12,* ☎ *071/22–17–55.* ▣ *Zł 4.* ☉ *Daily 10–3.*

Dining and Lodging

$$$$ ✕ **Karczma Piastow/Królewska.** This beautifully decorated estab-
★ lishment in the heart of Wrocław is divided into two parts: restaurant-nightclub and café–wine cellar. The restaurant offers a Polish and international menu. The *shashlik* (grilled beef and peppers) served with brown rice is particularly tasty, and the Renaissance-style wine cellar, Karczma Piastow, is a good place to relax on a hot summer's day. ⊠ *Rynek 5,* ☎ *071/72–48–96. AE, DC, MC, V.*

$$$ ✕ **Spiż.** This restaurant in the cellar of the town hall is the place to go for a mix of Polish and European cuisine. Heading the menu are *schabowy* (pork cutlet) with mashed potatoes and sauerkraut, and *golonka* (pig's knuckle). ⊠ *Rynek 9,* ☎ *071/44–52–67.*

$$$ ▦ **Dwór Polski** This hotel has well-lighted and attractively furnished rooms. ⊠ *Ul. Kiełbaśnicza 2, 50–108,* ☎ ⅲ *071/72–34–15. 28 rooms. Restaurant, bar. AE, D, MC, V.*

$$$ ▦ **Maria Magdalena.** This newly opened hotel is just 100 yards from the Old Town Square and offers excellent accommodations. The immaculate rooms have all the modern conveniences, including air-conditioning. ⊠ *Ul. Marii Magdaleny 2, 50–103,* ☎ *071/341–08–98,* ⅲ *071/341–09–20. 50 rooms. Restaurant, bar. AE, DC, MC, V.*

$$ ▦ **Hotel Europejski.** Renovations in this hotel have been sporadic, leaving half-old and half-new elements. The small and simple older rooms are more reasonably priced than the refurbished ones, and guests can still admire the exquisite lobby. ⊠ *Ul. Józefa Piłsudskiego 88, 50–017,* ☎ *071/343–10–71,* ⅲ *071/44–34–33. 74 rooms. Restaurant, bar. AE, DC, MC, V.*

Nightlife and the Arts

If you get tired of the bars around the Old Town Square try the **Kalambur** (⊠ Ul. Kuźnicza 29A, ☎ 071/343–26–50). This art nouveau café-bar is attached to a small, well-known theater; there is sometimes live music.

Teatr Polski (⊠ Ul. G. Zapolskiej 3, ☎ 071/343–86–53) is the occasional home of the Wrocław Pantomime Theater. **Wrocławski Teatr Lalek** (Puppet Theater; ⊠ Pl. Teatralny 4, ☎ 071/44–12–17) is widely regarded as the best puppet theater in Poland.

The most renowned of Wrocław's festivals are **Jazz on the Odra** (☎ 071/22–55–42), which has attracted an international group of performers for the past 25 years, and **Wratislavia Cantans,** a series of 24 concerts featuring Gregorian chants, German oratorios, operas, cantatas, and other choral performances. Concerts take place at different points in the city. Both of these festivals take place during the summer; ask IT or Orbis (☞ Visitor Information *in* Western Poland A to Z, *below*) for schedules.

The **Opera** (⊠ Ul. Świdnicka 35, ☎ 071/343–86–41) has performances in the Grand Opera House on plac Teatralny, south of the Rynek. Both **Operetka** (⊠ Ul. Piłsudskiego 67, ☎ 071/44–49–16) and the **Phil-**

harmonic (✉ Ul. Piłsudskiego 19, ☎ 071/442–001) host classical performances several nights a week.

Poznań

🟡 *300 km (186 mi) west of Warsaw, 170 km (105 mi) north of Wrocław.*

Set halfway between Warsaw and Berlin, in the middle of the monotonously flat Polish lowlands, Poznań has been an east–west trading center for more than 1,000 years. In the Middle Ages, merchants made a great point of bringing their wares here on St. John's Day (June 23), and the annual tradition has continued. (The markets have now been superseded by the important International Trade Fair, which has been held here since 1922.) Until the 13th century, Poznań was (on and off) the capital of Poland, and in 968 the first Polish bishopric was founded here by Mieszko I. It still remains the capital of the **Wielkopolska** (Great Poland) region.

Despite its somewhat grim industrial outskirts, Poznań is one of the country's most charming old towns; consider making a trip through western Poland if only to visit Poznań's majestic market square. Poznań may be only the fifth-largest city in Poland, but to a tourist it will feel larger than that. While the majority of sights are near the Old Town's impressive Stary Rynek (Old Market Square), other attractions are off in the sprawling maze of ancillary streets. Walking is not recommended here. Invest in some tram tickets and a city map with the transit routes marked; your feet will thank you.

Poznań's **Stary Rynek** (Old Market Square) mainly dates from the 16th century. It has a somewhat cluttered feeling, since the center is occupied with both 20th-century additions and Renaissance structures. Poznań residents will proudly tell you that the imposing, arcaded Renaissance **Ratusz** (town hall) at the center of the Old Market Square is the most splendid building in Poland. Its clock tower is famous for the goats that appear every day at noon to butt heads before disappearing inside. Legend has it that the clock maker who installed the timepiece planned to give a party on the occasion. He ordered two goats for the feast, but the goats escaped and started fighting on the tower. The mayor was so amused by the event that he ordered the clock maker to construct a mechanism to commemorate the goat fight. The Ratusz now houses a **Museum of City History,** which contains a room dedicated to Chopin. ✉ *Stary Rynek 1,* ☎ *061852–56–13.* 🎟 *Zł 4.* 🕐 *Sun.–Fri. 10–3.*

The tiny arcaded shopkeepers' houses in the Old Market Square date to the mid-16th century. Some of them now house the **Muzeum Instrumentow Muzycznycy** (Museum of Musical Instruments), where you can see Chopin's piano and a plaster cast of the maestro's hands. ✉ *Stary Rynek 45,* ☎ *061/852–08–57.* 🎟 *Zł4.* 🕐 *Tues. and Sat. 11–5, Wed. and Fri. 10–4, Sun. 10–3.*

A few blocks west of the old Town Square is the **Muzeum Narodowe** (National Museum), which has a good collection of Polish and Western European paintings. ✉ *Al. Marcinkowskiego 9,* ☎ *061852–80–11.* 🎟 *Zł 4.* 🕐 *Tues.–Sun. 10–3.*

After a visit to the museum, walk across Wolności (Freedom) Square to the beautiful **Biblioteka Raczyńskich** (Raczyński Library), built in 1829 by the aristocratic Raczynski family. 🎟 *Free.* 🕐 *Daily 9–5.*

Ostrów Tumski (Cathedral Island), an islet in the Warta River east of the Old Town, is the historic cradle of Poznań. This is where the Polanie tribe built their first fortified settlement and their first basilica in the 10th century. The present **Poznań Cathedral** was rebuilt after World War II in pseudo-Gothic style, but 10th- and 11th-century remains can be seen in some interior details. Directly behind the main altar is the heptagonal **Golden Chapel,** which is worth seeing for the sheer opulence of its romantic-Byzantine decor (1840). Within the chapel is the **mausoleum** of the first rulers of Poland, Mieszko I and Bolesław the Great. ⊠ *Ul. Mieszka I.*

Dining and Lodging

$$ ✕ **Kresowa.** Located on the main town square, this popular restaurant specializes in cuisine from the "kresy," or Poland's former Eastern territories (Lithuania, Ukraine and Belorussia) and is consequently known as "the Borderland restaurant." ⊠ *Stary Rynek 2,* ☎ *061/853–12–91. AE, DC, MC, V.*

$$$ ⌸ **Merkury.** This five-story, glass-front hotel is a standard Orbis product from the 1960s. Identical brown doors lead from long corridors into nearly identical rooms. Furnishings are in dark shades, but rooms have the usual Orbis standard of comfort. Its strong suit is convenience—an excellent location and good parking facilities. ⊠ *Ul. Roosevelta 20, 60–829,* ☎ *061/847–08–01,* F̲A̲X̲ *061/847–31–41. 203 rooms, 11 suites. Restaurant, bar, café. AE, DC, MC, V.*

$$$ ⌸ **Poznań.** This charmless, high-rise hotel, in the city center next to the railway station, has the familiar Orbis touch: rooms decorated in government-regulation brown with slightly outdated bathrooms. ⊠ *Pl. Andersa 1, 61–898,* ☎ *061/833–20–81,* F̲A̲X̲ *061/833–29–61. 485 rooms, 10 suites. Restaurant, bar, nightclub. AE, DC, MC, V.*

$$ ⌸ **Dom Turysty PTTK.** This hotel has only 18 rooms (of which 10 are singles), but its location, right at the center of the Old Town, makes it an attractive option—if you can get in. Rooms are comfortably furnished, with Polish folk elements, and the staff is friendly and well informed. ⊠ *Stary Rynek 91, 61–001,* ☎ F̲A̲X̲ *061/852–88–93. 18 rooms, 8 with bath. Restaurant, café. AE, DC, MC, V.*

$$ ⌸ **Lech.** This older hotel is near the university; it's a good base for exploring Poznań by foot. Rooms are on the small side but comfortably furnished. There is no restaurant service apart from breakfast, and the hotel bar sometimes attracts a rather rowdy crowd in the evenings. ⊠ *Ul. Św. Marcin 74, 61–809,* ☎ *061/853–01–51,* F̲A̲X̲ *061/853–08–80. 79 rooms, 1 suite. Bar. AE, DC, MC, V.*

Nightlife and the Arts

Stefan Stuligrosz's Boys Choir, the *Słowiki poznańskie* (Poznań nightingales), is one of Poznań's best-known musical attractions. ⊠ *Teatr Wielki, ul. Fredry 9,* ☎ *061/852–82–91.*

All the big hotels in Poznań have nightclubs with floor shows; the **Black Club** in the Hotel Merkury (⊠ Ul. Roosevelta 20, ☎ 061/847–08–01) is always crowded.

Filharmonia Poznańska (⊠ Ul. św. Marcina 81, ☎ 061/852–47–08) holds concerts in the beautifully restored Aula of the university, where the acoustics are excellent.

OFF THE
BEATEN PATH

WIELKOPOLSKI NATIONAL PARK – Nineteen kilometers (10 miles) southwest of Poznań on Route 430 is this beautiful national park. The pine forests are punctuated with 16 lakes; Lake Rusałka and Lake Strzeszynek have long beaches, tourist accommodations, and watersports equipment for hire. There are several interesting legends associated with the park—at the bottom of Lake Góreckie, for example, there is supposed to be a submerged town, and on still nights you can hear the faint ringing of the town bells.

Kórnik

⑨³ *20 km (12 mi) southeast of Poznań on Route 42.*

In this old town is a 18th-century **neo-Gothic castle,** which houses a museum full of antique furnishings, as well as a library of more than 150,000 rare books (including manuscripts by Mickiewicz and Słowacki). Note the magnificent wood-inlay floors. The castle is surrounded by Poland's largest **arboretum,** with more than 3,000 varieties of trees and shrubs. ☎ *061/817–00–81.* 🎟 *Zł 4.* ☯ *Tues.–Sun. 9–3, Sat. 9–4.*

OFF THE　　　**ROGALIN –** Head 20 km (12 mi) south of Poznán to this Baroque-era
BEATEN PATH　palace. It is now part of the National Museum in Poznán and includes a
　　　　　　　collection of 19th-century German and Polish art. The nearby English
　　　　　　　Garden contains some of the oldest oak trees in Europe. ☎ *061/813–
　　　　　　　8030.* 🎟 *Zł 4.* ☯ *Tues.–Sun. 10–4.*

Gniezno

⑨⁴ *50 km (31 mi) northeast of Poznań on Highway 5(E261)*

Lying along the Piast Route—Poland's historic memory lane running from Poznań to Kruszwica—Gniezno is the original capital of Poland and remains surrounded by towns whose monuments date to the origins of the Polish state. Legend has it that Lech, the founder of the country, spotted some white eagles nesting on the site; he then named the town Gniezno (nesting site) and proclaimed the white eagle the nation's emblem. On a more historical note, King Mieszko I made Gniezno the seat of the country's first bishop, St. Wojciech, after the king brought Catholicism to the Polish people during the 10th century.

★　The first **cathedral** in Gniezno was built by King Mieszko I before AD 977. The 14th-century building is considered the most imposing Gothic cathedral in Poland. On the altar is a silver sarcophagus, supported by four silver pallbearers, bearing the remains of St. Wojciech (Adalbert), the first bishop of Poland. At the back of the church the famous 12th-century bronze-cast Doors of Gniezno have intricate bas-relief scenes depicting the life of St. Wojciech, a Czech missionary commissioned to bring Christianity to the Prussians in northern Poland. Not everyone appreciated his message: He was killed by pagans. It is said that his body was ransomed from its murderers by its weight in gold, which the Poles paid ungrudgingly.

Housed in a characterless concrete school building in Gniezno, the **Muzeum Poczatkew Państwa Polskiego** (Museum of the Original Polish State) shows multimedia exhibitions (in five languages, including English) describing medieval Poland. ✉ *Ul. Kostrzewskiego 6,* ☎ *061/ 426–46–41.* 🎟 *Zł 3.* ☯ *Tues.–Sun. 10–4.*

En Route　Step back in time by wandering along the wood-paved streets and peer-
★　ing into the small wooden huts at the fortified settlement at **Biskupin,** 30 km (18 mi) north of Gniezno on route E261 toward Bydgoszcz. This 100-acre "Polish Pompeii" is one of the most fascinating archaeological sites in Europe. It was discovered in 1933, when a local school principal and his students noticed some wood stakes protruding from the water during an excursion to Lake Biskupieńskie. The lake was later drained, revealing a settlement largely preserved over the centuries by the lake waters. Dating to 550 BC, the settlement was surrounded by defensive ramparts of oak and clay and a breakwater formed from stakes driven into the ground at a 45° angle. A wooden plaque at the entrance shows a plan of the original settlement. The museum holds a yearly

festival, in the last week of September, which includes historic reenactments. ☎ *053/425–025.* ▣ *Zł 4.* ☉ *Daily 8–6.*

Toruń

★ ⑨⑤ *210 km (130 mi) northwest of Warsaw, 150 km (93 mi) east of Poznań.*

The birthplace of Nicolaus Copernicus, the medieval astronomer who
first postulated that the earth travels around the sun, Toruń is a beautiful medieval city. It is also one of the few Polish cities to have survived World War II relatively unscathed. The **Stare Miasto** (Old Town)
brims with ancient churches, civic buildings, and residences, with
Gothic burgher houses and a noted town hall blending harmoniously
with the Renaissance and Baroque of its later patrician mansions. It's
little wonder that in 1997 Toruń was listed by UNESCO as one of the
great historic cities of the world.

★ The **Muzeum Mikołłaja Kopernika** (Copernicus Museum), one block
south of the Old Town Square, commemorates Toruń's most famous
native son, who in 1617 wrote *De Revolutionibus Orbium Coelestium*
(*On the Revolutions of the Celestial Spheres*), explaining his theory of
a heliocentric universe. The museum consists of two houses: the house
at ulica Kopernika 17, where Copernicus was born (in 1473) and lived
until he was 17 years old, and the adjoining historic town house. The
rooms have been restored with period furnishings, some of which belonged to the Copernicus family. You can view his research equipment
and other exhibits associated with him. There is also a scale model of
Toruń, which is accompanied by a sound-and-light show (available in
English) telling the history of the city. ✉ *Ul. Kopernika 15/17,* ☎ *058/
270–38.* ▣ *Zł 4.* ☉ *Tues.–Sun. 10–4.*

Toruń's **Rynek Staromiejski** (Old Town Square) is dominated by the
14th-century **Ratusz** (town hall), one of the largest buildings of its kind
in northern Poland. There are 365 windows in the Ratusz, and the hall's
four pinnacles are meant to represent the four seasons of the year. Inside the Ratusz is the **historical museum,** which houses a collection of
painted glass, paintings, and sculptures from the region's craftsmen.
Look for the gingerbread molds, which have been used since the 14th
century to create the delicious treats for which Toruń is famous. ✉ *Rynek
Staromiejski 1,* ☎ *056/270–38.* ▣ *Zł4.* ☉ *Wed.–Sun. 10–4.*

Built in 1274, the Ratusz's **tower** is the oldest in Poland, although it
did receive some later Dutch Renaissance additions. You can go up into
the tower to enjoy a spectacular view. In the square outside the Ratusz is a **statue of Copernicus.**

NEED A BREAK?	In the same building as the Ratusz museum (entrance around the corner) is the atmospheric café **Piwnica Pod Aniołem,** which serves great coffee.

On the eastern side of the Old Town Square is **Pod Gwiazdą** (House
under the Stars). Built in the 15th century, it was remodeled in the 17th
century in the Baroque style. It now houses the **Far Eastern Art Museum,** which is worth visiting as an excuse to see the interior of the
house, especially the carved-wood staircase. ✉ *Rynek Staromiejski 35,*
☎ *056/270–38.* ▣ *Zł4.* ☉ *Tues.–Sun. 10–4.*

Kościół świelej Jana (St. John's Church) was built in the 13th–15th
centuries. This is where Copernicus was baptized. The **tuba Dei,** a 15th-
century bell in the church's tower, is one of the largest and most impressive in Poland. ✉ *South of the Rynek on ul. Żeglarska.*

In a pleasant park northeast of Toruń's Old Town stands the **Muzeum Etnografiszne** (Ethnographic Museum). Outside the museum are brightly decorated farmhouses that have been restored and filled with antique furnishings. The grounds have been designed to replicate life in the Bydgoszcz region (west of Toruń) in the 19th and early 20th centuries. ⊠ *Wały Sikorskiego 19,* ☎ *056/280–91.* ⌑ *Zł 4.* ⊙ *Tues.–Sun. 10–4.*

Dining and Lodging

$$$$ ✕ **Zajazd Staropolski.** This traditional Polish restaurant features ex-
★ cellent meat dishes and soups in a restored 17th-century interior. ⊠
Ul. Żeglarska 10/14, ☎ *056/260–60. AE, DC, MC, V.*

$$ ✕ **Restauracja Staromiejska.** Located in the old wine cellar of a 4th-
★ century building, the place has polished wood and stone floors, white-
washed walls, and red, brick-ribbed, vaulted ceilings. Enjoy the excellent
pizza (the owner is Italian) as well as Polish fare. ⊠ *Ul. Szczytna 2–
4,* ☎ *no phone. AE, DC, MC, V.*

$$ ✕ **Trzy Korony.** This restaurant, in one of the old houses on the square,
specializes in regional dishes, including many varieties of meat-filled
dumplings (*pyzy*) and thick bean soup (*zupa fasolowa*). ⊠ *Rynek
Staromiejski 21,* ☎ *056/260–31. AE, DC, MC, V.*

$$ ⌂ **Helios.** This friendly, medium-size Orbis hotel is situated in the city
center and contains a good restaurant. ⊠ *Ul. Kraszewskiego 1/3, 87–
100,* ☎ *856/250–33,* Ⓕ *856/235–65. 108 rooms. Restaurant, beauty
salon, sauna, nightclub. AE, DC, MC, V.*

$$ ⌂ **Kosmos.** A functional 1960s Orbis hotel, Kosmos is showing signs
of wear; however, one section of the hotel has recently been renovated.
It is near the river, in the city center. ⊠ *Ul. Popiełuszki 2, 87–100,* ☎
056/270–85. 59 rooms. Restaurant, bar. AE, DC, MC, V.

$$ ⌂ **Zajazd Staropolski.** This hotel is situated in three former tenement
★ houses off Rynek Staromiejski and is without a doubt the nicest hotel
in town. ⊠ *Ul. Żeglarska 10–14, 87–100,* ☎ *056/260–61,* Ⓕ *056/
253–84. 33 rooms. Restaurant. AE, MC, V.*

$ ⌂ **Hotel Polonia.** A favorite of Polish families, this antiquated hotel is
just across the street from the Municipal Theater near the Rynek. The
rooms are large, with high ceilings, and very simple. Note that no credit
cards are accepted here; payment is by cash only. ⊠ *Pl. Teatralny 5,
87–100,* ☎ *056/230–28,* Ⓕ *056/230–29. 46 rooms, 30 with bath.
No credit cards.*

Western Poland A to Z

Arriving and Departing

BY BUS
Long-distance PKS services from other Polish cities arrive at **Dworzec
Centralny PKS** (⊠ Ul. Kościuszki 135, ☎ 071/44–44–61 or 071/385–
22), diagonally opposite the main train station in Wrocław.

The **Dworzec PKS** bus station in Poznań (☎ 061/833–12–12) is on
ulica Towarowa 17/19, a short walk from the train station. Frequent
bus service is available to and from Kornik, and Gniezno.

Toruń's **PKS** bus station (⊠ Ul. Dąbrowskiego, ☎ 056/228–42) is east
of the Old Town. Take local Bus 22 to and from the station.

BY CAR
From the west, a four-lane divided highway extends most of the way
between Wrocław and the German bordertown of Cottbus. From War-
saw, the best route is to take the 8(E67) through Piotrków Tribunal-
ski to Wrocław.

Poznań, on the main east–west route from Berlin to Moscow, is eas-
ily accessible by car. The 2(E30), which leads from the border at Frank-

furt/Oder through Poznań and Warsaw to the eastern border at Tere-
spol/Brest in Belarus, is still mostly a two-lane road and is considered—
because of its curves and lack of shoulders—one of the most dangerous
roads in Europe.

BY PLANE

LOT offers daily flights from Warsaw to Wrocław. Special LOT buses
shuttle passengers from Starachowice Airport to the LOT office (⊠
Ul. Józefa Piłsudskiego 77, ☎ 071/343–90–31); buses leave from the
same point for the airport one hour before each flight. City Bus 106
will also take you the 10 km (6 mi) from the city to the airport.

Poznań's **Ławice Airport** is to the west of the city in the Wola district;
buses run regularly to and from the LOT office at Świelej Marcina 69
(☎ 058/852–28–47); allow about an hour for the journey.

BY TRAIN

Wrocław Główny PKP (⊠ Ul. Józefa Piłsudskiego, ☎ 071/68–33–33)
connects Wrocław by rail to all major cities in Poland, with frequent
service to and from Kraków (5 hours), Warsaw (6 hours), and Gdańsk
(7 hours). Trains also leave here for many cities in Western and Eastern Europe: Dresden, Berlin, Prague, Budapest, and Frankfurt. The station is in the city center, a 30-minute walk south of the Rynek.

The **Wrocław Nadodrze** (⊠ Pl. Powstańców Wielkopolskich) station
is the hub for local routes to the east and southeast, including Gniezno.

Trains run frequently from the modern **Poznań Główny** (☎ 061/869–
38–11) station to Szczecin (3 hours), Toruń (2½ hours), Wrocław (3
hours), Kraków (8 hours), and Warsaw (4 hours). International destinations include Berlin (4½ hours), Budapest (15 hours), and Paris (20
hours). The best way into the city center is to take a bus up the long
station approach road to ulica Świelej Marcina and turn right, or take
steps up to ulica Towarowa, turn back over the railway bridge, and
keep walking (the city center and bus station are straight ahead).

The **PKP** train station (☎ 056/654–72–22) in Toruń is south of the
city, across the Wisła River. You can get there on Bus 22. There is daily
service to and from Poznań (3 hours), Gdańsk (4 hours), Warsaw (3
hours), and Kraków (9 hours).

Getting Around

BY BUS

PKS offers comprehensive service in the region. Diagonally opposite
the main train station in Wrocław, **Dworzec Centralny PKS** (⊠ Ul.
Kościuszki 135, ☎ 071/61–81–22) serves local routes, with frequent
service to Jelenia Góra, Częstochowa, Łódź, and the spa towns of Kudowa, Duszniki, and Polanica.

BY CAR

Western Poland has good roads and plenty of gas and service stations.

BY TRAIN

You might want to come to the **Wrocław Świebodzki** (⊠ Pl. Orląt
Lwowskich) station just to admire the station building, which dates
from 1848. You can also catch local trains from here.

Contacts and Resources

EMERGENCIES

Wrocław, Poznań, and **Toruń** (☎ 999). **Late-night pharmacies: Wrocław**
(⊠ Pl. 1 Maja 7, ☎ 071/343–67–24); **Poznań** (⊠ Ul. 23 lutego 18,
☎ 061/852–26–25).

Wrocław: The **IT** office has good maps and English guidebooks (⊠ Rynek 14, ☎ 071/44–31–11) and is open weekdays 9–5, Saturday 10–2; **Orbis** is a good place to make train reservations (⊠ Rynek 29, ☎ 071/44–76–79). **Poznań: IT** (⊠ Stary Rynek 59, ☎ 061/852–61–56) sells the cultural guide **"IKS,"** which has lots of useful information, much of it in English, and is open weekdays 9–5, Saturday 10–2; **Orbis** (⊠ Ul. Marcinkowskiego 21, ☎ 061/853–20–52) sells train and bus tickets. **Toruń:** The **IT** (⊠ Ul. Piekary 37/39 ☎ 056/621–09–31) is open Monday–Saturday 9–4. **Orbis** (⊠ Ul. Mostwa 7, ☎ 056/217–14) has travel information and sells tickets.

SZCZECIN AND THE COAST

A dip in the Baltic Sea is a rugged but rewarding experience, which you can enjoy at a variety of resorts. Most foreign visitors in towns along the Baltic are Germans and Scandinavians looking for sunshine. In summer, duck the droves of Polish tourists and set yourself up in one of the smaller fishing villages.

Szczecin

96 *340 km (215 mi) west of Gdańsk, 515 km (325 mi) northwest of Warsaw, 240 km (150 mi) north of Poznań.*

The large port of Szczecin is on the Odra River just 48 km (30 mi) from the German border. Despite its somewhat industrial atmosphere, Szczecin's location and the overall friendliness of its inhabitants make it an interesting stop-off on your way to Germany or to towns on the Baltic coast. Ruled by several countries over the centuries, Szczecin (or Stettin in German) finally ended up as part of Poland after the Potsdam Conference in 1945. Although not exactly on the coast, Szczecin is separated from the Baltic Sea only by the Zalew Szczecinski (Szczecin Bay). Szczecin was remodeled during the 19th century on the Parisian system of radiating streets and is particularly pretty in spring, when the avenues along the Odra River glow with flowering magnolias.

Szczecin is rapidly regaining some of its former prominence as a Baltic port because of its close proximity to Berlin, which in 1999 will again become the capital of Germany. In fact, Szczecin still carries many reminders of its Teutonic heritage, including the grandiose **Zamek Ksiazat Pomorskich** (Pomeranian Princes' Castle), which was originally built during the 13th and 14th centuries. The past 300 years have not been kind to the castle, which fell into the hands of the Swedes, Prussians, and French, only to be ruined by carpet bombing near the end of World War II. Today the reconstructed castle is a cultural center housing art exhibits, an opera and concert hall, and the music department of the university. ⊠ *Ul. Korsarzy 1,* ☎ *091/434–02–92.* ⊡ *Zł 5.* ☉ *Tues.–Sun. 9:30–4.*

Housed in a Baroque palace and in an annex across the street, the **Muzeum Narodowe** (National Museum) in Szczecin is devoted mainly to art—older paintings, sculpture, and antiques (13th- to 16th-century Pomeranian), and some Polish pieces from the 17th century. The annex is devoted to modern Polish art. ⊠ *Ul. Staromłyńska 27/28,* ☎ *091/433–50–66.* ⊡ *Zł 4.* ☉ *Tues. and Thurs. 10–5, Wed. and Fri. 9–3:30, weekends 10–4.*

Dining and Lodging

$$ ✕ **Restauracja Balaton.** Named for the largest lake in Hungary, Balaton specializes in Hungarian cuisine at reasonable prices. The goulash soup served with bread is especially tasty and filling. The rustic, wood-

paneled atmosphere helps to ease the wait of the often slow service. ⊠ *Pl. Lotników 3,* ☎ *091/434–68–73. AE, DC, MC, V.*

$ ✕ **Restauracja Chief.** This seafood restaurant, in the more modern area of town, is cleverly decorated with stuffed fish, lobsters, and turtles on the walls; aquariums with live fish and turtles fill the corners of the two main rooms. The courteous staff serves fish dishes, as well as beef Stroganoff, and the mandatory pork cutlet. ⊠ *Ul. Rajskiego 16,* ☎ *091/434–37–65. AE, DC, MC, V.*

$$$ ⊞ **Radisson.** A favorite with German and Scandinavian businesspeo-
★   ple, this hotel offers all the usual comforts of a Radisson and more. The hotel even has a shuttle bus from the Radisson in Berlin (2 hours), which is also available to non–hotel guests. ⊠ *Pl. Rodła 10, 70-419,* ☎ *091/359–55–95,* ⬚⬚⬚ *091/359–45–94. 359 rooms, 10 suites. Restaurant, bar, indoor pool, exercise room, nightclub. AE, DC, MC, V.*

$$ ⊞ **Neptun.** This hotel offers comfortable, modern rooms, each outfitted with a large bathroom. ⊠ *Ul. Matejki 18, 70–530,* ☎ *091/424–01–11,* ⬚⬚⬚ *091/422–57–01. Restaurant, 2 bars. AE, MC, V.*

Kamień Pomorski

㊐ *90 km (55 mi) north of Szczecin.*

On the mainland, across the mouth of the bay from Świnoujście, sits the small town of Kamień Pomorski. Mysterious carved-wood idols can be found along its beaches, a reminder of the Slavic settlements that once existed here. The old walls that originally encircled the town are no longer complete, but portions have survived, including the gateway, **Brama Wolińska,** on the west end of the **Rynek** (market square). Also on the square is a well-preserved **town hall,** but the town's most impressive structure is its **late-Romanesque cathedral,** with a splendid Baroque organ. Frequent organ concerts take place in the cathedral, and there's a yearly International Organ and Chamber Music Festival in June and July.

Międzyzdroje

㊏ *112 km (66 mi) northwest of Szczecin.*

Every summer the coastal town of Międzyzdroje attracts thousands of vacationers, mostly Poles and Germans, who lie on the beaches, stroll on the boardwalk, and play on one of Poland's very few 18-hole golf courses.

Lodging

$$$ ⊞ **Hotel Amber Baltic.** This Austrian-owned and -managed high-rise hotel is a popular getaway for Germans. The rooms are slightly on the small side, but the outstanding views and the immaculate service compensate. Spend a weekend enjoying a swim in the Baltic (or the pool, if the weather is too cold), playing golf, or strolling along the beach. ⊠ *Ul. Promenada Gwiazd 1,* ☎ *091/328–1000,* ⬚⬚⬚ *091/328–1022. 192 rooms. 2 restaurant, bar, café, 2 pools. AE, MC, V.*

Szczecin and the Coast A to Z

Szczecin is the gateway to Poland's Baltic coast.

Arriving and Departing

BY BUS

Szczecin's **PKS** bus station (⊠ Pl. Grodnicki, ☎ 091/469–80) is right behind the train station. Check here for service to obscure towns along the Baltic coast. The bus to Gorzów takes two hours; the one to Międzyzdroje, 2½ hours.

BY CAR

To reach Szczecin and Świnoujście from western and southern Poland, take the E65 from Wrocław and Świebodzin via Gorzów Wielkopolski. From eastern and central Poland take the E75 to Toruń and then travel via Bydgoszcz, Piła, and Stargard Szczeciński.

BY PLANE

Passengers arriving by air in Szczecin can take a bus to the **LOT** office at Aleje Wyzwolenia 17 (☎ 091/433–99–26), which takes about 45 minutes.

BY TRAIN

Dworzec Główny (✉ Ul. Kolumba, ☎ 091/395) has service to and from the following cities: Warsaw (5 hours), Gdańsk (6 hours), Berlin (3 hours), and the small towns along the Baltic coast. The station is just south of the city on the river; take Tram 3 to reach the city center.

Getting Around

BY CAR

Generally the roads in this area are good, although the secondary roads can be poorly surfaced. The secondary road running nearest to the sea along the coast from Świnoujście through Kołobrzeg to Koszalin and beyond has picturesque views. In the summer season, many gas stations in small towns operate 24 hours a day.

Contacts and Resources

EMERGENCIES

Police (☎ 997). **Ambulance** (☎ 999).

VISITOR INFORMATION

Szczecin: Informacja Turystyczna (✉ Ul. Wyszyńskiego 26, ☎ 091/434–04–40); **Orbis** (✉ Plac Zwycięstwa, ☎ 091/434–51–54).

POLAND A TO Z

Arriving and Departing

By Bus

A number of companies operate buses between major European cities and Polish cities. Many travel nonstop, and what you lose in comfort you make up for in savings: The bus fare is roughly half the train fare. **Anna Travel** (✉ Ul. Jerozolimskie 54, Warszawa, ☎ 022/25–53–89) specializes in international bus travel.

By Car

In summer, the border crossing points into Poland from Germany and out of Poland to the East are notoriously lengthy. Green-card insurance, which covers collision damage outside one's country of residence, can be bought at the border and is necessary if you are bringing in your own car. Rental companies outside Poland often do not permit their cars to cross the border due to high incidents of theft (e.g., Avis Germany will not allow you to take its rental cars to Poland).

By Ferry

Polferries (Polish Baltic Shipping Company; ✉ ul. Chałubińskiego 8, Warsaw, ☎ 022/830–00–97) operates regular ferry service from Denmark (Copenhagen, Ronne) and Sweden (Malmo, Nynashamn, Oxelosund) to Świnoujście, Kołobrzeg, or Gdańsk. **Lion Ferry** (✉ Ul. Kwiatowskiego 60, Gydnia, ☎ 058/665–14–14) offers service from Gydnia to Karlskrona, Sweden.

By Plane
All flights from North America arrive at Warsaw's **Okęcie Airport** (Port Lotniczy), just southwest of the city. **Delta, American Airlines,** and **LOT Polish Airlines** offers direct service from New York (flying time is 7½ hours). Most major European airlines fly to Warsaw and also to secondary Polish cities such as Gdańsk, Kraków and Wrocław (☞ Arriving by Plane *in* Warsaw A to Z, *above*).

By Train
There are direct trains to Poland from major European cities. In Poland, Orbis and other international travel agencies like Wagonlit sell international rail tickets, as do all main city stations.

Getting Around

By Bus
The national bus company, **PKS,** and the private and much more pleasant **Polski Express** (☎ 022/630–29–67) offer long-distance service to all cities. You can reserve seats on Express buses, which often—except in the case of a few major intercity routes—get to their destination more quickly than trains. For really out-of-the-way destinations, the bus is often the only means of transportation.

By Car
Driving conditions in Poland continue to deteriorate as traffic density explodes. You will not yet find any Western-quality highways, although new east–west international highways are under construction and a few major roads (e.g., Warsaw–Katowice) are now entirely four-lane, divided highways. This is, however, still the exception rather than the rule. Horse-drawn traffic can still cause congestion even on major roads, and carts, pedestrians and cyclists make night driving particularly hazardous. If you can avoid driving in Poland, do so.

Poles drive on the right, and there is an overall speed limit of 100 kph (62 mph). The speed limit in built-up areas is 50 kph (30 mph); the beginning and end of these are marked by a sign bearing the name of the town in a white rectangle. At press time, the price of gas was about zł 23 for 10 liters of unleaded gas. Filling stations appear about every 40 km (25 mi) on major roads but can be difficult to find on side roads. They are usually open from 6 AM to 10 PM, although there are now increasingly many 24-hour stations, usually in cities. The **Polish Motoring Association** (PZMot; ☎ 022/ 629–83–36) provides tourist information about driving in Poland and **emergency** road help (dial ☎ 9637 country wide), as well as breakdown and repair services. If you break down in a remote area, you can usually find a local farmer who will help with a tractor tow and some mechanical assistance.

By Ferry
In the summer season, it is possible to take ferries or hydrofoils between various points on the Baltic coast. Two of the more popular routes are Szczecin to Świnoujście, near the German border on the coast, and Sopot to Hel, farther east north of Gdańsk.

By Plane
LOT Polish Airlines has daily domestic services linking many major Polish cities: **Warsaw, Gdańsk, Katowice, Kraków, Poznań, Rzeszów, Szczecin,** and **Wrocław.** Flying time in each case is no longer than about an hour. Compared with rail travel, flying is very expensive (although not by Western standards), and most airports are some distance from the city center. However, in a few instances, rail connections can be so

poor that flying is a real time-saver (this is especially true between Wrocław and Warsaw, and Rzeszów and Warsaw).

By Train

Polish trains run at three speeds: *ekspresowy* (express), *pośpieszny* (fast), and (the much cheaper) *osobowy* (slow). Intercity expresses between major cities are the most comfortable and include coffee and sandwiches in the price of the ticket. Only the first two categories have first-class accommodations, and you can reserve a seat only on express trains. *Couchettes* and sleeping cars (three berths to a car in second class, two berths in first class) are available on long-distance routes (e.g., Warsaw–Zakopane or Warsaw–Wrocław). Though restaurant cars are usually available on intercity trains and buffet cars on express trains, it is advisable when on a long trip to take along some food. Tickets can be bought at the station, through Orbis, or any travel agency. Tickets are issued for a given date, after which you get only two days' leeway to travel; thereafter they become invalid.

Contacts and Resources

Camping

You are allowed to camp only at recognized sites, but there are plenty of these. Standards vary; local branches of PTTK can provide excellent leads.

Car Rentals

A valid driver's license, issued in any country, will enable you to drive without a special permit. You do need green-card insurance, which can be purchased at the border, if you are driving your own car.

Booking a rental car in advance through rental companies in one's home country can often generate considerable savings. Cars with both manual and automatic transmissions are available, starting at about $450 a week (including insurance and unlimited mileage). Many major car-rental firms have offices at local and international airports and in towns and cities throughout Poland.

Avis Poland (⊠ Marriott Hotel, Al. Jerozolimskie 65/79 , ☎ 022/630–73–16). **Hertz** (⊠ Ul. Nowogrodzka 27, ☎ 022/621–13–60). **Budget** (⊠ Marriott Hotel, Al. Jerozolimskie 65/79, ☎ 022/630–72–80).

Customs and Duties

Persons over 18 may bring into Poland duty-free: personal belongings, including musical instruments; one computer; a radio; one camera with 24 rolls of film; up to 250 cigarettes or 50 cigars; ½ liter of spirits and 2 liters of wine; together with goods that are not for your personal use up to the value of $100. Foreign currency over the value of $2,500 may be brought in but must be declared, as should antique jewelry or books published before 1945 (to avoid possible problems when taking them out of the country). Further information can be obtained from **Customs Information** (☎ 022/650–28–73).

Guided Tours

SPECIAL-INTEREST TOURS

Many of the private tourist travel agencies in Warsaw arrange customized tours built around particular themes (☞ Guided Tours *in* Warsaw A to Z, *above*).

Language

Polish is a Slavic language that uses the Roman alphabet but has several additional characters and diacritical marks. Because it has a higher incidence of consonant clusters than English, most English speakers find it a difficult language to decipher, much less pronounce. Take a

phrase book and a pocket dictionary with you; the people you're trying to communicate with will at least appreciate the effort. The *Berlitz
Polish Phrase Book and Dictionary* is a good starting point.

Younger Poles are likely to speak some English, while their elders are
more likely to know French or German—and, of course, Russian,
which they will not admit to. In larger cities, English is increasingly
common, especially in hotels, restaurants, and tourism-related shops,
but English speakers in the countryside are still a rarity.

Mail

POSTAL RATES

Airmail letters to the United States and Canada at press time cost zł
1.50; postcards, zł 1. Airmail letters to the United Kingdom or Europe
cost zł 1.30; postcards, 90 groszy. Airmail Express costs an extra zł
2.5 flat charge and cuts the travel time in half. Post offices are open
weekdays 8–8. At least one post office is open 24 hours a day in every
major city.

RECEIVING MAIL

The main post office in every town has *poste restante* (general delivery) facilities. Friends and family who send you mail should write
"No. 1" (signifying the main post office) after the name of the city.

Money and Expenses

POLISH CURRENCY

The monetary unit in Poland is the *złoty,* which is subdivided into 100
groszy (gr). Since the currency reform of 1995, there are notes of 10,
20, 50, 100, and 200 złotys, and coins in values of 1, 2 and 5 złoty
and 1, 2, 5, 10, and 50 groszys. At press time, the bank exchange rate
was about zł 3.5 to the U.S. dollar, zł 3.0 to the Canadian dollar, and
zł 5.9 to the pound sterling. Foreign currency can be exchanged at banks
or at private exchange bureaus (*Kantor Wymiany Walut*), where rates
are usually slightly higher than at banks and service is swifter. With a
major credit card and a pin number, you can also get money from cash
machines, which you can find in most major cities.

WHAT IT WILL COST

At press time, the annual rate of inflation had fallen to about 15% annually. The złoty has strengthened and stabilized. The days when you
could exchange $50 on the black market and feel like a millionaire are
over. Although most goods and services are still cheaper than in the
West, they are gradually rising to European levels. On the other hand,
visitors have a greater range of options in selecting appropriate accommodations. Some top hotels still quote room prices in hard currency, but in the provinces simple rooms can be had for as little as $10
per night. Overall, you can still get very good value for your money in
Poland, and the farther you venture off the beaten track, the cheaper
your vacation will be.

SAMPLE COSTS

A cup of coffee will cost about zł 3–zł 5; a bottle of beer, zł 3–zł 7; a
soft drink, zł 2–zł 5; a 1½-km (1-mi) taxi ride, zł 6; a 240-km (150-
mi) train trip (first-class single), zł 40.

TAXES

A 7% value-added tax (VAT) is applied to hotel bills. In general, food
is also taxed at 7% and alcoholic beverages at 22%. There are also
taxes on airline tickets.

National Holidays

January 1; April 4–5, 1999 and April 23–24, 2000 (Easter Sunday and
Monday); May 1 (Labor Day); May 3 (Constitution Day); June 11 (Cor-

pus Christi); August 15 (Assumption); November 1 (All Saints' Day); November 11 (rebirth of the Polish state, 1918); December 25, 26.

Opening and Closing Times

Food shops are open weekdays 7–7, Saturday 7–1. Other stores are open weekdays 11–7 and Saturday 9–1, although more and more stores are staying open later and on Sundays. Banks are generally open weekdays 8–3 or 8–6. Museum hours are unpredictable but are generally Tuesday–Sunday 9–5.

Passports and Visas

U.S. and EU citizens do not require visas for entry to Poland (a valid passport will suffice). Canadian citizens must pay C$40 or C$80 for a single-or double-entry visa. Apply at the nearest Polish consulate. Each visitor must complete one application form and provide two passport-size photographs. Allow about two weeks for processing. Visas are issued for 90 days but can be extended once in Poland, through the local police headquarters.

Rail Passes

The **European East Pass** (☞ Train Travel *in* the Gold Guide)covers Poland, as well as the Czech Republic, Slovakia, Hungary, and Austria.

Student and Youth Travel

Almatur, the Polish student-travel organization, and **PTTK** are good resources. Substantial discounts can be gotten when traveling in Poland with **IYHC** (International Youth Hostel Card) and **ISIC** (International Student Identification Card) cards.

Telephones

The country code for Poland is 48. The city code for Warsaw is 22.

LOCAL CALLS

Phone booths which take calling cards have become widespread. They can be used for both local and long-distance calls. Cards, which cost zł 7.5 or zł 15, are available at post offices and most newspaper kiosks. When making a long-distance call, first dial 0, wait for the dial tone, then dial the rest of your number.

INTERNATIONAL CALLS

International calls can be made from post offices or first-class hotels, where you can use your credit card or pay after making the call. You can also dial direct to most European countries and to North America. Dial 0–0800–111–2122 to connect with **MCI** or call 0–0800–111–1111 for **AT&T** USA Direct. For **Sprint Global One,** dial 0–0800–111–3115.

Tipping

It is customary to round up on bills, for a total of not more than about 10% for waiters. For taxi drivers, round up to the nearest złoty or two. A tip of zł 2 per bag is in order for porters. Concierges and tour guides should get at least zł 5.

Visitor Information

Orbis is partially privatized and is still the main Polish tourist information office, with branches throughout the country. It specializes in booking reservations in its own hotels and in selling tickets for both domestic and overseas travel. **PTTK,** a nationwide network of tourist clubs, can provide extensive information for the budget traveler or visitor with a particular interest in the history of individual regions or the outdoors. Look for signs marked **IT** on or near the main squares of cities and towns for complete tourist information services.

6 Bulgaria

Bulgaria is "a land as big as the palm of one's hand," as its poets have often said. At the crossroads of Europe and Asia, once ruled by the Turks, the "Jewel of the Balkans" is an exotic and often confusing mix of cultures, where Eastern mysticism and mosques coexist with Slavic traditions and the deteriorating remnants of a Communist past. Mountains crowned by rugged hilltop monasteries, peaceful farmland villages dotting the fertile Danube plains, and a coastline strewn with miles of golden beaches and tranquil waterfront towns give undiscovered Bulgaria its intoxicating allure.

Updated by
Annie Ward

BULGARIA, A LAND OF MOUNTAINS AND SEASCAPES, of rustic unspoiled beauty and proud hospitality, lies in the eastern half of the Balkan Peninsula. From the end of World War II until recently, it was the closest ally of the former Soviet Union. "The forgotten corner of Europe," as locals still sometimes call it, Bulgaria was all but unknown to the Western world, save for media reports on its secret police and assassins, who were accused of the 1981 plot to kill the Pope. For this reason, the country always presented a rather mysterious and sometimes sinister image to Western travelers. This era ended in 1989 with the overthrow of Communist Party head Todor Zhivkov, when Bulgaria opened its doors to the West, readopted its former traditions and religion, and embraced the opportunity to present its true and unique character to the rest of the world. Since then, Bulgaria has struggled and suffered in its quest to institute democracy and a free-market economy. Many Bulgarians believed the "miracle" of Westernization would bring prosperity overnight. Instead, political and economic upheaval dashed the people's dreams, and since 1989, the government has changed hands seven times, primarily between parties composed of the former Communist leaders.

In the winter of 1997, massive unemployment, hyperinflation, rampant corruption, and growing bread lines turned the national apathy bred by political disillusionment into anger. Inspired by the new UDF (Union of Democratic Forces) president Peter Stoyanov, the people of Bulgaria took to the streets, surrounded the parliament building where members of the BSP (Bulgarian Socialist Party) were barricaded inside, and demanded new elections with shouts of "The BSP is Mafia . . . throw out the red garbage!" During the monthlong uprising, strikes and protests paralyzed the country, until finally the Socialists agreed to hold elections two years before the slated end of their term. In April of 1997 the people voted the UDF into power, marking the second time in nearly a decade that the country was not under Socialist rule. This new government has a tremendous task before it, and only time will tell if it can succeed in creating infrastructure out of chaos. The preliminary aims are to make Bulgaria a contender for membership in the European Union, to fight the omnipresent and all-powerful Mafia, and to revive the stagnant economy. (Taking steps to control Bulgaria's skyrocketing inflation, the International Monetary Fund helped institute a currency board in July 1997, which led to pegging the leva to the German mark.) Most Bulgarians now realize that meaningful reform may take years to implement, perhaps decades to succeed.

Yet having survived the recent turmoil, Bulgaria is once again a relatively peaceful destination in the Balkans. Though continuing economic depression makes life hard for locals, visitors will find Bulgarians exuberantly welcoming, especially to Western tourists (who are still few and far enough between to be regarded as fascinating foreigners) and the coveted hard currency they carry into the country. With gorgeous countryside, low prices, friendly people, thriving nightlife, and excellent cuisine, Bulgaria will not remain undiscovered for long. For adventurous souls who don't mind the discomforts of a country battling descent into the Third World (and wrestling with Cyrillic), Bulgaria provides not only an extraordinary vacation destination but a chance to see history in the making.

Founded in 681 by the Bulgars, a Turkic tribe from Central Asia, Bulgaria was a crossroads of civilization even before that date. Archaeological finds in Varna, on the Black Sea coast, give proof of civilization from as early as 4600 BC. Bulgaria was part of the Byzantine Empire from AD 1018 to 1185 and was occupied by the Turks from 1396 until 1878. Today, Bulgaria remains a dizzying blend of cultures, with its Eastern-influenced architecture, Turkish fast-food aromas, Greek ruins, Soviet monuments, and European outdoor cafés. Five hundred years of Muslim occupation and nearly half a century of Communist rule did not wipe out Christianity, and many lovely, icon-filled churches dot the countryside. The country's 120 monasteries, with their icons and numerous frescoes, chronicle the development of Bulgarian cultural and national identity.

The capital, Sofia, is picturesquely situated in a valley near Mt. Vitosha. Culturally and historically rich, the city has good hotels, a wide variety of restaurants, excellent ballet and opera, and a vibrant Mediterranean-style nightlife with scores of bars and discos. The interior landscape of the country offers magnificent scenic beauty, with tranquil forested ridges, spectacular valleys, and rural communities where folklore is a colorful part of village life. Veliko Turnovo, just north of the Balkan Range in the center of the country, was the capital from the 12th to the 14th century during the Second Bulgarian Empire and is well worth a visit for its medieval ramparts and vernacular architecture. Plovdiv, a university town reputed to be the intellectual center of the country, lies southeast of Sofia and has a particularly picturesque Old Town as well as one of the most well-preserved Roman amphitheaters in the world.

The Black Sea coast along the country's eastern border is particularly attractive, with secluded coves and old fishing villages, as well as wide stretches of sandy beaches that have been developed into self-contained resorts. Varna, the site of one of Europe's first cultural settlements, was once the summer beach playground for the entire Eastern Bloc but now draws a wider array of visitors. A thriving city in the winter as well, it is among the most important ports on the Black Sea.

Pleasures and Pastimes

Architecture

Old Bulgarian architecture is best seen in the country's towns and villages with cobbled streets, stone-vaulted bridges, and wooden houses. Hidden within the seemingly inaccessible solid walls, latticed windows, and heavy gates of typical houses in small mountain towns such as Bansko are delicate rooms with carved ceilings and colorful handmade rugs. Koprivstitsa and the Old Town of Plovdiv are known for their excellent examples of National Revival architecture, a 19th century style which helped reestablish Bulgarian artistic identity after the Turkish occupation. These houses are colorfully painted, often with ornately carved wooden ceilings and second floors that extend out over the first floors, supported by wooden pillars.

Churches, Monasteries, and Icon Paintings

Most Bulgarian churches and monasteries are monuments of the Bulgarian National Revival period (18th and early 19th centuries), a time of vigorous cultural activity and increased awareness of a national identity. The famous Rila Monastery is included on the UNESCO list of World Heritage Sites. The Bachkovo and Trojan monasteries are both well known for their splendid murals and icons, painted by Zahari Zograph and other great National Revival artists.

The tradition of the Bulgarian icon goes back to the 9th century, when the Bulgarians converted to Christianity. During and after the National Revival period of the 18th and 19th centuries, many icon-painting schools were formed. The schools of Bansko, Samokov, and Trojan produced

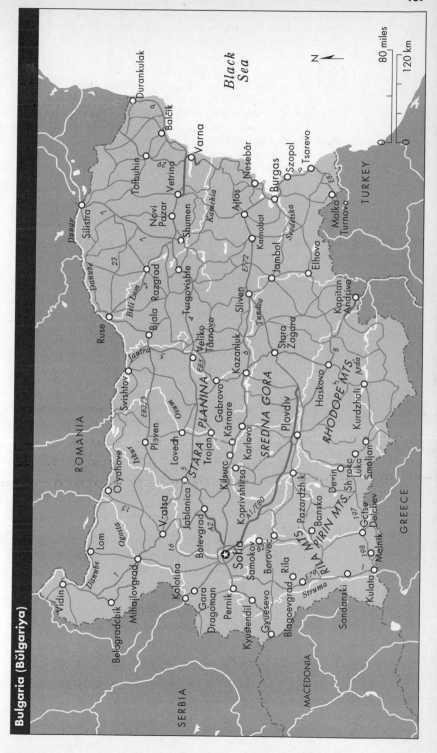

Bulgaria (Bŭlgariya)

Black Sea

Durankulak
Balčik
Varna
Tolbuhin
Vetrino
Nesebăr
Burgas
Szopol
Tsarevo
Silistra
Novi Pazar
Shumen
Ajtos
Karnobat
Malko
Turnovo
TURKEY
Kamchia
Razgrad
Turgovishte
Sliven
Jambol
Elhovo
Kapitan
Andnuo
Bjala
Veliko
Tărnovo
Kazanluk
Stara
Zagara
Haskovo
RHODOPE MTS.
Ruse
Gabrovo
SREDNA GORA
Plovdiv
Kurdzhali
Smoljan
Svishtov
Plaven
Trojan
STARA PLANINA
Kārnare
Karlovo
Pazardzhik
Devin
Luka
Loved
Kilsuc
Koprivshtisa
Shiroke
Orehove
Vratsa
Jablanica
Bolevgrad
Borovec
PIRIN MTS.
Gotse
Delchev
Melnik
Lom
Kolotina
RILA MTS.
Rila
Bansko
ROMANIA
Vidin
Mihajlovgrad
Gara
Dragoman
Pernik
Samokov
Blagoevgrad
Kulata
Sandanski
Belogradchik
Kyustendil
Gyueševo
SERBIA
MACEDONIA
GREECE
Sofia

80 miles
120 km

icons for the newly built churches and private homes. The biggest collections of icons are displayed in the Crypt Museum of Alexander Nevski Memorial Cathedral in Sofia and in the Museum of Art and History in Varna.

Dining

Balkan cooking revolves around lamb, pork, sheep cheese, eggplant, and other vegetables. Typical Bulgarian dishes include wonderful tomato, cucumber, and feta cheese salad (*shopska*), vine leaves stuffed with meat and rice (*sarmi*), and grilled meat balls (*kebapche*). Bulgaria invented yogurt (*kiselo mlyako*); excellent cold yogurt soups (*tarator*) are served in summer. Syrupy *baklava* and crepes stuffed with chocolate or nuts and honey (*palachinki*) are the favored desserts to round out a meal.

The national drink is *rakia* (brandy), made either from plums (*slivova*) or grapes (*grosdova*)—but vodka is popular too. Bulgarian wines are good, usually full-bodied, dry, and inexpensive. You may want to try the Bulgarian chardonnay, traminer, or muscat. Coffee is strong and is often drunk along with a cold beverage, such as cola.

Visitors have a choice between predictable, often uninspired hotel dining and the more adventurous outing to a local restaurant or café where the menu may only be offered in Cyrillic. In larger cities, international cuisine is easy to find, but in smaller towns the best bets are the small folk-style restaurants called *mehanas* that serve national dishes and local specialties. Dinner out in a mehana is considered a recreational experience. Bulgarians share tables with strangers (feel free to do this yourself—it's perfectly acceptable) and linger for hours over even the smallest of side salads while drinking rakia, smoking, and listening to loud music. (Restaurant turnover is practically unheard of—don't bother waiting if all the tables are full.) Calmer atmospheres are easily found in restaurants featuring more Continental cuisine.

CATEGORY	COST*
$$$$	over 20,000 leva
$$$	12,000 leva–20,000 leva
$$	7,000 leva–12,000 leva
$	under 7,000 leva

per person for a three-course meal, including tip but not alcohol

Hiking and Walking

Mount Vitosha and the mountains of the Rila, Pirin, and Rhodope ranges are good for walking. Nature lovers will appreciate Vitosha for its beautiful moraines, Rila and Pirin for their clear blue lakes, and the Rhodopes for their green slopes and rare plants. The Balkan range, which crosses the entire country, has splendid rocks and caves. Two of the most interesting are Ledenika and Magura, with their veritable sculptures of stalactites and stalagmites. Ledenika is about 200 km (124 mi) northeast of Sofia, while Magura is approximately 250 km (155 mi) north of the capital.

Lodging

Bulgaria offers a wide choice of accommodations, ranging from hotels—most of them dating from the '60s and '70s—to apartment rentals, rooms in private homes, and campsites. Although hotels are improving, all but the newest still tend to suffer from temperamental wiring and erratic plumbing, and it is a good idea to pack a universal drain plug, as plugs are often missing in hotel bathrooms. In moderate and inexpensive hotels, don't be surprised if strangely placed plumbing turns the entire bathroom into a shower. Flashlights and other battery-powered utilities are strongly recommended, as there are likely to be power outages in winter. Being prepared is especially important if you plan to rent a private room through a tourist agency; often these rooms don't even have towels. Quirks like these in accommodations give you a sense of the real Bulgaria.

Until recently, most hotels used by Western visitors were owned by Balkantourist and Interhotels. Many government-owned or -operated hotels are either recently privatized or on the verge of privatization. The conversion is expected to take up to five years, and hotels may be closed for renovation for extended periods or may be permanently shut down. We strongly urge you to contact hotels in advance to get the latest information. Most have restaurants and bars; the large, modern ones have swimming pools, shops, and other facilities. Popping up all along the coast are new, small, private hotels with far more personality than the ever-so-common large, nondescript older properties. Many of these small hotels are family houses in small towns and villages south of Burgas.

Socialist-era hotels often have a half-board policy; besides a Continental breakfast, you're given a coupon for either lunch or dinner; if you don't use the meal coupon, you are not reimbursed. If you refuse the coupons when booking a room—and most people do, since the meals are lackluster—your room rate should be lowered a bit. Hotel bills can be paid in either Western or local currency, but if you pay in leva, you must show your exchange slips to prove that the money was changed legally. Unless otherwise noted, all rooms have bath.

CATEGORY	SOFIA*	OTHER AREAS*
$$$$	over $200	over $75
$$$	$75–$200	$55–$75
$$	$40–$75	$30–$55
$	under $40	under $30

*All prices are for two people in a double room with breakfast.

Music

You can hear Bulgarian folk music at numerous folk festivals around the country, including the festival held in May in Koprivshtitsa and the late-September event held near Pamporovo, just south of Plovdiv. Bulgarian folk dances are performed to traditional music by dancers in brightly colored costumes, which differ according to the region of the country. Rhodope mountain music is eerie and beautiful, unfamiliar to most foreigners.

Spa Resorts

There are hundreds of mineral springs in Bulgaria. Their healing properties were well known to the ancient Romans. The spa hotels in the resorts of Sandanski and Velingrad have various traditional and new treatments, including manual therapy, acupuncture, phytobalneology, phytotherapy, and slimming cures. (Sandanski is a half hour from the Greek border crossing at Kulata; Velingrad is southeast of Sofia in the Rhodopes.) The Black Sea hydrotherapy centers in Sveti Konstantin, Albena, and Pomorie are famous for their healing mud. The mineral springs along the northern Black Sea coast turn the sea resorts into year-round spas.

Exploring Bulgaria

Bordered by Romania to the north (the Danube River forms the border), Serbia and the former Yugoslav Republic of Macedonia to the west, Greece and Turkey to the south, and the Black Sea to the east, Bulgaria is in the southeastern corner of Europe in the heart of the Balkan Peninsula. Geographically, Bulgaria can be divided into two basic regions: the Inland and the Black Sea Golden Coast. Inland you'll find one of Bulgaria's two chief attractions, its towering mountains, and on the Black Sea you'll find the other, its glittering seacoast.

Great Itineraries

Bulgaria may be small, but its nature and landscapes are strikingly diverse. If you have more than a week to tour the country, you'll be able to see most of it. If you have less than a week, you'll still get to see some major sights and get an impression of the country and its people. If two or three days are all you have, you'll have to choose between the mountains and the sea.

Numbers in the text correspond to numbers in the margin and on the Sofia map.

IF YOU HAVE 3 DAYS

Begin in **Sofia** ①–⑯ and spend the day in the central part of the city—be sure to visit the magnificent Hram-pametnik Alexander Nevski (Alexander Nevski Memorial Cathedral), the rich collections of the Natzionalen Istoricheski Musei (National History Museum), and some of the new art galleries. On the second day, head for ⚏ **Plovdiv.** Spend the morning walking around in Plovdiv's Old Town, and have a coffee on the terrace overlooking the magnificent Rimski Amfiteatur (Roman Amphitheater). On the third day, pass through the town of **Karlovo** to ⚏ **Koprivshtitsa,** where you can see some of the finest examples of typical old Bulgarian architecture. Or, instead of heading toward Koprivshtitsa, you can go to ⚏ **Borovec,** the oldest and the biggest mountain resort in Bulgaria, at the foot of Vrah Musala, the highest peak on the Balkan Peninsula.

IF YOU HAVE 5 DAYS

Spend a day in **Sofia,** and from there travel to ⚏ **Rila Monastir** (Rila Monastery), founded in the 10th century. Spend the night here, either in the local hotel or in one of the sparse monk's rooms in the compound, and leave the next morning for ⚏ **Bansko** by way of **Blago-evgrad.** In Blagoevgrad, spend some time walking around in the center of town. Next, continue on to Bansko, another museum town with charming National Revival houses. The third day, go hiking in the Pirin Mountains, and the next, visit the tiny village of **Melnik,** famous for its architecture, sandstone formations, lively taverns, and red-wine tasting in ancient caves. From Melnik, before going back to Sofia, you can visit the Rozhen Monastir (Rozhen Monastery), most of it decorated by unknown painters.

When to Tour

Summers here are warm, and winters are crisp and cold. If you're looking for sun, head to Bulgaria in July or August. Although this is Bulgaria's "high season," the only places you'll find crowds are the Black Sea coast and Sofia. Even when the temperature climbs in summer, the Black Sea breezes and the cooler mountain air prevent the heat from being overpowering.

Don't limit yourself to summer for a visit to Bulgaria, though—the coastal areas get considerable sunshine year-round. The inland areas, however, are wet during most of March and April.

SOFIA

Exploring Sofia

Bulgaria's bustling capital is set on the high Sofia Plain, ringed by mountain ranges: the Balkan Range to the north; the Lyulin Mountains to the west; part of the Sredna Gora Mountains to the southeast; and, to the southwest, Mt. Vitosha—the city's summer and winter playground—which rises to more than 7,600 ft. The area has been inhabited for about 7,000 years, but the first impression is of haphazard and thoughtless modern urban development. Driving in, don't be daunted by the surreal expanse of nightmarish Socialist-era block housing: It soon gives way to spacious parks, open-air cafés, and broad streets filled with an incongruous mix of pedestrians, Western sports cars, and archaic farmer's wagons laden with firewood. As recently as the 1870s Sofia was part of the Ottoman Empire, and one mosque still remains. Most of the city, however, was planned after 1880, and following the destruction of World War II, many of the main buildings were rebuilt in the Socialist style.

Numbers in the text correspond to numbers in the margin and on the Sofia map.

A Good Walk

Begin your tour in the heart of Sofia at the crowded and lively ploshtad Sveta Nedelya (St. Nedelya Square), named after the church, **Tzarkva Sveta Nedelya** ①, that dominates its south side. Behind the church, on the west side of bulevard Vitosha, is the **Natzionalen Istoricheski Musei** ②. On the north side of ploshtad Sveta Nedelya is the **Rotonda Sveti Georgi** ③, the oldest archaeological monument in Sofia. Heading east from here, you'll enter ploshtad Alexander Batenberg and see the huge Partiyniyat Dom, the former headquarters of the Bulgarian Communist Party—its architecture is reminiscent of the country's recent Communist history.

Near the southwestern corner of the square is the **Natzionalen Archeologicheski Musei** ④. Next to the museum is the **Mavsolei Georgi Dimitrov** ⑧. Across from the mausoleum is the former royal palace, which today houses the **Natzionalen Etnografski Musei** ⑩ and the **Natzionalna Hudozhestvena Galeria** ⑨. One block away on the left side of the street is **Tzarkva Sveti Nikolai** ⑪. From this church, walk down bulevard Tsar Osvoboditel, with its monument to the Russians, the Tsar Osvoboditel (Tsar Liberator), topped by the equestrian statue of Russia's Czar Alexander II. It stands in front of the **Narodno Subranie**, a building that still bears the scars of the January 1997 uprising, during which protesters lobbed stones from the plaza through the windows at the members of parliament barricaded inside. Behind it, just beyond ulitsa Shipka, you'll be confronted by the shining **Hram-pametnik Alexander Nevski** ⑬, where you can pause to browse through the outdoor antiques market. Here you should also take a look at the Crypt Museum inside. Across the square from the memorial church is a much older church, **Tzarkva Sveta Sofia** ⑫. Return to bulevard Tsar Osvoboditel through ploshtad Alexander Nevski. If you continue east, you'll reach **Borisova Gradina** ⑮.

From the park, walk south past the big sports stadium until you come to bulevard Dragan Tsankov. Next, turn down ulitsa Graf Ignatiev and head west to the monument of Patriarh Evtimij, a 14th century Christian patriarch. Take the boulevard of the same name until you reach the **Natzionalen Dvoretz na Kulturata** ⑯, where young couples meet and stroll, kids skateboard, and the elderly sit on park benches enjoying the spectacle.

Next, walk along bulevard Vitosha back to ploshtad St. Nedelya, and then follow bulevard Knyaginya Maria-Luiza toward the train station. On the right is the Tsentralen Universalen Magazin (Central Department Store). Just beyond this big store are the **Banya Bashi Djamiya** ⑥ and the **Tsentralnata Banya** ⑤, which are currently closed for restora-

Sofia

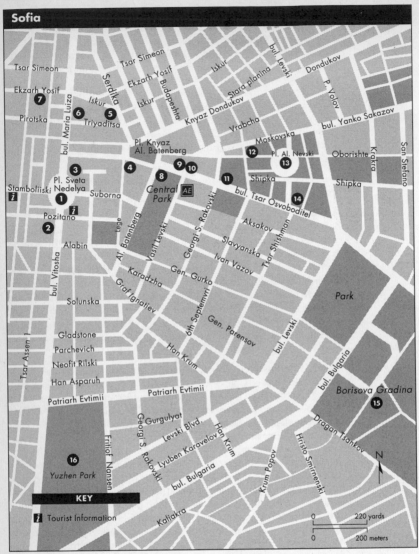

Banya Bashi
Djamiya, **6**

Borisova Gradina, **15**

Hram-pametnik
Alexander Nevski, **13**

Mavsolei Georgi
Dimitrov, **8**

Narodno
Subranie, **14**

Natzionalen
Archeologicheski
Musei, **4**

Natzionalen Dvoretz
na Kulturata, **16**

Natzionalen
Etnografski
Muzei, **10**

Natzionalen
Istoricheski Muzei, **2**

Natzionalna
Hudozhestvena
Galeria, **9**

Rotonda Sveti
Georgi, **3**

Tsentralna Sofiiska
Sinagoga, **7**

Tsentralnata
Banya, **5**

Tzarkva Sveta
Nedelya, **1**

Tzarkva Sveta
Sofia, **12**

Tzarkva Sveti
Nikolai, **11**

tions. Across the boulevard is the Tsentralni Hali (Central Market Hall), unfortunately also closed for renovations. Just west of the dilapidated Central Market Hall is the **Tsentralnata Sofiiska Sinagoga** ⑦, recently refurbished with gleaming Moorish domes and the largest chandelier in the Balkans. Turning left on ulitsa Ekzarh Yosif and walking west toward ulitsa Stefan Stambolov will immerse you in the crowds coming and going from the Zhenski Pazaar, the most fascinating outdoor bazaar in the city. With hordes of villagers hawking produce, pirated CDs, clothes, and homemade goods, this area is sensory overload and the perfect end to a full and fascinating day.

Timing

This walking tour covers a distance of about 5 to 6 km (3 to 4 mi) and will take about four hours to complete. If you visit the National History Museum, you'll need to allow one or more extra hours because there's so much to see. You can also combine a tour of Sofia with a short walk on Mt. Vitosha. To do this, you'll need six to seven hours. It's best to head for Vitosha during the week, as it's much less crowded than on weekends. Vitosha is usually covered with snow in winter (December–March). There are several ski lifts on the mountain, and rental skis are available.

Sights to See

⑥ **Banya Bashi Djamiya** (Banya Bashi Mosque). A legacy of Turkish domination, this 16th-century mosque is one of the most noteworthy sights in Sofia, with its imposing dome and elegant minaret. Built in 1576 by the Turkish architect Sinan, the mosque was named (*banya* means baths) for its proximity to mineral baths. The interior is closed to the non-Islamic public. ⊠ *Bul. Maria Luiza, across from Central Market Hall.*

☾🐾 ⑮ **Borisova Gradina** (Boris's Garden). If you look past the dilapidated benches, packs of stray dogs, and overflowing garbage dumpsters, you can imagine what the park was like before Bulgaria's recent depression. An empty lake, a dry fountain, and neglected statues of Communist leaders are surrounded by dense, overgrown woods and dirt paths—still a favorite spot for strolling. In summer, ice cream vendors, children riding around in battery-operated minicars, a cool outdoor disco, and a surprisingly pristine public pool with children's water slides bring life to the deteriorated park. ⊠ *Bul. Bulgaria between bul. Tsar Osvoboditel and bul. Dragan Tsankov.*

★ ⑬ **Hram-pametnik Alexander Nevski** (Alexander Nevski Memorial Cathedral). You may recognize this neo-Byzantine structure with glittering onion domes from the pictures that appear on almost every piece of tourist literature. It was built by the Bulgarian people at the beginning of the 20th century as a mark of gratitude to their Russian liberators. Inside are alabaster and onyx, Italian marble and Venetian mosaics, magnificent frescoes, and space for a congregation of 5,000. There's a fine collection of icons and religious artifacts in the **Cryptata na Hram Pametnik Alexander Nevsky** (Crypt Museum), representing Byzantine influence, Ottoman rule, and the National Revival period. On Sunday morning you can attend a service to hear the superb choir. In the area near and around the church, you may be harassed by one of the many ladies selling lace tablecloths. ⊠ *Pl. Alexander Nevski,* ☎ *02/87–76–97.* ▨ *50 leva.* ⊙ *Wed.–Mon. 10:30–5.*

⑧ **Mavsolei Georgi Dimitrov** (Georgi Dimitrov Mausoleum). A reminder of the recent Communist past, this building contained, until 1990, the embalmed body of the first general secretary of the Bulgarian Communist Party, who died in Moscow in 1949. His remains have been moved to the Central Cemetery, and there is talk of either converting the mausoleum into a museum or destroying it. It's not open to the public. ⊠ *Pl. Alexander Batenberg.*

⑭ **Narodno Subranie** (National Assembly). During the January 1997 uprising, CNN made this building famous by repeatedly broadcasting clips of Bulgarian protesters smashing and climbing through the windows and dragging the barricaded members of the Socialist parliament out into the plaza in a demand for new elections. On the western side of the building, you can still see damage from the uprising. Topped by the Bulgarian national flag, the squat, blocky building is adorned with an inscription reading "Unity makes strength," referring to the unification of the country in 1885, a few years after the defeat of the Turks. ⊠ *Bul. Tsar Osvoboditel at pl. Narodno Subranie.*

★ ④ **Natzionalen Archeologicheski Musei** (National Archaeological Museum). This museum is housed in the former Great Mosque. The 15th-century building itself is as fascinating as its contents, which illustrate the cultural history of the country up through the 19th century. ⊠ *Pl. Alexander Batenberg, behind the Sheraton Hotel,* ☎ *02/88–24–06.* ▦ *Free.* ☉ *Tues.–Sun. 10–noon and 2–6.*

⑯ **Natzionalen Dvoretz na Kulturata** (National Palace of Culture). This large modern building, filled with a complex of halls for conventions and cultural activities, is the main focus of **Yuzhen Park.** Its underpass, on several levels, is equipped with a tourist information office, shops, restaurants, discos, and a bowling alley. The park itself is a great place for people-watching. The section to the north is a favorite gathering spot for Sofia's youth, whizzing around on roller-blades, skateboards, bikes, and battery-operated minicars. ⊠ *Yuzhen Park, off bul. Vitosha,* ☎ *02/5–15–01.*

NEED A BREAK? | For an enormous Western-style cappuccino served in a soup bowl, apple pie with ice cream, or a slice of rich cheese cake with caramel sauce, try **Dvete Fucli** (⊠ 14, ul. Karnigradska), or "The Two Swanks," a tiny, homey café just off bulevard Vitosha.

⑩ **Natzionalen Etnografski Musei** (National Ethnographical Museum). Collections of costumes, handicrafts, and tools exhibited here in the former palace of the Bulgarian czar illustrate the rural lifestyle until the 19th century. ⊠ *1, pl. Alexander Batenberg,* ☎ *02/87–41–91.* ▦ *2,000 leva.* ☉ *Wed.–Sun. 10–noon and 1:30–5:30.*

② **Natzionalen Istoricheski Musei** (National History Museum). Priceless Thracian treasures, Roman mosaics, enameled jewelry from the First Bulgarian Kingdom, and glowing religious art that survived the years of Ottoman oppression vividly illustrate the art history of Bulgaria. Considered the most important museum in the city, it occupies the former Courts of Justice. The courts are due to return to this location as soon as a new home is found for the museum collection. ⊠ *2, bul. Vitosha,* ☎ *02/88–41–60.* ▦ *150 leva.* ☉ *Weekdays 9:30–4:30.*

⑨ **Natzionalna Hudozhestvena Galeria** (National Art Gallery). Here, in the west wing of the former royal palace, are paintings by the best Bulgarian artists as well as representative works—notably prints—from the various European schools. ⊠ *Pl. Alexander Batenberg,* ☎ *02/89–28–41.* ▦ *2,000 leva.* ☉ *Tues.–Sun. 10:30–6.*

③ **Rotonda Sveti Georgi** (Rotunda of St. George). These ancient remains are at the northeast side of ploshtad St. Nedelya, in the courtyard of the Sheraton Sofia Balkan Hotel. The rotunda was built in the 4th century as a Roman temple, destroyed by the Huns, rebuilt by Justinian, and turned into a mosque by the Turks before being restored as a church. Recent restoration has revealed medieval frescoes. It is not open to the public. ⊠ *Off pl. St. Nedelya.*

⑤ Tsentralnata Banya (The Central Baths). For years, this splendid building, once an Ottoman bathhouse, was left to disintegrate. Renovations began in 1997; at press time the baths were not yet open to the public, but visitors can taste the hot mineral water at the spring in the adjacent park. The building should be reopened in summer 1999. ⊠ *Bul. Maria Luiza at ul. Triyaditsa.*

⑦ Tsentralna Sofiiska Sinagoga (Sofia Synagogue). After decades of disrepair, the Moorish turrets and gilded domes of this 1909 synagogue have been beautifully restored. It is now one of the most spectacular buildings in downtown Sofia. ⊠ *Ul. Ekzarh Yosif and bul. Washington.* 🖼 *Free.* ☉ *Mon.–Fri. 9–5. Sat. open for services only.*

❶ Tzarkva Sveta Nedelya (St. Nedelya Church). This impressive church was built during 1856–1863. The structure was later altered by a Russian architect and, in 1925, was destroyed by terrorist action. The church was rebuilt in 1931. Today it's open to visitors, and services are held on Sunday. You may even get a peek at a bride—this is one of the most popular wedding spots in the city. ⊠ *Pl. Sveta Nedelya.* 🖼 *Free.* ☉ *Daily 7 AM–7 PM.*

⑫ Tzarkva Sveta Sofia (Church of St. Sofia). One of the oldest churches in the city, it dates to the 6th century, though excavations have uncovered the remains of even older structures on the site. Because of its great age and its simplicity, the church provides a dramatic contrast to the showy Alexander Nevski Memorial Cathedral nearby. While the church undergoes seemingly endless renovation, it's open to visitors, and services are held daily at 9:30 AM. ⊠ *Ul. Moskovska.* 🖼 *Free.* ☉ *Daily 9–1 and 2–5.*

⑪ Tzarkva Sveti Nikolai (Church of St. Nicholas). This small and very ornate Russian church—it has five gold-plated domes and a green spire—was erected in 1912–1914. Inside, mosaics depict favored Russian saints and czars. It's commonly called (surprise) the Russian Church. ⊠ *Bul. Tsar Osvoboditel.* 🖼 *Free.* ☉ *Daily 9–1 and 2–5.*

Dining

Near the influences of Western Europe and the Mediterranean as well as the Middle East, Sofia is a city teeming with exotic foods ranging from spicy Indian curries to Turkish *döner kebaps* (meat roasted on a spit). New restaurants and cafés offering high-quality but inexpensive cuisines from around the world are springing up everywhere. Still, for those who will brave the cigarette smoke and crowded seating for some local color, the most authentic and enjoyable experience is to be had in a *mehana* (tavern), where the music is loud, and Bulgarians relax for hours over rakia and traditional meals such as grilled pork sausages and french fries smothered in *cyrine,* a delicious variant of feta.

$$$$ ✕ **Krim.** This Russian restaurant serves the best beef Stroganoff in town and has a delectable caviar and lox platter that goes well with the superb selection of chilled vodkas. ⊠ *17, ul. Slavyanska,* ☎ *02/87–01–31. No credit cards.*

$$$$ ✕ **Nad Aleyata, Zad Shkafut.** In an old brick house, this small, casually elegant restaurant serves innovative Bulgarian and European cuisine. You can find such Bulgarian staples as *chushky biorek* (a pepper stuffed with cheese and deep-fried), as well as international offerings such as veal medallions and chicken Kiev. Popular with local diplomats, the restaurant has a large selection of salads and an excellent wine list, and the staff is accustomed to serving foreigners. ✉ *31, ul. Budapeshta,* ☎ *02/83–55–81. Reservations essential. No credit cards.*

$$$$ ✕ **33 Stoli.** Classy and intimate, this candlelit cellar has a changing menu specializing in European cuisine such as frogs' legs and Swiss fondue. The wine list is thorough, and the dessert tray is mouthwatering—try the *shokolade palachinka sus presni plodove* (chocolate crepe with fresh fruit). And yes, there really are only 33 *stoli* (chairs). ✉ *14, ul. Assen Zlatarov,* ☎ *02/44–29–81. Reservations essential. No credit cards.*

$$$ ✕ **Bai Gencho.** A favorite with Sofians, this traditional mehana provides the classic tavern experience with the added elegance of candles and a warm fireplace. The chef's specialty for two, *etspetsialitet na gotvachka za dvama* (mixed grill of sausages, steak, and shish kebabs), is a carnivore's dream. ✉ *ul. Kniaz Alexander Dondukov 15,* ☎ *02/81–74–54. Reservations essential. No credit cards.*

$$$ ✕ **Golden Dragon.** This small Shanghai restaurant near the opera house has attracted faithful regulars for years with its spicy dumplings and informal, friendly atmosphere. Don't expect a "No MSG" promise on the menu, but do expect tasty food and fast service. ✉ *166A, ul. Rakovski,* ☎ *02/88–80–30. No credit cards.*

$$$ ✕ **La Gondola Vinarna.** In a cellar just off bulevard Vitosha, this
★ *vinarna* (wine-tasting house) is the best place in the city for wine connoisseurs. The wine list includes all the outstanding bottled domestics, as well as towering carafes of excellent reds. Fill your plate (priced by weight after you've made your selections) from a buffet table laden with traditional salads and starters, such as *shopska salata,* exceptionally good *banitsa* (filo pastry filled with feta cheese and sometimes spinach), and *kiopolu* (puree of eggplant and tomatoes); if it's in season, don't miss the *tikvichki sus kiselo mlyako* (fried squash in yogurt). A pizzeria upstairs has the same wine selection but a less-expensive Italian menu. ✉ *16, bul. Vitosha,* ☎ *02/980–9493. No credit cards.*

$$$ ✕ **Mexicano (Casa del Arquitecto).** The menu is an odd couple of pseudo-Mexican and traditional Bulgarian fare; unless you're tempted by the off-kilter "burritos" with fillings like cabbage or white beans, you're better off with the Bulgarian choices, like the spicy moussaka. In summer, the beautiful candlelit patio—where guests dine outdoors under gigantic white umbrellas and a canopy of leaves—makes the inflated prices and snobby service more tolerable. ✉ *11, ul. Krakra,* ☎ *02/44–65–98 or 02/44–17–24. No credit cards.*

$$ ✕ **Art Club Lucky.** A trendy café and prominent Mafia hangout, this restaurant serves excellent pizzas, quiches, salads, and sandwiches, as well as a great selection of desserts and ice cream. Bright windows facing lively ulitsa Tsar Shishman make it an ideal spot for a daytime cappuccino and people-watching. ✉ *38, ul. Gurko,* ☎ *02/980–77–12. No credit cards.*

$$ ✕ **Baalbeck.** Though somewhat seedy looking, this Middle Eastern restaurant just off central ploshtad Slaveikov is favored by local businesspeople for its fast lunches of tasty falafel, hummus, and tabouleh. Sit downstairs for a quick bite from the bar, or dine upstairs if you want a fork and knife served with your *döner kebap* (spit-roasted meat). ✉ *6, Vasil Levski,* ☎ *no phone. No credit cards.*

Lodging

The following hotels maintain a high standard of cleanliness and are open year-round unless otherwise stated. Those on the higher end of the price range are comparable to luxury hotels in Western Europe, while those at the lower end will give you a taste of Bulgaria's Communist past with drab decor and the possibilities of faulty electricity and plumbing. If you want help finding a room, **Balkantourist** (✉ 1, bul. Vitosha, ☎ 02/87–51–92) can book you in a state-owned hotel.

$$$$ 🏨 **Castle Hotel Hrankov.** Escape the city to this 1996 luxury hotel 10
★ km (6 mi) from the city center in the suburban Dragalavci district, at the foot of Mt. Vitosha. Not only the most attractive and progressive hotel in Sofia, it also has the best fitness facilities; besides the squash and tennis courts and an Olympic-size swimming pool, it rents skis and has shuttles to the slopes. It's not exactly an authentic castle, but the turrets, gardens, and nighttime lighting make it a good facsimile. ✉ 53, Krusheva Gradina, Dragalevtsi 1415, ☎ 02/91–909, FAX 02/67–29–85. 360 rooms. 4 restaurants, pool, 2 tennis courts, squash, nightclub, casino. AE, DC, MC, V.

$$$$ 🏨 **Hotel Kempinski Zografski–Sofia.** Acquired in 1997 by the eminent
★ Kempinksi hotel chain, the former Inter-Continental is now a large, luxurious hotel whose large rooms have views of Mt. Vitosha. With audiovisual and simultaneous-translation facilities available, it is a prime option for business conferences. The hotel also has the most expensive restaurant in the entire country, Sakura, Bulgaria's one and only spot for sushi. ✉ 100, bul. James Bourchier, 1407, ☎ 02/68–32–51, FAX 02/68–12–25. 454 rooms. 5 restaurants, bar, minibars, room service, pool, finess center, shops, casino. AE, DC, MC, V.

$$$$ 🏨 **Sheraton Sofia Hotel Balkan.** The former Grand Hotel Balkan is a
★ first-class hotel with a central location that is hard to match. The building is a typically Socialist box, but the rooms are smooth, with large bathrooms. ✉ 5, pl. St. Nedelya, 1000, ☎ 02/981–65–41, FAX 02/980–64–64. 187 rooms. 3 restaurants, 3 bars, minibars, room service, exercise room, casino. AE, DC, MC, V.

$$$ 🏨 **Hotel Maria Luiza.** The closest thing Sofia has to a modern yet cozy bed-and-breakfast, this upscale private hotel has very bright, comfortable rooms; business facilities; an excellent downtown location with views of Banya Bashi Mosque and the Central Baths; and a friendly staff. ✉ 29, bul. Maria Luiza, 1000, ☎ 02/9–10–44, FAX 02/980–33–55. 21 rooms with bath or shower. Restaurant, bar, minibars, room service. AE, DC, MC, V.

$$$ 🏨 **Novotel Europa.** This member of the French Novotel chain is on one of Sofia's main boulevards, near the train station, and not far from the center of the city. Large, modern, but impersonal, it is better for business than for tourism. ✉ 131, bul. Maria Luiza, 1202, ☎ 02/3–12–61, FAX 02/32–00–11. 600 rooms. 2 restaurants, 2 bars, room service, exercise room, casino, meeting rooms. AE, DC, MC, V.

$$ 🏨 **Bulgaria.** Despite its central location, this small hotel is quiet and old-fashioned. The interior, with its marble staircase, arched windows, and low, wooden beds and lace curtains in the guest rooms, is charming. ✉ 4, bul. Tsar Osvoboditel, 1000, ☎ 02/87–19–77 or 02/87–01–91, FAX 02/88–41–77. 85 rooms with bath or shower. Restaurant, bar, café. No credit cards.

$$ 🏨 **Grand Hotel Sofia.** Just south of the Tsar Liberator monument, this central, five-story Interhotel, though comfortable and intimate, is a throwback to the Communist 1980s. The suites are quite modern, with separate offices, but in a standard room you may well be sleeping under a garish plaid coverlet. Try to nab a room in the front, where there are great views of the National Assembly. The retro '70s basement nightclub hosts amateur beauty contests with titles such as "Beauties of Bulgaria" and "Miss Striptease." ✉ 4, pl. Narodno Subranie, 1000, ☎ 02/87–88–21, FAX 02/88–13–08. 106 rooms. 2 restaurants, 2 bars, minibars, room service, exercise room. AE, DC, MC, V.

$$ 🏨 **Rila.** A central downtown location makes this a low-cost, if aesthetically challenged, alternative to the nearby Sheraton (☞ above).

Rooms are a bit garish, with red-and-orange color schemes, but the hotel does have all the essential facilities. Contemporary Bulgarian paintings (for sale) hang in the lobby. ⊠ 6, *ul. Kaloyan, 1000,* ☎ *02/980–88–65,* FAX *02/981–33–86. 138 rooms with bath or shower. Restaurant, bar, café, exercise room, casino. AE, DC, MC, V.*

$$ 🏨 **Serdika.** Centrally located in the University district, this clean and comfortable hotel is the place to stay if you're looking for a fun location—but not a quiet one. One of the city's best cinemas is right downstairs, and one of the newest and trendiest nightclubs, the Tequila Bar, is next door. Ask for one of the newer rooms, which have enclosed shower stalls (the rest have the open-shower setup). ⊠ *2, bul. Yanko Sakazov,* ☎ *02/44–34–11,* FAX *02/46–52–96. 140 rooms. Restaurant, bar, café. DC, MC, V.*

$$ 🏨 **Sun Hotel.** Cozy and comparatively inexpensive due to its lively but marginal neighborhood, this private hotel offers small but comfortable rooms in a beautiful old building with a cheerful, yellow facade scored with tiny wrought-iron balconies. Be alert outside: The Sun is directly across from the Luvov Most (Lion's Bridge), Sofia's most notorious red-light district and a prime area for pickpocketing. ⊠ *89, bul. Maria Luiza, 1000,* ☎ *02/83–36–70,* FAX *02/83–53–89. 16 rooms with bath or shower. Restaurant, bar, room service. No credit cards.*

Nightlife and the Arts

Nightlife

In a city that only a few years ago had just one discotèque, there is now a dizzying array of nightlife choices. Like the residents of neighboring Greece, Bulgarians love all-hours Mediterranean-style dance clubs. New nightspots are opening up every week, so consult the English-language **"Sofia City Guide,"** available at tourist agencies and the Sofia Sheraton, to find out about current hot spots. Upscale establishments are generally Mafia hangouts (unlike many Bulgarians, they have money to burn), but they are not a threat to tourists.

BARS AND NIGHTCLUBS

For live music, **Swingin' Hall** (⊠ 8, bul. Dragan Tsankov, ☎ 02/66–63–23), one of the first "Western" clubs to open in the city, is still a popular spot, though the bands most often play cover tunes of '80s heavy metal. **La Strada Jazz Club** (⊠ 4, ul. 6 na Septemvri, ☎ no phone) draws a sophisticated, arty clientele for jazz, blues, and modern alternative rock. The **703 Club** (⊠ 38B, ul. Gurko, at ul. Tsar Shishman, ☎ 02/981–97–75) is a contemporary bar with a trendy twentysomething crowd. If you can't find a seat, try one of the adjacent bars on the street, which is one of the best in the city for pub-crawling. The **Blaze Club** (⊠ 27, ul. Slavianska, ☎ 02/899–813), an acid jazz café by day, fills with trance music and dim lighting by night.

DISCOS

Neron (⊠ 1, pl. Bulgaria, ☎ 02/80–34–38), in the National Palace of Culture, is a flashy, mammoth, all-age underground disco popular with local Mafia. Metal detectors screen for guns as you enter, and you must check your mobile phone with your coat.

Spartacus (⊠ In the underpass at the junction of bul. Vasil Levski and bul. Tsar Osvoboditel, in front of Sofia University) is Sofia's first gay club, attracting the city's avant-garde, both gay and straight.

Aliby 2 (⊠ Yuzhen Park, ☎ no phone), wintertime sister disco to the favorite summer outdoor nightspot **Aliby 1** (⊠ Borisova Gradina, ☎ no phone), is the newest and hippest club. A college crowd gathers under the enormous tent for a carnival atmosphere and electronic music. Aliby

1 is open from June to mid-September, while Aliby 2 is open the rest of the year. One of the city's most chic and expensive discos, **Chervilo** (✉ 5, bul. Tsar Osvoboditel, just off ploshtad Narodno Subranie), or "Lipstick," draws Sofia's well-to-do twenty- and thirtysomethings. (When taking a cab, just tell the driver the disco's name.) In the smaller room, Sofia's best DJs take turns playing acid jazz and house music, and in the larger room, crowds dance to Euro-techno.

The Arts

The standard of music in Bulgaria is high, whether it takes the form of operatic, symphonic, or folk music, and it has started to attract international audiences with its close harmonies and colorful stage displays. Contact **Balkantourist** (Concert Office; ✉ 2, bul. Tsar Osvoboditel, ☎ 02/87–15–88) for general information.

Sofiska Durjhavna Opera (The Sofia National Opera and Ballet; ✉ 1, ul. Vrabcha, ☎ 02/987–7011) has excellent performances; stop by the box office (✉ 30, bul. Dondukov, ☎ 02/87–13–66) for a program.

You don't need to understand Bulgarian to enjoy a performance at the **Kuklen Teatur** (Central Puppet Theater; ✉ 14, ul. Gen. Gurko, ☎ 02/87–38–15), or the **Natsionalen Ensemble za Narodni Tantsi y Pesni** (National Folk Ensemble; check with Balkantourist [☞ Visitor Information in Sofia A to Z , *below*] for details).

Sofia seems to have a movie theater on nearly every street. All but a handful of out-of-the-way art-house theaters show recent foreign films in their original languages with Bulgarian subtitles. However, the only theaters where you will find comfortable seating and good sound systems are the **Serdika** (✉ 42, ul. Vasil Levski, directly across from the Levski monument, ☎ 02/43–17–97), **Modernun** (✉ 26, bul. Maria Luiza, ☎ 02/ 87–56–46), and **Dom Na Kinoto** (✉ 37, ul. Ekzarh Yosif, ☎ 02/88–06–76). Other theaters tend to have stiff wooden chairs and ripped screens.

Shopping

Department Stores

Sofia's biggest department store is the **Tsentralen Universalen Magazin** (Central Department Store; ✉ 2, bul. Knyaginya Maria-Luiza, ☎ 02/987–96–21), called TSUM for short. Here you'll find everything from cosmetics to furniture and gardening tools.

Gift and Souvenir Shops

There are good selections of arts and crafts at the shop of the **Union of Bulgarian Artists** (✉ 6, ul. Shipka), including ceramics and woodwork. The **Bulgarian Folk Art Shop** (✉ 14, bul. Vitosha) is a bit more expensive than the Union of Bulgarian Artists; besides crafts, there are traditional musical instruments and folk costumes. For more casual souvenirs, such as lace and T-shirts with Cyrillic logos, try **Sredec** (✉ 7, ul. Lege); **Prizma Store** (✉ 2, bul. Tsar Osvoboditel) is another source.

For recordings of Bulgarian music, go to the basement labyrinth market underneath the **National Palace of Culture** (☞ Exploring, *above*).

Markets

The quintessential shopping excursion in Sofia is to its outdoor produce and crafts markets. The most exotic and entertaining of these is the **Zhenski Pazaar** (Women's Market; ✉ ul. Stefan Stambolov, between ul. Tsar Simeon and bul. Slivnitsa), named for the swarms of women from neighboring villages who commute in daily to hawk everything from homemade brooms and lace to produce and used electronic equipment. With all the sights and sounds of bartering—sometimes a little overwhelming—the Zhenski Pazaar can give you a feel of the Middle East. Be wary of pickpockets.

One of the most popular crafts and souvenir-stall markets is **Nevski Pazaar,** just west of the Nevski Cathedral, where you can find everything from antique Greek coins to original icon paintings and old Russian whiskey flasks emblazoned with hammers and sickles. A little less touristy and slightly less pricey are the stalls in the underpass that runs under bulevard Vitosha just north of ploshtad Sveta Nedelya at ulitsa Trapezitsa, between the Sheraton and Central Department Store; here, the shopkeepers sell handmade lace, knitted sweaters and caps, and a variety of jewelry—new silver, as well as old Turkish jewelry.

Sofia A to Z

Arriving and Departing

BY CAR

From Serbia, the main routes are E80, going through the border checkpoint at Kalotina on the Niš–Sofia road, or E871, going through the checkpoint at Gyueshevo. From Greece, take E79, passing through the checkpoint at Kulata; from Turkey, take E80, passing through checkpoint Kapitan–Andreevo. Border crossings to Romania are at Vidin on E79 and at Ruse on E97 and E85.

BY PLANE

All international flights arrive at **Sofia Airport.** For information on international flights, call 02/79–80–35 or 02/72–06–72; for domestic flights, 02/72–24–14 or 02/79–32–21–16.

Between the Airport and Downtown: Bus 84 serves the airport, but it is crowded and impractical if you have a lot of luggage. The fare for taxis taken from the airport taxi stand is a flat fee of $20 (you can pay in dollars or the equivalent in leva) for the 10-km (6-mi) ride into Sofia. A much more affordable option (if you have local currency, can speak a little Bulgarian, and know where you're going) is an unofficial taxi from outside the airport doors, which will get you to the center of town for around 12,000 leva, less than half of what the official taxis charge. Be sure to agree on the fare before starting off.

BY TRAIN

The **Tsentralna Gara** (central station; ☎ 02/3–11–11 or 02/843–33–33) is at the northern edge of the city. The ticket offices in Sofia are in the underpass of the **National Palace of Culture** (✉ 1, pl. Bulgaria, ☎ 02/59–01–36) and at the **Rila International Travel Agency** (✉ 5, ul. Gen. Gurko, ☎ 02/87–07–77 or 02/87–59–35). There is a taxi stand at the station.

Getting Around

The main sights are centrally located, so the best way to see the city is on foot.

BY BUS

Buses, trolleys, and trams run quite frequently—between every five and 20 minutes. Buy a ticket (a single fare is 200 leva) from the ticket stand near the tram or trolley car and stop and punch it into the machine as you board (watch how the person in front of you does it). You can also pay the driver. Persons traveling with baggage or large backpacks are required by law to have both a ticket for themselves *and* a ticket for their baggage. If you or your bag is caught without a ticket, an on-the-spot fine of 2,000 leva will be issued. Trams and trolleys tend to get crowded, so keep an eye on your belongings and be alert at all times. The tourist information offices have full details of routes and times.

BY CAR

If you're staying near the city center, there's really no need for a car. Besides, driving in Sofia is no easy task—traffic is heavy and there are potholes everywhere.

BY TAXI

Daytime taxi rates are 300 leva per 1 km (½ mi), and 400 leva per km (after 10 PM. The most reliable way to get a taxi is to order it by phone; if you hail one on the street, make sure it is a company taxi with a phone number listed on the door. Some reputable taxi companies are **Taxi Plus** (☎ 1282); **Taxi Express** (☎ 1280); **Okay Taxi** (☎ 2121); and **Inex Taxi** (☎ 91919). To tip, round out the fare 5%–10%.

Contacts and Resources

B&B RESERVATION AGENCIES

Staying in private homes is becoming a popular alternative to hotels as a means of not only cutting costs but offering increased contact with Bulgarians. Some private homes offer bed-and-breakfast or bed only; some provide full board. In Sofia, contact **Balkantourist** (☞ Visitor Information, *below*).

CAR RENTALS

Eurodollar operates out of the Hotel Kempinski Zografski (⊠ 100, bul. James Bourchier, ☎ 02/68–32–51). **Avis** offices are downtown in the Sheraton Sofia Hotel (⊠ 5, pl. St. Nedelya, ☎ 02/988–81–67), and at the Sofia Airport (☎ 02/73–80–23). **Hertz** has a central reservation line (☎ 02/980–04–61) and an office at the airport (☎ 02/79–14–77). You can hire a car with a driver through **Balkantour** (⊠ 27, bul. Stamboliiski, ☎ 02/988–55–43) or through **Balkantourist** (⊠ 1, bul. Vitosha, ☎ 02/87–51–92).

EMBASSIES

United States (⊠ 1, ul. Suborna, ☎ 02/980–5241); consulate (⊠ 1, ul. Kapitan Andreev, ☎ 02/963–2022). **United Kingdom** (⊠ 38, bul. Levski, ☎ 02/980–1220). Canadians, Australians, and New Zealanders are on their own; they're normally referred to the British or American consulates.

EMERGENCIES

Ambulance (☎ 150). **Doctor:** Clinic for Foreign Citizens (⊠ 1, ul. Eugeni Pavlovski , Mladost 1, ☎ 02/75–361). **Fire** (☎ 160). **Pirogov Emergency Hospital** (☎ 02/5–15–31). **Police:** Sofia City Constabulary (☎ 166). **Pharmacies** (☎ 178 for information about all-night pharmacies).

GUIDED TOURS

Balkantourist (☞ Visitor Information, *below*) organizes all kinds of tours, from guided orientation tours of Sofia and environs, to various evening tours, such as a night out eating local food and watching folk dances or an evening at the National Opera, to over 20 types of special-interest tours (monasteries, spas, sports, etc.) of various lengths, using Sofia as the point of departure.

Visitor Information

Balkantourist (Head Office: ⊠ 1, bul. Vitosha , ☎ 02/43–331) is a travel agency as well as an information office, with offices in most major hotels. Also contact **Balkantour** (⊠ 27, bul. Stambolijski, ☎ 02/988–55–43), **Jamadvice** (⊠ 10, ul. Assen Zlatarov, ☎ 02/44–15–20), **Wagonlit Travel** (⊠ 10, ul. Legue, ☎ 02/980–81–26), or **Green Travel Agency** (⊠ 25, ul. Patriarh Evtimii, ☎ 02/981–4274, FAX 02/981–4275).

SIDE TRIPS FROM SOFIA

Boyana

10 km (6 mi) south of the city center. Hire a taxi or take Tram 19 from ulitsa Graf Ignatiev in central Sofia to the southwestern part of Sofia, where you can catch Bus 63 or 64. The trip takes less than an hour.

At the foot of Mt. Vitosha, this settlement was a medieval fortress near the beginning of the 11th century. Today it is one of Sofia's wealthiest residential neighborhoods. In this area is one of Bulgaria's most precious monuments, the tiny, medieval **Tzarkvata Boyana** (Boyana Church). Dating back to the 13th century, it is a historical treasure on UNESCO's World Heritage list for preservation. Unfortunately at press time it was closed for restoration (and will be for at least a decade), but a replica, complete with copies of the exquisite 13th-century frescoes, is open to visitors. This is usually a tour destination, but if you're coming by car, follow ulitsa Alexander Pushkin uphill until you can turn uphill onto ulitsa Sveti Kaloian, which branches out to ulitsa Brezovitsa. This will take you to ulitsa Boyansko Ezero, where you'll have to hike up the mountain to the church from the trail head. ▨ *Replica: 10,000 leva.* ☉ *June–Aug. Thurs.–Sun. 9–1 and 2–5; Sept.–May weekends 10–1 and 2–5.*

Dining

$$$ ✕ **Boyansko Khanche.** Local and national specialties are served in a typical Bulgarian setting with live folk music. ▨ *10, ul. Boyansko Ezero, near Boyana Church,* ☎ *02/56–30–16. AE, DC, MC, V.*

$$$ ✕ **Chepishev.** You can try Bulgarian specialties and listen to live folk music at this traditional Bulgarian *kurtchma* (tavern). ▨ *23, ul. Kumata, Boyana,* ☎ *02/55–08–88. No credit cards.*

Dragalevci

Hire a taxi or take Tram 19 from ulitsa Graf Ignatievto in central Sofia to the last stop, and switch to the Dragalevci Bus 63. You can also take Bus 66 or 93 from Hladilnika.

Picturesquely sprawled across the lower part of Mt. Vitosha, this was a slow-paced village just a few years ago. Today, it has been built up with modern homes and absorbed by the city, making it more or less a quiet suburb of Sofia.

In the woods above the village is the nearby **Dragalevci Monastir** (Dragalevci Monastery). It's currently a convent, but you can visit the 14th-century church with its outdoor frescoes. You can hike to the church from the Dragalevci bus stop (about 1½ km/1mi), or, to get there from downtown Sofia, take bus 64 or 93 from the Hladilnika bus station. ☉ *Thurs.–Sun. 10–6.*

A chairlift ride or two will give you stunning views of the area. The lift on ulitsa Panorama in Dragalevci takes you up to the Aleko resort; it costs 6,500 leva and runs from 8 to 5. From the terminus, walk over to the next chairlift to head farther up to the top of Malak Rezen. There are well-marked walking and ski trails in the area.

Dining

$$ ✕ **Vodenicharski Mehani.** Appropriately enough, the "Miller's Tavern" is made up of three old mills linked together. A folklore show and a menu of Bulgarian specialties give it a tourist-friendly but authentic atmosphere. Try the *gyuvech* (potatoes, tomatoes, peas, and onions baked in an earthenware pan). ▨ *ul. Panorama, at southern end of town next to chairlift,* ☎ *02/67–10–21 or 02/67–10–01. No credit cards.*

THE BLACK SEA GOLDEN COAST

The Black Sea, contrary to its name, is a brilliant blue and is warm and calm most of the time. Its sunny, sandy beaches are backed by the easternmost slopes of the Balkan range and by the Strandja Mountains. Although the tourist centers tend to be huge state-built complexes with a somewhat lean feel, they have modern amenities; and you can always escape them by heading to nearby fishing villages with traditional taverns, Roman and Byzantine ruins, and peaceful swimming coves. Slânčev Brjag (often referred to by its English name, Sunny Beach), the largest of the resorts, has plenty of children's amusements and play areas and is only a few minutes from Nesebâr, one of the most historic and tranquil small towns on the coast.

Begin your exploration of the southern Black Sea coast, famous for its sheltered bays and cliffs, in the industrial port of Burgas. From Burgas, you can visit the fishing villages of Nesebâr (with Sunny Beach), Sozopol, and Djuni. Lodgings tend to be scarce in these villages, so private accommodations, arranged on the spot or through Balkantourist, are a good option. Whatever resort you choose, all offer facilities for water sports.

Varna

470 km (282 mi) east of Sofia. It's easily reached by rail (about 7½ hours by express) or by road from the capital.

The ancient city of Varna, named Odyssos by the Greeks, became a major Roman trading center and is now an important shipbuilding and industrial city. With its beaches and tourism, Varna has a cosmopolitan flair, cultivated with events such as a yearly international film festival held in August. Though it is the third-largest city in Bulgaria, its older parts still possess a small-town charm. With wide, tree-lined boulevards, numerous gardens and parks, and a beachfront boardwalk, Varna is easily accessible to pedestrians. If you plan to drive from Sofia to Varna, allow time to see the **Pobiti Kammani** (Stone Forest) just off the Sofia–Varna road between Devnya and Varna. The unexpected groups of monumental sandstone pillars are thought to have been formed when the area was the bed of the Lutsian Sea.

The **Natsionalen Istoricheski Musei** (Museum of Art and History) is one of the great—if lesser known—museums of Europe. The splendid collection includes the world's oldest gold treasures, from the Varna necropolis of the 4th millennium BC, discovered in 1972, as well as Thracian, Greek, and Roman treasures and richly painted icons. ⊠ *On the corner of bul. Dimitar Blagoev and bul. Slivnitsa,* ☎ *052/23–70–57.* ◷ *Tues.–Sat. 10–5.*

Near the northeastern end of bulevard Osmi Primorski Polk are numerous shops and cafés; the same street leads west to ploshtad Mitropolit Simeon and the **Tsentralnata Tzarkva** (cathedral), built in 1880–1886. Take a look inside at the lavish murals. ☎ *No phone.* ⊡ *Free.* ◷ *Daily 7–6.*

Running north from the cathedral is ulitsa Vladislav Varnenchik, with shops, movie theaters, and eateries. Opposite the cathedral, in the Grada Gradina (City Gardens), is the 19th century **Starata Chasovnikuh Kula** (Old Clock Tower). In the very city center on the south side of the City Gardens and on ploshtad Nezavisimost stands **Natsionlana Teatur Stoyan Buchvarov** (Stoyan Buchvarov National Theater), a magnificent Baroque building. The theater was founded in 1921 and showcased some of Bulgaria's greatest actors.

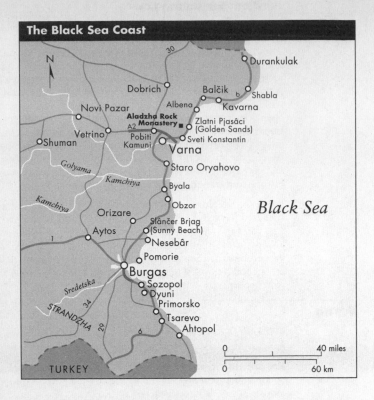

The Black Sea Coast

Durankulak

Dobrich · Balčik · Shabla
Albena · Kavarna
Novi Pazar
Aladzha Rock · Zlatni Pjasâci
Monastery · (Golden Sands)
A2
Vetrino · Pobiti · Sveti Konstantin
Shuman · Kamuni · **Varna**
Golyama
Staro Oryahovo
Kamchiya
Byala
Kamchiya
Orizare · Obzor
Aytos · Slânčer Brjag · ***Black Sea***
(Sunny Beach)
Nesebâr
1
Pomorie
Burgas
Sredetska · Sozopol
Dyuni
Primorsko
Tsarevo
Ahtopol
STRANDZHA
TURKEY

0 ___ 40 miles
0 ___ 60 km

On the corner of bulevard Knyaz Boris I and ulitsa Shipka you will see
the remains of the **Rimskata Stena** (Roman Fortress Wall) of Odyssos.
Bulevard Knyaz Boris I is another of Varna's shopping streets where
you can buy handcrafted souvenirs.

If you walk south along ulitsa Odessos to ulitsa Han Krum you will
find the remains of the **Roman Thermae.** These public baths dating from
the 2nd to the 3rd century AD are among the largest and most substantial
Roman ruins in Bulgaria. The site is now a hands-on museum, and visitors are free to wander among the ruins. ⊠ *1, ul. Han Krum,* ☎ *no
phone.* ☑ *2,000 leva.*

If you follow bulevard Primorski with the sea on your right, you will
reach the **Morski Musei** (Naval Museum), with its displays of the early
days of navigation on the Black Sea and the Danube. ⊠ *Graf Ignatiev
and bul. Primorski, just inside the park entrance,* ☎ *052/22–26–55.*
⊙ *Weekdays 8–5.*

⟳ From the extensive and luxuriant **Morska Gradina** (Seaside Gardens),
you can catch a great view over the bay. There are restaurants, an open-
air theater, and a fascinating astronomy complex with a natural science museum, an observatory, and a **planetarium.** ⊠ *Off Graf Ignatiev,
inside Primorski Park, just outside the entrance to the municipal beach,*
☎ *052/22–28–90.*

Dining and Lodging

$$$ ✕ **Bistro Rimski Termi.** Nestled in a quiet, private courtyard between
the port and the ruins of the Roman baths, this intimate mehana serves
well-prepared Bulgarian cuisine in a romantic tavern setting. Between
November and March it is prone to odd hours, but if you find it
closed, you can pick from the many similar-style restaurants that fill

the square around the Roman baths. ⊠ *4, ul. 8 na Noemvri,* ☎ *052/ 22–95–73.*

$$ ✕ **Horizont.** This restaurant in Morska Gradina has a good selection of seafood as well as a view of the Black Sea from its outside tables. It's not too busy during the day, but at night the live Greek music draws a crowd that dances between courses and stays long after the food is finished. ⊠ *Morska Gradina, just inside the main entrance to the park,* ☎ *052/88–45–30. No credit cards.*

$$ ✕ **Orbita.** This cheap hole-in-the-wall is extremely popular with the locals, who come here for the lentil soup, grilled kebabs with potatoes, and Bulgarian sausage in a pot. ⊠ *Hotel Orbita, 25, Tsar Osvoboditel, off Knyaz Boris I ,* ☎ *052/22–52–75. No credit cards.*

$$$ 🏨 **Černo More.** One of the best things about this modern Interhotel,
★   on the city's main drag leading to the beach, is the panoramic view from its 22nd floor. Rooms are somewhat sparse, though decorated with ocean-themed paintings. ⊠ *33, bul. Slivnitza Blvd.,* ☎ *052/23– 21–15 or 052/25–30–91. 230 rooms with bath or shower. 3 restaurants, bar, outdoor café, nightclub. AE, DC, MC, V.*

Sveti Konstantin

8 km (5 mi) north along the coast from Varna.

Sveti Konstantin, Bulgaria's oldest Black Sea resort, is small and intimate, spreading through a wooded park near a series of sandy coves.

Dining and Lodging

$$$ ✕ **Bulgarska Svatba.** This folky restaurant is on the outskirts of the resort; charcoal-grilled meats are especially recommended. In winter, try to reserve a table by the large wood-burning fire, where you will have an excellent view of the entertainment. ⊠ *Sveti Konstantin Resort,* ☎ *052/36–12–83. No credit cards.*

$$ ✕ **Manastirska Izba.** This eatery is modest but pleasant, with a sunny terrace. Try the meatball and shopska salad. ⊠ *Sveti Konstantin Resort,* ☎ *052/36–20–36. No credit cards.*

$$$$ 🏨 **Grand Hotel Varna.** This Swedish-built hotel has a reputation for
★   being the best hotel on the coast. It is only 150 yards from the beach and offers a wide range of hydrotherapeutic treatments featuring the area's natural warm mineral springs. Yearly upgrades enable the Varna to keep pace with brand-new hotels, but the luxury comes at a cost: It is no longer an inexpensive secret. ⊠ *Sveti Konstantin Resort,* ☎ *052/36–14–91,* 📠 *052/36–19–20. 325 rooms with bath. 3 restaurants, 6 bars, coffee shop, 1 indoor pool, 2 outdoor pools, 2 tennis courts, bowling, health club, squash, nightclub. AE, DC, MC, V.*

$$ 🏨 **Čajka.** Čajka means "seagull" in Bulgarian, and this hotel has a bird's-eye view of the entire resort from its perch above the northern end of the beach. ⊠ *Sveti Konstantin Resort,* ☎ *052/36–13–32. 130 rooms. No credit cards.*

Zlatni Pjasâci

8 km (5 mi) north of Sveti Konstantin.

In contrast to the sedate atmosphere of Sveti Konstantin, Zlatni Pjasâci (Golden Sands) is lively, with extensive leisure-time amenities, mineral-spring medical centers, and sports and entertainment facilities. Just over 4 km (2½ mi) inland from Zlatni Pjasâci is **Aladja Monastir** (Aladja Rock Monastery), one of Bulgaria's oldest, cut out of the cliff face and made accessible to visitors by sturdy iron stairways. To get there, take a minibus from the Zlatni Pjasâci bus terminal; it makes a run every two hours.

Albena

10 km (6 mi) north of Zlatni Pjasâci.

Albena, a 1970s resort, is between Balčik and Golden Sands. It is well known for its long, wide beach and clean sea. The contemporary conveniences come with only a minimal dose of local charm, inflated prices, and menus and street signs in German and Russian.

Dining and Lodging

$$ ✗ **Bambuka** (Bamboo Tree). This open-air restaurant serves seafood as well as international and Bulgarian fare. The *purzheni calamari sus chesun sos* (fried squid with garlic yogurt dip) is one of the best appetizers on the menu. ⊠ *Albena Resort,* ☎ *05722/24–04. No credit cards.*

$$ 🏨 **Dobrudja Hotel.** Albena's most luxurious hotel is large and comfortable, with a mineral-water health spa where you can relax in healing mud, enjoy a massage, or indulge in a curative bath. ⊠ *Albena Resort,* ☎ *05722/20–20,* ℻ *05722/22–16. 272 rooms with bath. 3 restaurants, 2 bars, coffee shops, 1 indoor pool, 1 outdoor pool, spa, exercise room. DC, MC, V.*

Balčik

35 km (22 mi) north of Sveti Konstantin, 8 km (5 mi) north of Albena.

Part of Romania until just before World War II, Balčik is now a relaxed haven for Bulgaria's writers, artists, and scientists. On its white cliffs are crescent-shape tiers populated with houses. Among them is the **Dvoretsa Balchik** (Balčik Palace), once the grand summer getaway for Romania's Queen Marie and her six children. Surrounding the palace are the beautiful **Botanicheska Gradina v Balchik** (Botanical Gardens), dotted with curious buildings, terraces overlooking the sea, and a small Byzantine-style church where the late Marie's heart was encased in a jewel-encrusted box. Her remains were returned to Romania when Bulgaria reclaimed the region during World War II. 🎫 *Free.* ☉ *Church: Tues.–Sun. 9–5; gardens daily 9–9.*

Slânčev Brjag

95 km (60 mi) south of Varna, 140 km (87½ mi) south of Balčik.

The enormous Slânčev Brjag (Sunny Beach) is especially popular with families because of its safe beaches, gentle tides, and playgrounds for children. During the summer there are kindergartens for young vacationers, children's concerts, and even a children's disco. Slânčev Brjag has come a long way since those immediately post-Communist years, but it remains a vast concrete expanse of eyesore architecture looming over a world-class beach. Overrun with tourists from Northern Europe, even the beachside restaurants serve more German schnitzel than Bulgarian shopska salata. Most people either love it or hate it.

Dining and Lodging

$$ ✗ **Hanska Šatra.** In the coastal hills behind the sea, this combination restaurant and nightclub has been built to resemble the tents of the Bulgarian rulers of old. It has entertainment well into the night. ⊠ *5 km (3 mi) west of Slânčev Brjag,* ☎ *0554/28–11. No credit cards.*

$ ✗ **Ribarska Hiza.** This lively beachside restaurant specializes in fish and has music until 1 AM. ⊠ *4, ul. Slanchev Brjag, northern end of Slânčev Brjag Resort,* ☎ *0554/21–86. No credit cards.*

$$ 🏨 **Globus.** Considered by many to be the best in the resort, this hotel
★ combines a central location with modern facilities. ⊠ *22, ul. Slânčev Brjag,* ☎ *0554/22–45 or 0554/20–18,* ℻ *0554/25–24 or 0554/29–*

21. *100 rooms with bath or shower. Restaurant, bar, coffee shop, indoor pool, exercise room. AE, DC, MC, V.*

$$ ⊞ **Kuban.** Near the center of the resort, this large establishment is just a short stroll from the beach. Worn flowered bedspreads and wicker coffee tables in the rooms spell out the casualness. ⊠ *Slânčev Brjag Resort,* ☎ *0554/23–09,* FAX *0554/25–24 or 0554/29–21. 216 rooms, most with bath or shower. 2 restaurants, 2 coffee shops. AE, DC, MC, V.*

$ ⊞ **Čajka.** Among the bargain hotels, the Čajka offers the best location—it's directly across from the best stretch of beach. ⊠ *8, ul. Slânčev Brjag,* ☎ *0554/23–08. 36 rooms, some with bath or shower. No credit cards.*

Nesebâr

5 km (3 mi) south of Slânčev Brjag (Sunny Beach) and accessible by regular excursion buses.

Just 10 minutes south of Slânčev Brjag (Sunny Beach) is a painter's and poet's retreat. Founded by the Greeks 25 centuries ago on a rocky peninsula reached by a narrow causeway, this ancient settlement exudes an aura of its past. Among its vine-covered houses are beautiful Byzantine ruins, richly decorated medieval churches, crumbling Ottoman bathhouses, and wooden National Revival homes. Quaint though not undiscovered, Nesebâr is densely packed with outdoor art markets, galleries, and ocean-terrace cafés where fried seafood is served in heaping portions. (It's not, however, well equipped for overnight visitors, so you're better off bunking in one of the modern resort towns.) There are many scenic vantage points from which you can watch local fishermen arriving in the harbor with the day's catch.

Burgas

38 km (24 mi) south of Nesebâr.

The next place of any size south along the coast from Nesebâr is the city of Burgas. Bulgaria's second main port on the Black Sea, Burgas is industrial and chaotic, with heavy traffic, chemical plants, several oil refineries, and huge ships anchored off its shore. Despite the noise, construction, and pollution, Burgas can provide a pleasant stay in its long **Primorski Gradina** (Seaside Park), expansive beach, and pedestrian alleyways winding through a lively city center.

Dining and Lodging

$$ ✕ **Cheren Peter.** Off the beaten track, this casually elegant and inexpensive restaurant is intimate, sparkling clean, and popular with locals. Relax over an excellent bottle of the local Burgas cabernet, and try the spicy moussaka, a layered meat-and-potato casserole. ⊠ *26, ul. Gurko,* ☎ *no phone. No credit cards.*

$$ ⊞ **Bulgaria.** This high-rise Interhotel is in the center of town. While the rooms aren't exactly upbeat—dark green, brown, and black predominate—it has its own nightclub with a floor show. ⊠ *21, ul. Aleksandrovska,* ☎ *056/4–28–20 or 056/4–26–10,* FAX *056/4–72–91. 200 rooms, most with bath or shower. Restaurant, nightclub. DC, MC, V.*

Sozopol

32 km (20 mi) south of Burgas.

Built on and around numerous Byzantine ruins, this fishing port was once Apollonia, the oldest of the Greek colonies in Bulgaria. With narrow, cobbled streets leading down to the harbor, it is now a popular haunt for Bulgarian and, increasingly, foreign writers and artists, who find private accommodations with locals in the rustic Black Sea–style houses, so picturesque with their rough stone foundations and unpainted wood slats on the upper stories. As romantic, historic, and quaint as Nesebar, Sozopol is more well known, and in September its tiny streets can barely contain the crowds that arrive for the **Apollonia Arts Festival**. To see the quieter side of the village, come in winter, when you will be one of few tourists and catered to like a king.

The Black Sea Golden Coast A to Z

Arriving and Departing

BY PLANE

There are daily 50-minute flights from Sofia and Plovdiv to Varna and Burgas on Balkanair (reservations in Sofia, ☎ 02/981–51–70).

BY TRAIN

It's a six- to eight-hour train ride from Sofia to Varna or Burgas.

Getting Around

Buses make frequent runs up and down the coast and are inexpensive. Buy your ticket in advance from the kiosks near the bus stops. **Bikes** are particularly useful for getting around such sprawling resorts as Slânčev Brjag (Sunny Beach)—though getting a hold of one is normally the stroke of luck of finding someone on the beachfront renting a couple out. A regular **boat service** travels the Varna–Sveti Konstantin–Golden Sands–Albena–Balčik route.

Contacts and Resources

GUIDED TOURS

A wide range of excursions are arranged from all resorts. There are bus excursions to Sofia; a one-day bus and boat trip along the Danube; and a three-day bus tour of Bulgaria departing from Zlatni Pjasâci (Golden Sands), Sveti Konstantin, and Albena. All tours are run by Balkantourist.

VISITOR INFORMATION

There is a Balkantourist office in most towns and resorts. **Albena** (☎ 05722/27–21, 05722/21–41, or 05722/28–34). **Burgas** (Hotel Primorets, ✉ 1, ul. Knyaz Batenberg, ☎ 056/4–54–96; ✉ 2a, bul. Svoboda, ☎ 056/4–81–11). **Nesebâr** (☎ 0554/58–30 or 0554/58–33). **Slânčev Brjag** (Sunny Beach; ☎ 0554/21–06, 0554/23–12, or 0554/25–10). **Sveti Konstantin** (☎ 052/36–10–45 or 052/36–14–91). **Varna** (main office, ✉ 3, ul. Moussala, ☎ 052/22–55–24 or 052/22–22–72; private accommodations office, ✉ pl. Slaveikov, ☎ 052/22–22–06). **Zlatni Pjasâci** (Golden Sands; ☎ 052/35–53–02 or 052/35–54–14).

INLAND BULGARIA

Inland Bulgaria is less well known to tourists than the capital and the coast. Adventurous travelers willing to put up with rustic hotel facilities and unreliable transportation (such as rickety buses traversing narrow mountain ridges) will be rewarded with unjaded hospitality and scenic beauty. Wooded and mountainous, the interior is dotted with attractive "museum" villages (entire settlements listed for preservation because of their historic cultural value) and ancient ruins. The region's folk culture, often pagan in nature, is a strong survivor from the past, not a tourist-inspired re-creation, and spending a few nights in a secluded mountain village can feel like a journey into the Dark Ages. The foothills of the Balkan range, marked *stara planina* (old mountains) on most maps, lie parallel with the lower Sredna Gora Mountains, with

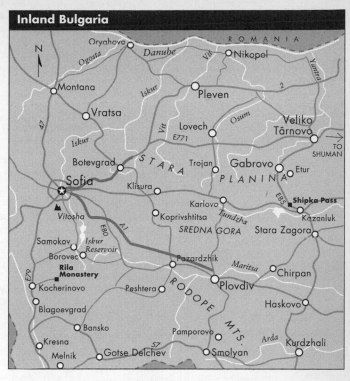

Inland Bulgaria

(map labels:) ROMANIA, Oryahovo, Ogosta, Danube, Vit, Nikopol, Yantra, Montana, Iskur, Pleven, 2, Vratsa, Lovech, Osum, Veliko Târnovo, E771, TO SHUMAN, Iskur, Vit, STARA, Botevgrad, Trojan, Gabrovo, Etur, Sofia, PLANINA, Klisura, Shipka Pass, Vitosha, Karlovo, E85, Kazanluk, Koprivshtitsa, Tundzha, SREDNA GORA, Stara Zagora, Samokov, Iskur Reservoir, A1, Borovec, Pazardzhik, Maritsa, Chirpan, Rila Monastery, Kocherinovo, Peshtera, RODOPE, Plovdiv, Blagoevgrad, Haskovo, Bansko, Pamporovo, MTS., Arda, Kurdzhali, Kresna, 57, Gotse Delchev, Smolyan, Melnik

the verdant Valley of Roses between them. In the Balkan range is the ancient capital of Veliko Târnovo; south of the Sredna Gora stretches the fertile Thracian Plain and Bulgaria's second-largest and most progressive city, Plovdiv. To the south, in the Rila Mountains, is Borovec, first of the mountain resorts.

Koprivshtitsa

★ *105 km (65 mi) from Sofia, reached by a minor road south from the Sofia–Kazanlak expressway.*

One of Bulgaria's showplace villages, Koprivshtitsa is set amid mountain pastures and pine forests, about 3,000 ft up in the Sredna Gora range. Founded in the 14th century, it became a prosperous trading center with close ties to Venice during the National Revival period 400 years later. The architecture of this period, also called the Bulgarian Renaissance, features carved woodwork on broad verandas and overhanging eaves, brilliant colors, and courtyards with studded wooden gates. Throughout the centuries, artists, poets, and wealthy merchants have made their homes here; many of the historic houses once inhabited by Ottoman landowners are open to visitors. The town has been well preserved and is revered by Bulgarians as a symbol of freedom, for it was here in April 1876 that the first shots were fired in the rebellion that led to the end of Turkish occupation two years later.

Dining and Lodging

$ ✕🖼 **Hotel Byaloto Kouche.** This charming inn uphill from the town square offers rustic rooms furnished in the traditional National Revival style, with woven rugs and low beds. One room has a fireplace; all have shared baths. An intimate restaurant offers traditional Bulgarian dishes. ✉ *Ul. Generilo 2, 2090,* ☎ *07184/22–50. 6 rooms without bath. Restaurant. No credit cards.*

$ ⛳ **Barikadite.** This small hotel is on a hill 15 km (9 mi) from Ko-
privshtitsa. Red, orange, and yellow bedspreads make rooms sunny;
the woven carpets and lace curtains add extra warmth. The local residents will willingly give directions and probably offer to show you the
way. ☎ 07184/32–42. *20 rooms with shower. Restaurant, bar, nightclub. No credit cards.*

Trojan

*At the village of Karnare, which is 17 km (11 mi) east of Klisura, take
the winding scenic road north over the Balkan range to the town of
Trojan, 93 km (58 mi) from Koprivshtitsa.*

The **Trojan Monastir** (Trojan Monastery) built during the 1600s, is in
the heart of the mountains. The church was painstakingly remodeled
during the 19th century, and its icons, wood carvings, and frescoes are
classic examples of National Revival art. While there's no phone and
no regular hours, you should be able to find someone to open the gate
in daytime.

Veliko Târnovo

*Travel north on the mountain road from Trojan until it meets High-
way E772, where you turn right for Veliko Târnovo, 82 km (50 mi)
from Karnare; 240 km (144 mi) from Sofia.*

In the 13th and 14th centuries, Veliko Târnovo was the capital of the
Second Bulgarian Kingdom. Damaged by repeated Ottoman attacks
and again by an earthquake in 1913, it has been reconstructed and is
now a museum city with panoramic vistas of steep mountain slopes
through which the idyllic River Jantra runs its jagged course.

This town ideally warrants one or two days of exploration. Try to begin
at a vantage point above the town in order to get an overview of its
design and character. **Tsarevec** (Carevec on some maps), protected by
a river loop, is the hill where medieval czars and patriarchs had their
palaces. The area is under restoration, and steep paths and stairways
now provide opportunities to view the extensive ruins of the Patriar-
chate and the royal palace. On summer nights, a spectacular sound-
and-light show presented here can be seen from the surrounding pubs.

On the Tsarevec and Trapezitsa hills are three important churches. On
Tsaravec are the **Tzarkvata Cheteridesette Machenika** (Church of the
Forty Martyrs), a 13th-century structure on Tsarevec, with frescoes of
the Târnovo school and two inscribed columns, one dating from the
9th century; and the **Tserkavata Sveti Dimitar** (Church of St. Dimitrius),
from the 12th century, built on the spot where the Second Bulgarian
Kingdom was proclaimed in 1185. The 14th century **Tzarkvata Sveti
Peter y Paul** (Church of Sts. Peter and Paul), on Trapezitsa, has vigorous murals both inside and out. ☎ *All churches: free.* ☺ *June–Sept.
daily 9–6; Oct.–May Tues.–Sun. 9–5.*

In the center of the town near Yantra Hotel is **Samovodene Street,** lined
with restored crafts workshops—a good place to find souvenirs, Turkish candy, or a charming café.

On ulitsa Rakovski is the **Museo Hadji Nikolai** (Hadji Nicoli Museum)
in what was once an inn. Part of a cluster of buildings from the National Revival period, this is one of the finest structures in town. At
press time the museum was closed for renovations, and there was no
projected reopening date. ✉ *17, ul. Georgi Sava Rakovski.*

Dining and Lodging

$$ ✕ **Bolyarska Izba.** In the center of the busy district just north of the river, this unpretentious mehana is packed with locals enjoying village specialties such as *mozuk* (brains fried in butter and garlic), *ezik* (tongue), *schkembay chorba* (spicy entrail soup), and *pachá* (head cheese). For the less adventurous, the menu has the more conventional national dishes as well. ⊠ *Ul. St. Stambolov,* ☎ *no phone. No credit cards.*

$$$ 🏨 **Veliko Târnovo.** In the historic heart of town, this modern Interhotel has good facilities. They may not have much personality, but the rooms are modern, with Western-style showers in the bathrooms. ⊠ *2, ul. Al. Penchev,* ☎ *062/3–05–71,* FAX *062/3–98–59. 195 rooms with bath or shower. 2 restaurants, bar, coffee shop, indoor pool, health club, nightclub. AE, DC, MC, V.*

$$ 🏨 **Yantra.** Looking across the river to Tsaravec, the Yantra has some of the best views in town, if not the most beautiful rooms—the aged wooden furniture and lace curtains are nothing special. Its decent restaurant has a fantastic balcony providing the best seats anywhere for the Tsarevec Hill summer light show. ⊠ *1, pl. Velchova Zavera,* ☎ *062/2–03–91,* FAX *062/2–18–07. 60 rooms, 45 with shower. Restaurant, bar, coffee shop. DC, MC, V.*

$ 🏨 **Etur.** Dark and sparse, with a state-owned atmosphere, this moderate-size hotel is a bargain because of its prime location for sightseeing (in town center, near the castle). While some rooms share showers and toilets, all rooms have sinks. ⊠ *1, ul. Ivailo,* ☎ *062/2–18–38. 80 rooms, 64 with shower. Restaurant, bar, coffee shop. AE, DC, MC, V.*

En Route If you leave Veliko Târnovo by E85 and head south toward Plovdiv, you'll go through the Shipka Pass, with its mighty monument on the peak to the 200,000 Russian soldiers and Bulgarian volunteers who died here in 1877, during the Russian-Turkish Wars. Continuing along N6, between the towns of Karlovo and Kazanluk, is the area called the Valley of Roses, hotbed of the flower industry. While most of the crop is harvested in early June, several fields of roses between Karlovo and Kazanluk are left for the benefit of tourists passing.

Plovdiv

174 km (104 mi) southeast of Sofia, 197 km (123 mi) southwest of Veliko Târnovo.

Plovdiv may be the quintessential Bulgarian city, with its colorful, well-kept National Revival buildings; progressive nightlife; and stunning ruins. Bulgaria's second-largest city is not only one of the oldest settlements in Europe, but it's now a major industrial, cultural, and intellectual center. Closed to cars to preserve the streets' original cobble work, the breathtaking, lantern-lit *starata grad* (Old Town) lies on the hillier southern side of the Maritsa River.

The **Natsionalen Etnografski Muzei** (National Ethnographic Museum) is in the much-photographed former home of a Greek merchant. It is an elegant example of the National Revival style, which made its first impact in Plovdiv; the museum is filled with artifacts from that fertile period. ⊠ *2, ul. Chomakov,* ☎ *032/22–56–56.* 🎫 *2,000 leva.* ☉ *Tues.– Sun. 9–noon and 2–5.*

Below the medieval gateway of Hisar Kapiya, the **Georgiadieva Kushta** (Georgiadi House) is a grandiose example of National Revival–style architecture, with its overhanging upper story, carved pillars, and intricate, painted floral decoration. It has a small museum dedicated to the 1876 uprising against the Turks. ⊠ *1, ul. Starinna,* ☎ *no phone.* 🎫 *2,000 leva.* ☉ *Wed.–Sun. 9:30–12:30 and 2–5.*

Steep, narrow **Strumna Street** is lined with workshops and boutiques, some reached through little courtyards. Beyond the jewelry and leather vendors in ploshtad Stamboliiski are the remains of a **Rimski stadion** (Roman stadium) that dates from the 2nd century. You can climb downstairs to the excavated pit, though recent wear and tear (read: litter and graffiti) diminish the atmosphere a bit. ⊠ *Ul. Saborna and ul. Knyaz Alexander I.*

The old **Kapana District** (⊠ Northwest of pl. Stamboliiski) has narrow, winding streets and restored shops and cafés. The exquisite hilltop **Rimski amfiteatur** (Roman amphitheater), only discovered and excavated in 1981, has been sensitively renovated and is open for exploration. In summer, this timeless setting is frequently used for dramatic and musical performances. ⊠ *ul. Tsar Ivailo.* ⌨ *2,000 leva.*

★

NEED A BREAK?   At the self-serve **Rhetora** (⊠ 8A, ul. T. Samodoumov, ☎ 032/22-20-93) the coffee is instant and the pastries shipped in, but the mediocrity of the snacks is far outweighed by the absolute beauty of the setting (and the dirt-cheap prices)—you can sip a drink while looking out over the Roman ruins.

The **Natsionalen Archeologicheski Muzei** (National Archaeological Museum) has a wealth of ancient Thracian artifacts from Plovdiv and the surrounding area. ⊠ *1, pl. Suedinenie,* ☎ *032/23-17-60.* ⌨ *1,500 leva.* ☉ *Tues.–Sun. 9–12:30 and 2–5:30.*

Dining and Lodging

$$$ ✕ **Puldin.** On a hill in the center of the Old Town, this folk restaurant has a romantic subterranean dining room complete with a waterfall. Order the excellent *pulneni chushki,* peppers stuffed with meat, spices, and rice, served with yogurt. ⊠ *3, ul. Knyaz Tseretelev,* ☎ *032/23-17-20. AE, DC, MC, V.*

$$ ✕ **Alafrangite.** This charming mehana in the Old Town is in a restored 19th-century house with carved wood ceilings and a vine-covered courtyard. A house specialty is *kiopolu* (vegetable puree of baked eggplant, peppers, and tomatoes). ⊠ *17, ul. Nektariev,* ☎ *032/22-98-09 or 032/26-95-95. No credit cards.*

$$ ✕ **Restaurant Starata Kushta.** In a Renaissance home in the Old Town, this restaurant presents traditional fare such as *cirene po shopski* (hot feta cheese with herbs, tomatoes, and peppers baked in an earthenware pot). ⊠ *19, ul. Nektariev,* ☎ *032/26-68-42. No credit cards.*

$$ ✕ **Verdi.** With vegetarian salads (unlike shopska, these have lettuce, cheese, and tomatoes), a variety of pastas, gourmet pizzas, and even homemade tiramisu, this spotless, modern Italian trattoria offers a good alternative to the standard Bulgarian vacation diet of heavy pork products and french fries. ⊠ *1, ul. Ponkovnik Bonev,* ☎ *032/65-03-69. No credit cards.*

$$$ ⊞ **Novotel Plovdiv.** The modern, well-equipped Novotel lies across the river from the new part of town, near the fairgrounds. There are large (for Bulgaria) beds, big windows, and up-to-date bathrooms. ⊠ *2, ul. Zlatyu Boyadzhiev, 4000,* ☎ *032/65-25-05 or 032/55-19-79. 322 rooms. Restaurant, pool. AE, DC, MC, V.*

$$$ ⊞ **Trimontsium.** This central Interhotel built in the 1950s is comfortable and ideally situated for exploring the Old Town. Rooms verge on old-fashioned, with polished wood furniture, heavy drapes, and unenclosed showers in the bathrooms. ⊠ *2, ul. Kapitan Raicho, 4000,* ☎ *032/2-34-91. 163 rooms with bath or shower. Restaurant. AE, DC, MC, V.*

$$ ⊞ **Hotel S and M.** Opened in 1997, this new, family-run bed-and-breakfast just outside the Old Town has bright, airy rooms with bay

windows. The owner's daughters serve a great complimentary breakfast of rich pastries, fruit, and yogurt. The hotel is just a few doors down from some of the city's trendiest bars. Advance room reservations are essential here. ⊠ *28, ul. Hristo Duckmedjiev, 4000,* ☎ *032/26–01– 35. 4 doubles with bath. Café. AE, MC, V.*

Nightlife

In the international tradition of university towns, Plovdiv has scores of bars, live-music venues, and discos. Almost all of the most popular places are clustered around the central pedestrain walkway that winds through the best shopping area, **bulevard Kniaz Alexander Battenberg.**

Borovec

Travel west along the E80 Sofia Road. At Dolna Banja, turn off to Borovec, about 4,300 ft up the northern slopes of the Rila Mountains; 109 km (68 mi) from Plovdiv.

This is an excellent walking center and winter sports resort, well equipped with hotels, folk taverns, and ski schools. The winding mountain road leads back to Sofia, 70 km (44 mi) from here, past Lake Iskar, the largest in the country. For information on trails and other facilities, contact the omnipresent Balkantourist office in Sofia (☞ Visitor Information *in* Bulgaria A to Z, *below*).

En Route On the way back to Sofia is the **Rila Monastir** (Rila Monastery), ★ founded in the 10th century by Saint Ivan of Rila, a prophet and healer. Cut across to E79, travel south to Kočerinovo, and turn east to follow the steep forested valley past the village of Rila. The monastery has suffered so frequently from fire that most of it is now a grand National Revival reconstruction, although a rugged 14th-century tower has survived. The atmosphere in this mountain retreat is heavy with a sense of the past—monks are still in residence, although some of the monks' cells are now guest rooms. You can see 14 small chapels with frescoes from the 15th and 17th centuries, a lavishly carved altarpiece in the new Assumption Church, the sarcophagus of Ivan of Rila, icons, and ancient manuscripts—a reminder that because of its isolation, the monastery was a stronghold of art and learning during the centuries of Ottoman rule. Sofia's Balkantourist office (☞ Visitor Information *in* Bulgaria A to Z, *below*) can make arrangements for overnight stays. ☎ *No phone.* ☒ *Free.* ☉ *Daily 9–6.*

Bansko

150 km (93 mi) south of Sofia via Blagoevgrad.

The houses in this small, picturesque town at the foot of the Pirin Mountains may seem inaccessible with their solid walls, latticed windows, and heavy gates—dating back to the days when Ottoman invaders would ride through on horseback, kidnapping local boys for military service in Istanbul and girls for the Sultan's harem—but the rooms inside these "fortresses" are delicate and beautiful, with carved ceilings and colorful handmade rugs. Generally, these homes are not open as museums, but by planning an overnight stay, or even politely asking, you may be able to see some interiors. The **Tzarkvata Sveta Troitsa** (Holy Trinity Church), built in 1835, along with the tower and the town clock, is part of the architectural complex in the center of the town.

Dining and Lodging

Privately owned bed-and-breakfasts can be found on almost every street, and the Vrah Vihren mountain is covered with large, sprawling ski resorts. The former offer small rooms and great home-cooked meals, while the latter are usually comfortable but lacking in charm. Reservations are only necessary at the height of ski season (March) and around New Year's, when Russian tourists descend in droves.

$$ ✕ **Dedo Pene.** A string of cowbells clangs as you open the heavy wooden door of this traditional *kurtchma* (tavern), and a waitress will pour you a glass of homemade red wine before you've even hung your coat on the rack. The walls are adorned with furs, stuffed bobcats, and handwoven rugs. Not for vegetarians or those with sensitive stomachs, this pagan tavern exudes authenticity (along with the aroma of uncured animal hides) and serves up hearty, gamey, medieval meat dishes. ✉ *Southeast corner of Tsentralnia Ploshtad,* ☎ *no phone.*

$$ ◫ **Pirin Hotel.** This popular hotel is large and modern but the plain wooden furniture and wool blankets have created a state-owned feel. ✉ *68, Tsar Simeon,* ☎ *07443/2536,* ☒ *07443/4244. 55 doubles, 7 suites. Restaurant, bar, coffee shop, exercise room. AE, MC, V*

Melnik

From Sandanski, head south down E79 about 8 km (5 mi); Melnik is west of E79.

"The village that slept for a century from drinking too much wine," according to local legend, Melnik is most famous for its fertile grape orchards, its wine aged in deep cellars, and its archaic ambience. Just north of the Greek border, this area was an important Byzantine fortress during the 12th through the 14th centuries. It developed rapidly again during the 18th century due to wine and tobacco trade but declined by the end of the following century. Today Melnik retains well-preserved houses of the National Revival period and is populated by fewer than than 400 permanent residents. Bulgarians and foreigners alike are charmed by the village's old-fashioned taverns, fire-warmed guest rooms, and cobblestone streets unmarred by such modern-world conveniences as electrical and phone wires. There's even a natural stone cave behind the village where you can taste wine straight from the barrel.

Rozhen Monastir (Rozhen Monastery), rising above the town, dates to the 12th century, but was rebuilt in the 16th century after being ravaged by fire. Within these protective walls is a church, dating from 1600. To reach it, you can either hike up the footpath, or hitch a ride on the bus that goes through Melnik roughly every hour (no fixed schedule) and get off at the first stop. A caretaker is normally around and will let you in; while there's no admission charge, it's a nice gesture to buy a few candles in the church.

Inland Bulgaria A to Z

Getting Around

Rail and bus services cover all parts of inland Bulgaria, but the timetables are not easy to follow, and there are frequent delays. Your best bet is to rent a car. To hire a driver, contact the Balkantourist office in Sofia (☞ Visitor Information *in* Bulgaria A to Z, *below*).

Contacts and Resources

Plovdiv (Balkantourist, ✉ 106, bul. Bulgaria, ☎ 032/55–38–48 or 032/55–28–07). **Veliko Târnovo** (Balkantourist, ✉ 2, ul. Al. Penchev, ☎ 062/30–571 or 062/33–971).

BULGARIA A TO Z

Arriving and Departing

By Boat

Modern luxury vessels cruise the Danube from Vienna to Ruse in Bulgaria. Hydrofoils link main communities along the Bulgarian stretches of the Danube and the Black Sea. For more information, contact Sofia's Balkantourist office (☞ Visitor Information, *below*).

By Bus

Some Bulgarian tourist agencies have regular round-trip bus service from Sofia to Victoria Coach Station in London. **ALMA TOUR-BG** bus service (⊠ 83, bul. V. Levski, Sofia 1000, ☎ 02/87–51–87 or 02/80–8–86) leaves London on Friday night, stops in Amsterdam the following morning, and reaches Sofia Monday morning. There is regular bus service from Sofia to most major Eastern European cities. Contact **Group Travel** (⊠ Hotel Novotel Evropa, 131, bul. Maria Luiza, Sofia 1202, ☎ 02/31–261), the best international bus company in the country; it has comfortable, modern, air-conditioned buses serving all parts Bulgaria, as well as the Czech Republic, Romania, Austria, Hungary, and other destinations as far away as Holland.

By Car

If you plan on driving into Bulgaria, be aware that border guards will stamp your passport to register that you have entered the country with a vehicle. No one but the holder of the stamped passport may leave the country with the vehicle, and likewise, the stamped passport holder may not leave the country without the vehicle—under any circumstances. If you have rented a car in Bulgaria and drive outside the border for a few days, make sure that when you cross back into Bulgaria the border guards realize the car is rented, or *pod naem* (pronounced poad nai-em). Otherwise, airport border guards may give you trouble—people have been known to miss flights—when you try to fly out of the country without the car that is registered in your passport.

By Plane

The major gateway to Bulgaria is **Sofia Airport** (☎ 02/79–80–35 or 02/72–06–72 for international flight information; for domestic flights, ☎ 02/72–24–14 or 02/79–32–21–16; for general information, ☎ 02/79–321), about 10 km (6 mi) northeast of the city. A word of caution: don't pack valuables in your suitcase when flying in and out of Sofia, as expensive items have a way of disappearing in customs and you may not realize the loss until you unpack.

FROM NORTH AMERICA

Balkanair (⊠ 437 Madison Ave., 32nd floor, New York, NY 10022, ☎ 212/371–2047), also called Balkan Bulgarian Airlines, flies from New York to Sofia twice weekly.

WITHIN EUROPE

You can fly from the capital cities of many Eastern European countries directly to Sofia. **Balkanair** (☞ *above*) flies from Budapest, Prague, and Warsaw. Transfer flights from these cities can be arranged through Balkanair with **CSA** (⊠ 9, ul. Saborna, Sofia, ☎ 02/88–55–58), **LOT Polish Airways** (⊠ 27, bul. Al. Stamolijski, Sofia, ☎ 02/87–45–62), and **Malev** (⊠ 19, bul. P. Evtimyi, Sofia, ☎ 02/981–50–91).

Lufthansa German Airlines (⊠ 9, ul. Saborna, Sofia, ☎ 02/980–4101) flies from Frankfurt to Sofia. **British Airways** (⊠ 56, ul. Alabin, Sofia, ☎ 02/981–7000) has nonstop service from London to Sofia three days a week.

By Train

From the Sofia **Centralna Gara** (Central Train Station; ✉ 112, bul. Maria Luiza, ☎ 02/31–11–11) you can book tickets for just about any destination in Europe, though certain routes are covered infrequently. Be careful not to book a ticket for a train that passes though a country you don't have a visa for, such as Serbia, because you will be unceremoniously booted off the train at the border. Trains cost about the same as buses, but are often overcrowded, smoky, and slow. There are three classifications of trains: *expresni* (express), *burzi* (fast), and *puticheski* (slow). If possible, always take the fastest train and pay a few dollars more for a seat reservation in first class (or else you may find yourself standing in the smoke-filled aisle for hours). Timetables are posted in every station listing *pristigashti* (arrivals) and *zaminavashti* (departures). For both domestic and international railway information, contact **Rila International Travel Agency** (✉ 5, ul. Gen. Gurko, Sofia 1000, ☎ 02/ 87–07–77 or 02/87–59–35).

Getting Around

By Boat

You can cruise between Black Sea resorts, as well as to Romania and Turkey. In Sofia, **Balkantourist** (☞ Visitor Information, *below*) can provide you with schedules and make reservations.

By Bus

In big cities, trams and buses are generally convenient, cheap, and easy to use. Buy tickets (130 leva–200 leva) at a kiosk or from the driver and cancel them on board. For longer bus trips between major Bulgarian cities, opt for **Group Travel** (✉ Hotel Novotel Evropa, 131, bul. Maria Luiza, Sofia 1202, ☎ 02/31–261) over other companies. For a small jaunt between towns, the sometimes unpleasant public buses may be the only way to go.

By Car

Driving in Bulgarian cities can be difficult, but once you hit the beautiful stretches of highway linking towns, it is definitely the best means of travel. For motorist information, contact the main office of the **Bulgarian Automobile Touring Association** (SBA; ✉ 3, ul. Pozitano, Sofia, ☎ 02/980–33–08). In case of breakdown, call 146.

Gas stations are spaced at regular intervals on main roads but may be few and far between off the beaten track. All are marked on Balkantourist's free driving map. Hotels, most tourist offices, and sidewalk book vendors also sell maps. Before buying a map, make sure that the names on it are in the Roman alphabet and not in Cyrillic.

PARKING

Bulgaria's parking laws are liberal, and if there isn't a place on the street, you can often park on the sidewalk. Just be sure you're not blocking a driveway or another car, and never park where there's a NO PARKING sign (a red circle with a line through it). When in doubt, check with the hotel or restaurant or sight you are visiting.

ROAD CONDITIONS

In cities, roads are generally poor, with lots of potholes. Main roads between towns, however, are generally well engineered, although some routes are narrow for the volume of traffic they have to carry. A large-scale expressway construction program is under way to link Bulgaria's main cities and towns. Completed stretches run from Kalotina—on the Serbian border—to Sofia, and from Sofia to Plovdiv.

RULES OF THE ROAD

In the bigger cities, trams, buses, and cars fight for the right of way without any clear rules, so drive defensively. Drive on the right, as in the United States. The speed limit is 50 or 60 kph (31 or 36 mph) in built-up areas, and 80 kph (50 mph) elsewhere, except on highways, where it is 120 kph (70 mph). Balkantourist recommends that you take out collision, or "Casco," insurance. You are required to carry a first-aid kit, fire extinguisher, and breakdown triangle in the vehicle. Front seat belts must be worn. The drunk-driving laws are strict—it is illegal to drive after you have had more than one drink. If pulled over by the police for any reason, be prepared for an on-site fine (read: *bribe*) of a subjective amount determined by the officer.

By Plane

Balkanair (reservations in Sofia, ☎ 02/981–51–70) has regular services to Varna and Burgas, the biggest ports on the Black Sea. Book through Balkantourist offices; this can take time, however, and overbooking is not unusual. Flights are much less organized than in the West; seats may be broken, and there are generally people standing in the aisles, smoking and passing bottles of rakia.

By Train

From Sofia there are six main routes—to Varna and Burgas on the Black Sea coast (overnight trains between Sofia and Black Sea resorts have first- and second-class sleeping cars and second-class *couchettes*, which are cheaper but less comfortable); to Plovdiv and on to the Turkish border; to Dragoman and the Serbian border; to Kulata and the Greek border; and to Ruse on the Romanian border. The main lines are powered by electricity. For information, contact **Rila International Travel Agency** (☞ Arriving and Departing, *above*).

Contacts and Resources

Car Rentals

Rental car prices vary widely in Bulgaria. The major companies, such as Hertz and Avis, generally charge upwards of $50 a day for mid-range rentals. Smaller, local companies charge as little as $8 a day, even with unlimited mileage, but you may find yourself behind the wheel of an old Russian Moskvich. Many cars have air-conditioning, but it is almost impossible to rent a car with automatic transmission. Car rental prices are comparable whether you make arrangements before your trip or on arrival. Three international car-rental firms have offices in Sofia and major towns. **Eurodollar** operates out of the Hotel Kempinski Zografski (✉ 100, bul. James Bourchier, ☎ 02/68–32–51). **Avis** offices are downtown in the Sheraton Sofia Hotel (✉ 5, pl. St. Nedelya, ☎ 02/988–81–67), and at the Sofia Airport (☎ 02/73–80–23). **Hertz** has a central reservations line (☎ 02/980–04–61) and an office at the airport (☎ 02/79–14–77). You can hire a car with a driver through **Balkantour** (✉ 27, bul. Stamboliiski, ☎ 02/988–55–43) or through **Balkantourist** (☞ Visitor Information, *below*).

You must obtain a green card from your car insurance company, as recognized international proof that your car is covered by International Civil Liability (third-party) Insurance. You may be required to show this card at the border. If you plan to leave the country, you must also have documentation from the rental company that proves the car is indeed rented (☞ Arriving and Departing by Car, *above*). Balkantourist recommends that you also take out collision, or Casco, insurance; the cost should be around $5 a day.

Customs and Duties

You may import duty-free into Bulgaria 250 grams of tobacco products, plus 1 liter of hard liquor and 2 liters of wine. Items intended for personal use during your stay are also duty-free. Travelers are advised to declare items of greater value—cameras, tape recorders, etc.—so there will be no problems with Bulgarian customs officials on departure. But beware: If you declare an item, such as a computer, when entering the country, you *cannot* leave the country without it. After declaring something, if you lose it or are robbed, you may be detained for hours of questioning at police headquarters.

It is prohibited to take works of art, church icons, and coins of particular historical or cultural value out of the country. All international restrictive regulations apply.

Emergencies

Ambulance (☎ 150). **Fire** (☎ 160). **Police** (☎ 166). In case of **breakdown** on the road, dial ☎ 146.

Guided Tours

SunShineTours (✉ 6, ul. Al. Zhendov, Sofia 1113, ☎ 02/72–35–79) offers special-interest tours for people of all ages.

Language

The official language, Bulgarian, is written in Cyrillic and is very close to Old Church Slavonic, the root of all Slavic languages.

In some resorts, railway stations, and airports, names and directions are spelled in the Roman alphabet. English is spoken in major hotels and restaurants but is unlikely to be heard elsewhere. It is essential to remember that in Bulgaria a nod of the head means "no" and a shake of the head means "yes." But there are people who are adopting the Western way, so you have to be careful.

Lodging

Bulgaria offers a range of lodging options, from luxury hotels to extremely inexpensive guest rooms in private homes. The following accommodation offices in Sofia can inform you of your options for almost any city in the country: **Balkan Tour** (✉ 27, bul. Stambouliiski, ☎ 02/987–7233), **Sofia Tours** (✉ 18, ul. Veslets, ☎ 02/802–238), **Marchella** (✉ 17, ul. Maria Luiza, ☎ 02/815–299), and **Balkantourist** (☞ Visitor Information, *below*). These companies can also provide information on camping, which is a popular alternative to hotel lodging, especially along the Black Sea during summer.

Mail

Letters weighing up to 10 grams to North America cost 860 leva; to the United Kingdom, 700 leva. Rates change constantly with inflation, so ask for the current price at the post office before sending mail. It generally takes around two weeks for mail to reach Western Europe and the United States.

RECEIVING MAIL

You can receive your mail through **Sofia Central Post Office** (✉ 6, ul. Gen. Gurko, Sofia 1000) if your letters are marked *poste restante*. You can also use the services of **DHL International** (✉ 8, bul. Tsar Osvoboditel, ☎ 02/88–23–09) or **International Post** (✉ 11, ul. Gen. Gurko, ☎ 02/81–32–96). To collect your mail, you will be asked to present your passport.

Money and Expenses

Most importantly, Bulgaria is still a true cash economy: There are only a few functioning ATMs in the entire country; most people look at traveler's checks as if they are funny, pretty, worthless pieces of paper; and there is little infrastructure for credit card use. To avoid getting stuck without cash, be sure to bring crisp, clean, unmarked, and untorn bills of hard currency with you to exchange at the many change bureaus.

You'll find that the favorable exchange rate makes prices extremely low by international standards. The greatest expense is lodging; expenses such as taxi and public transport fares, museum and theater admissions, and meals in most restaurants are quite low. A little hard currency goes a long way.

CREDIT CARDS

The major international credit cards are accepted in a few of the larger stores, and only in the most upscale hotels and restaurants. Even in these establishments the list of cards accepted may not always be correctly posted. Before you book a room or place an order, check to see whether you can pay with your card.

CURRENCY

The unit of currency in Bulgaria is the lev (plural leva). There are bills of 100, 200, 500, 1,000, 2,000, 5,000, 10,000, 20,000, and 50,000 leva. (Smaller bills still exist but, due to inflation, as of 1998 are no longer legal currency.) Although prices are sometimes quoted in dollars, all goods and services (except the most expensive hotels and international airline tickets) must be paid for in leva. It is illegal to import or export large amounts of Bulgarian currency. You may import any amount of foreign currency and exchange it at banks, hotels, airports, border posts, and the plentiful private exchange offices (which offer the best rates and no commission). Due to the recent phenomenon of counterfeiting, only new, clean bills will be accepted. Changing traveler's checks is always problematic: Though theoretically possible at a few select locations, such as the airport and some major hotels, commissions are exorbitant. In small towns, traveler's checks are *completely* worthless. ATMs are new on the scene and rarely work.

In summer 1997 the International Monetary Fund helped institute a currency board, which led to the pegging of the leva to the German mark. The value of the lev continues to fluctuate, however, and the exchange rate and price information quoted here may be outdated very quickly. At press time, the rate quoted by the Bulgarian State Bank was 1,800 leva to the U.S. dollar, 1,200 leva to the Canadian dollar, and 2,850 leva to the pound sterling.

SAMPLE COSTS

The following price list, based on costs at press time, can only be used as a rough guide. Trip on a tram or bus: 130 leva; theater ticket: 3,000 leva–7,000 leva; coffee: 500 leva; bottle of wine in a moderate restaurant: 4,000 leva–7,000 leva; museum admission: around 1,000 leva.

TAXES

Bulgaria has value-added tax (VAT). Its rate is 18%.

National Holidays

January 1 (New Year's Day); March 3 (Independence Day); April 10–11, 1999 and April 29–30, 2000 (Orthodox Easter Sunday and Monday); May 1 (Labor Day); May 24 (Bulgarian Culture Day); November 1 (Day of the Leaders of the Bulgarian Revival); December 24–26.

Opening and Closing Times

Banks are open weekdays 8:30–3. **Museums** are usually open 9–6:30 but are often closed Monday or Tuesday. **Shops** are open Monday–Saturday 9–7. Some shops are open on Sunday. A handful of *de-*

nonoshni magazini (day and night minimarkets) are open around the clock in the city centers.

Outdoor Activities and Sports

Bulgaria is a great destination for those who enjoy camping, hiking, and rock climbing. Taking advantage of the scores of mountains, the country has miles of beautiful trails, well-marked campsites, and excellent ski slopes. In summer, Black Sea beaches offer everything from parasailing to raft rides for kids. Boating is popular at Pancharevo, a lake 10 km (6 mi) outside Sofia. Questions about outdoor and sports activities throughout Bulgaria can be directed to Sofia's Balkantourist office (☞ Visitor Information, *below*).

Passports and Visas

All visitors need a valid passport. Americans do not need visas when traveling as tourists in Bulgaria for 30 days or less but are required to pay a $23 border tax upon entering the country. Other tourists, traveling independently, can also travel without a visa for up to one month. Many package tours are exempt from the visa requirements. All tourists are given a "statistical card." This must be stamped everywhere you spend the night and is collected at the border as you leave the country. If you plan on making reservations independently, without the help of an official agency, you are required by law to register at the local police station within 48 hours of entering the county, or risk a $100 fine upon departure.

Rail Passes

Bulgaria is not included in the Eurail network, but it is included in the **Balkan Flexipass** offered through **Rail Europe** (⊠ 226–230 Westchester Ave., White Plains, NY 10604, ☎ 914/682–2999 or 800/848–7245); a Bulgaria-only Flexipass is also available. However, train tickets are still so cheap that you should estimate your costs to decide if a pass is practical or necessary.

Student and Youth Travel

While student discounts are not generally offered in Bulgaria, prices are low enough to make budget traveling easy. There is a youth version of Rail Europe's Balkan Flexipass (☞ Rail Passes, *above*). For general information about student identity cards and youth hostels, *see* Students *in* the Gold Guide.

Telephones

Phone numbers in Bulgaria can be anywhere from four to eight digits, depending on whether it is an old line or a new digital one.

COUNTRY CODE

For international calls to Bulgaria, the country code is 359. The area code for Sofia is 2 from outside Bulgaria and 02 from within the country.

INTERNATIONAL CALLS

Calls to the United States can be made from the two types of calling-card phones, "Betkom" and "Bulfon," by using a local calling card to reach the international operator, and then a long-distance calling card to reach the States. They can also be made from your hotel, for a surcharge, or placed from a post office. In Sofia, direct-dial calls to the United States can also be made from the international phone office (½ block west of the main post office). To place a call using an **AT&T USA Direct** international operator, dial 00–800–0010.

LOCAL CALLS

Local calls cost 2 leva and can be made from your hotel, from pay phones, or from calling-card phones. Phone cards can be purchased at post offices, hotels, and numerous street kiosks.

Tipping
Tipping is expected especially by waiters, taxi drivers, and barbers, who usually get about 10%.

Visitor Information
Balkantourist (✉ 1, bul. Vitosha , Sofia 1040, ☎ 02/43–331), the leading travel company, covers the entire country. The Sofia office is the best equipped and has an English-speaking staff; since this branch handles bookings and contacts for the whole country, this may be your best resource. **Balkan Holidays International** (✉ 5, ul. Triaditsa, Sofia 1000, ☎ 02/88–37–39 or 02/83–25–45) provides information and booking services in English.

7 Romania

Bucharest, poised between Europe and the East, has begun to reawaken as a lively capital city. The pride of the nation's citizens, the Romanian countryside—among the most unspoiled in all of Europe—ranges from the forested Carpathian Mountains to the Danube delta, with its abundant waterfowl and wildlife, to the Black Sea coastline, dotted with sandy beaches and resort hotels. Transylvania, the mysterious Land of Dracula, is home to traditional towns and rural villages out of a medieval painting, while the Bucovina's beautifully frescoed churches and monasteries are unique cultural treasures in Romania's remote northern reaches.

HISTORICALLY, ROMANIA has not been the easiest place to visit as a tourist, but it is perhaps the most beautiful country in Eastern Europe, a last bastion of a medieval past long since lost elsewhere. The overthrow of the Ceauşescu regime in December 1989 started a continuing process of reform toward Western-style democracy and a market economy. These reforms are making for substantive changes for travelers: new, private, service-oriented hotels and restaurants; greater access to sights and cultural attractions; and the ability to interact directly with native Romanians. Bread lines, food shortages, empty store shelves, no stores at all—these are a thing of the past. The problems and inefficiencies that tourists may still encounter are often offset by the traditional hospitality and generosity that the Romanian people, once forbidden to speak with foreigners, are now free to express.

Updated by Kristin Rimington

Comparable in size to the state of Oregon, Romania is made up of three provinces: Walachia, Moldavia, and Transylvania. With a population of 23 million, Romania is a Latin island in a sea of Slavs and Magyars (it borders Ukraine, Moldova, Bulgaria, Serbia, and Hungary). Its people are the descendants of the Dacian tribe and of Roman soldiers who garrisoned what was the easternmost province of the Roman Empire. Constant Barbaric invasions, struggles against the Turks, the Austro-Hungarian domination of Transylvania, a once large and still existent Gypsy population, and a strong French cultural influence all contribute to present-day Romania's rich cultural stew.

It's easy to understand why Bucharest, with its own Arcul de Triumf and wide, tree-lined avenues, was once known as the "Paris of the East." The mythic land of Transylvania is the region of Vlad Ţepeş, the real-life prince upon whom the legend of Dracula was based. Its intact medieval villages are a trip back in time, with their town squares, churches, and surrounding Bavarian-style homes and shops reflecting the region's Hungarian and German ancestry. Many enchanting Orthodox monasteries, including some from medieval times with colorful frescoes on their outside walls, characterize the remote and mountainous region of the Bucovina. To the northeast of Bucharest lies the watery wilderness of the Danube delta. The rugged Carpathian Mountains, form a crown in the center of the country. The unattractive effects of industrialization are generally confined to the cities, with life in the countryside remaining picturesquely simple. Horse and cart are a popular means of transportation, horse-drawn plows a common sight, and folk costume everyday wear in the northern regions of Maramureş and the Bucovina.

Romania is one of Europe's poorest countries. Petty theft is a widespread problem, yet the streets are fairly safe at night. Romanians still have limited experience in dealing with foreigners and are sometimes envious of Westerners' wealth. Their efforts on your behalf may charm you, but they could also be cheating you. Tips, gifts, and even bribes are often expected, but use discretion or you may be regarded as patronizing.

Today you may roam as you wish and should feel free to wander through the beautiful countryside or discover old churches and buildings, museums, and crafts workshops. Be aware, though, that it is illegal to enter or photograph any bridge, building, transportation facility, or other site that would be considered of military importance. These sites are usually, but not always, marked.

Romania is a bargain for package tourists. Prepaid package holidays to ski, spa, and seaside resorts offer the best available standards at a very reasonable cost, though Romanian standards are not as high as they are in the West. Independent travelers often pay much more overall for their visit and find wide variations in quality. They must also be aware that there is a dual price system in which foreigners are charged a much higher price than Romanians; this higher price is not always displayed. Despite the recent governmental decision to discourage this practice, many hotels and museums continue the policy in order to survive. The country is currently privatizing its state monopolies, including its tourism industry. Much chaos has resulted from the restructuring, and visitors are likely to experience changes in prices, unreliable amenities, and varying quality of services. Nevertheless, conditions for visitors are constantly improving. More and better restaurants, cafés, and shops are opening in many of the larger towns.

Romania is likely to remain underexplored until the tourism industry develops and its serious economic difficulties are resolved. In the meantime, the package tourist is still assured a good price, while the intrepid independent traveler will experience a part of Europe rich in tradition, one that has in part escaped the pressures, complexities, and aesthetics of modern times.

Pleasures and Pastimes

Dining

Outside Bucharest, options are limited, and you should expect poorly cooked dishes based on pork or beef. Traditional Romanian foods include *mamaliga* (corn porridge), *sarmale* (cabbage rolls filled with meat and rice), and sheep cheeses. Vegetables and salads may be canned or pickled. If a main course is not offered, try *gustare,* a platter of hot or cold mixed hors d'oeuvres, or *ciorbă,* a slightly spicy and sour soup. Overcharging is a hazard outside the bigger restaurants with printed menus; ask for prices before ordering. Try to avoid less expensive *bufet expres, lacto vegetarian* snack bars, and *autoservire;* the food is normally unpleasant, and the sanitary conditions often leave something to be desired. Romanian coffee is served with grounds; instant coffee is called *nes.* Cappuccino is the closest to Western-style coffee.

If you are traveling independently, you may wish to take some food supplies with you. Vegetarians should know that there is a limited range of produce available outside Bucharest, especially in winter. But most towns have markets where local farmers sell produce at very reasonable prices (at least during summer and fall). Outside the major cities, many restaurants stop serving by 9 PM. Most restaurants open at midday. There are no dress rules as such; casual dress is usually appropriate.

Tap water should be considered unsafe. Old piping contributes to a high lead content in the water in many areas of Bucharest. Outside Bucharest there have been cases of cholera and hepatitis resulting from water consumption. Bottled water, referred to as *apa minerala,* is available in most restaurants and shops.

CATEGORY	COST*
$$$$	over $25
$$$	$15–$25
$$	$8–$15
$	under $8

All prices are per person for a three-course meal, including wine and tip.

Lodging

Lodging is simply not Romania's forte. In general a hotel will give you a chance to sleep in a decent bed and to shower, but don't look for style or ambience and don't be upset if you discover you are paying

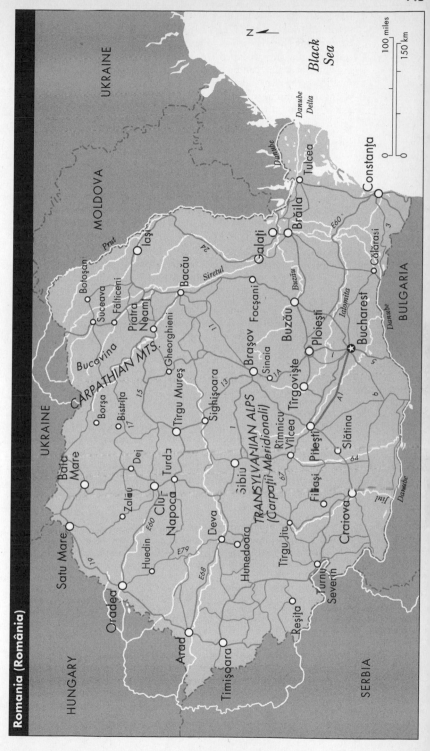

Romania (România)

Black Sea

Danube Delta

UKRAINE

MOLDOVA

UKRAINE

HUNGARY

SERBIA

BULGARIA

CARPATHIAN MTS.

TRANSYLVANIAN ALPS (Carpaţii Meridionali)

Bucovina

Constanţa
Tulcea
Brăila
Galaţi
Iaşi
Botoşani
Suceava
Fălticeni
Piatra Neamţ
Bacău
Gheorghieni
Focşani
Buzău
Ploieşti
Bucharest
Călăraşi
Braşov
Sinaia
Sighişoara
Rîmnicu Vîlcea
Tîrgovişte
Piteşti
Slatina
Tîrgu Mureş
Borşa
Bistriţa
Baia Mare
Zalău
Dej
Cluj Napoca
Turda
Sibiu
Deva
Hunedoara
Satu Mare
Huedin
Filiaşi
Tîrgu Jiu
Craiova
Turnu Severin
Reşiţa
Oradea
Arad
Timişoara

Prut
Siretul
Buzău
Ialomiţa
Danube
Danube
Jiul

100 miles
150 km

five times what a Romanian pays for a similar room. The Office of National Tourism (ONT; ☞ Visitor Information *in* Bucharest A to Z, *below*) ranks hotels with the international rating system of one to five stars, ranging from inexpensive to deluxe. Facilities, including plumbing and hot water, can be poor even in the top hotels and deteriorate rapidly as the overall level of the establishment falls. Ask to see your room first, and always ask at the front desk when hot water will be available. Unless otherwise noted, all rooms include bath or shower.

Book accommodations through private agencies, directly with hotels (many hotels require reservations by fax), or through tourism agencies. Discounts are available if you make prepaid arrangements through a travel agency abroad. Fly-drive holidays and other package deals often provide bed-and-breakfast accommodation vouchers. Most state-run places take vouchers; in deluxe hotels, you have to pay a little extra. Rooms in private homes can be booked through the ONT office and are a good alternative to hotels. Private citizens come to railway stations offering spare rooms (the signs read "camere libere"), but use discretion and be prepared to bargain. Inexpensive lodgings such as pensions and hostels are almost nonexistent. A few delightfully rustic cottages may be rented at ski resorts like Sinaia and Predeal. Details are available from Romanian tourist offices abroad.

CATEGORY	BUCHAREST*	OTHER AREAS*
$$$$	over $200	over $80
$$$	$125–$200	$50–$80
$$	$70–$125	$30–$50
$	under $70	under $30

All prices are estimates for a double room during peak season, including breakfast.

Shopping

Romania has experienced a dramatic increase in imported goods in the last few years. These items tend to be fairly expensive by Romanian standards and more expensive than they are elsewhere. For real bargains look for items produced in Romania, including handwoven rugs, sweaters, crystal and porcelain, and folk art like masks, embroidered decorations, painted eggs, and wooden statuettes.

Every town has an open-air market selling food and local merchandise, including unwanted home furnishings and crafts. *Artizanat* stores, found in most shopping areas and museums, sell local folk art. Keep all receipts, as tight customs restrictions prohibit exporting many items unless proof of purchase can be provided.

Walking and Hiking

Wherever you go, take time for leisurely walks. Hiking and backpacking are two of the best recreational activities in Romania. During the Communist era, Romanians were discouraged from vacationing outside Romania; as a result, a well-organized hiking system was developed. There are marked hiking trails throughout most of the mountains and villages in the countryside. Cabanas where you can stop for a drink and a hot meal can often be found along the trails. Hiking maps are available through the ONT (☞ Visitor Information *in* Romania A to Z, *below*), from street vendors in Bucharest, and in bookstores.

Exploring Romania

Great Itineraries

Numbers in the text correspond to numbers in the margin and on the Bucharest map.

IF YOU HAVE 3 DAYS

Spend two days touring 🏛 **Bucharest** ①–⑭: Explore the sights and sign up for tours of **Palatul Cotroceni** ⑬ and **Palatul Parlamentului** ①. If you have time, make the quick trip to **Snagov,** where you can picnic at the monastery. On your third day, journey to 🏛 **Sinaia,** the former summer retreat of the aristocracy, located within the Transylvanian Alps. Traveling here takes you through the area of Ploiești—the former center of Romania's oil industry—which was heavily bombed by the Allies during World War II. Rebuilt as a model communist city, it serves as an interesting contrast to the more remote towns and villages. In Sinaia take in the **Castelul Peleș** and the smaller **Pelișor.** If you have time, visit the **Sinaia Minastire.**

IF YOU HAVE 5 DAYS

Follow the itinerary above during your first three days, and after visiting 🏛 **Sinaia,** continue north toward Brașov, taking a side trip to **Castle Bran.** Along the way you'll see traditional Romanian villages. At **Brașov,** your final destination, explore the center of the city, an exquisite example of a medieval frontier town, as well as the Gothic church **Biserica Neagrǎ** and the large cobblestone square, **Piața Sfatului.** 🏛 **Poiana Brașov,** in the mountains above Brașov, is a resort area with a better selection of restaurants and hotels; you can take an evening ride in a horse-drawn wagon here. If you have time on your fifth day, hike the mountain trails around Poiana Brașov.

When to Tour

Bucharest is at its best in the spring and fall. The Black Sea resorts open in mid- to late May and close at the end of September. Winter ski resorts in the Carpathians are now well developed and increasingly popular, while the best time for touring the interior is late spring to fall. The Romanian climate is temperate and generally free of extremes, but snow as late as April is not unknown, and the lowlands can be very hot in midsummer.

BUCHAREST

The old story goes that a simple peasant named Bucur settled on the site where the city now stands. True or not, the name București was first officially used in 1459, by Vlad Țepeș, the real-life Dracula (known as Vlad the Impaler for his bloodthirsty habit of impaling unfortunate victims on wooden stakes). Two centuries later, this citadel on the Dîmbovița River became the capital of Walachia, and after another 200 years, it was named the capital of Romania. The city gradually developed into a place of bustling trade and gracious living, with ornate and varied architecture, landscaped parks, busy winding streets, and wide boulevards. Now, however, after decades of neglect and political turmoil, along with a severely destructive earthquake in 1977, only hints of its past glory remain.

Exploring Bucharest

The high-rise Inter-Continental Hotel dominates Bucharest's main intersection at Piața Universitǎții. Northward up the main shopping streets of Bulevardul Nicolae Bǎlcescu, Bulevardul General Magheru, and Bulevardul Ana Ipǎtescu, only the occasional older building survives. However, along Calea Victoriei, the flavor of Bucharest's grander past can be savored, especially at the former royal palace opposite the Romanian senate (formerly Communist Party headquarters) in Piața Revoluției. Here one also sees reminders of the December 1989 revolution, including the bullet holes on nearby walls. Modest, touching monuments to the more than 1,000 people killed in the revolution can be found here, and Piaţa Universităţii has a wall still festooned with protest posters.

South along Calea Victoriei is the busy Lipscani trading district, a remnant of the old city that sprawled farther south before it was bulldozed in Nicolae Ceauşescu's megalomaniacal drive to redevelop the capital. Piaţa Unirii is the hub of his enormously expensive and impractical vision, which involved the forced displacement of thousands of people. Cranes now stand eerily idle above unfinished tower blocks with colonnaded, white-marble facades. They flank a lengthy boulevard leading to the enormous, empty, and unfinished Palatul Parlamentului. With such a massive diversion of resources, it is not surprising that Bucharest is potholed and faded. But happily, the city continues to offer many places of historic interest, as well as cinemas, theaters, concert halls, and an opera house.

A Good Walk
Numbers in the text correspond to numbers in the margin and on the Bucharest map.

A tour of Bucharest should start with its most infamous point of interest, **Palatul Parlamentului** ①. From here it is just a short walk north, across the Dîmboviţa River, to Strada Iuliu Maniu to the historical core of the city, the **Curtea Veche** ②. The Curtea Veche now houses the **Muzeul Curtea Veche-Palatul Voievodal.** The Biserica din Curtea Veche, founded in the 16th century and the oldest church in Bucharest, stands beside the Curtea Veche and remains an important center of worship. Just across the road is **Hanul lui Manuc** ③. Nearby, **Lipscani** is a bustling area of narrow streets, open stalls, and small artisans' shops. In Hanul cu Tei, off Strada Lipscani, are many galleries, crafts boutiques, and gift shops. On Strada Stavropoleos stands the small but exquisite **Biserica Stavropoleos** ④. At the end of the street is the **Muzeul Naţional de Istorie** ⑤, which houses the National Treasury and the Columna Traiană (Trajan's Column) from Rome, commemorating the Roman victory over Dacia in 2 AD.

Turning north along the Calea Victoriei, you'll pass the military academy before reaching the **Biserica Creţulescu** ⑥ church on your left. Immediately north is a massive building, once the royal palace and now the Palace of the Republic, housing the **Muzeul de Artă al României** ⑦. Opposite the palace, in Piaţa Revoluţiei, was the former headquarters of the Romanian Communist Party. Before the revolution in December 1989, no one was allowed to walk in front of this building. During the uprising, the square was a major site of the fighting that destroyed the National Library, parts of the palace, and the Cina restaurant next to the **Ateneul Român** ⑧ concert hall.

Follow Calea Victoriei as far as the Piaţa Victoriei, where you'll find two fine museums. Opposite Calea Victoriei is the **Muzeul de Ştiinţe Naturale "Grigore Antipa"** ⑨. Next door is the impressive **Muzeul Ţăranalui Român** ⑩.

Şoseaua Kiseleff, a pleasant tree-lined avenue, brings you to the **Arcul de Triumf** ⑪. Still farther north lies Herăstrău Park, accommodating the fascinating collections of the **Muzeul Satului Romanesc** ⑫ as well as Herăstrău Lake.

TIMING
This walking tour of Bucharest could be done in as little as three to four hours. However, to have enough time to explore some of the museums, plan a full day. Most tourist sites don't open until 10 AM and

close at 4 PM. On Saturday, most shops close between 1 PM and 4 PM, while on Sunday almost all stores are closed. Museums are closed on Monday, some on Tuesday as well.

Sights to See

⓫ Arcul de Triumf (Arch of Triumph). A smaller version of the Paris landmark, the Arcul de Triumf was originally constructed of wood and stucco in 1922, to commemorate the Allied victory in World War I. It was then rebuilt in stone during the 1930s, when it was carved by some of Romania's most talented sculptors. ✉ *At the head of Şos. Kiseleff.*

❽ Ateneul Român (Romanian Athenaeum). The Ateneul concert hall with its Baroque dome and classical columns has survived much upheaval since 1888 and is still home to the George Enescu Philharmonic Orchestra. Renovations were winding up in 1998. ✉ *Str. Franklin 1.*

❻ Biserica Creţulescu (Creţulescu Church). Built in 1722 by the *boyar* (aristocrat) Iordache Creţulescu, this church is notable for its ornate carvings over the entrance and its decorative arches. The walls are adorned with frescoes by Tattarescu, a Romanian artist, which are a bit battered but still worth seeing. The exterior is currently undergoing repair. ✉ *Piaţa Revoluţiei,* ☎ *no phone.* ◷ *Daily 6 AM–7 PM.*

❹ Biserica Stavropoleos (Stravropoleos Church). This Orthodox church combines late-Renaissance and Byzantine styles with elements of the Romanian folk-art style. Inside are superb wood and stone carvings and a richly ornate iconostasis, the painted screen that partitions off the altar. The church is generally open daily from 6 AM to 7 PM. ✉ *Str. Stavropoleos.*

NEED A BREAK?
Near the Biserica Stavropoleos is the oldest surviving beer hall in Bucharest, **Carul cu Bere** (✉ Str. Stavropoleos 3, ☎ 01/6137560); it serves half-liter tankards of beer, appetizers, and Turkish coffee.

❷ Curtea Veche/Muzeul Curtea Veche-Palatul Voievodal (Old Wall/Old Wall Museum–Voievodal Palace). The court exhibits the remains of the palace built by Vlad Ţepeş in the 15th century. You can see the rounded river stones used in the early construction, later alternating with red brick, and later still in plain brick. Prisoners were once kept in these cellars, which extend far into the surrounding city. At press time, the museum was temporarily closed for restoration, scheduled to reopen early in 1999. ✉ *Str. Iuliu Maniu 31,* ☎ *no phone.* ▦.

❸ Hanul lui Manuc (Manuc's Inn). A renovated 19th-century inn, arranged in the traditional Romanian fashion around a courtyard, this now holds a hotel and restaurant (which is not recommended). Manuc was a wealthy Armenian merchant who died in Russia by poisoning—at the hand of a famous French fortune teller who, having forecast Manuc's death on a certain day, could not risk ruining her reputation. The 1812 Russian-Turkish Peace Treaty was signed here. ✉ *Str. Iuliu Maniu 62–64,* ☎ *01/6131415.* ▦ *Free.* ◷ *Daily 7:30–12:30.*

Lipscani. Developed around 1750, Lipscani is one of the oldest streets in Bucharest. It has retained much of its appearance since then; it continues to be filled with shops, cafés, open stalls, and artists' displays. ★ Of particular note is **Hanul cu tei,** an artists' alley near Boulevard Brătianu.

NEED A BREAK?
★ **Le Café de la Joie** (✉ Str. Lipscani 80–82, ☎ 01/3122910), an appealing French bistro, serves Romanian wine and gourmet coffee along with light French fare. It's open Monday through Saturday until 1 AM.

Bucharest (Bucureşti)

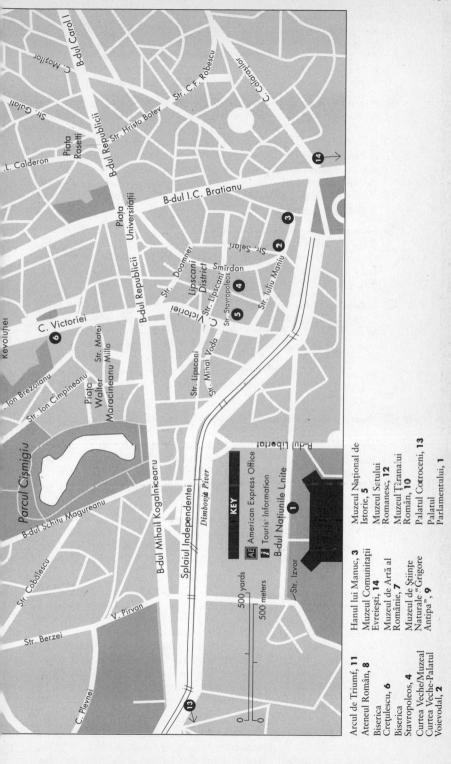

Arcul de Triumf, **11**
Ateneul Român, **8**
Biserica
Cretulescu, **6**
Biserica
Stavropoleos, **4**
Curtea Veche/Muzeal
Curtea Veche-Palatul
Voievodal, **2**

Hanul lui Manuc, **3**
Muzeul Comunitații
Evreiești, **14**
Muzeul de Artă al
României, **7**
Muzeul de Științe
Naturale "Grigore
Antipa", **9**

Muzeul Național de
Istorie, **5**
Muzeul Satului
Romanesc, **12**
Muzeul Țăranului
Român, **10**
Palatul Cotroceni, **13**
Palatul
Parlamentului, **1**

KEY

AE American Express Office

i Tourist Information

★ ⑭ **Muzeul Comunității Evreiești** (Jewish Community Museum). This museum traces the history of the Jewish people in Romania from AD 1000 through World War II. During the war, more than half of Romania's 750,000 Jews were killed in concentration camps established by Romania's police and military. The closest metro stop is Piața Unirii II. ✉ *Str. Mamulari 3,* ☎ *01/6150837.* ✇ *Free.* ☉ *Wed.–Sun. 9–1.*

❼ **Muzeul de Artă al Românie** (National Art Museum). Once the royal palace, this building now houses a fine collection that includes pieces by the sculptor Brâncuși and marvelous works from the Brueghel school. Much of this beautiful building was damaged during the events of December 1989, and it is now undergoing restoration; as a result, there are now only a few small exhibits on display. The majority of the original collection can be seen just down the road at Strada Calea Victoriei 111. ✉ *Calea Victoriei 49,* ☎ *01/6155193.* ✇ *3,000 lei, free Wed.* ☉ *Wed.–Sun. 10–6.*

❾ **Muzeul de Științe Naturale "Grigore Antipa"** (Natural History Museum). Natural wildlife exhibits from around Romania and the rest of the world are on display in realistic settings. The butterfly collection is particularly wonderful. ✉ *Șoseaua Kiseleff 1,* ☎ *01/4100581.* ✇ *3,000 lei, 1,000 lei Wed.* ☉ *Tues.–Sun. 10–5.*

❺ **Muzeul Național de Istorie** (National History Museum). This vast, somewhat dreary museum contains exhibits from the Neolithic period to the 1920s. The Treasury has a startling collection of royal crowns, weapons, plates, and jewelry dating from the 4th millennium BC up to the 20th century. This collection has a separate entrance and (steep) fee. ✉ *Calea Victoriei 12,* ☎ *01/6157056.* ✇ *Museum 6,000 lei, treasury 50,000 lei.* ☉ *Treasury Tues.–Sun. 10–5 (last tickets sold at 4); museum Wed.–Sun. 10–4.*

★ ⑫ **Muzeul Satului Romanesc** (Village Museum). This fabulous open-air museum near Herăstrău Lake is home to more than 300 authentic peasant houses taken from all over Romania, representing various regional folk styles. If you take pictures, there's a 10,000 lei surcharge. ✉ *Șos. Kiseleff 28,* ☎ *01/2229110.* ✇ *3,000 lei.* ☉ *Oct.–mid-May, daily 8–4; mid-May–Sept. daily 10–7.*

❿ **Muzeul Țăranalui Român** (Peasant Museum). In 1996, this became the first museum in Eastern Europe to receive the European Museum of the Year award. This enchanting building has displays of costumes, icons, and other items from rural life, including reconstructed interiors of two 19th-century wooden churches. ✉ *Șos. Kiseleff 3,* ☎ *01/6505360.* ✇ *3,000 lei.* ☉ *Tues.–Sun. 10–6.*

★ ⑬ **Palatul Cotroceni** (Cotroceni Palace Museum). One wing of this 17th-century, former royal residence is now used by the Romanian president and is off-limits to visitors. The remainder of the palace offers a wealth of history about the intimate lives of Romania's former royalty, with exhibits showing furniture, art, and personal effects. Reservations are required for tours (these are available in English). The palace is fairly far from the city center, but not too far from the Palatul Parlamentului (☞ *below*); it's easiest to get here by taxi. The closest metro stops are Armata Poporului and Politechnica. ✉ *Blvd. Geniului 1,* ☎ *01/2211200.* ✇ *40,000 lei.*

★ ❶ **Palatul Parlamentului** (Palace of Parliament). Formerly known as Ceaușescu's Palace, this mammoth building, among the largest in the world, was originally meant to house the Communist dictator Ceaușescu and his government offices. Construction began in 1984, was interrupted by the revolution in 1989, and resumed again in 1991. The building is still unfinished but is presently the home of the Romanian parliament. It is open to the public weekdays from 10 to 4 and weekends 10 to 2 except when the building is closed to visitors during conferences and other government functions. You can arrange for a guide; tours leave from the southern entrance of the palace and cost 30,000 lei, with a 30,000-lei surcharge for cameras and a 150,000-lei surcharge for video cameras. Tours can also be arranged through a travel agent (☞ Guided Tours *and* Travel Agencies *in* Bucharest A to Z, *below*). ⊠ *Blvd. Unirii,* ☎ *01/3113611 or 01/3120902 for tour information.*

OFF THE BEATEN PATH	**SNAGOV** – Snagov Monastery, a rustic cloister on a small island in the middle of Snagov Lake, is the reputed burial place of Vlad Țepeș, also known as Dracula, who, it is claimed, lies beneath the floor of the church. It's 40 km (29 mi) north of Bucharest; to get there from Bucharest, take the E60 north for about 20 minutes. Watch for a sign reading SNAGOV SAT. Turn right here and travel another 10 minutes, through the town of Snagov, until you reach the park area called Snagov Sat. You can rent a small rowboat here for the short ride out to the island. Simply row out of the canal into the lake and take a quick left. Both Snagov Sat and Snagov Island are great places for a picnic (your best bet for food). ☺ *Boat rentals daily 8–4.*

Dining

New restaurants featuring a variety of cuisines open in Bucharest almost daily, and many fast-food chains have invaded the capital. Some of the smaller kiosks should be avoided, but good, inexpensive meals can be found in many of the newer cafés. Always check your bill, as it is not uncommon for restaurants to try to overcharge foreigners.

$$$$ ✕ **Velvet.** One of the first deluxe restaurants to arrive in Bucharest, the Velvet offers an excellent mix of good service and a varied menu. There's a slant to luxury, with dishes such as lobster, shrimp, or pheasant; particularly notable is the chateaubriand. There is no official dress code here, but it's not the place for travel-crumpled grubbies. ⊠ *Str. Știrbei Vodă 4,* ☎ *01/6159241. Reservations essential. AE, DC, MC, V.*

$$$ ✕ **Café de Paris.** This restaurant's menu matches its splendid ambience. The salads are fresh, and the namesake steak, served in cream sauce, is exceptional. Try to hit the reasonably priced Sunday brunch. ⊠ *Str. Jean-Louis Calderon 33,* ☎ *01/3127013. AE, MC, V.*

$$$ ✕ **Casa Doina.** This historic restaurant, popular with the Bucharest elite between the wars, serves Romanian and international cuisines in a relaxing atmosphere. The menu includes seafood, stuffed cabbage rolls, and a variety of meaty entrées. ⊠ *Șos. Kiseleff 4,* ☎ *01/2223179. AE, DC, MC, V.*

$$$ ✕ **La Premiera.** For excellent Romanian food, head to this appealing restau-
★ rant for stuffed grape leaves, liver in cream sauce, or pork cutlets. The walls are decorated with scenes of Bucharest in the 1920s and 1930s. It's just behind the National Theater on Piața Universitatii. ⊠ *Str. Tudor Arghezi 16,* ☎ *01/3124397. Reservations essential. AE, DC, MC, V.*

$$ ✕ **Bistro Atheneu.** The atmosphere of this charming restaurant has over-
★ tones of a Parisian bistro, but the food is classic Romanian—liver in mushroom sauce, steak, and grilled chicken. Live classical music performed by small troupes of local musicians adds to the charm. ⊠ *Str. Episcopiei 3,* ☎ *01/6134900. Reservations essential. No credit cards.*

$$ ✕ **Piccolo Mondo.** One of the first restaurants to open in Bucharest after
★ the revolution in 1989, this mostly Lebanese place serves kabobs, hummus, tabouleh, and *fettouche* (a flavorful Middle Eastern salad);

there's also a sampling of Italian and Romanian items. ⊠ *Str. Clucerului*, ☎ *01/2229046. No credit cards.*

$$ ✕ **Sydney.** Lighting up Piața Victoriei, this Australian bar and restaurant offers a variety of grilled meats, a salad bar, and copious Mexican dishes. There is a wide choice of drinks, including many imported beers. The staff is friendly and helpful; this is a good choice for a late-night dinner. ⊠ *Calea Victoriei 222,* ☎ *01/6594207. AE, V.*

$$ ✕ **Tandoori.** To find this excellent Indian restaurant, you'll need to pass Piata Unirii and turn down a narrow side street. The temporary disorientation will be worth it; many of the chicken and vegetable dishes have spicy sauces, and the *raita*, a cucumber and yogurt salad, is especially good. This is one of a handful of restaurants that have both a smoking and no-smoking section. ⊠ *Str. Budai Deleanu 4,* ☎ *01/6234147. No credit cards.*

$–$$ ✕ **Casa Veche.** This restaurant's wood-oven pizzas make it a perfect spot for lunch or dinner. The large selection includes several vegetarian choices, like the four-cheese pizza with Brie, Camembert, mozzarella, and Romanian cheese. The ricotta and spinach pizza is also a good choice. ⊠ *Str. George Enescu 15–17,* ☎ *01/3125816. AE, MC, V.*

Lodging

New hotels continue to open in Bucharest, easing the strain on the shaky tourist infrastructure, but frankly, you seldom get what you pay for. Paying a large amount for an overnight stay does not guarantee the standards of a Western property, although some international chains are working hard to raise the bar. As a rule, budget lodgings are barebones; keep your expectations at the clean-bed level, and be prepared for unreliable plumbing.

$$$$ 🏨 **Athenée Palace Hilton.** After five years of construction and anticipation, this hotel reopened under Hilton management in 1997 as the first five-star hotel in Romania. Its immaculate, spacious rooms are the best in Bucharest, and the central location adds to its many advantages. From the marble-floored lobby to the sleekly modern rooms, this is still one of the ritziest places in the country. ⊠ *Str. Episcopiei 1–3,* ☎ *01/3151212,* 🖷 *01/3152121. 257 rooms, 15 suites. 3 restaurants, health club, business services, meeting rooms. AE, DC, MC, V.*

$$$$ 🏨 **Lido.** Conveniently situated in the center of the city, this prewar hotel was privatized and renovated to offer comfortable rooms and good facilities, including an outdoor swimming pool (closed for renovation at press time) and terrace. Rooms include air-conditioning and cable television. ⊠ *Blvd. Magheru 5,* ☎ *01/6144930,* 🖷 *01/3126544. 107 rooms, 12 suites. Restaurant, bar, pool, nightclub. AE, DC, MC, V.*

$$$$ 🏨 **Sofitel.** This Western oasis is on the edge of the city en route to the
★   airport. Rooms have a smooth decor in pastels like seafoam green and peach. Snag a spot on the front side of the hotel for a beautiful view of Herăstrău Park. You can also get a local health club membership. ⊠ *Blvd. Expozitiei 2,* ☎ *01/2234000,* 🖷 *01/2224650. 91 rooms, 12 suites. 2 restaurants, bar. AE, DC, MC, V.*

$$$ 🏨 **Minerva.** This is one of the few state-run hotels that make service
★   a priority. Rooms are comfortable and clean, if plain, and come with air-conditioning and television. ⊠ *Str. Gheorghe Manu 2–4,* ☎ *01/3111550,* 🖷 *01/3123963. 70 rooms, 13 suites. Restaurant, bar, meeting room. AE, DC, MC, V.*

$$ 🏨 **Casa Victor.** Though very simple, this is one of the better alternatives
★   to the expensive newer hotels. Each room includes cable television, a refrigerator, and an ample breakfast (served at any hour). It's within walking distance of the Arcul de Triumf, Herăstrău Park, and the Avi-

atorilor metro stop. ⊠ *Str. Emanoil Porumbaru 44,* ☎ *01/2221830,* FAX *01/2229436. 12 rooms, 8 suites. Restaurant. No credit cards.*

$ ⊡ **Triumf.** This comfortable hotel is on a small park near the Arcul de Triumf. It used to serve only the Communist elite; now, the rooms are filled with dark, severe, wood furniture. A few paintings bring a hint of decoration to some rooms. ⊠ *Şos. Kiseleff 12,* ☎ *01/2223172,* FAX *01/2232411. 97 rooms, 3 suites. Restaurant, bar, tennis court. V.*

Nightlife and the Arts

For information on bars, clubs, and all kinds of events in Bucharest, grab a copy of the free, weekly, English-language *Şapte Seare in Bucharesti*; its available in most hotels, airline offices, and Western-style bars and restaurants.

Nightlife

Bucharest nightlife has finally come into its own—new bars and clubs are opening throughout the city. The growing foreign population in the capital has resulted in an increase of Western-style bars, mostly owned by foreign investors. Nevertheless, as in restaurants, be sure to check prices ahead of time and look over your bill—it is common for foreigners to be overcharged. Also, remember that smoking is common but decent ventilation is not.

BARS

If you're looking for an Irish-pub atmosphere complete with darts and a variety of imported beer, try the **Dubliner** (⊠ Blvd. N. Titulescu 18, ☎ 01/2229473), a hot spot for the local expatriate community. The Dubliner's immensely popular younger-sister bar, the **Harp** (⊠ Piaţa Unirii 1, ☎ 01/4106508), has added a much-needed bar to the southern end of the city. For an English experience, head to the enjoyable **White Horse** (⊠ Str. G. Călinescu 4A, ☎ 01/6797796), a pub and restaurant that fills its tables nightly with foreigners and Romanians. For live music (for a small cover), including jazz and blues, make sure you visit the **Laptaria Enache** (⊠ Teatrul Naţional, Piaţa Universitatii, ☎ 01/6158508). This unique bar above the National Theater is a Romanian favorite. It moves outdoors to a sprawling roof terrace in warm weather.

CASINOS

With 16 casinos at last count, Bucharest offers plenty of opportunity for those who want to try their hand at gambling. One of the older and better known is the **Casino Victoria,** which also offers a dinner show. Gambling is available in both dollars and lei. Drinks are free, and there is no admission charge. ⊠ *Calea Victoriei 174,* ☎ *01/6505865.*

DISCOS

If dancing is part of your plan, head to the **Salsa You and Me** (⊠ Str. 11 Iunie 51, ☎ 01/3355640) for come-one-come-all Latin grooves. For a more Romanian feel, head to the Lipscani district, where you'll find the subterranean **Club A** (⊠ Str. Blanari 14, ☎ 01/6156853), a popular gathering place for university students who come to enjoy the crowded dance floor and the inexpensive beer—about $1 a liter.

The Arts

Generally, performance tickets can be purchased directly at the venue's ticket office or from your hotel, with a slight commission added. It's normally easy to get tickets without a prior reservation.

FILM

All of the foreign films in Bucharest are shown in their original language, with Romanian subtitles. Though the theaters are sometimes unkempt and the Romanian moviegoers a bit boisterous, going to the movies is still an excellent chance to catch a popular film (about six months after its major release) and view Romanians having a good time. There are several good theaters on Bulevard Magheru.

The **Filarmonica George Enescu** (George Enescu Philharmonic Orchestra), based in the Romanian Athenaeum, plays a variety of classical favorites. The music is top quality at inexpensive prices. Performances begin at 6:30 PM daily. ✉ *Str. Franklin 1,* ☎ *01/3156875.*

Sala Radio (Radio Hall) is a popular spot to hear the perennial classical music favorites performed by a variety of local and foreign musicians. Performances begin at 7 PM. ✉ *Str. Gen. Berthelot 62–64,* ☎ *01/6133769.*

OPERA AND BALLET

Opera Româna has some good productions, though not of the same quality you might find in Prague or Budapest. Performances start at 6 PM. The ballet and opera seasons overlap; both end in mid-June, so there is no regular summertime schedule. ✉ *Blvd. Kogălniceanu 70,* ☎ *01/6131857.*

Shopping

If you are interested in Western-style shopping, the **World Trade Center** (✉ Blvd. Expozitiei 2), next to the Sofitel, is a small shopping mall. There are several import stores, a music store, and a rather expensive *artizanat* selling Romanian folk wares.

ART AND CRAFTS

The **Apollo gallery** in the National Theater building (✉ Piața Universitatii) and the galleries in the **Hanul cu Tei** off Strada Lipscani sell art that you may legally take home with you.

For local folklore arts and crafts watch for the *artizanat* stores throughout the city, specializing in crafts made by Romanian peasants, including embroidered decorations, dolls, masks, and other items. While in the Lipscani area, make sure to look at the carpets, ceramics, and figurines found in the **Magazin Amintiri** (✉ Str. Gabroveni 20, ☎ 01/3144504).

CARPETS

Romania is well known for its handmade woven carpets. It is often difficult to take these out of the country unless purchased from an authorized retailer, such as **Covoare** (✉ Blvd. Unirii 13, ☎ 01/3362174). Be sure to hang on to your receipts.

CHINA, CRYSTAL, AND PORCELAIN

Romanian china, crystal, and porcelain tend to be fairly inexpensive and of good quality. **Sticerom S.A.** (✉ Str. Selari 9–11, ☎ 01/6157504; ✉ Str. Soarelui 3–5, ☎ 01/6144066) has a wonderful selection.

Bucharest A to Z

Arriving and Departing

BY CAR

There are three main access routes into and out of the city—E70 west from the Hungarian border, E60 north via Brașov, and E70/E85 south to Bulgaria. Bucharest has poor signposting and many tortuous one-way systems. While using a car in the city is not out of the question, it can be hair-raising; be prepared for aggressive, inattentive, and short-tempered drivers. It's common for people to park on the sidewalk.

BY PLANE

All international flights to Romania land at Bucharest's **Otopeni Airport** (☎ 01/2300042), 16 km (9 mi) north of the city.

Between the Airport and Downtown: Bus 783 leaves the airport every 30 minutes between 7 AM and 10 PM, stopping in the main squares before terminating in Piata Unirii. The journey takes an hour. Your hotel can arrange transport by car from the airport. Taxi drivers at the airport seek business aggressively and usually demand payment in dollars; the cost should be between $20 and $30 with tip, so bargain. There is also a shuttle service connecting the airport to the center of Bucharest. For $10 a person, **Sky Services** (☎ 01/2329691), takes passengers to Bucharest's main hotels and the train station; you'll need to call them to be picked up.

BY TRAIN

There are five main stations in Bucharest, though international lines operate from **Gara de Nord** (✉ Str. Gara de Nord at Str. Witing, ☎ 01/952). For tickets and information, go to the **CFR International** (✉ Domniţa Anastasia 10–14, ☎ 01/6132642).

Getting Around

Bucharest is spacious and sprawling. Though the old heart of the city and the two main arteries running the length of it are best explored on foot, long, wide avenues and vast squares make some form of transportation necessary. Tourist maps can be found in bookstores; they may also be available at tourism agencies, hotels, and from street vendors. It is generally safe on the streets at night.

BY BUS, TRAM, AND TROLLEY BUS

RATB surface transit may sometimes be uncomfortable and crowded, but service is extensive. A ticket (*bilet*) valid for one trip of any length can be purchased from kiosks near bus stops for 1,300 lei (though this rate goes up by 100–200 lei quite frequently); tickets do not allow transfers. Validate your ticket as soon as you board. There are also day and week passes (*abonaments*). More expensive *maxi taxis* (minibuses that stop on request) take fares on board. Bus stops are marked by blue-and-white signs; some bus stops have ticket booths where you can get a map of the bus and metro lines. The system shuts down at midnight but becomes scarce around 11 PM.

BY SUBWAY

The *Metrou* (metro) system is the best way to reach the city center from outlying areas; stations are marked with a blue-and-white "M" sign. While the four subway lines (blue [M2], orange [M3], and red and yellow [both known as M1]) are fairly comprehensive, only three stations— Piaţta Unirii, Universităţii, and Piaţa Romană, all on the blue M2 line—serve the downtown area. Subway trains usually arrive about 10 minutes apart and run 5 AM–11 PM. Try to get on at the rear of the train; the front section is like an express class, meaning the doors don't open at every station. Fares run about 2,500 lei for one round-trip ticket; change is available from kiosks inside stations, and you may travel any distance, although tickets are not good for transfers.

BY TAXI

Hail a moving **cab** (parked ones tend to charge more to make up for money lost while sitting idle), or phone 01/941, 01/953, or 01/985. Some dispatchers speak English, but it is a good idea to have the hotel or restaurant call you a taxi. Taxis are relatively inexpensive (less than $1 per km/½ mi), but be sure to check that there is a meter or negotiate a price before getting in.

Contacts and Resources

EMBASSIES AND CONSULATES
Canada (✉ Str. N. Iorga 36 ☎ 01/2229845). **United Kingdom** (✉ Str. J. Michelet 24, ☎ 01/3120303). **United States** (✉ Str. Nicolae Filipescu, ☎ 01/2104042).

EMERGENCIES
Police: (☎ 955 or 01/2229630). However, any serious problems should be addressed to your embassy, as the police force struggles with corruption. **Medical emergencies:** Medical care in Bucharest is still not up to Western expectations. You should look into evacuation insurance when traveling in Romania; your private health provider can usually make a recommendation. For minor difficulties your embassy or consulate may be able to help you. Some good, Western-style facilities have opened in the past few years, including **Bio-Medica** (☎ 01/2119674) and **Brimax** (☎ 01/617089). **Late-night pharmacies: Farmacia 14** (✉ Sos. Iancului 57, ☎ 01/2502172); **Farmacia 26** (✉ Sos. Colentina 1, ☎ 01/3367647); **Farmacia Magheru** (✉ Blvd. Magheru 18, ☎ 01/6596115). **Dentists: Novident** (☎ 01/3361223); **Dent–America** (☎ 01/2122608).

ENGLISH-LANGUAGE BOOKSTORES
Libris Noi (✉ Str. Halelor 1–3, ☎ 092/711820; ✉ Nicolae Bălcescu 18, ☎ 01/3143786) has a good selection of books in English.

GUIDED TOURS AND TRAVEL AGENCIES
Magellan Tourism (✉ Blvd. Magheru 12–14, ☎ 01/2119650, FAX 01/2104903) can help with travel arrangements. Another resource is **Romantic Travel** (✉ Blvd. Primaverii 47, ☎ FAX 01/3123056). The **Transylvanian Society of Dracula,** a division of the **Company of Mysterious Journeys** (✉ Str. G. Călinescu 20, Apt. 28, ☎ FAX 01/2314022), runs well-organized, fascinating tours in Bucharest as well as the rest of the country.

VISITOR INFORMATION
The English-language "What, Where, When Bucharest" is a helpful publication filled with information on sights and entertainment. It's published four times a year, and is available in most hotels, airline offices, and Western-style restaurants. The **Office of National Tourism (ONT)** (✉ Blvd. Magheru 7, ☎ 01/3140759, FAX 01/3120915) is a great all-around resource; the English-speaking staff can provide maps, brochures, and guided tours, as well as help with finding a hotel or a room in a private home.

THE BLACK SEA COAST AND DANUBE DELTA

The **Delta Dunării** (Danube delta) is Europe's largest wetlands reserve, covering 2,681 square km (1,676 square mi), with a sprawling, watery wilderness that stretches from the Ukrainian border to a series of lakes north of the Black Sea resorts. And it keeps growing—more than 47 square yards are added each year by normal silting action. As it approaches its delta, the great Danube divides into three channels. The northernmost branch forms the border with Ukraine, the middle arm leads to the busy port of Sulina, and the southernmost arm meanders gently toward the little port of Sfintu Gheorghe. From these channels, countless canals widen into tree-fringed lakes, reed islands, and pools covered with water lilies.

More than 80% of the delta area is water. It's a natural stopover for migratory birds, but the most characteristic bird is the common pelican, the star of this bird-watchers' paradise. Fishing provides most of

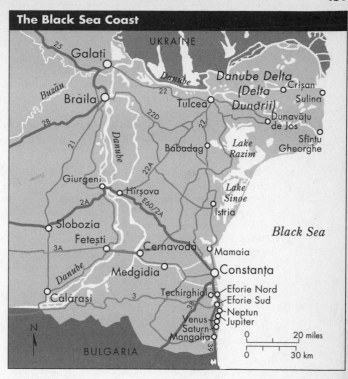

The Black Sea Coast

the area's inhabitants, many of whom are of Ukrainian origin, with a livelihood. One of the most common sights is a long line of fishing boats strung together to be towed by motorboat to remote fishing grounds. Smaller communities, such as Independenţa on the southern arm and Crişan on the middle arm, rent out the services of a fisherman and his boat to foreigners. The waters here are particularly rich in catfish, perch, carp, and caviar-bearing sturgeon.

Tulcea

277 km (172 mi) northeast of Bucharest.

The main town of the Danube delta, Tulcea is built on seven hills and influenced by Turkish architectural styles. Once a market town, it is now an important sea and river port, as well as the center of the Romanian fish industry. The **Muzeul Deltei Dunării** (Danube Delta Museum) provides a good introduction to the flora, fauna, and way of life of the communities in the area. ⊠ *Str. Progresului 32,* ☏ *40/ 515866.* ⊙ *Tues.–Sun. 11–4.*

Lodging

$$ 🏨 **Delta.** A spacious modern hotel on the bank of the Danube, this spot has good facilities. ⊠ *Str. Isaacei 2,* ☏ *040/514720,* 𝖥𝖠𝖷 *040/516260. 117 rooms. Restaurant, bar. V.*

En Route There are good roads to the Black Sea resorts from Tulcea that take you to **Babadag** via the strange, eroded Măcin Hills. It was here, according to local legend, that Jason and his Argonauts cast anchor in their search for the mythical golden fleece. Farther south is **Istria,** with impressive ruins of the settlement founded in 6 BC by Greek merchants. There are traces of early Christian churches, baths, and even residential, commercial, and industrial districts.

Mamaia

60 km (37 mi) south of Istria, 235 km (146 mi) east of Bucharest.

The largest of the Black Sea resorts, Mamaia is situated on a strip of land bordered by the Black Sea and fine beaches on one side and the fresh waters of Mamaia Lake on the other. The resorts have modern high-rise apartments, restaurants, and discos. There are cruises down the coast to Mangalia and along the new channel linking the Danube with the Black Sea near Constanţa. Sea-fishing expeditions can also be arranged for early risers, with all equipment provided.

Lodging

$$$$ ⊡ **Rex.** One of King Carol I's former residences, this is the largest and
★   grandest of all the hotels in Mamaia. In the 19th-century building, the rooms are spacious and clean, and the staff is very attentive. ⊠ *Mamaia,* ☎ *041/831595,* 𝖥𝖠𝖷 *041/831690. 102 rooms. Restaurant, bar, pool, exercise room. AE, DC, MC, V.*

$ ⊡ **Lido.** One of many newly built and moderately priced hotels, this complex is grouped in a horseshoe around open-air pools near the beach at the northern end of Mamaia. ⊠ *Mamaia,* ☎ *041/831555. 129 rooms. Restaurant, 2 pools. No credit cards.*

Constanţa

10 km (6 mi) south of Mamaia (a trolley connects the two), 225 km (140 mi) east of Bucharest.

Romania's second-largest city and one steeped in history, Constanţa has the polyglot flavor characteristic of so many seaports, with its cheek-by-jowl mix of modern life and antiquity. The famous Roman poet Ovid was exiled here from Rome in AD 8; a city square named for him provides a fine backdrop for a statue of the poet by the sculptor Ettore Ferrari. Behind the statue, in the former town hall, is one of the best museums in Europe, the **Muzeul Naţional de Istorie şi Arheologie** (National History and Archaeological Museum). Of special interest here are the statuettes of the *Thinker* and the *Seated Woman,* from the Neolithic Hamangian culture (4000 to 3000 BC). Collections from the Greek, Roman, and Daco-Roman cultures are generally outstanding. ⊠ *Piaţa Ovidiu 12,* ☎ *41/618763.* 🖃 *3,000 lei.* ☉ *Tues.–Sun. 10–6.*

Near the National History and Archaeological Museum (☞ *above*) is the **Edificiu Roman cu Mozaic** (Roman Mosaic; ⊠ Piaţa Ovidiu 1), a complex of Roman warehouses and shops from the 4th century AD, including a magnificent mosaic floor more than 21,000 square ft in area. The **Parcul Arheologic** (Archaeology Park; ⊠ Boulevard Republicii) contains fragments of buildings dating from the 3rd and 4th centuries AD and a 6th-century tower.

Dining and Lodging

$$$$ ✕ **Cazinou.** A turn-of-the-century former casino, this restaurant is decorated in an ornate, somewhat Art Nouveau-ish style; there's an adjoining bar by the sea. Seafood dishes are the house specialties. ⊠ *Str. Februarie 16,* ☎ *041/617416. No credit cards.*

$$ ✕ **Venetia.** The walls of this Italian restaurant off Ovidiu Square are
★   covered with Venetian scenes, and happily, the staff has absorbed some Mediterranean warmth. ⊠ *Str. Mircea cel Batrin 5,* ☎ *041/617390. No credit cards.*

$$$ ⊡ **Palace.** The large and gracious old Palace, near the city's historic center, has a good restaurant and a terrace overlooking the sea and the tourist port of Tomis. Rooms are clean but nothing fancy. ⊠ *Str.*

Remus Opreanu 5–7, ☎ 041/614696, ℻ 041/617532. 110 rooms. Restaurant. No credit cards.

En Route   A string of seaside resorts lies just south of Constanţa; the sandy beaches are the main draw, as the water is somewhat polluted. (People tend to rent paddleboats rather than swim.) **Eforie Nord** is an up-to-date thermal treatment center. A number of resorts built in the 1960s were given names evoking the coast's Greco-Roman past—**Neptune, Jupiter, Venus,** and **Saturn.** These amenity-rich resorts revolve around vacationers, and there are plenty of inexpensive hotels near the beaches. There are regular excursions from the seaside resorts to the Roman ruins of **Istria** and **Tropaeum Trajani.** You can also visit the **Podgoriile Murfatlar** (Murfatlar vineyards) for wine tastings.

The Black Sea Coast and Danube Delta A to Z

Arriving and Departing

BY CAR

The Black Sea is only 210 km (130 mi) from Bucharest. To get there follow route 3 out of Bucharest until you hook up to 3A, following this the remainder of the way to Constanţa.

BY PLANE

Tarom (☎ 01/6594125), the Romanian national airline, flies regularly to Constanţa from Bucharest. The flight takes only 45 minutes.

BY TRAIN

Trains leave Bucharest's **Gara de Nord** (✉ Str. Gara de Nord at Str. Witing, ☎ 01/952) for Constanţa at least 10 times a day; the trip takes roughly three hours.

Getting Around

BY BOAT

Regular passenger and sightseeing boats operate along the middle and southern arms of the Danube delta. Motorboats are available for hire, or rent one of the more restful fishermen's boats.

BY BUS

Sightseeing bus trips from the Black Sea resorts and Constanţa to the Danube delta, the Murfatlar vineyards, Istria, and the sunken city of Adamclisi are arranged by tourism agencies (☞ Visitor Information, below).

BY CAR

As bus service is infrequent, driving can be much more convenient. Roads are relatively well marked. The main route is the E87, which goes north from Varna Veche to Tulcea.

Contacts and Resources

EMERGENCIES

Late-night pharmacy: Farmacia 6 (✉ Blvd. Ferdinand 97, Constanţa).

VISITOR INFORMATION

Constanţa (✉ Danubius, Blvd. Ferdinand 22/36, ☎ 041/615836). **Mamaia** (✉ ATI–Carpaţi, Blvd. Tomis 46, ☎ 041/614861, ℻ 041/611429). **Tulcea** (Europolis; ✉ Str. Pacii 20, ☎ 040/512443).

BUCOVINA

Moldavia composes the northeastern section of Romania. During World War II, portions of Moldavia were annexed by the Soviet Union and still remain separate, both culturally and legally, from Romania to this day. Throughout history Moldavia has been home to some of

Bucovina

Romania's greatest poets, writers, and composers, including Mihai Eminescu, the national poet, and George Enescu, the national composer.

Bucovina—an area within Moldavia that is west of Suceava and north of Piatra Neamt—is a remote region that did not suffer the horrible suppression felt by the rest of the country under communism, in large part because the hilly land could not support large-scale agriculture. As a result, a visit to this area is like a step back in time: Farmers still use handmade hoes and ploughs, and homes are adorned with intricately carved wooden gables. The name Bucovina was first given to the area in the 18th century, when it was a part of the Austro-Hungarian Empire. It means "beech-covered land," and indeed the area is still filled with beeches.

Bucovina is also home to splendid medieval monasteries nestled in small valleys and on hillsides. Many date to the 15th century, when Moldavia was ruled by Prince Stefan Cel Mare, or Stefan the Great. During his rule, Stefan was engaged in ongoing battles with the Ottoman Turks. He was often successful in battle, and many of these monasteries were built in thanks to God for his achievements. They are noteworthy not only for their historical interest but also for the vivid frescoes that were painted on both interior and exterior walls in an effort to educate the illiterate Romanians of that period about their history. Even after centuries these colorful, detailed frescoes are impeccably preserved—UNESCO has added them to its "Catalogue of the World's Great Monuments."

There are more than 15 monasteries in Bucovina, so it would be difficult to see them all. Visits to Humor, Moldoviţa, Suceviţa, and Voroneţ will give you an idea of their exceptional beauty. The monasteries also offer dining and appropriately spare lodging (☞ *below*). There are small admission fees, and all monasteries will charge you a small amount to take photographs; donations in dollars are appreciated.

If you desire more conventional lodging, consider spending the night in **Suceava.** One hotel is the Suceava (⊠ 5 Nicolae Balcescu, ☎ 030/521079, ☒ 030/521079); a double room costs about $50. For a charming bed-and-breakfast with a wonderful restaurant, stay in **Suce-**

vița at the **Popasul Turistic Bucovina** (☎ 030/465389), right next to the Sucevița monastery; a double here costs roughly $30.

Voroneț

★ *41 km (25 mi) west of Suceava.*

The blues in the frescoes on the walls of Voroneț Monastery are so deep and penetrating that they have been given a color of their own: Voroneț blue. Erected in 1488 by Stefan Cel Mare, Voroneț is the most famous of all of the Bucovina monastic houses. Its frescoes include a detailed portrayal of the *Last Judgment,* in which Christ sits in judgment over those seeking entry into heaven. Among those turned away are Turks and Tartars, enemies of the Romanians during the medieval period. Voroneț is uninhabited, and very little remains of the original structure other than the church and a bell tower. To get here from Suceava, travel west on E576 until you reach the turnoff for Voroneț. From here it is about 5 km (3 mi).

Humor

8 km (5 mi) north of Voroneț, 41 km (25 mi) north of Suceava.

Humor is known for its deep shades of red, though some of the frescoes here have begun to fade from the weather. It is still possible to make out depictions of the *Return of the Prodigal Son* and the *Siege of Constantinople in 626*—only here the attacking Persians are revealed as Turks. Humor Monastery is also uninhabited, and it is surrounded by a wooden stockade. The turnoff for Humor Monastery is right across E576 from Voroneț Monastery (☞ *above*), making it a quick drive or a nice walk.

Moldovița

★ *32 km (20 mi) northwest of Humor, 103 km (64 mi) west of Suceava.*

Standing out as the focal point of the village, Moldovița was built in 1532 as a fortified monastery to provide a place of refuge for the villagers in case of Turkish attack. Constructed completely of stone, the monastery is still home to a group of nuns. Two of its best-known frescoes are the *Defense of Constantinople* (in 626) and the *Last Judgment.* In both cases sinners and villains are depicted as Turks. The throne of Prince Petru Rareș, who built the monastery, is on exhibit. From Suceava, travel west on E576 to 17A. From here journey north to the Moldovița turnoff. The monastery can provide lodging and meals. ☎ *030/336348.*

Sucevița

34 km (21 mi) northeast of Moldovița, 50 km (31 mi) northeast of Suceava.

Another example of a fortified monastery, Sucevița was constructed between 1581 and 1601. It is best known for the frescoes that adorn its inner and outer walls, including the *Ladder of Virtue,* which shows the 30 steps from Hell to Paradise, and the *Tree of Jesse,* which acts as a symbol of the continuity between the Old and New Testaments. There are still nuns in the monastery, and it houses a museum of monastic treasures. From Moldoviţa Monastery, return to 17A and travel north to the Suceviţa turnoff.

Bucovina A to Z

Arriving and Departing

BY BUS

Due to its remote location, Bucovina is best visited by bus on a tour arranged through an agency in Bucharest, which would provide a guide, as well as plan for lodging and dining (☞ Guided Tours and Travel Agencies *in* Bucharest A to Z, *above*).

BY CAR

With enough time, you could travel to Bucovina by rented car from Bucharest. Travel time is about eight hours each way. From Bucharest you would go north on E60 to Ploiesti. Follow 1b to Buzău, then E85 to Suceava.

BY PLANE

There are regular flights between Bucharest and Suceava on **Tarom** (☎ 01/6594125). However, this is not the best option for visiting Bucovina, as the monasteries are fairly spread out.

BY TRAIN

There is train service to Bucovina from the **Gara de Nord** (✉ Str. Gara de Nord at Str. Witing, ☎ 01/952) in Bucharest, though traveling this distance can be rather time-consuming and frustrating. Also, you will be left with few options for transportation upon arrival in Bucovina. If you do choose to take the train, get a sleeper car and try to travel by *expres* or *accelerat* service to help reduce the amount of time it takes; the trip will take between eight and 10 hours.

Getting Around

BY BUS

Bus service in this area of Romania is not very convenient or reliable. If you do choose to take a bus from Suceava or Piatra Neamt, you would be best off to shoot for one of the monasteries that are close to a few others and then hike from one to the other. Hiking trails are well marked, and trail maps can be picked up in Bucharest travel agencies.

BY CAR

Other than by organized tour, this is probably the best way to get around to the monasteries. It is possible to see them by traveling something of a loop starting at Voroneţ, followed by Humor, Moldoviţa, and Suceviţa. E576 is the main route.

BY TRAIN

Train access to the monasteries is fairly limited, though it is possible to travel by train to Moldoviţa from Suceava.

Contacts and Resources

VISITOR INFORMATION

Suceava (✉ Bucovina Travel Office, Str. N. Bălcescu 4, ☎ 030/221297).

TRANSYLVANIA

Transylvania, Romania's western province, offers travelers the chance to explore some of Europe's most beautiful and unspoiled villages and rural landscapes. The Carpathian Mountains, which separate Transylvania from Walachia and Moldavia, shielded the province from the

Turks and Mongols during the Middle Ages. Germans and Hungarians settled in Transylvania during this period, building many wonderful castles, towns, and churches. Since the 1980s many ethnic Germans have emigrated, but Transylvania, which was ruled by Hungary until 1920, is still home to a large Hungarian minority and to many of Romania's 2 million ethnic Gypsies. Many of the country's most beautiful tourist spots are found in Transylvania, but the lack of amenities outside the main towns makes traveling difficult. One solution is to base yourself in a major town like Sibiu or Braşov and take day trips into the countryside. An alternative is to travel north out of Bucharest along E60 and follow a loop, traveling first to Sinaia, then to Braşov, Poiana Braşov, Sighişoara, and Sibiu.

Sinaia

127 km (79 mi) northwest of Bucharest.

Prior to World War II and the abdication of the royal family, Sinaia was a summer retreat for Romania's aristocracy. A walk up the mountainside reveals many grand summer homes from this period. The first point of importance to be encountered is the **Sinaia Minastire,** or monastery. This is still a working monastery, with buildings dating to 1695; many of the monks living here are quite elderly, but some will be happy to show you around.

Just up the hill from Sinaia Minastire is **Castelul Peleş** (Peleş Palace), one of the best-preserved royal palaces in Europe. It served as the summer residence of the first Hohenzollern king of Romania, Carol I. Built in the latter half of the 19th century, it was the king's attempt to imitate the styles of his former homeland, creating a Bavarian setting in the mountains of Romania. The palace is ornately decorated, with intricate wood carvings and paintings of scenes from Wagner operas. Tours are available in English. ⊠ *2 Peleşului Str., up hill along Str. Manastirii,* ☎ *044/310918.* ⊟ *20,000 lei.* ⊙ *Wed.–Sun. 9–3.*

The **Pelişor** lies just above Peleş Palace (☞ *above*). This was the summer home of the second Hohenzollern king, Ferdinand. Though not as grand as the Peleş Palace, Pelişor has a lovely setting. Tours are available in English. ⊠ *Peleşului Str.,* ☎ *044/310918.* ⊟ *15,000 lei.* ⊙ *Wed.–Sun. 8–4.*

Beyond the Pelişor lies a Spanish-style **palace** created by Ceauşescu in an attempt to place himself above the royal family. It is not possible to tour the palace, but it is interesting to view and then hike the mountain path that begins just beyond, which was created as a private path for Ceauşescu.

In the center of Sinaia, just south of the Hotel Montana, is the **teleferic.** Here, from 8 to 4 each day, you may ride a cable car to the top of the mountain. Once there, you can look out over the grandeur of the Transylvanian Alps. You can take the cable car back down, or hike down the trail, which takes roughly two hours.

Dining and Lodging

$$$$ ✕🏨 **Mara Sinaia.** Opened in 1996, this is easily the grandest hotel in
★ Romania outside Bucharest. The service is superb, and all rooms are clean and spacious, with excellent views of the mountainside. The restaurant provides Romanian fare in an elegant atmosphere. The menu ranges from seafood to pork, beef, and venison. ⊠ *Str. Toporasilor 1A,* ☎ *044/310440,* 📠 *044/310651. 142 rooms, 6 suites. Restaurant, bar, pool, health club, casino. AE, MC, V.*

$ ✕⬚ Economat. This hotel was built in the same Bavarian style as the nearby Peleş Palace. Surrounded by mountains, it is simple, comfortable, and ideally located. Its restaurant offers traditional French cuisine in a very Germanic town—instead of schnitzel, you can try fondue, quiche, or steaming onion soup. ⊠ *2 Peles Str.,* ☎ *044/311151,* ☏ *044/313550. 36 rooms. Restaurant. V.*

....

OFF THE   **CASTLE BRAN –** Looming ominously in the shadow of Mt. Bucegi, Castle
BEATEN PATH   Bran is a gloomy though beautifully preserved fortress. Claimed to have
                been the castle of Vlad Ţepeş, Bran was actually a trading point during
                the Middle Ages (Vlad's castle lies in ruins farther west in the Argeş Val-
                ley). Tours in English are available through the castle. ⊠ *Str. Principală
                (Rte. DN 73); go north out of Sinaia for about 20 min; take the turnoff
                for Rişnov and travel until the road comes to a T. Go left and drive to the
                town of Bran.* ☏ *20,000 lei.* ☉ *Tues.–Sun. 8–4:30.*

....

Braşov and Poiana Braşov

43 km (27 mi) north of Sinaia, 127 km (79 mi) north of Bucharest.

Once an important medieval trading center and now largely industrial, Braşov is the third-largest city in Romania. Braşov's best sights can be found in the center of the city: **Piaţa Sfatului,** a large cobblestone square and the heart of the old Germanic town, is still surrounded in places by the original fortress walls. Built in 1420 and once the town hall, the large **Casa Sfatului** is in the center of the square and houses a historical museum. The square is surrounded on all sides by shops, cafés, and lively restaurants. ☉ *Tues.–Sun.*

Just off Piata Sfatului is the spiraling tower of the **Biserica Neagră** (Black Church), a Gothic masterpiece built in the early 15th century. It acquired its name after a fire in 1689 that left it with its current black, charred appearance. The church occasionally hosts classical-music concerts. Opposite the Black Church, and across Piaţa Sfatului, is **Strada Republicii.** This is a pedestrian street lined with some tempting shops, particularly the artizanat stores.

The best view of Braşov can be attained by riding the **Telecabina Timpa,** a cable car that runs from 10 to 6 daily, except Monday, to the top of Timpa. To get to the cable car you can walk through the old section of the city. Leave Piaţa Sfatului on Strada Apollonia Hirscher. Stroll along to the end of the road, taking a left on Strada Castelului. The next right is Strada Romer. Follow this until it ends and climb the stairs to the cable car.

A 10-minute drive or bus ride outside Braşov brings you to **Poiana Braşov,** a mountaintop ski resort area that was originally developed for foreigners and top Communist officials. Home to several good restaurants and hotels, it is the best base for visiting Braşov and the surrounding area. During the winter months Poiana Braşov has some of the best skiing in Romania, though trails are not groomed and ski lifts are limited. In summer, well-marked hiking trails wind along the breathtaking mountainside. Riding the cable car to the top of the mountain gives you a sweeping view of the Transylvanian plains.

Dining and Lodging

$$–$$$ ✕ Coliba Haiducilor. Walls decorated with hunting trophies, a large fireplace, waiters in peasant costume—all this strongly evokes a rustic hunting lodge. The menu includes boar, bear, and venison; traditional singing and dancing take you back to an earlier era. ⊠ *Poiana Braşov,* ☎ *068/262137. No credit cards.*

$$ ✗ **Sura Dacilor.** This restaurant was designed to resemble a Romanian
★ hunting lodge, with traditional peasant decor including wooden pan
flutes and hand woven rugs. Menu choices include garlic chicken and
a mixed grill. ⊠ *Poiana Braşov,* ☎ *068/262327. No credit cards.*

$–$$ ✗ **Stradivari.** This Italian-owned establishment includes both a pizze-
★ ria and a more expensive restaurant serving pasta and seafood dishes.
They didn't exactly take pains with the restaurant decor, but the pizzeria, in a basement with a curved ceiling, resembles a wine cellar. ⊠ *Piaţa
Sfatului 1, Braşov,* ☎ *068/151165. No credit cards. Closed Wed.*

$$$$ ⊞ **Alpin.** The location, at the highest point in Poiana Braşov, gives breathtaking views from most rooms. The hotel is very comfortable, clean,
and service-oriented. The rooms are somewhat dark, but this makes
the views from the small balconies that much more spectacular. ⊠ *Poiana
Braşov,* ☎ *068/262343, FAX 068/150427. 129 rooms, 4 apartments.
Restaurant, bar, pool, exercise room. AE, MC, V.*

$$ ⊞ **Casa Viorel.** Perhaps the best-kept secret in Romania, this private,
★ modern hotel is a true paradise. Every room is immaculate, with a bal-
cony and view of the mountains, and the service is superb. ⊠ *Poiana
Braşov,* ☎ *068/262024, FAX 068/262148. 10 rooms, 2 suites. No credit
cards.*

$$ ⊞ **Centrul De Echitatie.** One of this resort's best lures is its stable; you
can take wagon and sleigh rides or go horseback riding in the hills.
Each of the villas has a kitchenette; backwoods barbecues can also be
arranged. It is on the bus line to Braşov, and within walking distance
of all facilities in Poiana Braşov. ⊠ *Poiana Braşov,* ☎ *068/262161.
10 1- and 2-bedroom villas. No credit cards.*

Sighişoara

★ *121 km (75 mi) northwest of Braşov, 248 km (154 mi) northwest of
Bucharest.*

Long before you reach this enchanting place, you can see the profile
of Sighişoara's towers and spires. Towering above the modern town
is a medieval **citadel,** among the loveliest and least spoiled in Europe.
Walking up from the city center, you'll enter the citadel through the
197-ft-tall clock tower, which dates from the 14th century. The clock
still works, complete with rotating painted wooden figures, one for each
day of the week. The tower houses the town's **Muzeul de Historie** (History Museum), which includes some moving photographs of the 1989
revolution that led to the execution of Nicolae Ceauşescu and his wife,
Elena. From the wooden gallery at the top of the tower you can look
out over the town with its terra-cotta roofs and painted houses.

Opposite the clock tower is a small ocher-color house where the father
of Vlad Ţepeş, better known as Dracula, once lived. It is now a pleasant restaurant (☞ Dining and Lodging, *below*). Continuing uphill
along narrow, cobbled streets lined with faded pink, green, and ocher
houses, you'll come to a covered staircase, which leads to a 14th-cen-
tury Gothic church and a German cemetery.

Dining and Lodging

$$ ✗ **Restaurentul Cetaţ (Casa Vlad Dracul).** Known as the birthplace of
Dracula, this is the best place in town for a meal. On the first floor
you can drink draft beer at wooden tables. Upstairs, a cozy restaurant
serves good soups and traditional Romanian dishes. ⊠ *Str. Cosi-
torarilor 5,* ☎ *065/771596. No credit cards.*

$ ⊞ **Rex.** This new hotel has added a much-needed clean, modern es-
tablishment to the town. Though a few minutes walk from the center,
it is definitely the most appealing hotel in the city. ⊠ *Str. Dumbravei
18,* ☎ FAX *065/166615. 24 rooms. Restaurant. No credit cards.*

Sibiu

92 km (57 mi) southwest of Sighişoara, 271 km (168 mi) northwest of Bucharest.

Sibiu, known as Hermannstadt to the Germans, who founded the city in 1143, was the Saxons' chief settlement in Transylvania. Like Sighişoara and Braşov, the town has a distinctly German feel to it, even though there are few ethnic Germans left. The old part of the town centers on the magnificent **Piaţa Mare** (Great Square) and **Piaţa Mica** (Small Square), with their painted 17th-century town houses. In the Great Square is the **Biserica Romano Catolică** (Roman Catholic church), a splendid high-Baroque structure. The **Muzeul Brukenthal** (Bruken-thal Museum), is also on the Great Square. It has one of the most extensive collections of silver, paintings, and furniture in Romania. It also has an annex around the corner on Strada Mitropoliei.

Next to the Small Square you'll find the **Biserica Luthero** (Lutheran Cathedral), a massive 14th- to 15th-century edifice with a simple, stark interior in total contrast to that of the Roman Catholic church just a couple hundred yards away. On the outskirts of the town there is a large **Gypsy community,** with the ornate homes of the Gypsies' self-proclaimed leaders King Cioba and Emperor Iulian; Gypsies still live in the area.

Dining and Lodging

$$$ ✕▣ **Continental.** This hotel is the nicest Sibiu has to offer. Rooms are
★ clean and modern, and the staff is attentive. A large breakfast buffet is included with each night's stay. The restaurant serves a variety of well-prepared dishes, including trout, steaks, chicken, and a large fresh salad. ⊠ *Calea Dumbravii 2–4,* ☎ *069/218100,* 𝐅𝐀𝐗 *069/210125. 182 rooms. Restaurant, bar, casino. MC, V.*

Transylvania A to Z

Arriving and Departing

BY CAR
The main road from Bucharest is the DN1; the trip takes between two and four hours.

BY PLANE
There are regular flights from Bucharest to Braşov, Sibiu, and other major Transylvanian towns with **Tarom** (☎ 01/6594125). Traveling by plane is quite efficient, given the slow speed of train and bus services and the relatively inexpensive cost of air travel.

BY TRAIN
Train service from Bucharest is relatively frequent; the trip takes about three hours.

Getting Around

BY BUS
Bus trips to Transylvania are arranged by an increasing number of tourist agencies in Bucharest and Braşov (☞ Visitor Information, *below, and* Bucharest A to Z, *above*). There is an extensive network of local bus service in the region, but buses are often crowded, uncomfortable, and slow and should be used only for short distances, if at all.

BY CAR
Travel by car is perhaps the best way to explore Transylvania's rich rural life. The A1 highway is the quickest route between Bucharest and Piteşti; the DN7 leads to Rîmnica Vîlcea, and you can then take the E81 to Sibiu. The E60 links Bucharest to Braşov. Rental cars, with or without drivers, are available through tourist offices and major hotels.

BY TRAIN

Many Transylvanian towns are on international train routes, making train travel a good way to explore the region. Try to travel by *expres* or *accelerat* service; otherwise you may find that it takes several hours to cover just a couple of hundred miles. For domestic train information, call Bucharest's **Gara de Nord** (✉ Str. Gara de Nord at Str. Witing, ☎ 01/952).

Contacts and Resources

GUIDED TOURS

The **Transylvanian Society of Dracula** (✉ Str. G. Călinescu 20, Apt. 28, Bucharest, ☎ FAX 01/2314022) offers unique "Dracula" tours that combine locations figuring in Bram Stoker's *Dracula* with those associated with the historical figure on whom the novel is based.

VISITOR INFORMATION

Aro Palace Tourism Office (✉ Blvd. Eroilor 27, Braşov, ☎ 068/142840).

ROMANIA A TO Z

Arriving and Departing

By Car

You can drive into Romania from Hungary through the border towns of Satu Mare, Oradea, Varsand, and Arad. From Bulgaria you can enter through the boarder towns of Calafat, Giurgiu, Negru Voda, and Vama Veche. Driving into Romania can be a lengthy process. Border police are not very efficient, and the line to cross the border can sometimes take more than 24 hours.

By Plane

Most international flights arrive at **Otopeni** (☎ 01/2300042), the international airport just outside Bucharest. To catch an internal flight requires transferring to **Baneasa Airport** (☎ 01/2320020), which is about a five-minute drive from Otopeni. Bus service is available regularly between both airports for a small fee. You can also catch a taxi; taxi fare should be no more than $5. **Tarom** (☎ 01/6594125), the Romanian national airline, offers some flights from other countries to Arad.

By Train

Train service is available from Budapest and Sofia to Bucharest and all sites in between. Try to travel on a night train and rent a *vagon de dormit,* or sleeper. First class is worth the extra cost.

Getting Around

By Bus

Bus stations, or *autogara,* are usually located near train stations. Buses are generally crowded and far from luxurious—in fact, they can be downright horrible. Tickets are sold at stations up to two hours before departure. Local bus tickets can be bought at any stop; intercity bus tickets are sold only at the autogara.

By Car

PARKING

Parking in cities is normally a do-it-yourself affair; the one rule you must abide by is not to park in front of a blue sign marked with a red cross, or your car will be towed. Parking lots are few and far between; those that exist have attendants collecting a minimal fee, generally 2,000 to 3,000 lei. There are no parking meters; in fact, people often park on the sidewalk.

An adequate network of main roads covers the country, though the majority of roads only allow for a single lane in each direction. Roads have many potholes, and a few have not been paved at all. Progress may be further impeded by farm machinery, slow-moving trucks, horses and carts, or herds of animals. At night, the situation becomes doubly hazardous with poorly lighted or unlighted roads and vehicles.

Driving is on the right, as in the United States. Speed limits are 60 kph (37 mph) in built-up areas and 80–90 kph (50–55 mph) on all other roads. Driving after drinking any amount of alcohol is prohibited. Police are empowered to levy on-the-spot fines. Vehicle spot checks are frequent, but police are generally courteous to foreigners. Road signs are the same as those in Western Europe. If asking for directions, it's normally better to refer to major cities or towns along a road rather than the road's official number.

An International Driver's Permit is required for all drivers from outside the country for stays of more than 30 days (☞ Car Rental *in* the Gold Guide). Car insurance is also required and is included in the rental price (☞ Car Rentals, *below*).

By Plane

Tarom operates daily flights to major Romanian cities from Bucharest's Baneasa Airport (☞ Arriving and Departing by Plane, *above*). During the summer, additional flights link Constanţa with major cities, including Cluj and Iaşi. Be prepared for delays and cancellations. Prices average $100 round-trip. There are separate offices for international flights (✉ Str. Brezoianu 10, ☎ 01/6150499) and for domestic flights (✉ Str. Buzesti 59–61, ☎ 01/6594185).

By Train

Romanian Railways (CFR) operates *expres, accelerat, rapide,* and *personal* trains; if possible, avoid the *personal* trains because they are very slow. Trains are inexpensive and often crowded, with cars in need of repair. First class is worth the extra cost. A cheap *cuşeta,* with bunk beds, or a roomier *vagon de dormit* (sleeper) is available for longer journeys. It is always advisable to buy a seat reservation in advance, but you cannot buy the ticket itself at a train station more than one hour before departure. If your reserved seat is already occupied, it may have been sold twice. If you're in Bucharest and want to buy your ticket more than an hour ahead of time, go to **CFR International** (✉ Str. Domniţ Anastasia 10–14, ☎ 1/6132642). You will be charged a small commission fee, but the process is less time-consuming than buying your ticket at the railway station.

Contacts and Resources

B&B Reservation Agencies

It is possible to rent rooms in Romanian homes in Bucharest and in the Romanian countryside. This can be arranged through most travel agencies in Bucharest and through the **Office of National Tourism** (ONT; ☞ Guided Tours and Travel Agencies *in* Bucharest A to Z, *above*).

Car Rentals

Budget, Avis, and **Hertz** have offices in Bucharest; Budget generally has the best rates. There are also a few locally run operators, but they are largely undependable. Prices start at $100 per day and $400 per week for an economy car, with unlimited mileage, air-conditioning, and manual transmission. Car rental requires purchasing national automobile insurance, which is included in the price (☞ Getting Around by Car, *above*).

Avis (✉ Otopeni Airport, ☎ 01/2300054, FAX 01/2106912). **Budget** (✉ Hotel Dorobantilor, Calea Dorobantilor 1–7, ☎ 01/2102867, FAX 01/2102995). **Hertz** (✉ Otopeni Airport, ☎ 401/212–0122; ✉ Hotel Dorobantilor, Calea Dorobantilor 1–7, ☎ 01/211–5450, FAX 01/2106433).

Customs and Duties
ON ARRIVAL
You may bring in a personal computer and printer, two cameras, 10 rolls of film, one small camcorder/video camera and VCR, 10 video-cassette tapes, a typewriter, binoculars, a radio/tape recorder, a small television set, a bicycle, a stroller for a child, 200 cigarettes, 2 liters of liquor, and 4 liters of wine or beer. Gifts are permitted, though you may be charged duty on some electronic goods. Declare video cameras, personal computers, and expensive jewelry on arrival.

ON DEPARTURE
Make sure you have receipts for any artwork or antiques you may have bought; checks are sporadic, but it's best to be prepared.

Emergencies
Police (☎ 01/955). **Ambulance** (☎ 01/961), or contact your embassy or consulate.

Guided Tours and Travel Agencies
See Bucharest A to Z, *above*.

Language
Romanian is a Latin-based language similar to Italian. Travelers who speak another Latin language will find that they can easily understand quite a bit of Romanian. Most Romanians also speak at least one other language, usually French. It is not too difficult to find someone who speaks English, especially in Bucharest.

Mail
In Romania, post offices can be identified by yellow signs marked *Posta*. The main post office in Bucharest (☎ 01/6144054) is located at Strada Matei Milo 10.

POSTAL RATES
A letter to the United States or Canada costs 5,500 lei; a postcard costs 5,800 lei. Within Europe the rate is 4,050 lei.

RECEIVING MAIL
The safest way to receive mail in Romania is to have it sent to you at your hotel. First-class mail takes about two weeks from the United States and Canada. For quicker, tracked materials, contact **DHL International** (☎ 01/3123661).

Money and Expenses
COSTS
Inflation averaged around 150% in 1997; prices are constantly going up. Imported items are expensive in Romania due to the government's high import tax; hotel and restaurant prices can be as high as those in Western Europe. Despite this, Romania is still an inexpensive tourist destination, especially if you plan on leaving the capital. Museums, theater seats, and locally made items are still amazingly low priced.

CURRENCY
The unit of currency in Romania is the leu (plural lei). It is circulated in denominations of 500-, 1,000-, 5,000-, 10,000-, 50,000-, and 100,000-lei notes and 20-, 50-, and 100-lei coins. At press time, the

official exchange rate was approximately 8,100 lei to the U.S. dollar, 5,513 lei to the Canadian dollar, and 13,535 lei to the pound sterling.

Exchange rates are the highest at the *casa de schimb valutar* (exchange bureaus); ask for 10,000- and 50,000-lei notes. Be sure to hold on to all receipts to change your money back at the end of your trip, as it is needed to prove you didn't trade on the black market. The black market is a dangerous proposition; don't use it.

When you are owed change from a purchase, do not expect change for amounts less than 100 lei. If you plan to stay long in Romania, it's imperative you bring American dollars in small denominations ($1, $5, and $10 bills); a few dollars can be useful in many situations. Also note that you must buy international train tickets in hard currency, so be sure to save at least U.S. $50 for your trip out of the country.

CREDIT CARDS

Major credit cards are welcome in larger hotels and restaurants in Bucharest. Though they are becoming more common, they are not accepted in most independent establishments or in the countryside.

SAMPLE COSTS

A cup of coffee, 7,000 lei; museum entrance, 3,000–10,000 lei; a good theater seat, 10,000 lei; a 1-km (½-mi) taxi ride, 5,000 lei; a bottle of Romanian beer, 8,000 lei; a bottle of Romanian wine in a good restaurant, 30,000 lei.

TRAVELER'S CHECKS

Traveler's checks are almost useless in Romania: They're accepted only at banks, tourist offices, Bucharest's major hotels, and some exchange shops (look for signs in these shop windows). Banks usually charge a 5% commission, and tourist offices and hotels take a 5%–10% bite. Try to change a decent amount of traveler's checks into American dollars *before* you arrive, supplemented with a small bundle of traveler's checks in case of an emergency. Since you must travel in Romania with large sums of cash, it is absolutely imperative to stash your money in a safe place.

National Holidays

January 1; January 2; April 11, 1999 and April 30, 2000 (Orthodox Easter Monday); May 1 (Labor Day); December 1 (National Day), December 25–26, and December 31.

Opening and Closing Times

Banks are open weekdays 9–12:30. Exchange office hours vary, but most are open weekdays 9–5 and Saturdays from 9–1; some are open until 7 on Saturday and 1 on Sunday. **Museums** are usually open 10–6, closed on Monday (and sometimes Tuesday). **Shops** are generally open weekdays 10–6. Most state-owned shops close at 2 on Saturday, though an increasing number of private shops are staying open later to attract customers.

Passports and Visas

Americans need only a valid passport to enter Romania for up to 30 days, but border guards may try to extort money from you anyway: Be firm. If you're traveling on a British, Australian, or New Zealand passport, you must pay $31 for a 30-day tourist card when you cross the border. Canadians must pay $33. There is no application; you don't need any photos—just hand the border guard your money. They prefer U.S. dollars but will accept British pounds or German marks.

Rail Passes

Rail Europe (✉ 226–230 Westchester Ave., White Plains, NY 106 ☎ 800/438–7245, FAX 800/432–1329; ✉ 2087 Dundas E., Ste. 1(Mississauga, Ontario L4X 1M2, ☎ 800/361–RAIL, FAX 905/602– 4198) offers a Balkan Flexipass granting any five, 10, or 15 days of travel in one month; the pass costs between $152 and $317. A pass valid only for Romania is also available, allowing any three days of travel in 15 days; this pass costs $60. As rail prices are quite low in Romania, you should consider your itinerary to decide if a pass is a worthwhile expense.

Student and Youth Travel

Students can receive discounts to some museums and tourist attractions in Romania. Students are also able to take advantage of lower-priced student hotels in most larger cities, though these are usually in very poor condition. There is a youth-discount version of Rail Europe's Balkan Flexipass (☞ Rail Passes, *above*). A student identification is required to take advantage of discounts; the ISIC card (☞ Student Travel *in* the Gold Guide) usually works. For more information, contact the Office of National Tourism (ONT; ☞ Guided Tours *and* Travel Agencies *in* Bucharest A to Z, *above*).

Telephones

COUNTRY CODE

The country code for Romania is 40; when dialing from outside the country, drop the initial zero from the regional area code. The code for Bucharest is 01.

INTERNATIONAL CALLS

Direct-dial international calls can now be made from hotels, train stations, the phone company building on Bucharest's Calea Victoriei, and local post offices. To place long-distance calls out of Romania, dial 00, then the country code and number. To place a call from Romania via an **AT&T** USADirect international operator, dial 01–800–4288; for **MCI,** dial 01–800–1800; for **Sprint,** dial 01–800–0877. For international information, dial 971.

LOCAL CALLS

To make a long-distance call within the country, first dial 0, then the area code and number. In Bucharest, dial 931 for information. Operators do not always speak English.

Some public telephones can be accessed using 20-, 50-, and 100-lei coins; newer phones now require a phone card (*cartelă telfonică*), which can be purchased at the post office. Phone cards are available with values of 20,000, 40,000, 50,000, 60,000, and 100,000 lei. Local calls are quite cheap; a call within Bucharest, for example, costs about 20 lei a minute. You can also make local or international calls from the post office by ordering your call and paying at the counter. When your call is ready, the name of the town or country you are phoning is announced, together with the number of the cabin you proceed to for your call.

Tipping

Most Romanians are very poor tippers. Generally speaking though, services that cater to foreigners, especially restaurants, expect that you will tip 5%–10%.

Visitor Information

The **Romanian National Tourist Office** (ONT; ☞ Guided Tours and Travel Agencies *in* Bucharest A to Z, *above*) has been officially disbanded, although most offices both in Romania and abroad continue to use the name. Try to obtain information before arriving in Romania from the office in New York or London (☞ Visitor Information *in* the Gold Guide), for once you arrive in Romania it might be difficult. You can usually find a small tourism office in the local train station. These offices have limited information, and the staff may not speak English. To find the train station, follow signs leading to the GARA; it is usually well marked.

FURTHER READING

Since the revolutions of 1989–90, a number of leading journalists have produced highly acclaimed books detailing the tumultuous changes experienced by Eastern and Central Europeans and the dramatic effects these changes have had on individual lives. Timothy Garton Ash's eyewitness account, *The Magic Lantern: The Revolution of '89 Witnessed in Warsaw, Budapest, Berlin, and Prague,* begins with Václav Havel's ringing words from his 1990 New Year's Address: "People, your government has returned to you!" Winner of both a National Book Award and a Pulitzer Prize, *The Haunted Land* is Tina Rosenberg's wide-ranging, incisive look at how Poland, the Czech Republic, and Slovakia (as well as Germany) are dealing with the memories of 40 years of communism.

Also essential reading is *Balkan Ghosts,* by Robert Kaplan, which traces his journey through the former Yugoslavia, Albania, Romania, Bulgaria, and Greece; it is an often chilling political travelogue, which fully deciphers the Balkans' ancient passions and intractable hatred for outsiders. In *Exit into History: A Journey Through the New Eastern Europe,* Eva Hoffman returns to her Polish homeland and five other countries—Hungary, Romania, Bulgaria, the Czech Republic, and Slovakia—and captures the texture of everyday life of a world in the midst of change. Isabel Fonseca's *Bury Me Standing: The Gypsies and Their Journey* is an unprecedented and revelatory look at the Gypsies—or Romany—of Eastern and Central Europe, the large and landless minority whose history and culture has long been obscure.

Travelogues worth reading, though less recent, include Claudio Magris's widely regarded *Danube,* which follows the river as it flows from its source in Germany to its mouth in the Black Sea; Brian Hall's *Stealing from a Deep Place,* a lively account of a solo bicycle trip through Romania and Bulgaria in 1982, followed by a stay in Budapest; Patrick Leigh Fermor's *Between the Woods and the Water,* which relates his 1934 walk through Hungary and Romania and captures life in these lands before their transformation during World War II and under the Soviets. Though its emphasis is on the countries on the eastern side of the Black Sea, Neal Ascherson's recent, widely acclaimed *Black Sea* does touch on Bulgaria and Romania.

Forty-three writers from 16 nations of the former Soviet bloc are included in *Description of a Struggle: The Vintage Book of Contemporary Eastern European Writing,* edited by Michael March. Focusing on novels, poetry, and travel writing, the *Traveller's Literary Companion to Eastern and Central Europe* is a thorough guide to the vast array of literature from this region available in English translation. It includes country-by-country overviews, dozens of excerpts, reading lists, biographical discussions of key writers that highlight their most important works, and guides to literary landmarks.

Bulgaria

Bulgarian writers are less well known than their counterparts in other Eastern and Central European countries, and English translations are rare. Though their work is not specifically illuminating of Bulgarian life and culture, intellectuals such as Julia Kristeva, Tzvetan Todorov, and Elias Canetti (winner of the 1981 Nobel Prize for Literature, the first Bulgarian to be so honored) are all Bulgarian-born.

Czech Republic and Slovakia

With the increased interest in the Czech Republic in recent years, English readers now have an excellent range of both fiction and nonfiction about the country at their disposal. The most widely read Czech author of fiction in English is probably Milan Kundera, whose well-crafted tales illuminate both the foibles of human nature and the unique tribulations of life in Communist Czechoslovakia. Oddly, the Czechs never really took to the novels he wrote after leaving Czechoslovakia for France in the 1970s. *The Unbearable Lightness of Being* takes a look at the 1968 invasion and its aftermath through the eyes of a strained young couple. *The Book of Laughter and Forgetting* deals in part with the importance of memory and the cruel irony of how it fades over time; Kundera was no doubt coming to terms with his own forgetting as he wrote the book from his Paris exile. *The Joke,* Kundera's earliest work available in English, takes a serious look at the dire consequences of humorlessness among Communists.

Born and raised in the German–Jewish enclave of Prague, Franz Kafka scarcely left the city his entire life. *The Trial* and *The Castle* strongly convey the dread and mystery he detected beneath the 1,000 golden spires of Prague. Kafka worked as a bureaucrat for 14 years, in a job he detested; his books are, at least in part, an indictment of the bizarre bureaucracy of the Austro-Hungarian empire, though they now seem eerily prophetic of the even crueler and more arbitrary Communist system that was to come. Until recently, most of his works could not be purchased in his native country.

The most popular Czech authors today were those banned or harassed by the communists after the Soviet invasion of 1968. Václav Havel and members of Charter 77 illegally distributed self-published manuscripts, or *samizdat* as they were called, of these authors—among them, Bohumil Hrabal, Josef Škvorecký, and Ivan Klíma. Hrabal, who died in 1997, was perhaps the most beloved of all postwar Czech writers. He spent his entire life in his homeland, and was allowed to publish regularly; many claim to have shared a table with him at his favorite pub in Prague, U Zlatéyho tygra. His books include *I Served the King of England* and the lyrical *Too Loud a Solitude,* narrated by a lonely man who spends his days in the basement compacting the world's greatest works of literature along with bloodied butcher paper into neat bundles before they get carted off for recycling and disposal. Škvorecký sought refuge and literary freedom in Toronto in the early 1970s. His book *The Engineer of Human Souls* reveals the double censorship of the writer in exile—censored in the country of his birth and unread in his adopted home. Still, Škvorecký did gain a following thanks to his translator, Paul Wilson—who lived in Prague in the 1960s and '70s until he was ousted for his assistance in dissident activities. Novelist, short story writer, and playwright Ivan Klíma is now one of the most widely read Czech writers in English; his books include the novels *Judge on Trial, Love and Garbage,* and *The Spirit of Prague,* a collection of essays about life in the Czech Republic today.

Václav Havel, one-time dissident playwright and now president of the Czech Republic, is essential nonfiction reading. The best place to start is probably *Living in Truth,* which provides an absorbing overview of his own political philosophy and of Czechoslovak politics and history over the last 30 years. Also look for *The Art of the Impossible,* a selection of Havel's speeches and articles, *Disturbing the Peace* (a collection of interviews with him) and *Letters to Olga.* Havel's plays explore the absurdities and pressures of life under the former Communist regime; the best example of his absurdist dramas is *The Memorandum*, which depicts a Communist bureaucracy more twisted than the streets of Prague's Old Town.

Many observers, Ivan Klíma among them, have bemoaned what they view as the poor quality of writing since the revolution. Among the most prominent of the young writers is Jáchym Topol, whose *A Visit to the Train Station* documents the creation of a new Prague with a sharp wit that cuts the false pretenses of American youth currently occupying Prague.

Hungary

Hungarians have played a central role in the intellectual life of the 20th century, although their literary masters are less well known in the west than those who have excelled in other arts, such as Béla Bartók in music, and Andre Kertesz and Robert and Cornell Capa in photography (the latter two founded New York City's International Center of Photography).

Novelist and poet Dezső Kosztolányi was prominent in European intellectual circles after World War I and was greatly admired by Thomas Mann. His novels, including *Anna Édes* and *Skylark*, are known for their keen psychological insight and social commentary. Also worth discovering is novelist and essayist György Konrád, one of Hungary's leading 20th-century dissidents, whose *The Loser* is a disturbing reflection on intellectual life in a totalitarian state. The English writer Tibor Fischer's novels *Under the Frog* and *The Thought Gang* deal with life in contemporary Hungary. John Lukacs's *Budapest 1900: A Historical Portrait of a City and Its Culture* is an oversize, illustrated study of Hungary's capital at a particularly important moment in its history. For a more in-depth look at the city, András Török's *Budapest: A Critical Guide* offers detailed historical and architectural information, and is illustrated with excellent drawings.

Poland

For an introduction to Polish history and politics, check out *Heart of Europe: A Short History of Poland*, or the more detailed *God's Playground: A History of Poland*, both by Norman Davies. *The Polish Way* by Adam Zamoyski is another outstanding history of Poland.

Polish classics include the Henryk Sienkiewicz trilogy *With Fire and Sword, The Deluge,* and *Fire and the Steppe,* which describes Poland's wars with the Turks, the Swedes, and the Cossacks in the 17th century. *The Doll* by Boleslaw Prus depicts life in 19th century Warsaw.

Bruno Schulz wrote two volumes of stories—*The Street of Crocodiles* and *Sanatorium Under the Sign of the Hourglass*—about life in a Polish shtetl before World War II that, in their fantastical aspect, are not unlike the work of Franz Kafka. Eva Hoffman's *Shtetl: The Life and Death of a Small Town and the World of Polish Jews* takes a look at the complicated history of Poles and Jews. Australian Thomas Keneally's *Schindler's List* (originally titled *Schindler's Ark*)—half fiction, half documentary—tells the dramatic, moving story of Oskar Schindler, a German businessman who saved the lives of a thousand Polish Jews. The novel won the Booker Prize; Steven Spielberg's 1993 Academy Award®–winning film based on the book became perhaps the most widely seen movie about the Holocaust. Louis Begley's haunting 1991 *Wartime Lies* is the story of how a young Jewish boy and his aunt manage to stay one step ahead of the Nazis during the war. Tadeusz Borowski's *This Way for the Gas, Ladies and Gentleman* wryly explores the fate of the

Jews in Polish concentration camps under the Nazis. For stories about prewar Jewish life in Poland pick up any book by Nobel Prize winner Isaac Bashevis Singer.

Andrzej Szcypiorski's *The Beautiful Mrs. Seidenman* is a highly praised exploration of the Polish psyche, complex Polish-Jewish history, and notions of East Central Europe and Polish nationalism. The poet, essayist, and novelist Czesław Miłosz, winner of the Nobel Prize for Literature in 1980, is one of Poland's greatest writers. His major prose works include *Native Realm,* his moral and intellectual autobiography from childhood to the 1950s, and *The Captive Mind,* an exploration of the power of Communist ideology over Polish intellectuals.

Jerzy Andrzejewski's *Ashes and Diamonds*—the first of a trilogy and the basis for the Andrzej Wajda film of the same name—is a poignant account of Poland in the mid-1940s. Andrzejewski vividly captures this window in Polish history immediately after the war when partisans were still hiding in the fields and before the Soviets and their regime had fully entered the scene. Another excellent book is Eva Hoffman's *Lost in Translation,* an account of her Jewish-Polish childhood and subsequent sense of dislocation when she and her family moved to British Columbia. For lighter reading, Radek Sikorski's *Full Circle* is a personal coming-of-age story set in a small Polish town during the '70's.

Romania

Gregor von Rezzori, born in the Bucovina region of Romania to Austrian-German parents, has written two of the most moving memoirs of the 20th century: *Memoirs of an Anti-Semite* and *The Snows of Yesteryear.* Both offer richly detailed, coruscatingly honest recollections of his childhood and young adult life in Romania between the two world wars.

National Public Radio commentator Andrei Codrescu returned to his homeland to witness the December '89 revolution and offers his wry appraisal in *The Hole in the Flag: A Romanian Exile's Story of Return and Revolution.* One of the few Romanian novels available in English is Zaharia Stancu's *Barefoot,* a national classic about a turn-of-the-century peasant uprising. For an outsider's view of the country—one disputed by most Romanians—see Saul Bellow's novel *The Dean's December,* which alternates between Bucharest and Chicago. For profiles of Romania's most notorious character, read Radu R. Florescu's *Dracula: Prince of Many Faces* and Raymond T. McNally's *In Search of Dracula,* the first comprehensive histories of the myth and the actual historical figure.

Edward Behr's *Kiss the Hand You Cannot Bite: The Rise and Fall of the Ceauşescus* is a riveting account of the notorious Romanian dictator. *The Land of Green Plums,* by Herta Müller, depicts totalitarianism; it was written in memory of Müller's friends killed during the Ceauşescu regime. Also worth discovering: Norman Manea's *Compulsory Happiness,* an absurdist's view of Romania under the Ceauşescu regime, and his collection of short stories, *October Eight O'Clock.*

POLISH VOCABULARY

English	Polish	Pronunciation

Basics

English	Polish	Pronunciation
Yes/no	Tak/nie	tahk/nye
Please	Proszę	**pro**-sheh
Thank you	Dziękuję	dzhen-**koo**-yeh
Excuse me	Przepraszam	psheh-**prah**-shahm
Hello	Dzień dobry	**dzhehn dohb**-ry
Do you (m/f) speak English?	Czy pan (pani) mówi po angielsku	chee **pahn** (**pahn**-ee) **gyel**-skuu?
I don't speak Polish.	Nie mówi po Polsku.	nyeh **moohv**-yeh po-**pohl**-skoo
I don't understand.	Nie rozumiem	nyeh rohz-**oo**-myehm
Please speak slowly.	Proszę mówić wolniej	proh-sheh **moo**-veech **vohl**-nyah
Please write it down.	Proszę napisać	proh-sheh nah-pee-sahtch
I am American (m/f)	Jestem Amerykaninem/Amerykanką	**yest**-em ah-mer-i-**kahn**-in-em/ ah-mer-i-**kahn**-ka
English (m/f)	Anglikiem/Angielką	ahn-**gleek**-em/ ahn-**geel**-ka
My name is . . .	Nazywam się	nah-**ziv**-ahm sheh
On the right/left	Na prawo/lewo	nah-**prah**-vo/**lyeh**-vo
Arrivals/departures	Przyloty/odloty	pshee-**loh**-tee/ ohd-**loh**-tee
Where is . . .	Gdzie jest	gdzhyeh yest
the station?	Dworzec kolejowy	**dvoh**-zhets koh-lay-oh-vee
the train?	Pociąg	**poh**-chohnk
the bus?	Autobus	a'oo-**toh**-boos
the airport?	Lotnisko	loht-**nees**-koh
the post office?	Poczta	**poch**-tah
the bank?	Bank	bahnk
Stop here, please	Proszę się to zatrzymać	**proh**-sheh sheh too zah-**tchee**-nahch
I would like (m/f) . . .	Chciałbym/Chciałabym	**kh'chow**-beem/ kh'chow-**ah**-beem
How much?	Ile	**ee**-leh
Letters/postcards	Listy/kartki	**lees**-tee/**kahrt**-kee
By airmail	Lotniczy	loht-**nee**-chee
Help!	Na pomoc!	na **po**-motz

Numbers

English	Polish	Pronunciation
One	Jeden	**yeh**-den
Two	Dwa	dvah
Three	Trzy	tchee
Four	Cztery	**chteh**-ree
Five	Pięć	pyehnch
Six	Sześć	shsyshch
Seven	Siedem	**shyeh**-dem
Eight	Osiem	**oh**-shyem
Nine	Dziewięć	**dzhyeh**-vyehnch
Ten	Dziesięć	**dzhyeh**-shehnch

| | One hundred | Sto | stoh |
| | One thousand | Tysiąc | **tee**-shonch |

Days of the Week

Sunday	Niedziela	nyeh-**dzhy'e**-la
Monday	Poniedsiałłek	poh-nyeh-**dzhya**-wek
Tuesday	Wtrorek	**ftohr**-ek
Wednesday	Środa	**shroh**-da
Thursday	Czwartek	**chvahr**-tek
Friday	Piątek	**pyohn**-tek
Saturday	Sobota	soh-**boh**-ta

Where to Sleep

A room	Pokój	**poh**-kooy
The key	Klucz	klyuch
With bath/shower	Złłazienką/ prysznicem	zwah-**zhen**-koh/ spree-**shnee**-tsem

Food

The menu	Menu	**men**-yoo
The check, please.	Proszę rachunek	**proh**-sheh rah-**kh'oon**-ehk
Breakfast	Śnidanie	shnya-**dahn**-iyeh
Lunch	Obiad	**oh**-byat
Dinner	Kolacja	koh-**lah**-ts'yah
Beef	Mołłowina	voh-woh-**veen**-a
Bread and butter	Chleb i masłło	kh'lyep ee **mahs**-woh
Vegetables	Jarzyny	yah-**zhin**-ee
Salt/pepper	Sółł/pieprz	soow/pyehpsh
Bottle of wine	Butelkę wina	boo-**tehl**-keh **vee**-na
Beer	Piwo	**pee**-voh
(Mineral) Water	Wodę (mineralną)	**voh**-deh (mee-**nehr**-ahl-nohn
Coffee with milk	Kawę z mliekem	**kah**-veh **zmleyeh**-kem
Tea with lemon	Herbaté z cytryną	kh'ehr-**bah**-teh **ststrin**-ohn

CZECH/SLOVAK VOCABULARY

English	Czech/Slovak	Pronunciation

Basics

Yes/no	Ano/ne	**ah**-no/neh
Please	Prosím	**pro**-seem
Thank you	Děkuji	**dyek**-oo-yee
Pardon me	Pardon	**par**-don
Hello.	Dobrý den	**dob**-ree den
Do you (m/f) speak English?	Mluvíte anglicky?	**mloo**-vit-eh ahng-**glit**-ski?
I don't speak Czech.	Nemluvím česky.	nem-**luv**-eem ches-ky
I don't understand.	Nerozumím	neh-rohz-**oom**-eem
Please speak slowly.	Prosím, mluvte pomalu	**pro**-seem, **mloov**-teh poh-**mah**-lo

Please write it down.	Prosím napište	**pro**-seem nah-**peesh**
Show me	Ukažte mně	oo-**kazh**-te mnye
I am American (m/f)	Jsem američan/ američanka	sem ah-**mer**-i-chan/ ah-mer-i-**chan**-ka
English (m/f)	Angličan/angličanka	**ahn**-gli-chan/Ahn-gli-**chan**-ka
My name is . . .	Jmenuji se	**ymen** weh-seh
On the right/left	Napravo/nalevo	na-**pra**-vo/na-**leh**-vo
Arrivals	Přílety	**pshee**-leh-tee
Where is . . . ?	Kde je	g'deh yeh
the station?	Nádraží	nah-**drah**-zee
the train?	Vlak	vlahk
the bus/tram?	Autobus/tramvaj	**out**-oh-boos/**tram**-vie
the airport?	Letiště	**leh**-tish-tyeh
the post office?	Pošta	**po**-shta
the bank?	Banka	**bahn**-ka
Stop here	Zastavte tady	**zah**-stahv-teh **tah**-dee
I would like (m/f) . . .	Chtěl (chtěla) bych	kh'tyel (**kh'tyel**-ah) bihk
How much does it cost?	Kolik to stoji	ko-**lik** toh **stoy**-ee
Letter/postcard	Dopis/pohlednice	doh-**pis**-ee/poh-**hled**-nit-seh
By airmail	Letecky	**leh**-tet-skee
Help!	Pomoc	**po**-motz

Numbers

One	Jeden	ye-**den**
Two	Dva	dvah
Three	Tři	tshree
Four	Čtyři	ch'**ti**-zhee
Five	Pět	pyet
Six	Šest	shest
Seven	Sedm	**sed**-oom
Eight	Osm	**oh**-soom
Nine	Devět	**deh**-vyet
Ten	Deset	**deh**-set
One hundred	Sto	sto
One thousand	Tisíc	**tee**-seets

Days of the Week

Sunday	Neděle	**neh**-dyeh-leh
Monday	Pondělí	**pon**-dye-lee
Tuesday	Žterý	**oo**-teh-ree
Wednesday	Středa	**stshreh**-da
Thursday	Čtvrtek	ch't'v'**r**-tek
Friday	Pátek	**pah**-tek
Saturday	Sobota	**so**-boh-ta

Where to Sleep

A room	Pokoj	**poh**-koy
The key	Klíč	kleech
With bath/shower	S koupelnou/sprcha	s'**ko**-pel-noh/ **sp'r**-kho

Food

The menu	Jídelní lístek	**yee**-dell-nee **lis**-tek
The check, please.	Účet, prosím	**oo**-chet **pro**-seem
Breakfast	Snídaně	**snyee**-dan-ye
Lunch	Oběd	**ob**-yed
Dinner	Večeře	**ve**-cher-zhe
Bread	Chléb	khleb
Butter	Máslo	**mah**-slo
Salt/pepper	Sůl/pepř	sool/pepsh
Bottle	Láhev	**lah**-hev
Red/white wine	Červené/bílé víno	**cher**-ven-eh/**bee**-leh **vee**-no
Beer	Pivo	**piv**-oh
Mineral water	Minerálka voda	min-eh-**rahl**-ka **vo**-da
Milk	Mléko	**mleh**-koh
Coffee	Káva	**kah**-va
Tea (with lemon)	Čaj (s citrónem)	tchai (se tsi-**tro**-nem)

HUNGARIAN VOCABULARY

English	Hungarian	Pronunciation

Basics

Yes/no	Igen/nem	**ee**-gen/nem
Please	Kérem	**kay**-rem
Thank you (very much)	Köszönöm (szépen)	**kuh**-suh-num (**seh**-pen)
Excuse me	Bocsánat	**boh**-chah-not
I'm sorry.	Sajnálom	**shahee**-nah-lome
Hello/how do you do	Szervusz	**sair**-voose
Do you speak English?	Beszél angolul	**bess**-el **on**-goal-ool
I don't speak Hungarian.	Nem tudok magyarul	nem **too**-dock **muh**-jor-ool
I don't understand.	Nem értem	nem **air**-tem
Please speak slowly.	Kérem, beszéljen lassan	**kay**-rem, **bess**-el-yen lush-shun
Please write it down.	Kérem, írja fel	**kay**-rem, **eer**-yuh fell
Please show me.	Megmutatná nekem	meg-**moo**-taht-nah **neh**-kem
I am American.	Amerikai vagyok	uh-**meh**-rick-ka-ee **vud**-yoke
I am English.	Angol vagyok	**un**-goal **vud**-yoke
My name is . . .	Vagyok	**vud**-yoke
Right/left	Bal/jobb	buhl/yobe
Open/closed	nyitva/zárva	**nit**-va/**zahr**-voh
Arrival/departure	Érkezés/indulás	**er**-keh-zesh/**in**-dool-ahsh
Where is . . . ?	Hol van	hole vun
the train station?	a pályaudvar	uh pah-yo-**oot**-var
the bus station?	a buszállomás	uh **boose**-ahlo-mahsh
the bus stop?	a megálló	uh **meg**-all-oh
the airport?	A repülőtér	uh rep-ewluh-**tair**
the post office?	a pósta	uh **pohsh**-tuh

the bank?	a bank	uh bonhk
Stop here	Tlljon meg itt	**all**-yon meg it
I would like . . .	Szeretnék	**sair**-et-neck
How much does it cost?	Mennyibe kerúl	**men**-yibe kair-**ule**
Letter/postcard	levél/képeslap	**lev**-ehl/**kay**-pesh-lup
By airmail	Légi póstaval	**lay**-gee **pohsh**-tuh-vol
Help!	Segítség!	**shay**-geet-shaig

Numbers

One	Egy	edge
Two	Kettő	**ket**-tuh
Three	Három	**hah**-rome
Four	Négy	**nay**-ge
Five	Öt	ut
Six	Hat	huht
Seven	Hét	hate
Eight	Nyolc	nyolts
Nine	Kilenc	**kee**-lents
Ten	Tíz	teez
One hundred	Száz	sahz
One thousand	Ezer	**eh**-zer

Days of the Week

Sunday	Vasárnap	**vuh**-shar-nup
Monday	Hétfő	**hate**-fuh
Tuesday	Kedd	ked
Wednesday	Szerda	**ser**-duh
Thursday	Csütörtök	**chew**-tur-tuk
Friday	Péntek	**pain**-tek
Saturday	Szombat	**som**-but

Where to Sleep

A room	Egy szobá	edge **soh**-bah
The key	A kulcsot	uh **koolch**-oat
With bath/a shower	Fúrdőszo-bával/egy zuhany	**fure**-duh-soh-bah-vul/edge **zoo**-hon

Food

A restaurant	A vendéglő/az étterem	uh **ven**-deh-gluh/uz **eht**-teh-rem
The menu	A étlap	uh **ate**-lop
The check, please.	A számlát kérem	uh **sahm**-lot **kay**-rem
I'd like to order this	Kéem ezt	**kay**-rem etz
Breakfast	Reggeli	**reg**-gell-ee
Lunch	Ebéd	**eb**-ehd
Dinner	Vacsora	**votch**-oh-rah
Bread	Kenyér	**ken**-yair
Butter	Vaj	voy
Salt/pepper	Só/bors	show/borsh
Bottle	Üveg	**ew**-veg
Red/white wine	Vörös/fehér	**vuh**-ruhsh/**feh**-hehr **bor**-bore

Beer	Sör	shur
Water/mineral water	Víz/kristályvíz	veez/**krish**-tah-ee-veez
Milk	Tej	tay
Coffee (with milk)	Ávé/tejeskávé	**kah**-vay/**tey**-esh-**kah**-vay
Tea (with lemon)	Tea (citrommal)	**tay**-oh **tsit**-rome-mol
Chocolate	Csokoládé	chaw-kaw-**law**-day

ROMANIAN VOCABULARY

English	Romanian	Pronunciation

Basics

Yes/no	Da/nu	dah/new
Please	Vărog	**vuh** rahg
Thank you	Vă mulţumesc	vuh **mull**-tsoo-mesk
Excuse me	Scuzati-mă	**skoo**-zah-tsih-muh
I'm sorry.	Îmî pare rău	yumeh **pah**-ray
Hello/how do you do	Bunăziua	buh-**nuh**-zi-uah
Do you speak English?	Vorbiţî engleză	**vore**-bit-zyu ain-**glay**-zah
I don't speak Romanian.	Nu vorbesc romă neşte	new **vore**-besk rome-un-**esh**-tay
I don't understand.	Nu înţeleg	new **yune**-tsay-leg
Please speak slowly.	Vorbiţi rar	**vore**-bih-tsee rahr
Please write it down.	Scrieţi, vă rog	skrih-**eh**-tsee, **vuh** rahg
Please show me.	Indicaţi-ma vă rog	indih-**cah**-tsee, **vuh** rahg
I am American (m/f)	Sînt american/americanaă	syoont ah-meh-ri-**cahn**/ah-meh-ri-**cah**-nuh
I am English (m/f)	Sînt englez/engleză	syoont ahn-**glaze**/ahn-**glay**-zuh
My name is . . .	Mă numesc	muh **new**-mesk
Right/left	Dreapta/stinga	dray-**ahp**-tah/**stoon**-gah
Open/closed	Deschis/închis	**dess**-kiss/**yune**-kiss
Arrivals/departures	Sosiri/plecări	**so**-sir-ih/**play**-cuh-rih
Where is . . . ?	Unde este	**un**-day **ay**-stay
the station?	gara/staţie	**gah**-ruh/**staht**-zee-ay
the train?	trenul	**tray**-null
the bus/tram?	autobus/tramvai	**ahu**-toh-bus/**trahm**-va-hee
the airport?	aeroportul	air-oh-**por**-tull
the post office?	posta	**pahsh**-tah
a bank?	o bancă	uh **bahn**-cuh
Stop here.	Opriţi aici	uh-**prih**-tsih **ah**-ichih
I would like . . .	Aş vrea	ahsh **vray**-ah
How much does it cost?	Cît costă	coot **cohs**-tuh
a letter/postcard	o scrisoare/carte poştală	uh **scrih**-so-ah-ray/**kar**-tay **pohsh**-tah-luh
By airmail	Cu avion	coo ah-vee-**one**
Help!	Ajutor	ah-**zhoo**-tore

Numbers

One	Unu	**uh**-nuh
Two	Doi	doy
Three	Trei	tray
Four	Patru	**paht**-ruh
Five	Cinci	**chin**-chih
Six	Şase	**shah**-say
Seven	Şapte	**shahp**-tay
Eight	Opt	ahpt
Nine	Nouă	**nah**-u-ah
Ten	Zece	**zay**-chay
One hundred	O sută	uh **suh**-tuh
One thousand	O mie	uh **mih**-ay

Days of the Week

Sunday	Duminică	duh-**mih**-nih-kuh
Monday	Luni	**luh**-nih
Tuesday	Marţi	**mahr**-tsih
Wednesday	Miercuri	**meer**-kurih
Thursday	Joi	zhoy
Friday	Vineri	**vih**-nayrih
Saturday	Sîmbătă	**syume**-buh-tuh

Where to Sleep

A room	O cameră	uh **kah**-may-ruh
The key	Cheia	**kay**-ihuh
With bath/with shower	Cu baie/duş	koo **bah**-ih-ay/dush

Food

A restaurant	Restaurantul	rse-taur-**ahn**-tul
The menu	Meniul, lista	**may**-nih-ul, **lis**-tah
The check, please.	Plata, vă rog	**plah** tah, **vuh** rahg
I'd like to order this.	Aş vrea să comand acesta	ahsh **vray**-ah suh cah-**mahnd** ah-**ches**-tah
Breakfast	Micul dejun	**mick**-ul **day**-zjun
Lunch	Dejun, prînz	**day**-zjun, proonz
Dinner	Masa de seară	**mah**-sah day say-**ah**-ruh
Bread	Pîine	pih-**yune**-nay
Butter	Unt	uhnt
Salt/pepper	Sare/piper	**sah**-ray/**pih**-pair
Bottle	O sticlă	uh **stick**-luh
Red/white wine	Vin roşu/alb	vin **ros**-huh/ahlb
Beer	O bere	uh **bare**-ay
(Mineral) Water	Apă (minerală)	**ah**-puh (min-ay-**rahl**-uh)
Milk	Lapte	**lahp**-tay
Coffee (with milk)	Cafeá (cu lapte)	**cah**-fay-ah (koo **lahp**-tay)
Tea (with lemon)	Ceai (cu lămîie)	chay-**ah**-ih (koo luh-**myu**-ih-ay)
Chocolate	Cacao	kah-**cah**-oh
Plum brandy	Ţuică	Tsuh-**ih**-cuh

BULGARIAN VOCABULARY

Bulgarian is written in Cyrillic. The following chart lists only pronunciations written in Roman letters.

English	Pronunciation

Basics

English	Pronunciation
Yes/no	da/ne
Please	molya
Thank you (very much)	blagodarya
Excuse me	izvenete
I'm sorry.	sazhalyavam
Hello, how do you do	dobar den
Do you speak English?	govorite li angliyski?
I don't speak Bulgarian.	ne govorya bulgarski
I don't understand.	ne razbiram.
Please speak slowly.	molya, govorete bavno
Please write it down.	molya vi se, napishete go
Please show me.	molya vi se, pokazhete mi
I am American (m/f)	as sum amerikanets/amerikanka
I am English (m/f)	as sum anglichanin/anglichanka
My name is . . .	kazvam se
Right/left	dyasno/lyavo
Open/closed	otvoreno/zatvoreno
Arrival/departure	pristigane/zaminavane
Where is . . . ?	kade e
the station?	garata
the railroad/train?	zheleznitsa/vlaku
the bus/tram?	aftobus/tramvai
the airport?	letishteto
the post office?	poshtata?
the bank?	banka
Stop here	sprete tuk
I would like (m/f) . . .	bikh zhelal/bikh zhelala
How much does it cost?	kolko struva
Letter/postcard	pismo/poshtenska kartichka
By airmail	vazdushna poshta
Help!	pomosht

Numbers

English	Pronunciation
One	edin
Two	dva
Three	ri
Four	chetiri
Five	pet
Six	shest
Seven	sedem
Eight	osem
Nine	devet
Ten	deset
One hundred	sto
One thousand	hilyada

Days of the Week

Sunday	**ned**elya
Monday	po**ned**elnik
Tuesday	**fto**rnik
Wednesday	**sry**ada
Thursday	**chet**vartak
Friday	**pe**tak
Saturday	**sa**bota

Where to Sleep

A room	**sta**ya
The key	**klyu**cha
With bath/shower	sus **ban**ya/dush

Food

A restaurant	resto**rant**
The menu	**kar**tata, **men**yuto
The check, please.	**smet**kata
I'd like to order this	**osh**te **mal**ko
Breakfast	za**kus**ka
Lunch	**o**bed
Dinner	**vech**erya
Bread	hlyab
Butter	**mas**lo
Salt/pepper	sol/**pi**per
Bottle	**but**ika
Red/white wine	**cher**veno/**bya**lo vino
Beer	**bi**ra
(Mineral) Water	(miner**al**na) **vo**da
Milk	**miyu**ko
Coffee	**ka**fe
Tea (with lemon)	chay (s lim**on**)
Chocolate	za**har**
Plum brandy	**sli**vova

INDEX

NOTES

NOTES

NOTES

NOTES

NOTES

NOTES

NOTES